GOVERNMENT AND PEASANT
IN RUSSIA, 1861–1906

STUDIES OF

THE HARRIMAN INSTITUTE

COLUMBIA UNIVERSITY

The W. Averell Harriman Institute for Advanced Study of the Soviet Union, Columbia University, sponsors the *Studies of the Harriman Institute* in the belief that their publication contributes to scholarly research and public understanding. In this way the Institute, while not necessarily endorsing their conclusions, is pleased to make available the results of some of the research conducted under its auspices. A list of the *Studies* appears at the back of this book.

DAVID A. J. MACEY

GOVERNMENT AND PEASANT
IN RUSSIA, 1861–1906,

The Prehistory of the Stolypin Reforms

NORTHERN ILLINOIS UNIVERSITY PRESS

DEKALB, ILLINOIS 1987

A Note on Transliteration

The Library of Congress system of transliteration has been followed generally. All names are given in their Russian form, with the exception only of the tsars and their preeminent finance minister, whose name is more familiar as Witte than the more phonetically correct Vitte. As is customary, dates are recorded according to the Julian calendar, which was twelve days behind the Gregorian calendar during the nineteenth century and thirteen days behind in the twentieth.

© 1987 by Northern Illinois University Press
Published by the Northern Illinois University Press,
DeKalb, Illinois 60115
Manufactured in the United States of America
Design by Jo Aerne

Library of Congress Cataloging-in-Publication Data
Macey, David A. J., 1942–
  Government and peasant in Russia, 1861–1906
  (Studies of the Harriman Institute)
  Bibliography: p. Includes index.
    1. Agriculture—Economic aspects—Soviet Union—
History—19th century. 2. Agriculture and state—Soviet
Union—History—19th century. 3. Peasantry—Soviet
Union—History—19th century. 4. Soviet Union—
Economic conditions—1861–1917. I. Title. II. Series
HD1992.M19 1987   338.1'847   87-7684
ISBN 0-87580-122-6

Publication of this book was assisted by a grant from the Publications Program of the National Endowment for the Humanities, an independent federal agency.

CONTENTS

ACKNOWLEDGMENTS

I began working on the topic of the bureaucracy and the peasants almost fifteen years ago, at a time when the peasantry was just beginning to capture the interest of Russian history students. Today our numbers have grown tremendously. Over the years I have incurred innumerable debts. The most enduring has been to Leopold Haimson, mentor to a whole generation of students of pre-Revolutionary Russia, who has given me every possible support and encouragement, the full measure of which I will no doubt ever remain unaware. I would also like to thank Loren Graham and Marc Raeff for their many years of advice, criticism, and support. I have sometimes been unconscious of the intellectual influence of all three, though it is pervasive; and in no way should it be unacknowledged. Roberta Manning deserves a special word of thanks for her indefatigable energy in reading and rereading this manuscript during its various incarnations and for her incisive criticism. Richard Wortman's insightful comments were also greatly appreciated at a critical early stage. Of the many others who have either read and commented on my work or rendered other forms of support, I would particularly like to thank Bruce Lincoln, Dan Field, Dan Orlovsky, Richard Robbins, George Yaney, Ben Eklof, and Travis Jacobs. Last, I wish to express my very deep gratitude to Ruth Mathewson for her expert editorial assistance during a time of great need.

It is impossible to pursue the task of research without financial support. Like so many others who plow this field, I take pleasure in acknowledging the International Research and Exchanges Board, the Fulbright-Hays program, and the Soviet Union's Ministry of Higher Education for making possible my stays in Helsinki and the Soviet Union in 1973. I would also like to thank Columbia University's History Department, Russian (now Harriman) Institute, and Society of Fellows; the Whiting Foundation; and Middlebury College for various grants and fellowships that have enabled me to pursue my research and writing.

Were it not for the librarians and archivists of this world, the historian's task would, of course, be impossible. I would especially like to thank the staff of the Columbia University Libraries, particularly their Reference and Interlibrary Loan services and Department of Slavic Acquisitions, as well, of course, as the Russian (now Bakhmetev) Archive and its curator, Lev Magerovsky, for their invaluable assistance. Middlebury College's Interlibrary Loan staff proved especially helpful and provided important supplementary assistance in recent years. I am also grateful for the friendly cooperation of the staffs of the Harvard University Libraries, the New York Public Library's Slavonic Division, the Library of Congress, the Hoover Institution Archive and Library, the Department of Agriculture Library, the Helsinki University Library, the Lenin Library, the Library of Social Sciences in Moscow, and the Library of the Academy of Sciences in Leningrad. The time I was able to spend in the Central Historical Archive in Leningrad, and secondarily at the Archives of Ancient Acts and of the October Revolution in Moscow, was also of fundamental significance.

Finally, although words will ever be inadequate, very special appreciation is due my wife, Phyllis, and sons, Peter and Robert, who have had to put up with so much for so long and whose company I have too often had to forgo.

Back when I first ventured into the field of Russian agrarian history, Michael Confino gave a talk in the basement of McVickar in the old Russian Institute. When asked at the end why he had ended his studies of the peasantry and peasant agriculture with 1861 and changed topics, he replied that after 1861 the whole question became too complicated. Subsequently, I have come to understand what he meant, and I have frequently felt that both the complexities and the huge volume of available information were getting the better of me. If I have been able to add to our understanding of this period in any way, it is due to all those who have helped me climb out of the morass. I alone, however, must bear responsibility for the flaws that remain.

A *khutor* is only a tiny piece of land,
But it is mine forever,
Confidently, I plow the soil,
Confidently, I plant a small garden.
Without any fear of repartitions,
I cover all my land with manure.
I collect my belongings,
I fence all around.
Confidently, I clear away
What has become overgrown with my neighbor's weeds,
Confidently, I pick up stones,
Not sparing any effort.

—Pskov peasant, July 1917

INTRODUCTION

History leaves no traces. It only leaves consequences which have nothing in common with the circumstances which gave rise to them.

—Alexander Zinoviev, 1980

The peasantry is the true autocrat of Russia.

—Victor Chernov

Interpretations of the Stolypin Agrarian Reforms of 1906 have tended to reflect the political debates that surrounded their adoption. As a consequence, the Reforms have usually been seen as an ad hoc and primarily political response to the agrarian disorders and the widespread peasant demands for land that accompanied the Revolution of 1905.[1] Other interpretations have emphasized the underlying economic necessity of rationalizing or modernizing peasant agriculture.[2] Paradoxically, left- and right-wing critics of the Reforms, as well as Soviet historians, have generally adopted the "political" interpretation, whereas liberals, both Western and Russian, have often supported the economic and historically deterministic one. Recently, however, scholarly opinion seems to have converged on the political interpretation. Thus N. Riasanovsky, the author of the most popular American textbook on Russian history, asserts that the Stolypin Reforms "aimed at a break-up of the peasant commune and the establishment of a class of strong, independent, individual farmers—Stolypin's so-called wager on the strong and the sober."[3]

True, enactment of these Reforms was probably the most important *political* step taken by the tsarist government between 1861 and its demise in 1917. They were part of a comprehensive reform program designed to save the monarchy; to preserve, perhaps even to strengthen and consolidate, the social, economic, and political preeminence of the landowning nobility; and to transform the peasantry into a bulwark of the state.[4] As one group of land reformers noted in an early report, one of the "red threads" guiding the government's activity after 1906 was that "a transfer of noble land to the peasants on the same principles as those followed in 1861 would be tantamount to the destruction of the state."[5] In this context, the Reforms represented the final product of a long struggle by the tsarist government to avoid granting the peasantry an "additional" allotment of land and to develop a class of peasant farmers who would uphold the "sacred" institution of private property. More recently, the Reforms have been seen as but the latest manifestation of the tsarist government's long-standing efforts to impose "order" or "law" on the population, in this case by redefining rural property rights according to the legal and cultural concepts of educated, capital-city society.[6]

While acknowledging the very real merits of each of these approaches, my study seeks to broaden and deepen understanding of the Reforms by placing them in their joint political, economic, and sociolegal contexts. In this way, I hope to demonstrate that the Reforms had in fact been prepared gradually, during the half-century prior to the Revolution of 1905, in large part in response to a new awareness of Russia's economic backwardness and the necessity of stimulating the country's economic growth and development. Moreover, as I will argue, the Reforms were essentially ready for adoption before the outbreak of the 1905 revolution and before the entrance of Stolypin (after whom they were named) into the government.

At the beginning of the twentieth century, and despite the contemporary obsession with industrial development, agriculture still constituted the single largest sector of the Russian economy, producing approximately one-half of the national income and employing two-thirds to three-quarters of the population. Moreover, although Russia was edging slowly into the modern world, it was becoming increasingly clear that her agriculture could not yield the surplus needed to support an expanding industrial population or provide the raw materials for export in exchange for manufactured goods from abroad. As one observer noted in 1900, Russian agriculture was among the least productive in the entire civilized world: "the . . . conditions in which the . . . peasants are placed are such that, even having the most land per capita of almost any state in the world, it yields . . . the smallest quantity of grain, and that by a huge margin."[7] Indeed, the low level of productivity was undermining Russia's economic and fiscal stability and thus the military establishment that lay at the basis of her claim to great power status.[8]

"The land in Russia runs in long strips," wrote the Russian-born American journalist Maurice Hindus. "In the case of the peasant each strip is very narrow, anywhere between two and ten yards in width, and since [they] . . . are distributed over . . . as many sections as there are types of soil, the peasant had to lug all his tools from one field to another, and journey back and forth . . . whenever this or that crop demanded his attention. The strips are also separated from one another by dead furrows or ridges, which in the aggregate make up thousands of *dessyatins* of fertile soil that raise nothing but weeds, which spread freely to nearby fields, contaminate and often ruin crops."[9] Another American visitor, William English Walling, describes the view from the train window of the "fallow fields [that] indicate . . . the ancient three-field system." The peasants, he reports, could not afford crop rotation, and they lacked farm animals to utilize the crops and fertilize the fields. He likens the crude tools to those used by American pioneer farmers a century before; even the so-called new plow was "two or three generations behind the times."[10]

Indeed, the tsarist administration was in the unfortunate position of many third-world countries today of having simultaneously to face the four revolutions—demographic, agricultural, industrial, and political—that in the case of Europe's transition to the modern era had been spaced out over a century or longer.[11] In the agricultural sphere, this dilemma was reflected in the simultaneous demands for "land" reform, or extensification and "agrarian" reform, or intensification.[12] However, land reform, which was supported by both peasants and the political opposition, although resolving the political and social problem, left the underlying dilemma of productivity unsolved. Agrarian reform, on the other hand, would resolve the economic problem, but only in the long term. Of course, this dilemma, like many others facing the government in these years, is similar to that of other societies in the process of transition from feudalism to capitalism. As Marxists and economic liberals were to note at the end of the century, the problem was not so much the "development of capitalism" as its insufficient development. Meanwhile, for the peasants, of course, the issue was the transition from the "moral economy" of the premarket society to the "rational" economy of the market society.[13]

In its quest to balance the demand for economic growth with the equally imperative demand for political stability, Russia's rulers had traditionally adopted a short-term approach that was primarily extractive and fiscal in nature.[14] Beginning in the eighteenth century, they had made various attempts to intervene directly in the economic life of specific social groups in order to encourage changes that would increase their long-term taxpaying capacities. However, before 1861, Russia's privately owned serfs had been abandoned to the care of their noble owners and thus had been largely excluded from this kind of government-sponsored intervention. The government even avoided intervening in the economic life of the state peasantry,[15] even though they represented approximately half of the entire peasant population.

In the aftermath of the Emancipation, however, it became clear that the economic problems of rural Russia were directly related to larger political and social questions. In the 1860s, a number of bureaucrats began to move beyond the narrowly fiscal and extractive approach of their predecessors and to focus on the problem of economic development

and its relationship to political power. Placing agriculture and the peasantry at the center of concern, the government began to develop an agrarian policy that sought to reconcile the apparently "universal" laws of
economic development, based on individualistic and capitalist principles, with its conservative political values and its commitment to the
preservation of a patriarchal and autocratic social and political structure.[16] Thus, as we shall see, rather than simply copying one or another
Western model—whether Lenin's "American" or "Prussian" models or
any others[17]—the government tried to follow a unique and specifically
Russian course.[18]

The government's newfound concern for agriculture is often seen as
the product of a noble reaction. In fact, this course actually brought the
government into conflict with the majority of the nobility, for the agrarian program that was ultimately adopted was based on the assumption
that peasant agriculture would eventually replace that of the nobility.[19]
Even in the short run the reforms were widely perceived as harmful to
the economic interests of the traditional nobility. Thus, although it is
true that this new generation of reforming bureaucrats were a part of
tsarism's "counter-revolutionary convention,"[20] its members must also
be seen as "conservative renovators"[21] or "managerial modernizers."[22]
Indeed, the agrarian reforms finally adopted under Stolypin's name were
necessarily the product of a political compromise between government
and society that reflected the social conditions and political possibilities
of the period.[23]

Despite their tremendous economic and political significance, there
was in fact nothing particularly innovative about the Reforms' proposals
for the individualization and intensification of peasant agriculture. Similar ideas had been around since at least the middle of the eighteenth
century.[24] What needs explaining is why such a program of agricultural
rationalization was finally adopted during the second half of 1906. Expla-
nations for the tsarist government's apparent inability to enact reforms
necessary to its own survival take their cue from its repeated but ineffectual attempts to confront the problem of serfdom.[25] Thus, it has usually
been argued, the failure of such initiatives as well as the long delays that
eventuated between the identification of a problem and the adoption of
legislation were the result of bureaucratic inertia and inadequacy, the
arbitrariness and irrationality of the bureaucratic apparatus, and the political "influence" or "intrigues" of the tsar's advisers. Recent work in
the institutional and social history of the Russian bureaucracy has generally served to confirm this interpretation.[26]

The Stolypin Agrarian Reforms, like the Great Reforms of the 1860s,
were, however, a partial exception to this general picture.[27] Why were
they finally adopted? Why were they the only portion of Stolypin's larger
reform program to see the legislative light of day? To answer these questions, we must look at the bureaucracy not only as the executive instru-

ment of government but as an arena for the articulation and resolution of political and social conflicts. Thus, while acknowledging the economic and especially political influences on the Reforms' conception and ultimate adoption, this study will also emphasize the evolution of the ideas and concerns of the bureaucrats themselves and the ideological and cultural forces that shaped them.

In the final half-century of tsarist rule, the bureaucracy was influenced by two contradictory conceptions of government.[28] The first was the idea, developed in central and northern Europe, of the well-ordered police state (*polizeistaat*). Introduced under Peter the Great, it served to strengthen the traditional, patriarchal conception of autocratic rule; it saw the government's proper task as the regulation of virtually all aspects of social activity with the utopian goal of creating a perfectly ordered society. With the development of cameralist economic ideology in Europe, this new conception called for more than mere regulation and control and acquired a decidedly "interventionist" cast, calling on government directly to stimulate individual and social initiative to promote economic development.

The situation became more complex, however, during the nineteenth century with the expansion of the bureaucracy and the growth of legal education.[29] Under the influence of the German historical school of law, a new concept of government, known as the "rule of law" (*rechtsstaat*), began to develop. In theory, the two concepts were contradictory, the first implying an extension of the autocrat's authority, the second its limitation. In practice—at least for a period—the two notions tended to merge. As a consequence, the "rule of law" came to suggest to Russian officialdom not an autonomous legal system or a constitutional form of government, but simply a government operating through institutions, regular procedures, and laws. In short, what developed in Russia during the nineteenth century was neither a *polizeistaat* nor a *rechtsstaat* in the *original* sense of these terms, but what Marc Raeff has called a *reglamentsstaat*.[30] Moreover, these institutions and procedures were thought to enhance the tsar's authority, to the extent that they prevented individuals from acting as his "personal agents" (on the traditional autocratic model) or from exercising authority on their own initiative. Ultimately, however, these laws and institutions became very real limitations on the tsar's personal exercise of power.

By the second half of the nineteenth century, the underlying contradictions between the two models of government had begun to emerge. The result was considerable political conflict, as some members of the bureaucracy remained loyal to the older principles of the police state and personal rule by the tsar, while others adhered to the newer principles of rule through institutions and laws and even, in some cases, to a genuinely liberal conception of the "rule of law" itself.

The bureaucracy's view of its role was further complicated by conflicting visions of the government's social base and the social nature of its policies. Tsarist ideology had traditionally viewed the autocracy as a supraclass institution reconciling divergent social claims in the national interest. As the bureaucracy became professionalized, however, it expropriated this supraclass ideology, and some bureaucrats began to see themselves as members of a separate and virtually independent bureaucratic *soslovie*.[31] Further, despite their origin within the landowning nobility, individual bureaucrats became increasingly dependent on service as their primary source of income.[32] Accordingly, this bureaucratic ideology often manifested itself in antinoble policies.

The nobility, on the other hand, after its release from compulsory government service in 1762, increasingly tended to adopt the view that Russia was essentially a noble or gentry state in the sense that they saw themselves as its principal basis of social support. In this view, the government's primary task was the defense of noble interests and the preservation of the nobility as a *soslovie*. Nonetheless, it was not until after the loss of its serfs in 1861 that the nobility actively sought to develop a political role for itself in either central government or local administration.[33] At the same time, those segments of educated society who were disillusioned by the government's cautious solution to the peasant problem and the selfishness of the nobility also found their political voice.[34] Unlike the nobility, however, they placed the interests of the whole people or the nation ahead of those of any particular social or political group—a view that was in many ways a mirror image of the bureaucracy's supraclass vision of government and, indeed, derived from the same traditions of noble service.[35]

The bureaucracy, then, was influenced from within and without by conflicting ideas about the nature and role of government and its relationship to the various social and legal "estates." What is remarkable is that, despite the government's fragmentation by conflicting political ideologies, the Stolypin Reforms were ever adopted at all. That they were was in part a result of the bureaucracy's efforts to transcend the interests of particular social classes and to develop a genuinely supraclass program of national economic development. Indeed, as we shall see, the struggle between different bureaucratic factions was less over the actual course of Russia's agricultural development—a subject on which there was a surprising degree of consensus—than the bureaucracy's role in the reform and the degree to which the government should intervene in the economic life of the peasantry.

At the time of the Emancipation, the government's relationship to the peasantry continued to be predominantly noninterventionist in nature. Thus, although the bureaucracy initiated emancipation, its subsequent role in peasant social and economic life was conceived in terms of an essentially passive, protective, and paternalistic form of guardianship, or *opeka*.[36] However, no sooner had emancipation been promulgated than efforts to involve the bureaucracy directly in that life began. Paradoxically, the government was also beginning to view economic progress as an essential prerequisite to the preservation of social and political stability. As a result, its traditional policy of bureaucratic *opeka* acquired an increasingly interventionist cast. Implicitly, if not explicitly, the bureaucracy began to assume responsibility for the peasantry's entire way of life, including even its standard of living.[37] In its fully developed form, *opeka* in fact resembled a form of welfare statism or even state socialism. Indeed, *opeka* can provide a metaphor to describe the totality of tsarism's social policy during its final decades and to explain its seemingly obsessive drive to control all forms of spontaneous public activity.[38] The bureaucracy, meanwhile, saw this expanded conception of *opeka* as the essence of its service obligation, whether understood as a "duty" to state or society.

A final factor influencing bureaucratic attitudes toward reform was that central institution of Russian rural life—the peasant commune. The commune had become a subject of debate after the appearance of Baron von Haxthausen's famous book, *Studies on the Interior of Russia*, in the late 1840s.[39] Subsequently, it became the focus of almost all discussions of the agrarian question.[40] Paradoxically, both populists and Slavophiles supported the commune's preservation, the former because it appeared to be a link to the future, socialist society, the latter because it was an expression of the peasantry's innate "Russianness." Only the "conservative liberals"[41] and, later, the Marxists among Russia's Westerners favored its abolition.[42]

In the postemancipation era, the commune was responsible for a complex variety of tasks. It kept public order and arbitrated petty disputes, collected taxes according to the principle of mutual responsibility, and made the initial apportionment of land among its tax units or families. It also set the agricultural calendar, controlled agricultural practices, and preserved local customs. In most of Russia, it was, finally, the legal owner of its members' land and in some cases conducted periodical redistributions of land by means of partial and full repartitions. From the peasants' perspective, however, the commune's primary function seems to have been to resolve conflicts among its members and between them and nonpeasant society. For the government, on the other hand, the commune was symbolized by the periodical repartition and by its role in the *soslovie* system of administration; its primary function was as an instrument for preserving social and economic equality among its members, collecting taxes, and maintaining order. In the minds of government bureaucrats, the commune thus replaced serfdom as one of the two pillars of the Russian state—the other, of course, being the autocracy itself. At the same time, and in conjunction with the generally "historicist" cast of mind shared by almost all members of Russian educated society, the commune took on a mythical, almost sacred, significance that rendered it virtually impervious to change and repeatedly frustrated the efforts of those who sought to introduce rural or agrarian reforms.

Although the commune must therefore be at the center of our attention, that institution was in many ways a myth. Indeed, by the turn of the century, the government became less concerned with the question of preserving or abolishing the commune as an institution—though such debates were indeed part of the story—than with the broader social and political issue of abolishing the *soslovie* system, which served to isolate the peasantry and protect the nobility, and integrating the peasantry into the larger society on the basis of equality. Simultaneously, the government sought to stimulate the peasantry into conducting a more productive agriculture.[43] However, as we shall see, given the peasants' traditional hostility toward the outside world, the government's primary task in fact became that of winning their trust.[44] Paradoxically, in order to achieve this end, it would inevitably be forced to take into account the peasants' own attitudes and concerns and their understanding of "law." Thus, even as the government strove to prevent the granting of an "additional allotment" from the lands of the nobility by encouraging the peasantry to adopt more individualistic forms of property ownership and use,[45] its social policy, as embodied in the concept of *opeka*, came increasingly to reflect the commune's egalitarian and collectivist features, as educated society perceived them. In the last analysis, the government's own policies seem to have reinforced the peasantry's egalitarian dream of a final or "black" repartition that would redistribute all land equally among them—and may even have inspired it.

Under the influence of these varying pressures, political, economic, and cultural or ideological, government agrarian policy underwent two major overturns between the Emancipation and the Revolution of 1917, each responding to a major political crisis and each bringing a change in attitudes toward the nature of the government's role and the commune. Both were preceded by a long period of intrabureaucratic conflict over policy alternatives. The first culminated in the wake of Alexander II's assassination in 1881, when the government finally abandoned its so-called official liberalism and laissez-faire policies and both strengthened the commune and adopted a more interventionist approach toward the peasantry—a policy described by one observer as "official populism."[46] Nonetheless, this shift marked a critical first step on the path to that "perceptual revolution" that took place during the years immediately preceding the 1905 revolution and that finally led the government to abandon its reliance on the commune as the defender of social and political stability and to adopt the Stolypin Agrarian Reforms.[47] Thus began a new period that has been dubbed one of "official pseudo-Marxism."[48]

GOVERNMENT AND PEASANT
IN RUSSIA, 1861–1906

PART ONE
Background

It cannot be denied that the [Russian peasant]
commune offers immense advantages for the
inner social condition of the country. [It]
present[s] an organic unity and a compact social order not to be found anywhere else. Ow-
ing to the communes, there is no proletariat
in Russia today. As long as the institution of
the commune exists, a proletariat cannot
emerge. . . . On the other hand, one must also
admit that the basic principle of the commune, namely, the equal division of the land,
is not conducive to agricultural progress.
                    —August von Haxthausen, 1847

1

EMANCIPATION AND ITS
AFTERMATH, 1861–1900

The commune is a living principle among our peasantry. . . . We have to recognize its existence, its salutary and powerful influence on the peasant. . . . [Its abolition would] give rise to true chaos. . . . If we did not have such a communal system as now exists, we would have to create it; . . . With communal emancipation, the land will remain common property; consequently, there will be no difficulties with the organization of arable, pasture and other lands. [Moreover], as the population grows, the land will be repartitioned, and again all workers will receive land, and landlessness will . . . remain within its present limits. Such an order is not a utopian invention; it already exists on many well-organized noble estates.

—A. I. Koshelev, 1858

While liberating the peasants from bondage to their noble serfowners, it is impossible to create for them a new bondage to the commune; [rather] the development of a farmer economy should be evoked and encouraged among those small-scale peasant property owners who will be created by the new statute.

—N. A. Miliutin, 1860

The Emancipation Settlement

Any discussion of modern Russian history must begin with the emancipation of the serfs in 1861.[1] This is doubly important for the study of the Stolypin Reforms since, as has often been noted, these Reforms were both a return to the traditions of the Peasant Reform of 1861 and a final realization of the Emancipators' intentions.[2] Indeed, the bureaucrats who drafted the Stolypin Reforms repeatedly sought to establish the fidelity of their program to these traditions, although as we shall see, they were also motivated to solve some of the problems the Emancipation helped create.[3] From this perspective, the Emancipation's greatest significance lies not so much in its attempt to grant freedom to the peasantry, nor in its stimulus to overt political activity within the nobility, nor even in the institutional structure it imposed on the Russian countryside. Rather, it lies in the precedent that it set as an act of decisive government intervention in the social and economic affairs of the two most significant estates of the realm as it sought to resolve the serf or peasant problem in what it perceived as the national or supraclass interest.

Serious legislative work on emancipation was begun in March 1859 by a special Editing Commission created for the purpose by Alexander II. Despite the importance of its chairman, General Ia. I. Rostovtsev, as the executive agent of the tsar's will, the Emancipation's shape was largely determined by the work of a group of some sixteen "enlightened bureaucrats" within the Commission, led by N. A. Miliutin, who were united by their commitment to both the abolition of serfdom and the political, economic, and cultural progress of Russia.[4] They have also been described as "conservative liberals" in the sense that they sought to preserve the existing social and political order while supporting the development of an economically "liberal" individualism.[5]

The problem that had always faced the government when it contemplated emancipation was how to achieve the transformation of a private, customary, and unenforceable relationship between the peasantry and the nobility into a public, contractual, and enforceable one without provoking either a peasant uprising or a noble reaction or revolt. In the case of the peasantry, the government had long concluded that in addition to their freedom, the peasants would have to be granted land.[6] However, although the government considered it both necessary and possible to deprive the nobles of their labor force, expropriation of all their land in favor of the peasantry was inconceivable, not only politically but economically, since it was assumed that noble agriculture would remain a fundamental component of the Russian economy for the foreseeable future. On the other hand, even a partial expropriation would be impossible without some form of compensation. In order to resolve these complexities, it had also been decided that emancipation would have to be a gradual and evolutionary process, in which the government played the role of mediator.[7]

As a result of these preliminary decisions, when the Editing Commission met, its attention focused not on the peasants' ultimate acquisition of freedom but on the immediate and practical task of ameliorating their way of life during the transition period and preparing them for their eventual entry into the ranks of "peasant proprietors."[8] Two concerns, in particular, dominated the Commission's discussions: first, the land question and the regulation of the peasants' economic relationship with their former owners; second, the structure of rural administration and the government's role in it.

Insofar as the land question was concerned, one of the first problems the emancipators had to face was finding a way to legitimize the impending transfer of land from the nobility to the peasantry.[9] The nobles, of course, maintained that they owned their land on the basis of an absolute and inviolable private right and that there was no legal basis on which it could be taken from them.[10] Indeed, public recognition of this right had been one reason for so much autocratic wavering over the issue of emancipation. However, the noble interpretation of Russia's property laws came into direct conflict with the peasants' implicit labor theory of property, succinctly summarized in their oft-cited claim that although "we are yours, the land is ours."[11]

In attempting to reconcile these opposing conceptions of property rights, the Editing Commission took as its starting point what was referred to as "existing fact" and froze existing patterns of land distribution.[12] This meant that from that point on, the quantity of land allotted directly to the peasants for their support and subsistence could not be changed. To legitimize this action, it reverted to patrimonial theory, claiming that since the nobles' property rights originated in their service obligation to the tsar, the tsar continued to hold a kind of eminent domain or superordinate right over their land. In effect, this was the peasants' view as well. In any event, according to this theory, there were two kinds of property rights in Russia: first, an absolute or "full" right of property, which included an unlimited right of disposition. The noble's demesne, which the peasants cultivated for the nobility, fell into this category. Second, there was a conditional or limited form of property right, which restricted the owner's right of disposition and vested ultimate control in the state. This category applied to land that the peasantry cultivated on their own account.[13]

In theory, this was a judicious solution to a difficult social and political problem. Moreover, it provided a reasonably clear basis for the subsequent development of private-property rights in the Russian countryside as well as for the development of a private-property consciousness among the peasantry. However, as we shall see, the distinction between noble and peasant lands was never transformed into practice so that after emancipation, as before, the lands of any given village remained intermingled and interstripped with those of their former owners.[14] This, in conjunction with the fact that the peasants continued to work both their own and the nobles' lands, seems to have reinforced the peasants' belief that all the land they worked was their property and prevented the development of a private-property consciousness. On the other hand, the entire patrimonial fiction that was the basis of the distinction between noble demesne and peasant allotment was itself a violation of noble property rights. Thus, of course, the nobility feared that the government's solution might serve as a precedent for further breaches of these rights in the future, for example, if the population increased and the peasants needed more land.

Having established a legal framework for the subsequent division of land, the Commission decreed that, after the grant of personal freedom, the peasants would continue fulfilling their customary obligations to their former owners for a period of two years. During this time, the two parties were to reach voluntary agreements concerning the specific quantity and location of the land to be allotted to the peasants and the level of fiscal and labor dues owed in return. Beyond this, the peasants were required to cultivate the land given to them, known as their "allotment" (nadel), for either an additional seven years or until the commencement of the third, or redemption, stage of the process, whichever came first. By this measure, the Commission hoped to guarantee the nobles a constant supply of cheap local labor and the peasants a secure means of livelihood.[15]

During the third stage of the emancipation process, peasants were permitted to acquire legal title to their allotments. However, since they did not have the requisite funds, the government took upon itself the task of compensating the nobility and collecting both the sum loaned and the interest from the peasants. Similarly, because of Russia's precarious financial position after the defeat in the Crimea, the Commission had to see to it that the fiscal burden would not fall on the treasury all at once. In consequence, the initiation of this stage was left up to each individual noble, with or without the agreement of his former serfs. By granting the nobility this semblance of discretion, the Commission hoped to win their trust and persuade them of the advantages of redemption, which, in theory, at least, would make available a lump sum that could be used to convert their estates into capitalist, or free-market, enterprises, utilizing freely hired wage labor.[16] Meanwhile, the peasants were granted their allotments only in "permanent" use in order to encourage them to seek full ownership.[17]

With these provisions, the Emancipation laid the legal and economic basis for the peasantry's new status as "free rural inhabitants."[18] However, the peasants were not granted full legal equality with the other members of society. Rather, the peasantry was organized as an independent *soslovie*, with its own system of laws on the same basis as other *sosloviia*. This should not be surprising since a grant of full equality would have meant the abolition of the nobility's special rights and prerogatives and the establishment of a single national legal structure. On the other hand, the Commission saw the peasantry's legal isolation as but a temporary stage on the way to their eventual integration into an all-class society.[19]

Emancipation also required the abolition of the nobility's personal and arbitrary police powers over the peasantry.[20] Under serfdom, these powers had been exercised by the serf owner as a patrimonial privilege and more recently (at least in the government's view) as surrogate for a state apparatus. In devising a substitute, the Editing Commission initially intended to create an entirely new, all-class system of administration. In large measure because of noble objections both to any diminution of their status and to the power the preliminary drafts gave to the central bureaucracy, this project was soon abandoned. A compromise solution, adopted in 1864, provided for the establishment of a series of elective, all-class institutions of self-government at the provincial and county level known as zemstvos.[21] In retrospect, despite this setback, it seems that separating the task of administrative reform from the economic and legal issues may well have been a prerequisite for emancipation's adoption.[22] Indeed, as we shall see, several subsequent attempts at rural reform would be defeated precisely because of their association with projects of local administrative reform and the accompanying abolition of the *soslovie* system that they entailed. On the other hand, the adoption of the Stolypin Agrarian Reforms became easier when they too were separated from associated reforms of local administration.

In the absence of any administrative organization to take over the nobility's local responsibilities, the Commission once again began with "existing fact," guided by the lessons learned from some twenty years' experience administering the state peasantry.[23] First, it placed immediate responsibility for the maintenance of order and the collection of taxes within the peasant community on the peasant commune and its elected officials—a step that effectively transformed the commune into the lowest unit in the bureaucratic apparatus.[24] The Commission also created a new, exclusively peasant, administrative institution at the canton level to oversee several communes and a separate peasant court to handle minor civil disputes among the peasantry on the basis of local custom.[25]

Second, the Editing Commission created a new official, the peace arbitrator, who was charged with exercising the nobles' former responsibilities of moral guardianship and supervision.[26] This step was considered necessary in part because the Commission feared that without some external compulsion the peasants would refuse to pay their taxes and dues or work on their former owners' estates. In part, too, they felt that peasants were not yet ready to be left to their own devices, subject to the free play of market forces. Besides being charged with overseeing the Emancipation, these "guardian angels," as Rostovtsev had called them, acquired considerable authority to intervene in peasant affairs at the communal and cantonal levels.[27] Nonetheless, their powers were subject to some important limitations. In accordance with the newly adopted principle of the separation of powers, they were not permitted to exercise any strictly judicial authority. Equally important, they had no authority to intervene in the specifically economic or agrotechnical aspects of peasant life. The Commission wanted to avoid interfering in an area long regulated by custom.[28] This policy also reflected the government's traditionally fiscal or extractive approach to the peasants as a special kind of natural resource. By limiting its contacts with them to the administrative level, the government effectively treated them as a source of revenue rather than as economically productive individuals. As long as they were able to fulfill their fiscal responsibilities, it would be content to ignore the specifically economic arrangements that underlay their taxpaying capacities. Thus did the government continue its long tradition of nonintervention in the economic affairs of the peasantry. Nonetheless, the establishment of the peace arbitrators marked an important step in the bureaucracy's "invasion" of the countryside and its eventual assumption of a direct responsibility for the well-being of its rural inhabitants.[29]

While the Editing Commission devoted most of its attention to the problems of guiding the peasantry through the transition period between serfdom and freedom, discussion of the commune's different functions inevitably raised questions about its fate and the future development of peasant agriculture.[30] Here, almost all of the Commission's members assumed that economic productivity would be best served by a gradual replacement of communal agricultural and land-use practices, including the open-field strip system of compulsory crop rotation, by more individualistic and intensive forms of cultivation conducted on consolidated or integral holdings. Indeed, the entire redemption operation had an individualistic bias since it assumed a direct correlation between the size of the redemption payments and the quantity of land held.[31] However, the Commission's concern with fostering the growth of individual initiative and better work habits was subordinated to its larger concern with protecting the state's fiscal interests.

Thus, as part of its effort to strengthen the commune's authority and enhance its effectiveness as an administrative institution, the Commission gave legal sanction to two customary practices that were otherwise considered to be destructive of peasant initiative and sound agricultural practices: periodical repartitions of arable land, which were designed to equalize the taxpaying abilities of individual households as well as to enable communes to absorb future population growth from within and prevent the development of a rural proletariat; and mutual responsibility, which held the commune as a whole liable for the fulfillment of each member's fiscal and social obligations to the state. At the same time, in order to protect the peasantry as a whole and prevent both the encroachment of the peasants' former owners and the development of landlessness, it sanctioned existing forms of family and communal ownership of land wherever they existed rather than vesting such rights in the head of the household.[32] However, in keeping with the principle of nonintervention in the peasants' economic life, the Commission did not define these rights or regulate their execution beyond requiring a two-thirds majority for the approval of repartitions. In its view, local custom ought to regulate such matters.[33] Meanwhile, since some of the Commission's members regarded the peasants' allotment land as a special and inviolable land fund that had to be preserved for the benefit of the entire peasant *soslovie*, they placed limitations on the peasants' rights of disposal. As a consequence, any peasants who sought to claim title to and consolidate their holdings prior to the liquidation of the redemption debt had to obtain the commune's approval. Also restricted were the rights of whole villages to transfer to individual forms of landownership and use during the redemption period.[34]

Needless to say, discussion of these issues provoked some of the liveliest debates within the Editing Commission. Some members argued that simply by sanctioning these practices, the government was violating peasant custom and overregulating the peasant; they wanted to let the commune develop spontaneously in response to practical experience. Moreover, they argued, any regulations inevitably favored rich peasants who would be able to buy up land within the commune and then separate with it, thus depriving the rest of their fair share. Others, however, wanted to grant individual peasants an unlimited right to separate from the commune precisely because it would enable the prosperous peasant to escape from its slavery and conduct agriculture on a more progressive and profitable basis.[35]

In the end the Commission decided to permit the more innovative and "work-loving" peasant, who succeeded in liquidating his share of the redemption debt ahead of time, to claim title to his scattered strips and to consolidate them into a single compact parcel at any time. This right was embodied in the Redemption Statute's famous Article 165.[36] The Commission's hope was that such peasants would serve as a model for those who remained within the commune and encourage them to transfer to individualized forms of land-use in the future on the assumption that such forms would readily demonstrate their economic superiority to communal ones. However, they refused to sanction any government intervention that might influence the historical outcome of this competition.[37] This was indeed a period of "official liberalism."

From "Official Liberalism" to "Official Populism"

Despite the Editing Commission's essentially pragmatic approach and despite its attempt to impose a settlement that would satisfy the interests of all parties involved, it is not especially surprising to discover that their solution won few real supporters. For the peasants, emancipation was an anticlimax. They had been granted their personal freedom, together with such specific legal rights as the right to marry, conclude civil contracts, own land, and bring suit; but their relationship to their former owners continued much as before. As a consequence, large numbers of disillusioned peasants refused in the first two years to fulfill obligations to their former owners and engaged in other forms of disorder.[38]

The emancipation settlement also provoked conflict within the government. For even though the initial vision had been cast within an ideology of laissez-faire liberalism that seemingly abandoned the economic life of both peasant and noble to the fate of history and the "invisible hand" of the market, it soon became clear that such a policy was impractical. The very notion that there existed a state or supraclass interest, in conjunction with the interventionist precedent set by the Emancipation itself, made it impossible to abandon the peasantry to the individualistic pursuit of its own interests. Thus, although the Emancipation established institutional and juridical structures designed only for the peasantry's temporary protection during the transition from serfdom to freedom, their existence immediately became the focus of a political struggle within the bureaucracy. On one side were those who sought to preserve these structures and the entire emancipation settlement unchanged in order to inhibit the pace of social and economic change; on the other were those whose aim was to revise the settlement with a goal to encouraging the process of change and increasing agricultural productivity.[39] At the same time this struggle became intertwined with the emerging political conflict between the government and educated society and particularly the conservative nobility, which now attempted to recoup some of its losses.[40]

Operating at first in isolation on the local level, those nobles who were opposed to emancipation pursued a kind of guerrilla warfare against both government and peasantry and sought to exploit the negotiating process and revise the terms of the settlement in their own favor.[41] Later this opposition took a more political form as a small number of capital-city dignitaries sought to establish a form of oligarchic or aristocratic constitution that would draw local noble activists into the legislative process, at least on an advisory basis.[42] Despite their close personal and social ties to both tsar and bureaucracy, these Anglophile *frondeurs* did not succeed either in winning the tsar's support or in imposing their aristocratic program on the government. However, these efforts to defend and even expand noble influence did have an impact on bureaucratic attitudes toward the peasantry. As a consequence, some bureaucrats became avid supporters of increased government intervention that was designed to encourage the development of economic individualism. Meanwhile, those most closely associated with drafting the Emancipation Statutes switched positions, trying to preserve the commune as a defense against both noble revanchism and market influences, opposing any further government intervention.

The key figure in these changes was P. A. Valuev, one of the more interesting and important government figures in the second half of the nineteenth century. After the dismissal of the Reform's chief architects, including most notably N. A. Miliutin, Valuev was appointed interior minister in April 1861, an event that has usually been viewed as a virtual coup d'etat by the noble opposition.[43] Yet despite his reputation as a *frondeur*, Valuev, like the "enlightened bureaucrats" whom he replaced, was himself a conservative liberal. Like them, he was both committed to Russia's economic progress and development and resolutely opposed to all those who would relinquish the bureaucracy's legislative initiative or dilute the autocrat's authority. On the contrary, Valuev argued, it was "more important than ever for the government . . . to stand at the head of the social movement which is responsible for three-quarters of history."[44]

Although the maintenance of public order, particularly in the countryside, was one of his primary responsibilities as interior minister, Valuev did not see his task as merely a police matter; he viewed it in the broader sense of establishing, if not a well-ordered police state (*polizeistaat*), then a *reglamentsstaat*, that is, a unified and efficient system of laws and administration that could weld a diverse and fragmented Russian society into a single national and social community. Indeed, Valuev's concern for the integration of the various social and ethnic groups into one legal system and the development of social unity has a distinctly modern ring to it, even though its ultimate purpose was to strengthen the existing political order.

To achieve this goal, Valuev began in 1863 to submit a number of proposals to the tsar calling for representatives from educated, primarily noble society to participate as advisers in the legislative process.[45] As he saw it, government's problem was its isolation from society precisely at a time when government was more dependent than ever on the people. Consequently, while retaining its legislative initiative, the government had to reach beyond the bureaucratic *soslovie* and create a social constituency for itself, not only among the nobility but eventually even among the peasantry. At the same time, the government urgently needed to improve the quality of its information about the countryside.[46] In the short run, therefore, Valuev sought to draw the local landowning nobility into a consultative role in government in order to use their knowledge and expertise to improve the efficiency and effectiveness of the central government. He was not moved primarily by any commitment to constitutional principles, aristocratic or otherwise.

Valuev was not unconcerned about the gentry's fate. But his view of them was that, as the most educated and prosperous members of local society (and not as the members of a privileged legal estate), the local landowning nobility had a critical role to play as models for the newly emancipated peasantry. Moreover, because of their role as intermediaries between government and peasant, they were also a force for social integration. Any claims they had on the government in the future, he felt, would depend not on their social status but on their transformation into managers of productive capitalist enterprises.

Focusing on the peasantry, Valuev rejected the Editing Commission's notion that peasant custom was a sufficient force to preserve order. On the contrary, he argued, there was no such thing as peasant custom—only a multiplicity of peasant customs, the result of which was chaos. As proof, he cited the peasantry's low moral state, the widespread role of vodka in peasant community decision making, the complete absence among the peasantry of any understanding of public or state law, and the peasants' total lack of respect either for government authority or the personal and property rights of others.[47] Such a state of affairs threatened the social, political, and economic stability of the entire state. Thus, as early as September 1861, he called for new government intervention that would break down the peasantry's isolation, win their trust, and integrate them into the national community on an equal basis with other segments of the population. As he noted, although "the legislator's word must be the first word in the achievement of great reforms, it cannot be his last."[48] Two matters particularly concerned him: the nature of local administration and what Valuev's associate, P. A. Shuvalov, referred to as the "barbaric question of the commune."[49] In order to resolve them, Valuev conducted two campaigns: one designed to increase government authority in the countryside by subordinating the peace arbitrator to the central government and eventually by creating an all-class system of administration; the other, to raise agricultural productivity by encouraging the gradual dissolution of the peasant commune and the development of individualistic forms of ownership and use.

Despite every effort over the next seven years, Valuev did not succeed on either count. In large measure, this was due to the opposition of the extrabureaucratic Main Committee on the Organization of the Peasant Estate. This committee, which included Miliutin among its members and which was chaired by the tsar's brother, Grand Duke Konstantin, had been created to supervise the Emancipation's implementation and to act as its legal interpreter. As such it was the dominant force in determining agricultural policy down to 1881.[50]

Insofar as the peace arbitrators were concerned, the Committee viewed their independence and propeasant orientation as their greatest virtue and the very embodiment of the autocracy's supraclass approach to emancipation. Valuev's proposals, on the other hand, seemed likely to lead to the de facto restoration of noble authority in the countryside. However, the real issue, as both sides were aware, was achieving a proper balance between local initiative and centralized control or, in somewhat different terms, determining how much government intervention in rural life was necessary.[51]

In the end, the peace arbitrators were abolished in 1874 as a result of a compromise between the Grand Duke Konstantin and Valuev's successor as interior minister, A. E. Timashev. As a result, government authority withdrew to the county level, where a new institution, the Board of Peasant Affairs, was established, staffed by representatives drawn from the nobility and the zemstvos. In a concession to the Interior Ministry, it was permitted to appoint a "permanent member" to the board as its representative. However, the Committee of Ministers rejected a proposal that would have allowed the board to intervene in local economic matters.[52]

Valuev's other campaign, to encourage the individualization and intensification of peasant agriculture, was associated with his appointment as minister of state domains and the convocation, in 1872, of the Valuev Commission on the condition of agriculture. Following the model of the English crown commissions with their explicitly political tradition, both Valuev and his sometime-ally Shuvalov sought to use the Commission to exploit the growing public concern with the agrarian question and draw the local nobility into the legislative process.[53] However, as we shall see, Valuev's and Shuvalov's goals were quite different.

Insofar as the peasant commune was concerned, the initial opposition had been primarily theoretical in nature. To be sure, some enthusiastic serf owners had tried to replace open-field strip farming and the three-field system of crop rotation with more advanced methods. However, the attempts were few and far between and the successes fewer still. Certainly there had been no compelling economic need to drive either noble or peasant to change a routine that was sanctioned by tradition and served to mediate the peasants' relationship with their owners.[54]

Some of the same theoretical concerns had arisen at the time of the Emancipation, as we have seen. Yet once again there was no compelling reason for the government to intervene in peasant life in order to promote changes in their agricultural practices. In the aftermath of emancipation, however, opposition to the peasant commune and communal agriculture revived among the gentry, though on new and essentially selfish grounds. In part, this opposition was a consequence of the nobility's own conversion to the virtues of private property as they sought to defend their economic interests and prevent a second edition of the Emancipation and another compulsory expropriation of their land. In part, it arose from a fear that the commune might serve as an organizational basis for antigovernmental coalitions. It also reflected the concern of a small but growing number of economically progressive landowners who desired to cultivate their land on capitalist principles and who feared that the retention of the commune would restrict the supply of agricultural laborers available for hire.

Valuev's concerns, on the other hand, were considerably broader than those of the supporters of noble reaction. With the members of the Editing Commission, he assumed that individualized agriculture provided more incentives to cultivators and was more economically progressive and productive than the existing open-field strip system. He also shared their assumption that Russian agriculture, both noble and peasant, would eventually develop along western European lines. However, he was unwilling simply to allow peasant agriculture to evolve gradually in response to the general historical process, subject only to the moral and educational supervision of the peace arbitrators. Indeed, this kind of passive *opeka* was positively dangerous: as he once wrote, if "all Russia's agriculture were placed under [such] state supervision . . . then we would all starve."[55]

Once again, he urged the government to intervene, in this instance to accelerate the natural processes of economic change and encourage the transfer of the more enterprising peasants, the so-called *miroedy*, to compact plots of arable land that they could cultivate on an individual basis. Specifically, he proposed revising the Redemption Statute's Article 165 and extending the right of peasants to leave their commune, without the commune's approval, to those peasants who had not yet paid off their redemption debt. He also attempted to facilitate the transfer of whole communities to individualized forms of agriculture.[56] In his view, only when the peasantry was forced to submit to the atomizing and civilizing forces of the market would they be able to break out of their isolation and apathy and become supporters of stable and orderly government. However, in contrast to that of later reformers, his approach remained primarily legislative in nature, and both measures were proposed as purely voluntary procedures, which would have sharply limited their impact on peasant agricultural practices had they been adopted.

According to classical economic theory, encouraging the separation of individual peasants from the commune would speed up the process of social and economic differentiation among the peasantry. Valuev had long supported such developments on economic grounds, assuming that the agricultural successes of the enlightened and progressive minority would serve as a salutary model to the others and establish links between them and the rest of society. The mass of the gentry, on the other hand, generally opposed such developments lest these enterprising peasants compete with them for influence in the grain markets and in the countryside. As for the presumably inevitable development of a rural proletariat, Valuev saw such a prospect as a way of overcoming the labor shortage on larger gentry estates.[57]

The Commission, however, went even further and advocated measures limiting both general and partial repartitions of land as well as family partitions. It even proposed abolishing the commune as an administrative institution and establishing local self-government on an all-class basis. Even nobles like Shuvalov supported the latter proposal, seeing all-class government as a means for preserving noble hegemony.[58] However, Valuev also presumably supported it because of his long-standing assumption that the government could exercise better control over isolated or atomized individual peasants than peasants who were organized collectively.[59]

When the Commission's recommendations came before the Committee of Ministers, A. A. Abaza argued that despite the difficulties, the government had to take immediate action to encourage the development of individual peasant property ownership. He was supported by Interior Minister Timashev, who noted that such a policy was "the key to the country's future welfare."[60] In the end, the Commission's program received the support of the entire Committee, save only its chairman, P. N. Ignat'ev, who opposed any changes in the commune's structure on administrative and fiscal grounds. Subsequently, Alexander II approved the Committee's decisions and instructed the ministries to begin drafting appropriate legislation. Yet, despite Alexander's support, Valuev's proposals once again came to naught, in large part, no doubt, as a result of the Main Committee's opposition.[61] Even Miliutin, who once favored the commune's abolition, had now become convinced its preservation was necessary in order to protect the peasantry.[62]

The crux of the disagreement between Valuev and the Main Committee once again concerned the degree of government intervention in the peasants' economic life. In this instance, Valuev had argued, in effect, that time was running out and that the government had to intervene in order to speed up the rate of social and economic—and even political— change and thereby raise the peasants' agricultural productivity. The Main Committee, on the other hand, argued that a too rapid pace of change threatened the preservation of orderly and stable government and that the government had to slow it down. Thus, in contrast to the Editing Commission, which had looked on the Emancipation's various institutional and administrative arrangements as purely temporary measures that would allow for change in response to changing circumstances, the Main Committee came to look on them as if they were permanent. As a consequence, it resisted any attempts to change them, because it still saw these measures as the peasants' best means of defense against their former owners. The Committee's view, which was the very embodiment of the traditional concept of *opeka*, effectively became law in 1876 when the supposedly temporary emancipation legislation of 1861 was incorporated into the ninth volume of the *Digest of Laws* as part of the Statute on the Rural Estate.

Valuev, however, blamed the Commission's defeat not on the Main Committee but on the lack of governmental unity—a condition that Miliutin once described as Russia's de facto constitution[63]—in this case, the division of responsibility for the peasantry between the regular ministries and the extrabureaucratic Main Committee. Such disunity considerably complicated the task of reform not only by enhancing the political significance of bureaucratic rivalries but also by making reform dependent on both overcoming this fragmentation and building a constituency within the larger society.[64]

The Development of an "Agrarian Problem"

In the aftermath of Valuev's campaigns, the government's commitment to a policy of nonintervention in the economic life of the peasantry only increased its dependence on the peasant commune as a guarantor of social and political stability. As A. I. Koshelev noted at the time, the commune had the incomparable advantage of preserving for the peasantry "an inviolable land fund, guaranteeing forever shelter and a piece of bread."[65] However, toward the end of the 1870s, the government came under increasing pressure from both a political crisis at the center and an "agrarian problem" in the countryside. As a result, it had to assume a more active role in the affairs of the countryside. However, this took the paradoxical form of increasing its administrative reliance on the commune while expanding its commitment to individualistic forms of property ownership.

Although the political crisis was important in forcing the government to adopt a new approach, the growing sense of crisis that had enveloped peasant agriculture during these years determined the content of government policy.[66] The first signs of an agrarian problem had already begun to appear at the end of the 1860s. Reported in the press, the subject of both zemstvo petitions and reports from provincial governors, its existence had been trumpeted forth as part of the defense strategy in the 1871 trial of Sergei Nechaev and his revolutionary associates and then as a reason for convoking the Valuev Commission in 1872.[67] By the end of the decade, a number of statistical studies had appeared that seemed to confirm this thesis.[68] At the same time, rumors began to spread that either the tsar would finally give the peasants "real" freedom by granting an "additional allotment" of land or a "black repartition" or serfdom was going to be reinstituted.[69]

According to the government's critics, the key to this agrarian problem was "land-hunger" caused by the rapid growth of the peasant population and an even faster increase in the number of peasant households brought on by the gradual disintegration of the traditional, patriarchal family. The solution: a repeat of 1861 and the granting of an additional allotment.

Government opinion on the state of the countryside was mixed. Thus in 1872, during the convocation of the Valuev Commission to address the growing agrarian crisis, Valuev had claimed that the peasantry's impoverishment was much exaggerated. He even suggested, prophetically as it turned out, that the repeated assertion of such claims in the public press, without any governmental rebuttal, would create a situation in which the public would come to accept the existence of an agrarian problem regardless of the real circumstances.[70] Despite his warning, by the end of the 1870s the government itself seemed to have accepted society's judgment and conceded that there was indeed a problem.

Yet, from the government's perspective, the principal feature of this problem was not so much land-hunger as the rapid growth in peasant tax arrears and the development of a virtual crisis in tax collections. Fiscal concerns had already prompted the Finance Ministry to support Valuev's proposals for rural reform on more than one occasion. During the current political crisis, Finance Minister M. Kh. Reutern followed these precedents and once again called for the complete individualization of peasant landownership and land use with the goal of increasing the peasant's personal sense of responsibility and facilitating the sale of allotment land held by tax delinquents—a proposal subsequently supported by his successors, most notably N. Kh. Bunge, minister from 1881 to 1887. Paradoxically, despite such concerns, the government had actually raised direct taxes during the 1860s and 1870s.[71]

In explaining the origins of this tax-collection crisis, the government rejected the argument based on land-hunger, though it did acknowledge that there were, indeed, some peasants in some regions who suffered from a land shortage. Rather, it pointed to the widespread disparity between the quality (not quantity) of land initially allotted to the peasantry and the tax burden that those allotments were expected to carry. According to Grand Duke Konstantin, this disparity had arisen because the government had desired to recompense the serf owners not only for the land they were losing but also for their share of peasant earnings from nonagricultural sources.[72] Unfortunately, the low level of monetization within the rural economy and the lack of opportunities to earn cash income had seriously inhibited the peasantry's ability to meet their tax and other obligations. Even more important than the government's diagnosis of the problem, however, was that it seemed to have accepted the underlying assumption of both society and peasantry that it was the government's responsibility to resolve the agrarian problem.[73]

The Government Accepts Responsibility

In the face of the growing crisis, both political and agrarian, the government had to abandon the essentially passive approach of the past two decades and adopt a more interventionist agrarian policy. The tone was set by the Interior Ministry's Announcement on 17 June 1879 that declared that not only would there be no additional allotment but any increases in the area of peasant landownership would have to be made through individual purchases of land on the open market.[74] Thus did the government reject the precedent set by the Emancipation and commit itself to the defense of noble landownership and more generally to the principle of individual private property. At the same time, it also rejected the traditions of serfdom, according to which the noble landowner had provided just such an additional allotment when circumstances required.

Although nothing concrete was accomplished prior to the assassination of Alexander II in March 1881, M. T. Loris-Melikov, who was appointed interior minister and head of an extraordinary Supreme Executive Commission in 1880, did propose a series of measures that subsequently served as the agenda for the government of the new tsar, Alexander III. Some of these proposals merely revived those of the Valuev Commission; others, however, pointed in new directions. Among the new suggestions were the mandatory redemption of allotments for those peasants (some 15 percent) who remained in a state of temporary obligation, reduced redemption payments in areas where they remained out of proportion to peasant income, modification or elimination of mutual responsibility, and relaxation of some of the "temporary" restrictions placed on peasant mobility at the time of the Emancipation. In addition, he proposed that the government provide cheap credit for peasants who needed more land and that it ease restrictions on peasant migration from areas suffering from land-hunger.[75]

Loris-Melikov's agrarian program was first discussed by the Main Committee at the end of 1880.[76] Then, in early 1881, Finance Minister Abaza formed a commission to review the redemption operation. By early May, some two months into the new reign, the State Council had approved a number of Loris-Melikov's proposals, including reductions in redemption payments, cancellation of arrears, and a shift to mandatory redemption. In the final discussion of these measures, former Interior Minister Timashev drew attention to the underlying economic problem and called for the abolition of communal land use, which he saw as "an insuperable obstacle to any improvement in the peasants' material welfare."[77] Although Abaza's proposals did not find favor, Alexander III eventually approved the transfer of the remaining peasants to mandatory redemption and a reduction in redemption payments, totaling 20 percent of the yearly amount.[78]

The government did not limit itself to tax concessions, however, but went on to develop a number of Loris-Melikov's other proposals as well.[79] Taken together, these measures established the basic shape of the government's agrarian policy down to the revolution of 1905—and, in certain respects, beyond the revolution as well. However, in conformity to the new tsar's commitment to strengthening both autocratic power and bureaucratic prerogative, responsibility for this work now transferred to the regular bureaucracy. The Main Committee was abolished on 25 May 1882.[80]

The first concrete reform the new government adopted concerned the problem of migration.[81] Recognizing the urgent need to counteract peasant rumors, the Committee of Ministers rushed through a set of Temporary Regulations designed to bring the hitherto illegal and unregulated process of migration under control as well as to make land available in the east for the poorest, most land-hungry, and, potentially, most politically troublesome peasants, particularly the *darstvenniki*, who had received only one-quarter of the standard allotment in their region on their emancipation. The social and economic goals of these regulations, however, conflicted with their political goals. Thus despite the government's desire to alleviate rural overpopulation and land-hunger within European Russia, it also sought to protect landowning nobles from losing their source of cheap labor. Equally important, it was afraid that any steps to provide the peasantry with either free or even relatively inexpensive state land in the east might be interpreted as the equivalent of an additional allotment. The result therefore was a stalemate; for despite relatively liberal provisions for migrants once they arrived in the east, the requirements that had to be fulfilled before departure actually served to inhibit migration. In particular, a peasant family that had received permission to migrate was prohibited from selling its allotment to defray the many costs of resettlement and had to return it to the commune without receiving any compensation.[82] Finally, because of the government's fear of initiating a mass movement of peasants eastward, the regulations had only a restricted circulation.[83]

Subsequently a commission was formed within the Interior Ministry to work out the necessary administrative procedures for migration within European Russia: its chairman, P. P. Semenov (who had been a member of the Editing Commission at the time of the Emancipation), even proposed granting all peasants a right to migrate. However, D. A. Tolstoi's appointment as interior minister in 1882, and the opposition of the governors and a number of influential Slavophiles like D. F. Samarin, effectively foreclosed the possibility of any expansion in the scope of migration. As a result, these highly restrictive Temporary Regulations finally became law on 13 July 1889 virtually unchanged. Not surprisingly, the regulations did not succeed in stemming the flow of illegal migrants.

The other attempt to deal with the problem of the land-hungry peasant involved the establishment on 18 May 1882 of a peasant land bank to provide a source of cheap credit to peasants who wished to purchase additional land.[84] Like migration, this provoked considerable opposition, both at the time of the bank's formation and throughout its operation.[85] Again, as with migration, the political and economic motives behind the law came into conflict. In this case, what was at stake was whether such an institution would actually be able to extend credit to the land-hungry.

According to a minority within the State Council, the demand that the bank operate as an autonomous institution in accordance with standard banking practices would actually prevent it from helping the neediest peasants since only those who were already prosperous enough to make the down payment would be able to purchase land. Worse, such a requirement might actually encourage the development of kulak-speculators who would then resell or let out land acquired through the bank on usurious terms to their less fortunate fellow villagers.

The majority, on the other hand, argued that the government ought not to establish a land bank that served only a particular category of peasant since such a step would be tantamount to the creation of yet another government-sponsored system for the acquisition and redemption of privately owned land. That, however, would contradict the bank's political goal of convincing the peasantry that the government would not grant them an additional allotment, gratis. In contrast, by adopting a policy based on the principle that "only he who works and saves and not he who conducts his life in laziness, idleness and drunkenness" could expect to prosper, the government would help assure that "once he has land of his own, the peasant will respect not only his own property but also that of others, and he will come to protect its possession by every means available and, above all, will be the enemy of any kind of general repartition of land."[86] N. Kh. Bunge, the new finance minister, went even further. A former professor of economics, not a professional bureaucrat, Bunge was an almost fanatical supporter of individualized agriculture based on private property principles.[87] In his view the bank ought to function as a vehicle of land reform and actively "encourage the diffusion of private property among the peasants," both as a legal concept and in practice.[88]

Nonetheless, although many, including Valuev, had assumed that any such credit operation would be entrusted to private or local zemstvo institutions, the political delicacy of the whole land question persuaded the government that it alone had to take charge of the whole business. Only the government, it was argued, could exercise the necessary flexibility in "allowing various preferences and deferments in cases of necessity."[89] Of course, if the strictly private and contractual nature of the bank's relationship with its peasant clients were waived so as to protect the peasantry from the free play of the market, with its threat of foreclosure and an increase in the number of landless peasants, the bank would in effect be transformed into another Redemption Administration and would thus undermine the government's attempt to encourage the development of a private-property consciousness within the peasantry.

Not surprisingly, the bank did not fulfill all the expectations of its creators, though it did realize some of the fears of its critics. Thus, although it succeeded in making additional land available to the peasantry, the majority of its loans to individuals favored the better-off rather than the land-hungry. Nor did it take a tolerant attitude toward delinquents. On the other hand, most of its activity favored sales to peasant communities and associations. They were considered better risks than individual peasants since their debts were secured by the system of mutual responsibility. This was not such a contradiction as it might appear, however; for despite the very vocal support for individualistic forms of peasant land use, others within the government believed that peasant communes were *potentially* more economically productive than individual peasant holdings.[90] In part this was because they were presumed to share some of the benefits of large-scale agriculture, which, as most people at the time agreed, *pace* Marx, was the direction of agricultural evolution the world over. In part, however, it was also a reflection of contemporary populist claims that it was more effective to introduce technological changes in peasant agriculture on a communitywide than on an individual basis.

Finally, the government took up once again the question of local administrative reform. According to the evidence collected by the senatorial investigations of 1880 and 1881 as well as an 1880 survey of local government and zemstvo opinion initiated by the Main Committee, one of the principal causes of the agrarian problem was the chaotic system of local administration, which was divided among the bureaucratic apparatus, the zemstvos, and separate peasant institutions. In April 1882, a new commission, known after its chairman as the Kakhanov Commission, began work on administrative reform. It had the charge of creating a unified and hierarchical system that would integrate the zemstvos and render the local authorities more effective while extending the influence of the central government.[91]

The Commission was particularly critical of the *soslovie* system because it both perpetuated the peasantry's isolation from the rest of society, creating a virtual "state within a state,"[92] and failed to provide adequate supervision. Acknowledging that the past twenty years had been marked by a gradual evolution toward classlessness (*bezsoslovnost'*) in all areas of Russian life, the Commission nonetheless concluded that the peasantry still needed special protection. It therefore decided to retain the commune as an economic institution serving the peasantry alone. However, the Commission opposed direct government intervention in the peasants' economic life on the assumption that whatever changes were necessary could be fostered by improving their civil rights and the structure of rural administration—an approach subsequently adopted by political liberals at the turn of the century.

Insofar as the commune's administrative functions were concerned, on the other hand, the Commission proposed reorganizing them on an all-class basis by establishing a new administrative unit, to be headed by a new official (*volostel'*) who would have more or less the same rights and responsibilities as the former peace arbitrator and who would be directly subordinated to the county administration. In a partial concession to the local nobility, this official would be elected by the county zemstvo assembly.[93] However, the Commission's proposals were vigorously opposed by the assistant interior minister, I. N. Durnovo, and by the new minister, D. A. Tolstoi, who was responsible for closing the Commission on 1 May 1885.[94] In part, it seems, Tolstoi was unwilling to accept any reform that deprived the Interior Ministry of some of its local power. At the same time, he opposed the participation of the zemstvos in selecting the *volostel'*, preferring to have that official appointed from above and thus directly subordinate to his ministry.[95] Once again the cause of rural reform had fallen victim to the political fears associated with administrative change and the accompanying abolition of the *soslovie* order.

The closing of the Kakhanov Commission marked the defeat of those within the government who sought to encourage the spontaneous forces of social and economic change, although Bunge continued to push for the abolition of the commune until he was dismissed in 1887. Even so, given the custom of making exministers members of the State Council, this whole generation of conservative liberals was still able to make its opinions heard.[96] However, they remained a distinct minority, in large part because their arguments were still predominantly theoretical and because there were still no truly compelling economic or political reasons to abandon a quarter of a century's dependence on the commune.

New Forms of Government Intervention

The government's initial attempts to deal with the agrarian crisis, piecemeal as they were, marked a significant turning point in its policy toward the peasantry. They also represented a major step toward the abandonment of the laissez-faire or noninterventionist approach of the Emancipation era and the adoption of a more interventionist form of bureaucratic *opeka*. This process gained further impetus by a series of measures, initiated by Interior Minister Tolstoi, designed to expand the government's role in local administration, inhibit the role of market forces within the commune, yet foster individual economic initiative. Paradoxically, however, although he was critical of the commune as an economic institution, he ultimately strengthened the commune's administrative role and increased the government's reliance on it.

Along with the better known K. P. Pobedonostsev, Count D. A. Tolstoi is usually seen as the evil genius behind Alexander III's reign and the principal architect of the so-called counterreforms. As a consequence, both Tolstoi and the counterreforms with which he is associated are identified with a noble reaction. However, it would be more accurate to characterize Tolstoi as the leader of a statist reaction, for, even though many of his policies seemed to favor the nobility, his real goal, like Valuev's, was to strengthen the autocracy and to extend the bureaucracy's control over the rest of society.[97]

With respect to the peasantry, the problem for Tolstoi was not that there were too many constraints on peasant economic activity but that there were too few. Thus, in contrast to his ministerial predecessors, instead of encouraging spontaneous social and economic change, he attempted to slow down or even halt the rate of change and restore the harmony and prosperity of supposedly more idyllic times.

The most important of the measures initiated by Tolstoi was the establishment, in 1889, of a new official, the land captain (zemskii nachal'nik), in response to what he perceived as a breakdown of authority in the countryside and the failure of the Emancipation's experiment in peasant self-government.[98] The remedy for this situation was modeled on the autocratic principles of personal and absolute power and was vested with joint police, administrative, and judicial authority. In addition, he had the utmost flexibility in interpreting the law so as to make it conform to local conditions. Within his own district, the land captain was indeed a "little tsar."[99]

Of course, this contradicted Tolstoi's desire to establish a centralized, hierarchical, and uniform administrative system. In the name of bureaucratic regularization, the man whom one contemporary referred to as "a bureaucrat to the marrow of his bones"[100] had created an official whose reputation for independence and arbitrariness became notorious. However, it was Tolstoi's belief that the central government's supraclass interests would in fact be protected so long as these "knight servitors" were chosen from reliable men.[101] To this end the law required that these officials be nominated from among the local nobility by the county marshal. At the same time, however, the candidates needed confirmation by the governor and would be subordinate to the Interior Ministry after their appointment. Tolstoi himself died in April 1889, too soon to see his ideas implemented. Had he lived, he might well have sought to subordinate the land captain more fully to the Interior Ministry; but the systematic bureaucratization of this office was not begun until 1905.[102] Despite these contradictions, as his subordinate, V. K. Pleve, later commented, the land captain was to become the "primary cell of the state organism."[103] Thus began another stage in the bureaucracy's invasion of the countryside.

The land captain's principal responsibility was to supervise all aspects of peasant administration and justice, including the selection and functioning of peasant officials and the adoption of communal decrees. He was also charged with protecting the majority of weaker peasants against the depredations of the kulak and helping preserve the basic equality of all peasants within the commune. To this end, the land captain was expected, among other responsibilities, to enforce the government's prohibition on usury, which set the maximum interest for loans at 12 percent, as well as its ban on grain speculation in times of crop failure. He was also to ensure that family members fulfilled their moral obligations to one another.[104] The land captain was, indeed, the practical instrument of bureaucratic *opeka*.

There was one exception to the land captain's seemingly all-embracing powers: he had no authority to intervene in the peasants' economic life. A proposal that he regulate periodical repartitions was dropped quickly lest such a violation of the tradition of nonintervention delay the legislation's passage. In subsequent years, however, as we shall see, this and other tasks would accrue to the land captain's responsibilities, thus initiating the transformation of this official from a preserver of the status quo into an instrument of social and economic change.

Tolstoi's project did not, of course, go unopposed. Few of his fellow bureaucrats agreed that the breakdown in rural authority was the *sole* cause of the agrarian problem. Meanwhile, the minister of justice, N. A. Manassein, and the minister of the imperial court, I. I. Vorontsov-Dashkov, vigorously defended the liberal principle of the separation of powers introduced by the Great Reforms. In the end, the much revised final version of this project was defeated in the State Council by a vote of thirty-nine to thirteen. However, since Tolstoi had already won Alexander III's support, the latter approved the minority opinion; and the project became law in July 1889.

The Consolidation of the Commune

As part of his campaign to reestablish order in the countryside, Tolstoi was also responsible for inaugurating work on legislation to check the proliferation of unregulated family partitions and communal repartitions of land, reduce the number of early departures from the commune, and limit the sale of redeemed land.[105] Since 1861, most of these procedures required the commune's approval. In practice, however, the regulations had been almost completely ignored. Since the abolition of the peace arbitrators, they had also been virtually unenforceable. Moreover, the growth in the number of families in that period had outpaced the rate of growth of the whole population, in some areas by nearly four times.[106] Consequently, there had been a reduction in the average size of the family and an increase in the number of those with only one adult male worker. Tolstoi argued that such small, newly formed families were unable to benefit from a proper division of labor and, because they often lacked sufficient capital and adequate implements, suffered from low yields.

Moreover, one-worker families could not release labor to earn the off-farm income needed to raise cash for their taxes. These trends, he argued, if unchecked, could lead to the ruin of increasing numbers of peasant families and a rapid growth in the number of landless peasants.

In response to these same demographic processes, the number of repartitions had also increased, leading to smaller average holdings, more open-field strips, and increased fragmentation. Partial repartitions were even more of a problem. They were not subject to the commune's approval and were often conducted in the interests of its more powerful members with consequences similar to those accompanying the growth of family partitions. There was, in addition, a small but steady flow of peasants who were liquidating their share of the redemption debt and separating from the commune. The goal of such departures, however, was not the consolidation of strips and the improvement of agricultural practices, as the Emancipation legislation had intended. Rather, these peasants sought either to escape the burdens of mutual responsibility or to sell their land, in many cases to nonpeasants, and leave the commune altogether.

Taken together, these developments, Tolstoi felt, would reduce the amount of land available to the less prosperous peasants who remained in the commune and in the long term threatened both a general decline in agricultural productivity—perhaps even the ruin of entire villages—and a reduction in the peasants' taxpaying abilities. Like the Emancipation's framers and the government's populist critics, the Interior Ministry was haunted by the specter of widespread peasant impoverishment and landlessness, which they saw as the inevitable consequence of allowing the presumably "universal" laws of social and economic differentiation to operate in an unregulated market environment.

Meanwhile, under the influence of a rising revolutionary movement at home and such European developments as the revolutions of 1848, the Paris Commune of 1871, and the rapid development of labor movements and labor-oriented political parties, the government's fears about the social consequences of capitalism were paralleled by a new fear of socialism.[107] Rather like later Marxists, some members of the government seem to have begun looking on capitalism as but the precursor of a socialist order. After all, the same historicist or deterministic logic that argued for the inevitability of capitalist development in Russia bespoke the inevitability of socialism as well. Unwilling to accept this logic, the government was driven to find a third way that would enable it to reconcile the development of a modern industrial society with an autocratic social and political system.

In response to these fears, on 18 March 1886, the government enacted a law subjecting family partitions to more effective supervision by the commune and the county board for peasant affairs.[108] However, two related statutes—one abolishing partial repartitions and limiting general repartitions to once every twelve years, the other both prohibiting sales of allotment land to nonpeasants and subjecting *all* departures from the commune to the approval of both it and the newly established land captains by abolishing the second part of Article 165 of the Redemption Statute—did not become law until 1893.[109] This delay was due largely to the vigorous opposition of those conservative liberals of an earlier bureaucratic generation who now sat in the State Council. Even then, the legislation was only finally adopted under pressure from the fears aroused by the famine of 1891–1892 and the revival of gentry political activity as local zemstvos began petitioning the government for aid to combat the "deplorable" state of agriculture.[110]

The Interior Ministry's hope in proposing this legislation was in fact to give the peasant family a greater sense of security and continuity in the possession and use of its strips and thus to foster a private-property consciousness that could serve as the basis for improved methods of cultivation. However, the ministry's approach was contradictory, for at the same time it had specifically subordinated the interests of the individual "work-loving" or prosperous peasant to the collective interests of the family and the peasantry as a whole. Its concern with raising productivity continued to remain captive to its political fears—above all, to its fear of change itself.

When the State Council discussed this legislation, a minority of conservative liberals, including Kakhanov, A. A. Polovtsov, Bunge, Vorontsov-Dashkov, and Abaza, fought a strong rear-guard action in support of a more laissez-faire and individualistic approach.[111] In their view, the government's fears of peasant impoverishment were greatly exaggerated. They argued that peasants should be able to make rational, market-based decisions about the relative benefits of cultivating their strips within the commune; separating from it and setting up an independent economy; mortgaging their allotment to obtain capital for improvements; or selling their allotment in order to buy land privately or from the Peasant Bank, resettle in another province, migrate to Siberia, or even enter the industrial labor force, where they would help stimulate industrial development. Moreover, they claimed, the Interior Ministry's proposals would actually lead to results opposite from those intended. For example, the creation of a special allotment land fund for the exclusive use of the peasantry violated the private-property principles that the ministry was trying to foster: it might even raise peasant expectations of an additional allotment. Further, limiting purchasers of allotment land to the peasantry would encourage those village speculators (*zemlepromyshlenniki*) who gathered together peasant strips and then sold or rented them at a higher price.[112] At the same time, given the rapid growth in population, tying the peasant to his allotment land would speed up the process of fragmentation, exhaust the land, and thus destroy the peasants' taxpaying capacities.

Insofar as noble landowners were concerned, it was argued that the new regulations would prohibit them from acquiring allotment land, even to eliminate interstripping. As a result, they would have to compete with peasants for the purchase of nonallotment land, thus further impeding the development of more productive forms of both peasant and noble agriculture and forcing nobles to continue their dependence on more labor-intensive and exploitative methods rather than modernize their estates on the basis of freely hired agricultural wage labor.

Vorontsov-Dashkov, the only active minister in this minority, went even further and attacked the government's more than thirty-year dependence on the commune, arguing that it actually encouraged the formation of a proletariat rather than preventing it.[113] He did not advocate the immediate abolition of the commune, however; for he considered it useful as an administrative organ. But his proposals to develop small-scale peasant agriculture based on *otruba* and *khutora* were nonetheless radical in their anticipation of the Stolypin Reforms. Almost alone at the time, he offered a pragmatic and experimental approach that would change "the means of landownership gradually, beginning with those provinces and even counties which are most in need. . . . [Moreover, such an] experiment would serve as the best guide for the further development of the program."[114] However, the new interior minister, I. N. Durnovo, rejected this approach, arguing that he could not "concede even the idea of introducing a radical reform of the whole existing structure of peasant landownership . . . as a form of experiment—without the preliminary gathering and then . . . careful study of the evidence relating to it." Proper legislative methods, in his opinion, ruled out any action taken "on the basis of guesswork."[115]

On the other hand, Durnovo granted the commune's economic shortcomings and shared Vorontsov-Dashkov's suspicion that it was the embodiment of socialist principles.[116] Durnovo even agreed with Vorontsov that a "final transfer of peasants to individual forms of use . . . [though with the reservation of] the right of ownership to the whole community, would perhaps be most desirable in the future. . . ." However, Durnovo opposed any direct "governmental interference . . . fearing that as a result of the unfamiliarity of its administrative organs with the cultural and economic conditions of peasant life, [this] could bring harm rather than benefit."[117] There were also practical and political objections to what Durnovo called a "total economic revolution."[118] Not only did the government lack the fiscal, administrative, and technical resources to undertake such a reform: the creation of "compact holdings . . . would meet with insuperable difficulties . . . because the population is completely unprepared for this measure." Moreover, it would lead to an increase in the number of landless peasants. Thus, in Durnovo's view, the government had no choice but to adopt temporary and piecemeal measures that simply tried to achieve "the best possible regulation of communal landownership."[119]

Like the Emancipation's framers, the majority seemed to hold an almost sacred reverence for existing reality as an organic product of the historical process and attempted to enshrine it in the inviolable aura of custom or culture. With respect to the peasantry, in particular, this led them to argue, in effect, that the peasant did not possess free will and consequently could not be held personally responsible for his paralyzing dependence on routine. Yet, like Tolstoi, they were no longer content to confine law to the essentially passive function of reflecting that reality and permitting future change. In their view, its task was to intervene directly and to shape that reality.[120] Indeed, as Durnovo's argument makes clear, those who sought to regulate Russia's underregulated countryside and those who sought to foster the development of individualistic principles of property ownership and agriculture were equally guilty of intervening in peasant society. The difference between them was a question not so much of the degree of intervention that either would tolerate as it was of the goal—whether it was designed to liberate the peasant and encourage a spontaneous process of economic development or to slow the rate of change and preserve the traditional structure of peasant society. However, the very fact of regulation and the existence of the new bureaucratic office of land captain legitimized an interventionist interpretation of bureaucratic *opeka*—though still on the basis of traditional administrative assumptions. However, once such intervention was accepted in principle, it would only be a short step until the bureaucracy tried to influence the direction of change itself.

For the next decade, however, the laws of 1886 and 1893 served to reinforce the peasants' legal isolation, immobility, and traditional agricultural practices. In effect, the *soslovie* principle had been extended to every aspect of the individual peasant's existence, condemning him to near total civil and juridical dependence on the commune and reenserfing him to the land. In the process, the commune became transformed into a permanent and virtually inviolable feature of peasant society while its various functions as administrative unit, landowner, and land user became indissolubly linked, reinforcing its role as the government's principal instrument for the preservation of rural order. At the same time, the very adoption of these laws seemed to convince the government that nothing further need be done. Thus agrarian policy entered a period of stagnation and passivity that lasted down to the eve of 1905. Meanwhile, a series of new developments, symbolized by the appointment of S. Iu. Witte as finance minister on 1 January 1893, began to exert an influence on agrarian policy.

Government Policy and Local Opinion

The most important of these developments occurred during the second half of the 1890s, when Russia entered her age of industrial revolution. Responsibility for the sudden surge in industrial growth is usually placed on the Witte system, a series of policies that included railroad expansion, high protective tariffs, and a shift from direct to indirect taxation.[121] However, although apparently successful in stimulating the development of trade and industry, they also exacerbated the agricultural problems of both noble and peasant, at a time when both were already suffering from the catastrophic decline in grain prices that accompanied the worldwide agricultural crisis that began in the late 1870s.[122]

Meanwhile, at the end of 1892, in a sign of the new era, a commission that Tolstoi had organized to study the decline in agricultural prices and that was chaired by the assistant interior minister, V. K. Pleve, had issued a report recommending "more active state intervention" in rural affairs and calling for the formation of a new ministry devoted to the concerns of agriculture and the establishment of an agricultural council in which noble interests would be represented.[123] With respect to the problem of peasant impoverishment, the commission took a very broad view, citing in particular the rapid development of a money economy in the countryside over the past thirty years—a process that had taken a century or more in Europe—which had increased the peasants' need for cash income. However, many European nations and even the United States— which, like Russia, conducted a predominantly extensive agriculture— had doubled or tripled their productivity whereas Russia had remained stagnant. The commission thus proposed that the government try to raise peasant (as well as noble) income by providing agronomical aid, supporting peasant handicrafts, arranging migration to areas with surplus land, and otherwise remedying land-hunger where it was a problem. The Pleve commission also acknowledged the problems associated with communal forms of land use. However, it considered any changes in this area "too risky" and recommended only finding ways to balance the interests of enterprising individuals with those of the rest of the village.[124]

The most important consequence of Pleve's report was the establishment in March 1894 of a Ministry of Agriculture and State Domains and the appointment of A. S. Ermolov as its head.[125] Although this new ministry's narrowly technical focus led one fellow bureaucrat to refer to it scornfully as the Ministry of "Sand Dunes and Gullies,"[126] this step was of major significance; for it symbolized Nicholas II's abiding interest in the problems of the countryside.[127] It was also a major expansion in the scope of government activity.

A member of the landowning nobility, Ermolov was widely seen as society's representative in government.[128] As such, he was the leading edge of the noble reaction, or provincialization, that was to develop within the government over the next decade and a half.[129] Certainly his unparalleled knowledge of local conditions and his wide practical experience, much of it derived from the management of his own estates, distinguished him from the more limited specialists who had been gathering influence within the bureaucracy over the past century.[130] At the same time, he was a genuine exponent of the state's supraclass interest. Thus, in the aftermath of the 1891–1892 famine, he rejected the prevailing view of both the government and its critics that equated agriculture with grain cultivation and began calling for the formation of a large class of individual peasant proprietors who would practice highly intensive yet diversified forms of cultivation on *khutora* or *otruba*, thereby to guarantee the peasants a more stable income and to raise agricultural productivity. He also favored the elimination of all *soslovie* distinctions and the integration of the peasantry into the surrounding society on the basis of their common economic interest with noble landowners. Similarly, he supported the closest possible cooperation between government and society in agricultural matters and the establishment of regular lines of communication with the zemstvos for this purpose. More important, as a result of its technical specialization and Ermolov's recruiting policies, such views remained characteristic of this ministry down to the very end of the tsarist regime.[131]

Shortly after taking office, Ermolov polled the opinions of provincial zemstvo assemblies on improving the state of agriculture.[132] Not surprisingly, he avoided such sensitive political issues as local administration and the peasant commune and focused exclusively on economic and agronomical issues. The zemstvos responded in like terms, with requests for various improvements in the grain trade and in the provision of credit for meliorative work such as land reclamation. On the improvement of specifically peasant agriculture, however, they had little to offer. Certainly there was no reference to the problems of communal landownership or use. On the other hand, a majority of zemstvos favored increasing peasant landownership by purchases through the Peasant Bank, the rental of state or royal lands, or migration and supported measures to improve methods of cultivation. Clearly the perception of the agrarian problem within the liberal zemstvo segment of society conformed more or less to the prevailing view among the officials of the central government.

At the same time that the agricultural ministry was conducting its investigation of local opinion, Durnovo established within the Interior Ministry a commission charged with gathering the information Durnovo considered essential for the preparation of any future changes in peasant legislation. In the summer of 1894, the commission's chairman, Assistant Minister D. S. Sipiagin, sent out a questionnaire to specially organized provincial conferences consisting of local bureaucrats, marshals of the nobility, and other experts. Somewhat surprisingly, a significant number of questions addressed the problem of peasant land use, including the elimination of open fields and the partition of excessively large villages. Four even addressed the desirability of communal landownership and use, implying that the ministry itself actually favored individualized ownership and cultivation. Sipiagin also requested information on departures from the commune by former state peasants, who had not been affected by the recent subordination of this right to the decision of the commune.[133] How popular were independent, compact holdings among these separators? What was their impact on individual peasants and their former commune? The conferences were also asked their opinion of a law allowing the nobility's former serfs to execute such separations—a remarkable about-face since less than a year earlier the Interior Ministry had abolished that right.[134]

The local conferences were virtually unanimous in their support of the commune as a defense against landlessness and impoverishment and reiterated their approval of the 1893 law prohibiting free exit. The vast majority also opposed any law easing transfers to individual landownership on the grounds that it would lead to the "artificial" destruction of the commune.[135] Apparently officials and nobles in the countryside stood solidly behind Tolstoi's counterreforms.

In response to the growing local demand for government aid to landhungry peasants, at the end of 1894 Nicholas II issued a manifesto in which he proposed lowering the annual interest rate for Peasant Bank loans and extending the scope of the bank's activities by permitting it to purchase land directly, on its own account, for resale to the peasantry.[136] In subsequent discussions of the proposed legislation, Witte succeeded in increasing the size of available loans and reducing the initial deposit required in order to make more land available to landless and landhungry peasants. His proposal to offer land in hereditary rental to those peasants who still did not possess the means to purchase it was, however, rejected on the grounds that it opposed the trend toward individual forms of property ownership.[137] However, although some members of the State Council saw the gradual transfer of land from unproductive nobles to peasants as a natural and desirable phenomenon, so long as it was not artificially encouraged by the government, the majority was concerned with the way the peasants would interpret these new concessions and with their impact on the nobility. As a result, the proposed changes were introduced in the form of an experiment over a five-year period.[138]

Some minor changes also occurred in migration policies, including the organization in 1896, within the Interior Ministry, of a Migration Section charged with providing more accurate information about areas of settlement and eliminating some of the obstacles to safe transit and resettlement. Illegal migrants would be permitted to stay and even to receive government aid. Again concern about the impact such changes would have on the nobility's labor supply arose. Nicholas himself dismissed this fear as exaggerated. Witte raised a similar question about their impact on the supply of labor to industry, arguing that population pressure was itself a major stimulus to agricultural intensification. The changes did not, however, lead to a net increase in migration, since the number who returned from the east grew considerably. After a few years the government, therefore, reverted to the earlier, more restrictive, "Temporary Regulations," which remained in force until the eve of the 1905 revolution.[139] Beyond these relatively minor adjustments to the government's agrarian policy, nothing further was done to resolve the developing agrarian problem.

New Initiatives

Witte, however, was not satisfied with this turn of events. Back during the discussion of the 1893 laws expanding the authority of the commune, Durnovo had recommended the formation of a "special interdepartmental commission" to conduct a "general review of peasant legislation" that would "embrace every aspect of rural life and take up the . . . vital interests of the multi-millioned peasant population." Such a commission was to be composed of "local figures closely acquainted with the peasant question" who would engage in a "detailed study and resolution of all questions of peasant landownership," including "such fundamental questions as . . . communal landownership."[140] However, Durnovo apparently had second thoughts and subsequently persuaded the tsar to limit the inquiry to a simple review of legislation by the Interior Ministry, since all that was necessary was to reconcile existing laws with "life itself."[141] Durnovo's motives are not completely clear, the more so since he was himself critical of the commune. Apparently, he was afraid of arousing the "great opposition" to its abolition, symbolized by the new tsar, Nicholas II, who as late as 1902 declared that he would "never dare to put an end to the commune with a single stroke of the pen."[142] It is also likely that Durnovo and others within the government such as Pobedonostsev and Pleve were concerned about the constitutional implications of drawing the local nobility into such a review. Bureaucratic jealousies likely played a role as well, for peasant legislation had become the special province of the Interior Ministry's Rural Section (Zemskii Otdel) since the closing of the Main Committee in 1882. In any event, in the spring of 1898, Witte revived Durnovo's 1893 recommendation and called anew for a commission to investigate the needs of the rural population and review legislation on the peasants' property and sociolegal rights.[143]

Witte was and still is widely regarded as a one-sided proponent of industrialization who sought to develop Russia's industrial base by extracting the necessary capital from rural society.[144] To be sure, his motives in raising the agrarian problem were explicitly financial. Like his predecessors, he saw the agricultural crisis and the so-called agrarian problem primarily as crises in government tax collections. Modifying his commitment to industrialization and modernization was, however, his adherence to Freidrich List's system of "national economics," which was essentially a marriage of liberal economic theory and nationalist politics.[145] Considering Russia a part of Europe and subject to the same laws, Witte had no doubt that Russia's social and economic development would follow the same capitalist route as that already traveled by the West. Indeed, in his view, Russia at the turn of the century was already well on the way to completing its transformation from a natural economy, based on agriculture, to a monetary economy, based on trade and industry.[146] However, Russia's national interests, unlike the West's, demanded that the state continue to play a critical role in these developments.

Thus, in a variation on the popular aphorism, *"Bogat Ivan—bogat i pan"* (Where the peasant is prosperous, so, too, is the noble), Witte once remarked that "where the sheep are poor, so too are the shepherds," in effect agreeing with his fellow bureaucrats that the government still needed to maintain its tutelary role as "shepherd."[147] Indeed, despite his background in railroad management and private enterprise, Witte was a convinced supporter of the autocracy and its traditional supraclass approach to policy making.[148] In his view, the bureaucracy was the autocracy's only possible basis of support and power. As he put it, "not having opponents, the Russian supreme authority [has] no need of allies." Moreover, since the autocracy depended "on the whole population" and since its motto was "Everything is for the common good," it had nothing to fear from even socialism.[149] Witte's goal, indeed, was to utilize the autocratic power to avoid the all-too-visible costs of modernization as well as to preserve that political status quo that was the necessary condition for his policies. Applied to the peasantry, such an approach led him to reject his predecessors' laissez-faire policy of letting the rich get richer and the poor get poorer and to prescribe a uniquely Russian policy that, by combining civil equality with bureaucratic *opeka*, would assure a gradual and across-the-board improvement in the material well-being of all peasant strata.[150]

Witte's evaluation of Russia's historical and economic position at the end of the nineteenth century was in many ways quite remarkable. He certainly fit the mold of an "enlightened absolutist," as one commentator described him.[151] However, in seeking this "third way," he was attempting to unite three seemingly contradictory bureaucratic traditions: the "official liberalism" of the Emancipation era with its commitment to individual civil rights and spontaneous social and economic change, the older statist and interventionist tradition that had experienced a resurgence during the reign of Alexander III, and the newer tradition of "official populism" with its paternalistic emphasis on social equality.

Well aware that a successful fiscal policy and the overall health of the national economy depended on the taxpaying abilities and thus the welfare of the peasants, Witte had been concerned from the very beginning of his tenure as minister with their material and moral condition. Beginning in 1894, his annual budget reports had expressed concern for the rural economy and the welfare of both noble landowners and peasants.[152] He repeated his concern privately, in audience with the tsar. However, the peasants' overwhelming numbers and their position as the principal source of tax revenue soon made them the primary object of his attention. Indeed, for Witte, Russia was primarily a *muzhik*, or peasant, state, not a noble one. He even came to look favorably on the breakup of the nobility's huge landed estates and the eventual disappearance of the nobility from agriculture altogether. Like Valuev, he felt that the nobility's sole salvation lay in their *embourgeoisement*—in their becoming industrialists and bankers.[153]

At this stage, however, Witte, initially a supporter of the commune who had been turned against it by Bunge,[154] confined himself to drawing generally pessimistic conclusions about the probable state of future revenue collections. Like Valuev, however, he apparently did not believe there was a genuine agrarian crisis. In his view, the development of social and economic differentiation had caused the current problems. Thus, although the welfare of some peasants had improved, that of others had declined. Unfortunately, even though the latter group constituted only a minority of the peasant population, the public assumed that the minority's condition was characteristic of the peasantry as a whole.[155] Searching for ways to improve the peasantry's well-being and raise its agricultural productivity, Witte began, in 1898, to embrace the reform program of Russia's political liberals and to call for the abolition of the *soslovie*-based system of local administration and law.[156] Like the liberals, he assumed that ending the peasants' sociolegal isolation and expanding their educational opportunities would help them develop a sense of individual responsibility, increase their economic productivity, and thus give them a stake in society.

Despite the sensitive political nature of Witte's proposals, Durnovo's replacement as interior minister, I. L. Goremykin, the somnolent and indecisive "expert" in peasant legislation, did not object to them in principle. As this former conservative liberal himself pointed out, the regulations governing peasant society were, indeed, in a chaotic state. However, he agreed with Durnovo that all that was necessary was to bring the existing legislation into conformity with the principles under-lying the Emancipation Statutes—a task that not only belonged to the Interior Ministry but was already under way.[157] The implications of Goremykin's position were spelled out in more detail by Pleve, now imperial secretary. Thus, Pleve noted, since the "peasant way of life has its peculiar culture, which is sharply distinguished from the culture of the other classes *(klassy)* of the population," it was necessary to preserve the communal system of administration; the peasantry's isolated, *soslovie,* status; and the inalienability of allotment lands. At the same time, however, he believed that the peasantry should be free "to choose how they would utilize these lands."[158]

Following the suggestions of both Goremykin and Witte, the Commit-tee of Ministers proposed the formation of two commissions, one within the Interior Ministry to review legislation, the other, an inter-departmental commission, to investigate the economic and fiscal causes of rural decline. In the case of the legislative review, the Committee saw no need to delay any longer or to involve "society": there was already plenty of evidence available. Ever conscious of peasant tendencies to mis-interpret government intentions, the Committee kept the existence of the legislative review secret.[159] On the other hand, Durnovo, now chair-man of the Committee of Ministers, again postponed the convocation of a second, investigative commission. Learning of the delay, Witte wrote to the tsar a long letter of protest in which, for the first time, he spelled out his position on the agrarian question and called for immediate re-forms. The greatest evil in the peasant way of life, he wrote, was the absence of a firm legal structure. The peasant even lacked civil and prop-erty rights within his own family.

It is not enough to free him from the slaveowner—it is still neces-sary to free him from the slavery of despotism, to give him a legal system, and consequently also the consciousness of legality, and to educate him. . . . [But, at present,] the peasant is in thrall to the ar-bitrariness . . . of the land captain, the county police chief, the dis-trict police chief, the village police chief, the rural doctor, the canton head, the canton scribe, the teacher . . . every noble land-owner, [and] to the village assembly with its troublemakers.[160]

Under these circumstances, there was no incentive for the peasant to increase his productivity and improve his condition. Worse still, in times of crop failure, the government's provision of emergency food supplies made the peasants even more dependent on the government. Witte even implied that communal property ownership was incompatible with agri-cultural progress. Finally, he pointed out that the peasants' continuing poverty was a powerful weapon in the hands of the autocracy's oppo-nents.[161] Witte's efforts, however, came to nothing, for at the end of

December 1898 Durnovo once again persuaded the tsar to abandon the entire question until the tsar desired to reopen it—a delay that was to last for another three years.[162]

In part, the government's inertia is explicable in light of that "great opposition" that Durnovo feared that any attempts to modify the peasant commune and the related *soslovie* system of administration would arouse. In part, however, it was also a product of the growing conflict between the supporters of law and order within the noble- and rural-oriented Interior Ministry and its successive ministers, on the one hand, and the forces of social and economic change represented by Witte and his "capitalist" and proindustrialist Finance Ministry, on the other. The tsar's own well-known indecisiveness also contributed.[163] This inter-ministerial conflict came to a head during the tenure of that "superlative clerk," Pleve, who served as interior minister between 1902 and 1904[164] Yet, as we shall see, despite the important role this conflict played in obstructing needed reforms, in the realm of agrarian policy, Witte and Pleve and their two ministries were not nearly so far apart as they appeared.

We have already established that the Interior Ministry was, in fact, one of the principal defenders of the statist, supraclass approach. Pleve was no exception to this tradition. Indeed, he had been one of the principal supporters of the land captain legislation and a major force shaping the Interior Ministry's policies under Tolstoi and Durnovo.[165] Following this tradition, on taking office he set out to reform the entire system of provincial and county administration along these very lines. However, despite the tsar's support, Pleve's attempt at "bureaucratic imperialism" aroused the vigorous opposition of those—notably Witte and Ermolov—who stood to lose effective control of their local agents to the Interior Ministry. As a result, these proposals never saw the light of day, though they were subsequently revived by Stolypin in 1907.[166] Pleve's other major reform project involved the formation of a Council on the Local Economy designed to make society's knowledge and expertise available to the central government. Unlike earlier proposals, which had relied on the limited participation of "elected" representatives, Pleve's had a more statist orientation and depended exclusively on ex officio members such as marshals of the nobility, zemstvo board chairmen, and others appointed by the Interior Ministry who were "closely acquainted with the needs and interests of the local economy." It was also more successful, for this constitution, as it became known, was actually signed into law in March 1904.[167] However, Pleve's assassination on 15 July delayed its implementation until Stolypin revived it in 1908.[168]

Clearly, Pleve shared Witte's assumptions concerning the role of the autocracy and its importance in influencing social and economic developments, claiming that "there are perfectly sound grounds to hope that

Russia will escape the oppression of capital and of the bourgeoisie, and the class struggle."[169] Pleve, too, saw Russia as a *muzhik*-state.[170] At the same time, he was inclined to favor the landed nobility as the state's principal source of servitors and, thus, to some extent, of social support, though he was also prepared to allow a moderate influx of landowning capitalists into the nobility's ranks. Nonetheless, like Ermolov, Pleve gave preference to owners of medium-size properties within the nobility rather than the owners of huge latifundia. He also favored the development of a diversified agriculture.[171] Insofar as the peasantry was concerned, Pleve was no blind supporter of the commune. On the contrary, he already anticipated its replacement by individualized forms of landownership and use. However, he was vigorously opposed to any attempts to integrate the peasantry into a single unified legal system. In his view, the peasantry was not ready for such a change.

Thus, the principal issue in the dispute between the Finance and Interior ministries was not, as has usually been assumed, the fate of the commune as landowner or land user, nor even the development of a more individualized peasant agriculture. Indeed, the two ministries cooperated on limiting the institution of mutual responsibility in 1899 and then abolishing it in 1903 as a means of reducing the commune's harmful economic influence and encouraging a gradual individualization of peasant life.[172] Rather, the issue that separated them was the *soslovie* system itself. Witte saw peasant integration as the necessary first step toward the development of individualism, economic initiative, and national progress. Somewhat myopically, he did not see the political threat inherent in this policy; he foresaw grave political consequences only if the peasants continued to remain isolated. Pleve also desired agricultural progress, but, preoccupied with the problem of maintaining order and stability, he was more sensitive to its impact on both nobility and autocracy. Hence, he clung to the *soslovie* structure, to which the commune was linked, as the principal bulwark against the destruction of the existing regime. Thus the positions of these two ministers became polarized, with the Finance Ministry symbolizing a policy of bureaucratic interventionism and reform and the Interior Ministry a policy of bureaucratic passivity and piecemeal regularization.

However, in the face of the constantly growing political challenges to the autocracy, the views of both men were subject to change. Thus at a meeting with Witte in Yalta in October 1902, Pleve went so far as to express his willingness to accept even political reforms, provided only that the tsar initiate them.[173] Witte, meanwhile, abandoned his earlier distrust of educated society and turned to it for assistance in undertaking reforms. By 1905, he would even come to see the need for a representative system of government and would be largely responsible for urging the indecisive Nicholas to grant Russia a constitution. In sum, the difference between Witte and Pleve, both of whom, like Valuev and Tolstoi before them, believed that the autocracy had to initiate all change, lay in their respective opinions concerning the extent to which it was permissible for the government to "go to the people" in attempting to achieve reform. In the meantime, this interministerial conflict was responsible for embittering the political atmosphere within the bureaucracy and delaying much-needed rural reforms. Change would come only as a product of the perceptual revolution that was to take place within the bureaucracy during the first five years of the twentieth century. And only under the influence of these changes would the two ministries realize the similarities in their goals.

PART TWO
The Revolution in Perceptions

In recent years, a marked change [*povorot*] in the government's and society's views on the agrarian question has taken place.
—A. V. Krivoshein, 1911
The present legislative project [the version of the Stolypin Reforms before the State Council in 1910] is an exclusively bureaucratic product.
—S. Iu. Witte, 1910

2

THE FINANCE MINISTRY AND THE SPECIAL CONFERENCE, 1902–1904

Perceptual Revolution, Stage One

In the study of recent policy. . . there is a missing component: confidence in the people who are to gain from reform.

—D. Warriner, 1969

The first reform [of Danish agriculture in the late eighteenth and nineteenth centuries] was undertaken with the explicit intention of linking social equality with technical progress, one of the very few reforms of its time—perhaps the only one—of which this can be said.

D. Warriner, 1969

At the turn of the century, not only was Russian agriculture still based almost exclusively on the extensive cultivation of grain crops, but there had been no general improvement in the level of peasant agricultural practices and no significant increase in capital investment. As one observer noted, both the structure of Russia's rural economy and the methods of cultivation remained "almost completely medieval," some one to five centuries behind the rest of Europe.[1] To be sure, a market economy had begun to develop and both agricultural output and cultivated area had increased. Production had also increased in per capita terms, suggesting increases in both labor productivity and the peasant standard of living. Yet, as the population continued to grow, other indicators of peasant welfare were declining, including the average area of land and the number of working animals per household. Arrears in peasant taxes and redemption payments continued to increase. There were partial crop failures in 1897, 1898, and 1901.[2] Indeed, contemporaries considered the problem so serious that historians have generally assumed that peasant agriculture was in a state of severe crisis marked by soil exhaustion and a breakdown of the three-field system brought on by the peasants' exploitative methods of cultivation and exacerbated by the unequal social system.[3] The problem was conveyed most poignantly by a series of articles entitled "The Dying Village," published in 1902, by A. I. Shingarev, a zemstvo doctor in Voronezh Province and future minister of agriculture in the Provisional Government of 1917.[4] These trends seemed to reach a new level of urgency when, during a ten-day period in the spring of 1902, a series of violent peasant disorders that one historian has called a "miniature revolution" broke out in four neighboring counties of Poltava and Khar'kov provinces on the left bank of the Dnepr River in the Ukraine and then spread to a number of other provinces in the southern Ukraine and lower Volga regions.[5]

A New Generation of Bureaucrats

Under the pressure of these circumstances, along with the widening activity of the zemstvo opposition, the beginnings of industrial unrest, and the revival of a revolutionary movement, the agrarian problem increasingly took on the characteristics of a major national crisis.[6] Indeed, both within government and without, more and more people were beginning to see this crisis as a symptom of Russia's economic backwardness or underdevelopment vis-à-vis the Western nations. The liberal agricultural expert, P. Lokhtin, summarized the situation well: "For the most part of the Russian peasantry arable farming either does not yield sufficient grain for personal consumption or yields only a quantity sufficient for a frugal personal consumption such that no surplus remains either to feed livestock or to market."[7] With this growing awareness of the urgency of the agrarian problem a sea change took place in the attitude of society and the government toward the peasant commune as an agricultural institution. Beginning with the early 1890s, the ranks of the commune's opponents grew steadily;[8] by 1905, they would win a majority within the government and the liberal nobility. By 1906, an important segment of the conservative nobility also opposed the commune.

Inevitably, the increasing concern in educated society for peasant welfare brought forth renewed pressure on the government to grant an "additional allotment." The government's public response to this pressure was twofold. On the one hand, it reiterated its traditional dependence on the *soslovie* system of peasant administration and the peasant commune as the guarantors of rural order and peasant welfare in a series of official pronouncements proclaiming the inviolability of these institutions and of the peasantry's allotment-land fund.[9] On the other hand, the government created a series of new commissions charged with examining the scope of the agrarian crisis and developing appropriate solutions. The Stolypin Reforms of 1906 would be the final outcome of their work.

Compared to the government's traditional agrarian policy, which sought to slow down the pace of social and economic change by preserving the peasantry in a state of relative social and economic equality within their customary and essentially collectivist institutional framework, the Stolypin Reforms introduced changes that would constitute a virtual revolution. At the same time, however, as we shall see, these Reforms would preserve some important continuities with the past, most notably a commitment to bureaucratic *opeka* and an opposition to social and economic differentiation. In part, of course, these changes were a direct response to the revolutionary events of 1905–6. Yet, between 1902 and 1905, before the extent of peasant discontent had become clear, another kind of revolution took place in the bureaucracy's perception of the agrarian problem and the means by which change could be introduced into peasant society.

This revolution in bureaucratic perceptions was the product of a new generation of enlightened bureaucrats or agrarian experts who brought to the government a new spirit of realism and pragmatism. Among the forces shaping this new generation were a number of social and economic trends that had brought government and society closer together during the half-century following Emancipation. Principal among these were the new market forces unleashed by the Emancipation that had increasingly compelled landowning nobles to involve themselves directly in the management of their estates. The creation of the zemstvos in 1864 had encouraged a similar involvement in local administration. Then, in the aftermath of the agricultural crisis and the famine there was the "gentry reaction" as local noble society sought to protect its *soslovie* interests and privileges, first by petitioning the government for assistance and, increasingly, by organizing itself as an independent political movement either to win the government's cooperation or to offer alternative solutions.[10]

This reaction took a variety of political forms. One product was the emergence of a national zemstvo movement in the mid-1890s. By 1902, this somewhat amorphous entity, which contained within it an entire spectrum of political views from neo-Slavophile supporters of a traditional autocracy through aristocratic constitutionalists to constitutional liberals, had begun to crystallize into independent strands. The best known of these was the Union of Liberation, formed in exile in 1902 by a group of former "legal Marxists" and members of the professional intelligentsia in conjunction with liberal and progressive members of provincial society. Subsequently, the Union of Liberation would provide the nucleus for the formation of several political parties, including the "liberal" Kadets and the more conservative Octobrist party to its right.[11]

However, the most interesting group and the one most directly involved with the subsequent adoption of the Stolypin Reforms was composed of modernizing noble agriculturalists, the best known of whom, "the nobleman" N. A. Pavlov of Saratov Province, wrote for Prince Meshcherskii's paper, *Grazhdanin*, and served on a number of government commissions during this period. Pavlov, together with his brother, A. A.

Pavlov, who was on special assignment to the Interior Ministry, was a true representative of this gentry reaction. However, he based his defense of local noble interests not on the protection of their legal *soslovie* status and privileges but on their rights as individual owners of private property. For him, the nobility could survive only by becoming capitalist agriculturalists. In pursuit of these goals, Pavlov and a number of like-minded nobles from the Volga provinces would form a Union of Landowners in 1905 with the goal of harmonizing the economic interests of the modernizing noble with those of the peasants. Subsequently, many of these nobles, including Pavlov, would participate in the formation of the First Congress of the United Nobility in the summer of 1906. Finally, after almost half a century, the landowning nobility was beginning to organize itself politically for the defense of its interests.[12]

At the same time, the continuing growth and professionalization of the bureaucracy and its gradual expansion into the countryside gave the government closer and closer contact with rural life.[13] This led to a growing interchange of personnel between government and society at the local level and in St. Petersburg as well as between the latter and the provinces.[14] As a result more and more men in government possessed direct experience and knowledge of the problems of local agriculture and administration and of the peasantry.

At first, this new bureaucratic generation of agrarian experts comprised a small group of men, many of them relatively unknown. However, a few—V. I. Gurko, A. A. Rittikh, A. V. Krivoshein, and P. A. Stolypin, along with Witte, Ermolov, Polovtsov,[15] and others who belonged to the older generation of "conservative liberals"—were to play leading roles in the development and subsequent adoption of the Stolypin Reforms. Most were fairly young, born in the 1850s or 1860s and, thus, in their midforties or thirties at the turn of the century. Almost all had completed some form of higher education, usually at the law faculties of Moscow or St. Petersburg University or the Imperial School of Jurisprudence, though some had attended the more traditional Aleksandrovskii Lyceum. Usually, they had begun their service careers in local positions during the reign of Alexander III, some serving in the Interior Ministry as land captains or their equivalent. Some were marshals of the nobility, vice-governors, or governors. Others served in local branches of the judiciary or the agricultural ministry. Many had also had personal or service experience in the western borderlands and Poland, where individualized systems of landownership and land use were common, or had been involved in the resettlement of migrants from European Russia to Siberia. Gurko, for example, who participated in the modernization of his wife's estates in Voronezh Province, had also served for many years as a commissar for peasant affairs in Poland before transferring to St. Petersburg.

Rittikh had served in the Vladivostok office of the migration administration; Krivoshein, who also served in the Interior Ministry's migration department from its creation in 1896, was a frequent visitor to his family's estates in the west. Stolypin himself not only possessed estates in the west, which he operated according to modern and enlightened principles, but had begun service there as a marshal of the nobility and vice-governor for several years before being transferred to Saratov in 1904.[16]

What appears most significant about this contact with the West and Siberia is that these were areas where the commune either did not exist in the same form as in central Russia or was of relatively recent origin, while the West, in particular, was already in the throes of economic modernization. Under these influences, both the peasantry and nobility seem to have made a rapid adjustment to the market, developing a higher degree of individualism and initiative than elsewhere in the Russian Empire.[17] In addition, anyone involved in migration affairs must have become keenly aware of the penalties the communal system imposed on peasants who wished to relocate.[18] As a result, these men acquired a deeper understanding of peasant economic needs in a market-oriented environment and the political and social problems of rural society as a whole. Specifically, it seems that the more fluid social and institutional arrangements of these regions enabled them to look on such competitive social and economic relationships as a natural and viable form of social organization.[19] In consequence, they were less fearful of social and economic change and more open to experiments designed to foster the development of a less regulated society governed by the invisible hand of the market rather than by bureaucratic regulations. Indeed, in Poland, the local nobility had long been rubbing elbows with the peasantry on a basis of equality within the all-class *gmina*, the Polish equivalent of the Russian canton *(volost')*, thus demonstrating that it was indeed possible for the nobility to survive and to preserve its rights, privileges, and social prestige without the aid of a *soslovie*-based system of administration isolating the peasantry from other classes.[20]

After such service in the provinces, these men began to return to the capital during the 1890s and early 1900s. In part, this was a result of Witte's vigorous and wide-ranging search for expertise, which brought many nonnobles and academics into his ministry. In part, it was a result of a similar policy of reinvigorating the central government that was initiated by Pleve to recruit landowning nobles from local, provincial society. Meanwhile, the agricultural ministry had also begun assembling provincial landowners in its agricultural council as well as hiring and training growing numbers of technical experts. Initially, the most significant of these groups was Witte's "brain trust," which drew together career bureaucrats, both those from the various departments of the Finance Ministry and those pirated from other ministries, as well as a number of independent experts in society for whom he found positions.[21]

Perhaps the most important force that was to unite these rather disparate developments and provide the crucial link between government and society and, in particular, between this new generation of bureaucrats and the aristocratic constitutionalists and agricultural modernizers of both this and an older generation was the so-called Golovin salon.[22] The salon itself, one of St. Petersburg's most important during the 1890s and 1900s, was composed of both bureaucrats and landowning nobles. It had originated as a discussion circle during the immediate post-Emancipation period and from the first had been a consistent defender of beleaguered noble and agrarian interests. Many of its leading members combined their defense of the nobility with classical, laissez-faire liberal ideas. Others, however, were defenders of the peasant commune. During its long existence this circle underwent a number of metamorphoses. In its latest incarnation, it would be inspired in large part by opposition to Witte's fiscal policies.[23] Among its members were S. S. Bekhteev of Orel Province, one of the early initiators of the land captain legislation, though he opposed it in its final form, and a member of the agricultural ministry's railroad and tariff council since 1894;[24] a Slavophile and a former supporter of the commune, by 1905 he had joined the vanguard opposing it, as somewhat earlier had Senator A. V. Evreinov of Kursk Province and Prince Pavel D. Dolgorukov of Moscow, also members of the salon. All three, in addition to the salon's founder, Golovin, published books attacking the commune.[25] In addition, the salon included two assistant ministers in the agricultural ministry—A. A. Naryshkin and A. D. Polenov, also from Orel Province—and the zemstvo activists Count P. A. Geiden and A. N. Brianchaninov of Pskov. V. I. Gurko of Tver Province, later head of the Interior Ministry's Rural Section, was also a member.[26]

Golovin himself was rather an anomaly. A member of the older generation, former official in the Senate's Second (Peasant) Department, a Tver landowner and belle-lettrist under the name K. Orlovskii, he was an early supporter of peasant individualism and opponent of the commune. As such, he represented one of the few surviving links to the conservative, economic liberals of the Emancipation and immediate post-Emancipation eras. Despite his opposition to Witte's fiscal and tax policies, Golovin shared Witte's belief in the domestic and international benefits of economic growth and industrial development for Russia.[27] Indeed, since the early 1890s, Golovin had, like others within educated society, been searching for ways in which the government and the forces of order could derive some political benefit from Marxist philosophical and historical insights into the process of economic development. In

1896 he published a detailed analysis of recent works by P. B. Struve, G. V. Plekhanov, and A. Skvortsev entitled *Peasant Without Progress or Progress Without the Peasant.* [28] However, what is particularly interesting about Golovin and some of the other conservative liberals in his salon is that they had adopted an essentially materialist approach to the analysis of Russia's historical development that brought them closer to the legal Marxists than to those like Witte who remained within the "liberal" tradition with its focus on juridical and legal issues and on the development of individual civil rights. Most interesting of all, late in 1904, Golovin published a lengthy work of political history and theory that was based on European developments since the French Revolution.[29] In its final chapter, devoted to Russia, he called for the development of a new political program that not only foreshadowed many of the government's actions during the course of 1905–6 but also gave an extremely accurate description of the way the government would eventually prepare and enact its agrarian program under Stolypin. Golovin also included an electoral project that later served as a model for the government when it first began to consider constitutional reforms in the fall of 1904.[30]

In addition to these social and economic factors, two other developments played a role in the emergence of the perceptual changes being studied here: the first of these was the "information revolution" that the almost exponential growth in the quantity of data available about rural society over the course of the previous quarter of a century had produced. This was a result, in part, of the government's increasing need for knowledge about rural society upon which it could base policy decisions. More important was the role of "society" and particularly the zemstvos and their statisticians who produced large numbers of increasingly sophisticated studies, including household censuses and family budget studies, and who not only led the way for all of Europe but also pioneered many of the statistical techniques involved.[31] However, despite all the advances in knowledge, it is important to point out that in many ways the countryside remained a "terra incognita."[32] The government did not even know the exact size of its provinces.[33] Moreover, since very few private holdings had been surveyed, it is unlikely that the nobility had any precise idea of the size or boundaries of their landholdings—a situation that the continued intermingling of peasant and noble lands and the indeterminacy of the borders between them had complicated.

The second influence in the emergence of these bureaucrat reformers was the general intellectual environment in the last third of the nineteenth century.[34] Without undertaking either a formal intellectual history of this period or a genealogy of ideas, we can mention the influence of two schools of thought on the new generation. The first of these derived from Germany and from the traditions of historicism and statism initiated by Hegel and then spread into various academic disciplines, including history, law, and economics. Especially important was F. C. von Savigny, the creator of a German historical school of law that developed a strong Russian following.[35] The second derived from France and was associated with Auguste Comte's concept of positivism. It, too, had a powerful influence on the academy in Russia.[36] In the period under consideration, these two trends served to reinforce each other and, in particular, to emphasize an organic, gradual, and evolutionary (historicist) approach to the problem of change. At the same time, the Hegelian influence combined with Russia's historical experience to glorify the state and its historical role both in the past and in the future. For many Russian bureaucrats, Prince O. E. L. von Bismarck and his self-proclaimed program of state socialism epitomized this trend. A third trend, though one that was almost always subordinate to the other two, was classical, British economic liberalism with its individualistic, anti-state traditions. However, given the importance of the state in the Russian context, this trend was more strongly reflected in its French form, physiocracy, which placed more emphasis on agriculture than did Adam Smith, though even for Smith the development of agriculture was the first and "natural" step along the path to economic development.[37] The development of Marxism in the second half of the nineteenth century subsequently reinforced the materialist cast of this Anglo-French economic theory.

All of these trends influenced a number of late nineteenth century thinkers, both Russian and non-Russian, who were to have a major impact on forming the ideas of Russia's university students, particularly in the faculties of history, law, administration, and economy. Among the thinkers who seem to have had greatest influence were such men as the Russian jurist N. M. Korkunov; the German economist F. List and his Russian disciple, the "Titan of scientific thought," D. I. Mendeleev; and the British social theorists John Stuart Mill and Herbert Spencer. Korkunov has been described, along with that éminence grise of this period, Pobedonostsev, as the ideologue of autocracy and of the reign of Alexander III in particular.[38] The reflection of this strain of thought is most clear in the spell that Alexander III's figure and personality cast on government figures during the reign of his successor Nicholas II.[39] List, and Mendeleev after him, was most notable as an ideologist of economic modernization and specifically industrial development. At the same time, List placed his theory of economic development within the context of an extremely powerful nationalism. His was, indeed, a "national system" in which the state was to play the dominant role and was the principal beneficiary.[40] Spencer's theory of social Darwinism, with its concept of the "survival of the fittest" and its profound animosity toward all forms of socialism, also found a very powerful echo in Russia.[41] John Stuart Mill, the representative of classical liberal economics rather than the supporter of social-welfare legislation, also enjoyed some popularity in these circles.[42]

There are several paradoxes involved in the Russian adoption of these ideas. In the first place, all of these thinkers linked their ideas to "liberal" or "constitutional" political forms, whereas in Russia these ideas became the property of those who in the main defended the autocratic state even while favoring some form of historically progressive social and economic change. Second, both Comte and Hegel played down the role of individuals in history, emphasizing the impersonal or "spontaneous" forces at work that were independent of individual volition. However, those Russians influenced by their systems of thought rejected this particular feature and asserted the importance of human, "conscious" volition in historical change—and this is true not only of the radical intelligentsia but of the government bureaucrats whom we will be considering. Thus, one constantly finds an uneasy tension between their understanding of the spontaneous or deterministic forces of change and their unwillingness to abandon themselves to them and thus their insistence on preserving a role for conscious human activity or voluntarism.

The new generation of bureaucrats thus combined the laissez-faire liberal and individualistic economic perspectives of the Emancipation's framers and subsequent government reformers with the similarly liberal and individualistic but more materialist and economics-oriented perspectives of the modernizing noble agriculturalist reaction. Moreover, this combination of influences was to serve as a basis for the otherwise unprecedented alliance between conservative noble landowners and reform-minded government bureaucrats in 1906. Their common ground was a commitment to economic modernization. However, their primary emphasis was not on industrial modernization, as was the case with Witte and the Finance Ministry and the majority of progressive society, but on agricultural modernization, which was seen as the necessary first step toward both the development of industry and the progress of Russia as a whole. In this sense, then, these men offered an agrarian alternative based on liberal economic theory and a belief in spontaneously generated change to the industrially oriented and state-dominated "Witte system." Paradoxically, however, they shared with both Witte and the bureaucracy as a whole the newly developed commitment to an interventionist form of *opeka*, one that would for the first time interfere directly in the peasants' economic life.

Of course, reformers had always existed within the bureaucracy. However, their programs were seldom successful. What distinguished this bureaucratic vanguard of agrarian experts from their reform-minded predecessors like Valuev and the enlightened bureaucrats of the 1850s was that in the growing political crisis they conducted a campaign of persuasion that converted virtually the entire government, and eventually even Nicholas himself, to their view of the agrarian problem and its solution. They also succeeded in building an alliance with like-minded forces within the landowning nobility. Paradoxically, as we shall see, it was Witte, Russia's leading industrializer, who was primarily responsible for initiating this propaganda campaign and carrying it through to completion.[43]

The first steps on what would be a long and tortuous path to reform came in January 1902, some three months *before* the outbreak of the peasant disorders in Poltava and Khar'kov provinces, when Witte's efforts to persuade the tsar to reopen discussion on the agrarian question finally achieved fruition. Indeed, within the course of some eight days, the tsar authorized the formation of two commissions: the first, an Editing Commission within the Interior Ministry that was charged with reviewing peasant legislation; the second, an interdepartmental conference under Witte's leadership that was to investigate the condition of agriculture.[44] The public, of course, looked on the creation of these two bodies as yet another sign of the conflict between the Ministries of Interior and Finance. However, the division of labor between them had already been established in 1893 during preliminary discussions of these proposals. Indeed, as we have seen, Durnovo had already established a commission within the Interior Ministry to review peasant legislation in part as an alternative to a public investigation into the state of agriculture. Under Goremykin's leadership, that commission accomplished little beyond the publication of some collections of relevant laws.[45] Thus its reactivation in 1902 did not of itself signify any major change of attitude in the ministry or by the tsar. It was rather a by-product of one of the tsar's periodical requests for information.[46] In response, the Committee of Ministers had called on the current interior minister, D. S. Sipiagin, to draw up plans for a review of peasant legislation. However, despite the tsar's apparent support for this undertaking, on 20 February 1901, Durnovo had succeeded in postponing even this moderate initiative. Sipiagin seemed unconcerned, since he did nothing to follow through on his recommendations until Durnovo informed him of the delay almost a year later. Only at that point did Sipiagin's interest revive. Finally, on 14 January 1902, Sipiagin announced the formation of an Editing Commission that would undertake such a review. However, his rather desultory interest offered little hope that this body would have any significant impact on government agrarian policy.[47]

A much more promising initiative was the tsar's authorization, on 22 January 1902, after nearly a decade of delay, of a Special Conference on the Needs of Agriculture under the chairmanship of none other than Witte himself.[48] Oddly, it was Sipiagin who had persuaded the tsar to authorize the formation of such an investigative commission. Apparently, Sipiagin was in this instance acting on Witte's behalf.[49] Indeed, the two men were longtime friends and allies; in the view of many, they were united by a common quest to establish a "bureaucratic dictatorship" and exclude society completely from the realm of policy formation and decision making.[50] At first, however, Witte was not very optimistic about the conference; in an audience with the tsar, he questioned whether it could bring about any significant improvement in peasant welfare. In his view, only a sharp reduction in taxes could provide any real relief. However, such a cut would require in turn a reduction in the size of Russia's armed forces by one-quarter to one-third of their current strength. Unfortunately, Witte noted, such an approach was impossible in the face of the arms race, or "peacetime war" (*mirnoi voiny*) as Witte termed it, then existing in Europe. Despite these misgivings, Witte nevertheless agreed to head the new investigative body, on condition that he be granted a completely free hand both to choose its members and to draw up its agenda.[51]

Despite this apparent harmony between the two ministries, as the preparatory sessions of the Special Conference got under way in March Sipiagin seemed to have second thoughts. Thus, even though he had assured Witte in the tsar's presence that the Special Conference would be free to discuss any questions that arose, including any currently under consideration within the Interior Ministry, he now tried to prevent Witte from raising questions that related to the Emancipation Statute. Such questions, Sipiagin claimed, belonged more properly to his ministry's Editing Commission.[52] Subsequently, however, these relatively mild indications of conflict were transformed into overt hostility when, after Sipiagin's assassination in April, Witte's arch bureaucratic enemy, V. K. Pleve, was appointed interior minister.

In the two years before his own assassination, Pleve would take every opportunity to elevate the Interior Ministry's Editing Commission ahead of Witte's Special Conference. He would be responsible for launching a campaign of harassment against a number of the Special Conference's local committees, some of which their noble members had transformed into major public forums for the liberal opposition within the zemstvos.[53] Paradoxically, during these years Witte, a longtime opponent of the nobility, would become politically dependent on them, and Pleve, their supposed supporter, would become their prosecutor.

Despite the aura of conflict that surrounded these two investigations, their contradictory procedural and substantive approaches to the problems of rural reform, and the tsar's congenital indecisiveness, it was nonetheless within these two bodies that the new perceptions of rural society first achieved their full articulation. As a result, the long-standing theoretical opposition to the peasant commune as an agricultural institution would finally become an issue of practical politics.

The Special Conference on the Needs of Agriculture

The Special Conference had been instructed to investigate the needs of Russian agriculture in general and to consider measures for its benefit and for the benefit of that part of the national labor force engaged in it.[54] As finally constituted, the Conference operated on two levels: a central conference presided over by Witte and a series of county and provincial committees. The central body functioned from 2 February 1902 until 30 March 1905 and held a total of ninety-eight sessions. During this period, its activities encompassed two stages: the first examined special areas of concern and considered individual projects of reform; the second, which began on 8 December 1904, discussed the Conference's program and conclusions.

The range of topics covered was immense and underlined the complexity both of the problems facing the government and of the possible solutions. Nineteen persons initially participated, if somewhat sporadically, in its working sessions, though by the time the Conference closed, the numbers had increased considerably. Selection of the individual members primarily emphasized their professional interest in or association with agriculture and the problems of rural Russia. Some, however, clearly received appointments only because they had strong opinions on these issues. Among them were such reform-minded officials as Vorontsov-Dashkov and Ermolov, and others active in right-wing political circles such as Assistant Interior Minister A. S. Stishinskii. Pleve was also a member.[55]

Among members no longer actively serving in the ministerial branch of the government but still involved in state affairs were a number of equally qualified but more socially illustrious figures, including genuine experts, large landowners, and dignitaries (sanovniki), the best known of whom were Polovtsov and P. P. Semenov[-T'ian-Shanskii], the only surviving member of the Emancipation's Editing Commission, who had sat on numerous commissions over the years and who was also an internationally acclaimed geographer, statistician, and agrarian expert.[56]

In addition to the regular members, some ninety other persons participated in the Conference's discussions in order to provide specific, often technical, information. This group was drawn primarily from the three domestic ministries though some also came from private banks, railroads, universities, and zemstvos, as well as other ministries. Two of the most important participants during the early stages were Rittikh, a member of the Finance Ministry on special assignment to Witte himself, and Gurko, the de facto head of the Interior Ministry's competing Editing Commission. The most frequently called witness was N. N. Kutler, director of the Finance Ministry's Department of Direct Taxation, who would become Witte's agricultural minister in 1905 and still later a representative of the Kadet party in the Second and Third Dumas. One of Witte's most important collaborators during these years, Kutler was himself a member of the new generation of bureaucrats. Born in 1859, he attended Moscow University in the Faculty of Law and upon graduation practiced law for a few years before joining the Finance Ministry in 1882. Initially, Kutler served in a variety of local posts in Moscow and Simbirsk provinces, returning to the capital in 1892.[57]

After devoting some initial sessions to organizational questions and to the establishment of the Conference's field of competence, the members turned on 9 February to the problems of gathering local materials on the contemporary state of agriculture. Interior Minister Sipiagin was the first to propose forming provincial level conferences for this purpose. Polovtsov went further and suggested that committees be created at the county level as well so as to increase the value of the information gathered. He also expressed the hope that their findings would be available to the Interior Ministry's Editing Commission in order to assure some degree of coordination between it and the Special Conference. Sipiagin, however, opposed such an unwarranted interference in his ministry's business. Diplomatically, Witte agreed with him. Nonetheless, the Conference adopted Polovtsov's general proposal, with some modifications, and as a result more than six hundred local committees formed during the course of 1902.[58] As it turned out, the materials they collected were indeed used by the Editing Commission.[59]

The Conference then went on to discuss procedures for selecting the members of these local committees. With the usual government disdain for elective forms of representation, they decided that members of these local committees would be appointed from the local bureaucracy and zemstvo executive boards (in the thirty-four provinces where these existed) by the provincial governors. In addition, the governors could appoint anyone interested in or engaged in agriculture who might prove valuable. Not surprisingly, the opposition members of the zemstvos' elected assemblies were highly critical of this approach. Nonetheless, in view of the Interior Ministry's opinion a mere ten years earlier that such "consultations" were a threat to the preservation of the autocracy, the mere convocation of these committees was indeed a notable occasion, and it was so received by provincial "society."[60]

V. I. Kovalevskii, a former agronomist and now assistant finance minister, compiled the draft program for both the Special Conference and the local committees with the assistance of both bureaucratic and academic experts. The Special Conference discussed the program in two sessions held on 23 and 25 March. Once again Sipiagin defended his ministry's prerogatives and refused to allow the inclusion of any questions that might impinge on its review of peasant legislation. Witte also had to defend himself against Ermolov, who attempted to include questions implicitly critical of the Finance Ministry's fiscal and tariff policies toward agriculture over the preceding decade. Despite these conflicts, a program of forty questions was finally worked out, and the tsar approved it on 12 May 1902. However, only twenty-seven questions were to be addressed to the local committees. Drawn up before the outbreak of the peasant disorders in Poltava and Khar'kov provinces, the questions were sufficiently broad not to inhibit discussion. In the main, they focused on problems raised by the emergence of a money economy and the gradual modernization, industrialization, and specialization of rural life then under way. Only one broached the subject of reducing open-field cultivation and resettling peasants on separate parcels of land. Excluded from local consideration were questions that went beyond purely local concerns and for which the government already had sufficient data. Also excluded were questions that had political significance, including one addressing the nature and scope of government aid to zemstvos and other local organizations involved in agricultural improvement, and others suggesting reforms in the system of peasant justice and administration, the establishment of a new economic-administrative unit, and limitations on and the equalization of local tax burdens. After the settlement of these procedural questions, the Special Conference began its discussion of various substantive questions of rural reform.[61]

Extensification or Intensification: Kutler's Experimental Approach

The moving force behind the Special Conference once it started functioning was, of course, Witte, the chairman; he was present at every one of its plenary sessions. At first, however, he did not commit himself to any particular approach to the agrarian problem either in public or before the Conference. Nonetheless, during the opening days of substantive discussions, Witte revealed his ideas indirectly. Thus, among the very first materials presented was a proposal that, although prepared by Kutler and submitted in the name of the Department of Direct Taxation of which he was head, Witte had initiated.[62] The project, "Proposed Measures for the Improvement of Peasant Land-Use . . . ,"[63] took as its starting point a project that D. P. Semenov, the brother of P. P. Semenov [-T'ian Shanskii], a former assistant administrator of the Section of Rural Economy and Agricultural Statistics in the agricultural ministry and currently a member of the Statistical Council of the Interior Ministry, had compiled in 1899.

Semenov's project, which had been widely circulated within the bureaucracy when it was first compiled,[64] had raised two concerns that lay at the very heart of the government's dilemma: first, whether the communal system of peasant land use could, in fact, provide a satisfactory source of peasant income; and second, whether it would be possible to improve peasant agriculture without changing existing forms of land use. Semenov's answer took the form of a choice between policies that embodied diametrically opposed social assumptions. On the one hand, the allotment land fund could continue to be regarded as the principal source of income for the entire peasant *soslovie*, in which case the government would have to continue the traditional policy of protecting the peasantry from proletarianization and landlessness. However, given the growing number of peasants who either were landless or lacked a sufficient quantity of land to farm independently, such an approach would, at one point or another, require the government to grant an "additional allotment." On the other hand—and this was Semenov's preference—the allotment land fund could be looked at as a source of income only for that portion of the peasantry that could derive an adequate standard of living from it. In this case, the government would have to undertake only a single and final redistribution of allotment land among peasants capable of supporting themselves from agriculture.

Semenov's approach to the agrarian problem was thus very similar to that of the laissez-faire liberals, since it would have eliminated the various *soslovie* restrictions on peasant landownership and placed all members of the peasantry at the mercy of the market. However, in order to prevent the possibility of an excessive fragmentation of landholdings or the accumulation of land in the hands of the more prosperous, Semenov did propose setting minimum and maximum limits on the size of peasant holdings. He was less concerned about the increase—considered inevitable—in the number of landless peasants such a measure might produce, claiming that this would create no more of a problem than that presented by those landless peasants and rural and urban wage laborers who already existed.

After such a reorganization of peasant landownership patterns, Semenov assumed that the peasants would begin transferring to improved forms of land use on a voluntary basis, without need of any further government intervention. However, the government would need to provide some assistance both to the newly landless who wanted to migrate to state lands and to those who remained on the land and sought to improve their economies.[65] Semenov optimistically calculated that accomplishment of the proposed changes was possible in ten to fifteen years, arguing that any further postponements or delays would only lead to increased complications and costs.

According to the Department of Direct Taxation, the problem with Semenov's project was that it had all but ignored the economic deficiencies of existing forms of land use, to the point even of considering open-field systems inevitable. The Department attributed this failure to the widespread assumption that Russian agriculture would continue to be extensive in nature for the foreseeable future. As a consequence, Semenov, like members of the opposition movement, had placed exclusive blame for the peasants' agricultural distress on land-hunger.[66] However, if one focused on the problem not of land-hunger but peasant land-use practices, then it became possible to consider other alternatives, notably the shift by the peasantry to more intensive and productive forms of agriculture.

The Department acknowledged that there were innumerable obstacles to the successful implementation of such a policy. In particular, it pointed to the peasants' exaggerated attachment to the land, itself a major cause of the excessive fragmentation of their holdings and the predatory and destructive forms of cultivation practiced on them. Worse still, the peasant's reverence for the land had been incorporated into existing legislation and was responsible not only for placing limitations on his civil rights but for undermining both public and private attempts at agricultural improvement. As a consequence, the individual peasant was subject to the arbitrary will of the commune and effectively deprived of the right to cultivate his land and receive the benefits of his own labor. Thus, in accordance with Witte's publicly stated views, the Department concluded that any long-term improvement in the state of peasant agriculture depended in the last analysis on a revision of peasant legislation. However, noting that even well-intentioned laws could be both ineffective and dangerous, the Department was unwilling to postpone the adoption of a new agrarian program until the Interior Ministry's review of legislation was complete. As a consequence, it proposed a highly innovative exit from what was by now a very familiar stalemate.

The Department's project* began by noting the many examples of successful agricultural improvement already accomplished within the existing legal framework, particularly those undertaken with the aid of the zemstvos. To the Department, this indicated that the peasants were well aware of the deficiencies in their existing systems of land use and the steps necessary to eliminate them. The Department also pointed to the many spontaneous efforts by peasants to overcome economic hardships either by migrating to the east or by eliminating open fields and consolidating their holdings—even though such efforts were often unsuccessful. On the basis of this evidence, it concluded "that a large part of the peasantry does not reject the assistance offered to them [by individual zemstvos] for the improvement of the existing structure of land use." Nonetheless, winning the peasants' approval for such im-

---

*To avoid any confusion between this project and the later Kutler project, which was discussed at the end of 1905, this project, compiled within the Department of Direct Taxation, will be referred to henceforth as *the Department's project*.

provements was a slow process. However, once they had witnessed a number of successful examples, they were quickly persuaded to introduce similar improvements themselves. Consequently, there was, in fact, "no reason to suppose that the contemplated measures . . . would not lead, although not immediately, to useful results."[67]

The Department then went on to make a number of specific proposals for the intensification of peasant agriculture, ranging from the elimination of open fields between neighboring villages and nonpeasant owners and the breaking-up of large villages and culminating with the complete elimination of open-field agriculture within each independent village and the formation of compact holdings (*otruba* and *khutora*). However, it was not sufficient, in the Department's view, simply to grant peasants their land in individual ownership and then rely on their spontaneous desires for the subsequent transfer to improved forms of land use. Indeed, the Department believed that granting peasants title to their land without providing for the simultaneous elimination of open fields would, in all probability, encourage the accumulation of land by more prosperous peasants at the expense of their weaker neighbors. As a consequence, the government would have to intervene in order to ensure that such changes in land utilization practices were, in fact, accomplished. However, its role ought to be confined to the drafting of legislation that would facilitate this process by eliminating the material sacrifices currently involved. Indeed, the experience of other European countries suggested that, although major legislation had always accompanied such reforms in land-use practices, it had also always contained elements of compulsion that had provoked potentially dangerous dissatisfaction and popular disturbances. Consequently, it would be more prudent merely to regulate the formal aspects of the process, indicating its final goals and purposes and some of the methods appropriate to the improvement of peasant land use. The final decision on the adoption of specific measures ought, however, to be that of local institutions, which could then tailor them to local conditions and the particular desires of the peasants concerned. Similarly, the initial decision about whether or not to leave the commune should not be obligatory but the choice of the individual peasant. However, the government would have to make special arrangements so that landless peasants forced out of the commune by these changes would be able to acquire land from the Peasant Bank since such "weak" peasants would not be suitable candidates for migration, as Semenov had assumed.

Finally, for the execution of its reform program, the project proposed the organization of special county-level institutions under the direction of the local marshal of the nobility and consisting primarily of land captains,[68] assisted by surveyors and agronomists. An interdepartmental commission would supervise the entire procedure and would also resolve whatever problems and misunderstandings arose during implementation. The government would bear the costs.[69]

Having made these proposals for what amounted to the total restructuring of peasant agriculture, the Department then addressed some of the practical problems involved in their implementation. In particular, it emphasized the time and the cost of such a project as well as the demands for trained personnel it would make. In order to meet the inevitable objections raised by such a vast undertaking, the Department recommended that it be introduced gradually, in the form of a limited experiment, to allow the practical impact of the various measures to be examined in detail prior to making a total commitment. An additional advantage in adopting such an experimental approach was that there would be no need of any preliminary legislative changes. And, echoing Polovtsov's hopes, the Department expressed its belief that the information gathered from such an experiment would prove valuable for the Interior Ministry's concurrent review of peasant legislation.

The project's most notable innovations were its reinterpretation of peasant psychology and its commitment to empirical and experimental methods of implementation. At the same time, the project represented a judicious balance between demands for the increased development of individualism and a continued reliance on an interventionist bureaucratic *opeka*. In each of these respects, it accurately foreshadowed the gradualism and voluntarism that were to characterize the Stolypin Reforms themselves. It also demonstrated a highly sophisticated understanding of the obstacles and complexities involved that critics were to deny the government even after several years experience of implementing the reforms in the post-1906 period. Particularly significant, given the degree of support for the commune and opposition to change that still existed within the government, was the project's pragmatic emphasis on the economic problems of communal forms of land use rather than on the communal system of administration or landownership. At the same time, the project expressed the growing sense of urgency within the government and demanded immediate action. This explains in part its attempt to combine the traditional government commitment to directed change with a "liberal" faith in the power of organic and spontaneous social and economic forces.[70]

Indeed, the Department's project already evinced a new conception of the role of both government and law by arguing in effect that only direct and active involvement of the government could solve the agrarian problem. However, this involvement did not primarily concern the traditional task of enacting legislation designed to impose order from above. Rather, it was concerned with practical activity—with the actual process of propagating and realizing a reform program that reflected the spontaneous and voluntary desires of the peasants themselves, that sought to acquire the necessary knowledge directly from that activity and then to convince through demonstration.

This approach of course, followed the model of the actual process of change, as observed within peasant society itself. It also echoed Vorontsov-Dashkov's proposals of the early 1890s. However, given the attitudes that still prevailed within both government and society, this was, indeed, a revolutionary approach. It not only assumed that the agrarian problem was in the last analysis a product of the peasants' consciousness or attitudes, but also that such attitudes had continued to develop and were now in a position to influence the government in its selection of a program of agrarian reform. In effect, the Department's project attempted to divine the wisdom of the "Owl of Minerva" before it was too late to reap the political, economic, and social benefits. However, although the old myth of "peasant ignorance" was now abandoned, a new myth was in the making: that the government's role was simply to realize those economic and social potentialities for change that were already manifesting themselves in reality and to mobilize the peasantry's own spontaneous, even preconscious, desires for such improvements.

Despite, or perhaps even because of, these innovations, the project itself received a rather desultory reception when it was discussed in the plenary session of the Special Conference. Nonetheless, in May 1902, Witte succeeded in having it transferred to a special commission for further examination. Apparently, the Conference had accepted the project's two basic, if implicit, theses: that the real issue in the agrarian crisis was the problem of communal land use, and only secondarily that of communal landownership; and that practical measures would probably be more successful in the resolution of that crisis than legislation alone.[71]

V. N. Kokovtsov, then assistant finance minister, directed the special commission set up to examine the Department's project. The commission comprised two ideological groups: a majority of five who opposed the commune, including Kokovtsov, Kutler, and Kovalevskii;[72] and a minority of three who supported it, most notably D. P. Semenov and Stishinskii.[73] Not surprisingly, this commission adopted the Department's proposals, but it delayed their realization by conducting an independent study of some ten to twenty counties to determine the nature of existing inadequacies in land use and their causes and to draw up appropriate measures for their resolution. The results of their work were reviewed on 16 November 1903. The Interior, Finance, and agricultural ministries then devised jointly a program for the realization of the proposed experiment. The ministries chose seven provinces and instructed each governor to select two villages in his province for the experiment as well as suitable officials to carry it out. Work was to begin in the summer of 1904. Unfortunately, this remarkable experiment went no further, either because of the reluctance of the Interior Ministry and the governors who had been placed in charge of it[74] or, more likely, because of the onset of the war with Japan. In any case, the outbreak of revolution at the beginning of 1905 was to render the entire experiment irrelevant.

As a consequence, the significance of these initiatives lies not in what they achieved but in their having outlined the basic problems confronting the government as it tried to resolve the agrarian problem and, even more important, the shape such reforms would eventually have to take. However, at this stage in the bureaucracy's deliberations neither the Department's project nor its underlying assumptions had achieved the necessary political support within either government or society to permit their acceptance as the basis of a new governmental agrarian policy.

Rittikh, the Commune, and the Family Farm

After its consideration of the Department of Direct Taxation's Project, the Special Conference continued to emphasize the commune's economic role as an agrotechnical or land-using institution and to a lesser extent its juridical role as landowner. Thus it shifted attention away from the more traditional, "liberal," concern with the commune's administrative role within the *soslovie* system and the related problems of peasant civil rights. As a result, it devoted most of its time to the discussion of practical measures that would have the most immediate impact on the level of agricultural productivity and the development of a market-based individualism among the peasantry. At the same time, Witte launched what amounted to a massive propaganda campaign designed to undermine the almost mythical belief in the commune's social and political benefits and, in particular, its sacred and symbolic role as guarantor of the status quo.

To this end, Witte directed Rittikh to compile a work specifically devoted to the socioeconomic and psychological consequences of the peasantry's dependence on the commune as landowner and user and as administrative unit. Completed during April 1903 and published at the end of the year under the auspices of the Special Conference, this work amounted to 215 pages of sustained assault upon the commune in all its aspects as well as upon contemporary social attitudes toward that institution. In addition, it included a 9-page conclusion detailing measures to ease peasant departures from the commune that was subsequently adopted as the program for the final stages of the Special Conference's deliberations, beginning in December 1904.[75]

Rittikh was, as we have seen, a member of the new generation of bureaucrats. His first appointment had been to the Interior Ministry's Rural Section. Subsequently he was sent to Vladivostok, where he was in charge of Far Eastern migration. Transferring to the Finance Ministry's Department of Direct Taxation, Witte's headquarters for rural reform, he became Witte's special assistant for agriculture. Later, he was to become the principal official in charge of implementing the Stolypin Reforms within the agricultural ministry. He also served as tsarist Russia's last minister of agriculture, from 12 January to 27 February 1917.[76]

The first part of Rittikh's work summarized traditional attitudes toward the commune and examined the nature of periodical repartitions. On the basis of the available evidence, Rittikh concluded that the commune had failed to fulfill the expectations of both government and society. Indeed, the commune had not only not prevented the formation of a rural proletariat; it had encouraged the formation of both a "rich" minority and a "poor" majority within each commune. Indeed, although Rittikh declined to generalize, he presented a picture of the commune as an institution that was dominated by the kulak or *miroed* (literally, "commune-eater"), the moneylenders, and land speculators who held the other peasants in thrall by their monopoly on petty credit. They used this power to exploit the repartitional mechanism and the system of mutual responsibility in order to accumulate communal land at the expense of the weaker members of the commune. They then rented this land back at a higher price to those land-hungry and landless members of the commune from whom it had originally been taken, thus subjecting them to even further exploitation. At the same time, he argued, these practices had led to a decline in agricultural productivity.[77]

Rittikh's interpretation, of course, ran counter to the overwhelming weight of contemporary government and public opinion. However, the real novelty of his analysis was that it contradicted the conclusions of many of the sources on which his study was based. Thus, drawing much of his evidence from populists and others who supported the commune and who therefore tended to minimize its negative consequences, Rittikh had built up a devastating case against that institution along lines very similar to those that the Marxist critics of neopopulism had adopted in the preceding decade.[78] However, what Rittikh did not directly bring out, though it was implicit in his argument, was that this polarization between "rich" and "poor" peasants was, in fact, only the superficial manifestation of a more basic conflict between the principles of individual and collective property ownership.

Rittikh's work was not, however, limited to destroying the "myth of the commune," for he was also interested in finding practical alternatives to the existing communal system of agriculture. Thus he discussed the viability of small-scale, individual property ownership based on an evaluation of both Russian and European evidence, primarily from the German Rhineland, Belgium, and France. And once again he contradicted prevailing assumptions by concluding that notwithstanding the supposed social and political benefits of the commune the individual peasant family farm was, in fact, an entirely stable and completely viable economic institution. Nor was there any evidence to indicate that this form of landownership and use was inevitably bound to disintegrate and produce that much dreaded polarization of the peasantry into a landless proletarian majority and a prosperous and land-rich minority. The problem, however, was finding a way to make the transition from communal to individual forms of land use.[79]

Rittikh then turned to a discussion of the second part of Article 165 of the Redemption Statute of 1861, which had been eliminated in 1893 and which had required that when a peasant prepaid the amount due for the land granted at the time of emancipation with the intent of separating from the commune, that is to say of claiming individual title to his strips, he be granted, so far as was possible, a single compact parcel of land.[80] Rittikh, however, disagreed with both Kutler and the members of the Interior Ministry's Editing Commission and opposed restoring the Article to its original form. In Rittikh's view, there was no need to link individual title claims for a share of the commune's land to a simultaneous physical separation of that land in the form of a single, integral parcel. The increased security of tenure that would follow from simply granting the peasants legal title to strips that remained in open-field use was itself sufficient to lead to an immediate rise in productivity. Rittikh's position on this issue, which was eventually to become a key part of the Stolypin Reforms, was based on laissez-faire, liberal, and individualistic assumptions and a commitment to gradual, spontaneous, and organic change. Thus Rittikh also argued that both title claims and physical separations from the commune should be initiated voluntarily by each individual peasant and executed on the basis of mutual agreement between the two parties. He was particularly insistent that separations not be made obligatory for the commune, for not only might the commune's interests be harmed, but obligatory separations could prove especially damaging to the interests of the separator. For even after separation, such peasants would remain dependent on the commune for the continued use of both pasture and other common lands. Moreover, separators would need to preserve the goodwill of the commune so that they would be able to leave their cottages and other buildings within the central community until they had firmly established themselves on the new land and were in a position to transfer them.

As for the implementation of these reforms and the negotiation of such "amicable agreements," Rittikh proposed that the land captains, as the officials closest to the peasantry, take charge.[81] Should agreement nonetheless prove impossible, Rittikh did allow for separations on an obligatory basis, though he clearly felt uneasy with this solution and suggested that in such cases the separator receive financial compensation from the commune instead. Acknowledging the doubts that had been expressed by the Interior Ministry's local conferences in 1895 as to the possibility of a successful outcome to such proposals, he warned that the land captains would have to exercise extreme caution. At the same time, offering government loans to help those peasants who chose this course could ease the process of separation. Finally, he recommended granting land titles not in the name of the family but of the head of the household, thus assuring the most complete individualization of property rights possible.

Despite his underlying concern with the problems of communal land use and peasant agricultural productivity, Rittikh directed his attention primarily to developing a private-property consciousness within the peasantry. However, like Kutler, he sought to achieve this goal not by the traditional route of granting the peasantry full and equal civil rights but by gradually dividing up the commune's land into individually owned holdings—first on paper, as it were, though ultimately in physical reality as well. Moreover, the evidence indicated that peasant small-holdings in both Europe and Russia were also more productive than large-scale forms of landownership. Indeed, Rittikh argued, the evidence from Western Europe suggested that it was the very absence of individual property rights that was responsible for the high level of unrest currently plaguing the Russian countryside:

> When peasants received stable rights to the lands they owned, then all unrest among them ceased; small-scale landed property, apparently, is [not only] one of the most reliable foundations of the civil legal order. . . ; the whole cultural power of the country and . . . its economic and political strength is built on [it].[82]

Besides all these reasons for supporting the development of small-scale property ownership in Russia, there was the even broader question of popular or public morality and the dangers that flowed from the current state of lawlessness in the countryside. The situation was so bad, indeed, that not only did the peasants violate existing laws with impunity but they now automatically rejected the instructions and advice of the law's representatives and executors in favor of their opposite. However, according to Rittikh, this state of affairs had arisen not because of the peasant's innate ignorance or backwardness, as was often charged, but because of the law's complete lack of conformity to the needs of the people. Moreover, if this situation were allowed to continue, the peasant would only be further convinced that every manifestation of authority had to be opposed. Rittikh quoted one commentator's observation that such a situation ultimately creates "a fatalistic world outlook as to the necessity of evil. . . , [so that] the peasant begins to believe in the rule of evil. . . . [T]he absence of rights to land is equivalent to the absence of land [itself]."[83] Thus, Rittikh concluded, law had to conform more closely to needs in order to carry any authority—a conclusion that was similar to Kutler's and that recalled the assumptions of the Emancipation's framers some forty years earlier to the effect that it was society, history, or "life itself" that was the source of law, not the autocratic government.[84]

Rittikh then confronted the traditional fear that any breach of the commune would immediately produce a rapid increase in the size of the proletariat. He argued that, even with the commune, the seasonal ebb and flow of labor between country and city, which depended on the conditions of both domestic and international markets, not to mention the existing surplus of urban labor, had already created a dangerous situation of urban unrest and unemployment. However, guaranteeing the peasantry firm rights of property ownership would actually alleviate this situation, since profitable agricultural employment would become available to a larger proportion of the peasantry than was at present possible. And to reinforce his argument, he pointed out that despite the universal dread of enlarging the size of Russia's urban proletariat, Arthur Young, the noted English authority on agriculture at the time of the French Revolution, had long ago observed that a large rural proletariat was an even greater threat to political stability than an urban one.[85]

Rittikh's commitment to laissez-faire economic liberalism also led him to favor the elimination of all restrictions on the disposability of peasant allotment land. And once again he countered traditional fears by arguing that far from leading to an increase in the exploitation of the peasantry by the kulaks, such a measure would actually reduce their influence by encouraging urban dwellers and other nonpeasants to move to the countryside and acquire land and thus to serve as a stabilizing force. In addition, the higher cultural level of these newcomers would help diffuse improved agricultural techniques and raise the standards of rural administration. Moreover, Rittikh argued, it was completely false to assume that were the peasantry to have complete freedom to dispose of their land, they would be rapidly transformed into landless proletarians. On the contrary, they already possessed an exaggerated faith in the land that would not only be strengthened by granting them complete authority over it but would place them in an even stronger position to resist kulak exploitation.

In a final affirmation of his faith in small-scale individual landowner-ship, Rittikh resolutely opposed any policy that might encourage the concentration of land in the hands of a wealthy, or bourgeois, peasant minority. On the contrary, he composed a paean to the peasant that recalled the populists of an earlier era and prefigured by a number of years the appearance of those ideologists of the peasant family farm who were associated with A. V. Chaianov and his organization and production school of economic theory[86]:

It is important for the state that a certain quantity of land be owned
by a population which personally applies its labor to the land. . . .
These small-scale property-owners who personally work on the
land also constitute a healthy foundation of the state organism—
"which is fed by its roots."[87]

Thus, rejecting the attitudes and policies dominant within the bureaucracy during the reign of Alexander III, Rittikh, like both Marxists and
liberals, succeeded in demonstrating not only that the commune was not
the much desired preserver of order but that it was itself in the process
of disintegration brought on by the inexorable forces of social and economic change that were beyond the power of mere laws to halt. Moreover,
these forces were responsible for the peasantry's increasingly rapid polarization into mutually hostile economic classes. Using the same empirical data that the revisionist Marxists had used in their assault on the
dogmas of orthodox Marxism, Rittikh also rejected the inevitability of
rural differentiation.[88] However, Rittikh based his defense of free will
not on philosophical principles but on traditional assumptions concerning the power of law and the role of the bureaucracy in defending the
autocracy's interests. Thus, in place of class differentiation, he proposed
the development of a system of small-scale peasant landed property that
would not only solve the economic problem but would simultaneously
provide a new social, economic, and political foundation for the traditional autocratic and supraclass state. The superordinate mechanism of
bureaucratic *opeka* would therefore counterbalance his seemingly wholehearted commitment to an atomistic form of individualism and would
act as the unifying force. In effect, Rittikh thus offered Russia a "third
way" that avoided the evils of both capitalism, with its class conflict,
and socialism with its abolition of private property.[89]

   In two respects, Rittikh's proposals were considerably more radical
than those of his fellow bureaucrats. On the one hand, his enthusiasm
for the peasant family farm suggests that he might already have abandoned the assumption that noble agriculture would continue to play a
leading role in the national economy—an assumption that had guided
the government's agrarian policy since before the Emancipation. On the
other hand, by setting the maximum norm for peasant landownership at
twenty-five desiatinas per person per village, he had declared his opposition to the development of large-scale peasant holdings, or farmer-type
economies.[90] Indeed, far from trying to drive a wedge between the strong
and the weak, as the government's critics often charged,[91] Rittikh's proposals, like Kutler's, attempted to adopt measures that would reduce the
size of both rural and urban proletariats with the goal of reducing existing conflicts and avoiding future ones. Reflecting the provincialization
of the bureaucracy that had taken place during the preceding decades,

Rittikh also abandoned the government's traditional fetish for adopting legislation that had to be applied uniformly throughout the Russian Empire in favor of what would become a new fetish for the unique and the local that would allow flexibility in the implementation process.

The Local Committees and the Commune: The Development of Political Support

Rittikh's assault on the commune was not Witte's only weapon in the struggle to overcome the apparently implacable political opposition to rural reform. Since the mid-1890s, Witte had sponsored a variety of studies designed to provide an empirical basis for his campaign to reeducate government and society and to win the political support necessary to effect a change in the government's agrarian policy. Moreover, the new generation of bureaucrats widely read all of these works. Thus, as part of his campaign to abolish mutual responsibility, Witte had commissioned N. K. Brzheskii, a student of financial law who had written on that institution in 1895, to study its relationship to the growth of peasant tax arrears.[92] He subsequently submitted this study, completed in 1897, for the degree of doctor of financial law at St. Petersburg University. Brzheskii, who was at the time a member of the Finance Ministry's Department of Direct Taxation and later its assistant director, then published a short study of the relationship between the commune and peasant economic insecurity that appeared in 1899 with the design of bolstering Witte's campaign for the creation of a commission on the agrarian problem.[93] In it, Brzheskii expressed his belief in the paramount importance of small-scale peasant agriculture to the national economy. Subsequently, he wrote a variety of journal articles critical of the commune, many of which appeared in his Ministry's journal, *Vestnik Finansov*.[94]

Witte also commissioned two works by P. Lokhtin, the well-known expert on European and Russian agriculture. The first, which appeared in 1903, was a study of changes in the size of the sown area in Russia over the preceding twenty years; it demonstrated that within the next ten to fifteen years Russia would run out of free land that could be brought under cultivation.[95] Thus, he concluded, it was imperative to initiate steps to increase the level of productivity. Lokhtin's second work for Witte was a statistical analysis of the repartitional mechanism designed to demonstrate its role in the creation of a landless proletariat within the existing communal system.[96] Finally, Witte was responsible for enabling the Danish agronomist and Peasant Bank official A. A. Kofod to complete his investigation of peasant *khutora* within European Russia.[97] Completed and published in 1904, this work examined the origin and development of these farms as an example of the peasantry's spontaneous attempt to improve agricultural productivity and thus as a practical alternative to open-field or communal forms of land use. Kofod's study also served to show the importance of the role of example and demonstration in converting peasants to new forms of land use. After the adoption of the Stolypin Reforms, Kofod would become an important technical adviser and head of the Reform Inspectorate.

Important as these studies were, the work of the local committees of the Special Conference proved even more significant. These committees were responsible for assembling a vast amount of material on local agricultural conditions in the most ambitious investigation of local conditions ever undertaken in Russia. At the same time, they had a major social and political impact since they brought the largest number of local figures together to discuss the affairs of government since the Legislative Commission appointed by Catherine II in 1767.[98]

The committees themselves were convoked at the end of May 1902. The course of the next three months witnessed the formation of a total of 618 committees in European Russia, Poland, the Caucasus, Siberia, the southeastern steppe, and Turkestan, 536 on the county level. Approximately 12,500 people participated in their work. At the provincial level, half of the members were appointed ex officio, the other half having been selected by the governors. On the county level, the proportion of officeholders was considerably lower, averaging only a quarter of the members. Of those who served on the county and provincial levels within European Russia whose social status is known, slightly more than a quarter were bureaucrats, half of them members of the Interior Ministry, mainly land captains. An almost equivalent proportion identified themselves as nobles, though not all owned land; and slightly under a quarter were members of zemstvo assemblies or their staffs and thus also predominantly noble. The proportion of zemstvo members in the thirty-four provinces with these institutions was, of course, higher, with one-third at the county level and slightly less in the provincial committees. Zemstvo members and employees constituted an absolute majority in 1 provincial and 49 county committees. Only 240 county and 6 provincial committees invited any peasants to participate and, as a result, only 13 percent of the overall membership were peasants. Not surprisingly, about half of the peasants were village or canton elders.[99]

What is noteworthy about these committees, however, is not that a high proportion of nobles participated but that an absolute majority was held by nobles who were outside the bureaucratic apparatus. Given the political potential of these committees, it is all the more surprising that there was such a high proportion of zemstvo members, though only some twenty-three committees actually attempted to exploit their position or to become involved in the larger political and constitutional struggles that were just then beginning to gather momentum and take on national significance.[100] Even so, the Special Conference played an important role in the politicization of the provincial nobility and the development of the liberal opposition both within the zemstvos and without.[101] Its primary purpose, however, was to provide the government with information about the state of both local agriculture and local opinion. In this respect, the work of the local committees served as a kind of public opinion poll. This was the function that Witte sought to exploit in order to further the cause of rural reform. In this sense, it can be said that Witte and the "liberal" minority within the nobility shared a common perspective. At the same time, however, neither Witte nor the liberal nobles had developed a coherent program of reform.

The first county-level committees began collecting materials in August 1902. After local discussion, these data, together with the reports of the county-level committees, were sent on to the provincial conferences for further discussion. By the end of July 1903, this complex process was complete for the European provinces and all the evidence and recommendations were assembled in St. Petersburg.[102] These materials, published in fifty-eight volumes, appeared the same year, one for each province or administrative division; 491 complete sets of this material were subsequently distributed to various members of the bureaucracy at all levels of the administration as well as to selected marshals of the nobility, zemstvo executive boards, individual scholars, and others.[103] In addition, twenty-three volumes of topical summaries covering European Russia were published, 1,359 sets of which were similarly distributed.[104] A general digest of the summaries was also issued in one volume.[105] Finally, a brief pamphlet that purported to express the committee's majority and minority conclusions on the most important questions submitted to them summarized the entire work of the committees.[106] Never had the products of an official government investigation achieved such widespread public distribution.

Although the fifty-eight volumes of local materials remain the single best source of information on the opinions of both local officials and inhabitants as well as on the condition of agriculture and the peasantry in each locality during the postemancipation era, it is unlikely that more than a handful of people actually examined all of them in any depth. In the impact of this paper onslaught on government and public opinion, the one-volume digest and the twenty-three topical summaries must have been of much greater significance. A group of sixteen bureaucrats from both the agricultural and Finance ministries and presumably sympathetic to Witte's approach to the agrarian problem prepared the summaries.[107] The work proceeded under Rittikh's general direction; he himself compiled the two most politically salient summaries—those on peasant land use and the peasant sociolegal structure.[108] In addition,

Rittikh composed what can only be described as a propaganda tract, which appeared first in the 21 December 1903 issue of *Vestnik Finansov* and then as a separate pamphlet at the beginning of 1904—fourteen brief pages claiming to summarize the essence of those fifty-eight volumes. He presented the local committees' recommendations in two short paragraphs:[109]

> To aid the transfer of rural communities to personal ownership and individual *khutora*, granting to individual peasants the right to separate their allotment land from communal land use without requiring the consent of the commune.
>
> To eliminate the peasantry's isolation in civil and personal law according to *sosloviia*, particularly in the area of administration and justice.[110]

What is most significant about these conclusions is not so much their content—though that is important—but the fact that the recommendation to individualize both peasant landownership *and* use had been placed ahead of the one favoring the abolition of the peasantry's *soslovie* status and their equalization and integration. Clearly, this decision was taken deliberately in order to shift attention, even if only slightly, away from the sensitive political issue of the commune's administrative role within the *soslovie* system and toward those more practical economic concerns that had been raised earlier by both Kutler and Rittikh. As such, the decision reflected both a shift in Witte's political strategy in deference to the prevailing political mood within the government and the conservative majority of the nobility as well as the broader perceptual revolution that was then in progress. However, unlike the other materials that have been discussed, Rittikh's pamphlet was designed to persuade not by the presentation of factual data but by its demonstration that widespread support for these changes already existed within the local nobility and bureaucracy. However, in seeking to realize this political purpose, Rittikh's conclusions seem to have seriously, and presumably intentionally, misrepresented the actual positions taken by the local committees. Indeed, not only were their conclusions incomparably more complex and, therefore, more difficult to interpret than Rittikh represented, but the Special Conference's entire attempt to give the economic issues of land use and landownership precedence over the juridical and political issue of peasant rights was a similarly deliberate simplification.

Fortunately, the claim that the committees' opinions were misrepresented can be supported without reading the entire fifty-eight volumes. They have been analyzed by several independent authors who, although differing in approach, nonetheless enable us to judge the accuracy of Rittikh's interpretation of local opinion. At the same time, these analyses provide us with a deeper insight into the workings of this vast opinion poll as well as the changes that had taken place in provincial public opinion since the mid-1890s.

The most detailed analysis of the local committees' opinions on the issue of peasant landownership and land use was the one-volume digest prepared by S. I. Shidlovskii on the basis of Rittikh's own summary volume on that subject. Shidlovskii was himself a member of the new generation of bureaucrats. He was born in 1861, the year of the Emancipation; had been graduated from the Imperial Aleksandrovskii Lyceum; and then moved to the countryside, where he undertook the modernization of his own relatively large landholdings, sought to encourage improvements in peasant agriculture, and became active as a liberal in the local zemstvo. In 1900 Shidlovskii entered the Finance Ministry and became a member of the board of the Peasant Bank. In 1905 he would become head of the Department of Agriculture in the agricultural ministry. Subsequently, he became a left Octobrist and was elected to the Third Duma in 1907.[111] Shidlovskii was also responsible for compiling the Conference's summary volumes on the zemstvos and on land taxation and the volume on the problems of surveying and land seizures, which painted a very grim picture indeed of the absence of law and order in the critical sphere of property ownership.[112]

Given Rittikh's somewhat extravagant claims in the *Vestnik Finansov*, one is surprised to learn from Shidlovskii's digest that only a mere 160 of the 531 committees formed in European Russia had even raised the question of the commune as an economic institution. Despite such a moderate level of interest, Shidlovskii interprets this to mean that the commune was the one issue that was basic to the whole purpose of the Special Conference. Tabulating the opinions of these 160 committees, Shidlovskii goes on to note that 47 actually favored the preservation of the commune either in its current form or with some minor legislative adjustments, presumably along the lines of those being worked out within the Interior Ministry's commission. At the other end of the spectrum, however, a total of 96 committees expressed some form of hostility toward the commune. The suggestions made for its improvement were, however, quite varied, though a majority of 52 could be said to have been fairly strongly in favor of establishing individual forms of ownership and use, including 10 committees that specifically recommended the formation of *khutora*. The other 44 committees were more restrained and simply recommended legislative changes to make transfers to individual forms of ownership easier, though without adopting any compulsory measures for the abolition of communal land use. Of the remaining committees, 14 adopted a completely laissez-faire approach and opposed any government intervention on either side of the question, preferring to let the problem of peasant land use resolve itself. Finally, 3 committees took refuge in a call for still further study.[113] I. V. Sosnovskii, who compiled the summary volume on landownership, confirmed these figures. However, Sosnovskii indicates that only 3 committees favored the abolition of the commune.[114]

Thus, by the Conference's official count, less than one-fifth of the European committees had actually favored the development of *khutora* as a solution to the agrarian problem. Clearly, both Rittikh and Shidlovskii had manipulated the evidence in order to give the impression of a much higher degree of opposition to the commune than actually existed. Curiously, when it came to the local committees' opinions concerning the *soslovie* issue, neither Shidlovskii nor Rittikh, on whose summary volume Shidlovskii again depended for his data, gave any numerical compilations. Rather, they were both content merely to assert that a majority of the committees favored integrating the peasantry into the general civil order. As a consequence, it is impossible to confirm their assertions without recapitulating their work. However, their reticence suggests that here, too, they may have manipulated the evidence.[115]

Another tabulation that reached quite different conclusions was that by the highly respected P. P. Semenov[-T'ian-Shanskii]. Semenov, now reputedly a defender of the commune, had been dissatisfied with the official figures and had set about compiling his own summary, though it, too, was published under the Conference's auspices in 1905. Limiting himself exclusively to the question of peasant land use, Semenov focused on the 372 committees within the Great Russian provinces where communal forms of landownership predominated. In these committees, Semenov found that 205 committees had raised the land-use question. Of these, 121 had favored preserving the commune as it was, though a few called for some minor legislative adjustments; 27 chose to leave the question to local initiative; only 53 favored a gradual and voluntary transfer from communal to individual ownership. According to Semenov, only 4 committees advocated the commune's immediate abolition. Clearly, these figures were less favorable than even Shidlovskii's. However, for the sake of delicacy, Semenov refrained from stating outright that a majority of the committees did *not*, in fact, want to abolish the commune.[116]

Among the more strictly independent surveys of the Special Conference's work, M. Tolmachev's specifically avoided the critical issue of the commune and its relationship to peasant landownership and land use. In Tolmachev's view, the issues were so complex and the differences of opinion so wide that any attempt to tabulate them would be meaningless. However, he did note that a majority of the committees, including both supporters and opponents of the commune, often within the same committee, opposed any "artificial," that is, bureaucratic, violation of or interference with the communal structure. Any changes, they felt, should develop spontaneously, on the initiative of each individual commune.[117]

Another student of the Special Conference was the well-known economist and statistician, and a founder of the liberal Union of Liberation, S. N. Prokopovich. Prokopovich chose to examine the issues before the local committees from an explicitly "liberal" viewpoint and as a result did not even discuss the questions of communal landownership and land use. For him, the critical questions were those of education, zemstvo self-government, land-hunger, and peasant civil rights, in that order. Other so-called liberal sources disagree somewhat with his choice. Nonetheless, the opposition movement among both the nobility and the zemstvos did focus its attention primarily on the more highly charged political questions of providing an "additional allotment" and of granting peasants equality of status.[118]

Undoubtedly, the most valuable summary was that compiled by A. I. Chuprov, the liberal economist and supporter of the commune who in the aftermath of the famine of 1891 had coauthored for Witte a highly controversial study of the famine's impact.[119] Chuprov showed the way in which the different committees' positions on the commune were determined by the history and geography of their localities. And instead of following Witte's propagandists and polarizing the issue as a choice between the commune and the *khutor*, he illustrated the complete range of possibilities available to the peasantry.[120]

Thus, according to Chuprov's calculations, a total of 245, or almost 40 percent, of the 618 committees had raised the issue of the commune. Excluding some 14 committees in the northwest and in Siberia that represented certain geographical exceptions, Chuprov found that 27 committees favored easing transfers from communal to individual ownership of land by allowing them to be approved by a simple rather than a two-thirds majority of householders; 57 wanted to grant individual members of the commune the right to exit from the commune with land; 13 advocated prohibiting repartitions altogether and transferring the allotment land to its de facto possessors; 19 favored a gradual and unconstrained transfer to individual (household) tenure; 3 more recognized such transfers as desirable but opposed giving them legislative approval. However, at the same time, a number of these same committees continued to support the commune in a modified form and held various reservations that would have excluded them from the ranks of those who wholeheartedly favored its abolition. In addition, Chuprov counted 71 committees that supported the commune, a high proportion of which were in the north, where landed relations were less complex and land-hunger less severe than in other areas. Finally, he identified 25 committees that advocated governmental neutrality and the selection of appropriate forms of landownership and use by the peasants themselves.

Thus, according to Chuprov's final summary, only 138, or one-fifth, of the committees could be considered opponents of the commune, leaving 81 supporters and 26 undecided. Of those opposing the commune, however, only 109 favored the separation of peasant allotment land to individual compact holdings or *khutora*; only 36 of these would allow such separations on the unilateral demand of the separator.

One issue, emphasized by Chuprov's summary, and to a lesser extent by Tolmachev's—and reflected in the Conference's own publications— was that whatever its position on the commune, provincial opinion was almost unanimously hostile toward all forms of bureaucratic *opeka* and resolutely opposed any form of government intervention in the economic life of the peasantry, particularly if directed toward the destruction of the existing communal order. Not surprisingly, the only exceptions to this near unanimity were the Interior Ministry's land captains. Underlying this popular sentiment were two assumptions that are already quite familiar: first, the liberal belief in evolutionary, spontaneous, and self-directed modes of rural development; and second, a very realistic appreciation of the great compexity of the problem and the tremendous practical difficulties facing any attempt to change existing structures. The first of these assumptions was also, of course, in part a reflection of local society's traditional suspicion of the bureaucracy. Similarly, the second assumption received support from traditional noble fears and a desire to inhibit any change lest it harm their own interests. At the root of both assumptions, however, lay the equally familiar and deeply rooted fear that all change, but particularly "artificial" change, would provoke widespread opposition from the mass of peasants, who were supposedly ardent adherents of the commune and its repartitional system of land tenure. At this point, it would seem, the various works commissioned by Witte had yet to make their impact.

In sum, it seems clear that Witte and his coworkers had, indeed, distorted the evidence. According to all of the sources, only a minority of the local committees had even expressed an opinion on the commune, and an even smaller proportion had actually favored transfers from communal to individual landownership and use.[121]

One must also acknowledge, however, that a significant shift had taken place in the opinion of provincial "society" and, to some extent, of provincial officialdom since the last attempts to survey local opinion in the mid-1890s. Clearly, the possibility and desirability of potentially far-reaching changes in the peasants' social and economic existence, if not yet direct government involvement in these matters, was now receiving serious consideration. On this latter point, indeed, Witte and the local committees were still in general agreement, in large part because of their mutual hostility to the Interior Ministry. Witte had not, however, abandoned his broader commitment to bureaucratic *opeka* and the necessity and desirability of government intervention. It is also important to note that the local committees were responsible for bringing to public attention those members of local society who were themselves supporters of reform.

Of course, the activities of the Special Conference and its local committees also testified to the perceptual changes that were taking place within the bureaucracy itself. Indeed, under the influence of Rittikh, Kutler, Kofod, and others, Witte himself had publicly shifted the focus of his concern away from the issue of peasant civil rights and toward more immediate and practical measures for the individualization and intensification of peasant agriculture. His shift was indicative of a more general trend within the bureaucracy, which now began to abandon its long-standing flirtation with laissez-faire liberalism and, in particular, its philosophical idealism, and to adopt a set of assumptions based on a more naturalistic and materialistic approach. More important, these changes would provide the basis for the later convergence of the proposals of the Special Conference with those of its competitor, the Editing Commission. On the other hand, despite Witte's attempt to demonstrate his solidarity with local opinion, a considerable gulf continued to separate the Special Conference's vision of reform from that of the local committees.

Meanwhile, although Witte had not completely abandoned his earlier support of peasant equalization and integration, this program was subsumed by the opposition movement's concurrent public campaign for the establishment of an all-class unit of self-government (canton zemstvo), a measure that even Pleve did not completely oppose.[122] Of course, although the opposition movement continued to regard juridical reform and integration as prerequisites for agricultural improvement, such measures were also considered concomitants of political reform. Thus, quite apart from the "constitutional" precedent that the Special Conference's sponsorship of so massive a consultation with public opinion provided, Pleve was undoubtedly right in considering the local committees a threat to both bureaucratic hegemony and the autocratic principle. It is not surprising, therefore, that he launched a campaign of political repression and harassment against some of these committees' more overt expressions of "disloyalty." However, the Imperial Manifesto of 26 February 1903 announcing the abolition of mutual responsibility had already signaled the eclipse of the Special Conference. This document, although mentioning the government's investigations of the agrarian problem, had completely ignored Witte's Special Conference and referred only to the Interior Ministry's Editing Commission and its rather narrowly defined search for "measures to ease the departure of individual peasants from the commune."[123] At the same time, the Manifesto had reaffirmed "the inviolability of the communal structure of peasant landownership." In similar fashion, the publication of Rittikh's "conclusions" in *Vestnik Finansov* preceded by just eighteen days an 8 January 1904 ukase that once again asserted the inviolability of both the commune and the *soslovie* system.[124] As late as 31 December 1904 a circular letter to the provincial governors from the new interior minister, Prince Sviatopolk-Mirskii, confirmed these principles yet again and reasserted the continuing significance of the Interior Ministry's review of peasant legislation.[125]

Witte, of course, immediately tried to minimize the political nature of his Conference's activity. Yet, by attempting to use his de facto alliance with the noble and zemstvo oppositions to further his campaign for rural reform, he inevitably drew the Special Conference directly into the broader political and constitutional conflict that was brewing between the Interior Ministry and the zemstvos. In so doing, Witte not only helped to perpetuate and deepen the conflict between his own ministry and the Interior Ministry, but also made his political task that much more complex. Among the consequences would be a general hardening of government opposition to reform, Witte's own dismissal from the Finance Ministry, and his "promotion" to the virtually powerless post of chairman of the Committee of Ministers in August 1903, and, finally, the sudden closing of the Special Conference itself at the end of March 1905.[126]

The Commission of the Center: Intensification and Intervention

Some years before the convocation of the Special Conference, and after Nicholas's rebuff to his attempts to form an interdepartmental commission on the agrarian question, Witte had supported a proposal from V. I. Kovalevskii, then director of the Department of Trade and Manufacturing, to form a commission to investigate the causes for the economic decline of the central black-earth provinces of European Russia. This commission had a rather odd parentage. Its immediate precursor was Kovalevskii's own conference on the grain trade, but it was also an outgrowth of a discussion circle formed, with Witte's approval, within the Finance Ministry in 1897 that had included participants from outside the government. However, even though this new commission was known as the "Kovalevskii Commission" and included both Kovalevskii and Kutler among its official members, its chairman was A. I. Zvegintsov of the Interior Ministry. It functioned from 1899 to 1901. The "Commission of the Center," convoked by the tsar on 16 November 1901 under the chairmanship of Kokovtsov, then assistant finance minister, then took up the same theme. As its rather awkward title explained, it was charged "with studying the question of changes in the well-being of the rural population between 1861 and 1900 in the central agricultural provinces compared with other regions of Russia."[127]

What is particularly interesting about both the Kovalevskii and the Kokovtsov commissions is that even though they had been created under Witte's protection, they nonetheless became instruments in the hands of his political enemies. Thus, the Golovin salon in effect took over the Kovalevskii Commission. Golovin himself, Bekhteev, and Polenov were members of the commission. As a result, when it had completed its work, it published a volume of statistics, prepared by Polenov, that supported those critics, particularly within the conservative nobility, who saw Witte as the evil genius behind the nobility's declining economic position.[128] At the same time, however, the Kovalevskii Commission echoed Witte's own criticisms of the *soslovie* system, attacking the arbitrariness of the peasants' legal, civil, and juridical situation; the persistence of customary law; and the obsolescence of their administrative and court systems—all of which it considered harmful to the peasants' economic interests.[129]

Witte initiated the Kokovtsov Commission, which replaced the Kovalevskii Commission, out of disillusionment with the latter's conclusions. The Commission itself did not meet for formal discussions until October 1903. In the two-year interim, Kutler and the Department of Direct Taxation were to collect appropriate data. Then, after the formation of the Special Conference, it became in effect an adjunct of that body, serving as a kind of preparatory commission.

When the Commission finally met in plenary session, its members included the usual government figures, such as Zvegintsov and Gurko from the Interior Ministry; Bekhteev and Polenov from agriculture; and Kokovtsov, Shvanebakh, and Kutler from Finance. Four of them had also served in the Kovalevskii Commission. However, in a significant departure from recent bureaucratic practice, the Commission also invited fifteen chairmen and three members of provincial zemstvo executive boards and one member of a provincial zemstvo assembly to attend, drawing predominantly from the provinces of the agricultural center, the Volga, and the Left Bank of the Ukraine. Among them were D. A. Olsuf'ev of Saratov, later active in the United Nobility, and A. A. Pavlov also of Saratov, brother of the well-known spokesman for the modernization of noble agriculture. The majority, however, would subsequently become active in the zemstvo congresses of late 1904 and 1905 and would join the Kadet or Octobrist parties.[130]

At Kokovtsov's invitation, the zemstvo members presented their views in a memorandum that appeared simultaneously in a number of periodical publications.[131] This memorandum, together with the Commission's published statistical materials, then became the principal subject of discussion. What is most interesting about the zemstvo memorandum, beyond its predictable criticisms of Witte's financial policies and his niggardliness toward the agricultural ministry, was that it was in complete agreement with Witte's 1899 budget report, his most detailed public statement on the agrarian problem to date. Thus, like Witte, the zemstvo members urged the government to abolish the *soslovie* order and to integrate the peasantry into the general sociolegal structure.[132]

However, with respect to the peasantry's economic problems, the zemstvo representatives adopted a more traditional approach and placed the principal blame on land-hunger, which, they argued, prevented the peasantry from applying its labor productively. Their solutions were similarly traditional: an expansion in the sale of land to the peasantry through the Peasant Bank, with limits placed on the quantity of land purchasable by any one peasant; a reform of the Migration Administration and an increase in the scale of peasant resettlement to the east; and the encouragement of long-term renting. Finally, reflecting the changes in both the zemstvos' political mood and its perception of the agrarian problem since the 1890s, they raised the question of the commune. However, to avoid becoming bogged down in controversy, the memorandum avoided the question of communal landownership and focused exclusively on the strictly economic issue of communal land use. This decision represented a major perceptual innovation, for it finally made explicit what had been so far only implicit in the approach of Kutler, Rittikh, and the Special Conference: namely, that the highly wasteful and unproductive three-field system of crop rotation in conjunction with the open-field strip system of cultivation was all but universally characteristic of peasant agriculture whether the land were held in communal or individual tenure. Having established this point, the memorandum went on to propose the development of small-scale peasant property and the formation of individual family farms as well as more general measures such as the dispersion of large villages, the right of free departure from the commune, and the unrestricted disposability of peasant allotment land as a solution to the problem of low peasant productivity. Thus, despite their criticisms of Witte's fiscal policies, the opinions of these zemstvo representatives corresponded with the Special Conference's one-sided interpretation of local opinion.[133]

The Kokovtsov Commission's discussions ranged over all these issues. What is most remarkable, however, was the agreement among the governmental and nongovernmental members. Its conclusions identified a number of new concerns shared by these two groups, including a sense of urgency that counseled against the long, slow process of cultural and legal reform and favored the adoption of more immediately practical economic measures;[134] the peasants' excessive and often exclusive dependence on agriculture and the need to supplement their income by encouraging the development of various outside sources including seasonal or migratory employment, domestic handicrafts, and local processing industries;[135] the importance of land-hunger as a cause of rural poverty and the necessity of granting special concessions to those peasants with the least land, presumably *darstvenniki*, since granting an "additional allotment" across the board was both "unthinkable and impracticable";[136] the problem of "relative" land-hunger and the necessity of eliminating those obstacles—social, economic, political, juridical, or psychological—that prevented peasants from increasing the productivity of their land;[137] a willingness to consider measures to reorganize the configuration of peasant holdings to eliminate the problems of communal land use and the sanitary and fire hazards that particularly troubled large, compact villages;[138] and, finally, the need for cooperation between government and society through the use of the zemstvos as the local executive organs of agricultural reform and the provision of governmental financial assistance.[139]

The one issue that broke this unanimity was the seemingly minor question of the inalienability of peasant allotment land. This issue split the Commission into two major groups. The zemstvo members and seven of the bureaucrats, including Zvegintsov and Kutler, voted in favor of free disposability of allotment land, and the other five government figures voted to preserve it. In fact, this issue was far more significant than it appeared, for it served as a touchstone for determining different members' attitudes to the more complex problem of change itself. Thus the majority of the commission's members, including a majority of the government's representatives, supported the laissez-faire, liberal principle of free and spontaneous social and economic change and a minority, all from the government, but including such otherwise strange bedfellows as Kokovtsov and the three members of the Golovin salon, clung to the principles of bureaucratic *opeka*. Gurko, then head of the Interior Ministry's Editing Commission on peasant legislation, considered this question so critical that he was either unable or unwilling to declare himself and so abstained.[140]

The Kokovtsov Commission did not go beyond these general considerations to offer any more specific or practical proposals, since it did not want to encroach on the work currently under way in the Interior Ministry on the revision of peasant legislation or in the Finance Ministry on the review of the Peasant Bank charter and the problem of rural credit in general. Nor did any specific actions follow the Commission's adjournment. Nonetheless, its conclusions reflected the changes that were taking place in the perception of the agrarian problem within both government and society. Most significant, perhaps, was the forthright recognition that traditional solutions such as the sale of land through the Peasant Bank and the expansion of migration were inadequate so long as they remained within the existing structures of the *soslovie* system and an extensive agriculture. In consequence, the Commission proposed as an alternative a joint policy of individualizing and intensifying peasant agriculture and integrating the peasantry into the larger society. Moreover, it also broke with the traditional assumption that such changes were of necessity the product of a long and gradual process of development and began to look on intensification as a purely economic process that could be promoted independently of other changes—an approach that was in sharp contrast to the mood of the Special Conference's local committees.[141] Meanwhile, by separating the issue of intensification from the larger complex of social, cultural, and psychological developments usually associated with modernization and by identifying it as the source of agricultural progress and development, the Kokovtsov Commission came close to the conclusions already reached by Kutler in the Department of Direct Taxation's 1902 project and by Rittikh. In due course, these perceptions would have a significant influence on the direction of the government's agrarian policy.[142]

In the meantime, the Kokovtsov Commission presented its report to the Special Conference, which discussed it at several sessions in January 1904. However, chastened by the Interior Ministry's campaign against the Conference's local committees and his own dismissal from the Finance Ministry, Witte sought only to avoid controversy and to keep the Special Conference out of the political limelight. Consequently, and despite the close affinities between the Kokovtsov Commission's conclusions and the proposals that had been worked out by both Rittikh and Kutler, Witte effectively confined the Conference's attention to the issue of reducing the peasants' tax burden.[143]

Yet, even here Witte had to retreat, for although he had long supported the abolition of redemption payments as a means of undermining the legislative rationale for the commune's preservation and, thus, as an indirect way of abolishing the commune itself, he found himself constrained from supporting even this relatively moderate proposal since it had been framed as a criticism of his financial policies by Shvanebakh and the zemstvo members of the Commission. As a result, the Kokovtsov Commission's proposals were scaled down to the single, extremely modest recommendation to lower redemption payments in the central provinces.[144]

The establishment of the Special Conference had been a victory for Witte; mutual responsibility had been abolished early in 1903; and a consensus was developing between the reform-minded members of both government and society. Yet, Pleve and the Interior Ministry had completely overshadowed Witte in the search for a solution to the agrarian problem. We must, therefore, turn our attention to that ministry and to the Editing Commission that alone appeared blessed with the tsar's favor.

3

THE INTERIOR MINISTRY AND THE EDITING COMMISSION, 1902–1904

Perceptual Revolution, Stage Two

The antithesis of utopia and reality . . . is a fundamental antithesis revealing itself in many forms of thought. . . . "It is the eternal dispute . . . [according to Albert Sorel] between those who imagine the world to suit their policy, and those who arrange their policy to suit the realities of the world. . . . " A concrete expression of [this] antithesis . . . is the opposition between the "intellectual" and the "bureaucrat."

—E. H. Carr, 1939

If it is possible to apply Marx's observation about the harm of an insufficient development of capitalism to any country in Europe, then, certainly, it is to us, to Russia.

—K. F. Golovin, 1896

The Editing Commission's contribution to the cause of agrarian reform has not had wide acknowledgment[1] in part because it had to accommodate its new understanding of the agrarian problem to political realities, in part because of the rivalry between the Interior and Finance Ministries and between Pleve and Witte. Yet the underlying assumptions and final implications of its work were virtually identical to those of Witte's brain trust and the Special Conference. Indeed, one could argue that the Editing Commission was even more influential than the Special Conference and the agricultural ministry. For whereas the Commission's members comprised men drawn from the Interior Ministry's Rural Section, most of whom belonged to the new generation of bureaucrats, several of its key members, including D. I. Pestrzhetskii, Assistant Interior Minister A. S. Stishinskii, who belonged to an earlier generation; and its de facto head, V. I. Gurko, would play a major role in winning the support of the conservative nobility, who by and large had hitherto supported the preservation of the commune.

Charged with reconciling existing peasant legislation with the principles of the Emancipation so as to bring it into closer conformity with both the actual "needs of life" and the welfare of the state, the Editing Commission would review four areas: peasant administration, land use and peasant civil rights, peasant economy, and peasant courts.[2] It accomplished nothing of note until Pleve took over from the assassinated Sipiagin in May. Shortly thereafter Gurko became director of the Rural Section, effective from September, and was placed in charge of the Commission's agenda, under the purely nominal supervision of Stishinskii. Gurko's instructions were extremely vague: Pleve offered little in the way of recommendations beyond some casual comments, occasioned by the disorders on the Left Bank of the Ukraine that spring, linking the commune with socialism and private property with the preservation of order. Nonetheless, he remained committed to the commune as part of the *soslovie* system of administration and as the guarantor of order.[3] Thus, by default, it was the ideas of Gurko and his appointees that determined the outcome of the Commission's work.

Gurko: An Economic Approach

Gurko himself was an exemplary representative of the new generation of bureaucrats. Born in 1862, he had attended the Juridical Faculty of Moscow University. After graduation, he spent some ten years in Poland, first as a commissar for peasant affairs and then as assistant to his father, Field Marshall I. V. Gurko, governor-general of Poland. When Pleve received an appointment as imperial secretary in 1894, Gurko moved to St. Petersburg and became a member of the Imperial Chancellery, a body that exercised an important behind-the-scenes role in shaping legislation that passed through the State Council.[4] However, it was in direct response to his Polish experiences that Gurko developed his general conception of rural society and its relation to national policy, though his work as architect of a model economy on his wife's estates in Voronezh Province undoubtedly influenced his views as well.[5] His earliest ideas were embodied in two works, one on noble landownership and local reform, the other on the Vistula region.[6] In 1901, a series of articles, "Agriculture and Peasant Off-farm Earnings," in *Novoe Vremia*, a progovernment newspaper of reformist orientation, demonstrated that, like Rittikh, Kutler, and others within the bureaucracy, Gurko had undertaken a fundamental reinterpretation of the agrarian problem and was already a staunch opponent of both the commune and the entire *soslovie* system.[7]

Insofar as the current crisis was concerned, Gurko argued that the fall in grain prices after the onset of the agricultural crisis in the midseventies, in conjunction with the development of a money economy and the government's fiscal policies, had led to a decline in the peasants' monetary income while vastly increasing their need for cash to buy goods and pay taxes. As a result, despite some minor tax reductions, there had been a rapid increase in arrears of both direct taxes and redemption payments.

One consequence of these developments was a reduction in the size of community grain reserves as they were gradually sold off to help meet this increased demand for cash. Thus, by the time of the widespread crop failure of 1891–92, the peasantry had been rendered virtually defenseless.

The traditional explanation for many of these problems was, of course, peasant land-hunger. However, among the worst affected, according to Gurko, were not the land-hungry or landless peasants, usually categorized as the poorest segment of the peasantry, but those who relied exclusively on agriculture for their source of income yet who, because they owned more land, were generally considered better off. On the contrary, he noted, the geographical incidence of what amounted to a "cash famine" among the peasantry, as reflected by both tax arrears and declining grain reserves, indicated that arrears were greatest and reserves lowest where allotments were largest, and vice versa.[8] He explained this apparent paradox by observing that the central and southeastern regions were still undergoing the painful process of transformation from a natural to a money economy. In consequence, the peasants' precarious financial situation and poor agricultural techniques made it unprofitable for them either to expand or intensify production. At the same time, there were few off-farm sources of income. The agrarian problem, then, was a result not of land-hunger or soil exhaustion or even a crisis in the productivity of the three-field system but of a shortage of peasant cash income. Ultimately, therefore, it was also a product of Russia's inadequate economic development.[9]

Following List and Mendeleev, Gurko advocated solutions that assumed that agriculture would continue to play a crucial role in the national economy though in tandem with the development of industry. Thus, he rejected such traditional approaches as increasing peasant land-ownership either with the aid of the Peasant Bank or by facilitating peasant migration eastward because he considered the nobility's estates highly productive and a valuable source of income for surrounding peasants who were employed to cultivate and most commonly to harvest their crops. Rather, he proposed to expand the peasants' opportunities to take off-farm employment to supplement their income by improving noble agricultural techniques and establishing more agricultural processing industries on noble properties. At the same time, he proposed to reduce taxes and equalize the tax burden by replacing indirect taxes on such items of peasant consumption as matches and kerosene, which placed the greatest burden on the peasant poor, with an income tax—a proposal more commonly associated with the liberal opposition because of its implicit assault on the nobility's *soslovie* status and the advantages that it derived from the current system of direct taxation.[10]

A fervent supporter of individual property ownership as the source of all economic progress, Gurko supported his opposition to the commune by contrasting the exhausted and impoverished agricultural center and southeast, where communal landownership prevailed and the market economy was weakly developed, with the vigorous and more prosperous west and southwest, where individual ownership predominated and the market economy had penetrated more deeply. He was one of the first to point out that the commune had not only failed to prevent the formation of a landless proletariat but had actually encouraged its development as well as the development of a wealthy minority of kulaks—that bête noire of the nobility—who accumulated land at the expense of the poor by controlling the repartitional mechanism. Without referring to the spontaneous peasant transfers to *khutora* in the west and northwest, he argued that the peasants' failure to separate from the commune and claim individual title to their holdings in central Russia was in fact due not to a lack of desire but to the legal obstacles placed in their way by the abolition of Article 165 of the Redemption Statute. Yet, like so many others at this time, Gurko opposed the actual destruction of the commune, noting that the transfer to individual ownership in other countries had always been a long, slow process. Rather, what the government had to do was to make such transfers practicable. At the same time, he was unwilling to abandon the peasant completely to the market, since that would accelerate the process of social and economic differentiation. Thus he supported the establishment of both maximum and minimum norms for peasant landholding as well as the retention of existing prohibitions on the alienation of allotment land to nonpeasants, thereby preserving a role for the traditional, passive variety of bureaucratic *opeka*.[11]

Despite his membership in the bureaucracy, Gurko was also a *frondeur* and spokesman for the growing "noble reaction" that characterized these years. He was particularly critical of the state's ever-expanding bureaucratic apparatus and its increasing separation from the land, as manifested by the diminished role of landowning nobles in government, though, as we have seen, this had recently begun to change. Indeed, Gurko's entire approach was imbued with a profound sympathy for the noble landowner.[12] Yet, his greatest concern was not for those nobles who owned Russia's largest estates and *latifundia*, but for those medium-scale or farmer-type economies in the 50 to 150-desiatina range. In his later writings, he became even more critical of this stratum of the nobility, urging an expansion in the proportion of the more productive farmer-type holdings at their expense.[13] On the other hand, although he did not shrink from attacking Witte's fiscal policies, his criticism of the proindustrial excesses of the Witte system was quite moderate, and he acknowledged the very real national benefits of Witte's forced march to industrialization, despite its one-sidedness. Indeed, he went even further and called for a similar singlemindedness and concentration of resources in order to stimulate the development of agriculture.[14]

Insofar as the agrarian problem was concerned, Gurko's approach had much in common with that of Witte and his assistants. However, like Witte, Gurko was at this time more interested in problems of peasant administration and civil rights than in questions of peasant landowner-ship or land use.[15] As a consequence, he had yet to declare himself pub-licly in favor of *khutorizatsiia*. However, on other issues, these men diverged sharply. Quite apart from the conflict between their two min-istries, it is not, therefore, very surprising that they were unable to join forces in pursuit of their common goal while they headed competing investigations.[16]

The Editing Commission

Given the Commission's "bureaucratic" and juridical approach, it was to be expected that when its projects were finally published at the begin-ning of 1904 the liberal members of government and society alike sharply criticized them for leaving the peasant commune and the *so-slovie*-based system of local administration virtually unchanged—and thus for having failed to solve the agrarian problem.[17] The sharpening conflict between government and society and the growing confrontation between the Interior Ministry and the zemstvo opposition only made a dispassionate evaluation of the Commission's work even less likely. True, the only proposed changes in these two critical areas implemented the tsar's moderate recommendations, in the Manifesto of 26 February 1903, to facilitate "the separation of individual peasants from the com-mune."[18] But in its approach to the peasants as a single undifferentiated class—it had interpreted its mandate as calling for uniform statutes ap-plying equally to *all* peasants irrespective of the historical or geographi-cal origin of their legal status—it did represent a definite, if preliminary, step toward the eventual integration of the peasantry into a single socio-legal structure.[19]

The public reception of the Commission's work, however, contrasted sharply with Gurko's evaluation of its significance. Indeed, Gurko in-forms us in his memoirs that from the very beginning he had intended to use his position to initiate the abolition of both the peasant commune and the *soslovie* system of administration and to integrate the peasantry into the general sociolegal order. However, in the face of his own minis-try's seemingly implacable support for these institutions as well as the generally conservative political atmosphere within the government as a whole, he had deliberately "camouflaged" these goals within a primarily "economic" proposal for the establishment of "a rational system of land tenure [use]" that emphasized "productivity." In the long run, however, this would itself have brought about the complete individualization of the peasant way of life through the formation of *khutora* and the development of an all-class system of local administration.[20] Yet, it was precisely this concentration on "economics" that was most significant.

The government report of 14 January 1902 authorizing the Interior Ministry to introduce changes in the existing peasant legislation had also required that the Editing Commission preserve those underlying principles that had governed the drafting of the Emancipation legislation some forty years earlier. According to Gurko these were "the isolation of the peasant *soslovie* and the special [*soslovie*] system of peasant self-government . . . , the inalienability of peasant allotment lands, and the immunity of the basic forms of peasant landownership from any forcible change dictated by law."[21] To most government officials, of course, such a directive would have prohibited any of the changes that Gurko envisioned. Gurko, however, reinterpreted those principles in such a way that he not only legitimized the Commission's proposals, but placed them in ideological continuity with the legislation of both the emancipation and the counterreform eras. His arguments were contained in his introductory survey to the Commission's work, which also appeared separately in *Pravitel'stvennyi Vestnik* (Government Herald) on 10 and 11 January 1904.[22]

Gurko began by trying to learn from the government's past mistakes and, particularly, from the failure of the counterreform legislation either to resolve the agrarian problem or to influence the direction of social and economic change by means of prescriptive legislation.[23] Thus he sought to focus on the original motivations behind the preservation of the *soslovie* system and the commune. The Emancipation, he argued, had retained these two institutions in part to protect the peasants' customary way of life from those sudden or artificial changes that would follow from direct government intervention. However, he pointed out, the intent of their preservation had not been to provide a means of prohibiting spontaneous social and economic change. On the contrary, it had been considered a purely temporary expedient that would serve to prepare the peasantry for their eventual and, it was assumed, inevitable transformation into individual peasant-proprietors and their integration into a universal and egalitarian civil legal order. Thus at issue was not a prohibition against change, as was conventionally believed, but against the use of legislative coercion to introduce change from above. However, having made a perfectly valid point, Gurko pushed this interpretation beyond its legitimate limits by claiming that the prohibition against legislative coercion also prevented the government from placing any restraints on individual peasants who wished to transfer either to another *soslovie* or to improved forms of land use outside the commune. On the contrary, "the law," he wrote, "had to give all strong, intelligent . . . individual peasants the opportunity to apply their talents, to spread their wings, though [only] in such a way that their growth is not at the expense of the whole peasantry but follows a separate course. To assume that every peasant must without fail devote his whole life to agriculture is manifestly unfounded."[24]

This expression of Gurko's commitment to economic individualism may suggest the somewhat paradoxical policy of splitting the peasantry into two strata: the strong and intelligent, who would be free to leave their *soslovie* and prosper in nonagricultural occupations; and the weak and ignorant, who would remain within the existing system and continue to engage in agriculture. In fact, however, what was involved was not Gurko's attempt to favor the "strong and intelligent." Rather, it was an attempt to reconcile his commitment to individualism and economic development with the traditional assumptions of bureaucratic *opeka*, which regarded the kulak as an evil and disruptive force within the commune and sought to preserve the peasantry's basic social and economic equality within both commune and *soslovie*.[25]

These same concerns were apparent in Gurko's argument for retaining the recently adopted law prohibiting the free disposability of peasant allotment land. Thus, on the one hand, he noted that equalizing the rights of allotment land ownership with those of private property would result in the vast majority of the peasants' losing their land and would lead to the disappearance of the very land that alone could provide for the needs of the average peasant family. At the same time, he sought to expand the application of the inalienability principle to provide for the protection of small-scale individual property ownership against the seemingly ineluctable processes of capital accumulation and concentration. In both cases, Gurko tried to reconcile the development of economic individualism with the prevention of social differentiation and thereby to balance the state's need for social stability with the needs of economic development.[26]

As for the commune itself, Gurko pointed out that more than forty years of debate had failed to resolve the essentially theoretical question of whether communal or individual ownership were more economically advantageous. As a consequence, the Commission shifted attention away from the commune as a juridical institution and adopted a pragmatic and empirical approach similar to that simultaneously being adopted by Kutler, Rittikh, and the zemstvo members of Kokovtsov's Commission of the Center. He noted that under present conditions both communal and individual forms of ownership placed insuperable obstacles in the way of individual development and agricultural improvement. Consequently, the peasants' economic welfare depended not on the form of property ownership but on the level of their prosperity, which in turn depended on the productivity of the land. Civil rights should therefore be considered a consequence of economic prosperity and cultural development, not a prerequisite for their development. In 1909, in a different context, Gurko would phrase more pithily this challenge to conventional liberal political ideas. "We must keep in mind," he would say then, "that their [the peasants'] weakness and their drunkenness do not depend on themselves, that these qualities of theirs are the result of the totality of social phenomena among which they live and act."[27] Consequently, Gurko argued, the Commission's task was not to introduce changes in the legal rights of peasants but to focus its attention on the practical task of eliminating practical restraints on their agricultural activity—such as open fields and the fragmentation of holdings into strips—and creating opportunities for peasants to exercise freedom of choice in their economic affairs.

By reinterpreting the "fundamental" principles upon which the Commission's work was to be based and by restoring the Emancipators' original intentions to the forefront of attention, Gurko had also been forced to challenge the bureaucracy's assumption not only that change was a consequence of government intervention but that the very function of government was to determine what changes were most desirable and then to impose them from above. In place of this joint fantasy of autocratic power and political liberalism, Gurko had adopted an economic and deterministic approach that was very similar to the economic materialism of contemporary Marxists, both Orthodox and Revisionist. According to this approach, change was the result not of the conscious designs of the supreme legislator but of spontaneous social and economic processes. To be effective, laws had to reflect both popular consciousness and popular needs. Indeed, like the "enlightened bureaucrats" of the Emancipation era, Gurko and his fellow members of the new generation of bureaucrats shared the Hegelian belief that "what is real is rational" and concluded that it was the legislator's task to draft laws that reflected the rational content of that reality rather than laws that imposed themselves on it from above. However, like their competitors within the Special Conference, Gurko and the other members of the Editing Commission began the task of rural reform by focusing on existing reality, or, as they now called it, "life itself," though not in order to prevent change, as had been the case in the past, but to encourage it and to identify the obstacles that stood in its way.

The Commission's specific responsibilities, as Gurko described them in his survey of the Commission's work, were to place the customary peasant courts on a firm legal foundation that would reflect the peasants' legal consciousness and permit both the speedy apprehension of criminals and the proper resolution of property disputes, define more clearly rights to various forms of allotment land, encourage the development of

individual initiative and the application of improved agricultural methods and forms of land use, regulate property relations between peasants
and neighboring landowners, and provide a firm basis for the development of a consciousness of the rule of law and a respect for the rights of
others.[28]

On the surface, the Commission's work appeared to remain within the
bureaucracy's traditional juridical perspectives. Indeed, its most urgent
concern was the necessity of establishing the "rule of law" in the countryside or, more accurately perhaps, of imposing the government's conception of law on the peasantry, particularly as it concerned the
acquisition and subsequent protection of individual property rights. This
concern—which, as the materials published by the local commissions of
the Special Conference demonstrated, was shared by educated provincial
society—was, of course, traditional within the Interior Ministry.[29] It had
been given renewed emphasis by the 1902 disorders in Poltava and
Khar'kov provinces. However, the Commission had adopted an entirely
new approach to the problem of maintaining order, casting it in terms
completely different from the traditional approach, which focused on
such issues as peasant cunning, ignorance, and laziness or the activities
of revolutionary parties.

Gurko began by noting that, in general, the peasant had not yet developed a private-property consciousness. In analyzing the origin of this
problem, he took a deterministic, sociohistorical approach. The peasantry's attitude toward property rights, he argued, was a direct outgrowth of
serfdom and the almost total absence of accurately surveyed and clearly
demarcated boundaries that was one of its consequences. For centuries,
the peasant had thus not only been prohibited from owning land; the
land that he cultivated was itself physically united with that of his noble
owner, who alone possessed the right of disposition over it. In consequence the peasant had become completely dependent on his owner for
all economic needs, including land, fuel, construction materials, and
pasture. Such circumstances, of course, could not and did not prepare the
peasantry for the property rights inherent in the redemption operation.
This situation was only compounded by the Emancipation, which not
only did not change these fundamental relationships but actually prevented the peasant from separating himself physically or economically
from his former owner. The perpetuation of open-field landownership
and land use by both peasants and noble landowners, in conjunction with
the continued absence of boundary markers, and the complete failure of
both the Emancipation Statute and the officials who implemented it to
establish a clear and concise structure of property rights only further
exacerbated the problem. Moreover, this situation had remained unchanged down to the present, despite several later attempts to make the
necessary legislative adjustments. These deficiencies were then further

compounded by the internal operation of individual peasant communities, many of which, whether they held their land in individual or communal tenure, actually redistributed it at will in response to changes in the size of their population. It was therefore only natural, in the Commission's view, that the peasant would be inclined to continue taking what he needed from what was now the property of others and then using it as his own. And, indeed, illegal land seizures, plowing, pasturing, and wood cutting had become widespread, affecting not only the peasants' former owners but anyone who owned land in the immediate neighborhood. Inevitably this had also given rise to those notorious and interminable legal struggles over property rights that succeeded only in clogging the courts, exacerbating social tensions, and in general hindering the development of a stable and productive agricultural life.[30]

However, as part of its argument to demonstrate the existence of a material basis for the reforms it would propose, the Commission, like Kutler and Rittikh within the Special Conference, pointed out that despite these obstacles the peasantry had in some areas already begun to develop a private-property consciousness.[31] The primary stimulus for this development, it held, was the redemption operation, which, by requiring payments from individual peasant households in accordance with the actual quantity of land in their use, had encouraged them to view their share of the communal allotment as their individual property. In support of its argument, the Commission pointed to the large number of communes, particularly in central Russia, that had never had a full or a partial repartition of land since the Emancipation, demonstrating that the peasants within such communes considered their share of the common allotment to be their de facto property. Second, there was the widespread practice of executing repartitions not on the relatively egalitarian basis of the actual number of males or the total number of "mouths" in the household but on the basis of the number of "revision souls"—in effect, those peasants in a village, or their immediate successors, who had been the original recipients of allotment land and who, presumably, looked on the commune's land as their own. This assumption was confirmed, in the Commission's eyes, by the recent growth of intravillage conflicts over the basis on which to execute the next repartition; such conflicts, they argued, demonstrated not the strength and vitality of the communal principle, as its supporters claimed, but the clear presence of a private-property consciousness among the defenders of the revision soul principle.[32]

Thus, the Commission's task was redefined in more narrowly economic terms as one of drafting legislation to encourage the immediate and spontaneous development of economic independence and initiative that would both foster the peasantry's legal consciousness as well as provide a basis for the broader program of modernizing peasant agriculture and integrating the peasantry into an expanding capitalist economy.[33]

Of the Commission's six projects, that on peasant allotment land compiled by P. P. Zubovskii and A. I. Lykoshin is of greatest interest. Both men belonged to the new generation of bureaucrats. Of Zubovskii, little is known except that he was a member of the clerical *soslovie* and entered government service in 1888, presumably at the local level as was then customary. According to Gurko, Zubovskii was one of the bureaucracy's earliest exponents of *khutorizatsiia*.[34] Lykoshin on the other hand was a noble landowner with estates in several provinces. A graduate of the Imperial School of Jurisprudence, he began his career in the Ministry of Justice. His interest in peasant affairs had already led him to publish a long article favoring individual over family landownership that had attracted Gurko's attention.[35] Two others who helped draft the allotment land project were A. V. Krivoshein, a man of mixed but nonnoble background, who, as we shall see, played a key role in influencing the final shape of the Stolypin Reforms; and S. D. Rudin, a landowner from Simbirsk Province, a trained surveyor and a principal figure in some of the technical issues associated with changing the configuration of peasant landholdings.[36]

What is most remarkable, however, is not so much the project itself as Gurko's discussion of it in his introductory survey as well as the analyses of specific articles that were included in the accompanying materials. For in both cases, rather than confining themselves to giving a brief survey of the project and the motivations behind it, as might have been expected, all of Gurko's fourteen-page commentary and much of the supplementary materials actually emphasized *khutorizatsiia* and the various obstacles that stood in the way of implementing such a policy.[37]

Since an improvement in peasant welfare was considered a prerequisite to any and all changes in property rights, the problem facing the project's compilers was that such an improvement was hindered not so much by the laws they were directed to revise as by the practical obstacles inherent in the existing pattern of land use and the unproductive expenditures of energy associated with it. In Gurko's opinion, the only escape from poverty was "a transfer to individual land use on consolidated *otrubnye* holdings. The very substantial obstacles presented to this course surely can not serve as a basis for refusing to take every possible means to realize this ideal system in practice."[38]

The problem was determining the means to achieve this ideal. One approach would be to issue a decree granting peasants individual title to the strips of land that they cultivated. However, Gurko felt that the consolidation of these strips into *khutora* could not be accomplished by legislative means. On the one hand, the costs involved in relocating the household plot and cottage were insurmountable. On the other, such resettlements were made impossible in much of Russia, particularly in the agricultural center and south, by the scarcity of surface water. Even more important, only government or zemstvo assistance over a prolonged period of time could overcome some obstacles, such as problems associated with the mutually reinforcing systems of common grazing for livestock and compulsory crop rotation, both characteristic of peasant agriculture whatever the form of landownership. Peasant agriculture had to be considered as an organic whole, as a historically formed ecosystem. These systems were

the necessary consequence of the totality of local soil and climatic conditions and, in particular, the average level of the country's general culture and the intellectual development of the popular masses. In a word, communal and individual forms of peasant landownership . . . are a naturalistic structure of land use which has been worked out historically on the basis of local peculiarities.[39]

On the other hand, Gurko pointed to areas, such as the western provinces, that not only possessed the geographical and cultural conditions necessary for a successful conversion to *khutora* but had already entered the initial stages of such a transformation on the initiative of the villages themselves. Such developments were "organic," "creative," and "vital," since they sprang from a happy conjunction of local conditions, material and cultural, that together had shattered the old unity of collective and individual economic interests and produced a new consensus as to the necessity of forming individual, separate, and integral holdings. Unfortunately, this process had not begun in the rest of the empire. In part, this was due to the absence of such necessary prerequisites as a developed network of roads, security of property and person from both wild animals and "evilly-intentioned persons," and more intensive forms of land use that could stall-feed enough livestock to provide an adequate supply of manure for fertilizer. "The transfer to an economy based on *otruba* and *khutora*," Gurko concluded, "is possible only as a result of a complete revolution in the entire system of agricultural practice." But for such a revolution to occur, there had to be a "substantial intellectual development in the proprietor himself." Moreover, there were many other regions where such a fundamental and sweeping change would neither conform to local conditions nor to "the real needs of the population." Such a change "would not meet with sympathy among the peasants; on the contrary, it would provoke their opposition."[40] There was also little hope of success for a policy based on purely voluntary transfers by whole villages, since "the majority of the population is always and everywhere unfailingly disposed to adhere to ancient customs, and the endeavors of individual householders who possess greater enterprise to persuade the community to adopt any kind of innovations, no matter how rational, remain in vain."[41]

However, Gurko did not hold the commune responsible for this state of affairs. Inevitably, peasant communities had adopted that system of land distribution and utilization that best conformed to the capabilities of its members. Unfortunately, the prevailing open-field strip system of compulsory crop rotation was quite primitive. It not only prevented individual peasants from improving their methods and intensifying their production as long as they remained within the village: it virtually eliminated any possibility of subsequent improvements. Material and cultural necessities had thus created a vicious circle that could only be broken "with the mass shift of the population from simple to more complex economic systems."[42]

Since legislative force was precluded, and voluntary transfers of whole villages were unlikely, the only alternative left open to the Commission was to make it easier for individual peasants to claim title to their strips and consolidate them into one compact unit. However, Gurko was not solely concerned with opening up opportunities to individual peasants. He also hoped that, in time, "when the peasantry is convinced by the example of individual proprietors that the separation of strips to one place is of value for their economic welfare . . . [there will] appear among them a general trend in this direction."[43]

Indeed, the process by which social and economic change would be diffused gradually and spontaneously in response to personal observation and practical experience was, in fact, central not only to the entire conception, structure, and execution of the Editing Commission's proposals, but also to the later Stolypin Reforms themselves. *Individual* separations of land into compact parcels were, thus, but the first stage in the eventual transfer of the entire peasantry to individual ownership and use. The *khutor* was "the final goal which . . . must be kept in mind in reorganizing peasant land use. . . ."[44] Thus it is clear that, despite the relatively limited nature of its final legislative proposals, the Commission's ultimate intent was, in fact, to set in motion a major, self-sustaining process of social and economic change designed to transform the entire structure of Russian peasant agriculture and therewith to provide a basis for the modernization of the national economy.

Despite its commitment to facilitating the separation of individual peasants from the commune, the Commission had at the same time to ensure that this could be accomplished without disrupting the economic life of the village as a whole. In addition, adoption of a number of meliorative measures short of full *khutorizatsiia* would be necessary in order to eliminate some of the most harmful agrotechnical problems affecting the peasants who remained within the commune, particularly the extreme distances that often separated a peasant's strips from one another and from his dwelling. One such possibility was a provision permitting the partition of large villages into smaller units, which subsequently could be divided into *otruba* or *khutora*.

Yet another problem involved finding ways to encourage whole villages to approve the departure of individuals and small groups. As Gurko acknowledged,

> It will be extremely difficult to influence the majority of householders in a village by administrative measures. The fact of the matter is that even if it were possible to separate by force, against the desires of the majority of householders, that part of the allotment land being relocated, it is obvious that it would be impossible to protect those who have relocated from the hatred of that majority and from the . . . persecution to which the aforesaid minority would inevitably be subjected by the majority.[45]

Indeed, accusations that the government was applying undue pressure would become so widespread once the Stolypin Reforms had been enacted that it is important to emphasize Gurko's conviction at this stage that compulsory procedures would undermine everything that the Commission hoped to achieve. Only on the condition of widespread public sympathy would it be

> possible to protect that rural peace between individual groups of peasants which is so necessary in rural life and in general to create those overall conditions of order and calm without which no phenomenon rooted in life can develop, and above all to promote an increase in the population's well-being—the final goal pursued in this work.[46]

The Commission's proposals, like those of the Special Conference, thus rejected all measures that might serve to generate any more social conflict within the village than already existed. "Divide and rule" strategies clearly played no part in either of their plans.

The Commission's position vis-à-vis social differentiation within the peasantry is, of course, critical for an understanding of the social content not only of its own proposals but also of the later Stolypin Reforms themselves.[47] Its discussion of this issue took place in connection with the problem of establishing a ceiling on the accumulation of allotment land by a single peasant proprietor or household. On the one hand, it recognized that the gradual transformation of peasant agriculture from a natural to a money economy would encourage the formation of a group of prosperous peasants and the development of ever greater property inequalities. At first glance, therefore, it might have seemed desirable to place limitations on the concentration of allotment land in order to protect the weaker peasant majority from losing their land to speculators and kulaks. On the other hand, it noted that any attempt to prevent such an inevitable development would only serve to inhibit the operation of that fundamental economic law of nature that demonstrated that the accumulation of wealth was one of the most powerful instruments of economic and cultural progress. The Commission was also guided by more general political considerations that similarly counseled a noninterventionist stance, since prosperous peasants, who naturally sought to uphold private property principles in their own self-interest, were also a crucial element in the defense of the existing social and political structure. Yet, allowing the process of property accumulation to develop unrestrained would lead only to the creation of a large group of landless peasant laborers for whom there were already insufficient opportunities for employment.[48] Indeed, in the Commission's view, the principal source of peasant income would for a long time remain the land, and particularly the peasants' own allotment lands. The traditional concern with making cheap labor available for noble estates was clearly not a major concern; as Gurko himself had pointed out earlier in his article in *Novoe Vremia*, and as the 1902 disorders demonstrated, noble estates could not absorb the quantity of labor that was already available. Consequently, the concern for preserving rural order by improving peasant welfare took precedence over any concern for noble welfare on this issue.

The Commission now faced a dilemma, for although at this stage of Russia's economic development it should be concerned to encourage the development of individual forms of peasant landownership, it also had to assure that such processes not harm the interests of the peasantry as a whole. In the final analysis the Commission felt that maintaining social and political stability in the countryside was even more important than allowing the immutable laws of economics to have free reign. On these grounds, it decided in favor of adopting maximum norms for allotment-land ownership.

In attempting to reconcile the differing interests within the peasantry to the government's advantage, the Commission's preponderant concern was thus not—as is so often argued—the encouragement of social and economic differentiation but rather the protection of the vast masses of the peasant population. It was timid, perhaps, yet pragmatic and certainly in conformity with the traditional concerns of bureaucratic *opeka*. Furthermore, in attempting to calculate the particular interests of the parties involved, the Commission specifically rejected the possibility of its establishing any such standard as "absolute justice." Rather, the merits of each party's claims had to be balanced—a demand that conforms perfectly to the traditional image of the bureaucracy as the instrument of a supraclass autocracy whose task was to mediate between and reconcile conflicting interests.[49]

To prevent the fragmentation of peasant holdings—as undesirable as concentration from economic, social, and political standpoints—the Commission also proposed setting lower limits on the size of allotment landholdings. However, since it had already been demonstrated that laws alone were powerless to prevent peasants from partitioning their allotments, the Commission proposed supplementing such legislation with incentives to form khutora and otruba in the hope that these new forms of property would render family partitions economically undesirable. In addition, it hoped that the creation of new credit institutions would enable individual peasant households to provide financial compensation to those of its cadet members who sought to leave the nest and establish independent households.[50]

Given the extreme urgency of the agrarian problem and the impossibility of relying on purely legislative action, when it came to the government's role, the Commission adopted a much broader view than was customary, even within the Interior Ministry, in the hope of speeding up the process of change. Specifically, it recommended that the government assume part of the financial burden of the changes by making loans for agricultural improvements available on special terms, granting tax relief to those who wanted to establish khutora, and providing technical workers to assist in digging wells where surface water was inadequate. In addition, it proposed hiring professional land surveyors to execute the practical aspects of the program, under the direction of the Ministry's provincial executive boards. However, keenly aware of the problems of implementing government policy at the local level as well as the defects in its own administrative apparatus, it foresaw the necessity of establishing an effective system of supervision, since "mistakes and deliberate irregularities in the work [of the surveyors] is an almost commonplace phenomenon that, of course, undermines the trust of the local population in them."[51] Once again, the Commission underlined the need to foster trust between the government and the peasantry as a means of winning popular respect as well as support for its reform program.[52]

There was one notable lacuna in the Commission's work, for neither the projects themselves nor the supporting materials made any reference to the establishment of peasant landownership on the basis of the individual head of household rather than the family, though Rittikh's work on the commune had included such a measure.[53] The Commission's failure to deal with this issue can be explained only by the exigencies of bureaucratic politics and the continuing hold of traditional notions about the peasantry's moral character—the fear that were title to be granted to the head of the household he would quickly squander the family patrimony in exchange for vodka. The prevailing view held that the peasant family continued to perform a vital protective function very similar to that of the commune and was perhaps the last bastion upon which the traditional form of bureaucratic *opeka* could depend. Despite the Commission's avoidance of this issue, however, there is no doubt that the rest of its proposals could have been realized at the time, for they were pragmatic proposals, par excellence.

Pleve, the Local Conferences, and the Search for Support: Tradition and Change

When the Editing Commission completed its work in October 1903 Gurko submitted his introductory survey to Pleve for transmission to the tsar.[54] It received approval on 26 October, just two days after the last session of Kokovtsov's "Commission of the Center," which, as we have seen, had reached strikingly similar conclusions.

Pleve's covering report to the tsar ignored the more far-reaching implications of the Editing Commission's proposals and, in words taken almost verbatim from Gurko's survey, emphasized the Commission's continuity with bureaucratic tradition as reflected in the three underlying principles that had supposedly guided its work. He also gave a thoroughly traditional interpretation of the Commission's historical, deterministic, "organic," and materialistic analysis of the peasant way of life, reiterating customary objections to the use of legislative force in attempting to change that way of life; faith in the spontaneous development of the historical process; as well, of course, as his Ministry's paramount concern with strengthening the peasants' "sense of legitimacy and respect for the rights of others."[55]

It is not clear whether Pleve shared Gurko's goals or whether he simply did not see the implications of the Commission's work. However, Pleve's subsequent comments before the Committee of Ministers when procedures for the local review of the Commission's projects were discussed suggest that he was ignorant of them.[56] These discussions, held on 25 November and 2 December 1903, also demonstrate the continuing conflict between Witte and the Interior Ministry as well as the sensitive political and constitutional issues involved even in reforms as limited as these seemed in Pleve's presentation.

Even though he was no longer finance minister, Witte caviled at the Commission's failure to discuss the financial costs of the reforms and their implications for the state budget. He also attacked the Commission for having failed to utilize any of the materials generated by his Special Conference, not to mention the summary volumes being prepared by

Rittikh, some ten of which were directly relevant to the peasant question. Because of what he saw as the "undigested" nature of the Editing Commission's projects, Witte therefore opposed sending them to provincial conferences lest they become the focus of a new round of political conflict between the government and educated society. Instead, he proposed creating yet another interdepartmental commission to undertake a preliminary review of the projects—a familiar obstructionist gambit of bureaucratic politics.

The state comptroller, General P. L. Lobko, shared Witte's objections and raised the question of the proper constitutional relationship between tsar and society with respect to agrarian reform since the three principles of *soslovie* isolation, the inalienability of allotment land, and the inviolability of the commune had not received the tsar's official approval and were, therefore, open to discussion in the proposed conferences. Thus, if the government wished to retain the initiative it would first have to get these principles sanctioned by "imperial authority."

In response, Pleve reasserted the continuity between the Commission's projects and existing legislation. Rather than introducing any new principles, he argued, they sought merely to harmonize the existing statutes, bringing them into "strict order on the basis of the practices of the Ruling Senate and peasant institutions" and filling in any gaps.[57] Moreover, he foresaw the development of an even more serious political problem if it were decided neither to publish the projects nor submit them to local discussion since both steps had been promised in the Commission's program and the public was already eagerly awaiting them. In the end, Pleve was victorious and the acceptance of the final stage of the Editing Commission's work was marked by the simultaneous publication of the first part of Gurko's survey in the 9 January 1904 issue of *Pravitel'-stvennyi Vestnik* and a ukase establishing the provincial conferences and setting out the terms on which the projects would be discussed.[58]

Of course, the Interior Ministry's projects had not provided a solution to the agrarian problem. On the other hand, they accurately reflected the limits of what was possible, given the prevailing political mood within the government as a whole. Moreover, the frequent charges of bureaucratic isolation that its critics leveled at the government completely failed to recognize the degree to which society's interests were, in fact, represented within it. Just as the government was often guilty of failing to distinguish between the shades of opinion existing within educated society, so was society at fault for failing to discern the quite considerable cracks that were beginning to develop in the government monolith.

Not surprisingly, Gurko, disappointed by the public response, began to assume the role of propagandist for *his* solution to the agrarian problem. In 1904 he spoke before a number of the anti-Witte "economic banquets"

organized by influential members of government and society in the hope
of influencing government policy. On one such occasion his attempts to
clarify the Commission's projects received an unfavorable response, and
he was criticized for his opposition to the commune. Worse still, after a
speech to one of the Commission's provincial conferences in his native
Tver Province, he was even attacked in Pleve's presence as a "typical"
representative of the liberal bureaucracy—hardly an accurate characterization in the sense intended by the traditionalists responsible.[59]

The year 1904 was not an auspicious one for rural reform. At the end
of January, the outbreak of the Russo-Japanese War claimed the attention
of central and provincial administrations. However, the tsar had specifically ordered that the Commission's work not be interrupted.[60] Some
fifteen governors had already met, on 25 January (one day before the
Japanese surprise attack on Port Arthur), at the Interior Ministry in St.
Petersburg to draft a discussion program and establish procedures for
selecting members of the proposed provincial conferences. (A second
meeting of the remaining governors, scheduled for February, never took
place.) On 6 February Pleve confirmed these proposals.[61]

The provincial conferences met sporadically during the course of 1904
and early 1905. However, by the time the Rural Section had begun to
assemble its findings, Pleve had been assassinated and the political situation had changed dramatically. As a consequence, only two incomplete
volumes of summaries were finally published, and then only at a point
in 1906 when they might help persuade a still reluctant government of
the political support that existed for such a radical program of rural
reform as was then under consideration.[62] According to the evidence
contained in these volumes, some 2,041 members attended the forty-
three conferences for which there are data. Almost half were government
officials; one-third were members of or were appointed by the local corporations of the nobility; the rest were selected by the governors from
the membership of county-level zemstvo assemblies or were invited to
participate by the governors although they did not belong to these categories. Not surprisingly, virtually two-thirds owned land and met the
property qualifications for the various local electoral or appointive posts.
More than half had some higher education. Thus, despite the relatively
small scale of this "opinion poll" compared to the numbers involved in
the local committees of the Special Conference, these participants were
remarkably well educated, deeply involved in local agriculture, and represented the local bureaucracy and nobility in about equal measure. Together, their opinions undoubtedly serve as an accurate barometer of the
bureaucracy's traditional social constituency.[63]

The responses to two questions on the conference's agenda are of particular interest. The first, "Should peasants be encouraged to establish
independent *khutor* economies . . . ," elucidated almost universal ap-

proval, as did the second, "Should legal requirements be eased for transfers from communal to individual landownership."[64]

The results of this survey contrast sharply with those obtained by the Interior Ministry from the very similar grouping of provincial officials and nobles that, just ten years earlier, had supported the commune almost unanimously and rejected any attempts to encourage the development of individual ownership. The responses also contrast sharply with those of the local committees of Witte's Special Conference in demonstrating significantly greater support for a government-sponsored program of gradual *khutorizatsiia*. What is not clear is the degree to which these conclusions reflect the pressure of the peasant disorders that erupted in February 1905 and heralded the development of a widespread agrarian movement such as had not been seen since the spring of 1902. However, it appears that most of the provincial conferences' resolutions passed either during 1904 or the early months of 1905. And although there was some increase in disorders during this period, the conferences certainly reached their decisions before the full seriousness of these events became clear.[65] Nonetheless, the results of the Editing Commission's survey signaled a fundamental shift in political mood within both provincial officialdom and noble landowners.[66]

An early indication of this change came as a result of a conference on migration policy called by Pleve in response to the 1902 disorders in the Left Bank Ukraine.[67] Despite the usual conflict with Witte, as well as with the Siberian Railroad Committee, whose head, A. N. Kulomzin, chaired the conference and whose primary concern was the problems of Siberia rather than European Russia, this conference succeeded in issuing a set of Temporary Regulations that were adopted on 4 June 1904. They included a number of innovations reflecting Pleve's ideas, some of them already expressed in the Editing Commission. Most important, for the first time the migration of land-hungry peasants from central Russia was specifically encouraged as one solution to the problem of peasant poverty and the preservation of rural order. Thus, the regulations broke with previous practice, which had required departing peasants to return their share of land to the commune without compensation, and now permitted peasants who owned land on an individual basis to sell their land either to the community or a fellow villager; peasants in villages with communal tenure could similarly sell their household plot and the commune would be required to recompense them for their arable land— in effect, an early acknowledgment that it was, indeed, their property rather than the commune's. To facilitate migration by the poor, various forms of government assistance also became available. Finally one article gave migrants, regardless of whether they initially chose communal or individual tenure, the right to separate their share of the new land into compact holdings (*khutorskie otruby* as the law actually called them), thereby bringing the ideas of the perceptual revolution into the legislative realm for the first time.[68] Of course, these measures could have no significant impact on the agrarian problem within European Russia. However, they did signal the government's first attempt to experiment with such innovations. Certainly it was easier to do this on newly or recently settled land than to embark on a full-scale reform on lands that had been settled and cultivated for centuries and were encumbered with all kinds of conflicts and disputes—a consideration that also influenced Peasant Bank policies. However, the war with Japan postponed the implementation of these regulations until 1906.[69]

Like the other members of this new generation of bureaucrats, Gurko and his co-workers within the Editing Commission had set forth a program of agrarian reform that sought to "emancipate" the individual peasant by gradually eliminating the deficiencies of communal land use and landownership. Moreover, it is clear that at this stage in the struggle to develop a new agrarian policy, the Finance and Interior ministries were fundamentally of one mind in their perceptions of the agrarian problem, at least at the subministerial level. At the heart of this agreement was their effort to demonstrate the existence of a material and cultural basis upon which a reform could build. Indeed, their proposals were conceived as a direct expression of existing and potential developments. They also shared a new conception of the government's role that was based on a pragmatic, experimental, and interventionist approach to rural change. Their hope was to develop a program that would mirror the actual processes by which agricultural improvements were diffused among the peasantry and that would at the same time legitimize the government's participation in the process of initiating and encouraging change. In this way the government would be able to participate in the determination of its own fate while stimulating the peasantry to follow a similar path of self-determination. Thus was launched the new myth of peasant spontaneity that would in due course come to replace the myth of the commune as a justification of government policy. And once again we see the paradox of a government policy that strove to harmonize the new interventionism of bureaucratic *opeka* with the individual freedom and initiative of laissez-faire liberalism—or, in the language of their revolutionary Marxist opponents, to harmonize rational egoism and economic determinism, consciousness and spontaneity. Indeed, like their Marxist opponents, these bureaucrat-reformers also sought to outwit Hegel's "Owl of Minerva" by first predicting the future and then acting as its midwife. Despite this perceptual unity between two otherwise inimical ministries, it would only be acknowledged during the final stages of the Special Conference's activity, beginning in December 1904.

4

THE SPECIAL CONFERENCE, DECEMBER 1904 TO MARCH 1905

Perceptual Revolution Consolidated

Reason is not an independent historical factor. It acts only under the influence of those conditions which are established by the external world.

—K. F. Golovin, 1896

Throughout the world, the small-scale economy is more profitable than the large, and science, the doctrine of political economy, which passes a harsh judgment on the future of small-scale industrial production in the struggle with large, makes an exception in the realm of agriculture.

—A. V. Krivoshein, 1908

Japan's declaration of war on Russia on 26 January 1904 proved to be the first in a series of developments during that year that led to the outbreak of revolution in the next. As is so often the case, and, indeed, as Pleve apparently hoped, the onset of war initially served to heal social antagonisms and to provoke a surge of patriotism throughout the country. This relative calm, in part the product of the Interior Ministry's repressive measures, was broken only by Pleve's assassination on 15 July and the widespread jubilation that it provoked even in some conservative circles. Despite the fact that this event marked the end of an era, it was not until the appointment of Prince P. D. Sviatopolk-Mirskii as Pleve's successor that the political atmosphere began to heat up.[1]

Mirskii, who had served as an assistant interior minister until Pleve's appointment in 1902, was currently governor-general of Vilna, in Poland. There was a complex struggle over the choice of Pleve's successor, and the tsar waited six weeks before making an appointment. However, when he finally offered the position to Mirskii at the end of August he declined, in part because of poor health but also because he was a staunch opponent of his predecessor's policies, particularly Pleve's opposition to the political activities of the zemstvos. Given Mirskii's well-known advocacy of reform, the reason for the tsar's choice is not completely clear. However, it appears that Nicholas waived his own preference for Assistant Interior Minister B. V. Stürmer, who favored a continuation of Pleve's repressive police policies, under pressure from influential figures at court for whom the Empress Dowager, Maria Fedorovna, acted as spokeswoman.[2]

In the event, the tsar finally convinced Mirskii to take the post and promised support for reform. Mirskii took office on 16 September. However, even before he left Vilna, he started giving interviews to foreign newspapers in which he talked of granting greater freedoms, particularly to the zemstvos. Then on his arrival in the capital he made his famous speech to a group of high officials in the Interior Ministry. In it he noted that "fruitful government activity" has to be "based on sincere and trustworthy relations" with society. Shortly thereafter the Associated Press quoted him as saying that the essence of his policies would be the "good of the people."[3] The contrast between his ideas and Pleve's was so sharp that the speech provoked a storm in the press. Thus was launched the "era of confidence" that the editor of *Novoe Vremia* dubbed a "Spring."[4]

Mirskii subsequently presented to the tsar a report that contained a number of proposals for reform, the most significant of which would enlarge the State Council by admitting members elected from society. This proposal, although it had a venerable genealogy, as we have seen, appears to have been based most recently on the ideas set forth in a memorandum by Golovin that Mirskii also submitted to the tsar.[5] At the same time, Mirskii effectively gave his tacit approval for the meeting of a zemstvo congress in Moscow on 2 November. This congress of zemstvo constitutionalists and members of the newly formed Union of Liberation eventually drafted an address to the tsar calling for constitutional reforms. This was followed on 15 November by a four-day conference of local marshals of the nobility in St. Petersburg that, although of major significance as a political event, had no immediate impact because of its internal political divisions. Subsequently, among the zemstvos a campaign began to address the tsar with demands for reform.[6]

Meanwhile, in early December, Mirskii's own proposals for reform were brought before a special conference made up of ministers, other high officials, and *"les oncles,"* as the royal family's grand dukes were called. This resulted in the publication on 12 December of a ukase drafted in the main by Witte and Baron E. Iu. Nol'de, the administrator of the Committee of Ministers' Chancellery, in which the tsar proclaimed his principal concern to be the improvement of the peasant way of life and promised to help the peasantry realize that status of "free rural inhabitants with full legal rights" that had been recognized as their due by the Tsar-Liberator, Alexander II. Then, acknowledging the contributions of both the Interior Ministry's Editing Commission and the Special Conference, Nicholas expressed the hope that their work would result in appropriate legislation.[7]

Despite this expression of concern for the peasantry, the ukase did not include Mirskii's plan to include elected representatives in the State Council, nor did it include another of Mirskii's proposals, the transfer of peasants from communal to individual tenure.[8] Thus did Mirskii's attempt to build a regime based on trust go down to defeat even before it had begun. The fall of Port Arthur came only six days later. Mirskii lasted exactly another month, when he was replaced by A. G. Bulygin after the "Bloody Sunday" massacre in which members of a peaceful demonstration of workers, led by Father Gapon, tried to deliver a petition to the tsar and were shot down on the square in front of the Winter Palace.

The ukase had not, of course, signaled any change in the government's official policy toward the commune.[9] Rather, under pressure from the growing confrontation with the liberal opposition movement, the government had shifted the focus of attention back to sociolegal issues. The ukase even suggested the peasantry's eventual integration "with the general legislation of the Empire." In the face of political crisis, the once sensitive issue of *soslovie* isolation had lost some of its significance. Paradoxically, despite the extension of political rights to society in 1905 and the grant of full civil rights to the peasantry in 1906, this issue would continue to be a source of conflict, particularly, as we shall see, between the provincial landowning nobility and the Stolypin government. At this stage, however, the tsar was still a long way from taking any decisions concerning the fate of the sacred and inviolable commune—an institution as fully suffused with symbolic significance as the very autocracy itself.

The Memorandum on the Peasant Problem

On 8 December 1904, Witte's Special Conference began meeting in a series of plenary sessions that represented the culmination of nearly three years of carefully staged activity.[10] Its goal was to review the conclusions of its local committees and discuss the program that Rittikh had appended to his 1903 work on the commune.[11] The agenda's formal organization was in accord with the pamphlet summarizing the opinions of the Conference's local committees.[12] However, as part of Witte's critique of the Editing Commission's work, the discussions themselves were organized around the questions submitted by the Commission to its own provincial conferences.[13]

Just before the Conference reconvened, Rittikh had elaborated on his program in a *Memorandum on the Peasant Question* (which appeared under Witte's name).[14] The organization of this essay focused on seven specific questions all concerned with the peasantry's status and the problem of integration: peasant administration, peasant justice, civil law, criminal law, the commune, family ownership, and freedom of departure from the commune—the last three topics being subsumed under the category of private law.

Designed as part of Witte's ongoing campaign to publicize these issues, the *Memorandum* reflected the concerns of the local committees and the new political climate. Indeed, its concentration on questions concerning the peasantry's sociolegal status and the problem of integration suggested that Witte was once again pursuing a strategy of winning allies for his program of reform among the liberal opposition movement within the zemstvos. As a consequence, the *Memorandum* seemed to reemphasize, on the surface at least, the conflict between Witte and the Interior Ministry. However, in its treatment of the commune it also confirmed the continuity between Rittikh's ideas as worked out in 1902 and 1903 and those developed by Gurko's Editing Commission.

The *Memorandum* reiterated traditional arguments that the commune encouraged rather than prevented the formation of a proletariat; encouraged the accumulation of land in the hands of the few; created disputes, discord, and economic disorder; promoted egoism, indifference, and apathy with respect to the agricultural work at hand; inhibited the rationalization of agriculture on market-based principles; and had nothing in common with free organizations of cooperation that were based on private property.[15] However, to these it added one traditionally held only by the older generation of conservative liberals but now revived both by the Conference's local committees and in an important work by A. P. Nikol'skii, a member of the Finance Ministry, a participant in the final stages of the Special Conference, and future agricultural minister.[16] Thus, going beyond the populist argument that saw in the commune the seed of a socialist future, this argument attacked the commune as a "socialist bacillus" that prevented the development of a private-property consciousness. At this point the argument was more hypothetical than real. However, in the aftermath of the agrarian disorders of 1905, as we shall see, the issues would quickly become polarized into a conflict between the commune and private property, between agrarian forms of capitalism and socialism, and this argument would become an important weapon in the battle to win support for a program of reform.[17]

As a solution to the problems inherent in the commune, Witte's *Memorandum* again adopted a slightly different emphasis, reflecting both Nikol'skii's views and the liberal sentiments of the zemstvo opposition movement. It urged the Special Conference to develop legislation that would transform the commune into a "free and voluntary union" of those peasants who wished to remain within it while allowing the free departure of those who desired to own their land on an individual basis.[18] As for the hallowed principle of communal inviolability, it noted merely that this was violated as much by a policy of "forcible" preservation as it would be by a policy of "forcible" destruction. The *Memorandum* also proposed that government and society cooperate in realizing the necessary reforms by granting peasants financial and material incentives, including the abolition of redemption payments. Finally, it favored preserving the special *soslovie* status of small-scale peasant property so as to prevent its purchase by nonpeasants and establishing a limit on the quantity of allotment land that could be owned by a single household to prevent its concentration in the hands of a rich minority.

Although it proposed a thoroughgoing policy of *khutorizatsiia*, most of Witte's *Memorandum* subordinated the agrotechnical and economic problems of peasant land use and ownership to sociolegal issues. This reflected Witte's awareness that the government had to build a new constituency within the increasingly powerful liberal segment of society. Nonetheless, those sections of the essay that directly addressed the economic problem differed only in their forthrightness and degree of detail from the almost identical solution set forth by Gurko in the Editing Commission. They were also, of course, a concise summary of Rittikh's own conclusions. Despite this attempt to appeal to liberal opinion, which included some barbed comments on the land captains—a particular bête noire of Witte's—the preservation of *soslovie* restrictions on the acquisition and disposability of peasant allotment land appeared to be the only political alternative to the social anarchy of the market or the legal arbitrariness of the existing situation. Thus, even Witte found himself compelled to support at least this vestige of the bureaucracy's traditional, regulatory form of *opeka*.

The Special Conference

The Special Conference met regularly from December 1904 through March 1905.[19] Despite the apparent shift of focus from economic to sociolegal issues, only nine of its twenty-eight sessions focused on legal and administrative questions. The voting on these issues demonstrated that the vast majority of the members of this broadly conceived interdepartmental conference generally supported Witte's program of peasant integration.[20]

The remaining nineteen sessions, beginning on 15 January 1905, emphasized the commune, family ownership, and free departure. The discussion of these issues provoked somewhat greater conflict. Yet, even so, all fourteen questions on these topics were discussed, and the Conference's decisions on the first thirteen were passed on to a special editorial subcommission before they were to be returned for a final vote.[21] From these discussions, it is clear that the Conference had reached a consensus on these issues as well. Then, on 30 March, it was suddenly adjourned under the pressure of changing political circumstances and the tsar's ambivalent relationship with such a strong personality as Witte, both of which were exploited by his opponents, who did not favor the Conference's newly developed sociolegal approach and its attempt to build bridges to the opposition movement.[22] As a result, final recommendations were adopted only with respect to the questions of peasant administration and courts. Subsequently, the Conference's work would be transferred to a new conference on "strengthening peasant landowner-ship" under the chairmanship of I. L. Goremykin, Witte's principal bu-reaucratic enemy since Pleve's death.

Despite the sudden end to its work, the Conference's members had agreed that legal obstacles to the free development of peasant landown-ership and use be eliminated;[23] government and society cooperate in encouraging peasants to adopt improved forms of land use short of form-ing *khutora*, though without exerting any legislative pressure; individual peasants be granted a categorical right to separate from the commune with their land at the next repartition or at other times either if several households desired to separate or with the voluntary agreement of both parties; and every adult male peasant be granted a unilateral right to leave his community at any time without his land. The members also agreed in principle to limit administrative interference in the freedom of communes to execute repartitions and adopt community resolutions, though they could not agree on specific details.[24]

The one issue that split the proponents of reform from their more traditional colleagues was a proposal to replace family ownership with individual ownership by the head of household.[25] An equally controver-sial proposal to grant peasants the right to dispose freely of their allot-ment land on leaving the community remained unresolved at the abrupt closing of the Conference.[26] Despite such widespread agreement, how-ever, the sessions devoted to these questions frequently turned into vit-riolic exchanges between Witte and Stishinskii and on one occasion between Witte and his old adversary and soon-to-be successor, Goremy-kin.[27] Yet even in conflict, these men seem to have been united in a common purpose. Stishinskii's position is somewhat difficult to deter-mine. As recently as 15 November he had stated privately that "the abolition of the commune . . . will be worse than the total defeat of Rus-sia by the Japanese for then the peasant population will revolt."[28] Yet within the Conference his various statements did not reflect such an extreme position. On the contrary, in that forum he simply argued, on purely formal and legal grounds, that the commune as the officially rec-ognized redeemer of the land allotted to it at Emancipation was a juridi-cal person and corporate owner of that land and that its rights had to be placed ahead of its individual members, who were merely allocated land for their temporary use. This hardly matched Khvostov's more impas-sioned defense of the commune when he attacked the "cosmopolitans" for their slavish adoption of Western ideas and claimed that "true Russians will never become reconciled to the abolition of the commune, to the destruction of the commune, or to the destruction of the peasantry's family way of life."[29] At the heart of Stishinskii's disagreement with the reformers was the contradiction that existed between the intentions of the Emancipation's framers, as expressed in specific articles of the Statute, and the Senate's subsequent interpretations.[30] Indeed, this issue lay at the very heart of the perceptual revolution within the bureaucracy and would continually reappear as discussions proceeded—hence the importance of invoking the "spirit of 1861" to promote any reform. Yet, the practical impact of the legal issue was negligible, for the bureaucratic supporters of both individual and communal ownership were in fact united on the one real issue of importance: the impossibility of using legislative or administrative force against the commune, which, both parties agreed, continued to attract widespread peasant support.[31]

What was at stake here was the practical question of deciding whose interests were to be given precedence: the commune's or the individual peasant's. Thus, even though he declared himself a supporter in theory of the *khutor* system, Stishinskii nonetheless argued that the rights of the commune ought to have precedence.[32] However, the vast majority favored individual rights. Yet this conflict, too, proved inconsequential. For, in the final analysis, all members of the Conference were agreed that no matter what measures were finally taken, it was politically imperative that intravillage conflict be prevented or at least kept within manageable bounds. This was a very special problem, for, as Witte himself noted, on any given question "peasants only rarely reach agreement amongst themselves; more accurately, there are always two sides, each of which has its calculations, motives, and reasons."[33] Stishinskii himself observed that whenever communal assemblies made decisions about repartitions, they were always "prejudiced decisions."[34] There could, therefore, be no absolute or "arithmetical" calculation of justice, as Gurko's commission had observed and as Witte frequently had cause to remind the Conference's members. The only alternative was to make as many allowances as possible for the rights of both parties, while taking steps to limit disputes within the villages themselves.[35]

All members appeared to agree about Russia's future economic development. The tenor had been set by Witte in the first session on the commune: "The peasant question," he noted, "is in essence a political question to which it is therefore necessary to relate with particular caution."[36] For emphasis, the threat to noble landownership posed by the events of 1902 in Poltava and Khar'kov provinces and the current outbreak of peasant disorders that had begun in February 1905 were alluded to more than once.[37]

Reflecting the shift in focus from economic to juridical issues already noted in the *Memorandum*, Witte now linked the peasant question and the issue of economic development together within the framework of the conflict between private and socialist forms of property ownership. According to Witte, the state itself was responsible for the peasant's lack of a private-property consciousness. After reading the peasant requests for more land that had begun to pour in to the central government, he was convinced, he said, that the peasants sincerely believed that the land allotted them in 1861 was ultimately owned by the state. Consequently, he deemed it no naive request when peasants asked the government to repeat the 1861 experience and grant them an "additional allotment" of land from the estates of the nobility. Such a conclusion, he believed, was inevitable—confirmed by the peasants' very unanimity on this score.[38] Thus the only way to save the noble's land—and Witte was no friend of the nobility—was to focus on the problem of peasant consciousness and take measures to develop a respect for private property. The commune, of course, hindered such a process. Thus, in order to avoid granting an additional allotment, the sole alternatives were to maintain the status quo and resort to the Malthusian solution for land-hunger or to grant the peasant civil rights so as to enable those who so desired to find nonagricultural occupations while permitting those who remained to redistribute the existing peasant land fund in a more productive manner.[39]

Those members of the Conference who addressed themselves to these questions were more or less in agreement with Witte—including even Stishinskii. Some, however, as we have seen, were of the opinion that a private-property consciousness was already developing. For Rittikh the evidence demonstrated that individualized ownership was, in fact, the eternal peasant "dream."[40] Lykoshin maintained that a consciousness of private property had begun to develop as a consequence of the 1893 laws limiting repartitions. Moreover, he argued, private property was the wave of the future.[41] Witte's goal or model was France: "would to God that our Russian peasants were in the same situation as the French"—that mythical nation of peasants. Private property, he argued—and more and more people within the government and the nobility were beginning to agree with him—guaranteed political stability. Indeed, he went on, as recently as 1870–71 France had demonstrated that, despite the turmoil after her defeat by Germany and the establishment of the Paris Commune, despite even the existence of extremist political parties, she was ultimately more stable even than Russia. To this paean even Goremykin agreed, noting that small-scale peasant landownership had now stabilized in Western Europe and fragmentation was slowing.[42] Even the carping Stishinskii was persuaded that the "future of the Russian peasantry" lay in the development of *khutora*, which, far from being a dream, was a real possibility.[43] Witte, however, argued that although the *khutor* might be the "ideal" solution, all such talk was meaningless since it took place in a vacuum; he warned the Conference that the legislator did not have a tabula rasa on which he could impose whatever he desired with a "stroke of the pen."[44] On the contrary, the problem was a truly practical one.[45]

The fears traditionally aroused among the commune's defenders by such visions of Russia's future were explicitly held up to ridicule by Prince L. D. Viazemskii, the conservative head of the *Udel* administration that supervised the imperial family's properties. Echoing the argument of that segment of the landowning nobility that had been converted to the virtues of a capitalist agriculture conducted within a free market system, he claimed that even if the abolition of the commune destroyed the nobility's traditional source of labor, the release of peasant cadet sons unable to count on the commune for an allotment of land at the next repartition would be quite adequate to assure a continuous supply of wage laborers. Meanwhile, the resulting increases in the productivity of noble agriculture would offset any increase in labor costs. Furthermore, he argued, even those fears associated with the possible development of a rural proletariat were pointless since that entity already existed within the commune.[46]

Of course, the Malthusian alternative was politically impossible, and Witte and Evreinov frequently harped on the cataclysmic consequences that would result from inaction.[47] Consequently, Evreinov argued, since Russia had already entered her capitalist era and since the preponderant source of the country's wealth was small-scale landed property, the government's slogan vis-à-vis the peasantry should be "get rich" (*nado bogatet*).[48] Such a viewpoint, of course, not only recalls the famous slogan *"enrichissez-vous"* uttered by Guizot during France's Bourgeois Monarchy in the 1840s; it also echoes the previously cited peasant maxim, *"Bogat Ivan—bogat i pan"* ("Where the peasant is rich, so too is the noble").[49]

Greater or lesser emphases on individual civil rights and sociolegal reform or on the rights of the commune were thus subsumed by a near unanimous recognition not only of the need for reform, but even of the specific direction such reform was to take: the gradual transformation of peasant Russia into a country of small-scale peasant proprietors—in short, *khutorizatsiia*, though the term itself was not used—and the development of more intensive, specialized, and diversified forms of cultivation. And although the Conference's members almost universally proscribed administrative force, as we have seen, all were of the opinion that the government had no choice but to take an active role not only by enacting the necessary legislative changes to permit such developments, but by intervening positively through the provision of necessary material resources such as credit and personnel.[50]

Harbingers of the Future

We should consider separately here the views of Rittikh and Gurko, which differed considerably from those of the other Conference members and from each other's. For they were the principal articulators of the revolution in perceptions and would later play key roles in transforming those perceptions into reality.

During a discussion of separations from the commune, Rittikh addressed the problem raised by the term *khutor* and the direction that it was assumed agricultural land-use practices ought to take in the future. In an earlier discussion, the Conference had decided to omit this term so as not to exert undesirable pressure on the peasantry by implying that the government favored such a solution. Moreover, some felt that the *khutor* was but one possible form of improvement that, as was widely acknowledged, was in itself unsuited to many areas of Russia.[51] The problem also arose when Witte himself proposed excluding the term on the grounds that requiring separations specifically to *khutora* might in fact restrict the peasant's freedom to separate his land from the commune.[52]

Basing his views on A. A. Kofod's recently completed study of *khutora* in Russia's western provinces,[53] and elaborating on his discussion of this question in his writings for the Special Conference, Rittikh noted that when peasants first separated their land from the commune they formed *otruba*—that is, they consolidated their open-field strips into compact parcels of land in one, two, or three fields. In this way, their land was effectively withdrawn from the communal system of compulsory crop rotation. Not until later did they transform the *otrub* into a *khutor* by constructing a new cottage and outbuildings on the consolidated land. The essence of this process, for Rittikh, was "gradualism." Moreover, the actual means by which it was finally accomplished were quite varied. Consequently, Rittikh concluded, requiring both separations from the commune and transfers to *khutora* to be executed in a single process, at the whim of the separator, went completely against practical experience. Rather, consolidations of land after separation should be required only "as far as possible" in one place. By permitting peasants to adopt intermediate forms of *otruba*, the formation of the more agriculturally desirable *khutora* could follow naturally, rather than being imposed on a peasantry that was often still unaware of its material benefits.[54]

Subsequently, while discussing the right of peasants to separate from their villages other than at the time of repartition, Rittikh set forth a model for a two-stage process of separation that would involve first "the transformation of [the peasant's] allotment into [his] personal property" and second, "the separation of the property in nature."[55] Even though this proposal was the essence of flexibility and spontaneity and was designed to reflect "life itself," it generated sharp criticism by Witte, Viazemskii, and Stishinskii. In their view simply allowing peasants to separate from the commune by granting them title to their strips while leaving them physically within the existing system of open-field land use would not only lead to all kinds of disputes and economic problems but create major obstacles to subsequent attempts to eliminate open fields by either individual peasants or the commune.[56] Nonetheless, the two-stage provision would subsequently be part of the Stolypin legislation.

Gurko's proposal was in complete contrast to Rittikh's evolutionary and gradualistic approach. But, like Rittikh's, it was, eventually, to become a part of the Stolypin Reforms. Gurko presented his proposal in a long speech on 22 January 1905 in which he outlined his views on the whole peasant problem.[57] His argument on this occasion, however, contrasted completely with the assertion, in his memoirs, that the real focus of his concern was peasant civil rights and integration, though it was in conformity with the Interior Ministry's and Witte's concern with rural poverty and with the primarily economic orientation of the Editing Commission's work. Thus, Gurko noted, despite all the attention the Conference had devoted to the questions of peasant administration and courts, the supreme problem was economic: the need "to assure [the peasant] the possibility of material enrichment and moral development."[58] State power and local stability were dependent on the successful development of these two processes. But since they depended in turn on the elimination of the commune, the failure of the government to adopt measures for its dissolution would throw Russia into a state of complete rural disorder and state powerlessness.

Gurko went on to demonstrate the already widespread existence of a private-property consciousness among the peasantry, using data on repartitions compiled by his Editing Commission's provincial conferences. Combining this evidence with statistics on the quantity of allotment and nonallotment land already held in individual ownership, he concluded that communal landownership was a practical reality only for a minority of the peasant population. Indeed, communal landownership was a myth whose existence was only perpetuated by the artificial support of the law. "Life itself" had already evaded the law and was rapidly moving toward the commune's complete abolition, at least in those regions where the income from land exceeded the combined total of redemption payments and taxes due. Gurko concluded, therefore, that legislative fiat could, indeed, abolish communal landownership not only because over one-half of the peasantry already owned their land de facto on an individual basis but also because, in the central provinces, for example, the agricultural way of life of those communities that practiced repartitioning was indistinguishable from that of those that did not. Therefore, the government could intervene in the "historical process" and enact the appropriate legislative changes without fear. Referring specifically to those communes that had not executed a repartition within the past twenty-five years, Gurko proposed that they be immediately recognized as owning their land de jure on an individual basis.[59] Here, too, Gurko's position had shifted considerably since 1903. However, even this relatively mild form of legislative coercion, which, ostensibly at least, sought merely to acknowledge what already existed, met a unanimous rejection by the other Conference members.

Yet Gurko went even further down the path of government intervention. Like the other reformers of his generation, as we have seen, he considered landownership secondary to the universal problem of communal land use, which was independent of legal forms. Without a solution to this problem, all other efforts would be in vain. And, here, no simple legislative measure could succeed in eliminating regressive land-use practices. As Gurko had pointed out before, on the basis of Kofod's work, the solution to this problem lay with livestock rearing and the need to provide better fodder—by stall feeding, for example. Nevertheless, he considered the struggle to eliminate communal land use not only feasible but necessary. Rejecting such traditional approaches as granting an additional allotment or encouraging migration on a large scale, he argued that they would be harmful both to the country as a whole and to the very peasants such measures were designed to aid. To Gurko, it was essential for Russia to preserve a differentiated and multileveled agrarian structure. In contrast to other reformers, to him noble landholdings remained an important part of the future. He repeated his earlier argument: if they were eliminated, the peasantry would lose opportunities for wage labor, and, therefore, a vital source of income. Moreover, noble agriculture was an important vehicle for the diffusion of improved agricultural techniques among the peasantry since it used more intensive methods of cultivation.

Increases in peasant productivity could not, however, be legislated. Rather, as the rest of Europe had demonstrated, the transition to intensive forms of agriculture was possible only "under the iron pressure of necessity."[60] However, the transfer to a more intensive agriculture need not be a long-drawn-out process. On the contrary, if the government committed itself to intensification, if the bureaucracy involved itself directly in economic affairs, if "the whole of our governmental activity [were to] be imbued by the idea of promoting the development of Russian agriculture by every possible means" on the pattern of its current promotion of industry, then the desired goals could be achieved.[61]

With this speech, Gurko became the most forceful proponent of direct government intervention designed to intensify peasant agriculture and introduce individual property ownership, in that order of importance. However, at this time, his was not the only, or even the preponderant, voice in the growing chorus for reform. But his newly developed sense of urgency reflected the changing political situation, which had clearly forced him to abandon his earlier gradualism in favor of vigorous state interventionism.[62]

Conclusion

The closing of the Special Conference on 30 March 1905 marked the beginning of another stage in the ongoing bureaucratic process of developing a program of rural reform. Before considering this new stage, it is important to note that it was in this Conference that the new agrarian policy of "intensification" was finally elaborated not only as a response to the country's deep need for a policy of economic growth but also as an alternative to the government's own traditional but ineffectual policies of "extensification." Equally important, intensification offered an alternative to the increasingly radical forms of extensification demanded by the opposition movements and the peasantry, all of which involved some form of "expropriation" or "additional allotment" of noble and other nonpeasant lands—in effect, a "black repartition."

Much of the disagreement that did occur in the Conference both reflected and perpetuated the traditional conflict between the Finance and Interior ministries. Nevertheless, a nearly unanimous majority of the Conference's members, including even the recalcitrant Stishinskii, in effect adopted the vision of reform that both Rittikh and Gurko had originally set forth between 1902 and early 1904. Agreement on principles transcended the differences of detail. And it must be reemphasized that the members of that Conference represented a broad cross section of dignitaries and bureaucratic and nonbureaucratic officialdom, almost all of them recognized as agrarian experts of one kind or another. And this consensus included significant elements of the government's traditional social constituency within the local administration and the provincial landowning nobility and even, though to a lesser extent, within the liberal opposition movement centered in the zemstvos.

The scope of what I have termed a perceptual revolution, it is clear, extended far beyond the bureaucracy. Moreover, there was a reciprocity of influence. For as the government reached deeper into the countryside in pursuit of its regulatory function and its search for knowledge and came into ever closer contact with economic and social reality, in turn both "society" and even the peasantry influenced the bureaucracy. In the absence of any wider political forum, the bureaucracy became a locus of social and political conflict. At the same time, noble landowners, who had increased their involvement in and dependence on agricultural production, had begun to flex their political muscles in response to new pressures for the rationalization of agriculture, both noble and peasant, and the growing threat the peasants posed to their property rights. Although the nobility's *embourgeoisement* was limited, however, it nonetheless signaled the appearance, both within government and without, of a new political force committed to classical "economic" liberalism—in contrast to the "political" liberals who took a primarily juridical and "idealist" approach to politics. However, in the face of the near universal ideological, political, and quasi-religious support for the commune that had existed at the turn of the century and that continued to be reflected in the attitudes of the tsar and diehards like Khvostov, the bureaucratic reformers in the three domestic Ministries of Finance, Interior, and agriculture independently adopted the conceptual strategy of distinguishing among the commune's functional components, separating the agrotechnical problems of land use from the more sensitive and symbolic issues of landownership and the *soslovie* system (though under the growing influence of the liberal opposition movement sociolegal concerns were again in the forefront, without however changing the underlying economic rationale of the argument). Proposing economic solutions to economic problems, they thus sought to foster agricultural progress within existing legislative and institutional structures. In practice, this meant encouraging individual peasants to leave the commune, consolidate their holdings into agricultural units as compact as possible, and begin to farm their land independently.

Most of the proposals for agricultural individualization advanced by the Emancipation's framers and other reformers during the second half of the nineteenth century specifically aimed at liberating the prosperous peasant or kulak from the mediocrity of the commune. Now it was apparent that siphoning off the most productive elements from the commune would only worsen conditions for those who remained without resolving the underlying political and economic problems. Indeed, what distinguishes these latest bureaucratic proponents of individualization was that they directed their proposals at the average and even below-average peasant. Thus, although individual separations from the commune were considered but one step toward the commune's eventual dissolution, the social content of this policy was not designed to encourage the concentration of land and the formation of a minority class of prosperous peasants on farmer-type economies in the twenty-five to fifty-desiatina range; rather it was to benefit the entire peasantry as a social class. Here Gurko was the exception in favoring such large-scale peasant holdings as well as small and medium-scale noble landowners. However, he shared the others' concern for the average and even the poor peasant. Thus, although these bureaucrats had adopted the economic and developmental orientation of classical liberalism, they sought at the same time to reconcile their commitment to economic individualism with the government's traditional policy of bureaucratic *opeka* and its commitment to the preservation of equality within the peasant *soslovie*. In this sense, these bureaucrats, like their populist and neopopulist political opponents, were hoping to escape from the stagnation of the present and to encourage Russia's modernization while avoiding the social dislocations associated with capitalism. In effect, they were searching for a third way. True, they vehemently opposed the abolition of private property as foreseen by socialism, and under the pressure of the events of 1905 this concern would supersede both economic and civil rights concerns. But their continuing adherence to traditional forms of *opeka* and their opposition to both social differentiation and the free operation of market principles in peasant agriculture in fact pushed the government in the direction of state socialism. Moreover, with respect to the peasantry, the government's commitment to private property was compatible with the kind of "socialism" characteristic of French artisan circles in the first half of the nineteenth century and reflected in the writings of Proudhon and others, as N. Kh. Bunge had once pointed out.[63] This paradoxical similarity between the government and its agrarian socialist opposition was a familiar dilemma to another passionate laissez-faire liberal, Polovtsov, who derisively referred to Russia's bureaucrats as her "first socialists."[64]

Similarly, the proposals of these bureaucratic reformers were distinguished in the political realm by their belief that the establishment of a *universal* system of small-scale individual peasant property ownership and cultivation, with its inevitable atomization of the peasantry, on the French or Danish models, would in fact preserve social and political stability better than existing arrangements.[65] And this too was in the tradition of bureaucratic *opeka*, since the atomization of the peasantry would enhance and protect the bureaucracy's claim to its privileged social status and its exclusive right to represent society and initiate government policy. Despite its self-serving aspects, however, the vision of this new generation of bureaucratic reformers was ultimately a national vision, one that had developed in response to what was perceived as a national crisis. Moreover, in conformity to the growing noble role in and influence on government during these years, this vision also represented an "agrarian" alternative to the industrially oriented policies of the past decade and a half.

Ideology, theory, and myth had thus been conquered in large measure by an increase in the practical and empirical knowledge of reality—a process that had begun in the nineteenth century and that was more or less completed prior to the appearance of the more genuinely political forces galvanized into life by the onset of revolution in 1905. The first stage of the revolution in governmental agrarian policy had been accomplished.

In the coming months, both political urgency and the conservative instinct for self-preservation would supersede these new perceptions. But they would do so only for some of the figures involved and only for some of the time. Traditional beliefs in gradual and organic change would reassert themselves in conjunction with the new belief in the capacity of governmental intervention to develop preexisting tendencies for change—though this would prove a rather unstable association. The ultimate fate of the Rittikh-Gurko proposals, however, depended on the outcome of subsequent political conflicts and the mobilization of sufficient social and political support. But their fundamental assumptions and basic propositions would remain unchanged. Indeed, they never received any significant reconsideration in the light of the changed political circumstances. Before the Revolution of 1905, the economic and social content of the government's new agrarian policy had, in fact, been fully articulated.

PART THREE
The Revolution in Policy

Given unity, the government would gain
strength, but then the administration would
become a dense wall between society and
authority to the undoubted harm of both. To
escape from this situation, and at the same
time to establish a current of democratiza-
tion, there is only one possible course—a
regularized summoning of informed people
from the provinces to the capital.
                        —K. F. Golovin, 1905
So ended the long-drawn out, almost one-
and-a half century, romance of the government and the nobility with the commune.
                        —I. V. Chernyshev, 1918

5

THE REVOLUTIONARY CHALLENGE, APRIL 1905 TO JANUARY 1906

Compulsory Expropriation versus the Sacred Right of Private Property

For me, the Sovereign's word is law.
>   —I. L. Goremykin, 1915

There is insufficient basis . . . to contrast the positions of . . . Kutler and Gurko.
>   —I. V. Chernyshev, 1918

. . . The marshals of the nobility [of Khar'kov Province, meeting in a conference convened by the governor] pointed to the necessity of replacing communal land use in the countryside with individual land use and equalizing the rights of the peasant *soslovie* with the rights of other *sosloviia*. . . . [However] everyone acquainted with the countryside knows how zealously the peasants strive to preserve their ancient forms of land use. . . . [Thus, even though] the law allows such transfers . . . it is impossible to permit the forcible abolition of the commune.
>   —General A. P. Strukov, 27 January 1906

The closing of the Special Conference in March 1905 and the simultaneous appointment of that stubborn defender of autocracy, I. L. Goremykin, to head a new conference to discuss "measures for the strengthening of peasant landownership" signaled the reappearance of those fears that had attended the Valuev and Kakhanov proposals in the seventies and eighties.[1] In the short term, far from increasing pressures for what would become known as the Stolypin Reforms, the onset of revolution and the rapid growth of new political challenges to the government's authority actually led the bureaucracy to fall back on traditional stopgap measures to alleviate the immediate needs of impoverished peasants.[2] Indeed, as we shall see, in the wake of a new and more violent upsurge of peasant disorders in October and November 1905, the government would even consider the compulsory expropriation of noble lands as a solution to the "peasant problem"—a proposal that was radical in political terms but economically traditional in its reliance on extensification rather than intensification. This decision to reject the innovations of the Special Conference undoubtedly derived strength from the argument that they had been formulated in an era of relative calm and were designed to solve the agrarian problem only over the long term. In the maelstrom of 1905, however, the paramount need was for measures that would produce immediate results without threatening rural stability by launching an assault on the commune. At the same time the cause of agrarian reform fell victim to a chain of associations linking the dissolution of the commune, the integration of the peasantry through the abolition of the *soslovie* system of administration, and the growing public demand for a constitution. Thus were the spokesmen for agrarian change once again pushed aside in times already too full of change.

In response to these political limitations, the Goremykin conference was to devise "immediate" and "practical" measures for the "stabilization of the peasant landed structure" on condition that private (that is, noble) property be preserved. It was also to propose measures to improve the cultivation of allotment land, to assist land-hungry peasants either to migrate eastward or purchase additional land from the Peasant Bank, and to set off peasant allotment lands from neighboring properties so as to "consolidate in the popular consciousness a conviction of the inalienability of all private property."[3]

However, over the subsequent six months, and despite the huge increase in peasant disorders, which reached a peak in June, the agrarian problem seems virtually to have lost the government's attention.[4] In part, this is explicable in terms of the government's immediate political concern with the problems of sovereignty and constitution. But in part, the widespread myth of peasant loyalty that prevailed among the ruling classes encouraged it. Despite the growing unrest they believed that the peasant not only remained loyal to the tsar but might even be his only remaining source of social support in these desperate times.[5] Thus, although the peasantry's concerns were regarded as important, the government appears to have felt that they could be deferred while more momentous political matters were dealt with.

Over the summer and fall of 1905, the government's agrarian policy therefore confined itself to preserving the "inviolability of [the nobles'] private property"—a task that was occasioned by the immediate peasant threat to these lands and by the increasingly strident demands of liberals, socialists, and peasants to satisfy the peasants' land-hunger by a repeat of 1861—an "additional allotment" of land to be taken largely from the domains of the nobility.[6] The adoption of a number of repressive police measures designed to restore a semblance of law and order in the countryside reflected this most directly.[7] At this early stage, however, the government's defense of "private property" was more a defensive reaction to the concerns of the landowning nobility than an expression of commitment to a political ideology or a theory of economic development.

The appointment of Goremykin, Semenov[-T'ian-Shanskii], Stishinskii, D. F. Trepov, Prince Shcherbatov, the Slavophiles D. A. Khomiakov and F. D. Samarin, and a number of other conservatives did not augur well for a more constructive approach to the peasant problem.[8] Goremykin's 22 April report to the tsar set the traditionalist tone:

[Our goal] must be to ease the separation of peasants with that share of the allotment land due them in private property . . . [with the proviso that] legislative measures for the reform of the commune must "in every way possible avoid changes in the government's regulation of peasant landownership and abrupt intervention by forcible measures in the historically-formed landed way of life of the rural population."[9]

In addition, Goremykin called for the creation of a more centralized and unified government and the concentration of all departments concerned with agrarian policy, including the agricultural ministry, the Peasant Bank, and the Interior Ministry's Migration and Rural Sections, within a new body to be known as the Main Administration of Land Organization and Agriculture (*Glavnoe Upravlenie Zemleustroistva i Zemledeliia*, referred to hereafter as GUZiZ). He also proposed the formation of a Committee on Landed Affairs to be composed of six ministers, under the tsar's chairmanship, that was to issue general guidelines for the conduct of peasant land and migration policies.[10]

These organizational changes were not, however, Goremykin's idea. They were the product of a joint initiative by Krivoshein,[11] then head of the Interior Ministry's Migration Section, and D. F. Trepov. A military man and noble landowner from Orel Province, Trepov assumed the newly created post of governor-general of St. Petersburg in the immediate aftermath of the massacre of workers on Bloody Sunday, 9 January 1905. From this post, which after May he held in addition to those of chief of police and assistant interior minister, and from his subsequent position as palace commandant in October, Trepov exercised enormous political influence and effectively became the de facto dictator and head of the government during these months of government paralysis and indecision. He was also a member of the "star chamber," a group of government bureaucrats who would come together to defend the autocracy in the aftermath of the workers' general strike in October.[12]

This first of several attempts to centralize the various agencies concerned with peasant affairs within a single bureaucratic organization was not especially successful. On the one hand, the Finance Ministry undermined it, refusing on fiscal grounds, as well perhaps for reasons of bureaucratic jealousy, to abandon its supervision of the Peasant Bank. At the same time, reflecting Witte's own ambivalence toward the nobility, it opposed the Bank's transfer to a ministry that, in its previous incarnation, had traditionally been regarded as pronoble. On the other hand, the Interior Ministry had presumably opposed the transfer of its Rural Section since this agency was central to its own task of maintaining order in the countryside. Even the far less controversial transfer of the Interior Ministry's Migration Department to the GUZiZ, although approved, was delayed until 19 September 1905.[13] As a consequence, the only other change to be adopted was the renaming of the agricultural ministry as the GUZiZ on 6 May 1905.[14] Nonetheless, the Goremykin Conference had initiated a process of functional specialization that would continue and that would prepare the ground for the eventual dominance of the more economically oriented GUZiZ over the more politically motivated Interior Ministry during the implementation of the Stolypin Reforms.[15]

Beyond this and the compilation of a set of instructions for the new ministry, Goremykin's Conference accomplished little. The instructions do, however, indicate the Conference's position on a number of the crucial issues raised earlier. For example, it expressed its tacit agreement with the opposition movement by acknowledging that land-hunger was, indeed, a major cause of peasant unrest.[16] However, its proposals were confined to such traditional measures as encouraging peasant migration to state land and the sale of land through the Peasant Bank, as the tsar had wished.[17] Even a proposal to form *khutora* on state lands ignored the issue of replacing communal forms of peasant land-ownership with individual ones, suggesting merely that such holdings be held in temporary possession or permanent use.[18]

However, a minority of the conference—Gurko, G. V. Glinka, Kutler, and A. I. Putilov, all members of the new generation of bureaucrats—succeeded in expressing its opposition to the commune, thereby keeping alive an alternate viewpoint.[19] Indeed, Gurko even submitted his proposal that those communes in which there had been no repartitions over the preceding twenty-five years be legally recognized as having transferred from communal to individual tenure. Of course, this proposal was rejected, just as it had been by Witte's Special Conference. Thus the final version of the instructions to the new ministry expressed the majority's opinion that the fate of the commune should remain with "the natural order of things" and once again proclaimed the commune's "inviolability."[20] The only concession toward the commune's opponents was to extend to peasants who wished to leave the commune the provisions of the 6 June 1904 regulations on migration, which had made it possible for peasants to receive compensation from the commune for their share of the land when they left.[21] The only other positive expression of government agrarian policy during this period was an imperial command of 14 July 1905 removing restrictions placed on Peasant Bank activity as a result of the war with Japan.[22]

Thus, in the face of the immediate challenges posed by the revolution, the government had reasserted its commitment to the preservation and consolidation of the peasant commune as a unit in the *soslovie* system of administration and an instrument of bureaucratic *opeka*. At the same time, it reverted to the more traditional policy of facilitating the departure of those enterprising and prosperous peasants who were disturbing its internal tranquility. Indeed, Goremykin later argued that the departure of such peasants would, in fact, strengthen the communal order—an argument that had been fashionable in the years following Emancipation.[23]

Bureaucracy versus Nobility: The Migulin and Kutler Projects and "Compulsory Expropriation"

Russia's massive naval defeat by Japan, widespread discontent in the countryside after a major crop failure in the late spring, a constant round of worker strikes, and growing demands for a constitution from the opposition movement had marked the summer of 1905. Finally, on 6 August, in an effort to reach a compromise with the liberal opposition movement among the zemstvos and provincial nobility, the government made public its proposal for the establishment of a consultative assembly, known as the Bulygin Duma after A. G. Bulygin, the interior minister who had replaced Prince Sviatopolk-Mirskii. Not surprisingly, most of the opposition movement reacted negatively both to the assembly's lack of legislative power and to the highly restrictive franchise, which gave a large voice to the presumably loyal peasantry but virtually excluded the intelligentsia and the factory workers. The zemstvo congress held the following month expressed its dissatisfaction with these proposals and called for further reforms—a demand that produced a split that would lead to the formation of the Constitutional Democratic (Kadet) party in the middle of October.

In early October, under pressure from a general strike of workers, students, and professional and white-collar employees, the shutting down of the railroads, and the election of a workers' soviet in St. Petersburg, Nicholas turned once again to his nemesis, Witte, for support. The price of government weakness was high, for on 17 October, the tsar found himself compelled to issue a manifesto that granted civil liberties to virtually all groups in the population, extended the franchise to those previously excluded, and transformed the consultative assembly into a legislative body with genuine powers of initiative.[24] Two days later, the tsar issued another ukase establishing a new Council of Ministers designed, at least in theory, to create a unified government capable of dealing with the new Duma. Witte became its first chairman, or prime minister.[25]

Witte's return to power marked the beginning of a new course in government policy that combined both immediate repression and substantive reform—a policy foreshadowing Stolypin's essentially similar but better known program that would be characterized by the phrase "repression and reform."[26]

Paradoxically, the publication of the October Manifesto, which had been designed to calm both workers and intelligentsia, produced the opposite effect on the peasantry, stimulating a new wave of peasant disorders.[27] Indeed, in confirmation of the government's seemingly obsessive fear that the peasantry would inevitably misinterpret its proclamations, the Manifesto seems to have been interpreted by them as having granted not merely civil rights but complete "freedom" to take whatever they needed from surrounding noble landowners, including even their land. Under the pressure of these events and the growing sense of panic that was aroused by the fear of a new *Pugachevshchina*, the siege mentality that had already helped prepare the ground for the political concessions of 17 October now succeeded in pushing the government's agrarian policy in a more politically "radical" direction. And once again, it was to be Witte who was to function as the visible, and therefore highly vulnerable, symbol of a government apparently ready to adopt an agrarian program that threatened to undermine the social, economic, and political position of the very landed nobility that supplied many of its highest officials and had traditionally constituted its most significant basis of social support.[28]

Witte had already signaled the first sign of a new direction in his 9 October memorandum to the tsar on the urgent problem of peasant land-hunger. The author of the memorandum, however, was the former general and political liberal, V. D. Kuz'min-Karavaev, to whom Witte had turned for advice on returning from the peace conference with Japan in Portsmouth, New Hampshire.[29] In it, Witte proposed a partial distribution of state and Peasant Bank lands as well as the expropriation of a portion of the privately owned lands already rented by the peasantry, with appropriate compensation to be arranged through some kind of government-sponsored redemption operation. However, these critical October days saw Witte absorbed in issues of constitutional and civil reform and in negotiations with various factions of the liberal opposition who might join his cabinet. As a result, one should not see Witte as having committed himself to the argument that what the peasantry suffered from most—and what was therefore the principal source of rural unrest—was land-hunger, or to a specific program of reform. Rather, Witte's proposals represented an attempt to test the political mood within the government as well as to establish a basis for cooperation with the liberal opposition by setting forth a program that went part way toward meeting their demands.[30] Subsequently, however, government agrarian policy took a more radical and practical turn.

After the collapse of Witte's negotiations with liberal society, and under the influence of the increasing peasant disorders, a sense of panic spread in the court and the government as well as in provincial noble society.[31] Inspired by a new urgency to identify the causes of this upsurge in rural unrest, government officials became increasingly willing not only to accept the traditional explanation of land-hunger but also to see the necessity for immediate measures that would involve some form of expropriation or additional allotment. Under these pressures, none other than Trepov, now palace commandant, was to declare to Witte in a well-known (perhaps apocryphal) conversation some time toward the end of October that "I myself am a noble landowner and will be very happy to give away half of my land since I am convinced that only on this condition will I preserve the second half for myself."[32] Immediately after this conversation, Nicholas handed Witte a copy of a project on compulsory expropriation that was sponsored by Trepov and instructed Witte to discuss it in the Council of Ministers.[33]

P. P. Migulin, a young professor of financial law at Khar'kov University and frequent critic of Witte's fiscal policies, had composed the project. Its most important proposal, and the one that aroused greatest attention, provided for the compulsory expropriation of some 20 to 25 million desiatinas of state and privately owned land for distribution to the peasantry by means of what Migulin called a state-sponsored program of "obligatory redemption" based on a "just compensation" of approximately one hundred rubles per desiatina.[34]

Such a policy, he asserted, had both economic and fiscal justification. However, it was on purely political and pragmatic grounds that he finally argued for its adoption since, in his view, "the majority of landowners will gladly agree to the alienation of [part of] their land in favor of the peasant even at extremely moderate prices in order to preserve the remaining part and [thereby] to restore good relations with the neighboring peasants. . . . " Only by granting an "additional allotment," he added, could the current "pogrom" (sic) in the countryside be halted.[35]

Elaborating on these ideas in the press, he pointed out that he was not "solely concerned here with the interests of private landowners or even of peasants."

> We are speaking about *the interests of all Russia*. Russia needs a well developed large- and medium-scale agriculture . . . maintained in the hands of individual property owners. To accomplish this the peasantry has to be calmed. . . . [Meanwhile] the development and improvement of peasant agriculture requires the creation of small-scale peasant holdings . . . with the aid of additional allotments. . . .[36]

Migulin then urged the government to implement his plan immediately—prior to the convocation of the Duma. Only by taking such a forthright position, he argued, could the government recapture its policy-making initiative from society and counteract those peasant rumors, spawned by the October Manifesto, that the tsar had been forced to capitulate to the landowners, who only wanted to retain possession of all their lands.[37]

Despite this emphasis on expropriation, it is clear from Migulin's explanatory note that this proposal was part of a much broader vision that sought to link the political need for decisive action with the necessity of developing a long-term solution that would encourage Russia's economic growth.[38] Indeed, for Migulin, the primary issue was, as it was for Trepov, the preservation and extension of private property, which, he argued, would strengthen the "links between the cultivator and the land he works . . . [and guarantee] the calm in the countryside that is evident wherever large numbers of small-scale landed proprietors have a stake in preserving it.[39]

Thus, in order to avoid what he saw as a Russian edition of the French Revolution's assault on "feudal" property and property owners, Migulin set forth a plan that combined the innovative policies of individualization and intensification with the traditional policies of extensification. (He also added a pet project of his own—the provision of insurance against crop damage caused by the weather.) Specifically, he proposed a resettlement of European Russia's surplus population on the free lands of Russian Asia, the rationalization and intensification of agriculture within European Russia, an expansion of agriculturally based industries, and an increase in peasant landownership—especially of pasture land, which he saw as the critical first step toward the development of a more intensive agriculture and the elimination of a major source of conflict between peasants and noble landowners.[40]

When he presented his project before a congress of the recently formed Octobrist Party the following February, Migulin was more explicit. The entire program, he noted, was itself but a prerequisite to the voluntary transformation of the entire peasantry from a system of communal land-ownership to one based on individualistic principles. Clearly, Migulin's awareness that the tsar remained unwilling to consider any proposals that directly threatened the integrity of the commune, even though the tsar was prepared to consider measures of expropriation, dictated the failure to include such a statement in earlier versions of his project. On the other hand, Migulin had now retracted his proposal for the compulsory sale of noble land to the Peasant Bank. Such a step, he felt, was unnecessary by virtue of the close conformity between the price the Bank actually paid for noble land and the "just" price he had initially proposed, though he retained compulsory expropriation as a principle of state policy.[41]

Despite the cogency of his arguments and the breadth of his vision, despite even the support of Trepov and the tsar, the Council of Ministers nonetheless rejected Migulin's proposals unanimously at the end of October—an event Migulin had in fact anticipated.[42] Witte gave two reasons for this rejection. On the one hand, under the influence of both a certain pronoble sentiment and a concern for the principle of legality, the Council wanted to preserve the inviolability of private property as an absolute principle of government policy. On the other hand, there were some in the Council who sought to avoid taking precisely this kind of unilateral action in a realm that it considered the proper concern of the Duma lest they undermine the government's ability to work with that institution and with the liberals within it. In addition, the widely held belief that when the Duma met it would be dominated by loyal and conservative peasants who would resolve this issue in a way that was acceptable to both government and nobility influenced the Council.[43]

Despite this rebuff, Migulin's project was nonetheless transferred to a new conference headed by Kutler that was charged with reworking the proposals into a form suitable for submission to the upcoming Duma.[44] Apparently, some ministers, including Witte, continued to see expropriation as a possible basis for cooperation with both the peasantry and the liberals. Meanwhile, the Council of Ministers felt compelled to take some immediate measures to relieve the current crisis. Thus, in a ukase published 3 November 1905, the tsar "granted a favor (*milosti*) to the peasant population," as Witte phrased it,[45] by reducing redemption payments for most categories of peasants by one-half from 1 January 1906 and abolishing them completely as of 1 January 1907.[46] This "favor" accompanied another ukase authorizing an increase in the Peasant Bank's capital and a reduction in interest rates so that it could purchase additional land and expand sales to the land-hungry peasantry. An indirect reference to the Kutler conference also noted that these measures were, however, only interim steps, to be followed by others, as yet unspecified, that would be directed to the specific needs of the land-hungry.[47] Finally, on the same day, 3 November, the tsar issued a Manifesto calling for a peaceful and legal solution to the problem of peasant welfare and warning that those responding to his earlier request for suggestions to improve peasant welfare should make sure that their proposals did not violate the interests of other, nonpeasant landowners. Significantly, this Manifesto did not mention "the inviolability of private property."[48]

Then, on 16 November 1905, the Finance Ministry took specific steps to implement the new Peasant Bank policies, appealing to the county zemstvos for assistance. To this end, it called for the election of special commissions composed of persons "closely acquainted with local conditions," one half of whom were to be peasants.[49] This matter was considered so urgent, indeed, that the county zemstvo executive boards were instructed to function as surrogates until the commissions themselves could be formed; in those cases in which the zemstvos refused to cooperate, the local marshal of the nobility was to form the appropriate commission.[50] Assignment of these tasks to such local, nonbureaucratic institutions rather than to organs of the central government was somewhat unusual. However, although it reflected the continuing inadequacy of the government's own administrative organization at the county level and below, it also demonstrated the influence of Witte's continuing policy, after the announcement of a Duma, of achieving a measure of reconciliation with the liberal opposition by involving "society" directly in the government's activities.

Established to ensure that the Peasant Bank's activity was conducted in accordance with the overall goals of the state's agrarian policy, these zemstvo commissions were also to serve as intermediaries between peasants and private landowners to facilitate direct purchases of land. To these ends, the commissions were to advise the Bank about the appropriateness of proposed purchases as well as the needs of the local peasantry. We do not know how many of these commissions were actually formed, though there is evidence that society's response to such prosaic, local, and seemingly "nonpolitical" tasks was sporadic and insignificant.[51] Consequently, as we shall see, the head of the Land Banks would have to dispatch his own appeal some six weeks later, urging the local marshals of the nobility to form such commissions in their area.

In the meantime, while the Kutler conference began the task of revising Migulin's proposals, Migulin himself was seeking wider support for his proposals. Already on 2 November, presumably after learning that his project had been rejected, Migulin wrote directly to Witte briefly outlining his proposals.[52] This was followed on 15 November by an oral presentation of his program before the tsar in General Trepov's presence.[53] Apparently, Nicholas was still willing to consider a policy that included the principle of expropriation. A few days later Migulin took his ideas before the newly formed Union of Landowners (*Soiuz Zemlevladel'tsev*) in Moscow, where, despite a vote against expropriation, he received some support for his project, including his concept of expropriation, on condition only that he eliminate the word *compulsory* from it. His most outspoken supporter at that meeting was none other than General A. P. Strukov, himself a large landowner recently returned from Tambov and Voronezh provinces, where he had commanded one of the infamous "punitive expeditions" dispatched to suppress peasant unrest.[54]

Meanwhile, during this period, Witte received several other independent suggestions favoring a policy of expropriation. In a private conversation in December, Vice Admiral F. V. Dubasov, just returned from a punitive expedition to Chernigov and Kursk provinces, endorsed the idea of compulsory expropriation as a way of preserving what remained. Moreover, with Strukov, Dubasov urged the immediate adoption of appropriate legislation prior to the convocation of the Duma as the only way to avert the widely anticipated renewal of peasant disorders in the spring.[55] In addition, the government received a number of petitions from various groups of local nobles that expressed support for the tsar should he decide to alienate a portion of their lands.[56] Although nothing came of Migulin's proposals at this time, it was against this background that the notorious "Kutler Project" came before the Council of Ministers at the end of December 1905.

The Kutler project on the "expansion and improvement of peasant landownership" was, in fact, a revised version of Migulin's project that A. A. Kaufman, the well-known agrarian expert, had prepared with Rittikh's assistance.[57] Impressed both by the way the abolition of redemption payments in November had been ignored by the peasantry and by the continued increase in the number of peasant disorders throughout the rest of that month, Kutler had apparently become convinced that some form of compensated expropriation was indeed necessary.[58] As a consequence, the new project retained the principle of expropriation, subjecting Migulin's other proposals to minor modification. In Kutler's view, expropriation was necessary primarily because it was important for the government to reserve this right:

> Too stubborn an insistence on the principle of the inalienability of private property . . . can lead . . . to the proprietors' losing everything under conditions that would be extremely destructive for themselves and the whole country.[59]

At the same time, however, the project's explanatory note repeated Migulin's argument that only eliminating open fields and the communal system of land use could produce a solution to the low productivity of peasant agriculture and to the broader agrarian problem. However, since this would take a long time and would require both a general increase in the peasants' cultural level and the development of personal and social independence, there was no choice but to take preliminary but decisive action that could produce rapid results even within the existing structures of landownership and use. Thus, the project proposed first that the government take steps to expand the area of peasant landownership both by sales of privately owned land through the Peasant Bank and by the selective expropriation of nonpeasant lands. These measures would not only be of economic value to the peasantry, since they would bring some immediate relief and contribute to the elimination of the most extreme cases of land-hunger; they would also be of political value to the state, since they would undermine peasant expectations of an additional allotment.[60]

Inevitably, Kutler's project, like Migulin's, became identified with compulsory expropriation. Nonetheless, Kutler only planned to use expropriation as a supplement or "corrective" to the more important task of selling land through the Peasant Bank. To this end, the project established an order of priorities in which state- and other institutionally owned lands would be the first targets for expropriation. Only when these sources proved inadequate for the needs of local peasants would the government turn to noble lands, and then only those properties already rented by peasants. Land that was a part of the noble demesne and that the proprietor himself actually cultivated would be considered only in exceptional cases, and land growing specialized crops or utilizing advanced and intensive methods was completely exempt. Finally, the project offered a somewhat more generous rate of compensation than that proposed by Migulin.[61]

At the same time, in seeking a way for the government to begin the practical task of agrarian reform, the Kutler project borrowed from a project that had been compiled by Gurko's Editing Commission and then transferred to the GUZiZ. This provided for the elimination of open fields between peasant and nonpeasant landowners. The commission saw this measure as an important first step toward increasing the peasants' productivity, developing their respect for others' property, and reducing a frequent source of conflict in the countryside.

Meanwhile, to implement these reforms, the Kutler project developed another idea of Migulin's and proposed the formation of a central land committee, its members to be divided equally between government officials and Duma representatives, that would supervise and coordinate the various agencies involved in reform, including the Peasant Bank. In addition, "land commissions" would be formed at the provincial and county levels that would include elected representatives from the zemstvos, local landowners, and the peasantry.[62]

Although all its modifications to the Migulin project seemed in principle to have considerable support within governmental circles, the Council of Ministers rejected the "more moderate" Kutler project on 6 January 1906, and it again returned to the GUZiZ for reconsideration.[63] The Council also called for more repressive measures in the countryside as well as for a reform of peasant administration and an improvement in general cultural conditions.[64] Almost simultaneously, a tremendous furor arose over the whole question of compulsory expropriation within the provincial gentry: Who, they asked, was behind this attempt to destroy the landowning nobility and even the autocracy itself? Indeed, as subsequently became clear, a sharp change in political mood had taken place within the bureaucracy and the palace between October 1905, when Trepov and the tsar first considered Migulin's project, and January 1906, when Kutler's version of it came before the Council of Ministers.

To understand this change of mind and thus chart the shifting directions of government agrarian policy, we must now turn to an analysis of the opposition that began to develop within court and government circles not only to the whole concept of expropriation, but also to the entire trend of government thinking that saw land-hunger as the root of the agrarian problem.

Nobility versus Bureaucracy: The Counterattack

It is understandable that during the threatening months of November and December 1905 the tsar was increasingly beset by indecision and thus at the mercy of similarly panic-stricken advisers. Yet, even at the autocracy's lowest point, a small but significant group of opinion makers remained unshaken in their support of the absolute inviolability of the nobility's landed property and categorically opposed to any policy of concessions in the face of the growing peasant unrest. Moreover, as the defenders of the traditional order began finally to organize for their own defense and that of the tsar and the autocracy, their influence began to grow.

Predictably, the first move in the noble counterattack—which sought to develop an alternative to expropriation and extensification or the expansion of peasant landownership through traditional means—came from the Golovin salon, long opposed to Witte and his policies.[65] More surprising was the emergence of Gurko, still head of the Interior Ministry's Rural Section, as one of the principal spokesmen and leaders in this campaign.

Gurko first set forth his argument in a brief memorandum written in response to the Migulin project and then circulated privately in late November 1905.[66] At this stage, however, he confined himself to attacking the various proposals for "compulsory expropriation" and exposing the contradictions inherent in the very concept of an additional allotment. Granting it, he said, would actually exacerbate the peasants' problems. Any increase in the area of land at their disposal would, given the low level of agricultural technique, lead to a decline in their own well-being and in the country's productivity and wealth. On the other hand, Gurko acknowledged that from their perspective, it could justifiably be argued that the entire peasant population was to some degree land-hungry though such a claim assumed—incorrectly in his eyes—that agriculture was the sole source of peasant income. Nonetheless, because much of the peasantry held this view, if the government were to adopt a policy of granting additional allotments, every peasant community would have to be regarded as an active contender for an increase in its landholdings. Not only would such demands be impossible to meet, but limiting such a measure to the so-called land-hungry would provoke

even more dissatisfaction among those peasants who were not so classi-
fied—a state of affairs that could only lead to even more undesirable
political consequences.

Thus, Gurko argued, the existing state of rural social relations would
not, in fact, permit the government to limit its distribution to the merely
"land-hungry" but would ultimately oblige it to parcel out every piece
of available land to the peasantry—in effect, to execute that mythical
black repartition. Even so radical a measure as this, however, would,
according to Gurko's calculations, increase the peasants' holdings only
by approximately half a desiatina per soul—an insignificant amount in
view of their real economic needs. More important, it would lead to a
rapid increase in peasant impoverishment since the abolition of nonpeasant holdings would eliminate all sources of outside agricultural income.
And this, in turn, would lead inexorably to the destruction of the domestic market and a drastic decline in both industrial production and urban
employment. In addition, there would, of course, be a considerable reduction in the size of Russia's grain exports—a major source of state income.
The final consequence of such an agrarian policy, therefore, would be
complete state bankruptcy.[67]

On more directly sociopolitical grounds, Gurko attacked the government's neo-Slavophilism—its identification of the empire's strength and
social stability with the traditional concept of Russia as a *muzhik*-state
in which a conservative peasantry, loyal to the tsar and cultivating its
own land within the commune, would more than outweigh the unstable
urban population. On the contrary, he believed, the distribution of all
land to the peasantry would generate complete disorder as peasant became pitted against peasant and village against village in a struggle initiated by the prosperous, who sought to acquire for themselves the
greatest possible quantity of the limited supply of land—a paradox already evidenced in 1905. The consequences would be similar, moreover,
in the case of a partial expropriation that granted an additional allotment
only to the neediest peasants since the lands usually proposed for this
form of distribution were already rented by peasants. Their expropriation
would, therefore, merely deprive one category of peasants, the prosperous, in favor of another, the land-hungry. Either way, Gurko argued, the
outcome would be a "universal civil war." Increased migration would
similarly fail to provide any solution to the problem. Thus Gurko rejected any policy that sought its base of social support within the land-
hungry peasantry. In his view, the state's only viable source of support
among the peasants lay with its strongest elements.

Gurko resoundingly attacked Witte's government for its confusion and
inconsistency in considering expropriation. Indeed, not only was expropriation without precedent in the history of organized states, it had not
even received any extended and widespread discussion by the different

classes (*klassy*)—by nobles, zemstvo members, prosperous peasants, trad-
ers, industrialists, or even workers—such as had preceded the Emancipation of 1861. As a consequence, he charged, the whole country stood
united in fear before Witte's dictatorial government and its arbitrary
policies (though he was not unmindful of the fact that the events of the
past months had finally shaken the country out of its traditional rut and
held out at least the possibility of the right kind of change). He also
criticized Witte for ignoring the implications of the ukase of 3 November
abolishing redemption payments. For, as Gurko was one of the first to
realize, this ukase, by removing the last remaining obstacle to the liquidation of the peasant commune, had opened up the possibility of a totally
different approach to the agrarian problem, as we shall see.

Taken as a whole, Gurko's was a cogent, convincing, and "intelligent"
argument, as the tsar was himself to note. What was most surprising,
perhaps, in the light of conventional criticisms of the government's in-
effectiveness in these declining years of the Empire, was Gurko's highly
informed analysis of the very real social, economic, and political problems that had to be dealt with in the formation and enactment of government policy. Equally significant was his recognition that the economy—
a crucial factor—was a complex and interrelated whole, obviously capitalist and united by the market, in which actions taken in one realm
could not but have their reactions in others. Indeed, as has been suggested earlier, this analysis included no small degree of insight derived
both directly and indirectly from Marxist sources—to the point where
Gurko not only accepted the Marxist diagnosis that what Russia suffered
from was an insufficiently developed capitalism, but also foresaw what
Lenin himself was later to predict, if incorrectly—a civil war within a
peasantry that had been polarized into two hostile classes. At the same
time, Gurko had also given a relatively accurate forecast of the fate that
actually befell Russian agriculture and the national economy in the years
after the October Revolution.

Gurko's perceptive critique, however, was but the first volley in what
quickly developed into a sustained assault by the landed nobility, within
the government and without, on proposals for the compulsory expropriation of private land. And although, in deference to the prevailing political prejudices, he had only hinted in a footnote at the necessity of
abolishing the commune, other expressions of opposition to the Migulin,
and later the Kutler, projects began to link their dedication to the inviolability of private property with attacks on the commune itself. Thus, on
17 November 1905 the Union of Landowners was one of the first such
groups to adopt a resolution recognizing that adherence to the principle
of communal landownership had been a tragic mistake and demanding
the commune's destruction in the name of the defense of the holy right
of property.[68]

Among the first to come forward with a program to save private property was D. I. Pestrzhetskii. One of Gurko's coworkers within the Interior Ministry's Rural Section, he had some seventeen years' experience in peasant affairs.[69] He made his debut as *fidei defensor* in December 1905 with a series of three articles that appeared in *Vestnik Finansov*, the house organ, oddly enough, not of his own ministry but of the competing Finance Ministry.[70] Reprinted in book form the following month,[71] they were quickly followed by two more series of articles in the newspaper *Novoe Vremia*, for which he, like other bureaucrats interested in reform, wrote frequently on agrarian questions.[72] However, unlike his superior, Gurko, who did not publish his own programmatic suggestions until the spring of 1906, Pestrzhetskii declared himself openly from the beginning.

In contrast to Gurko, but like both Migulin and Kutler, Pestrzhetskii argued in his articles in *Vestnik Finansov* that a solution to the agrarian problem would require the immediate adoption of a twofold program combining an increase in the area of peasant land use with the transfer of peasant agriculture from extensive to intensive forms of cultivation. In the first part of his program, which did not, however, call for any form of expropriation, his proposals were reasonably traditional and included an increase in migration to Siberia, the purchase of both private and *Udel* land (which belonged to the imperial family) through the Peasant Bank, and the institution of hereditary rents—measures that even Gurko did not oppose in this form. However, Pestrzhetskii noted, the effectiveness of even these modest provisions would be hindered by the very poverty of those landless and land-hungry peasants for whom they were primarily intended. Consequently, he proposed in addition a number of measures that would permit such peasants to acquire the capital necessary to take advantage of these policies, most notably through the mortgage or sale of their allotment land.[73]

Such measures, however, were for Pestrzhetskii, as, indeed, they had been for Migulin and Kutler, only palliatives. In his view, the only real escape from what was, indeed, a completely untenable situation for the peasantry lay in the intensification of peasant agriculture and an individualization of peasant landownership and land use. And it was to this that the bulk of his project was devoted. As proof of this contention, and basing himself primarily on Petr Lokhtin's highly respected comparative survey of Russian agriculture, Pestrzhetskii first gave a brief outline of agrarian history in England, Germany, Austria, Denmark, Finland, Sweden, and France (with an aside on Japan), from all of which he deduced the historical and economic "necessity of a transfer from communal to personal land use by the abolition, as far as possible, of open fields and the concentration of small plots into larger *otruba*."[74] Then, basing himself on Kofod's work and the data on repartitions recently collected by the Rural Section, Pestrzhetskii went on to demonstrate "that agrarian evolution in Russia follows the same course as in the rest of the civilized countries of the world."[75] "In Russia," he therefore concluded, "an intensive economy must begin with [the encouragement of] small-scale peasant holdings, which can be cultivated by the family without resorting to hired labor."[76] At the same time, he expressed hope that the rise of the new constitutional political order would free the country's best talents from the ranks of the bureaucracy, thereby enabling them to apply themselves to practical activities, including agriculture.[77]

Thus, not only did Pestrzhetskii reject traditional arguments about Russia's historical uniqueness (*samobytnost'*), which he believed were used as a shield for intellectual ignorance and laziness and indicated the lack of any desire to study the subject at hand; he attacked the widespread isolationism of contemporary Russian studies on the history, political economy, and psychology of the peasantry since such an approach only inspired the creation of ingenious and improvised theories that were, in his view, without foundation. Indeed, he argued, unless Europe's accumulated knowledge in this realm were integrated into Russian thought, such ignorance could lead to cataclysmic consequences, as the present situation already threatened.[78]

Rejecting both the classical theory of liberal economics, which counselled against state intervention in economic matters, and the Spencerian version of this ideology with its concept of a war of all against all, Pestrzhetskii argued that these theories did not describe the actual historical record of the West European states. Moreover, under present circumstances, both domestic and international, such a passive approach to the economy was impossible. Rather, he urged immediate governmental intervention to implement his proposals for both extensification and intensification. At the heart of his program was the specific demand, first proposed by Gurko, that the holdings of peasants who belonged to communes that had had neither general nor partial repartitions during the past twenty or thirty years automatically transfer into individual property and that those peasants whose communes had conducted repartitions within this period obtain the right to claim title to their strips.[79]

Some three weeks later, Pestrzhetskii reiterated his demands in the last of his *Novoe Vremia* articles. On this occasion, however, he placed the government's future tasks more specifically within the context of the ukase of 3 November 1905 abolishing redemption payments and in effect described the course the government would actually follow until the dissolution of the First Duma in early July 1906:

By January 1, 1907, two laws must be published: 1) on the transformation of strips of communal land into the personal property of individual householders on their demand; and 2) on the reduction of open-field possessions into *otrub* holdings (*kommassatsiia*). This latter law must be applied in localities with both communal and individual forms of ownership.[80]

Beyond his opposition to expropriation, the proposal to abolish communes that did not execute repartitions, and the desire—derived from J. S. Mill—to see local life reinvigorated, Pestrzhetskii's most interesting idea, though it too was not original to him, was his adoption of List's and Mendeleev's mercantilistic notions of a "national economy" and the demand for direct government intervention not only in industry, but also in agriculture—a view shared by Gurko and Witte. Interventionism had, of course, always been explicit or implicit in government activity; what was new was that it was only now advocated with respect to peasant agriculture. Even more remarkable, in the aftermath of 1905, was that this perspective would rapidly win new adherents not simply among those bureaucrats who were resolved to take an active role in determining the future fate of Russia but among the landowning nobility as well.

Thus, although Pestrzhetskii was undoubtedly seeking to advance his own version of a program for the resolution of the agrarian or peasant problem as an alternative to the Migulin and Kutler proposals, his writings also reflect the state of the bureaucratic mind and its remarkably high level of sophistication and expertise. At the same time, Pestrzhetskii's program, which combined modified forms of both extensification and intensification, established the basis for a compromise between those within the government who supported either one or the other. Meanwhile, the subsequent reprinting of the conclusion to his *Vestnik Finansov* articles in an unprecedented "bibliographical" article in the January 1906 issue of the Rural Section's journal suggests that even though Gurko may initially have blocked the publication of these articles, he had now recognized their political value.[81]

Gurko himself finally appeared in print a few months later in a pamphlet entitled *Fragmentary Thoughts on the Agrarian Question* that was basically an expanded version of his November memorandum.[82] This work is particularly important for an understanding of Gurko's position and the role his ideas played not only in consolidating government and noble opposition to expropriation, but also in setting the stage for subsequent developments in the realm of government agrarian policy.

In this pamphlet, as in his earlier memorandum, Gurko expressed far less interest in setting forth a specific program of agrarian reform than he did in establishing the underlying principles of state policy within the context of a broader vision of national economic development. Above all, he sought to liberate the government from what he saw as its panic-stricken subordination to the immediacy of special interests and its narrow self-protectiveness. Consequently, he began by rejecting the entire conceptual framework within which partial concessions were urged as a means to preserve what remained.

He then turned to the larger question of Russia's economic development. Seen from this perspective, it was clear that increased peasant prosperity depended on the country's overall level of wealth. However, as he pointed out, before wealth could be more equally distributed, it had first to be accumulated. Therefore, he argued, since Russia was the poorest country in Europe, her first task had to be one of increasing her national wealth even if it were inevitable that such a policy would initially lead to an increase in inequality—or even to landlessness. However, in a predominantly agricultural country such as Russia, economic growth ultimately depended on increasing the productivity of the soil. Thus Gurko came back full circle to the problem of peasant poverty, which he identified as the root cause of Russia's poverty. Having already rejected land-hunger as the source of this problem, he now identified the main obstacle to improving peasant welfare as "routine"—an all-pervasive and deadening routine that was institutionalized in the commune's system of compulsory crop rotation. However, because communal land-use practices were designed to operate on the level of the lowest common denominator, only the energetic few could overcome this routine. Indeed, this situation in itself was sufficient to show that granting an additional allotment would subject the entire country's agriculture to the same principle, thereby producing general impoverishment rather than general improvement.[83]

In expanding on his earlier proposals for agricultural intensification on the West European model as the sole way out of the present dilemma, Gurko acknowledged that it might well prove impossible for Russia to achieve such highly intensified forms of agriculture as had been developed in northern and western Europe. Yet, he argued, Russia was undoubtedly capable of achieving some degree of improvement. Here, Gurko focused on the one resource in the agricultural economy that was available in abundance: labor. Unused labor power, thus, became the key to intensifying Russia's agriculture and breaking out of her poverty. Hence Gurko's primary goal: to provide every inhabitant with sufficient work rather than with more land.[84]

In accordance with the vision of an ideal structure for Russian agriculture that he had first presented to the Goremykin Conference at the end of 1905, Gurko divided agricultural undertakings into three categories: first, small holdings of less than 50 desiatinas, which would supply the consumption needs of the peasant family and utilize all of its labor power; second, medium-size farms with between 50 and 150 desiatinas, in which the owners would engage in personal labor yet would also hire outside workers in order to cultivate the land fully; and third, large-scale enterprises with from 150 to 1,000 desiatinas, where the owner would be

involved only as an administrator, if at all, and the entire work of cultivation and administration would be the domain of hired laborers and
other employees. Increased size, in Gurko's view (and here he differed
significantly from Rittikh and others within the government), corresponded to increased productivity—under optimal circumstances and
within the specified limitations. Indeed, in the Russian case, he noted,
in which both knowledge and capital were in short supply, small-scale
properties were the least favorable subjects for intensification. In terms
of labor productivity it was in fact the medium-size holding that was
most efficient because the owner himself set the example and encouraged
higher productivity by the hired labor than was possible if they were
merely supervised, as was the case for holdings in the largest category.
Yet, in the overall socioeconomic structure, Gurko considered the small-
scale properties of greatest importance since they also supplied labor for
medium-size and large estates. Furthermore, insofar as they provided a
substantial share of their own consumption, such workers were more
independent of their employers than mere agricultural day laborers.
Thus, Gurko argued, the large-scale landowners were dependent on the
peasants rather than the reverse, at least so long as the peasants had some
minimal basis for their own independence.[85] It should also be added that
although 50 desiatinas may seem rather large for peasant holdings, this
figure was clearly only intended to suggest a ceiling. Indeed, in the south-
east and among the Cossacks, holdings already approached this limit.

What Russia needed then, according to Gurko, was a better balance of
these three kinds of agricultural undertakings. Comparing Russia to
France and Germany, he proposed an increase in the proportion of mid-
dle-size holdings at the expense of the two extremes. Despite appear-
ances, Gurko was not simply a spokesman for the selfish political
interests of Russia's parasitic class of truly large landowners. Indeed, he
vigorously attacked the noble *latifundia*-type enterprises on economic,
social, political, and even moral grounds, going so far as to imply that the
landowner who failed to apply either his knowledge or capital to his
property forfeited his right to that property on the grounds of state interest. For Gurko, the state had the right to adjust the structure of landownership in such a way as to encourage the growth of national wealth as a
whole, on the basis of the most productive use of the soil as reflected in
yields.[86]

In order to achieve the desired expansion of landownership in the middle range of from 50 to 150 desiatinas, depending on the region, Gurko
proposed the adoption of a progressive land tax that would indirectly
force the owners of the largest estates, which were both the least productive and the least likely to sell, either to intensify their cultivation or to
sell their land. However, he distinguished such measures from "expropriation," since the noble landowner had the alternative option of modernizing his economy.[87]

Although Gurko advocated the breaking-up of large *latifundia* to create more efficient agricultural units, he opposed government intervention to combine small-scale properties into larger ones lest such a step lead to a reduction in their number. Rather, he claimed, with the end of the redemption operation in sight, the entire peasantry would soon automatically become property owners on the basis of civil law and would, therefore, have the right to dispose freely of their share of it. This alone, in his opinion, would help solve the problem of land-hunger by encouraging that "natural [process of] class differentiation within the peasantry which even now is universally observed." Thus, the weak would sell to the stronger and migrate to free lands in the east or to the cities, encouraging the concentration of land and thereby increasing its productivity.

As Gurko acknowledged, he had, indeed, changed his position and rejected his earlier support for the traditional *soslovie* principle of preserving an inalienable fund of allotment land for the exclusive and eternal use of the peasantry—even at the risk of offending those whom he respected. He believed that in the long term such a policy would result in the beneficial destruction of the commune and its eventual replacement by the individually owned *khutor*, though even this, he admitted, would not completely rule out the possibility that the government might have to provide more land to the peasantry.[88] Nonetheless, for Gurko, the *khutor* was the "crown of small-scale landownership which until now has unfortunately been [regarded as] an ideal achievable in Russia only in the distant future."[89]

Gurko's vision of the future combined an updated version of the Enlightenment's belief in unlimited progress with the optimism of the classical economists. Like Witte, Pestrzhetskii, and Rittikh, not to mention Russia's Marxists, he assumed that Russia's economic development would follow Western Europe's. Moreover, his faith in this process led him to expect that gradual industrialization and urbanization would ultimately provide a solution to the Malthusian problem of overpopulation, as they had in the West. Even more important, however, his program was practicable, since it was finally on the political agenda by virtue of the manifesto of 17 October 1905.[90]

Despite Gurko's sympathy for the landowning nobility, and notwithstanding a superficial similarity between its concerns and his own, his proposals in fact had little in common with the traditional perspectives of that class. Rather, he reflected the still somewhat inchoate interests of a relatively new class of modernizing noble agriculturalists. Indeed, his was only one of many voices raised in behalf of an economic future that was strictly bourgeois in the sense that a *fronde* of noble landowners engaged in agriculture as an occupation and acting for the first time in defense of their own "economic" or "class," as opposed to status or *soslovie*, interests would take the first steps. In the historical sense, then, this phenomenon, which was an expression of the classical economic liberalism of Adam Smith and subsequent advocates of laissez-faire, was a progressive one. Moreover, unlike Pestrzhetskii and others who supported individualization and intensification primarily on the historicist grounds of inevitability, Gurko left far more scope to the influence of "free will" and to man's ability to participate in the determination of his own future—a perspective not in fact so different from that of Russia's "revolutionary" intelligentsia.

From this vantage point, Gurko then went on to argue that a major problem with government policy to date lay precisely with its traditional, noninterventionist forms of bureaucratic *opeka;* since the Emancipation, the exercise of this prerogative had in effect led to a form of state socialism, though in the long run it was becoming nothing more than administrative despotism *(proizvol).* As a consequence, the government had failed even to achieve its main goal of supporting the peasants' economic well-being. In the last analysis, therefore, it was the collectivist and egalitarian orientation of *opeka* that was responsible for reducing the entire peasantry to its present state of extreme poverty. Now, however, it was time for the collectivism and egalitarianism in *opeka* to yield their places to the new principle of individualism. Any return to collectivism or cooperative principles such as socialist theory proposed was for Gurko a matter only for the distant future.

It was this traditional form of *opeka* that Gurko rejected. However, when it came to the question of the government's immediate role, he argued that even though it was impossible to establish a particular economic order ex nihilo on the basis of either political ideas or legal norms, as political liberals hoped, state intervention could act to modify the economic structure in conformity with such organic and objective external necessities as climate, topography, and geology. Whereas previously the government had acted in a conservative manner and sought to preserve the given order—existing reality or life itself—current circumstances called for "radical" and "decisive" intervention by the government, whatever labels—capitalist or socialist—critics might give them.[91]

Yet, although asserting his commitment to a voluntaristic approach and a pragmatic methodology, Gurko did not abandon his equally strong belief in a deterministic form of economic materialism, a contradiction that he shared with segments of the revolutionary intelligentsia. Thus, he remarked at another point in his argument that he did not "in the least lose sight of that incontestable proposition that any and every durable political structure is the invariable logical consequence of the economic structure which predominates in the country."[92]

Within the contemporary political context, of course, Gurko was defending a version of the status quo—though one that recognized and even embraced gradual and organic change. Thus, in urging the government to take measures to expand medium-scale landownership, he was motivated not only by their economic significance but also by their political function.

For the preservation of the existing order it is necessary immediately, without losing a single day, to create an economic bridge between the poor ignorant masses of the population and its upper, prosperous, but thin strata. Without the presence of these intermediary links . . . we will not be in a position to defend our state order, to defend the rights granted by the Manifesto of October 17th. Either we will fall anew under the police-bureaucratic regime or we will be present at the complete collapse of our entire social order.[93]

He also retained the traditional perspectives of the bureaucratic servitor:

I have in view not the interests of individual strata of the population and still less the interests of individual personalities, but the interests of the entire country in its totality, since I am deeply convinced that what is beneficial for the entire country is in the final analysis beneficial to every one of its inhabitants.[94]

In sum, what Gurko sought to achieve was the elimination of that historic split between Russia's educated elites and her popular masses by introducing those necessary *corps intermediares* of eighteenth-century liberal political theory, in this case a middle class of agriculturalists, within an individualized and fully integrated sociolegal structure based on economically determined social classes. At the same time, he combined the bureaucracy's traditional supraclass perspective with a new, interventionist version of *opeka* designed specifically to encourage the economic development and modernization of Russian society. This goal was to be achieved by means of a government-sponsored policy of agricultural intensification that would be applied at every level of landownership.

Thus was the campaign against expropriation launched, waged, and, as we shall see, eventually won. More immediately, as we saw, Gurko's campaign was largely responsible for the rejection of the Migulin and Kutler projects by the Council of Ministers. Clearly, whatever support had existed within the government for such an extreme measure as the expropriation of private landed property had evaporated.

The arguments of "experts" such as Gurko and Pestrzhetskii were not, however, the only factor influencing responses to the government's proposals for expropriation. A surge of confidence within both court and government as the army began returning from Manchuria and turned to the task of domestic repression also marked December and January. The first sign of a change in the government's fortunes came with the suppression of the armed workers' uprising in Moscow, which was completed by 19 December. There followed a growing number of equally successful "punitive expeditions" to quell peasant disorders beginning the same month. And both of these developments were followed by a rapid decline in the number of peasant uprisings and worker demonstrations and strikes.[95]

This newfound confidence was reflected in a number of ways. In January, Vice-Admiral Dubasov retracted his earlier support for expropriation.[96] Similarly, General-Adjutant Panteleev expressed his support for "inviolability" in a January 1906 report on the suppression of rural disorders in Kursk Province.[97] Then on 27 January, General Strukov submitted to the tsar a series of brief memoranda that opposed compulsory expropriation and supported the inviolability of private property in terms that directly reflected Gurko's arguments.[98] Meanwhile, the Congress of the Marshals of the Nobility, which met in Moscow from 7 to 11 January 1906, passed a resolution stating that the "decision of the agrarian question must be established on the basis of the principle of the inviolability of private property."[99] Finally, as a result of a campaign launched by the Congress among the local corporations of the nobility, dozens of petitions went to St. Petersburg opposing expropriation and supporting the inviolability of private, noble property.[100]

In the midst of this concern over the Migulin and Kutler projects, local society was suddenly galvanized by a circular dispatched on 9 January 1906 by the administrator of the two Land Banks, Putilov, apparently at Witte's direction, to all marshals of the nobility urgently calling on them to act on the Finance Ministry's appeal of 16 November and form local commissions, with the participation of peasants, in order to determine, in consultation with local nobles and others, what lands were best suited for transfer to the land-hungry. Whereas the earlier appeal had been all but ignored, Putilov's circular caused a tremendous stir among the provincial nobility, who were now becoming more conservative and who feared that it heralded the start of a unilateral bureaucratic solution to the agrarian problem by the proverbial stroke of the pen. The emotions the "Putilov Affair" aroused also helped fuel the change of mood in the provinces, and objections to such government intervention merged with the marshals' petition campaign.[101]

All of these developments, of course, influenced Nicholas. In addition, he had undoubtedly been swayed by such personal factors as the German kaiser's remark, relayed to him toward the end of December by Finance Minister Kokovtsov, that a policy of expropriation would be the "purest Marxism."[102] In any event, the tsar began reexpressing his own support for the inviolability of private property. He did so first by writing in the margin of Witte's 10 January 1906 report summarizing the government's discussions on the agrarian problem to date, that he "did not approve" of the Kutler project and that "private property must remain inviolable."[103] Thus, as early as the second week of January 1906, Nicholas too had felt compelled to reject the threat that "expropriation" presented to the traditional social order and to side with the nobility—though not, as in the case of Louis XVI in the France of 1789, as the country's first noble, but rather as her first landowner.

Subsequently, Nicholas reaffirmed his commitment by making similar remarks to a peasant delegation from Kursk on 18 January and to delegations from the nobility of Vladimir, Tula, and Tambov provinces during the month of February.[104] By the end of March 1906, he had apparently regained sufficient confidence both in the strength of the regime and in the loyalty of the peasantry to express "confidence that the peasants . . . love [me]" though he also expressed his utter contempt for the peasantry's demands for land, which he sanguinely felt could be held in check by the army.[105]

Not surprisingly, responsibility for the initiation of the proposals for compulsory expropriation and particularly the Kutler project has usually been placed on Witte—the nobility's universal scapegoat. Certainly Witte must share some of the responsibility. However, he shifted it to Kutler, who shifted it back to Witte or to Kaufman. Nevertheless, Kutler was the first to be sacrificed to this change of mood: he was forced to resign as head of the GUZiZ on 4 February 1906. The tsar's distaste for him was so great, indeed, that he was deprived of the customary appointment to the State Council, just as Sviatopolk-Mirskii had been one year earlier. Yet, to the very end, he insisted that his project had had the tsar's personal backing.[106] Witte himself remained in office only another two and a half months before being removed on the eve of the First Duma's convocation at the end of April.

Some within the government, however, continued to believe that the political situation was such that the government had no alternative but to adopt a policy of compulsory expropriation. Apart from Kutler, who was on his way out of office, the most notable example was Witte himself, who continued to argue that even though expropriation had been rejected, all the evidence suggested that the peasants sincerely believed that they suffered from land-hunger and possessed some rights to non-peasant lands—particularly those they had been renting continuously and for which they had paid rents far exceeding the value of the land itself. As a consequence, he argued, the government would eventually have to adopt some form of compulsory expropriation if only to forestall the resurgence of peasant disorders anticipated for the coming spring.[107] Subsequently, in a special conference to revise the Fundamental Laws that was held under the tsar's chairmanship at the beginning of April, Witte again noted that "there will undoubtedly be a law which allows

the [compulsory] expropriation of private property in favor of the peasants. After a few months the tsar will have to confirm such a law . . . or
the entire peasantry will rise up against the supreme authority."[108]

However, it seems clear that neither Witte nor Kutler believed that
expropriation was anything more than a political strategy designed to
gain the support of the peasantry or win the cooperation of the opposition parties by accepting, in principle, their agrarian programs. Certainly, neither man believed that expropriation could provide a solution
to the agrarian problem itself.[109] Moreover, extensification could be combined with policies that favored either preservation or dissolution of the
commune. Witte's prediction was wrong, at least in its timing. The revolt that he anticipated took another eleven years to come to pass.

Meanwhile, throughout the remainder of 1906, a great many bureaucrats and nobles rushed into print with their own programs of agrarian
reform, often extremely well thought out, all calling for the individualization and intensification of peasant agriculture as an alternative to compulsory expropriation. They are of interest only insofar as they reflect
the state of the bureaucratic mind during these months, for none of their
authors was to have any direct influence in shaping the government's
agrarian policy. Similarly, several government departments entered the
fray, publishing collections of statistical data designed to support the
argument that extensification was unrealistic and that the only alternative was for the government to promote intensification.[110]

Despite the arguments of men like Gurko and Pestrzhetskii, and despite having officially rejected compulsory expropriation as the principal
component of its agrarian policy, the government continued to share a
modified version of the opposition's argument. Thus it continued to believe that at least a portion of the peasantry suffered from land-hunger
and that it was the government's responsibility to extend the area of
landownership for at least some of those who fell into that category. The
ukase of 3 November authorizing an expansion in the quantity of land
acquired and sold by the Peasant Bank was only the most explicit expression of this commitment.

Conclusions

This entire episode emphasizes the indecisiveness that beset both the
tsar and the government as a whole as they were faced with a choice:
they could take the immediate steps proposed by some panic-stricken
dignitaries and local gentry to resolve the political crisis and prevent the
potential defection of the peasantry into the ranks of the revolutionary
parties, or they could develop a more durable solution to the underlying
economic problems, as was proposed by Rittikh, Gurko, and a number
of other officials. Faced with this choice, the government initially split

into two major camps, one supporting immediate measures designed to increase the area of peasant landownership, an approach that conformed to traditional assumptions about the nature of the peasant or agrarian problem; the other supporting the innovative, if less immediately effective, policies of individualization and intensification, based on the new assumptions introduced by the perceptual revolution, though with a new emphasis on developing the peasantry's respect for private property by transforming them into property owners themselves.

Initially, in the 1902–4 period, in deference to the widespread support that existed for the commune, the campaigns for individualization and intensification had focused on the economic and agrotechnical issues of eliminating open fields and communal forms of land use and the development of integral, compact holdings. These measures were seen as prerequisites to the establishment of economic prosperity, which would lead in its turn to changes in peasant consciousness and thus create the order necessary to foster national economic progress. However, under the pressures generated by the October Manifesto—particularly by the threat that peasant disorders and expropriation projects posed to noble lands—this relationship reversed: the importance of granting peasants property rights to their allotment land was now given primary emphasis as the most effective means of instilling the virtues of property ownership and creating a new basis for the establishment of order, both of which were seen as necessary prerequisites to an increased peasant prosperity and national economic development. In this context, the individual claims of title to strips within the commune were seen as a first step toward the ultimate economic goal of intensification as an alternative to extensification. Ironically, in retrospect, the proponents of intensification were right. For it seems clear that the preservation of the existing order would ultimately have been better served by a program that emphasized real economic changes rather than one that placed its emphasis, at least initially, on changes in the peasants' legal consciousness.

Thus, although the existing political crisis and the immediate threat to noble property determined the terms of the conflict, the underlying issues remained those of the prerevolutionary period—specifically, of choosing between extensification and intensification as a solution to the peasant problem. At the same time, as our analysis of the proposals for "compulsory expropriation" has demonstrated, both Migulin and Kutler shared many of the same perspectives as their opponents. Similarly, Pestrzhetskii had incorporated some measures of extensification into his proposals. Indeed, everyone who offered up a reform program during this period combined both approaches. What distinguished them was only the emphasis that they placed on one or the other. Indeed, as we have seen, no one within the government supported only one approach. On the one hand, complete dependence on expropriation would have brought the government very close to implementing a populist form of agrarian socialism based on the commune and the black repartition, as Gurko charged. On the other hand, not even Gurko depended exclusively on a policy of transforming peasants into individual property owners or even on the broader one of intensification. Kaufman, who was directly involved in the government's reform activities at this time, even claims to have heard Gurko say that he was willing to consider some forms of compulsory expropriation so long as the purpose was to "improve," that is, intensify, peasant landownership rather than "broaden" it.[111] Moreover, as we have seen, even those who supported extensification did so largely from political rather than economic motives. However, under the intense political challenges posed by these critical months, the issues became polarized in the minds of many government figures and nobles so that individualization and intensification came to be identified with the preservation of the nobility's private property and the survival of the existing tsarist regime, and expropriation and extensification were identified with the revolutionary overthrow of tsarism and its replacement by a socialist agrarian order, based on the peasant commune. Indeed, for Gurko and the members of the Golovin salon and their sympathizers within the landowning nobility, the issues were even more sharply drawn as a choice between private property and the commune, between tsarism and socialism, since they assumed that the abolition of private property in agriculture would quickly lead to its abolition in other areas of the economy as well.

The role of Nicholas II—the autocrat—was, of course, critical to the adoption of any agrarian program. However, unconvinced of the need for such a radical reform as the replacement of the commune by individualized forms of agriculture, he had seemed for a time almost ready to capitulate before the growing demands for a "compensated expropriation" as the only means to preserve at least a portion of the nobility's holdings. Although he had rejected this alternative (though he was briefly to entertain it once again in the summer of 1906), it is not clear at what point he accepted the alternative of individualization.[112] Thus, in commenting on Witte's report of 10 January, Nicholas had expressed his approval for measures to develop the peasants' respect for private property that would permit them to claim title to their land on an individual basis and to separate that land into a single compact parcel. Whether Nicholas was at this point aware of the implications such a policy would have for the commune is not, however, clear. More important than the commune, however, was the nature of the government's relationship to rural society and the degree to which government could safely intervene in the organic process of historical development in the determination of its own future.

This question of government intervention and the role of legislative force also found itself reflected in the conflict over the Migulin and Kutler projects. At the time, of course, the paramount need had been to respond to the peasant challenge in as politically dramatic and visible way as possible. Meanwhile, a new form of decisiveness that was built on self-confidence rather than fear was developing. However, these new partisans of order were also critical of the existing system, characterizing it as an obsolete police state or *polizeistaat*, in the seventeenth and eighteenth century sense of that term. In its place, they sponsored a more modern, interventionist form of bureaucratic *opeka* that would abandon its association with collectivist and egalitarian principles and require the government to take the initiative and prepare the conditions necessary to foster the development of economic individualism in agriculture along laissez-faire and capitalist lines. Such was the form that the tsarist government's oldest and most recalcitrant problem, with all of its inherent contradictions, took at the beginning of the twentieth century.

In his memoirs, Gurko claimed that even in 1904 he had been a wholehearted supporter of social Darwinism's "wager on the strong":

A system devised to assist the weak and to protect them from the strong only corrupts the activity of the strong and weakens the weak. The progress of mankind has resulted from the work of the strong. . . . Left to themselves, the weak elements might perhaps perish, but their demise would have little significance for human progress and for the vital strength of a people and its government; in fact, their removal might even be beneficial.[113]

However, when it came to drafting projects, Gurko was compelled to subordinate his rather extreme views on this and other matters to the more moderate opinions of his colleagues.

The conflict over bureaucratic intervention was not, however, easily resolved. As a consequence, in the shadow of the upcoming Duma, the government continued to vacillate for some months more, since many within both the government and the "unofficial" government surrounding the tsar continued to oppose directed governmental change in the peasant way of life—a fact of which the bureaucracy's proponents of intervention were fully cognizant.

6

THE WITTE GOVERNMENT, JANUARY–APRIL 1906

The Development of a Government Agrarian Policy

How often a King is ruled by a minister; how many ministers by their secretaries.
—Johann Goethe, 1774

The idea of transferring Russian peasants into small-scale property owners was propagandized by S. Iu. Witte [while] the land reform projects . . . [were prepared by] Gurko.
. . .

—A. A. Kaufman, 1908

In his report of 10 January 1906 to the tsar summarizing the discussions of the Council of Ministers on the problems of rural reform, Witte had detailed the Council's arguments against the Kutler project, repeating, in essence, those already made by Gurko and others. The members had agreed that the government should enact no major new measures before the Duma was convened.[1] However, this expression of respect for the newly created legislature, although sincere among some members of the Council of Ministers and their ministerial subordinates, obscured a series of sharp disagreements not only within the bureaucracy but between it and both the State Council and the "unofficial" government centered around the tsar's court—disagreements that would persist right up to the opening of the Duma on 27 April.

However, after the tsar's decisive rejection of compulsory "expropriation," these disagreements, at least in the Council of Ministers and the subministerial forces within the three "domestic" Ministries of Interior, Finance, and agriculture involved in agrarian reform, no longer involved the general shape of the government's agrarian policy. Indeed, despite the differences of emphasis between Witte, on the one hand, and Gurko and Krivoshein, on the other, they seem to have agreed on a program that represented a compromise between the extremes of extensification and intensification—a program that combined the provision of more land for the neediest, granted on the basis of individual principles of ownership, with a gradual dissolution of the commune and the individualization of peasant landownership and land use. However, given the threat to noble lands posed both by expropriation and peasant disorders, primary emphasis, as we shall see, now lay on the development of a private-property consciousness within the peasantry as the first step in this process. Nonetheless, despite this basic agreement, particularly the agreement to preserve noble property from compulsory expropriation—the only part that had so far received the tsar's support—many, including the tsar himself, were clearly ambivalent. Thus, for example, even Witte, who had long supported the gradual replacement of the commune by individual forms of property ownership (though only as part of a comprehensive plan of reform), not only had doubts as to whether what was in theory an excellent idea could work in practice but continued to believe that the government would have to adopt some form of compulsory expropriation either to satisfy the demands of the liberal opposition or to calm the peasantry.[2]

However, although the Council of Ministers and the subministerial officials were in basic agreement over content, they did not agree on the proper strategy to adopt vis-à-vis the Duma. To begin with, there was the procedural question: Should the government take the initiative and enact its program before the Duma met? Or should it wait and present its program to the Duma for its approval? Or should the Duma be allowed to initiate its own agrarian program? These constitutional questions were further complicated by the fact that the government had no idea what to expect from the upcoming Duma. This uncertainty was strengthened by continuing confusion over the nature of its own social basis and support. For example, despite having begun the task of equalizing all members of society before the law by granting new civil and political rights to nonnoble *sosloviia,* the government's official policy of defending private, that is, noble, property implied, on the other hand, that it had abandoned its traditional supraclass role as mediator between conflicting social interests in favor of one that depended on and reflected the interests of the landowning nobility.[3] Meanwhile, there were those who considered it imperative for the government, under the new constitutional regime, to win support among the political parties. There were still others who considered that the government's most reliable basis of support remained the peasantry. Ultimately, of course, positions on this issue depended on each bureaucrat's answer to another, more personal, question: Whom or what was he serving, the tsar, the bureaucracy, the nobility, the peasantry—or even the nation as embodied in the Duma, which implied a commitment to the rule of law?

Witte's report expressed many of these conflicts and the dilemmas they posed for the development of a unified agrarian policy. Nonetheless, the Council did take steps to set the bureaucracy on the path of preparing projects that would realize the Council's compromise program. Pointing out that concern for improving the conditions of peasant land use had been virtually abandoned after the closing of his Special Conference by Goremykin in March 1905, in fitting revenge Witte now proposed closing Goremykin's conference—a proposal the tsar accepted—and concentrating such discussions within the Interior Ministry.[4] Meanwhile, since the 3 November 1905 abolition of redemption payments had established a legal basis for the transfer of peasant allotment land from communal to individual ownership and use, the GUZiZ was charged with drafting legislation to facilitate this process for immediate enactment, prior to the opening of the Duma.[5]

The Council of Ministers met again on 24 January to discuss what it considered the central issue before the government—the integration of the peasantry into the general sociolegal order. Indeed, it was argued, all other aspects of the government's broader program of rural reform depended on the solution to this question, including the reform of local administration, the creation of a small zemstvo unit at the canton level, abolition of the land captain, tax reform, and unification of the judicial system.[6] Moreover, to the extent that all these measures, not just the agrarian reform, were considered part of the bureaucracy's unfinished business—indeed, many of them had been on the agenda since the 1860s—the Council felt obliged to rush them to completion and to enact them prior to the Duma's convocation—the more so because they were highly contentious and would undoubtedly become a source of conflict between the government and the Duma were they to be submitted for the latter's approval.[7]

Over the three months before the Duma's convocation, the government's chancelleries thus became a hive of activity. Agrarian reform, in particular, was concentrated in a series of commissions, the two most important being one within the GUZiZ under Krivoshein's de facto leadership and one in the Interior Ministry under Gurko.[8]

The Krivoshein Commission

The Krivoshein commission had initially formed under Kutler's leadership to reconsider the Migulin and Kutler projects. Its members included Rittikh, Kaufman, Gurko, and Nikol'skii.[9] At first, there was considerable conflict, with Kutler's only support coming from his subordinates within the GUZiZ. Krivoshein alone among them maintained his independence. Then, on 19 January he joined the larger Gurko faction in their attack on the whole concept of expropriation.[10] This was the first time Krivoshein had taken sides and expressed himself unequivocally on this sensitive political issue. Subsequently, he took over the leadership of the commission, which then went on to reject the Kutler project even before its author had to resign his post as agricultural minister, in part at Krivoshein's instigation, on 3 February.[11]

Krivoshein, with the tsar's support, then received an appointment to succeed Kutler as head of the GUZiZ. However, Witte, intensely hostile to Krivoshein because of his associations with D. F. Trepov and Goremykin, persuaded the tsar to make this an interim appointment until on 27 February Witte succeeded in replacing him with the more acceptable Nikol'skii. In the meantime, the Krivoshein commission went on to reconsider the whole question of a government agrarian policy. Its first move was to discuss a series of projects generated by opposition to the Migulin and Kutler proposals; these were associated with a plan for the tsar to issue a manifesto in defense of private property to still the rumors generated by the recent flirtation with expropriation.[12] However, the most important part of its work would be the drafting of a law authorizing the creation of a network of local land-organization commissions, based on a memorandum that had been prepared earlier by Krivoshein.[13]

Krivoshein came from a rather unusual background. Descended from mixed Voronezh peasant and Polish-Catholic noble stock, and son of an artillery officer, he was born in 1857 in Warsaw and grew up in that city.[14] He attended St. Petersburg University, first in the Faculty of Natural Science, later in the Juridical Faculty. While there, he established contacts with the world of merchants and industrialists that led to his marrying the daughter of Savva Morozov in 1892, thereby making him one of the few bureaucrats with family links to this class—some of whom, like G. A. Krestovnikov,[15] were supporters of agrarian reform. He worked first as a Moscow legal adviser to one of the railroads; in 1884 he transferred into state service. Among other posts, he served in the Interior Ministry's Rural Section and later as a commissar of peasant affairs in Poland. Returning to St. Petersburg in 1891, he specialized in peasant affairs and established good relations with Goremykin, Sipiagin, and Stishinskii, though not Pleve, whose policy toward the zemstvos he, like Gurko and the liberal Sviatopolk-Mirskii, opposed. Later, he rejoined the Interior Ministry and subsequently became an assistant head of its Rural Section, and then head of the newly formed Migration Department. As we have seen, he also participated in the Witte and Goremykin Conferences. Appointed an assistant administrator of the GUZiZ, he would leave that position to become head of the land banks in the Finance Ministry in October 1906. Meanwhile, on 6 May 1906, he received an appointment to the State Council. In 1908, he would become chief administrator of the GUZiZ and as such the chief executor of the Stolypin Reforms.

Branded a careerist by all commentators, Krivoshein had avoided taking any principled stand on the agrarian problem until he sided with

Gurko in January 1906. Prior to that time, he had apparently been a passive supporter of the commune, possibly because he was not himself an estate owner: his initial contact with rural life had been limited to vacation visits on the estate of a school friend in Poland. However, his years as a commissar of peasant affairs in Poland presumably left their mark, as they had on Gurko. Moreover Krivoshein apparently continued his visits to the western borderlands. Thus Gurko reports that Krivoshein's change of convictions in 1905 came about as a result of personal observation.[16] In any event, although he was a little older than some of the other agrarian reformers, he may be considered a member of the new generation of bureaucrats. Certainly, his ideas, as we shall see, directly reflected the revolution in bureaucratic perceptions.

During the period following the October Manifesto, Krivoshein belonged to that informal group of government officials dubbed the "star chamber"; it included D. F. Trepov and N. V. Pleve. Krivoshein was also close to the newspaper *Novoe Vremia*. Like Gurko, he had composed his memorandum in response to the government's flirtation with compulsory expropriation. Transmitted to the tsar by Trepov, Nicholas expressed approval for the memorandum's argument in early February 1906.[17] Krivoshein's memorandum repeated many of Gurko's arguments, including his claim that land-hunger was only a secondary cause of the peasant disorders and his emphasis on the supreme necessity of preserving the inviolability of private (noble) property. In addition, Krivoshein had called for immediate repressive measures.[18] Apparently, Nicholas had supported Krivoshein for the post of agricultural minister primarily because of his forthright stance in support of both private property and a strong and decisive government.[19]

With respect to agrarian policy, Krivoshein's memorandum noted that all measures to raise the general level of peasant welfare were primarily of a cultural nature and thus had to be conceived in the long term. Yet, he argued, time was of the political essence. Only by taking immediate action to assist the neediest peasants could the government reestablish order in the countryside and forestall a second *Pugachevshchina* in the spring. Specifically, he urged the adoption of a multilevel approach to the agrarian problem that would meet these political criteria yet satisfy the very diverse needs and problems of different sections of the peasantry in different localities. To this end, he proposed that the government provide material aid for the formation of *otruba*, petty credit to expand domestic industries to supplement peasant income during the winter, and grants for the purchase of improved agricultural implements. In addition, land would become available to the neediest peasants through the Peasant Bank or the expansion of migration.[20]

Dismissing familiar objections to reform proposals based on their cost, Krivoshein contrasted the wastefulness of the government's current expenditures on emergency food relief with the long-term benefits that would accrue from the investment of identical sums to raise the productivity of peasant labor. He similarly dismissed another argument repeatedly cited as a reason for postponing any action: the lack of detailed information on specific conditions in the countryside. In his view, the information already accumulated as a result of past studies was sufficient. But even if it were not, he urged the government to abandon its customary procrastination, its alluring declarations and promises, and its interminable conferences and commissions. It was high time to adopt a purposeful program of government action.

Beyond this sense of urgency and purpose, Krivoshein's principal contribution to the business of agrarian reform was his proposal for the immediate creation of a network of special collegial commissions, under the direction of the GUZiZ, composed of both governmental and nongovernmental members. Such organizations would serve both as that ministry's local agencies and as the executive organs of the government's agrarian policy. Commissions of this type, he argued, were indeed the only practical means by which the government could gather the data necessary for effective action. Moreover, they would provide the basis of a decentralized decision-making process, which he regarded as the only feasible one for the government to follow. Equally important, the establishment of local commissions would satisfy the urgently felt need to take immediate and decisive action.[21] Krivoshein's proposal was not, of course, original. It had already been suggested by Migulin and Kutler and even put into partial practice by the Finance Ministry. However, his specific vision of the way an agrarian policy would develop as an outgrowth of local activity was new.[22]

Activity, indeed, was the essence of Krivoshein's approach. The mere vision of the government in action was in itself conceived to be of major propaganda value in retaining peasant loyalty. Moreover, Krivoshein claimed, the specific content of the local commissions' activities, although as yet undetermined, would, in fact, be self-actualizing, would develop out of the very process of activity itself. Indeed, he argued, the principal danger facing the government as it decided on the adoption of a rural reform program lay not with such an experimental and pragmatic approach but with policies like expropriation that sought to solve the agrarian problem at a single stroke.

Krivoshein's commission drew up its conclusions on 31 January and 7 and 10 February 1906. Predictably, it expressed unwavering support for the principle of inviolability and recommended the immediate publication of a strongly worded manifesto spelling out the government's readiness to take immediate retribution against those who violated private property rights.[23] On the basis of Krivoshein's memorandum, it also proposed the formation, within the GUZiZ, of a central Committee on Land

Organization, which would include zemstvo representatives, and a network of local commissions at both the provincial and county levels authorized to take immediate steps to improve peasant land organization. Provincial commissions would consist of twelve or thirteen members; county commissions would have fifteen or sixteen. Of the latter, six were to be elected by the local population, including three from the peasantry. The remainder were to be appointed ex officio from among local government officials, noble corporations, and zemstvo administrative boards. Within this framework, the real work would be executed by the county commissions, which it was proposed should first assist land-hungry peasants who wanted to purchase land or migrate, and then help any peasants who wanted to improve their methods of land use, especially by eliminating open fields and common lands and partitioning large villages. The local commissions could also provide various kinds of financial and technical support.[24]

The commission's proposal to establish such a network of commissions represented a major expansion of bureaucratic power at the local level and provided for a degree of direct, continuous, and regulated government intervention in the day-to-day conduct of local agricultural life that was without precedent. Moreover, these commissions were considerably more bureaucratic in nature than the zemstvo commissions sponsored by the Finance Ministry that had so aroused the fears of the conservative gentry in the aftermath of the Putilov circular in early January. Nonetheless, they did provide for the participation of elected representatives, which would give local society an opportunity to work with the government on what was after all the most important question of the day.[25]

In an apparent concession to a now resurgent nobility seeking to defend its *soslovie* privileges, the commission's other proposals concentrated on economic and agrotechnical issues in isolation from the more general though related sociolegal issues of the peasantry's *soslovie* status and local administrative and court reform. Perhaps in deference to the tsar's views on this issue, it also avoided any direct attacks on the commune. Rather, the problems associated with communal landownership and land use were here subsumed by the ostensibly neutral designation *land organization (zemleustroistvo)*—a term that had already been used in the agricultural ministry's title and that could describe either intensification *or* extensification and even be extended to include the reorganization of noble properties. However, there was no question within the Krivoshein commission about its primary commitment to intensification.[26]

In fulfillment of its original mandate to reconsider the overall shape of the government's agrarian policy, the Krivoshein commission concluded its work by calling on the appropriate government departments to prepare specific legislation, for enactment prior to the Duma, to facilitate peasant transfers to individual ownership and to *khutor* forms of land use, permit the granting of mortgage loans on allotment land, reorganize and expand migration, transfer all appropriate state property to the GUZiZ as a fund to assist the land-hungry, and reform agricultural rents. In addition, Gurko and Krivoshein submitted a minority opinion in which they proposed the unification of the peasant and noble land banks and their transfer to the GUZiZ.[27]

The Krivoshein commission thus combined the earlier proposals of Gurko and Rittikh with the compatible elements of the Migulin and Kutler projects into a more moderate compromise package that reflected the growing bureaucratic consensus. Similarly, the demands of Gurko and Krivoshein for decisive executive intervention, once the enabling legislation had been adopted, were modified by the commission's majority to allow a larger role for gradual and spontaneous processes of organic change in response to the nobility's traditional fears that government interference in local, and particularly peasant, life would further exacerbate an already sensitive political atmosphere.

The Council of Ministers expressed its preliminary support for the Krivoshein commission's proposals on 10 February 1906.[28] In the course of the Council's discussions, however, it became clear that the ambiguity of the term *land organization* was beginning to create jurisdictional problems. Accordingly, it formally separated the process of reorganization into two independent stages and, reversing its initial distribution of responsibilities, charged the drafting of legislation on title claims to the Interior Ministry, which had the advantage of already possessing a network of local agents. The more narrowly defined agrotechnical work of consolidating the peasants' strips into compact parcels and improving forms of cultivation became the responsibility of the GUZiZ. To provide the GUZiZ with the necessary local agencies to carry out this work, it also proposed placing the land-organization commissions under its authority—a step that was seen as making unnecessary the transfer of the Peasant Bank to the GUZiZ as a means of providing it with local agents.[29]

At a subsequent meeting of the Council of Ministers, Finance Minister I. P. Shipov was directed to draft a reform of the Noble and Peasant Land Banks to bring their activities into conformity with the operations of the agriculture and Interior ministries.[30] At this meeting, however, while conceding the fiscal argument for retaining the Land Banks within the Finance Ministry, Krivoshein insisted—accurately, it turns out—that for any agrarian reform to be successful, all the agencies involved had to be subordinate to a single ministry, in this case the GUZiZ, to ensure unity of action. Once again, however, this particular proposal was defeated.[31]

On 24 February 1906, the Council of Ministers finally approved the commission's proposals for the creation of local land-organization commissions and agreed that such a demonstration of government decisiveness might well serve to calm the peasantry.[32] However, some objections also arose. On the one hand, it was suggested that, by arousing false hopes among the peasantry, such intervention might actually produce the opposite result from the one intended. A second criticism was more procedural and sought to preserve some room for cooperation between the government and the Duma, noting that the final goals of the land-organization commissions' work would only become known after the Duma had drafted an agrarian program of its own. As a consequence, any government action taken prior to this time was likely to be interpreted as having preempted the Duma and predetermined the outcome of the whole question. There was also some concern that the land-organization commissions might fall under the control of chairmen who would then take the opportunity to enact policies developed by extremist parties.[33]

In light of these considerations, the Council proposed that the local commissions confine themselves to the task of increasing peasant landownership. At the same time, in order to preserve the Bank's independence, it suggested that their role be limited to a purely advisory one. They would assume additional responsibilities only at the specific request of the local governor or zemstvo assembly, still only on an advisory basis and within the limits of available funds. In part, traditional fears about government intervention in rural society seem to have motivated the council's modifications of the Krivoshein commission's proposals. Its members were also reluctant to impose a program of individualization and intensification on provincial society because such measures, which were widely regarded as purely long-term solutions, were not particularly urgent. For this reason, and because they ultimately involved a radical restructuring of the existing sociolegal order, such measures were seen as lying within the Duma's jurisdiction.[34]

Insofar as the Peasant Bank was concerned, the Council supported its traditional fiscal independence. However, the Council's members were ambivalent toward the idea of providing additional land for the land-hungry, even though it had already formally adopted such a policy back in November. The Council also expressed fear that if the Peasant Bank were transformed into an instrument of the government's agrarian policy, the nobility's fiscal interests would ultimately be sacrificed to those of the state. The Council was similarly ambivalent about the structure of the local commissions, and although it sought to protect the rights of the local nobility, it also tried to preserve the government's policy-making initiative. Thus, it eliminated local representatives from the Committee on Land Organization. In a similar vein, the Council made one final change, at Krivoshein's request, that would permit the GUZiZ to appoint one of its own officials to each local commission as a "permanent member"—a change that would take on major importance after the eventual adoption of the Stolypin Reforms themselves.[35]

The Council's deference to the upcoming Duma was paradoxical, as we have seen. As the Duma elections approached, the tsar himself remained optimistic about the fundamental loyalty and conservatism of peasant delegates, but not everyone in the highest levels of government shared his blind faith. As early as 9 October 1905, Witte had considered it risky to place any hopes in the Duma on this score.[36] More recently, on 20 February 1906, A. N. Kulomzin in a letter to the Council's administrator, N. I. Vuich, had characterized any lingering faith in a Duma solution to the agrarian question as a gamble, pure and simple. At the same time, he denounced Krivoshein's proposals and called instead for more repression; even so, he opposed the publication of an imperial manifesto against peasant violations of private noble property because of the extremely volatile situation in the countryside. In these circumstances, he wrote, no matter how carefully or decisively the tsar expressed his will, the peasants would interpret his words, as always, according to their own subjective perception of their interests—in this case in all likelihood as a declaration in support of compulsory expropriation on the model of the liberal Kadets' agrarian program.[37] Despite these arguments, the Council finally recommended the publication of a manifesto in support of private property. However, the tsar himself eventually decided that it would be inappropriate, apparently accepting Kulomzin's argument.[38]

The Council went on to approve the establishment of its watered-down version of the Krivoshein commission's proposals for local land-organization commissions.[39] However, the 4 March 1906 ukase authorizing their establishment and the establishment of a Committee on Land Organization in St. Petersburg was issued by the tsar, who with Trepov had supported Krivoshein's original proposal on this subject, without its having been submitted to the State Council for the usual preliminary discussion.[40] As a result, when, later in the month the new head of the GUZiZ, Nikol'skii, submitted a budget request to the State Council for funds to set up even these much modified commissions, the whole proposal generated renewed criticism.[41]

Nikol'skii's initial request was to establish commissions during the course of 1906 in about half the counties of European Russia, 60 of which would possess a full roster of functions while the remaining 240 would be limited to giving aid to the Peasant Bank. Funds were also requested for the establishment of 17 provincial commissions and the Committee on Land Organization itself. In preliminary discussions by the State Council's United Departments, a minority of seven members opposed the institution of these organs prior to the opening of the Duma and expressed their doubt that there were sufficient personnel available for the government to fulfill these tasks. The United Departments, therefore, reduced the request by more than 1 million rubles to 1.8 million rubles. In the State Council's general session, a minority of thirty-nine members drawn from all positions on the government's political spectrum, including Goremykin, Ermolov, F. F. Trepov, Bulygin, Stürmer, Shvanebakh, Stishinskii, Nikol'skii, Chikhachov, and P. P. Semenov [-T'ian-Shanskii], supported immediate approval of the reduced requests. In their opinion, "the entrance of the government into the task of land organization in the localities [was] very important as the sole means of giving the agrarian question a direction in conformity with the views of the government."[42]

On the other hand, a majority of forty-six members, also drawn from across the political spectrum—including Sol'skii, Polovtsov, Panteleev, Durnovo, Kulomzin, and Terner—rejected the very idea of such a bureaucratic invasion of provincial life. More pragmatically, however, they argued against the introduction of local commissions on the grounds that the government's legislative projects on land organization would not even be ready until after the Duma had convened. This position then derived reinforcement from the argument that if the Duma were to approve a contrary policy, such as granting an additional allotment, a completely different kind of organization would be required. Clearly, there were many in the government, in addition to Witte, who believed that compulsory expropriation might still become necessary.[43] The tsar, however, confirmed the minority opinion on 26 April 1906, one day before the opening of the Duma. As a result of the reduced appropriation, however, only 184 commissions were authorized for that year.[44] The first opened in relatively short order on 15 July 1906 in Sumskii County, Tula Province.[45]

Despite these limitations, the ukase of 4 March 1906 nonetheless laid the foundation for the establishment of the first large-scale administrative organization designed to deal exclusively with the peasant question. Eventually, these commissions would be transformed into the executive arm of the Stolypin Reforms, in which role they would finally realize the potential that was inherent in the post of land captain. The bureaucracy's invasion of the countryside was continuing apace.

The Peasant Land Bank

The only other legislative project to be adopted during this pre-Duma period was a law revising the rules governing the Peasant Bank's operation that enabled it to purchase more land at its own expense for sale to landless and land-hungry peasants, rather than, as in the past, only to those who could afford a considerable down payment in cash.[46]

A Finance Ministry commission meeting simultaneously with the Krivoshein commission compiled this project. When it was submitted to the State Council in early March, it, too, provoked sharp criticism. Specifically, the United Departments objected to the Peasant Bank's becoming an instrument of government agrarian policy and to the government's committing itself, before the Duma was convened, to a policy of expanding peasant landownership, which—whether or not it were compulsory—was, it argued, tantamount to a policy of "expropriation." In effect, it was claimed, the Finance Ministry was pursuing an independent agrarian policy. Witte rejected this charge. On the contrary, he asserted, not only was the government completely opposed to compulsory expropriation, but it had not even reached any conclusions as to the overall shape of its agrarian program—a claim that, as we have seen, was not strictly true since the Council of Ministers had as early as mid-January effectively committed the government to enacting a compromise program combining intensification and extensification prior to the Duma's convocation. The United Departments did not, however, agree with Witte, for they held that the proposed changes would, in fact, transform the Peasant Bank from an autonomous and independent credit institution into an institution of "state" agrarian policy that would inevitably place state or peasant interests ahead of those of the landowning nobility—a charge that the nobility would repeatedly level at the Peasant Bank in succeeding years, with some justice.[47]

When the project came before the State Council's general session, a number of members reiterated Gurko's earlier assault on the entire concept of extensification, arguing that such a policy might in fact worsen the situation by legitimizing the concept of land-hunger and forcing the government to accept the responsibility for eliminating it. Indeed, they strongly implied that such a government-sponsored operation to expand peasant landownership, even if conducted on individualistic principles, had, in fact, distinctly socialist overtones. From a somewhat different perspective, some members charged the government with underwriting its own cash-flow crisis with the nobility's debts.[48]

In the end, the State Council substantially modified the bill's technical details and reduced the amount of money to be made available to the Peasant Bank from 250 million rubles to 100 million. Moreover, the Bank was permitted to purchase land only in exchange for short-term, interest-bearing notes rather than for cash.[49] This bill became law on 21 March 1906.

The State Council's filibustering considerably weakened the final versions of these laws on local land-organization commissions and the Peasant Bank. As such they constituted a rather tentative approach to the tasks of agrarian reform. Moreover, the opposition aroused indicated that—although Witte and the subministerial officials working in the various drafting commissions were in general agreement on the content of the government's agrarian policy—there was no such agreement within the larger government. As a consequence, as we shall now see, Witte's government, which had been losing the tsar's favor ever since the Kutler project episode, was unable to gain approval of any other aspects of its program. Thus it had to change its strategy from one of enacting laws prior to the opening of the Duma to one of preparing legislation for submission at its opening session.

The Gurko Commission

The final project to be prepared by the Witte government as part of the reform program it had planned to enact prior to the opening of the Duma focused on the issues of individualizing and intensifying peasant land-ownership and use. In the eyes of the government, as we have seen, the ukase of 3 November 1905 abolishing redemption payments, which had been intended as a financial concession to soothe an aroused countryside, had prepared the ground for and signaled the end of that period of transition from serfdom to freedom and from "feudalism" to capitalism. The Gurko commission had the charge of drafting legislation to deal with this new situation.[50]

From the beginning, the members of the Gurko commission agreed on the critical importance and desirability of equalizing the peasants' status with that of the other classes of the population and, in particular, of introducing private-property principles and encouraging the consolidation of peasant open-field strips into compact holdings. In addition to Gurko, Nikol'skii, Rittikh, Pestrzhetskii, Lykoshin, and Zubovskii were widely known within the bureaucracy to hold similar opinions in these respects, all formulated prior to the revolutionary events of 1905–6. Ia. Ia. Litvinov also belonged to this group, though his convictions were of more recent vintage.[51]

The Gurko commission saw its work not simply as codifying the legislative consequences of the ukase of 3 November but also as defining the rights of peasants to their allotment land in general and eliminating whatever legislation restricted such rights.[52] In effect, this meant restoring to its full effect Article 36 of the Emancipation Statute—which permitted peasants to claim title to their strips and separate from their communes without any restrictions—but without restoring the second part of Article 165, which had required that such strips be simultaneously consolidated "as far as possible" into a single, compact parcel.[53] This, of course, meant that the commission had accepted as its point of departure Rittikh's distinction and separated the process of individualization into two stages by making the act of claiming title independent of and prior to the actual reorganization of the strips themselves.

Beyond "regularizing" what it perceived as the new legal situation, the commission also saw an important link between its work and the government's commitment to making more land available to land-hungry peasants. It was particularly concerned that such extensification would remain a dead letter unless additional steps could be taken to enable peasants to raise the capital necessary to purchase additional land from the Peasant Bank. Similarly, peasants who were not land-hungry but who sought to transfer to an *otrub* or *khutor* or obtain agronomical aid to improve their land-use practices also needed capital to finance such undertakings. Yet, the commission noted, the peasants did possess one form of capital: their allotment land. Under the existing *soslovie* limitations, however, they could not mortgage this land, both because it was supposedly only in their temporary possession and because the government had been afraid that if large numbers of peasants defaulted, not only would redemption payments to the state be jeopardized but the dispossessed peasants would inevitably swell the ranks of the proletariat. However, the abolition of redemption payments had now removed the fiscal rationale for that prohibition, if not the social one. Even so, the right to claim their share of communal land meant very little since each peasant's allotment was fragmented into strips that were scattered throughout the commune and were, moreover, subject to changes in both size and location with each repartition.

In fact, the commission concluded, what the peasant possessed as a result of the 3 November ukase was only a right to a share in the communal land at the discretion of the community as a whole. One solution therefore might be to grant individual peasants a fixed quantity of land in their eternal possession, independent of the community's will. Then it would be possible for the individual peasant to realize his new property rights by selling or mortgaging his share of allotment land with the assurance that neither its quantity nor its location could change at the commune's whim. To achieve this goal, the commission proposed drawing up legislation that would enable peasants to sever all ties—personal, juridical, and economic—with the commune.[54]

Not surprisingly, the commission described its goal in the liberal phraseology typical of the government's critics in the pre-Revolutionary period as well as of men like Nikol'skii and Witte within the bureaucracy as transforming the commune from a compulsory union of peasants, established in the state's fiscal interests, into a voluntary one, designed to serve their own interests. However, although committed to liberalism in the economic sphere, the commission's members, like most bureaucrats, rejected its political program, at least as represented by the Kadet party. On the other hand, the commission's emphasis on individual property rights and its implicit opposition to the commune reflected the reformers' recent change in political strategy, which was dictated by the necessity of building an alliance with the landowning nobility whose support now appeared critical to the adoption of their program.

Although they agreed on the commission's objectives, Rittikh and Pokrovskii subsequently split with the other members over the procedures for implementing them. The majority, considering its work as merely regularizing an already existing situation, argued, along with the Council of Ministers, that its proposals be enacted immediately, prior to the convocation of the Duma. Indeed, the only innovative aspect of the commission's work, in their view, was the elimination of those "practical difficulties" preventing the peasant from exercising his right of departure—a task that required them simply to develop procedures for determining the specific quantity of land due. Although Rittikh and Pokrovskii were concerned about violating the Duma's prerogatives by taking such precipitous action, they were even more concerned about the threat it posed to the commune's integrity. As a consequence, they sought to balance its rights with those of the individual peasant. The majority, however, responded that the adoption of their proposals would only be "temporary" and would not therefore threaten the commune's integrity since the Duma would review the whole question.

The stand taken by Gurko and the majority was, of course, opportunistic and based on legalistic quibbling. Juridically speaking, their position was indeed justifiable. However, there was then no legal requirement that the proposed measures, once enacted, be reviewed by the Duma, as there would be under the Fundamental Laws after the Laws' adoption on the eve of the First Duma. At the same time, as Rittikh and Pokrovskii pointed out, the majority's recommendations were in fact little short of revolutionary in their potential impact on the peasantry's economic life. And, indeed, the potential for fundamental social change inherent in the commission's proposals was perfectly obvious to all its members. After all, for a number of years they had themselves been in the vanguard demanding just such radical rural reforms.

Having lost this procedural point, Rittikh, occasionally supported by Smirnov or Pokrovskii, came into repeated conflict with the commission's majority as he continued his efforts to balance the economic interests of the weak against the strong, of the commune against those who left it, as well as what he saw as the nation's long-term economic interests against shorter-term, political goals.[55] His arguments and the commission's responses are of particular interest, for not only did the issues involved lie at the very heart of most later criticisms of the Stolypin Reforms but it was this commission's work that largely determined the final shape those Reforms took.

The essence of the commission's final project is to be found in its first two articles, which, based on the Gurko/Pestrzhetskii formula, provided that in those communities in which there had been no general repartition during the past twenty-four years, individual peasants should gain the right to claim title to that arable land that was in their actual possession as their "personal" property. Peasants who lived in communes that had conducted general repartitions within this period also received this right. However, the quantity of arable land due them was not what was in their actual possession. Rather, their share had to be recalculated on the basis of the relative sizes of their family and the commune at the time of application. In subsequent articles, the commission decided that since the individual peasant could not be denied the right to exit, such requests could be approved by a simple majority of the communal assembly or, failing that, by an obligatory decree issued by the land captain. The project also included provisions for the separation of such land to *otruba* and *khutora*. Finally, it introduced two innovations that breached the *soslovie* limitations on allotment land ownership by permitting peasants who took advantage of the proposed law to claim title to their share of such land to mortgage it to the Peasant Bank. The Bank could acquire such lands, though only for resale to other peasants.[56]

At the heart of Rittikh's disagreement with the other members of the commission was the complex problem of determining what share of communal land was due each individual peasant on separation from the commune. Thus, Rittikh opposed the division of communes into two groups according to the twenty-four-year criterion, for he held that, although some communes may not have conducted a general repartition in the course of that time, they might conduct one in the future.[57] Yet the adoption of such a rule would permit those peasants who had accumulated surplus land over the years to separate with more than their fair share, irreparably damaging the interests of the remaining peasants if the commune were to execute a general repartition at some later time. As a consequence, Rittikh opposed the element of coercion that was contained in the legislative recognition of this de facto and possibly temporary situation. Rather, he sought to develop a framework that would cover both kinds of communes and that would enable both the individual peasant and the commune to reach decisions about their respective landed rights on a totally free and voluntary basis. As he put it, he wanted to give the commune an equal right "to fight for its existence and to take measures against the plundering of communally-owned land without at the same time depriving those separating of their legal right."[58]

The commission's rejection of Rittikh's position does not, however, mean that the majority did not share his desire to protect the weak from the strong. Rather, they had as their motivation what they perceived as the immediate political benefits of their project for the development of the peasants' legal consciousness. Consequently, they sought to frame the project in such a way that it would have as rapid an impact as possible. They rejected Rittikh's attempt to apply an "ideal" or "absolute" standard of justice in favor of a realistic and pragmatic approach based on a relative concept of justice. Nonetheless, the majority did agree that if peasants who separated from communes that practiced repartitions were to have their share of land determined on the basis of what was in their actual possession in the same manner as those who separated from non-repartitioning communes, this too could lead to an "artificial decomposition" of the commune. For in such circumstances "all households which on the basis of their personal composition expect a reduction in the quantity of land at their disposal with the next repartition would immediately petition for separation and in general there would remain [in the commune] only those who expect to receive an addition of land with [the next] repartition."[59]

Those who stayed would, of course, then be frustrated since peasants with surpluses would have withdrawn land that would otherwise have been available for redistribution from the common pool. As a consequence, the repartition would lose its significance and the commune would be destroyed. And even the commission's majority considered such a significant step possible only as the outcome of a law passed by the Duma. On the basis of these arguments, therefore, the majority recognized actual use as a valid criterion only for communes that had not executed a general repartition over the preceding twenty-four years.[60]

Similar issues arose when the commission sought to establish a criterion apart from use to determine the quantity of land due peasants who separated from those communes that had executed repartitions. They considered several alternatives. One possible solution was to calculate shares on the basis of the historical record of a particular family's land use and its fiscal contribution toward the total redemption debt. This approach was truly one of "absolute justice" as it was also of "formalism." However, it was rejected on the incontrovertible grounds that in practice it would be impossible to establish an exact historical record of either a particular family's land use or its contributions to the redemption debt, since the necessary records were either inaccurate or nonexistent.

Another alternative was to require that with each title claim the procedure for a repartition be followed in order to determine the quantity due, though without actually executing the repartition. A major objection to this proposal was that a commune could select a method that would be intentionally damaging to the interests of those claiming title. However, since the commission recognized that the entire procedure of claiming title could arouse significant social conflict, it rejected any measures that would enable the stronger party, in this instance the commune, to frustrate or damage irrevocably the rights of the weaker, individual members. Quite apart from such considerations, however, the procedure for executing repartitions, even without its practical realization, was so complex that to have to execute it with the receipt of each petition was inconceivable, particularly in the case of large villages or in areas where migratory labor was well developed. The net effect of such a proposal would in fact be to delay the whole procedure—itself a violation of individual rights. Consequently, the majority decided to adopt the criterion utilized in the last repartition as a basis for calculation.

In seeking to apply this principle in practice, the commission proposed that those peasants whose family size had not changed as well as those whose families had increased since the last repartition should receive only that quantity of land in their actual use. Where family size had decreased, the commission recommended calculating the quantity of land due according to the criteria applied at the last repartition, though on the basis of the *new* family size. However, so as not to violate the economic integrity of their holdings, they suggested that the surplus be retained until the next repartition, when it would revert to the community. Such a procedure, the commission's majority held, would best protect the interests of both parties. Insofar as those peasants whose family size had increased would be penalized, it was argued that the benefits of claiming title more than compensated for the quantity of land lost.[61]

Later, the commission reversed itself on the issue of surpluses and argued that the quantity of land involved in the case of peasants who separated with more than their due was in most cases too insignificant to damage the interests of the community as a whole. Consequently, there was no reason to break up the economic integrity of the separating peasants' plots by demanding the return of the surplus. Furthermore, the problem of deciding when to cut off the surplus as well as the fact that the family could retain the surplus until the next repartition, no matter how far off it was, would only lead to an exacerbation of relations between such peasants and the commune. Indeed, the prospect of losing the surplus might even influence the peasant to retract his title claim altogether. On these grounds, then, they finally agreed to require the individual peasant to compensate the community financially for the surplus.[62]

On the question of determining a basis for establishing a fair price for the surplus land, the majority agreed that compensation should be paid not at the current local land prices but at the initial, and therefore considerably lower, redemption price. This was deemed just for both parties, since it was at this rate that the land had, in fact, been redeemed by the commune. Indeed, since there had been both reductions in the scale of redemption payments and abolitions of arrears, the commune would actually receive an additional benefit, since the total amount it had paid since the onset of redemption would therefore be less than the original price. Of course, this calculation excluded the very substantial interest payments. Similarly, the individual peasant would benefit by acquiring land at lower than market rates. True, it would perhaps be even fairer to have calculated the price according to the actual total redeemed. However, the lack of proper records made such a calculation impossible.[63]

At issue here was once again speed, with Rittikh defending a spontaneous and gradual pace that was unacceptable to the majority who, without using any direct legislative pressure, sought to do everything within its power to remove all obstacles to the process of claiming title.[64]

Rittikh and Smirnov also opposed the proposal that when peasants received title to their strips, their boundaries be marked out and recorded.[65] Again, of course, there was the problem of community rights—but in this instance the concern lay primarily with the long-term economic interests of the individual peasants, the community, and even the state as a whole. Thus Rittikh argued that the individual peasant should have the right to claim title only to an "abstract quantity" of land, with the actual physical delimitation of its boundaries, "in nature," being postponed until the various strips had been consolidated into one or several parcels. In this way the government would not be perpetuating and "freezing" open-field land use either by peasants who owned land on individualistic principles or by those who remained in the commune. This procedure would also enable a community to avoid the innumerable difficulties that would confront it if in attempting to regulate its economic affairs it subsequently found itself faced with large numbers of individually owned but scattered strips within its borders that could only be relocated with the specific approval of their owners. Rittikh's ultimate goal, once again, was to give precedence to long-term economic interests as against the immediate political interest in expanding individual property rights and developing a consciousness of private property among the peasantry.[66]

The majority of the commission, however, favored the more immediate and practical political benefits. Yet, despite their emphasis on the presumed advantages of individual ownership, the majority had its own economic rationale. In its view, the physical realization of the title claim was more beneficial to the peasant since only in this way could he actualize its true value as capital—through sale or mortgage.[67]

Of course, it might be argued in Rittikh's behalf that since a peasant would probably realize a still higher sale price were his land to be physically delimited in one compact parcel, an "abstract" share might perhaps have been more valuable even than delimited but scattered strips. However, an "abstract" share would clearly not facilitate mortgages or security of tenure and therefore would not encourage agricultural improvement, which was, of course, a goal common to both the majority and the minority. Furthermore, claiming title on this basis might result in a purely paper change with no practical consequence—a problem that had long bedeviled government administrators. On balance, then, the majority decision to mark the change in tenure status in a practical way, despite certain later problems, was in all probability a sound economic, and an even sounder political, choice.

In their final shape, the commission's proposals sought to permit the individual peasant to claim title to his share of the commune's allotment land at any time while seeking to balance the interests of the various parties in as reasonable a manner as was possible. At the same time, despite the emphasis that has been placed here on the issue of property rights, all members of the commission saw title claims as but the first stage in a process that was designed eventually to encourage peasants to give up the communal system of land use and transfer to more individualized and intensive forms.

The new interior minister, P. N. Durnovo, sent the completed project to the Council of Ministers on 19 February 1906. Not surprisingly, that body approved it on 5 March with only Prince Obolenskii expressing opposition.[68] What is surprising is that five days later, on 10 March, the tsar also approved the project.[69] The significance of his approval is, however, more difficult to determine. On the one hand, it is clear that the tsar had committed himself to a policy of dissolving the commune with the goal of establishing individual property ownership among the peasantry and protecting the nobility's property rights. Yet, despite this expression of unity, and despite even the tsar's support, the United Departments of the State Council rejected the Gurko commission's project on 18 March, twenty-three votes to seventeen, and subsequently buried it. The majority's objection was not, however, to the project's assault on the peasant commune, but to the attempt to enact such legislation prior to the opening of the Duma. By a small majority the United Departments now refused to allow the government to enact any more measures of agrarian reform before the assembly was convened. In their view, the passage of such a law, which affected matters so essential to the peasant way of life, was not merely premature; it would effectively predetermine the whole issue of agrarian reform as well as exacerbate the already delicate political situation in the countryside.[70] It has been argued that the minority, which supported Gurko's proposal, did so on the Machiavellian principle of "divide and rule" in the hope that it would encourage social differentiation and create conflict between rich and poor peasants, thereby taking pressure off the government.[71] Although this may, indeed, have been true of some members, it seems an unconvincing characterization of the minority as a whole. Certainly, as we have seen, this sentiment had nothing in common with the motivations of those who had drafted the project—even though it is true that in theory Gurko favored the strong over the weak. However, Gurko, the consummate bureaucrat, was also well aware that the state interest precluded such an approach.

In any event, the United Departments' opposition was a clear reflection of Witte's declining authority within the government. And, in the face of this opposition, Witte was forced not only to withdraw the project completely but also to abandon his initial strategy of adopting an agrarian program prior to the Duma.[72] In this respect it is clear that the tsar's support of the Gurko commission project, although significant in terms of his acceptance of the implied program, had little political significance in the face of the strong disagreements within the government concerning its relationship to the Duma. Subsequently, Gurko himself resubmitted the project in May to the new Council of Ministers under Goremykin's chairmanship only to have it rejected once again.[73] Nonetheless, as we shall see, this did not signify the end of the project's history, for a revised version of this same project would be submitted to the First Duma in early June for its consideration.

The Nikol'skii Commission

At the same 5 March session in which the Gurko project had been approved, the Council of Ministers had established a new commission to coordinate the preparation of all the government's projects on rural reform. However, reflecting the changing mood within the government and the growing opposition to Witte, the Council changed its strategy and now proposed to present its projects to the Duma's opening session.[74] The commission, chaired by the new head of the GUZiZ, Nikol'skii, had ten members, many of whom had already been involved in the preparation of reform projects in one or another of the commissions already discussed.[75] It was in this commission, which met for the first time on 10 March, that a comprehensive approach both to the agrarian question and to the broader problem of rural reform was finally synthesized.

The commission began by dividing the government's task into two functionally independent parts: those *soslovie*-related problems of civil rights and local administrative and judicial reform, and the more specific economic and agrotechnical problems associated with the commune in its functions as land user and landowner.[76] This separation of the sociolegal issues from the agrotechnical ones would play a major role in facilitating the adoption of the future Stolypin Reforms. In the agrotechnical sphere, the commission identified three areas in need of immediate government action: *zemleustroistvo*, by which was now meant the rationalization of peasant landownership and land-use patterns, the expansion of peasant landownership, and the intensification of peasant agriculture by means of agronomical aid and extension services including an expansion of subsidiary rural industries of the factory or handicrafts type designed to raise the overall level of labor productivity in the countryside.[77]

The Nikol'skii Commission drew on the work of all the preceding commissions, including Gurko's Editing Commission and Witte's Special Conference. In conformity to the new division of labor, it charged the Interior Ministry with presenting to the Duma either a statute on peasant rights to allotment land or, if there were not enough time, a summary of the proposed main principles, accompanied by an explanatory note; a statute on peasant administration and civil and personal rights; and one on passport regulations. The Finance Ministry was to prepare the bill on the Peasant Bank that, in fact, became law on 21 March. The GUZiZ, meanwhile, was to draft two bills, one on the renting of privately owned land, and the other on the reorganization of allotment land and the rental of state land. Finally, the Ministry of Justice was to draft a bill on the reorganization of peasant courts in conjunction with a general reorganization of local justice.[78]

Despite having incorporated most of the significant proposals made since 1902, the Nikol'skii Commission noted that these proposals alone "should not be seen as all that would be required to raise peasant welfare."[79] Therefore, the commission, reflecting the predominantly agricultural orientation of its members as well as the growing anti-Witte tendency within the government, launched into a sharp criticism of existing government policy, noting that it was "extremely important that . . . the financial-economic policy of the state be directed in conformity with the interests of the agricultural population and agriculture." It went on to urge that Russia's industrial activity be directed in such a manner that it "would increase the demand for rural labor and assure the production of more valuable agricultural products."[80] The commission also recommended the adoption of measures to develop agricultural education, expand rural credit of various types, and develop local means of communication. In effect, the commission was arguing for the government to adopt a wide variety of measures of a more general and cultural nature to supplement the proposed reforms in the peasants' sociolegal status and their landownership and land use.[81] In its opinion, only a combination of these measures "could assure real prosperity and lasting economic success for the peasant population and lessen the severity of the problem of peasant land-hunger. . . ."[82]

The commission then added a postscript in which it argued that the peasant problem should be viewed as a totality, rather than fragmented into a series of isolated "peasant problems" according to the particular category of peasant involved—an apparent attack on those like Gurko and Krivoshein who tended to see the peasantry in terms of economically differentiated classes and to develop a series of different strategies for each group within it. In this sense, it seems, the Nikol'skii Commission represented a step back toward the government's traditional policy of a "wager on the whole peasantry."[83] At the same time, it urged the government to commit itself to a more unified perspective and to the adoption, in effect, of a national program of economic development. Such a stance was, of course, appropriate to a commission composed principally of members from the GUZiZ, all of whom tended to see all agriculturalists, noble and peasant alike, as the victims equally of an economic policy that had emphasized industrial development at the expense of agriculture. The solution, it was argued, lay with an across-the-board reform that would benefit all the victims. At the same time, the commission was concerned that the various reforms it was proposing be considered as part of a comprehensive "plan" that in order to be effective would require all of its components to be set in place.[84]

Notwithstanding its criticisms of the so-called Witte system, on 25 March, Witte extended the tenure of the Nikol'skii Commission. It continued its coordinating work with the addition of Gurko, now an assistant interior minister, and Litvinov, his replacement as head of the Rural Section, who together bolstered their ministry's otherwise meager representation; and Putilov, Nikolaenko, and Gardov for the Finance Ministry.[85] One of the products of this commission's subsequent activity was the formation of yet another commission within the GUZiZ. Known as the Rittikh commission, it was to prepare a project for presentation to the Duma on the "improvement and broadening of peasant landownership." It met between 26 March and 18 April.[86] The project compiled by this commission spelled out specific procedures for various forms of "qualitative" land reorganization designed to eliminate some of the undesirable aspects of communal land use and developed existing proposals on increasing migration and on the sale of land to land-hungry peasants, both directly by the state and through the Peasant Bank.[87]

Insofar as this commission's work was not submitted either to the Council of Ministers or the State Council during the remaining weeks of Witte's premiership, a detailed analysis will be postponed until our discussion of the legislation that would be submitted to the First Duma. However, what is most interesting about it in the present context is the importance that it gave to the "quantitative" task of increasing the area of landownership of land-hungry peasants as it sought to reach some kind of compromise with the liberal parties in the Duma and the peasants themselves. Needless to say, it repeated Gurko's now familiar arguments against expropriation. However, it went on not only to acknowledge the existence of land-hunger but to accept figures developed by the Kadet economist, Professor A. A. Manuilov. On the basis of his work, the commission concluded that in the central black-earth zone, where land-hunger was most severe, a total of 18 million desiatinas would be needed in order to bring all peasants up to the norms established in 1861. Of this, 4 million desiatinas would come from lands currently rented by the state to more prosperous peasants. The remaining amount, it was argued, could be obtained without resorting to expropriation simply by relying on sales of privately owned land through the Peasant Bank. For, according to the commission's calculations, based on the rate at which the Peasant Bank had purchased land in the past, the additional 14 million desiatinas could be acquired within a mere five-year period. At the same time, the commission was at pains to point out that its proposals were directed at strengthening small-scale peasant agriculture by making land available to the land-hungry and those with "dwarf" holdings, not at developing those medium-scale holdings of the "farmer" type favored by Gurko.[88] This, indeed, was the essence of the Witte government's compromise policy of combining intensification and extensification, presented within a single project.

The deliberations of all these commissions were generally completed prior to the opening of the First Duma. However, after the replacement of Witte, Durnovo, Nikol'skii, and Shipov, respectively, by Goremykin, Stolypin, Stishinskii, and Kokovtsov on the very eve of the Duma's opening session—a step that had in fact been in preparation for some time and that signified in one form or another Goremykin's final victory over Witte—these projects were not submitted as planned. When the Duma opened, the new Goremykin government appeared before it without a coherent policy or program. Ironically, however, it would subsequently submit the work of those same Rittikh and Gurko commissions to the Duma as its own proposals for a new agrarian policy. Moreover, it was the work of these two commissions that was eventually incorporated into the Stolypin Reforms and helped determine their final shape.

7

THE MOBILIZATION OF SUPPORT, APRIL–JUNE 1906

Bureaucracy, Duma, and United Nobility

Our country above our estates.
—V. I. Gurko, 1906

To air the mustiness of bureaucratism, it is certainly best to summon fresh people from the land who are directly acquainted with the life of the country.
—K. F. Golovin, 1905

The competition between personal and collective tenure will be made more complicated in Russia by the habitual competition between "great" and "small" property, "great" and "small" culture.
—A. Leroy-Beaulieu, 1893

After the Kutler affair, the tsar had rapidly begun to lose whatever faith he once had in Witte, a process facilitated by men such as Goremykin, Krivoshein, the Trepovs, Durnovo, and Shvanebakh, who did their best to discredit him.[1] Nonetheless, on 23 April, his final day in the government, Witte presented the Nikol'skii Commission's comprehensive program of rural reform to the tsar, including the Gurko and Rittikh commission projects and new projects on the equalization of the peasantry and the reform of local judicial and administrative institutions. Surprisingly, Nicholas approved the program and passed it on to Witte's replacement, Goremykin.[2] Goremykin, however, did not introduce these or any other reform projects in the Duma either on the day it opened or during the entire month of May. And when on 6 June and 10 June the Gurko and Rittikh projects would finally be submitted to the Duma, it clearly was not with any expectation that they would receive serious discussion, let alone approval.

The answer to the question—why such passivity after months of preparation—lies primarily with the government's mood when the Duma opened and thereafter. Unfortunately, evidence for this crucial period is sparse. However, it seems clear in retrospect that the government viewed the opening of the Duma as inaugurating a new period of uncertainty and indecision. With the Kadets comprising the single largest Duma faction—some 40 percent of the members—it is not at all surprising that the government became apprehensive about what it now foresaw as the approaching confrontation. However, as Witte himself noted in his letter of resignation to the tsar, it was "the peasant question" that would in fact "determine the entire character of the Duma's activity."[3] Meanwhile, as a result of decisions made back in the fall of 1905, the government also faced a Duma some 45 percent of whose members were themselves peasants. In the face of these circumstances, the government found itself split between hard-liners and conciliators. Goremykin, Stishinskii, Shvanebakh, Shirinskii-Shikhmatov, and Gurko saw this confrontation primarily in terms of the land question and the preservation of the nobility's property rights and hoped that the Duma would soon be dismissed; Izvolskii, Stolypin, von Kaufman, Kokovtsov, and even Trepov (though only Izvolskii remained completely consistent) sought to develop a working relationship with the parties of the center, primarily the Kadets and the Octobrists. However, as the Duma's agrarian debates progressed and the number of peasant disorders rose, the government's faith in the supposedly conservative peasantry and the conciliators' hopes for the Duma began to crumble, and once again the specter of expropriation loomed ominously before the government, in effect transforming the confrontation between it and the Duma into one between tsarism and socialism, as Goremykin was to note.[4]

The First Duma

To the extent that the government had a policy during the Duma's first weeks it appears to have been one of procrastination. Indeed, Nicholas seems to have chosen Goremykin not simply because he was a loyal and faithful servant, but also, perhaps unconsciously, in the hope that his legendary lethargy would delay the moment of decision. Moreover, although Goremykin was reputedly a "peasant expert," he was not himself an advocate of any specific program. Indeed, he had been one of the sponsors of the counterreforms in the 1880s, and as interior minister in the 1890s had opposed any review of peasant legislation as unnecessary.[5] On the other hand, there were some possible advantages to be gained from adopting such a position. For, by waiting for the Duma to make the first move, the government would not only be able to make the Duma seem responsible for whatever confrontations occurred, but could use such a confrontation to help unite its own ranks and define the future course of its own activities.

On the basic content of the government's agrarian policy, the tsar and the ministerial bureaucracy appear to have been in agreement. However, there were still those within the government who continued to support

Witte's policy of making political concessions to the liberals and the landless and land-hungry peasantry that would include a commitment, at least in principle, to a limited degree of compulsory expropriation. There was disagreement over the degree of acceptable government intervention and initiative in the countryside—an issue also related to the government's approach to the Duma. And there was a split between the members of the new cabinet, none of whom had participated directly in formulating the government's program, and those agrarian experts at the subministerial level who were the program's actual creators. The most vociferous and outspoken member of this group of course was Gurko. Indeed, during the Duma's early days, he was not only acting interior minister until Durnovo's replacement, P. A. Stolypin, took up his post; he also sat in on the Council of Ministers' sessions, where he seems to have functioned as the Council's expert on agrarian reform as well as a defender of those proposals, including of course his own, that had already been approved by the tsar.[6]

The government did not have long to wait before the Duma declared itself. On 6 May, in response to the meaningless generalities of the tsar's throne speech, the Duma issued to the tsar an address in which it virtually arrogated to itself the role of a constituent assembly and demanded a new cabinet that the Duma could trust. In addition, it called on the government to respect the law, enact immediate administrative reforms, and adopt legislation on all the key issues, including, of course, the land question. Specifically, the address called for the distribution to the peasantry of land drawn from the holdings of the state, the royal family, and various religious institutions as well as for the compulsory expropriation of land from private noble landowners. Two days later, the Kadet party introduced its "project of the forty-two," which called for the compulsory expropriation and redemption of private landed property.[7]

Goremykin replied on 13 May in a speech drafted by none other than Gurko who, after discussions in the Council of Ministers, was also responsible for editing the final copy.[8] Predictably, the speech defended the bureaucracy's traditional prerogatives in those areas of legislative initiative considered vital to the survival of the regime, above all, the land question. Rejecting out of hand all proposals for compulsory expropriation and reiterating the government's commitment to the inviolability of private property, Goremykin argued, in tones distinctively Gurko's, that the issue was one of principle. For even if expropriation were strictly limited, having once violated private property rights the government would subsequently be powerless to prevent its application not only to peasant lands themselves but *"to all other forms of property as well"* (emphasis added). Moreover, he argued, it would be totally inconsistent for the government to protect the property rights of one group only to deny it to others.[9]

The issue, however, went beyond merely preserving the rights of particular classes, for private property was "throughout the entire world, and at all stages in the development of civil society, the cornerstone of the public welfare and social development, the fundamental principle of national life without which the very existence of the state [is] unthinkable."[10] This was particularly important in Russia's case since the basis of its power was its agricultural population: "The prosperity of our fatherland cannot be achieved as long as the necessary conditions for the progress and prosperity of agricultural labor, the basis of our entire economic life, are not assured. In view of its significance for the state, the peasant question is the most important of those [questions] now subject to a solution. . . . [Only] the development of agriculture . . . will increase national productivity and general welfare."[11]

Such were the terms in which the government chose publicly to define itself. Thus it sought to preserve the existing political order and defend its continued right to exist in the face of the revolutionary challenge. Goremykin concluded, "the might of the state, its international power and domestic prosperity rest immutably on an executive authority whose activity is regularized and governed by the principles of law."[12] Such an authority the government intended to defend.

Meanwhile, Goremykin's positive suggestions for rural reform essentially repeated the Nikol'skii Commission's program as submitted to the tsar by Witte.[13] However, although he embraced many features of the liberal program, including the equalization and individualization of peasant civil and property rights and the reform of local justice and administration, he reasserted the traditional claims of a paternalistic bureaucratic *opeka*, arguing that the government had no intention of abandoning some 85 percent of the population of European Russia to the arbitrary fate of the market, as had been the case in the decades following emancipation. Rather, as long as the peasantry remained a *soslovie* it would continue to be the subject of special government concern and protection; and its legal status would, of course, continue to embody some of the features of its centuries-long "isolation" despite a simultaneous policy of integration. Goremykin similarly reasserted the government's traditional commitment to a policy of gradualism, noting that "it is also necessary to be cautious in this matter in order to avoid rude shocks to the historically and uniquely formed peasant way of life"—a caveat that could apply equally to proposals for expropriation as well as those directed against the peasant commune. But the government's policy of nonintervention did not mean that it should not implement its own legislation.[14]

Immediately after Goremykin's Duma speech, Gurko took advantage of his own presence at the Council of Ministers' sessions to resubmit his commission's project for the Council's consideration. Once again, however, he was rebuffed. According to Gurko, whose account of this episode is the only one we have, his principal opponent was none other than Goremykin himself, though it seems likely that Kokovtsov and Stishinskii also opposed him. Goremykin's objections, it seems, were the same as those already expressed by the State Council in March, that this project, with its image of sudden change at the stroke of a pen, was too coercive. Stolypin, meanwhile, though he had officially presented the project, had declined to defend it before the Council, in all likelihood because he was unwilling to commit himself on so complex and sensitive a matter at the beginning of his new career in St. Petersburg.[15]

Nonetheless, despite these disagreements, six days after Goremykin's speech, and in direct response to the Duma's debates on the agrarian question, the government finally came forward in the persons of Stishinskii and Gurko to expound in greater detail its fundamental opposition to the direction the debates were taking. We do not know who drafted Stishinskii's speech. Both Rittikh and Krivoshein were probable candidates. However, the nature of the argument suggests that Gurko himself may have been involved. He and Stishinskii had been close colleagues within the Interior Ministry and were soon to be politically linked through their association with those nobles and dignitaries who were simultaneously organizing the first Congress of the United Nobility—a relationship described later in more detail.[16] In any event, in his speech, Stishinskii repeated the standard arguments against expropriation and linked them with the new perceptions about rural society to which he himself had only recently converted. Reflecting the moderate and gradualist approach characteristic of the GUZiZ, he offered essentially the same package of reforms that the Nikol'skii Commission had put together. Above all, he argued for the paramount importance of private-property ownership for the state and for the absolute necessity of preserving *"zakonomernost"*—a notion that united respect for legal precedent and for the overall continuity and regularity of government activity with the traditional, historicist, and organic approach to changing the peasant way of life. In his view, therefore, the only way to bring about improvements in peasant welfare was for the government to accelerate the process of agricultural intensification that had already begun to spread eastward from its source in the western borderlands. However, he was also careful to note that, although "there is no doubt that the future of our small-scale agriculture lies in the development of this movement," the formation of *"khutor*-type *otruba"* (sic) is only possible where local conditions permit.[17] On the other hand, he noted, more and more peasants were attempting to transfer to individual forms of landownership and use. Consequently, the government should encourage these developments. In the meantime, communes that had not executed any repartitions during the past twenty-five to thirty years ought to be prohibited from undertaking them in the future so as to strengthen the peasants' sense of private property.[18]

Stishinskii's speech was reasonable, balanced, and passionless and showed little understanding of his audience. In contrast, Gurko's, although it covered the same ground, was one-sided and full of passion and, even though he made an attempt to appeal to his audience, insulted it. The speech itself is seldom referred to. Yet it is deserving of special consideration, for it was at once an emotional, last-ditch political appeal to rally support behind the government and an unwitting exposure of the near hoplessness of the government's situation, the baffling complexity of the problems that it sought to resolve, and the intractable contradictions it had to face. It also included a tragically prophetic vision of the future if the government failed to stave off revolution.

Goremykin had officially commissioned the speech, presumably because Stolypin's inexperience prevented him from delivering the speech himself. However, as a result of Stolypin's last-minute objections to its content, Gurko agreed to present his ideas not as the official view of the Interior Ministry but as his own personal opinion.[19] Apparently, Stolypin wanted to leave the question of expropriation open as a basis for possible negotiations with the Duma liberals.

After such a disclaimer, Gurko went on to present statistical evidence in support of the government's contention that there was not enough private and state land in European Russia for expropriation and redistribution to have any significant or positive economic impact on peasant welfare. On the contrary, he concluded, the impact would be a negative one. Even if the government were only to adopt a partial expropriation, as was recommended in the Kadet party's project, ultimately it would have to redistribute all such land in the interests of equity. Then "all peasants who owned more than four desiatinas of land would end up being forced to yield the surplus to other landowners." Indeed, were the entire rural population to be included in this distribution, the total quantity of land available to each male peasant would actually be even less than four desiatinas. Of course, he continued, "we all know that peasant holdings are extraordinarily diverse, that they differ not only within individual provinces, counties, and cantons, but also within the boundaries of each commune." As a result, approximately one-quarter of the entire peasantry in fact owned land in excess of fifteen desiatinas per household and one-half of these owned land in excess of twenty desiatinas. Given an average of three males per household, this amounted to more than five desiatinas per male soul. Gurko then appealed to the peasant delegates in the Duma, who, he seems not unreasonably to have assumed, fell into the category of owning four or more desiatinas—and by implication to the inhabitants of the Great Russian plain beyond the Duma walls:

Delegates of the Russian landed peasantry, remember those four desiatinas, remember this figure! Let it be indelibly engraved in your memory! Remember that any program of compulsory expropriation of privately owned lands is indissolubly linked with the removal from part of the peasant population of some share of the land in its use; remember also that under no circumstances can a single inch of land be added to that of all those peasants who already possess these four desiatinas.[20]

Clearly, Gurko sought to drive a wedge between the different strata of an already economically differentiated peasantry, a theme that he retained throughout the speech. However, his real purpose was primarily political; he sought to undermine the argument for expropriation and win support for the government's program. Indeed, in his view, the government was engaged in a life-and-death struggle with the opposition to win over the peasantry or, at the least, that portion of it that owned in excess of four desiatinas.

For Gurko, either the state was based on the universal principle according to which land was the object of private ownership or on its opposite, the idea that "land is God's gift, that it belongs to everyone who wants to work it."[21]

Until now all nations in the world have recognized land as the object of private ownership. Certainly, it is on this basis that a level of agriculture developed and became firmly established which assured the states of Western Europe their general progress, their economic prosperity. Some now affirm that this is an old principle, that the principle of private landed property has become obsolete, that Russia is fated to reveal the new truth (slovo) to the whole world, to reconstruct on new principles a decayed social system.[22]

In the face of this challenge, the government was, in effect, obliged to shoulder the almost messianic mission of saving Europe from socialism, a goal that originated with and was the mirror image of the revolutionary parties' equally "messianic" goal of establishing socialism in Russia.

Seen in these polarized terms, even a partial expropriation of land such as the Kadets proposed was equivalent to socialism. Moreover, expropriation would lead inevitably to a state of universal equality, the most extreme fragmentation of land, the transformation of agriculture into a universally small-scale industry, and the complete destruction of the country's productive forces, both agricultural and industrial. However, what Russia needed in order to prosper, in Gurko's eyes, was not expropriation, or an increase in the quantity of land—which would simply perpetuate its dependence on an unproductive monoculture of grain—but an increase in productivity. (Diversification indeed remains an urgent problem in many underdeveloped countries as well as in the Soviet Union today.) To hammer his point home, he insistently raised the specter of crop failure and famine as the alternatives to this path, as "that risk to which the entire peasant population is subject with the transfer of all land into its ownership."[23] Intensification, indeed, was the historical task that now faced Russia. The government, he asserted, ought therefore to follow this "universal" path of economic development that the other European states had already traversed. For the Russian government, however, the task was more urgent and was complicated by the simultaneous problem of remaining at the political helm.

Gurko then turned to one of the crucial elements in the whole developmental equation: the productivity of peasant labor. Rejecting the popular argument that the peasants needed more land on the grounds that there was only sufficient work in the countryside to keep some 25 percent of the peasant population fully employed, he pointed out that even a total expropriation of private landowners could not provide work for all of the remaining 75 percent. Meanwhile, in "all developed countries this surplus is applied to other spheres of human activity, spheres in which the scope for the application of human labor is unlimited and which can therefore absorb a greater quantity of labor than the land." In France, Gurko noted, only 46 percent of the population was occupied in agriculture, in Germany 35 percent, and in England only 15 percent. Yet, one of the consequences of this occupational shift from agricultural to nonagricultural occupations was "that those who remain on the land must produce grain not only for themselves but also for those working in other occupations. Certainly on this is founded the ethical basis of the right to own land. . . . Those who remain on the land are obligated to produce more grain than they themselves consume. Only by adopting such a course can the problem of rural over-population be solved."[24] Hence, although expropriation may produce some economic relief in the short term, in the long run there could be no historical alternative to intensification, the potential fruits of which far exceeded those of expropriation. Such a policy had therefore to be adopted at the earliest opportunity.

If the Kadet program attracted the peasants because of a belief that it was populist or socialist, they were mistaken, he said. The basis of the "ruling socialist theories" was concentration; however, that of the Kadets' agrarian reforms was fragmentation. Thus, he argued, not only did the Kadet program have nothing in common with socialist economic principles, but the Kadets erred in assuming that an egalitarian distribution of land would automatically result in an equalization of individual incomes and an increase in national income sufficient to provide the population with a higher standard of living.

Indeed, Gurko accused the Kadets of having drafted their project solely to win the peasantry's political support. However, he himself realized only too clearly that the struggle for power would ultimately be fought and won precisely at the level of peasant attitudes. Unfortunately for the government:

The masses of the people are not in a position to investigate this complex question of political economy. Influenced by their conviction that the quantity of land at the disposal of the Russian state, even within the limits of European Russia, is so great that it is sufficient for almost twenty—and some think even for one hundred—desiatinas per soul, many peasants strive with all their might to realize a "black repartition." Certainly, there is no force that could convince the ignorant, indigent man that he will in the final outcome be impoverished rather than enriched by an increase in the property at his disposal. . . . But people who are acquainted with political economy and who are aware of the universal laws lying beyond human control which guide the complex national economy cannot doubt that this would be the case.[25]

In the historical perspective of some seventy years, and with certain reservations regarding his strictures as to the viability of a "peasant economy," Gurko's general position still seems to have the weight of historical proof on its side. Yet he and the rest of the government could clearly see the impasse that faced them—the need to take peasant expectations into account, no matter how irrational they might appear from the economic viewpoint of the state as a whole. Thus, it is hardly surprising that the government was reluctant to submit its proposals to the Duma. This awareness also explains in part the desire of some members of the government to enter directly into the practical task of reform in the belief that, by its actions, the government would win popular support even in the face of revolutionary rhetoric.

In trying to refute the charge that he spoke simply in defense of noble interests, Gurko criticized those landowners who eagerly sold their arable lands. He noted ironically that the Kadet project would, in fact, better serve the selfish and short-term interests of most of those landowners who, in the face of the agrarian disorders, wished nothing more than to abandon their land at the earliest possible opportunity and to realize a profit. Only a minority was prepared to engage in intensive, capitalist forms of agricultural exploitation. But it was they who better served both the long-term interests of the country as a whole and those of the peasantry. Indeed, the political and economic importance of such noble agriculturalists was so great that Gurko challenged the rest of the nobility to take on a new sense of mission and service. Their obligation was not to turn their land into money but "out of a patriotic sense of duty" to invest their money in their land "to raise the productivity of its soil as a prerequisite for an increase in national prosperity."[26] Identifying the principle of private property ownership with freedom, a word which he sardonically noted "resounds incessantly within these walls," he attacked those political liberals who based freedom solely on civil rights:

> Any kind of complete realization of freedom is conceivable [only] . . . with the possibility of developing completely freely, in conformity with the each man's natural aptitudes, his acquired capabilities in a sphere of human activity chosen by himself. The fragmentation of all land into tiny subsistence plots with a prohibition against increasing these plots beyond a definite limit—this is the most despotic limitation of man's freedom, the limitation of his economic freedom and his freedom of initiative and practical activity. This is nothing but an enslavement of the peasantry to the land, a new serfdom with no exit, which in the nature of things must be more and more aggravated as the size of each person's landed possessions is continually reduced with the natural increase in population. The State Duma, an assembly of the elected representatives of the population of the country who are concerned with the affairs of state, cannot be guided in its discussions by feelings alone, no matter how exalted and unselfish. The State Duma must discuss every measure, not only from the perspective of its immediate results, but also carefully elucidating all of its final consequences.[27]

In the last analysis, therefore, the struggle was between thinking men, rational men, civilized men, and the peasants with their "blind spontaneous craving to possess the noble's land," though even they, Gurko believed, "would be convinced by experience" within a very few years.[28]

For all its eloquence, Gurko's speech had little immediate impact on the peasant-dominated Duma. Nor, indeed, did the government submit its projects on agrarian reform for the Duma's consideration until another three weeks had passed. In the interim, a third force intervened that served to break the impasse between government and Duma and helped galvanize the government into action. That force was the First Congress of the United Nobility, which began meeting for a week on 21 May 1906, just two days after Gurko's speech to the Duma.

Bureaucracy and Nobility: A New Alliance

This Congress was the final outcome of a number of social and political forces active during the critical years of 1905 and 1906. Its organization was, moreover, of vital political significance, for it represented the first appearance of the nobility on the public stage as a self-consciously political force. At the same time, by serving as a kind of umbrella organization uniting the political right, it became the only such organization to maintain a continuous and significant political influence at the national level until the regime's final collapse in 1917.[29]

Among the forces responsible for the organization of the United Nobility, most significant was the formation, during late 1905 and early 1906, of a host of noble and promonarchist associations of self-defense in response to the peasant disorders that spread through the countryside after the October Manifesto. Some of the better-known, if evanescent, groupings on the national level were the Fatherland or Patriotic Union, the Union of Russian Men, the All-Russian Union of Landowners, the All-Russian Union of Landed Proprietors, the Nobles' Circle, and the Russian Monarchist party. At the same time, a variety of unions and law-and-order parties proliferated at the provincial level.[30] However, the most important feature of these organizations was not their institutional form or particular political views but their deeply interlocking memberships.

The impetus for the formation of a national organization of nobles developed in response to the government's flirtation with the Migulin and Kutler projects; it gained momentum in the spring of 1906 after the Putilov circular and in conjunction with the campaign against expropriation initiated by the Congress of the marshals of nobility. However, the initial attempts foundered on the conflict between the marshals' liberal and Octobrist-oriented leadership, which was opposed to an exclusively government-initiated agrarian reform, and the more conservative and progovernment forces behind the other organizations, both in the capital and in the provinces.

In consequence, no practical steps were taken until the end of April, on the eve of the convocation of the Duma. At that time, the marshals of the nobility were shunted aside and the newly formed organization fell under the control of a combination of groups—provincial landowners, most notably from Saratov and Orel provinces; capital-city dignitaries with close ties to the government, the court, and provincial society; and a number of bureaucrats.[31]

Traditionally, of course, relations between bureaucrats and the provincial landowning nobility had been characterized by mutual antagonism. Now, however, the revolutionary threat had enabled those who had access to both groups to establish a link between them. Equally significant, the memberships and interests of these groupings overlapped in such a way that the members of one of them, the Golovin salon, tended to assume a central role as both initiators and mediators among these otherwise diverse interests. Moreover, when one examines the role of this intermediary group in the formation and subsequent conduct of the First Congress, it quickly becomes clear that its influence was out of all proportion to its numbers. Indeed, to the extent that the United Nobility's membership was theoretically limited to those elected directly by the local nobility, the role of those who were either self-appointed or coopted must also be regarded as disproportionate.

On the policy level, the critical link uniting these capital-city figures with provincial noble landowners was their activism. As loyal supporters of the autocracy and the existing socioeconomic order, many of these activists can be characterized both as conservatives and as reformist-modernizers. Although they supported government interventionism in society and the participation of society in government, they were not in the main supporters of a government that was truly representative of the population. In their view, the nobility ought to have the preponderant voice. Many of them therefore also opposed the Duma as it was presently constituted. Together, these men formed a new, politically conscious, and "creative minority" within the broader and generally inert nobility and bureaucracy. At the same time, however, they belonged to a long tradition of autocratic reformers. They, too, sought to preserve the existing order by means of a vigorous and active government that would undertake significant reforms, most particularly in agriculture, as a prerequisite to a more general modernization that would in due course usher Russia into the twentieth century. Thus, despite the particularistic overtones of this alliance, it nonetheless preserved elements of a national or supraclass perspective on Russia's social, economic, and even political future.[32]

Ultimately, this pressure group assumed that the nobility would change from a privileged legal estate into an economic class. Its success, however, would depend on the support it could win among those provincial landowning nobles invited by Gurko's Duma speech to adopt a new version of state service based on classical economic liberalism's concept of self-interest. And since this was not forthcoming, it is not very surprising that this alliance was to prove fragile and evanescent, both in theory and in practice. It would survive, and could survive, only as long as these public figures, bureaucrats, and modernizing noble agricultural-ists held a leading role in the United Nobility. And so it was that, even before the Second Congress met in November of the same year, these self-appointed activists were rapidly superseded by more tradition-minded representatives from the provinces who began to exert increas-ingly powerful pressures for a restoration of the status quo ante and rejected such innovative proposals for the reform and development of Russia's agriculture as an all-class activity uniting the interests of both peasant and noble. For the duration of the First Congress, however, this alliance remained reasonably intact.[33]

The First Congress opened 21 May. On 23 May, it began discussing a draft version of its agrarian program that had been prepared by a special commission appointed by the Congress's preparatory committee. The commission's nine members included Bekhteev and Pestrzhetskii.[34] The principal issue for the agrarian commission, as it had been for Gurko, was that of the existing order versus socialism, of the inviolability of private property versus compulsory expropriation. Not surprisingly, the commission identified private landownership as the "bearer of progress" and reiterated Gurko's Duma appeal to the landowning nobility to return to state service. In the eyes of the program's framers, not only did private property serve an essential cultural and state function, but noble landowners fulfilled a similar role as a source of cadres for local self-government and the "service estate" in general. Moreover, besides being the most educated elements in the countryside, their intimate knowledge of local conditions made them more influential than the urbanized intelligentsia.[35]

The agrarian commission's proposals, of course, sought to prevent the government from adopting any program that included compulsory expropriation.[36] Meanwhile, its alternate program essentially conformed to the proposals already worked out by the Nikol'skii Commission in Witte's cabinet and supported by Goremykin. Thus, for those villages that had sufficient land, the commission proposed "a better and more complete utilization of the existing allotment area," including "transferring peasants to a multi-field rotation, better cultivation and fertilization of land, granting individual peasants rights to allotment land, and bringing the plowman closer to the plowland." Specifically, this would involve transferring the peasantry "from communal to personal-property ownership, the partition of large villages, the abolition of intra-allotment open-fields and the adoption of the *khutor* system" of land use. At the same time, the commission recognized that the government and the zemstvos would have to take the initiative for such improvements, since "throughout the world, the transfer of peasants to improved systems of cultivation originates with a powerful pressure from above." Ultimately, however, the key to success would lie with "a more complete utilization of peasant labor."[37]

With respect to those households that were "actually land-hungry"— some 1.2 million of them, mainly in the Ukraine and southwest—the commission proposed increased migration and the "purchase of privately owned land." Indeed, it noted that there was no need to adopt a policy of compulsory expropriation to satisfy their needs, since an average of more than three and a half million desiatinas of privately owned land went on the market each year. Consequently, if the peasants could mortgage their allotments to the Peasant Bank, most of that land would ultimately transfer to peasant hands.[38]

And, lest one is tempted, along with the United Nobility's critics, to see in this program nothing more than a skillful attempt to drive a wedge between the rich peasants and the poor, thereby to distract them from the so-called first social war with the nobility, the draft specifically characterized any action that might set one portion of the peasantry against another as undesirable. Indeed, existing levels of intrapeasant conflict were considered unacceptable. Echoing the apocalyptical language of Gurko's Duma speech, the commission noted that: "Even now the agricultural and Interior ministries are receiving demands from individual peasant communities calling for the forcible expropriation of lands from neighboring villages and from peasants who own only two or three desiatinas per soul." Thus, were the path of expropriation to be adopted, it was already possible to foresee that "When all privately-owned lands [have been] divided up, a civil war will begin for the equalization of allotment lands."[39]

Of course, from the viewpoint of the individual noble, the desire to prevent his own land from being expropriated must often have prevailed over any broader concern for domestic peace, let alone economic or social development. Nonetheless, the draft program accurately expressed the views of that minority within the landowning nobility that was beginning to see itself as an economic, and essentially agricultural, class. Moreover, its members increasingly identified their economic, political, and social interests with those of a rejuvenated state that had similarly, and simultaneously, acknowledged its own primarily agricultural nature. Rather than basing their social position on the exclusively juridical principles of their *soslovie* status, these "new men" saw a new role for themselves in which their economic function would justify their privileged status—indeed, could alone justify it. This position, of course, explains their customary antipolitical bent and their divorce from the more politically liberal members of the nobility in the Octobrist and Kadet parties and in the United Nobility itself. The minority status and ultimate powerlessness of these new men, even within the United Nobility, are only further corroborated by the subsequent failure of organizations such as the Union of Landowners and the Union of Landed Proprietors that were specifically intended to represent their views.[40]

Meanwhile, it is clear that those who drafted the agrarian commission's proposals were closely associated with those forces in the government who opposed compulsory expropriation and supported the immediate enactment of a program combining individualization, intensification, and extensification. The conclusion seems inescapable that these forces had made a deliberate effort to manipulate the United Nobility into supporting their program as a way of breaking the stalemate that existed within the government.

The First Congress, which met in Stishinskii's quarters in the GUZiZ, continued the pattern established in its planning committees and invited a great many nondelegates to attend, again with an advisory voice. Among them were such familiar names as Lykoshin, Bekhteev, Pestrzhetskii, Bobrinskii, Golovin, Naryshkin, Volodomirov, Sergeev,

Gurko, and Stishinskii himself as well as observers from the Nobles' Circle. There followed the election of Bobrinskii as chairman and appointments of Sergeev as secretary and Volodomirov, Brianchaninov, and Zybin as members of the four-man secretariat. New lists of nobles coopted into the Congress were read off at almost every subsequent session. Apparently, the leadership was trying to draw in as many representatives of nobles' organizations as possible in order to strengthen the image of the Congress as representative of all elements of the "first estate."[41] Indeed, according to the figures of the United Nobility, eventually, the 135 nondelegate "advisers" outnumbered the 114 duly elected delegates, who represented some twenty-nine provinces. Among these advisers the bureaucratic contingent was very active. After a break in the evening session on the second day, Count V. F. Dorrer, the extreme rightist, introduced Gurko to loud applause, noting that his now famous speech before the Duma three days earlier had been the government's first successful move vis-à-vis that institution.[43]

After the presentation of the agrarian commission's draft program by Pestrzhetskii, Baron A. A. Pillar-fon-Pil'khau of Lifland and a member of the St. Petersburg Union of Landed Proprietors was the first to support its proposals. His was the voice of the modernizing noble agriculturalist, though one who lived in a region that was economically and socially far in advance of the rest of the country. Such Baltic barons coexisted with a free peasantry that had long ceased to live under the communal system. Thus in his eyes, the main evils of peasant agriculture were "the commune and open-field landownership." The remedy: abolish the commune, that "breeding ground of socialist bacillae." Nor was it essential for the entire peasantry to be provided with land after the commune was dissolved, since the market forces of supply and demand would satisfactorily regulate the ensuing development of a free labor market. The Baron clearly spoke from experience when he repeated the German version of "*Bogat Ivan . . .*": "*Hat der Bauer Geld, hat's die ganze Welt*" (If the peasant is rich, so is the whole world). However, he also spoke as a member of his *soslovie* when he urged the nobility to become actively involved in the proposed agrarian reform, since only they possessed the experience necessary to ensure its success.[44]

The views expressed during the remainder of the discussion are familiar. Not surprisingly, most speakers—though by no means all, as we shall see—sought to deny the existence of peasant land-hunger and, therefore, to undermine the argument for expropriation, no matter from what source. Early in the discussion, Prince A. P. Urusov of Tula observed that "fear is a poor adviser." However, fear was clearly behind the rhetorical excesses of those who defended private property and opposed the commune and socialism. Given the polarized alternatives, it is clear why those who adhered to a position of "no compromises" tended to side with the bureaucratic faction—and there were many hard-liners at the First Congress.[45] In contrast, as we shall see, the more politically oriented nobles shared many of the assumptions of the liberal opposition movement and of those in the chancelleries who had supported the Migulin and Kutler projects and who, like Witte and Stolypin, favored a compromise approach toward the Duma.

In any event, as Pillar-fon-Pil'khau and Pavlov noted, it was socialism that was the enemy: to defend private property was to defend the monarchy and to attack socialism.[46] The nobility was not, therefore, simply defending its own narrow *soslovie* interests; it was also defending the national interest. N. E. Markov of Kursk, the leader of the infamous right-wing Union of the Russian People and later a member of the Third and Fourth Dumas, delivered one of the most inflammatory speeches in support of the agrarian commission's report. According to Markov, "poverty" was at the root of the agrarian problem; any solution had to create the necessary material conditions for the successful application of peasant labor.[47] Pavlov blamed the current problem on "laziness"—"the mother of stealing, murder, violence [and] depravity."[48] Yet he did not refer merely to the peasant—but to the whole country, to government and society, high and low. By implication, the noble landowner, too, was branded as lazy in his desire to own land yet not to work it.[49]

Brianchaninov, nominally a member of the Octobrist party, and Count P. S. Sheremetev of Moscow, looked first at the nobility's political "image" rather than at the substance of the agrarian program. Both expressed the view that in order to defend themselves in the political arena—and to avoid appearing as the selfish defenders of exclusive interests—they had to adopt a program that went halfway toward the peasant's needs, even to the point of compensated expropriation where the state interest was at stake.[50]

Count Olsuf'ev of Saratov, who had earlier supported the reform projects being prepared within the Goremykin government, took an interesting compromise position. Like Bekhteev, he argued that no single solution could be uniformly applied to Russia as a whole. Rather, the problem had to be approached at the local level, with the aid of local investigations of the peasantry's needs. Then, turning to the problem of land-hunger, he urged the Congress to recognize what was, in fact, staring it in the face—that land was already, and, indeed had long been, in the process of being transferred from the nobility to the peasantry. However, this spontaneous movement, which he considered might even be a sound one, had to be organized along rational and legal lines. Only under such conditions would it be possible to preserve those good relations between peasant and noble that, he claimed, already existed. As he put it, "If [my] land is torn away from me by force I will become an enemy of the peasants; in the opposite circumstances I will remain their friend."

Thus he urged the nobility to compromise, to sell a part of their land to the peasants, and to support the government's agrarian proposals.[51]

Prince A. A. Krapotkin in part echoed Olsuf'ev's views, as he sought to interpret the peasants' perspective:

Secluded in the commune, the peasants see enemies in all the sosloviia around them since no sosloviia work with them or know their interests; when the land became overcrowded, the nobles and the bureaucrats and the clergy became [their] enemies. . . . [As a consequence] revolutionaries stepped in and replaced [us] as the people's leaders. [Thus,] we must return to the people . . . we must say that the darstvenniki and the landless who were deprived of their [full] share in 1861, who have not enjoyed the benefits of the [Emancipation] Manifesto, should be satisfied.[52]

Although this latter idea was a minority opinion, nevertheless, his analysis of the peasantry's social relations with the nonpeasant was historically sound. So, too, was his analysis of the nature of the newly developing patron-client relationships that mediated the peasants' contact with the surrounding society.[53]

Count A. A. Uvarov, the former bureaucrat and zemstvo activist from Saratov and, later, nonparty Octobrist deputy in the Third Duma, expressed a different perspective. He was one of the first at the Congress to argue for the organization of an alliance of noble and nonnoble landowners, large and small, that would defend the principle of private property against those who demanded expropriation.[54]

Contrary to what one might expect from an assembly of nobles traditionally hostile to the bureaucracy, suspicion of bureaucratic solutions was rarely expressed. In part, this was obviously due to the important role that bureaucrats had played in the Congress and in the drafting of the agrarian program. In part, however, it was because these nobles needed the government and were afraid it would side with the Duma. Thus, the task of agrarian reform was usually conceived as a joint undertaking of both government and society.[55]

The speech by A. I. Zybin of Nizhni-Novgorod, later secretary and member of the Permanent Council of the United Nobility and one of the nonbureaucratic members of the agrarian commission, reflects the common perspective of the commission's bureaucrats, notables, and noble-activists:

By the expressions "agrarian problem," "agrarian reforms," etc., I do not mean the relatively narrow problem of peasant land-hunger . . . but the much broader problem . . . of raising and ensuring the welfare of the peasantry as a laboring agricultural class [and that is but one part of the] . . . still broader problem of improving all of

Russia's agriculture . . . and [thus strengthening] the state's power and [prosperity]. . . . The entire peasantry awaits, and has waited a long time, and awaits feverishly, the realization of promises repeatedly handed down from the throne, and every delay, even on grounds of the need to link peasant reforms with other, essentially similar, economic reforms, may be understood by the peasantry as a desire only to delay the matter and may evoke a sharp critical protest.[56]

Zybin, too, opposed an "additional allotment" both on principle and out of fear of provoking a civil war within the peasantry. In its place he argued in favor of the commission's program of individualization and intensification, citing John Stuart Mill's famous quotation from Arthur Young in support.[57] At the same time, he rejected a single uniform solution imposed from St. Petersburg, since it could not address the peculiar conditions of each locality. Thus, although acknowledging that reform was the government's responsibility, he also favored the participation of local public forces since "in each individual case, local men know best what is necessary for the welfare of the people, and the local nobility, jointly with the peasantry, in the name of mutual interest, must successfully introduce all the proposed reforms." The nobility, he said, "must not be afraid, must not flee from the aroused crowd, but by a wise word and by orderly and proper actions draw it to our side. . . . The peasants possess great common sense, they understand perfectly well who talks with them and how, and value it very much when one talks to them in a human manner, and they also know their interests better than the legions of bureaucrats—for example, the representatives of the Peasant Bank—watching over them." "The state," he concluded, should put the implementation of reform "into the hands of nobles and peasants, without interfering in its details, and providing only the general principles and appropriate means."[58]

In the discussion of the agrarian program itself, most of the criticisms came from a centrist position and were directed against statements that assayed either a general interpretation of the contemporary crisis or referred to land-hunger.[59] In opposition to these criticisms, however, a number of nobles, including Prince Kurakin of Iaroslav and Count Olsuf'ev, fought a rearguard action in defense of the concept of land-hunger and even favored an additional allotment.[60] However, those who opposed making any concessions won the day, and every reference to land-hunger was removed from the draft.[61] Meanwhile, on the grounds that certain subjects implied the existence of land-hunger, an article on migration was also rejected.[62]

Count Dorrer also acknowledged the existence of land-hunger but urged the government to abandon its concentration on land as the sole source of peasant income and to consider industry as another field of employment. The program repeats this sentiment: "In general, the welfare of the peasants does not depend directly on the extent of landownership."[63] A speech by Senator S. P. Frolov, who owned land in several provinces, including a model estate in Tambov, seems to have been part of the bureaucracy's pressure tactics. He began by summarizing the Nikol'skii Commission program that the Goremykin government and the tsar had endorsed, referred to Pestrzhetskii's articles, and stressed the need to eliminate restrictions established by the "counterreforms" of 1893. He then proposed granting full property rights in land to peasants in conjunction with an equalization of all civil rights, complete freedom of departure from the commune, and establishment of the conditions necessary to make that decision feasible. However, these rights, he argued, should be granted not by "forcibly violating the commune, but by depriving it of the character of a compulsory union prescribed by law, by letting life itself, in conformity with the demands of the various localities and distinctive conditions, freely decide the question of its further existence." Further, he proposed assisting the land-hungry by expanding both migration and the activities of the Peasant Bank; adopting measures to establish *khutora*, not only to encourage a consciousness of private property, but also to facilitate the improvement and intensification of land use; extending petty credit; providing more education; and establishing a "strong authority" that could protect individual rights as well as punish violators swiftly.[64]

Discussion of land sales to the peasantry and the role of the Peasant Bank inevitably evoked, and would continue to evoke, a very mixed response. The variety of opinions that went into the writing of the agrarian program was evident. Zybin and the notorious General Strukov, a former member of the Interior Ministry, marshal of the nobility in Ekaterinoslav, and an elected member of the right wing of the State Council, not only expressed the nobility's traditional hostility to the Peasant Bank; they asked whether the Bank's policies might not ultimately lead to the peasants' losing their land as well.[65]

Pestrzhetskii, however, defended the sale of land to the peasantry as consistent with the overall development of private property rights and the preservation of private landed property in general. He also supported the subdivision of large and unproductive properties as one way to increase the number of more productive peasant smallholdings—a position first developed by Gurko in 1905.[66] On the other hand, A. I. Lykoshin, also of the Interior Ministry, maintained that such large-scale transfers of land to the peasantry were undesirable on economic grounds since they would end the beneficial personal influence exercised by private landowners over neighboring peasants. Lykoshin joined with Strukov and Zybin in supporting continued restrictions on the alienability of peasant lands. Otherwise, he said, the peasantry would in due course be cheated out of its lands by the "non-Russian" Jews![67]

Lykoshin apparently had more confidence than his fellow nobles that the Peasant Bank could both preserve its character as a credit institution and become an instrument of the government's agrarian policy. Volodomirov supported him and proposed subordinating the Bank to the Committee on Land Organization. This proposal was part of the program's final draft. At the same time, the Congress urged the Bank to calculate the purchase price of properties according to prevailing market prices rather than the lower standard of peasant income. A reduction in the rate of interest on loans to peasant purchasers was also recommended. Finally, the customary *soslovie* limitations on the peasants' right to dispose of their property was maintained in the face of some opposition, thus continuing the long tradition of bureaucratic *opeka*.[68]

Although the Congress of nobles certainly expressed ideas that served its own vested interests, the final result—in large measure because of the concerted efforts of a determined activist minority—was a program that coincided very closely with the one that, it must be emphasized, had *already* been worked out within the bureaucracy. Thus were the interests of both noble and peasant harmonized with raison d'état.

Ultimately, however, neither the bureaucratic group nor the hard-liners within the Congress could claim complete victory. Dissatisfied with the right's denial of land-hunger and its retention of *soslovie* limitations on allotment lands, a group of some forty nobles submitted a special minority opinion. Advocating a program of long-term economic development that would lead to a gradual dissolution of the commune and the movement of peasants from agriculture into industry and trade, it called on the government to take immediate action to deal with land-hunger—on the basis of local studies. In this view, such action was the only way to pacify the peasantry. Among those who signed this manifesto of "political realism" were Olsuf'ev, Uvarov, Prutchenko, Sergeev, Zybin, and Prince Krapotkin.[69]

In the end, these disagreements were sufficient to prevent the agrarian program from being finally edited, adopted, approved, or published.[70] However, the Congress did adopt and publish an "Address to the Tsar" that had been drafted by another sub-committee.[71] The opinions expressed in this document corresponded quite closely to the opinions of those members of the Congress who had signed the "minority opinion" on the agrarian question. Most significantly, three points integral to the minority's argument—all of them expressly excluded from the draft of the agrarian program submitted to the editorial subcommission—were incorporated in the final published version of the address: total freedom of property ownership, an end to bureaucratic *opeka* in the countryside, and necessary expansion of peasant landownership through migration and government credit, a provision that implicitly at least acknowledged the existence of land-hunger though it did not, of course, resort to expropriation.[72] It is not clear how this minority was able to win the adoption of these points by a Congress whose majority had already rejected them during its discussions of the agrarian platform. Nor is it possible to determine why the final version of the address expressed them more clearly and emphatically than even its first draft had. However, since the specific wording of the address was not subject to discussion in open session, the final result was a product not of the Congress, but rather of its editorial commission. This commission consisted of Zybin, Naryshkin, Prutchenko, Pavlov, Prince Urusov, Prince Shcherbatov, Count Dorrer, and Count Olsuf'ev. Of these, four—Count Olsuf'ev, Prutchenko, Prince Urusov, and Zybin—signed the minority opinion on the agrarian question; three of the other four members, Naryshkin, Pavlov, and Dorrer, are also known to have agreed with it.[73]

Conclusions

Such, then, was the somewhat paradoxical outcome of the United Nobility's First Congress. Clearly, there were more conflicts than its organizers had anticipated. These divisions, in conjunction with the crucial determining role played first by the Congress's planning committees and later by its subcommissions, explain why the address—the only official statement of the Congress's position—contradicted the views of a majority of its members on the volatile issues of land-hunger and extensification; and, similarly, why it sought to substitute a more rigorous application of laissez-faire principles for the traditional policy of bureaucratic *opeka*. After the tsar expressed his appreciation for the address, it appeared in the public press.[74]

Of more significance was the endorsement by a majority of those who attended the Congress of direct government intervention to resolve the agrarian problem and a gradual abolition of the peasant commune. On the other hand, and also in agreement with the bureaucracy's proposals, the most active and vocal members opposed compulsory procedures of enactment, though they did anticipate the use of incentives to encourage peasants to participate in the reform process.[75] Such an expression of support for the government's program, although incomplete and temporary, nonetheless seemed to be sufficient to break the stalemate that existed within the government and to give both it and the tsar the confidence necessary to follow through on Goremykin's speech of 13 May. Thus, after more than a decade of bureaucratic politicking and procrastination, the government seemed about to commit itself to a program of agrarian reform.

In the meantime, on 23 May, the *Trudoviki*, the newly formed peasant faction in the Duma, submitted their own "project of the 104" out of disgust with what they considered the weakness of the Kadet proposals. They called for the expropriation of all private, state, and institutional lands above the amount that could be cultivated by personal labor and its transfer into a national fund for distribution to anyone who wished to cultivate it with his own labor, with compensation paid by the state, not the peasantry.[76]

Over the next two weeks, individual members of the Goremykin cabinet began private discussions to determine whether it might be possible to form a coalition cabinet with the Kadets.[77] Then on 5 June, the Duma's debate on the agrarian question, which had focused entirely on the Kadet project, came to an end, and an agrarian commission was formed to work out a project of land reform.[78] On the following day, the Socialist-Revolutionary party introduced its own project, the "project of the 33," which sought to develop the earlier Trudovik project. It called for the total abolition of private landownership, that is, the complete socialization of all land.[79] It is in this context, and in the aftermath of the support expressed by the First Congress of the United Nobility for the government's program,[80] that the Interior Ministry submitted two draft statutes to the Duma. Four days later, on 10 June, the GUZiZ submitted its "Draft Statute on the Improvement and Broadening of Peasant Landownership."[81] Thus did the Gurko and Rittikh commissions present their proposals as the government's official policy and introduce them into the legislative process. More surprisingly, the objections of those few who continued to oppose the elimination of the commune as well as those who opposed direct bureaucratic intervention had finally been overcome.[82]

8

CONSENSUS, COMPROMISE, AND OBSCURITY, JUNE 1906

A small proprietor . . . who knows every part of his little territory, who views it all with the affection which property, especially small property, naturally inspires, and who upon that account takes pleasure not only in cultivating but in adorning it, is generally of all improvers the most industrious, the most intelligent, and the most successful.
—Adam Smith, 1776

First, the commune's common tutelage over its members must be weakened; second, no matter what, the fragmentation of peasant arable land into narrow strips must be abolished.
—S. T. Semenov, peasant writer, 1911

Once the Interior Ministry submitted its two draft statutes and the GUZiZ submitted its statute to the First Duma, the government's agrarian policy entered a new stage. The government's motives for introducing them were complex. On the one hand, it is clear that they were submitted as part of a broader political strategy that sought to establish the terms on which the government might begin to cooperate with the Duma, or at least the moderate parties within it, primarily the Kadets.[1] On the other hand, however, the government was once again beginning to waver, for almost simultaneously it had also taken the first step toward preparing for the Duma's dissolution by obtaining the tsar's preliminary approval for such a measure on 7/8 June. Of course, both Goremykin and the government as a whole had long recognized that it might be necessary to dissolve the Duma if it tried to overthrow the "Fundamental Laws" and violate the sacred right of private property. Yet, it must also be acknowledged that many members of the government were perfectly sincere in their desire for cooperation. Thus, although it offered the Duma a final opportunity to redeem itself, if the bills were rejected the government would be in a position to use such a rejection to justify a subsequent dissolution. Moreover, there were members of the ruling circles who still had to be convinced of the necessity for it.[2]

On the surface, of course, it might seem that there was little hope of approval of the government's bills. Nonetheless, there is some basis for believing that they were in fact submitted in all sincerity. After all, the government's program was a serious and reasonable proposal. Moreover, since the Duma's agrarian commission included people from educated society whose background was not, after all, very different from that of the bureaucrats themselves, it is not unreasonable to assume that they might at least have recognized the program as a genuine attempt to deal with the agrarian problem and thus at least a starting point for further discussion. Indeed, the only issue separating the government's agrarian experts from those of the Kadet party, which now included both Kutler and Kaufman, was their respective positions not on the economic merits of intensification or extensification but on the *principle* of expropriation. Moreover, even on this issue they were not so far apart as it might appear. For although the Kadet party was committed to the principle on political grounds, in fact its expropriation program was quite moderate.[3] On the other hand, although the government's experts rejected the principle, they were nonetheless committed to increasing the quantity of land at the peasants' disposal on a more or less equivalent scale. And within the privacy of the government chancelleries, even expropriation, sometimes disguised within the concept of the state's right of eminent domain, was considered acceptable as long as the goal was intensification rather than simply the relief of land-hunger. In their view, the agrarian problem could not be "solved" simply by giving the peasants land, in whatever manner it was transferred.

It is also important to realize that the two ministries submitting these drafts to the Duma were operating in political circumstances that contrasted sharply with those in the years immediately preceding the Revolution of 1905. Whereas earlier the Finance and Interior ministries had been competing for control over the government's agrarian policy, by 1906 cooperation was more the rule. This is not to say that there were no differences between the drafts submitted by the Interior Ministry and the GUZiZ to the Duma. However, they were simply differences of emphasis between drafts compiled as part of a single agrarian program whose individual components were designed to complement each other.

The Interior Ministry's Draft Statutes

The two draft statutes submitted by the Interior Ministry to the Duma on 6 June 1906 were collectively entitled Draft Statutes on Landed Communities Owning Allotment Lands and Acts on Allotment Lands.[4] The daily press published extracts from their joint explanatory note and the drafts themselves—though after considerable delay and invariably without comment. The public, preoccupied with the more exciting battle between the government and the Duma, paid almost no attention to them.[5]

According to the explanatory note, the intent of the drafts was to reconcile existing legislation with the ukases of 3 November 1905 by defining "allotment land" and then elucidating the law as it would apply to it after the termination of the redemption operation on 1 January 1907. However, in addition to such "regularization," as this procedure was called, Gurko's new commission had to draft a statute that could appeal to the liberal opposition. Thus it also sought to reconcile these laws with the October Manifesto and the Election Statute, both of which had brought the government closer to equalizing the peasants' civil rights with those of other social classes and integrating them into the general sociolegal order. The note also claimed that the government would shortly submit to the Duma a series of bills for the reform of local administration and courts at all levels—on an all-class basis.[6] At last, under pressure of the events that had given rise to the October Manifesto and the establishment of the Duma, the government had apparently placed the abolition of the peasant's *soslovie* status and the *soslovie* system of administration on its public political agenda.

While seeking to develop individual principles of property ownership and use among the peasantry and inculcate a respect for the property rights of others, the Gurko commission also found itself compelled to reach a compromise between its own commitment to change and the traditional opposition to government intervention. The commission therefore rejected the original proposal—adopted in March and strongly supported by Gurko—to eliminate all *soslovie* restrictions on the peasants' rights to their allotment land, particularly their right of disposal. In its current view, such restrictions had to be retained since the state's interest in preserving this category of land in a special and permanent land fund administered by the state for the exclusive use of the peasantry superseded even its interest in protecting the "sacred" principle of private, that is, noble, property. Thus, the commission now proposed prohibiting the sale of individually owned allotment land to nonpeasants except under special and limited circumstances; subjecting rentals and sales of allotment land owned by communities to administrative approval; and prohibiting both the attachment of allotment land by private suit and the holding of mortgages on allotment land by private persons or institutions. The commission also placed limits on the amount of allotment land that could be owned by one person to prevent its concentration in the hands of a wealthy minority of peasants.[7]

Interestingly, the justification for these continued restrictions was a traditional economic argument, which Gurko had previously abandoned in his struggle to defend the principle of private property as an absolute right, and which Rittikh, using the latest evidence from Germany and France, had also rejected. Thus, it was now argued, limitations on the peasants' right to dispose of their allotment land were necessary because "small-scale peasant landownership in Russia is still insufficiently firmly established and still cannot exist independently and develop normally without some state support."[8] Indeed, "left to circulate freely on an equal basis with other private property, small-scale peasant landownership proves short-lived and gradually disappears, yielding its place to landed property of another character."[9] Although the commission thus retained the *soslovie* principle and the bureaucracy's traditional form of *opeka* over the peasantry, it also sought to reconcile them with the general civil law, though without violating either the state interest or the sacred "peculiarities" of peasant life. As a consequence, these restrictions were only to apply to peasants who continued to live and cultivate their land within the commune. Peasants who had physically separated from the commune, on the other hand, could dispose of it freely. In this way, the commission hoped to convince traditionalist critics that the government's program of agrarian reform was, in fact, a gradual and organic one and would not lead to a "fundamental breach" in the peasant way of life.[10]

Despite these attempts to conciliate the bills' liberal *and* conservative opponents within the government and without, the fundamental criterion guiding the commission's deliberations remained that of the state or national interest. And that involved trying to achieve a balance between individual freedom and state control. Thus, although the commission sought to instill a consciousness of private property in the peasantry for both political *and* economic purposes, it simultaneously tried to limit its anarchic consequences by subordinating individual or private interests to the public or "social" interest. Once again, the government was trying to pursue the contradictory task of stimulating the growth of individualism and individual initiative by means of governmental intervention. In the process of searching for that third, Russian, path between capitalism and socialism, the bureaucracy thus had to combine its traditional policy of bureaucratic *opeka* with the sponsorship of a far-reaching agrarian reform that required massive state involvement.

The core of the two bills, however, concerned the right of free exit from the commune. Here again the commission sought to draft its proposals in such a way as to meet the demands of such disparate groups as the Duma liberals and the conservative activists of the United Nobility as well as those who opposed any kind of government-sponsored change. Not surprisingly, the commission regarded the problem of free exit as primarily an economic issue, the ramifications of which the GUZiZ draft submitted to the Duma four days later would tackle. However, the explanatory note did introduce a major innovation: that the allotment land of those peasants who separated from the commune be held not as family or household property but as individual or personal (*lichnoe*) property. Family ownership, it was argued, not only discouraged independence and enterprise, but was an obstacle to successful land organization, since it made decisions dependent, not on the head of the household, but on the entire family. It also hindered the peasant's ability to obtain credit, since loans were not usually given to families but to individuals. Similarly, "the absence of a personal stake (*sobstvennost'*) in allotment holdings hinders the rural population from developing correct views on private property in general." Indeed, the note explained in one of the government's most candid public statements in this period:

The new political order in our fatherland calls for . . . an economic structure resting upon principles of personal and private property and on respect for the property of others. Only by this means will be created everywhere that mass of small and middle proprietors who are loyal to the state order which preserves their vital interests. At the same time, the new political structure, which elevates [the role of] personality in the state, demands that considerable scope be given to the independence and enterprise of individual persons.[11]

On the other hand, the note said, as long as the two existing forms of peasant landownership—communal and individual—existed, no single legislative act could effect any essential changes in them, let alone abolish them. Furthermore, such an act, if undertaken, would not meet with peasant sympathy, but "would even evoke opposition . . . since a fundamental . . . rupture in the existing peasant land system, sanctified as it is by antiquity, would not in many cases accord with local peculiarities or with the current needs of the population." Here was another attempt to appease those who opposed any coercive government intervention—followed immediately by an attempt to appease those who favored granting peasants mobility and civil rights: "even though these forms of land use are inviolable they can in no way be compulsory for individual members of landowning communities. . . ." And there followed a statement that could have been taken directly from the mouth of Nikol'skii or Witte or even from the liberal opposition press:

Therefore, landowning communities must be completely free unions such that every member who does not wish to subordinate himself to the existing form of land use in the community has the full possibility, with the support of law itself, to liquidate his property relations with the community and exit from it at any time.[12]

Free exit, in fact, meant the peasant's ultimate right to remove himself and his land physically from the community. It was thus seen as dependent on the peasant's ability to dispose of his allotment land without economic loss. For those peasants who already owned their land on an individual basis, there was no real obstacle. For those living under the system of communal ownership, however, it was a different story. There the problem was, as we have seen, to determine what proportion of the total allotment was due an individual peasant who wanted to sever his economic ties to the commune. This issue had already occasioned considerable debate, some of it reviewed in the note by way of explanation.[13] It was Gurko's opinion that prevailed now. The bill itself began with the following article on a change he had been the first to propose:

> Communities with communal land use in which there have been no general repartitions of arable fields executed in the course of twenty-four years are considered to have transferred to individualistic (uchastkovoe) forms of land use, and each householder acquires the right of personal property to the arable plots in his permanent [not rental] use.[14]

According to the Interior Ministry's own calculations, this article would transfer to individual ownership about half the peasant communities then owning their land, de jure, on communal principles. Thus, while resolving the question of how to determine the quantity of land due them from the communal allotment at the time of their departure, the article would substantially increase the number of peasants owning land on an individual basis.[15] On the face of it, and certainly on legal grounds, there was no precedent for such an act of legislative arbitrariness and coercion. Yet the Interior Ministry's rationale was pragmatic in the extreme and logically unexceptional in considering that failure to repartition over a twenty-four-year period represented the "silent agreement of a majority" of the heads of family to the community's de facto transfer to individual household possession.[16] This article was not therefore coercive in the formal sense, though its ultimate implications were, to be sure, revolutionary.

Similarly, members of communities that had executed repartitions were also to gain the right of free exit at any time.[17] Again, however, the bureaucracy's concern was to defend itself against the charge of dangerously disrupting rural life:

> There is no need to fear . . . that such a measure will destroy the commune. This can occur only where the commune itself has already decayed . . . [and] a majority of its members have already outgrown this form of land use and are striving to transfer to improved forms of economic management which are impossible under communal land use. On the other hand, the commune cannot be destroyed artificially if communal principles are still firm and vital in the consciousness of [its] members.[18]

Such were the dogmas of the new era.

The division of the process of separation from the commune into two distinct and independent stages was, as we have seen, a direct reflection of the desire to imbue as many peasants as possible with individualistic principles. But it also shows the gradualist and evolutionary approach to land organization that Rittikh and others favored. Ultimately, however, it conformed to the division of labor established between the Interior Ministry—responsible for legal, political, administrative, and legislative aspects of the question—and the GUZiZ—responsible for agriculture, both noble and peasant. At the same time, the Gurko commission's drafts reverted to an older ministerial tradition by treating the important issue of property ownership in the same bill as the much broader issues of the peasant's political and civil rights and the administration of rural life. Thus, for example, they included Witte's pet scheme, also advocated by the liberal opposition: the elimination of almost all forms of *opeka* over the peasantry including the abolition of the land captains and their ubiquitous supervisory powers over the administrative life of the commune, and the transfer of all other functions of local administration to the local land-organization commissions. This was indeed a revolutionary proposal coming from the Interior Ministry's Rural Section, which supervised the land captains.[19] If enacted, it would also have been the government's greatest concession to the liberal opposition since the granting of the October Manifesto. Of course, this did not mean the end of *opeka*. For even as the bills anticipated the abolition of its traditional, largely passive manifestations, the entire effort to bring agrarian reform to the village represented a new and far more pervasive and interventionist form of *opeka*.

Taken together, the two bills represented not only a consensus but also a compromise between the different factions within the bureaucracy and government as well as between them and the political groupings within the larger society. Moreover, the tsar had approved them. Yet, these bills included measures that were not to be enacted for another four years, most notably the twenty-four-year provision. Still others, including the local administrative reforms, were never to be realized at all.[20] In retrospect, of course, it is clear that there was little chance that the Duma would support the proposals. However, this does not diminish the sincerity of the government's efforts to achieve a compromise in this area. At the same time, they represented another stage in the growth of the government's confidence and assertiveness. Moreover, as part of its counterattack the government had also clearly resolved on a radical reform of the existing order—if only to preserve it the better.

What was noteworthy, however, was the total lack of political response to these two bills, which, when introduced some five months later in a simplified and more moderate form, were to be accused of decreeing the abolition of the commune. One must therefore conclude that those later evaluations were the product of the different political mood within the liberal opposition—one that was heavily influenced by the rage of disillusionment that followed first the closing of the Duma and, five months later, the government's unilateral enactment of its own agrarian program. For one cannot truly claim, even for these 6 June bills, that they decreed the legislative abolition of the commune.

The GUZiZ Draft Statute

Four days after the Interior Ministry submitted its bills to the Duma, the GUZiZ submitted its own "Draft Statute on the Improvement and Expansion of Peasant Landownership." It was the work of the Rittikh commission, established by Witte's government in April, and had constituted part of the Nikol'skii Commission's recommendations that the tsar had approved on the eve of the Duma's convocation. Subsequently the Committee on Land-Organization reworked it and the Council of Ministers approved it on 7 June. The final choice of a title was in itself significant, representing the government's two-pronged attack on the agrarian problem: *Improvement* referred to the reformist policy of land reorganization or intensification; *expansion*, to more traditional policies of increasing the area of peasant landownership, or extensification.[21] Thus, like the Gurko commission's bills, this too represented a compromise between the different factions within the government as well as an attempt to appease those groups with which the government felt it might be able to work in the new constitutional political order.

The draft's explanatory note began by declaring that neither policy had been stressed over the other; it was concerned with both the "quantitative and qualitative" improvement of landownership and use. But the ordering of the draft's sections gave the lie to this neutrality. Moreover, the note devoted its opening pages to the now conventional disquisition on the evils of communal land use and pointed out that the peasants were themselves well aware of the obstacles it presented to agricultural improvement. (The bill also noted that communal land use was "a source of misunderstanding between neighbors and under certain conditions serves as a means for the economic exploitation of the weaker neighbors by the stronger.") Somewhat further on, the statute's aim was stated more frankly, and in almost Leninist terms, as encouraging intensification and agricultural development by eliminating "the vestiges (*perezhitki*) of the past," as they were reflected in the open-field system of strip cultivation and existing legislation. In order to achieve such a goal, the draft acknowledged the need for "active state assistance," for even though "a certain initiative" would be demanded of the peasant population, the realization and execution of that initiative would be the responsibility of "government agents." It was they who would actualize the peasants' own will and thus serve as the very midwives of history.[22]

Starting where the Interior Ministry's bills left off, the GUZiZ bill set forth five procedures for the "qualitative" improvement of allotment landownership: (1) the break-up of large and complex communities into small ones on demand of a simple, rather than the existing two-thirds, majority; (2) the separation of land to newly formed villages and parts of villages on demand of no fewer than ten householders or one-fifth of the total number, whichever was smaller; (3) the separation of *otrub* plots for individual peasants at the time of repartition; (4) the conversion of whole villages to *otrub* plots on demand of a two-thirds majority; and (5) the elimination of open fields and common pastures between villages and neighboring private owners on demand of one of the parties.[23] In each of the five procedures, the initiative for change was to come from either of the parties involved. Where the parties reached a voluntary agreement, government agents would act strictly as technical advisers and were specifically forbidden to intervene directly. Where, however, there was no agreement, government agents were to take a more decisive role—in conformity, of course, with the rights, needs, and desires of the parties involved. Specifically, they were to support those peasants whose interests were closest to its own, which, in practice, meant those who were more "progressive," and possibly also more compliant. In either case, however, all surveying was to be executed at government expense.[24]

Equally significant, although the bill established an appeals process that any one of the parties could initiate, that process now became subject to administrative rather than civil procedures as had earlier been proposed, thus opening the process to bureaucratic exploitation. The reason for this decision was, of course, that of speed, particularly in light of the peasants' "factious" and "litigious" nature. At the same time, however, the Rittikh commission was concerned not only to avoid provoking intravillage conflict, but to eliminate whatever conflict did arise during the land reorganization process as rapidly as possible.[25]

Thus, in contrast to the more political focus of the Interior Ministry's bills, the first section of the GUZiZ bill laid the legislative groundwork for the transformation of the existing system of open-field strip cultivation into one that would ultimately be characterized by compact and enclosed plots of land. The process itself was conceived in gradualist, evolutionary, and spontaneous terms and was broken into stages that, at this time, emphasized the partition of large villages into smaller and more rational units. At the same time, the GUZiZ bill sought to achieve the quickest possible elimination of open-field strip cultivation by consolidating individual strips into an *otrub* without involving itself in the far more complex task of resettling peasants on those plots and forming *khutora*. Nonetheless, the bill conceived its task more as a collective process of community development than an individualistic process of community destruction.

The bill's second section took up the question of expanding peasant landownership, and the explanatory note set forth the bureaucratic perspective on this problem, subordinate as it was to the task of improvement. Surprisingly, its position was by no means so completely negative as might have been expected in the wake of the furor over the Migulin-Kutler proposals. Indeed, the very first sentence stated that, in addition to land acquired by the Peasant Land Bank, all state-owned land (with the exception of valuable forest land), as well as any additional land purchased by the state, would be placed at the government's disposal in order to help resolve the agrarian problem. However, the note also pointed out that, although valuable, such measures had only limited worth given "the peasants' acute need for land" and once again categorically rejected expropriation as an adequate solution. Having nonetheless acknowledged the seriousness of peasant land-hunger—seen here as a geographical rather than a social phenomenon—and the necessity of addressing that issue, it also noted that most of the privately owned land available for sale was already being rented to peasants. Unfortunately, it was seldom rented to the neediest so that the truly land-hungry peasant had to seek access to such land through intermediary renters, often at grossly inflated rentals. Even when whole villages or voluntary peasant associations (*tovarishchestva*) rented land, they usually excluded the poorer members. Thus "the actual renters are not those members of a community whose economic condition is especially impaired and merits the special concern of the government, but the strongest, the most substantial elements." In order to put the state's limited supply of land to most effective use, the government would therefore have to limit its availability to those peasants most in need.[26] At the same time, and in conformity to the principles on which the earlier bills had been based, it mandated that such land be sold to the peasantry on private-property principles rather than rented, since renting only encouraged the exploitation of the poor by the rich, furthering the polarization of the population into two groups—the propertied and the propertyless. Similar considerations were to govern the disposal of land by the Peasant Bank. Here, then, was the first stage of the government's attempt to meet the needs of the land-hungry without resorting to expropriation.[27]

A second measure vital to this aspect of the government's program projected an expansion in railroad construction in order to increase accessibility to the vast and underpopulated state-owned forest and taiga zones in the north, northeast, and Siberia. This would accompany a general reform and expansion of migration in conjunction with vastly increased expenditures on material aid by the state. Yet even this measure was insufficient, for the majority of land-hungry peasants were concentrated in the central and southern regions of European Russia where the state owned little land. However, although it might be argued that here, at least, the peasantry's needs could only be met by expropriation, the note proposed instead to rely on the sale of privately owned land to the peasants either directly or through the Peasant Bank.[28]

However, as we have seen, there were many, both within the government and without, who claimed that the Peasant Bank was incapable of administering such a huge program of sales to land-hungry peasants in accordance with the overall goals of the government's agrarian policy. The GUZiZ did not agree with this assessment and set out to dispute the four charges usually leveled against the Bank: (1) the neediest peasants did not have the resources to pay a deposit; (2) the Bank's activities were not coordinated with those of other government departments; (3) they were on too small a scale to have any significant impact; and (4) they provoked rapid increases in land prices and encouraged uncontrolled speculation.[29]

Reviewing the Bank's history since 1882, the explanatory note asserted that over the past decade and a half the Bank had had two major goals: to help expand peasant landownership in general, without any special consideration for the land-hungry; and to encourage the development of small-scale landed property. In practice, however, these goals had been subordinate to the more pragmatic task of serving as an intermediary between the private landowner, who wished to sell his land, and the peasant. However, the ukase of 3 November had changed these circumstances. Now, the Bank could grant loans up to the full value of the land being purchased, thus eliminating the first and most practical objection. Similarly, the Bank's historical independence was about to come to an end, and from this point on its policies would have to conform to the overall goals of the government's agrarian policy.[30]

The problem of the scale of the Bank's activity was more complex. However, in response to this objection, the note now proposed to focus the Bank's primary attention on the *darstvenniki*, who had received an incomplete allotment at Emancipation, and on those peasants who had been forced to abandon agriculture by the rapid growth of population and resulting shortages of land. Indeed, it argued, the Bank could, in fact, acquire the 14 million or so desiatinas of land needed to assuage such land-hunger in the center and the south and distribute it in the course of a mere five-year period.[31]

Finally, the note argued, rising land prices were not a sign of failure but a response to that "whole series of changes in the economic life of the country" that had occurred in the past decade. At the same time, the rise had been exacerbated by the fact that nearly 40 percent of all Bank sales had been to members of the nobility—a circumstance that would have to be eliminated. Nevertheless, the telling point was made that, although the increase in land prices had been excessive, the continued peasant demand for land demonstrated that from their perspective at least agriculture was still a profitable undertaking. Finally, with regard to speculation, the commission hoped it could be brought under control by the local land-organization commissions.[32]

While discussing these ways of dealing with peasant land-hunger, the note emphasized that the government's goals were "not the development of medium-scale landed property of the farmer-type, but putting the already existing small-scale landownership in good order"—thus specifically rejecting the suggestion that its proposals were designed to favor the more well-to-do peasants. At the same time, it excluded from the category of land-hungry those peasants who were so poor that they no longer owned the inventory necessary to conduct their own economies— that is, those landless or virtually landless households that obtained their income primarily from wage labor. This was, of course, at once a forthright recognition of the existing economic situation and a rejection of those utopian attempts to turn the clock back to a supposedly more idyllic period in which every rural inhabitant had cultivated his own plot of land. Even if the government sold land to such peasants, they would be unable to cultivate it. Moreover, they would then have to resell the land, thereby encouraging the three evils of speculation, rising prices, and concentration that the government hoped to eliminate. Furthermore, the inclusion of this category of peasant within a government program to expand peasant landownership would prevent it from helping those needy and equally deserving peasants who were actually conducting their own economies.[33]

On the other hand, even though it excluded the landless wage laborer, the concept of land-hunger was still considered applicable to the entire class of agriculturalists, which was defined to include everyone—peasants, nobles, or town dwellers—who personally conducted his own economy and "whose way of life was indistinguishable from that of the peasantry."[34] This, of course, reflected the bureaucrats' conception of the Empire's population in terms of its economic function, and therefore as consisting of classes rather than *sosloviia*. However, this reconceptualization, which for the agricultural modernizers of the United Nobility was a product of the revolution of 1905, was for the government more the consequence of some forty years of economic development and the cumulative wisdom that reflection upon it had produced. Yet, the inclusion of this provision in this draft represented another advance for the proponents of integration as well as one more basis for a compromise with the Duma.

This new conceptual framework, in effect, divided rural inhabitants into two economic categories: those who owned some land and the necessary inventory—the agriculturalists; and those who owned little or no land and insufficient inventory—the wage laborers or rural proletarians. Yet, even though the GUZiZ bill started with this fact, for reasons that reflected both the political demand for social stability and the traditional supraclass approach embodied in *opeka*, it made every attempt to assure that the balance between these two classes did not alter to the detriment of either, or to that of the state as a whole. At the same time, the bill sought to forestall the development of a class of prosperous landowning peasants. Consequently, much of the rest of the draft was devoted to establishing the means necessary to prevent sudden changes or imbalances in the existing social structure. On such measure, and potentially the most important, was the establishment of limits on the size of peasant holdings—a measure seen as a necessary consequence of the limited supply of land at the government's disposal. Further, since the existing ceilings on purchases of Peasant Bank land were considered too high, the local land-organization commissions were to establish new, lower ceilings.[35]

In contrast to the Gurko commission statutes, the GUZiZ statute extended the *soslovie* limitations on allotment landownership to include land purchased by peasants from the state or from the Peasant Bank; this was in the interest of preventing a "mass transfer of land from persons cultivating it with their own labor to persons conducting an entrepreneurial economy. . . ." Such a provision, it was argued, not only was in the "direct interests of the peasants . . . of private individuals" but, more important, it served the "broad state goal of guaranteeing the laboring agricultural population a stable source of the means necessary for its existence." One final precaution adopted in this, the state's, interest, was to set restrictions on the Bank's ability to recover arrears in payments by making repossession and sale by auction procedures of last resort.[36] In effect, this would have made such payments closer in form to the recently abolished system of redemption payments and subjected their collection to the same procedures as direct state taxes. Here the traditional form of bureaucratic *opeka* continued to reign supreme over laissez-faire principles of individual freedom—with all the familiar implications. Here, too, were reiterated the same concerns enunciated by Witte and Pleve, Westerners and Slavophiles, Marxists and Populists: to follow the Western path of economic development and, by learning from the West's experience, to avoid both political and social revolution.

The third and final section of the GUZiZ bill spelled out the responsibilities of the local land-organization commissions charged with executing the government's program. What was most notable in this section was the very significant expansion of their responsibilities, even prior to the formation of the first commission. In effect, this bill restored those functions that had originally been proposed by the Krivoshein commission back in February. At the same time, it placed increased emphasis on the professionalism, skill, and technical training of the local executors of reform. Indeed, the tasks facing the land-organization commissions were perceived to be of such importance and complexity in their juridical, economic, and political aspects that it was considered essential for all members of the county level commissions to be freed from all other official duties so that they could devote themselves exclusively to its affairs. It was also considered desirable that some members have higher legal or agronomical training. However, because of the costs involved and the absence of a trained pool of potential applicants, these qualifications were only recommended.[37]

Such, then, was the government's agrarian program. In part, as we have seen, the political exigencies of the government's relationship with the Duma and the peasants had dictated it. However, it also came about as a consequence of internal pressures exerted by those bureaucrats who were most vociferous in the defense of the existing system of private-property ownership and who succeeded in exploiting the political power of the United Nobility's First Congress to demonstrate the existence of real and significant social support for their arguments. Finally, of course, this consensus was also the product of those longer-term economic realities with which the bureaucracy had been grappling for decades. All of these strands can be identified in the bills examined previously.

The bills of the two ministries did differ in one significant respect. Gurko succeeded in incorporating into the Interior Ministry's bills his proposal to transfer to individual household ownership all peasant communities that had not executed general repartitions within the preceding twenty-four years by legislative fiat. The GUZiZ bill adopted the less radical, more spontaneous and evolutionary approach shared by Rittikh and his coworkers that emphasized agrotechnical improvements and community development over *khutorizatsiia* and the complete social—and therefore political—atomization of the peasantry. On the other hand, the radical proposal to abolish the *soslovie* character of peasant landownership, which both Gurko and Rittikh had supported, was now rejected in favor of preserving some of the more traditional forms of bureaucratic *opeka*, in conjunction with its new, more interventionist form—all in the state interest. Finally, these measures, all of which focused on transforming the peasantry into individual property owners and intensifying their agriculture, were combined with a moderate policy of extensification designed to aid those land-hungry peasants and others in the countryside whose holdings were their primary source of livelihood.

Conclusions

One cannot say that the government's program, submitted to the First Duma at this particular juncture, made any truly significant concessions to that revolutionary-minded institution. On the contrary, as we have demonstrated, the basic outlines of the government's policy had been determined many years before. It is nonetheless true that the recent modifications in it, intended to avoid the presumed evils of instantaneous modernization—to avoid, indeed, the upheaval for which the reforms, as finally enacted, were to be held responsible—were designed in part to appeal to those political groups that opposed "abrupt changes in the peasant way of life."[38]

Meanwhile, after the submission of these bills to the Duma, negotiations between the government's more liberal or conciliatory ministers and the Kadets and Octobrists continued. However, in the face of growing rumors of a reconciliation with the Duma, the United Nobility's leaders sought audiences first with Stolypin and then with Goremykin to prevent the government from making any concessions and to argue for the dissolution of the Duma. The government responded by issuing a report on the agrarian question on 19 June that, in language strongly reminiscent of Gurko's, once again decisively rejected expropriation as an alternative.[39]

In this report, Goremykin tried both to reconcile the various aspects of the government's policy and to demonstrate its political good faith. But the report was also intended as a final challenge to the now virtually defunct Duma as well as a propaganda stroke designed to win the peasantry away from the Socialist-Revolutionary party and the independent Trudoviki and convince them of the government's sincere efforts to solve the agrarian question. The government's program, thus presented, appeared not simply as a plausible alternative to the more radical bills before the Duma; rather, it appealed directly to the peasantry as an economic class, though one made up of different categories with different needs. Nor was the inclusion of measures for the expansion of peasant landownership merely a response to purely demagogic and immediately political concerns—though these of course existed. On the contrary, there was strong support within the government for just such measures based on more dispassionate, economic grounds.[40] In this respect, the government's program represented a compromise within its own ranks between the polarized alternatives of expropriation and inviolability and their supporters. Nonetheless, these same issues continued to be a source of conflict within the government even after the 19 June report, even after the Duma's dissolution on 9 July and the victory of those such as Shvanebakh, Shirinskii-Shikhmatov, and Gurko who opposed concessions on political grounds, and even after the dismissal of Stishinskii, Shirinskii-Shikhmatov, and Goremykin.[41]

It is evident, then, that, on the one hand, a consensus had been reached on an agrarian policy that combined intensification with an extensification that stopped short of expropriation—a consensus that even Gurko shared. On the other hand, the political circumstances continued to foster a polarized view of the agrarian problem in terms of "concessions" or "no concessions" such that a government-sponsored policy of expropriation continued to appear attractive to some members of the bureaucracy on political grounds.

PART FOUR
The New Agrarian Policy

The fact is that the peasant *can* be an innovator, and there is ample evidence that through underpropitious circumstances he has become one, even if not on a large scale. . . . But to enlarge these pockets [of innovation] so as to encompass a country's entire agriculture, initiative, enthusiasm, and above all appropriate resource allocations must be provided by planners, economists, and national governments to a degree comparable to that accorded to industrialization. . . . Hence . . . the existing imbalance in the treatment of industry and agriculture must be redressed so that industry *and* agriculture may constitute, as indeed they must, the base upon which an effective national economy must rest.
—W. Ladejinsky, 1964

[The ukase of 9 November] is only one of the links in a broadly conceived plan directed to raising the productivity of the countryside and improving the welfare of the peasant, a plan, consistently and persistently being realized by the government.
—A. I. Lykoshin, 1910

9

THE INTER-DUMA PERIOD AND STOLYPIN, JULY-AUGUST 1906

Consolidation of an Agrarian Policy

These questions can only be resolved appropriately if you yourself stand at the head of the matter and surround yourself with people selected for this [purpose]. If your grandfather, Emperor Alexander II, had not acted so in the business of the peasants' emancipation, then we would have retained serfdom until the present day.

—S. Iu. Witte, 1902

Land reorganization . . . is the necessary basis for the improvement of the peasant way of life and the improvement of agriculture which is, perhaps justly, cited as the axis of the government's entire domestic policy.

—P. A. Stolypin, 1907

P.A. Stolypin's appointment as prime minister on 9 July 1906 is usually seen as a decisive turning point in the development of the government's agrarian policy. In consequence, the period between his appointment and the enactment of the ukase of 9 November 1906 on the individualization of peasant landownership and land use has received little attention. Hence, this decree and the others with which it became associated have become known collectively as the *Stolypin Reforms*. Yet a change in the government's first minister—who described himself as a newcomer to the capital[1]—was hardly likely to have had any major impact on all the political, social, and economic forces determining the content of the government's agrarian policy. Indeed, it seems very probable that even if Stolypin had not become prime minister, the government would have adopted more or less the same program of agrarian reform. On the other hand, Stolypin's social and political background do seem to have facilitated its passage though it is also important to note that this was the only part of the government's larger program of reform to be so enacted and to win the approval of both legislative houses.

The dissolution of the First Duma was due in large measure to its support for a program of compulsory expropriation that seemed to the

government to be the embodiment of agrarian socialism. However, although its dissolution was a symbolic and decisive act, it was only finally
decided at the last minute. Even then, rumor had it that soon after he
entrusted the decree to Goremykin, the tsar had misgivings and sought
to postpone its implementation.[2] Certainly, members of his entourage
had feared such a change of mind. On the other hand, during the Duma's
last days and for some time after its closing, Stolypin revived and continued negotiations with representatives of the political parties to form a
coalition cabinet.[3] The willingness of both Stolypin and the tsar to
entertain some form of "compulsory expropriation" as part of the government's agrarian program reflected the government's spirit of compromise.[4] Another indication was the removal of two of the most right-
wing members of the cabinet—Stishinskii, the head of the GUZiZ, and
Shirinskii-Shikhmatov, the Ober-Prokuror of the Holy Synod. Of still
greater moment, the former post—a crucial one for the government's
future agrarian policy—remained vacant until 27 July, a total of nearly
three weeks, until Prince B. A. Vasil'chikov finally received an appointment to that position.[5]

In time, it became clear that the closing of the First Duma had failed
to galvanize the population into a new *Pugachevshchina* as so many had
feared.[6] This led not only to the complete discrediting of Trepov, who
had been the most powerful proponent of the conciliatory approach to
the Duma, but also to the breakdown of negotiations to form a coalition
cabinet.[7] However, as the political atmosphere cooled, a more dispassionate consideration of government policy became possible. From late July
and early August, one can observe the growth of a new kind of bureaucratic and governmental self-confidence as Stolypin began constructing
a comprehensive program of reform well before the new Duma was due
to meet on 20 February 1907.

In the critical arena of agrarian reform, this newfound confidence first
manifested itself when Stolypin pushed through a series of measures by
means of the notorious Article 87, culminating with the ukases of 9 and
15 November 1906.[8] Indeed, it was on the basis of these extraordinary
measures to preempt all alternative solutions to the agrarian problem—
and on the policy that prevailed—that Stolypin was to earn much of his
reputation. At last, "the abolition of the commune" was law. This was
the government's last gamble to win over to its side the peasantry—all
of the peasantry.

P. A. Stolypin and Prince B. A. Vasil'chikov

Stolypin is known for his calmness, strength, and self-confidence, even
in the face of great personal danger, and for his early adherence to an
agrarian policy that was hostile to the commune and favored intensifi-

cation on the model already developed by Witte, Rittikh, Gurko, and Krivoshein. (His ideas were closest to Rittikh's and Krivoshein's.) A member of the new generation of bureaucrats, he was born into a noble family in 1862 and owned a number of properties, none of great size, in five provinces.[9] He received his education at St. Petersburg University, where he studied in the Faculty of Natural Sciences. After the award of his degree in 1885, he entered the Statistical Section of the Ministry of State Domains and two years later became county marshal of the nobility in Kovno County, Kovno Province.[10] Ten years later, he was the provincial marshal of the nobility in that province, holding that post until his appointment as governor of the neighboring province of Grodno in 1902. Subsequently, he became governor of Saratov, where he remained until his transfer to St. Petersburg in 1906.

During his fifteen years in local office in the western borderlands, Stolypin, by all accounts, not only executed his responsibilities faithfully, but also demonstrated a deep interest and involvement in rural life and a distinct zeal for the improvement of both peasant and noble agriculture. One such project frequently recalled was the organization of an agricultural society and the opening of a retail outlet for improved agricultural implements and supplies. At the same time, he was deeply interested in the management of his own estates.[11]

It was on this basis that Stolypin subsequently claimed for himself the title of "social activist" (obshchestvennyi deiatel') rather than government official (chinovnik).[12] To the extent that this description is an accurate one, Stolypin symbolized that unification of government and society that had contributed to the development of the perceptual revolution and, ultimately, to the adoption of an agrarian reform based on its new vision of rural society. Moreover, Stolypin's appointments as governor, first in Grodno, and then in Saratov, had been made by Pleve as part of his policy of drawing into government new men from the provincial landowning classes.[13] Despite his long years in the provinces, Stolypin was, nonetheless, well connected at court through his wife, who was the sister of A. B. Neidgardt. In addition to being a member of the court, Neidgardt was a member of the United Nobility from Nizhni-Novgorod Province and an elected member of the State Council.[14]

In direct response to these experiences Stolypin reached his own conclusions about the agrarian and political problems facing Russia and the solutions they required. While in Grodno, he had chaired the local committee called into existence by Witte's Special Conference. And even as he followed Pleve's instructions to depoliticize these committees, he declared himself an opponent of open-field land use and a supporter of khutorizatsiia in conjunction with the development of such fundamental extension services as petty credit and agricultural education.[15] Even then Stolypin had seen the relationship between these issues and Russia's political fate. Thus, comparing Russia to Germany, he commented that there would be no socialist revolution in Germany because it had a widely developed network for the dissemination of agricultural knowledge—a system that he saw as the basis of a secure and conservative agricultural class. At the same time he noted that the formation of a landless proletariat was a particular danger to be avoided.[16] And lest this be thought to be mere theory to Stolypin, one has only to recall that he was an avid observer of German peasant farmers, or *khutoriane*, during his yearly trips through Prussia when he visited one of his Kovno properties on the German border.[17]

In setting forth his views before the Grodno committee, Stolypin was especially outspoken, locating the root of the economic—and ultimately the political—problem in the system of open-field strip cultivation. In these western regions, moreover, the problem was further complicated by the custom of *servituti* that gave peasants gleaning and grazing rights on noble properties after the harvest in addition to water rights. To eliminate these twin evils, he proposed that the government enact its own program of reform that would gradually achieve this goal.[18]

Stolypin repeated and elaborated upon his Grodno observations during his governorship in Saratov, where he confronted for the first time not only the institution of communal landownership but also the urban and rural revolutionary components of the broader political equation. His annual report to the tsar for 1904, which was submitted in early 1905 at the start of the political crisis, carefully drew the link between economics and politics. As Stolypin noted, communal landownership was the fundamental obstacle to the enrichment and improvement of the peasant population and its way of life. It was also the principal cause of that dependence and the paralysis of personal initiative that were almost universally evident. In contrast, individual property ownership, which was its natural opposite, "serves as the guarantee of order, since the small-scale proprietor is that unit on which the stability of the state is built."[19] Then, addressing the problem of class differentiation within the peasantry, he added, "at the present time the more powerful peasant is usually turned into a kulak, an exploiter of his fellow villagers." The solution, however, was not to increase the quantity of land available for renting, as was often proposed, since that only exacerbated social tensions:

If another outlet were given to the energy and the initiative of the best forces of the countryside, and if the possibility were given to the work-loving slave of the land to receive—at first temporarily as a kind of trial, and then to claim for himself—an individual parcel of land cut-off from the lands of the state or the Peasant Bank . . . then, side by side with the commune, where it was still vital, would appear an independent and prosperous peasant, a stable representative of the land.[20]

In effect, he was proposing to set the opposing forms of land use in competition with one another, much as those who had drafted the emancipation had once envisaged, in the conviction that individualistic forms would ultimately triumph by the force of example. Moreover, his proposals already combined the three elements of reform—individualization, intensification, and extensification, with the aide of state and Peasant Bank land—that he would eventually be instrumental in enacting. To this extent, Stolypin's ideas in 1905 foreshadowed the compromise agrarian policy that we saw worked out under Witte and that became the government's policy under Goremykin. Indeed, more often than not, as we have seen, compromise was what usually resulted from the tsarist government's decision-making process as it tried to reconcile conflicting social interests in accordance with its traditional supraclass perspectives.

One year later, and after much first-hand experience with the problem of peasant revolution and its suppression in one of Russia's most revolutionary provinces, Stolypin had this to say in an 11 January 1906 report to Interior Minister Durnovo written in direct response to a request to every governor for information on the causes of local peasant disturbances—a request that was motivated by a desire to refute those who blamed such unrest exclusively on land-hunger:

> The root solution to the problem [of political unrest] will consist in the creation of a class of property owners, that basic cell of the state, who are by their own nature the organic opponents of all destructive theories. . . . Without abolishing by force that commune to which the people are accustomed, everything possible should be done to further individual transactions with the aid of the Peasant Bank, to allow allotment land to be sold and mortgaged and to help such small-scale landowners with credit. Then the most able of the peasants would be changed from kulaks and extortionists into advanced workers. The commune is now corrupted and terrorized by the depraved youth and such a commune is hardly made richer by the inexpensive acquisition of surplus land.[21]

As for the question of causes, Stolypin agreed with most other governors that revolutionary propaganda was the immediate cause of rural disorder. Yet, although eight governors saw land-hunger as a contributing factor, Stolypin joined the majority of ten who saw no relationship between the disorders and land-hunger—an analysis based on the frequent observation that those peasants who owned land were often more active in disturbances than those who did not.[22]

As Durnovo's 29 January 1906 report to the tsar summarizing these opinions pointed out, the governor of Saratov saw the general level of rural poverty as the root cause of unrest.[23] Meanwhile, Stolypin's ideas on a possible solution had evolved since his last report. He no longer believed that an expansion of Peasant Bank sales, even if on the basis of individual ownership, could, of itself, solve the problem. It was, however, a "necessary palliative" that would give the government a much needed respite.[24] Once again, we see Stolypin taking a pragmatic position that was a compromise between extremes.

Thus it is clear that, long before his arrival in St. Petersburg, Stolypin had been a convinced partisan of individual forms of landownership and use who saw in their expansion the ultimate solution to Russia's economic and political crisis. At the same time, he showed himself to be a strong executive, experienced in agricultural and local life, who, having acquitted himself well as a provincial administrator, had also acquired an appreciation of the power of compromise, propaganda, and action.

Stolypin's apparently unsought rise to power, beginning with his appointment as interior minister on 25 April 1906, had no relation to his views on agriculture and rural reform. It was rather the result of his personal qualities, particularly his insistence on governmental strength and decisiveness and his ability to exploit the propaganda value of a given situation to best advantage—what one writer referred to as his love of "both the phrase and the pose."[25] His words before the provincial committee on the needs of agriculture in Grodno already contained a hint of this. Indeed, Nicholas had been acquainted with Stolypin's administrative accomplishments for some time. In his March 1905 report to the tsar, Ermolov had praised Stolypin's activities in suppressing disorders.[26] This was followed by a laudatory report submitted by Trepov about Stolypin's activities in Saratov during the summer of 1905 and his role in the famous "Balashov incident." Apparently Stolypin had entered a rebellious village in Balashov County alone and unarmed and succeeded in quelling the revolt by his mere presence and his complete fearlessness before the armed peasants.[27] Then, in October 1905, Prince Obolenskii, Ober-Prokuror of the Holy Synod and a friend of Witte, proposed Stolypin for the post of interior minister in Witte's cabinet on the basis of Obolenskii's own presence in Saratov at a similar incident.[28]

In the same vein, Durnovo's report to the tsar had focused primarily on Stolypin's attitudes toward government, noting that Stolypin had proposed the "consolidation of authority by way of a steadfast and undeviating governmental policy," and only secondarily on his proposals for "a radical reform of peasant land organization."[29] The tsar saw Durnovo's report on 4 February. In his own report to Durnovo, Stolypin had waxed eloquent on the inefficiencies and weaknesses of the local administration and its failure to act as a bulwark against revolution. In his view this was, in part, a result of the political confusion that had followed the sudden appearance of the October Manifesto. The ensuing highly charged atmosphere had persuaded both police officers and land captains that everything was permissible, leading to a de facto abolition of local authority as these officials fled the scene. Meanwhile, the appearance in the Petersburg chancelleries of a *chinovnik* "movement" that began to present its own demands and even threatened to strike had exacerbated this loss of local control.[30] Only overcoming this crisis of confidence and eliminating its weakness and confusion, Stolypin wrote, could restore order.[31]

Clearly, Stolypin stood out among Russia's provincial governors as a supporter of authoritative government and of private property. It is not, therefore, particularly surprising that the tsar should turn to him to fill the position of interior minister when he finally lost trust in the old guard at the center. Paradoxically, it was none other than Goremykin who proposed Stolypin for the job.[32] Such, then, were the circumstances surrounding Stolypin's rapid elevation from governor to interior minister in a little more than three years and from interior minister to prime minister in a little less than three months. More important for the cause of agrarian reform, the tsar had found in Stolypin his counterpart to Alexander II's Rostovtsev.

In light of the October Revolution, a legend of almost mythical proportions has grown up around Stolypin in which he is seen as tsarist Russia's savior and last hope.[33] Part of this legend would have us believe that Stolypin had a comprehensive program of reform designed to bring Russia into the twentieth century.[34] To what extent, however, did Stolypin himself have such a program? It has already been noted that his opinions on rural reform were not original and were already held by the bureaucracy as a whole at the time of his appointment. (Indeed, on more than one occasion, and even after 9 July, Gurko had cause to suggest that Stolypin was less than a wholehearted supporter of the Gurko/Rittikh program with which his name became associated.[35]) On the basis of the evidence, the answer to this question must be that he did not, in fact, have a program of his own. In the realm of agrarian reform as well as in the realms of civil and political rights and administrative and court reform, the so-called Stolypin program had already been drawn up and in some cases even turned into draft laws while Witte was still premier.[36] Yet although Stolypin may have to be denied the title of innovator, one has nonetheless to recognize his strenuous efforts in getting that program adopted, for, as we shall see, it was he who successfully fused the entire program with a political philosophy that was sufficiently persuasive to a significant portion of government and society for a long enough time to win legislative approval for its agrarian section. Of course, this was in part a formality since by that time the government had been busily implementing the reform for some four years.[37]

A second question is considerably more complex: What were Stolypin's relations with the United Nobility? How did they affect the situation? Here, it is clear that the very same socioeconomic and political forces that had sent noble landowners from the Volga region into the national political arena during the First Congress of the United Nobility had also raised Stolypin to national office. Moreover, as governor in Saratov he was in close contact with the local nobility during the troubled period prior to the convocation of the First Duma and was highly appreciated for his spectacular success in suppressing revolution. Of special significance were his contacts with Counts D. A. Olsuf'ev and A. A. Uvarov, both among the founders of the United Nobility and both members of its minority, which had called for government measures to deal with land-hunger—though short of expropriation—and for a gradual abolition of the commune.[38]

Beyond noting Stolypin's links to the Saratov nobility and the First Congress of the United Nobility—as well as his connections with the new bureaucratic generation—it would be wrong to conclude that the United Nobility was the determining force behind government policy. Rather, they were only one of many forces—though an important one—influencing government decisions. On the other hand, Stolypin's ties with that organization undoubtedly enhanced his image within the conservative circles around the tsar and thus his ability to defend the bureaucratic program of reform. In this way, both Stolypin and the United Nobility gained power from their association.

On 9 July 1906, in the Manifesto accompanying the closing of the Duma, the tsar had expressed the government's program in terms of his inexorable will. It called for order and calm first, then reform, stressing an improvement in peasant welfare. In recognition of economic and political necessities, it proclaimed that "where the land is overcrowded the Russian plowman will receive legal and fair means to extend his holdings without damage to the property of others." The tsar also called on the members of other *sosloviia*, by which he meant primarily the nobility, to aid in "this great task."[39] For the first time, the tsar had recognized publicly the peasants' need for land. Moreover, even though the proposed measures fell far short of compulsory expropriation, this was a political point of no small importance to Nicholas since he sought to maintain respect and loyalty in part through consistency.

The rest of July and part of August passed primarily in political negotiations between the government and representatives of the middle-of-the-road political parties aimed at creating a coalition cabinet. Discussions broke down, however, as a result of the intransigence of both parties.[40] Nonetheless, it was during this period that both the tsar and Stolypin are recorded as having acknowledged the political necessity of at least some form of expropriation, the former in a meeting with members of the imperial family, the latter in a conversation with the chairman of the United Nobility, Count Bobrinskii.[41] Meanwhile, on 15 July, *Novoe Vremia* recorded a rumor leaked from the GUZiZ that the project submitted to the Duma in June was likely to be subjected to a radical revision, if not complete withdrawal, and that the Kutler project would be submitted in its place.[42]

Despite the significance of such concessions to the political moderates, Stolypin's willingness to consider a partial expropriation of noble lands, with compensation, was not a deviation from the government's agrarian program as sketched out by the Nikol'skii Commission and approved by the tsar. Indeed, as we have seen, government policy had never been only a simple choice between abolishing the commune or resorting to compulsory expropriation. On the contrary, since the rejection of the Kutler project in early January 1906, it had been committed to a compromise program that would combine both intensification and extensification in some form.

Rather, Stolypin's motivation was a desire to win over the moderate opposition. Thus, one should not take his comment to Count Bobrinskii about expropriation completely at face value. According to A. I. Guchkov, the chairman of the Octobrist party, the agrarian program Stolypin presented to him and Prince N. N. L'vov during their discussions was in two parts. The first and more important was "the replacement of communal by individual peasant landownership." As Guchkov noted, Stolypin

> attached enormous importance to the spread of small-scale and middling peasant property in Russia, but his reform plans went further. Once a class of sturdy [*krepkie*, in the sense of stable and enduring but not necessarily prosperous] peasant-proprietors had been created, he proposed then to give them access to culture and independence by the introduction of the canton zemstvo, a vigorous expansion of the school network, the development of meliorative credit, etc.

The second part stressed an overall expansion of peasant landownership. In Stolypin's words,

> There is no limit to the aid and privileges which I am ready to grant to the peasantry in order to lead it on to the path of cultural development. I want to contribute in every possible way to an increase in peasant landownership, and in this respect I agree with the Kadets. I only deny a *large-scale compulsory* [emphasis added] expropriation of privately-owned lands.[43]

In Guchkov's eyes, Stolypin's approach to the whole problem was not simply one that sought to defend the narrow class interests of the noble landowners, despite the fact that Stolypin was himself a member of that class. Rather, he approached it from the perspective of the general interest of the state—just such a supraclass position as had been taken before him by Witte. Witte, of course, had paid dearly for this, as would Stolypin.

Stolypin's theory of agrarian reform was that of the "stake in society"; his goal, an increase in Russia's national strength and international prestige. However, as Guchkov noted, in the process of achieving these goals, Stolypin "understood that the interests of the nobility could suffer from this—but he said 'Let the nobles reorganize their own economic affairs. That is their business.' "[44] This remark, with its slightly hostile attitude toward those nobles who were not directly involved in the economic exploitation of their estates, was, in fact, characteristic of Stolypin. The same attitude was typical of others, too, such as N. A. Pavlov, the Saratov landowner and propagandist for the intensification of noble agriculture, and that active minority that had been behind the First Congress of the United Nobility, as well as bureaucrats such as Rittikh, Krivoshein, and even Gurko. Indeed, the rapid eclipse of that minority of agriculturalist-modernizers in later congresses, as well as the failure of Pavlov's scheme for an organization of landed proprietors based strictly on class principles, prefigured the later troubles that would beset Stolypin himself within the bureaucracy, in court circles, and with the United Nobility.

Then, on 20 July, in the midst of Stolypin's negotiations with the Octobrists, the United Nobility once again intervened in an effort to prevent any changes in the cabinet, to reiterate its opposition to expropriation, and to voice its support for the Gurko project.[45] As a result of this, as well as the difficulties of reaching an agreement with Guchkov and L'vov, negotiations to form a coalition cabinet once again stopped. Nevertheless, Stolypin did not completely abandon his attempts to reach some kind of agreement with the center parties; for shortly thereafter, on 27 July 1906, Prince B. A. Vasil'chikov became the new head of the GUZiZ—an appointment that was designed to leave at least some room for compromise.

An extremely wealthy noble landowner, Prince Vasil'chikov had a career remarkably similar to Stolypin's.[46] Born in 1863, a graduate of the Imperial School of Jurisprudence in St. Petersburg, Vasil'chikov had entered the Ministry of Justice in 1881. Three years later, however, he moved back to his home province of Novgorod, where he was elected county marshal and, in 1890, provincial marshal of the nobility. Serving there for ten years, he became governor of neighboring Pskov from 1899 to 1904 and then worked with the Red Cross. He was also a member of the United Nobility. He owned property in Kovno Province and like so many others involved in agrarian reform during these years had become familiar with the western borderlands, where communal landownership was all but nonexistent. His extended residence in the northwest undoubtedly also familiarized him with that spontaneous evolution from communal to individual forms of ownership that was already beginning there.[47] Already in his 1900 report to the tsar as governor of Pskov, he had expressed his opposition to the commune.[48] Like Gurko and other noble modernizers, he valued a diversified agricultural economy, composed of landed property on every scale, from large to small.[49] In this respect, of course, his views were also very close to those held within the GUZiZ and by its former head, A. S. Ermolov.

What is most remarkable about his appointment, however, is not simply that his views on the agrarian question were very similar to those of Stolypin and others in the bureaucracy. It is rather that in addition to favoring the extension of private property principles to the peasantry, he supported an increase in their landownership through a program of voluntary purchases that would also protect noble interests.[50]

Thus like so many who had preceded him into office, Vasil'chikov considered the government's agrarian policy since the Emancipation not only completely misguided, but also the very cause of the problems now facing the country. Yet he, too, rejected the idea that change could result from "a single stroke of the pen." What was needed was "a period of systematic legislative activity . . . [to provide] laws . . . not only in order to regulate landed relations directly but also to create finally in *Rus'* a truly free and creditworthy citizen-agriculturalist with the ability to work." One way to help achieve this goal was to accelerate the transfer of land to the peasantry so that "every householder-agriculturalist could have the possibility of extracting from his industry the means of his own subsistence and that of his family by conducting a rational economy on his holding."[51] However, he was critical of the GUZiZ draft statute, which had been submitted to the Duma, for having granted too much power to the local land-organization commissions. In his view, this was an encroachment on peasant rights that was totally without legal precedent.[52] These objections augured future conflict with his superior, Stolypin.[53]

Meanwhile, Vasil'chikov saw the government's immediate task as one of setting its agrarian policy on the correct course so as to eliminate the possibility of further agrarian disorders. The key to this new policy was in his view a more rational organization of peasant landownership. And although he saw land-hunger as only one of the causes of peasant unrest, he believed additional land should become available to those peasants who had suffered most at the hands of the Emancipation settlement. Such provisions were, however, no substitute for the adoption of a broad program of land reorganization in conjunction with a reform of migration policy.[54]

Like Stolypin, Vasil'chikov was a political appointee. Consequently, he too made no substantive contribution to the shape of the government's agrarian policy beyond acting as a spokesman for it. Nonetheless, during his less than two years in office, he was able to identify one of the key weaknesses that would beset the implementation of the government's program, namely, insufficient financial resources. For even though the GUZiZ would undertake the main work of agrarian reform, its success would ultimately depend on the Finance Ministry, whose ministers had not, in his view, been especially generous in the past. Sheer short-sightedness, he suggested, and as Gurko also later suggested, kept the Finance Ministry from seeing that an investment in agrarian reform would eventually eliminate those huge and unpredictable expenditures incurred by the provision of emergency food supplies during times of crop failure.[55]

The Government Takes the Initiative: Article 87 and Agrarian Reform

The first major move by the new government was to use the extralegislative provisions of Article 87 to establish the—infamous—"field courts-martial," those roving military tribunals that were dispatched into provincial Russia as part of the government's policy of "repression." This step demonstrated the government's—and the tsar's—newly found confidence. Indeed, in this respect, Nicholas wrote to Stolypin on 14 August expressing his conviction that only "exceptional laws" could convincingly demonstrate government decisiveness.[56] Stolypin felt the same way about agrarian reform, and he hoped that a similar approach in this area would effectively preempt the political parties of the left, win back the peasantry into the tsarist camp, calm public opinion, and, as a result, produce a more moderate Duma. The attack on Stolypin and his family at his home on 12 August 1906—an attack that ironically could not have been better timed to bolster his political program by bestowing on him a mystical aura of invincibility—further galvanized this strength and purposefulness.[57]

Stolypin spelled out his joint policy of repression *and* reform in two government reports on 15 August and on 24 August. The second but more politically important of these dealt with the establishment of the field courts-martial and sought to relate them to the government's future plans for reform. Here Stolypin elaborated on the government's new, "centrist" approach—one that would become institutionalized in the legislative and political systems established by the "coup d'état" of 3 June 1907 dissolving the Second Duma and introducing a new and more conservative electoral law. Rejecting the policy of vacillation that had characterized the preceding months, Stolypin set forth the principle of "meeting force with force" as the only way for the government to retain its identity and justify its existence as a state. However, the new policy focused not so much on specific acts of rebellion against the government, whether agrarian disorders or urban strikes, as at the "villainous" agitation that fomented them.[58] To be sure, such outbreaks met armed force. But the government's primary concern was bringing the propagandists, the instigators, those who sought to prevent it from following its appointed path, to justice by "legal means."[59]

In establishing the field courts-martial as a means of restoring order, the government did not, however, confuse the means with the ends. In Stolypin's view, the government's true raison d'être lay not in self-protection, but in positive productive activity to eliminate the causes of existing problems.[60] Referring indirectly to the tsar's meeting with the Council of Ministers in early August in which everyone except the tsar and Stolypin had called for the establishment of a dictatorship,[61] Stolypin confronted the issue of repression versus reform head on. His report categorically rejected both the reactionary position, which urged postponement of all reform until law and order had been restored, and the liberal position, which urged immediate reforms on the assumption that "illegalities" would disappear of their own accord as a consequence of reform. This latter position was rejected on the grounds that the "revolution" could not be spirited away by reform since what it wanted was not reform but the "destruction" of the existing order. And once again the conflict was portrayed in polarized terms, only this time as a struggle between "monarchism" and "socialism."[62]

By rejecting the extremes, the government had perforce to occupy a centrist position and to follow a policy that could command the widest possible governmental and public support. Repression and reform were, therefore, to be pursued simultaneously, with "reform" directed toward the creation of a new order based on legality and freedom.

These August reports also sketched out the positive aspects of the reform program that Stolypin was to attempt to follow over the course of his five years as prime minister. The report of 15 August dealt exclusively with the Imperial Command of 12 August on the sale of the royal family's (*Udel*) lands to the state and discussed the political significance of "expanding peasant landownership." The 24 August report took up the question of all the other rural reforms currently in preparation. They were divided into two categories: those to be submitted for consideration by the State Duma and State Council and those that "because of their great urgency must be enacted immediately." At the same time, in order to conciliate the liberal opposition, he claimed that any "partial solutions" that the government might adopt, which would in any case only involve problems already discussed by one of the tsar's manifestos, "would not restrict the freedom of future legislative bodies or of those [reforms] whose direction is already predetermined. Among these tasks, the problems of land and land organization have priority." The report went on to summarize the initiatives the government had already taken to expand peasant landownership. It then proposed a number of other measures, including the establishment of civil equality and inviolability of person, freedom of religion, universal education, and reforms of local administration and courts. Third on the list after civil and religious rights was "the improvement of peasant landownership"—the government's alternative to expropriation.[63]

The decree on *Udel* lands was in fact the first of a series of laws designed to make land available for the land-hungry peasantry.[64] When the tsar first proposed this measure at a meeting with some of the members of his family on 30 July, he made it clear that the political situation and the agrarian movement had required the government to take the initiative in providing additional lands for the peasantry. Such land would have to come not only from the state and from the tsar's personal holdings (*kabinet*), but also from the sale of 1.8 million desiatinas of the Imperial family's land, currently being rented to peasants. At this meeting the issue remained undecided.[65] The tsar raised the subject again with his family on 9 August, this time with the participation of Stolypin, Kokovtsov, Prince Vasil'chikov, Prince Kochubei, and Baron Frederiks, the minister of the imperial court. On this occasion, despite objections, the tsar won approval for the measure.[66] Such was the first definitive, though largely symbolic, step toward a government solution to the agrarian problem.

This was followed on 27 August 1906 by a ukase making state lands that were currently rented to peasants available for sale to the land-hungry.[67] On 19 September 1906, lands belonging to the tsar in the Altai region were transferred to the GUZiZ for distribution to migrants.[68] All told, these three ukases made approximately nine million desiatinas of land available to the peasantry. Along these same lines, an imperial command of 21 October 1906 granted owners of various categories of entailed lands the right to sell portions of such land to peasants.[69] The government also enacted a number of measures designed to provide privileged financial assistance for those who purchased such land in individual ownership. Finally, on 14 October 1906, interest payments on current and future Peasant Bank loans were lowered from 5r.75k and 5r.25k to 4r.50k per 100 rubles over a period of 55½ years. It also reduced rates for short-term loans, which were higher. Further, the State Treasury would reimburse any financial losses the Bank might suffer as a result of these reductions—though this proposal never received any further development.[70]

As a supplement to these efforts to expand peasant landownership, a commission was formed in early September to draw up regulations permitting peasants for the first time to mortgage their allotment land to the Peasant Bank.[71] The results of this commission's work eventually became law on 15 November 1906. As finally adopted, this law permitted peasants to borrow money against *individually* owned allotment land for the purpose of buying land, resettling on new land, migrating, or upgrading land use by easing transfers to more intensive forms of land-ownership.[72] The terms of the loans were comparatively good, though they discriminated in favor of peasants who had already consolidated their strips into a single, compact holding. Such peasants could receive loans up to 90 percent of the land's value rather than only 60 percent in the case of lands still held in open fields. The limit on loans for all other purposes was 60 percent of value when the property was consolidated into a single parcel, and 40 percent when it was not. The maximum size of such loans was three thousand rubles. At the same time, so that the Bank would not be used to concentrate land in the hands of a prosperous minority, there was a limit on the quantity of allotment land that could be acquired with the aid of Bank loans, so that the total amount of allotment land held by any one household, including what was already owned, could not exceed the amount that the personal labor of the purchaser and his family could work. The agricultural, Interior, and Finance ministries would determine the specific amount jointly.[73]

Despite these genuine efforts to increase the area of peasant landown-ership, from the perspective of the poorer peasants supposed to benefit from it, even these conditions were likely to prove beyond their reach. To be sure, such an approach conformed to the government's overwhelming emphasis on the individualization of peasant land use. However, these laissez-faire elements of government policy conflicted with the new in-terventionism of bureaucratic *opeka*. More important, the traditional requirement that the Peasant Bank, as a credit-mortgage institution, pro-tect the security of its loans prevailed over its function as an instrument of agrarian policy, and this new source of credit never became truly effec-tive—a poor omen for the Finance Ministry's future relationship to agrarian reform.[74] The fiscal conservatives from that ministry also suc-ceeded in preventing the law of 15 November 1906 from being put into effect until both the Duma and the State Council finally approved it in 1912. Finally one must note that although the Peasant Bank was rela-tively successful in selling its land, less than a quarter of a million desiatinas of state land was ever sold to peasants.[75]

Meanwhile, on 9 August 1906, the same day the tsar approved the sale of the royal family's lands to the state—a measure Gurko did not com-pletely approve of[76]—Gurko was once again named to chair yet another commission, or rather series of commissions, to prepare legislation for the expansion of peasant landownership, the equalization of peasant civil and political rights, the reform of peasant administration, and the reform of peasant property rights. And, in what must by now have become a familiar ritual, the commission's first session was set for 2:00 PM on 11 August 1906, "in frock coats."[77] Not surprisingly, the commission had almost no creative role to play beyond the formal work of reordering previous drafts into new packages, for the members of this commission had already discussed every one of the ideas included in the bills it prepared long before it ever met. Indeed, the explanatory notes prepared for the Council of Ministers copied long segments verbatim from earlier documents and materials. Gurko himself subsequently maintained that this was indeed the sole contribution of these commissions he chaired.[78] Simultaneously, a new GUZiZ commission headed by Krivoshein began work on a set of instructions to the local land-organization commissions that had been authorized on 4 March 1906.[79] Together, these two commissions were responsible for drafting the legislation that eventually constituted the so-called Stolypin Reforms.

Even though the government had apparently finally decided on a course of action and had even begun to enact it into law, Stolypin and Vasil'chikov continued to consider a number of additional measures. Sometime in August, at their joint request, the notorious P. P. Migulin received an invitation to join the GUZiZ and prepare a series of bills in his areas of special interest, including measures to expand migration, introduce a "homestead" law on the American model, provide the peasantry with an additional allotment, make pasture land available to villages, and establish a state agricultural bank. At this time, Migulin noted, Stolypin was still "dreaming" of giving the land-hungry peasantry, particularly the *darstvenniki*, an "additional allotment."[80]

Simultaneously, the Gurko commission was preparing the first of its bills, On Broadening the Landownership of Land-Hungry Peasants. One of this bill's most innovative proposals was a measure that would have made state subsidies available to land-hungry peasants for the purchase of land from the Peasant Bank.[81] Subsequently, it prepared a bill on peasant civil rights that was presented to the Council of Ministers on 30 August 1906 and enacted as the ukase of 5 October 1905, On the Abolition of Some Limitations in the Rights of Rural Inhabitants and Persons of Other Formerly Taxable Estates. Its last bill, unassumingly entitled On the Addition of Some Decrees to the Existing Law Concerning Peasant Landownership and Land Use, was presented to the Council of Ministers on 1 October and enacted into law as the notorious ukase of 9 November 1906.

There is little information available to explain the delay between the establishment of the new Gurko commission in mid-August and the final adoption of its bills in October and November. However, since Gurko found time to go abroad for two weeks at the end of August to visit his sick mother, one gets the impression that summer vacations were in part responsible.[82] Another factor was the heavy workload of the Council of Ministers beginning in September as it sought to rush legislation through by means of Article 87. Part of the delay, however, seems to have stemmed from the uncertainty surrounding Stolypin's continuing hopes of reaching some kind of compromise with the moderate liberals. There was also a final effort to save the commune led by the Slavophile F. D. Samarin. Then, shortly after the publication of the ukase of 5 October, the United Nobility learned not only of Migulin's projects, including the one on granting an additional allotment, but also of the Gurko commission's project on broadening peasant landownership. In this context, the flurry of ukases regarding state, *Udel,* and *kabinet* lands, together with Stolypin's sale of some of his own land, must have made them think these measures were merely a prelude to similar sacrifices expected from the gentry. As a result, they once again sought to dissuade the government from adopting measures to assist land-hungry peasants and to urge the passage of the law that was eventually adopted on 9 November.[83] Independent of such pressures, however, Migulin's drafts had run into strong opposition within the government, particularly from Krivoshein, Kokovtsov, and Glinka as well as by others in the "unofficial" government around the tsar. Only Vasil'chikov and Stolypin supported them.[84]

As a result, all of Migulin's bills were rejected, as was the Gurko commission's related project—though the latter was subsequently revived and reconsidered by yet another commission at the end of May 1907 that was devoted specifically to the land-organization problems of *darstvenniki.*[85] Once again, however, it fell victim to its political opponents, who continued to believe that adopting a law devoted specifically to "land-hungry" peasants would set a dangerous precedent. Nonetheless, other legislative enactments would incorporate most of its proposals.

While the question of special measures for the land-hungry was still being debated, however, on 19 September, the GUZiZ's Committee on Land-Organization Affairs issued a detailed set of regulations, by administrative fiat, based on the 10 June draft submitted to the First Duma as modified by the new Krivoshein commission.[86] These instructions are particularly important because they embodied that pragmatic and experimental methodology that had inspired the creation of the land-organization commissions in the first place. Indeed, until the passage of the Land-Organization Statute of 29 May 1911, the entire work of these commissions was to be conducted on just such a basis, guided only by administrative directives adopted outside the constitutionally established legislative process. Furthermore, as Krivoshein had himself proposed, the process itself would in large measure determine the ultimate goals.[87] The government's first steps toward what promised to be a fundamental restructuring of peasant society and agriculture thus bore a decidedly provisional and experimental cast.

In anticipation of the adoption of the new Gurko commission's draft on the expansion of landownership for land-hungry peasants, the Instructions began by charging the land-organization commissions with undertaking, in cooperation with the zemstvos and other local governmental departments, a detailed study of the economic condition of all classes in their county and, in particular, of peasant land needs. Clearly, the restoration of the government's confidence, in conjunction with the rightward swing within the zemstvos themselves, had led it to lose its earlier fear of encroaching on zemstvo prerogatives.[88] More generally, the land-organization commissions were to acquaint the peasantry with their functions and goals and the occasions on which they could render assistance. The intent of this preliminary work was to provide the knowledge and data to meet the land needs of the worst-off and then to offer preferential aid to help them purchase additional land.[89]

The commissions were then to assist in the sale and rental of Peasant Bank and state lands to peasants (though during the 1906 and 1907 field periods they actually concentrated on the liquidation of Peasant Bank land; only in 1908 would state land receive increased emphasis).[90] In cases in which peasants acquired land from the Bank or, with its assistance, directly from private landowners, the commissions were to play the same strictly advisory role the 4 March statute had assigned them. However, they had somewhat greater authority if they and the Bank agreed on the desirability of a sale. Then they were to identify the most eligible buyers and work out an appropriate agreement.[91] Eligible peasants were those whose basic income came from agriculture and who possessed their own inventory, but members of other *sosloviia*, including even nobles, whose principal source of income derived from personal agricultural labor were also eligible. However, when it came to setting priorities in obtaining land, the traditional, protective concerns of *opeka* prevailed over the principles of laissez-faire individualism. Thus, first to be considered were those land-hungry and landless peasants who had continuously rented the land being sold; next, land-hungry peasants whose allotments bordered such land; third, peasants who were purchasing the land to eliminate unproductive features such as open fields or poor configurations. Only after the needs of these three groups had been met were peasants who agreed to resettle on the acquired land and form *otruba*, *khutora*, or new villages to be considered. In the sale of *Udel* and state lands, the land-hungry and those members of the army or navy reserves who had served in Manchuria during the Russo-Japanese War were to receive preference, especially those soldiers who had been wounded.[92]

The commissions were to perform similar advisory functions with respect to purchases of land both directly from private landowners and from the state. In the interim, those state lands that remained unsold were to be rented, without public bidding, to rural communities and peasant associations and, in the case of small plots, to individual peasants and persons of other estates on a yearly basis. In addition, the commissions were to work with the Migration Administration in the resettlement of peasants on state lands in Asia, particularly by distributing information on the general conditions of settlement and the availability of unsettled land.[93]

Such were the land-organization commissions' primary tasks. Together, they restored most of the responsibilities originally assigned them by the first Krivoshein commission back in February. They also confirmed the government's intention, at least in 1906, of offering real and significant assistance to the poorer and land-hungry peasants rather than merely to the strong and sturdy or even the kulak. On the other hand, there is no denying the equally obvious fact that the government was placing predominant emphasis on the individualization of peasant agriculture.

In addition to helping in the expansion of peasant landownership, the commissions were responsible for introducing, at the peasants' request, measures that fell more strictly within the agrotechnical category of land reorganization. More detailed than in the 10 June project, these included the partitioning of land between villages united into one community or between parts of single villages, the separation of the more remote lands of a village for the formation of new villages, the separation of holdings from communally owned lands to become the property of individual householders, the transfer of communities from communal to individual tenure and the apportionment of open-field strips or the distribution of all lands in *otruba* or *khutora*, the apportionment of individually owned open-field strips into *otruba*, the partition of communally owned land for transfer to multifield rotation, and the partition of open-field allotment lands between adjacent properties or in the common use of peasants and private landowners. Where the formation of individual, compact holdings involved the relocation of cottage and garden plots, well-sinking, or other expenses, the commissions were to provide surveyors and financial assistance. In this connection, the commissions were also responsible for distributing A. A. Kofod's brochure, "Settling on *khutora*," and other pamphlets, in order to familiarize peasants with the merits of individual ownership and use.[94]

When it came to forming *otruba* and *khutora*, the role of the local commission was primarily to persuade the parties to reach a voluntary agreement by discovering the true desires of each through interviews in the village, and, then, to work out all the details. However, if they could not reach agreement, the commission was to adopt mandatory procedures and make the fairest and most expedient arrangement possible. If local conditions made separation impossible, they were to describe the obstacles. The commission's proposals and those of the local land captain were then to be presented to the parties concerned and sent (along with their complaints) to the local congress of land captains. If the congress approved the proposal, the land captain was to execute it with the aid of the land-organization commission's surveyor.[95]

Reflecting the government's priorities at the time, land reorganization initially took second place to land sales. However, as the peasants began responding to the government's program, it began to take on greater significance, eventually becoming the core of the government's agrarian policy.[96] But even at this stage, and even though the proposed procedures were highly technical and devoted primarily to the reorganization of field boundaries, and, thus mainly a surveying operation, the members of the land-organization commission and the land captains had considerable powers of discretion. The intent was to assure the greatest possible flexibility in harmonizing the abstract requirements of centrally determined laws with the actual requirements of local conditions. It is also clear that there would be considerable opportunities for abuse, since so much depended on the character and personality of the officials involved.[97] On the other hand, at least during the early years, conflicts between the various agencies of the Interior, agricultural, Justice, and Finance ministries, each of which was involved at different stages of the process, would hinder the Reforms' implementation. As a consequence, the commissions had considerably less than a decisive voice in matters that were their direct concern, though this situation too changed gradually.[98]

A final aspect of the commissions' work, considered to be of vital importance by the government, was the provision of loans to peasant householders, in addition to those available from the Peasant Bank, to defray the costs of transferring buildings or constructing wells, dams, drainage ditches, and roads when such improvements had an educational value for nearby peasants. The maximum loan obtainable directly from the commissions' own funds was 165 rubles. Where the improvements had special demonstrative value for the surrounding peasantry or the peasants were too poor to repay the loan, a special provision allowed for the amount to be awarded as a nonreturnable grant.[99]

Implicit in the whole conception and procedure of reform, the concern for diffusion by practical and successful example subsequently led to the creation of model farms and the organization of visits by parties of peasants; it was also fundamentally linked to the bureaucracy's need to demonstrate the integrity of the Reforms. Honesty, as it were, was the only possible policy in this last-ditch attempt to win the peasantry's trust and its political loyalty.

In sum, and despite the limitations of these measures, one cannot doubt that the government sincerely intended to assist both the needy and the average peasant. Moreover, as land reorganization took an increasingly central role in the government's reform program, the availability of loans, as well as agronomical aid, became of ever greater concern.[100] After all, the government was well aware that the Reforms' success ultimately depended on their economic impact.

Of course, critical to the whole process were the social composition and qualifications of the commissions' members. The most important person on the commission was the permanent member, appointed by the GUZiZ to serve as the administrator, and the local land captain. It was these men who carried out the practical work. The other members were considerably less important and often did not even participate in the commissions' work. They included the local marshal of the nobility, the chairman of the zemstvo board, an official of the judiciary, the tax inspector, and, when appropriate, a member of the local *Udel* department. In addition, the commissions included three members elected from the zemstvo assembly and three peasants, selected by lot at the canton level, who received two-hundred rubles each a year as compensation. Interested parties or their representatives also had the right to attend commission sessions. Other government officials could attend commission meetings by invitation as advisers. A quorum, however, consisted of only five members, including at least one from each of the elected groups.[101]

The regulations governing the commissions' activities constituted in effect a set of collective bargaining procedures. Moreover, they allowed considerable scope for the expression of local interests and the participation of the parties concerned. To be sure, the government's voice was most likely to dominate, usually in favor of individuals and groups who desired to separate from the commune, though there were exceptions. However, the final outcome in any dispute would depend, in part, on the degree to which the public actually participated in the commissions' work. These commissions thus represented a first step toward developing more cooperation and trust between Russia's "We and They."

After the issuance of these instructions, on 5 October 1906, the government published what might well be considered the most revolutionary of all its reforms—the law on peasant civil and political rights. Drafted by the Gurko commission and submitted to the Council of Ministers on 30 August, it won approval with very few changes and was sent to the tsar for his approval.[102] This law represented the government's first real step toward the equalization of the peasantry with the other social estates, though it had been foreshadowed by the Manifestos of 6 August and 17 October 1905 granting the peasantry political rights. Specifically, the ukase granted peasants equal rights with members of the nobility to enter state service (though still with some exceptions) together with complete freedom to enter educational institutions, the parish clergy, or monasteries. Peasants could also remain members of their village communities even if they took up nonpeasant occupations or transferred to another *soslovie*. They had complete freedom of mobility although residence permits (*vidy na zhitel'stvo*) continued to be required. Once again, peasants could gain direct election to the zemstvos without the confirmation of the governor, a right taken away in the zemstvo counterreform of 1890.[103] Finally, the ukase included a number of truly "regularizing" measures that eliminated several of the minor regulations applied to one or another of the several legally distinct groups within the peasantry.

However, though the government eased these restrictions, it continued to regard the peasantry as one *soslovie* within a system of *sosloviia*. One need only cite the requirement, imposed at the height of the counterreforms, that the village assembly approve family partitions of land. This requirement was retained at the specific request of the Council of Ministers, though it was not immediately apparent from the ukase itself.[104] Nevertheless, the ukase was clearly a major step toward integration—an issue that had caused considerable agitation in the years before 1905, particularly because of its association with the entire *soslovie*-based system of local administration. Now, as a consequence of the revolutionary events of the past year and a half, not only was integration acceptable, but, as the ukase itself declared, "the legislation defining the structure of local administration and courts will [itself] be subject to a radical review."[105] However, this statement was itself a harbinger of the government's ultimate failure to enact those administrative reforms, for it was a much-watered-down version of Gurko's original declaration that "the abolition of anomalies in the juridical condition of rural inhabitants, which flow from the special order of their *soslovie* institutions, both administrative and judicial, is possible only in conjunction with a radical reform of these institutions and their replacement by others."[106] Clearly, it had been Gurko's assumption that these reforms would be instituted on an all-class basis as was the case in all the bills submitted in due course to the Duma. For the moment, however, the Council of Ministers still had reservations, and those measures that it did introduce were something of a compromise.

Nonetheless, this law contained the essence of the liberal approach to the agrarian problem as it had been proposed by both Witte and the zemstvo opposition as well as by Gurko in the years prior to 1905. Clearly, the senior officials within the bureaucracy, who had initially been most opposed to that program, had finally recognized its value— even if it did not provide a completely adequate solution. At the same time, the bureaucracy sought to preserve certain aspects of the *soslovie* system as part of its continuing policy of *opeka*, though one based on a new set of perceptions, which it shared with society, on the nature of Russian rural life and the direction of its future development.

Finally, on 1 October, the Gurko commission submitted its bill on peasant property rights and land use to the Council of Ministers. A majority approved it on 10 October, though Kokovtsov, Prince Vasil'chikov, and Prince Obolenskii opposed introducing this law prior to the reconvening of the Duma by means of Article 87, and the tsar confirmed it on 9 November 1906.[107] Thus had the long struggle to initiate the individualization and intensification of peasant agriculture as a first step toward creating the conditions for economic growth and political stability achieved fruition. Whether the timing of this act was a product of the bureaucratic process or an attempt to present the upcoming Second Congress of the United Nobility with a fait accompli is unclear.[108] However, in response to the government's action, the United Nobility called an emergency Congress. Held between 14 and 18 November 1906, it had a strong antigovernmental mood that sharply distinguished it from the First Congress. As a result, the United Nobility decided not to express any official support for this law.[109]

The law itself consisted of four sections.[110] The most important dealt with title claims by individual peasant households to communally owned arable land and the consolidation of such land, held in personal (*lichnoe*) property, into an *otrub* or *khutor*. This was the basic two-stage procedure introduced by Rittikh to give as flexible, spontaneous, and evolutionary an approach as possible to what was, indeed, but the first step toward a total reoganization of the peasant way of life. However, as we saw, claiming title, the first stage in this process, had taken on political significance when the peasant movement and the government's proposals for compulsory expropriation threatened noble property. As a consequence, greater emphasis was now placed on this stage as a way of developing the peasants' respect for the property rights of others.

Thus, at the heart of this ukase was a modified version of the Gurko/Pestrzhetskii rule according to which peasants in communes where there had been no general repartition over the preceding twenty-four years could claim title to that portion of the community's arable land that was in his actual use, including the household plot. On the other hand, in communes that had so repartitioned, the peasant could also receive the amount in his actual use, but only until the next general repartition. At that time, if there were more land in his use than would be due, on the basis of the criteria adopted at the last repartition and the number of allotment units in his family at the time of application, he could receive title to the surplus only on condition that he compensate the community for its full value, determined according to the average redemption price at the time of its initial allotment. Failing this, surpluses would revert to the community.[111]

Together, these measures were considerably more moderate than the original program set forth by Gurko and incorporated into the draft submitted to the First Duma on 6 June 1906, but they conformed very closely to the version worked out in February and March 1906. Rittikh's attempt at that time to moderate these measures still further was ignored. Once more, the conflicting forces within the bureaucracy and the government had produced a compromise. And even when the Law of 14 June 1910 reinstated Gurko's more extreme version of this rule and provided for the automatic transfer to individual ownership of communes that had not executed general repartitions during the preceding twenty-four years, the de jure acknowledgment of this de facto situation still depended on at least one peasant's petitioning for title to his share.[112] The law of 9 November also guaranteed the rights of separating peasants to a share of common forest or pasture lands.[113]

Needless to say, it was the Interior Ministry and its land captains who were in charge of implementing the more "politically" significant procedure of claiming title. Ideally, a community decision adopted by a simple majority would approve such claims. Failing that, the land captain could approve them. In either case, one could appeal to the county congress of land captains. Subsequent appeals were permissible only in cases that violated the law or in instances of the county congress's exceeding its authority.[114]

Not surprisingly, the only change the Council of Ministers made in its 10 October discussion of the draft law was to transfer the appeals process from the courts and the civil process, where its authors had once again placed it, to the administrative process, thus restoring one of the strongest provisions of the GUZiZ's June project. This step ensured that decisions would better accord with government intentions; and, more significantly, it would also, as Gurko had earlier argued, help speed up the appeals process and convince what was assumed to be a skeptical peasantry that the government really meant business.[115]

Overall, the government's intent was, of course, to ensure the quickest possible satisfaction of the individual separator's legal rights in the face of potential community opposition. This emphasis on the primacy of individual rights, which characterized all the legislation, was, of course, entirely new. At the same time these articles opened the door to administrative abuse and the possibility that decrees issued by the land captain could be used in cases in which there was no peasant initiative.[116]

Other provisions of the law concerned the second stage of the reform process—the more immediately agrotechnical, though also political, separation of strips already held as personal property to *otruba* or *khutora*. Again, the project followed the decisions adopted during February and March and achieved a reasonable compromise between the divergent interests of the parties involved. Thus, any peasant who had claimed title to his share of the community land could, at any time, demand that the community exchange these open-field strips of arable land for a parcel of comparable value—if possible in one compact holding. However, if such demands did not coincide with a general repartition and if the county congress, on the advice of the local land-organization commission, had upheld the community's decision that the separation would be inconvenient or impossible, then the community would be obliged to satisfy the peasant's requests by a cash payment instead. If the peasant did not agree to this, the canton court was to resolve the dispute. Should the separator continue to be dissatisfied, he could retain his strips within their former boundaries. However, at the next general repartition, all peasants who had claimed title to their strips or expressed an intention to do so would be obliged to consolidate them, on the demand of one of their number or the community, as expressed in a decree passed by a simple majority. At such times the community would not be permitted to make cash payments in lieu of land. Again administrative procedures would resolve disputes. Of course, the land captains held the principal decision-making powers in this process. However, the land-organization commissions, governed by the 19 September instructions worked out under Krivoshein's leadership, would handle the technical aspects of separations. Peasants who claimed title through this process would possess the same rights as those who held their land in individual, household tenure.[117]

The law also simplified the procedures by which peasants in communes where land was held in individual, household ownership could obtain proof of title. Paradoxically, this was a more complex process than that confronting holders of land in communal tenure and one that involved local notarial institutions. Once such proof had been obtained, however, these peasants could also begin the voluntary process of consolidating their strips into a single unit.[118]

One of the law's more radical measures borrowed from Rittikh's earliest proposals abolished the traditional system of family or household ownership of property, though only for those peasants who already lived in communities that did not own their land on a communal basis and those who had claimed title to their strips. Thus the head of household now achieved recognition as the legal owner of all forms of peasant personal property.[119] This was, of course, a logical consequence of the very concept of personal property and was at the same time of both economic and political benefit. It was also, however, that feature of the law that was subsequently to raise the most controversy within government circles.[120]

Finally the law provided for the transfer of whole communities from communal and individual, household tenure to ownership in *otrub* fields on the decision of two-thirds of the householders. It is important to note, however, that separation to *khutora* still required unanimous consent, since it involved the transfer of household plots on which the peasants' cottages and gardens were located. Nonetheless, this provision marked a distinct break with the past, since under the previous legislation even a transfer to *otruba* had required unanimous consent. Granting those minorities who opposed such resettlement the right to compensation and to bring civil suits protected their interests.[121]

In comparing this law to the GUZiZ draft of 10 June, as well as the instructions of 19 September, it is clear that the title claims and separations of individual peasants received far greater emphasis than did group or community procedures, reflecting the changed political atmosphere and the government's newfound interest in the immediate political gains it hoped would result from a rapid increase in the numbers of peasants owning land on an individual basis. At the same time, however, the law's overall shape and emphasis reflected the bureaucracy's fear that the peasants might not want to take advantage of the government's legislation either to leave the commune or even to claim title to their share of allotment land. Hence—and quite apart from potential opposition to its proposals within the bureaucracy and the government—there was a clear recognition of the need to act as cautiously as possible where the peasants were concerned. Thus, the commune was not "abolished," even in cases in which there had been no general repartition during the preceding twenty-four years. The initiative resided in the peasants themselves. On the other hand, of course, the legislation had not accomplished the impossible task of preventing local officials from exerting their own pressures in that direction. Similarly, with the formation of *otruba* and *khutora* and the severance of the peasant's economic and agrotechnical links to the commune, the main emphasis was on individual and spontaneous initiative—even though it was obvious that transfers of whole communities to new agricultural forms was a simpler technical process than separations by individuals and small groups. Indeed, repeated cases of such separations could well prove counterproductive if they antagonized the community as a whole. However, the government's initial emphasis on individual procedures also reflected the tentativeness of its approach; for these "pioneering" reorganizations, it was hoped, would serve as a model for those who remained in the commune.

Clearly, then, the government had major reservations about the peasants' response to the legislation despite the sanguine predictions made earlier that they would welcome the concept of individual or personal property ownership. In this sense, the ukase of 9 November was an experiment, a kind of opinion poll of peasant attitudes, the results of which would lead the government to revise its legislative and administrative procedures. The subsequent development of the Reforms bears out this interpretation. The history of the bureaucracy's methodological approach to agrarian reform also corroborates it.[122] Indeed, the ukase was the very embodiment of that provisional and experimental approach to knowledge first spelled out by Vorontsov-Dashkov and that subsequently became an important part of the perceptual revolution as reflected in the work of Kutler, Krivoshein, Rittikh, and Gurko. Thus had the government finally enacted the policy of individualizing peasant landownership that had been gestating since before the Emancipation. It was, indeed, a "second Emancipation."[123]

10

CONCLUSION

Consolidate the depths!

—P. A. Stolypin, 1909

I think it is completely impossible to force peasants to such an expression of their will [as reflected by the statistical data on implementation]. This is clear to anyone who knows rural life.

—A. A. Rittikh, 1909

The Stolypin Reforms were, as we have seen, conceived both as a solution to the economic and political crises of a modernizing country and as part of a more comprehensive program of national economic development that focused on the need to increase agricultural productivity. Contrary to traditional interpretations, these Reforms were not, however, either a simple "wager on the strong and sober," or as some have suggested the kulak, or a mere abolition of the commune. Nor were they simply an attempt to save noble landownership and the nobility as a *soslovie*. On the contrary, they were a wager on the whole peasantry that was conducted on the basis of an entirely new conception of the national interest. Moreover, in the long term, they assumed the complete disappearance of the nobility as a privileged *soslovie* of landowners and the formation of a single agricultural class.[1] Thus, by means of a gradual, spontaneous, and individualistic process that was designed to convert a tradition-bound and routine-oriented peasantry to the benefits of modernization and rationalization, every peasant—the average or middle peasants and the land-hungry, in addition to the notorious kulak—was to have an opportunity to separate his land from the commune in order to cultivate it more efficiently, in one compact unit, and thereby to exercise his full individuality and initiative. On the other hand, those who pre-

---

Portions of this chapter appeared in different form in David A. J. Macey's "Bureaucratic Solutions to the Peasant Problem: Before and after Stolypin." In R. C. Elwood (ed.), *Russian and East European History: Selected Papers from the Second World Congress for Soviet and East European Studies.* Published by Berkeley Slavic Specialists in Berkeley, California, 1984.

ferred to remain within the commune—although not encouraged—could continue to do so. Indeed, the commune was deliberately allowed to remain in existence, though only on a free and voluntary basis. What the Reforms did was to allow those who wished to leave the commune, whether merely to legitimize an already de facto departure, to take up nonagricultural employment, or to resettle in Siberia or on state or privately owned land purchased from the Peasant Bank in European Russia, to do so without financial loss. Migration was also seen as beneficial to those who stayed behind since it would reduce the surplus population in areas of greatest hardship.[2]

For those who left and those who remained, the government had indicated its willingness to make the choice both juridically and economically feasible. Indeed, without its aid, withdrawal from the commune would have been virtually impossible for all but the richest peasants. Insofar as the notorious ukase of 9 November was concerned, however, the government did not see it as the only, or even the principal, means to achieve its goals. Rather, its purpose was to establish the juridical basis for a subsequent rationalization of peasant land organization and use. Making it lawful for peasants to leave the commune was only a first step, politically important in the immediate struggle to protect noble property rights and to fight socialism, and also of direct economic significance for the peasantry and the country as a whole. But without the provisions for land reorganization, the political goals could not have been achieved, the underlying economic causes of the whole agrarian crisis would have remained unaffected, and the ukase of 9 November 1906, the Law of 14 June 1910, and the effort to increase the area of peasant landownership would all have proved meaningless. At the same time, of course, although the commune was allowed to survive, the reformers assumed that the process of legalized, voluntary withdrawal, which was now being encouraged, would eventually lead to its dissolution. Gradualism and spontaneity, indeed, were the very essence of the government's proposals, in large measure because almost all those associated with the development of the Reforms had rejected the use of legislative force as inimical to the achievement of their goals.

The government's immediate concern, as we have seen, was with the political problems of calming and stabilizing the countryside and creating a strong foundation of social support for the new constitutional order. As in generations past, there was a well-nigh unanimous agreement within the bureaucracy and the government that whatever reforms were adopted would have to be introduced gradually lest sharp and sudden changes in the peasants' customary way of life excite more unrest than the state could withstand. The rapid spread of peasant disorders and violence during 1905 and 1906 seemed to confirm the wisdom of this approach. In the face of this unrest, the government temporarily discarded schemes that foresaw a long period of gradual development in favor of measures that would produce an immediate impact on the political crisis in the countryside. Yet, sudden strokes of the legislative pen remained out of the question; the only alternative therefore was to adopt some form of immediate economic relief. But even then, the government did not ignore long-range concerns. Indeed, it was precisely these concerns that eventually led the government to reject the otherwise popular policy of a partial expropriation of noble land.

Since it was recognized that all levels of the peasantry had grievances, the only feasible program was the one eventually adopted: to provide land for those who needed it and to rationalize land-use practices for those who already had enough. To deal with both the short-term political crisis and the long-term economic crisis, the government thus adopted a policy that combined extensification and intensification, thereby rejecting the prevailing opinion within both the political opposition and the peasantry, which saw more land as the sole solution.

Despite its sudden conversion to the ideology of private property, the government was in fact both unwilling and unable to commit itself to a totally laissez-faire conception of capitalist development and its concomitant, a free and unregulated process of social and economic change. In large part, this was because it had still not lost its fear of social and economic differentiation and the growth of a landless proletariat, either rural or urban. At the same time, although some have argued that the government sought to use the Reforms to break up the so-called united front of the peasantry that formed during the agrarian disorders in 1905–6, in fact it refused to adopt measures that would deliberately set one section of the peasantry against another and thus increase rural frictions. But it was clearly willing to exploit such an ideology to win support from within the two major moderate political parties, the Kadets and Octobrists, as well as the provincial nobility in general. Thus, although it sought to encourage what it recognized as a spontaneous and natural development toward individual, capitalist forms of agriculture, it hoped to utilize these developments to the state's advantage—and in the last analysis for its own preservation. Such a stance, of course, compelled the government not simply to retain but even to strengthen its policy of bureaucratic *opeka* over the peasantry by increasing the level of government intervention, at least in the short term. Social and political considerations thus restrained whatever pressures existed for an immediate dissolution of the commune and encouraged the preservation of both it and the *soslovie* system in order to protect those peasants who might not succeed as independent cultivators and/or who were unwilling to abandon a marginal agriculture and find work in nonagricultural occupations.

To these ends, the government retained the 1893 law prohibiting peasants from selling allotment land to nonpeasants, thereby preserving the state's traditional allotment land fund as a resource for the peasantry as a whole. At the same time, it imposed limitations on the accumulation of both allotment and Peasant Bank land by any one household in order to prevent weaker peasants from being forced into the ranks of landless wage laborers. Indeed, there can be no question but that the government wished to avoid flooding the cities with hordes of landless peasants. It was only too well aware that the opportunities for employment there were inadequate to absorb such a massive influx—though it hoped to increase such opportunities by encouraging industrial development and by creating new consumers in the countryside.

The guiding principle of the Reforms was, then, a combination of autocracy and freedom, of law and spontaneity, of continuity and change. A passage from the Interior Ministry's explanatory note to the version of the ukase of 9 November 1906 submitted to the Second Duma—as was required by the Fundamental Laws—early in 1907 embodies this almost utopian fusion of the seemingly incompatible:

At the basis of all living phenomena there always lies the principle of regularity. Life does not allow jumps and sudden shifts from one phenomenon to another. Law must also be subordinated to the same general principal of continuity, since law, by standardizing the relations which arise from the soil of actual life, is in essence nothing but a reflection of life. Intelligent legislative activity must therefore always be based on a deep respect for the country's historical past and must seek not to break its connections with it but to develop and improve the principles worked out by it. This is especially true with respect to the sphere of landed juridical relations, which in all countries are formed in the course of a slow historical process and are always distinguished by comparative immobility and stability . . . . [Moreover] the agricultural class . . . is everywhere the most conservative, the most loyal to the country, the most alien to innovation. With respect to this class, therefore, it is essential to preserve legislative continuity and consistency,. . . [since] sudden violations of the peasants' landed way of life can evoke undesirable shocks in the whole multi-millioned organism of the peasant soslovie.[3]

The note then turns from the abstract to the concrete:

Both the communal and household forms of landownership have been firmly rooted in the legal consciousness of the peasant and have not yet lost their vitality. This eliminates any possibility of either their complete abolition or of essential changes by a single decree of the law. Such measures would not be met with sympathy from the peasants and would even evoke their opposition, since a radical and total break in the existing forms of landownership, which have been consecrated by time, would not in many instances conform to local peculiarities or to the actual demands of the population.[4]

The explanatory note from the version of the ukase submitted to the Third Duma, similarly noted that

At the very basis of the ukase of November 9, 1906 lies the idea . . . that it is desirable to allow the question of the commune to be decided by life itself and that it is inexpedient to adopt any artificial means either for the support or the abolition of the commune.[5]

In the same way, despite the government's concern to expand private property principles, the property rights finally granted were far from absolute. Thus peasants who claimed title to their strips received them in "personal" property, which meant little more, in fact, than the right to mortgage or sell them, though this was in itself an important new right.[6] Certainly the peasant could not cultivate them independently of other members of the commune or make decisions regarding their use without the commune's approval. Similarly, at different stages of the land reorganization process, the property rights of individual peasants could be violated in the interests of better forms of land organization.[7] And even when land was consolidated into *khutora*, such land maintained its *soslovie* and "allotment" character as "personal" property— which granted only the right to its individual possession and use, subject to state and community restrictions, and excluding mineral rights. Such land, therefore, always remained distinct from the "private" property of other *sosloviia*.[8]

Despite these limitations, the government was nonetheless genuinely committed to the development of individualistic and capitalist forms of peasant agriculture as it was to raising its productivity. Thus, at least at first, land reorganization focused almost exclusively on the formation of *khutora*, to the point where the political interest in this form of landownership and use frequently overrode what was economically rational for either the individual peasant or the specific locality. This preference was reinforced by the simultaneous policy of equalizing the peasantry's legal and political rights with those of other members of society, which implied atomizing the peasant class rather than driving a wedge between the prosperous minority and the impoverished majority. As the Council of Ministers concluded on 10 October 1906, the goal of all of the government's measures was the calming of the population and the creation of "that strong union of small and medium-scale property owners which everywhere serves as the support and cement of the state order."[9] Thus, the government's leading expert on agrarian reform, A. A. Kofod, noted, when peasants resettled on *khutora*, one of the first consequences was a virtually complete loss of social consciousness as they devoted all their attention to the new property. But, when their social consciousness returned, as it would after they had stabilized their new undertaking, it would be the consciousness of a property owner with a stake in the existing order. This, then, was the ultimate value of the *khutor*, that "cell" from which a healthy social organism was to grow. It would transform the peasant from a discontented social critic into a partisan of law and order and the status quo.[10] Furthermore, as Valuev suggested a half-century ago, atomization could well prove to be a more effective means of social control and a more appropriate instrument of bureaucratic *opeka* than the collectivistic and corporate commune, since the latter tended, at least in times of crisis, to unite the different peasant strata against their common external enemies.

One must also acknowledge that the government had intervened decisively in the course of rural and peasant life. The entire process of land reorganization was itself an expression of the bureaucracy's continuing custodial policy of *opeka*. Yet, as has been repeatedly emphasized, this was a new, interventionist form of *opeka* that was based on the bureaucracy's changed perception of rural society and its adoption of a new and experimental approach to the formation of government policy. Indeed, it was the ideology of bureaucratic *opeka* that enabled the government to combine its respect for the organic totality of the present as a historical product of the interaction between the material and cultural environments with its urgently felt need for fundamental change. Moreover, the government had built its entire program of reform around the claim that it merely sought, by its intervention, to foster the development of those seeds of change that it—and not it alone—believed it had discerned in the present. A new myth, the myth of peasant spontaneity, replaced the traditional myth of the peasant commune.

Of course, the enactment of a reform program does not guarantee its successful implementation. Although the subsequent fate of the Reforms does not concern us,[11] it is worth noting that they did appear to have struck a responsive chord within peasant society. Even some of the government's critics, many of them acknowledged experts in agrarian and peasant affairs, came in due course to recognize this.[12] Insofar as the reformers themselves were concerned, the Reforms' results seem to have confirmed their initial assumptions and expectations. Thus, the government repeatedly expressed its amazement at the scale of the peasant response, comparing it to the Muscovite state's formative period between the fourteenth and sixteenth centuries and describing it as a modern "gathering of the Russian lands."[13] However, despite the intentionally experimental approach, the accumulation of local experience seemed less to shape the subsequent legislative and administrative evolution of the Reforms, as their proponents had claimed it would, than to buttress ideas already developed by the central administration—though that in itself must be considered a favorable judgment not only on the government's program but also on the effectiveness of at least this branch of the bureaucracy. As a consequence, the government gradually increased its support for individual peasants against the commune by expanding the number of occasions on which mandatory procedures could be applied.[14] At the same time, the government continued to eschew coercive measures designed to increase the pace of peasant separations and consolidations. As the Interior Ministry noted in a circular dated 21 January 1909,

> The whole essence of the law . . . is based exclusively on the voluntary consciousness of the population as to the benefits which would accrue to them from a transfer to personal landownership and does not give any right to the administrators to exert any kind of pressure on them. . . . [Coercive] measures are, thus, completely illegal and at the same time not only will not achieve the desired goals but even must be recognized as harmful, since they will break the peasants' trust in and sympathy for the government's land reorganization work. . . . In choosing the means to realize the ukase of November 9 . . . government organs can only explain to the population the significance of the transfer to individual forms of landownership and acquaint peasants with the procedures and the political and juridical consequences . . . but they can not in any way force those persons or . . . anyone else to transfer to personal property, an act which . . . depends on the personal inclination of each individual peasant.[15]

Indeed, it was argued, the reforms had already achieved such a momentum that force was not even necessary. Krivoshein described the voluntary principles on which the Reforms were based as the "red thread" guiding the government's entire work. On the other hand, his chief technical adviser, Kofod, was inclined to argue in favor of more legislative coercion, though to no avail.[16]

As the political crisis began to pass and in part in response to peasant reactions, the government shifted attention away from the more radical, individual procedures and placed increasing emphasis on community measures that looked to the eventual reorganization of whole villages—clearly a more efficient approach in terms both of personnel use and peasant convenience.[17] So, too, was the "khutoromania" of the early years moderated, and the government showed itself increasingly willing to allow the formation of intermediate forms of land organization such as otruba.[18] Even Stolypin abandoned his initial preference for separating kulaks and *miroedy*, which he saw as a means of liberating the commune from their exploitation while encouraging them to apply their talents directly to the cultivation of the soil, and expressed increasing concern for all peasant strata. In this respect, Gurko's dismissal from the government on charges of corruption at the beginning of 1907—a curious parallel to Miliutin's dismissal after the Emancipation of 1861—and the subsequent domination of the reform apparatus by Krivoshein, Rittikh, Kofod, and the technical experts from the agricultural ministry led to a more egalitarian approach to rural economic development. And while remaining committed to the peasant family farm on the French model of a "republic of peasants," the government increasingly began to envision Russia as a land of consumer cooperatives on the Danish model.[19]

In conjunction with these shifts in emphasis, the level of cooperation between government and local society increased, and attempts were made to persuade both local zemstvos and agricultural societies to assist in providing agronomical aid and establishing cooperatives.[20] However, these possessors of local knowledge were, in the main, the self-same members of the "third element" who had aroused the ire of both the government and the provincial nobility before the revolution of 1905. As a result, their relations with the government continued to be stormy.[21] Meanwhile, Krivoshein revived his earlier efforts to involve elected members from the zemstvos in the work of the agricultural ministry's council.[22] Before long, agronomical aid and the establishment of a full range of agricultural extension services were regarded as fundamental to the success of the entire attempt to increase agricultural productivity.[23] The reforms were clearly becoming increasingly "integral" or "integrative" in their approach, embracing rural society in its totality.

The laws were gradually extended so that by 1911 they applied not just to peasant allotment lands, but to all categories of peasant-owned lands. Thus, too, after the partial breach in the *soslovie* principle of inalienability that had permitted the mortgaging of allotment land to the Peasant Bank as well as its sale to nonpeasants in cases of default, peasants who consolidated land held on the basis of both allotment and private property rights into one unit could equalize the rights of the allotment portion with those held on a "private" basis. In a similar way, the application of the reform legislation to the properties of "anyone whose way of life was indistinguishable from that of the peasant agriculturalist," regardless of his legal status, became possible. In addition, the properties of both nobles and public institutions could be drawn into the reorganization process in order to facilitate the elimination of open fields.[24] Thus, although the government still had no intention of abandoning either *opeka* or the *soslovie* character of peasant allotment land, there was some further weakening of traditional *soslovie* principles. This paralleled a growing recognition of the role urbanization and industrial development could play in absorbing the inevitable flow of proletarianized peasants—though the government continued to do its best to slow that process to a minimum.[25]

In the final analysis, the Reforms seem to have been well conceived, particularly when judged according to recent reevaluations of current attempts at agrarian and land reforms in underdeveloped countries.[26] Above all, the government sought to retain as large a proportion of the rural population on the land as was possible and to depend primarily on labor-intensive methods to achieve the desired increases in productivity. Such an approach also suggests that the tsarist bureaucracy was not so universally benighted as its many critics have assumed. On the other hand, it is often argued that the peasant revolution of 1917 and the peasants' ultimate success in realizing their age-old dreams of a *"chernyi peredel'"* ultimately proved that the government's program of agrarian reform was flawed from the outset. Such a conclusion does not necessarily follow, however, for the peasants' seizure of private land and their return to the commune, which took place in the context of war, revolution and civil war, and the complete breakdown of both the market and civil authority, must be considered independently of their attitudes toward either the commune or the Stolypin Reforms. Moreover, as George Yaney has pointed out, once the civil war was over in 1920, new and spontaneous forces that once again encouraged individual peasants to leave the commune and set up family farms began to develop.[27]

Of course, it might also be argued that the government's commitment to such a gradual modernization of the rural economy as the Stolypin Reforms embodied was doomed by its very ambivalence, that it is impossible to flout the "inevitable" laws of social and economic development and expect to reap the economic benefits of a capitalist-style modernization while rejecting its social and political consequences. In seeking to answer this argument, I can only point out the ahistorical nature of any effort that tries to evaluate past events within a polarized framework and confines historical alternatives to either capitalism or socialism, Prussian or American models, extensification or intensification. Moreover, given the power of the tsarist state and its tradition of intervention, there is no reason to believe that the government's historical balancing act was inherently impossible. In this connection, it should be pointed out that there are certain similarities between the tsarist government's approach and that of its Soviet successor, for both believed in the state's ability to influence those "inevitable" laws of economics in the interest of larger social and political concerns. Today, of course, all political authorities do this, regardless of their ideological orientation. Stolypin, who once described the government's agrarian policy as "state socialism," as well as other members of the bureaucracy, knew well the distinction between the theoretical and the possible and, like all politicians, sought to extend the latter's limits. Paradoxically, this resulted in an ideological stance that combined determinism and voluntarism in ways that closely resembled the revolutionary ideology worked out by V. I. Lenin and the Bolshevik faction of the Russian Social Democrats. The label, *official pseudo-Marxism*, indeed seems an apt description of bureaucratic ideology during this era.

In a conversation with A. A. Polovtsov on 14 April 1900, Witte had alluded somewhat pessimistically to the tsar's repeated refusal to take up the question of rural reform. In response to Polovtsov's comment that Witte himself had nonetheless actively and vigorously pursued this issue, Witte noted that he could "not meddle in everything. I am already accused of doing that too much. But even I doubt that a man will be found who would dare to introduce that transition from communal to individual ownership which is necessary for economic development."[28]

Stolypin had in fact dared, though he was not ultimately to achieve his goals. That he was even able to win the enactment of the agrarian reforms was, however, a product not so much of his own political role, though that was important, as of the perceptual revolution that had taken place in agrarian policy at the beginning of the twentieth century. And that in turn was a product of the social, economic, and political changes that developed in the aftermath of the Emancipation. Another major factor was, of course, the Revolution of 1905, though as we have seen its initial impact was rather to delay the adoption of a new agrarian policy. Later, however, that policy came to be seen as an imperative of the 1905 Revolution itself, for it was the Revolution that helped generate both the necessary governmental decisiveness and the equally necessary social support. Thus, as I have attempted to demonstrate, in circumstances in which the tsar's will was not manifest (in contrast to the situation at the time of the Emancipation), the decision to adopt a program of reform and the content of that program were shaped both by the political and economic exigencies of Russian history as well as by the government's relationship with the landowning nobility and the peasantry and its pragmatic and "naturalistic" understanding of the historical process, as reflected in the peasantry's material way of life and consciousness.

However, as with the Emancipation, it was the very conjunction of these forces that produced an agrarian reform that was both traditional and revolutionary and represented a compromise between the extremes of the revolutionary period: between extensification and intensification; abolition of the commune and its preservation; integration and the perpetuation of an isolated and exclusive legal, or *soslovie*, status; bureaucratic *opeka* and peasant spontaneity; revolution from above and evolution from below. Ultimately, the legal acrobatics that accompanied the government's attempt to foster radical changes within a framework set by the conservative principles of continuity, regularity, and precedent and the government's fear of administrative force may well have impeded the Reforms' implementation, as Kofod himself has argued.[29] And here, it seems, the expanding legal consciousness of the government's ministers, with its inherent cautiousness, was, indeed, in contradiction with the realities of Russia's economic and agrarian life, which seemed to demand a more radical, less traditional approach.[30] Moreover, as we have seen, the conjunction of economics, politics, and bureaucratic ideology was to prove short-lived as the United Nobility withdrew its support for the government's agrarian reform and then helped defeat the reform of local administration.

Within the continuities imposed by these larger historical forces, I have, nonetheless, tried to establish the critical role played by the bureaucracy in the formulation and enactment of the Stolypin Agrarian Reforms. The new generation of bureaucrats, born in the 1860s, who had attended institutions of higher learning and had entered government service at the provincial level during the reign of Alexander III, was the dynamic force behind this final attempt to stimulate the spontaneous development of individual and social initiative. It was they who were responsible for constructing the program. It was they who steered it through the government chancelleries. It was they who won over a critical segment of the landowning nobility. It was they, finally, who persuaded Nicholas of the necessity of enacting these reforms. For, in the last analysis, Nicholas alone possessed the power to make them a reality. Indeed, beneath the superficiality of changing political structures and ministerial leaders, there endured a continuity of both problems and personnel that determined the final shape of those reforms. Thus, it seems, we must entertain a new conception of at least this segment of the bureaucratic *soslovie*, no longer an impenetrable "wall" between society and the tsar, but a creative innovator, responsible even to society's pressure for change.

However, it is also clear that the Stolypin Agrarian Reforms represented a very special case. Thus, although the preceding conclusions are, indeed, accurate, one must be exceedingly cautious about using them as a basis for making broader generalizations about either the overall effectiveness of the Russian bureaucracy or the direction of Russia's development on the eve of World War I.[31] Indeed, it is precisely because the formulation and adoption of the Stolypin Reforms appear to have been exceptions to the rule that they are so important. Therefore, the extent to which the results of this analysis are applicable to other segments of the governing apparatus will have to be evaluated anew in each instance.

NOTES

ABBREVIATIONS

AHR	*American Historical Review*
CASS	*Canadian-American Slavic Studies*
CMRS	*Cahiers du Monde Russe et Soviétique*
CSSH	*Comparative Studies in Society and History*
EAIVE na	*Ezhegodnik agrarnoi istorii Vostochnoi Evropy na . . . .*
FOG	*Forschungen zur Osteuropäischen Geschichte*
GDSO	Gosudarstvennaia Duma, *Stenograficheskie Otchety*
GSSO	Gosudarstvennyi Sovet, *Stenograficheskie Otchety*
HIA	Hoover Institution Archive
IZ	*Istoricheskie Zapiski*
IZO	*Izvestiia Zemskago Otdela*
JGO	*Jahrbücher für Geschichte Osteuropas*
JMH	*Journal of Modern History*
KA	*Krasnyi Arkhiv*
OsNSKhP	Osoboe Soveshchanie o nuzhdam sel'sko-khoziaistvennoi promyshlennosti
Otchet za	*Otchet po deloproizvodtsvu Gosudarstvennago Soveta za . . . .*
PSZ	*Polnoe Sobranie Zakonov Rossiiskoi Imperii, III-e sobranie.*
RACU	Russian Archive, Columbia University
SEER	*Slavonic and East European Review*
SPB	St. Petersburg
Spravki MVD	*Spravki k vnesennomu Ministrom Vnutrennikh Del, 27 oktiabria 1903 g. za No. 29157, delu o poriadke predvaritel'nago obsuzhdeniia proektov novykh zakonopolozhenii o krest'ianakh* (SPB, 1903)

Trudy redkom	Trudy redaktsionnoi komissii po peresmotru
	zakonopolozhenii o krest'ianakh. 6 vols. (SPB,
	1903–4)
Trudy VEO	Trudy Vol'nago Imperatorskago Ekonomicheskago
	Obshchestva
TsGAOR	Tsentral'nyi Gosudarstvennyi Arkhiv Oktiabr'skoi
	Revoliutsii
TsGIA SSSR	Tsentral'nyi Gosudarstvennyi Istoricheskii Arkhiv
	SSSR, Leningrad
Vestnik Finansov	Vestnik Finansov, Promyshlennosti i Torgovlia
VID	Vspomogatel'nye istoricheskie distsipliny
VMUSI	Vestnik Moskovskogo Universiteta: Seriia Istoriia

Introduction

1. For example, G. T. Robinson, *Rural Russia under the Old Regime: A History of the Landlord-Peasant World and a Prologue to the Peasant Revolution of 1917* (Berkeley, 1932), pp. 169–242; S. M. Dubrovskii, *Stolypinskaia zemel'naia reforma: Iz istorii sel'skogo khoziaistva i krest'ianstva Rossii v nachale XX veka* (Moscow, 1963), pp. 5–129.

2. For example, G. Pavlovsky, *Agricultural Russia on the Eve of Revolution* (London, 1930), pp. 61–242; A. D. Bilimovich, "The Land Settlement in Russia and the War," in *Russian Agriculture during the War,* ed. A. N. Antsiferov et al. (New Haven, 1930), pp. 301–43; B. Brutzkus, "The Historical Peculiarities of the Social and Economic Development of Russia," in *Class, Status and Power,* ed. R. Bendix and S. M. Lipsett (Chicago, 1953), pp. 523–29.

3. N. Riasanovsky, *A History of Russia,* 4th ed. (New York, 1984), p. 414. Compare L. Volin, *A Century of Russian Agriculture: From Alexander II to Khrushchev* (Cambridge, Mass., 1970), p. 105; R. T. Manning, *The Crisis of the Old Order in Russia: Gentry and Government* (Princeton, 1982), pp. 205–92; D. Atkinson, *The End of the Russian Land Commune 1905–1930* (Stanford, Calif., 1983), pp. 41–70.

4. The most extreme form of this approach argues that the Stolypin Reforms were designed to defend the class interests of the landowning nobility and create discord among their seemingly united peasant opponents by splitting the peasantry into two groups: a minority of prosperous and productive peasant proprietors with a "stake" in the existing structure of society who would serve as a buffer between the noble landowners, and the majority of impoverished and near landless or proletarianized peasants who would constitute the second group. Unfortunately, such interpretations explain the government's actions in exclusively class terms. However, that a government policy benefits a specific social class does not necessarily indicate that that class succeeded in influencing the government to adopt the policy in question or that the government was primarily motivated by a desire to satisfy that class's interests. Indeed, without denying the existence of class interests or the possibility of a close relationship between government policy and the interests of specific classes, it must also be noted that virtually any action taken by any government can be identified as benefiting some groups at the expense of others. Moreover, the special interests concerned are usually quick to claim responsibility for such actions in order to enhance their

political appeal and bolster their own sense of importance. Similarly governments play on such interests to win political support. Thus, despite their value, class-based analyses can also obscure and even preclude the possibility of autonomous government action.

5. TsGIA SSSR, f. 1291, op. 31 (1907), d. 115, l. 6.

6. G. L. Yaney, *The Systematization of Russian Government: Social Evolution in the Domestic Administration of Imperial Russia, 1711–1905* (Urbana, 1973); and Yaney, *The Urge to Mobilize: Agrarian Reform in Russia, 1861–1930* (Urbana, 1982).

7. P. Lokhtin, *Sostoianie sel'skago khoziaistva v Rossii sravnitel'no s drugimi stranami* (SPB, 1901), p. 227.

8. In 1902, S. Iu. Witte commented to Nicholas on the necessity of reducing military expenditures in order to resolve the agrarian problem ("Dnevnik A. A. Polovtsova," KA, 3 [1923], 115). In 1857, the economist L. V. Tengoborskii similarly warned Alexander II. J. W. Kipp and W. B. Lincoln, "Autocracy and Reform: Bureaucratic Absolutism and Political Modernization in Nineteenth-Century Russia," *Russian History* 6:1 (1979): 10.

9. M. Hindus, *The Russian Peasant and the Revolution* (New York, 1920), p. 83.

10. W. E. Walling, *Russia's Message: The True World Import of the Revolution* (New York, 1908), pp. 182–83.

11. T. H. von Laue, "Imperial Russia at the Turn of the Century," *CSSH* 3 (July 1961): 353–67; D. W. Treadgold, *The Development of the USSR: An Exchange of Views* (Seattle, 1964), pp. 359–88. The following comparative and interdisciplinary works in a huge field have proved especially useful: P. Dorner, *Land Reform and Economic Development* (Baltimore, 1972); and E. Boserup, *The Conditions of Agricultural Growth: The Economics of Agrarian Change under Population Pressure* (Chicago, 1965). On peasants: T. Shanin, ed., *Peasants and Peasant Societies* (Baltimore, 1971); R. Redfield, *"The Little Community" and "Peasant Society and Culture"* (Chicago, 1965); M. Nash, *Primitive and Peasant Economic Systems* (San Francisco, 1966); E. R. Wolf, *Peasants* (Englewood Cliffs, N.J., 1966).

12. On the distinction between "land" and "agrarian" reform, see E. H. Tuma, *Twenty-six Centuries of Agrarian Reform: A Comparative Analysis* (Berkeley, 1965), pp. 8–14; D. Warriner, *Land Reform in Principle and Practice* (Oxford, 1969), pp. xiii–xx; and R. King, *Land Reform: A World Survey* (Boulder, 1977), pp. 3–25.

13. E. P. Thompson, "The Moral Economy of the English Crowd in the Eighteenth Century," *Past and Present* 50 (February 1971): 76–136; J. C. Scott, *The Moral Economy of the Peasant: Rebellion and Subsistence in South-East Asia* (New Haven, Conn., 1976). Cf. S. L. Popkin, *The Rational Peasant: The Political Economy of Rural Society in Vietnam* (Berkeley, 1979), pp. 1–31, 243–52. On the role of agrarian structures in shaping the contemporary world, see B. Moore, Jr., *The Social Origins of Dictatorship and Democracy: Lord and Peasant in the Making of the Modern World* (Boston, 1966); T. Skocpol, *States and Social Revolutions: A Comparative History of France, Russia and China* (New York, 1979), pp. 112–57; and E. R. Wolf, *Peasant Wars of the Twentieth Century* (New York, 1969). On the role of the peasantry in Russian history, W. S. Vucinich, ed., *The Peasant in Nineteenth Century Russia* (Stanford, 1968). On the relationship between peasant ideals and government policy, D. Field, *Rebels in the Name of the Tsar* (Boston, 1976), pp. 208–15; and K. A. Wittfogel, *Oriental Despotism: A Comparative Study of Total Power* (New Haven, 1957), pp. 179–81, 278–79, 340–43.

14. The following works on economic growth and development have been es-

pecially useful: A Gerschenkron, *Economic Backwardness in Historical Perspective: A Book of Essays* (Cambridge, Mass., 1962) pp. 119–97; Gerschenkron, *Continuity in History and Other Essays* (Cambridge, Mass., 1968) pp. 140–248; A. A. Skerpan, "The Russian National Economy and Emancipation," in *Essays in Russian History: A Collection Dedicated to George Vernadsky*, ed. A. D. Ferguson and A. Levin (Hamden, Conn., 1964), pp. 161–229; R. W. Goldsmith, "The Economic Growth of Tsarist Russia, 1860–1913," *Economic Development and Cultural Change* 9:3 (1961): 441–75; A. Kahan, "Government Policies and the Industrialization of Russia," *Journal of Economic History* 27:4 (1967): 460–77; P. Gregory, "Economic Growth and Structural Change in Tsarist Russia: A Case of Modern Economic Growth?" *Soviet Studies* 23:1 (1972): 418–34; Gregory, "Russian Industrialization and Economic Growth: Results and Perspectives of Western Research," *JGO* 25:2 (1977): 200–18; O. Crisp, *Studies in the Russian Economy Before 1914* (London, 1976), pp. 5–54; J. Nötzold, *Wirtschaftspolitische Alternativen der Entwicklung Russlands in der Ära Witte und Stolypin* (Berlin, 1966). Compare T. H. von Laue, *Why Lenin? Why Stalin? A Reappraisal of the Russian Revolution, 1900–1930* (Philadelphia, 1964); and A. Walicki, *The Controversy over Capitalism: Studies in the Social Philosophy of the Russian Populists* (Oxford, 1969).

15. .This changed with the Kiselev Reforms of 1837–1841, though even then intervention was quite limited. N. M. Druzhinin, *Gosudarstvennye krest'iane i reforma P. D. Kiseleva*, 2 vols. (Moscow, 1946–1958), 2:41–63, 233–48, esp. p. 236; Druzhinin, "Kiselevskii opyt likvidatsii obshchiny," in *Akademiku Borisu Dmitrievichu Grekovu ko dniu semidesiatiletiia: Sbornik statei* (Moscow, 1952), pp. 351–72; and R. E. McGrew, "Dilemmas of Development: Baron Heinrich Friedrich Storch (1766–1835) on the Growth of Imperial Russia," *JGO* 24:1 (1976): 71.

16. Compare Druzhinin, *Gosudarstvennye krest'iane*, 2:573; McGrew, "Dilemmas of Development," pp. 68–69; J. W. Kipp, "M. Kh. Reutern on the Russian State and Economy: A Liberal Bureaucrat during the Crimean Era, 1854–1860," *JMH* 47:3 (1975): 437–59; and J. A. Armstrong, *The European Administrative Elite* (Princeton, 1973), pp. 47–72.

17. V. I. Lenin, *Collected Works*, vol. 12 (Moscow, 1962), pp. 238–42, and vol. 15 (Moscow, 1963), pp. 139–40. The "Prussian" path involves the preservation of noble landownership and increased dependence on an impoverished peasantry and the American, the elimination of all forms of feudalism and the free development of a farmer economy on the basis of individual private property. Other alternatives include the English model, which involved the preservation of noble landownership, the expropriation of the peasantry, and the development of tenant farming; the French, based on small-scale peasant landownership; and the Danish, established on cooperatives. Compare A. A. Kofod, *Bor'ba chrezpolositseiu v Rossii i za granitseiu* also issued as *Zemleustroistvo v Rossii i v drugikh stranakh* (SPB, 1906); Lokhtin, *Sostoianie sel'skago khoziaistva; The Consolidation of Farms in Six Countries of Western Europe, International Journal of Agrarian Affairs* 1:4 (1952): 6–61. See E. Kingston-Mann, *Lenin and the Problem of Marxist Peasant Revolution* (New York, 1983), especially pp. 101–27 on different paths to capitalism. M. Kovalevskii, "Sudby obshchinnago zemlevladeniia v nashei verkhnei palate," *Vestnik Evropy*, 1910:6, pp. 71–3, argues for the irrelevance of the American model.

18. Compare L. G. Zakharova, "Pravitel'stvennaia programma otmeny krepostnogo prava v Rossii," *Istoriia SSSR* (1975): 30–31; Zakharova, "Redaktsionnye komissii 1859–1860 godov: uchrezhdenie, deiatel'nost'. (K istorii 'krizisa verkhov')," *Istoriia SSSR* 1983:3: 69; and T. Shanin, *Russia as a "Developing Society,"* vol. 1 of *The Roots of Otherness: Russia's Turn of Century* (London, 1985).

19. D. A. J. Macey, "Agriculture," in *Dictionary of the Russian Revolution*, ed. G. D. Jackson and R. Devlin, (Westport, Conn., forthcoming).
20. A. A. Peshekhonov, "Ukaz 9 noiabria o vydelenii iz obshchiny," *Trudy VEO* 2:6 (1906), 5.
21. D. T. Orlovsky, *The Limits of Reform: The Ministry of Internal Affairs in Imperial Russia, 1802–1881* (Cambridge, Mass.: 1981), p. 3.
22. J. H. Kautsky, "Revolutionary and Managerial Elites in Modernizing Regimes," *Comparative Politics*, July 1969, 441–66; and Kautsky, *The Politics of Aristocratic Empires* (Chapel Hill, 1982), especially pp. 348–59.
23. Compare Zakharova "Pravitel'stvennaia programma," pp. 45–47. On terminological problems, see A. J. Rieber, "Alexander II: A Revisionist View," JMH 43:1 (1971): 42–58.
24. M. Confino, *Domaines et seigneurs en Russie vers la fin du XVIIIe siècle: Étude de structures agraires et de mentalités économiques* (Paris, 1963); Confino, *Systèmes agraires et progrès agricole: L'assolement triennal en Russie aux XVIIIe–XIXe siècles: Étude d'économie et de sociologie rurales* (Paris, 1969); and Yaney, *Urge to Mobilize*, pp. 165–68, who describes this interest as an obsession and labels it a "checkerboard fantasy."
25. For example, A. Presniakov, "Samoderzhavie Aleksandra II," *Russkoe Proshloe* 1923:4: 3–20.
26. W. M. Pintner and D. K. Rowney, eds., *Russian Officialdom: The Bureaucratization of Russian Society from the Seventeenth to the Twentieth Century* (Chapel Hill, 1980); D. K. Rowney, "The Study of the Imperial Ministry of Internal Affairs in the Light of Organization Theory," in *The Behavioral Revolution and Communist Studies*, ed. R. Kanet (New York, 1971), pp. 209–31; D. T. Orlovsky, "Recent Studies of the Russian Bureaucracy," *Russian Review* 35:4 (1976): 448–67; M. Raeff, "The Bureaucractic Phenomenon of Imperial Russia," AHR 84:2 (1979): 399–411.
27. G. A. Hosking, *The Russian Constitutional Experiment: Government and Duma, 1907–1914* (Cambridge, 1973); M. S. Conroy, *Peter Arkad'evich Stolypin: Practical Politics in Late Tsarist Russia* (Boulder, 1976); A. V. Zenkovsky, *Stolypin: Russia's Last Great Reformer* (Princeton, 1986).
28. The following ideas are based primarily on M. Raeff, "The Well-Ordered Police State and the Development of Modernity in Seventeenth- and Eighteenth-Century Europe: An Attempt at a Comparative Approach," AHR 80:5 (1975): 1221–43; Raeff, *The Well-ordered Police State: Social and Institutional Change through Law in the Germanies and Russia, 1600–1800* (New Haven, 1983), pp. 181–257; Raeff, "The Bureaucratic Phenomenon," pp. 399–411; Orlovsky, *The Limits of Reform*, pp. 1–12; and H. Whelan, *Alexander III and the State Council: Bureaucracy and Counter-Reform in Late Imperial Russia* (New Brunswick, 1982), pp. 17–37, 83–97. Compare A. J. Rieber, "Bureaucractic Politics in Imperial Russia," *Social Science History* 2:4 (1978): 399–413.
29. R. S. Wortman, *The Development of a Russian Legal Consciousness* (Chicago, 1976), pp. 9–50.
30. Raeff, "Bureaucractic Phenomenon," p. 409.
31. The concept of a bureaucratic *soslovie* was suggested by A. A. Polovtsov in "Dnevnik A. A. Polovtsova" KA 3 (1923): 98, 139; and P. A. Valuev in V. V. Garmiza, "Predlozheniia i proekty P. A. Valueva po voprosam vnutrennei politiki (1862–1866 gg.)," *Istoricheskii Arkhiv* 4:1 (1958): 150. The bureaucratic service class increasingly saw itself in almost Hegelian terms as the "universal class," independent of yet mediating between other social groups. At the same time, it was constantly trying to overcome its isolation from "educated society"—and therefore from its own origins—in order to stem the growing conflict between

them. Thus, paralleling its attempt to reconcile laissez-faire individualism with autocracy, the government repeatedly tried to reconcile the centralized system of bureaucratic absolutism with the participation of society in both local administration and government decision making at the center.

32. On the sociology and mentality of the bureaucracy, in addition to works already cited, see especially M. Raeff, "The Russian Autocracy and Its Officials," *Harvard Slavic Studies: Russian Thought and Politics* 6 (1957): 77–91; Raeff, "L'état, le gouvernement et la tradition politique en Russie imperiale avant 1861," *Revue d'Histoire Moderne et Contemporaine* 1962:9, pp. 295–307; D. K. Rowney, "Higher Civil Servants in the Russian Ministry of Internal Affairs: Some Demographic and Career Characteristics, 1905–1916," *Slavic Review* 31:1 (1972): 101–10; S. Monas, "Bureaucracy in Russia under Nicholas I," in *Russia: Essays in History and Literature,* ed. L. H. Letgers (Leiden, 1972) pp. 100–16; W. B. Lincoln, *In the Vanguard of Reform: Russia's Enlightened Bureaucrats, 1825–1861* (DeKalb, Ill. 1982); S. F. Starr, *Decentralization and Self-Government in Russia, 1830–1870* (Princeton, 1972) pp. 3–50, 292–354; W. E. Mosse, "Aspects of Tsarist Bureaucracy: Recruitment to the Imperial State Council, 1855–1914," SEER, 57:2 (1979): 240–54; Mosse, "Aspects of Tsarist Bureaucracy: The State Council in the Late Nineteenth Century," *English Historical Review* (April 1980), pp. 268–92; Mosse, "Russian Bureaucracy at the End of the Ancien Régime: The Imperial State Council, 1897–1915," *Slavic Review* 39:4 (1980): 616–32; Mosse, "Bureaucracy and Nobility at the End of the Nineteenth Century," *Historical Journal* 24:3 (1981): 605–28; Mosse, "The Tsarist Ministerial Bureaucracy, 1882–1904: Its Social Composition and Political Attitudes," CASS 18:3 (1984): 249–67; Mosse, "Russian Provincial Governors at the End of the Nineteenth Century," *Historical Journal* 27:1 (1984): 225–40; D. C. B. Lieven, "The Russian Civil Service under Nicholas II: Some Variations on the Bureaucratic Theme," JGO 29:3 (1981): 366–403; Lieven, "Bureaucratic Liberalism in Late Imperial Russia: The Personality, Career and Opinions of A. N. Kulomzin," SEER 60:3 (1982): 413–31; Lieven, "Bureaucratic Authoritarianism in Late Imperial Russia: The Personality, Career and Opinions of P. N. Durnovo," *Historical Journal* 26:2 (1983): 391–402; Lieven, "Russian Senior Officialdom under Nicholas II: Careers and Mentalities," JGO 32:2 (1984): 199–223; R. G. Robbins, Jr., "Choosing the Russian Governors: The Professionalization of the Gubernatorial Corps," SEER 58:4 (1980): 541–60; Armstrong, *European Administrative Elite*; Armstrong, "Old Regime Administrative Elites: Prelude to Modernization in France, Prussia and Russia," *International Review of Administrative Sciences* 38:1 (1972): 21–40; Armstrong, "Old-Regime Governors: Bureaucratic and Patrimonial Attributes," CSSH 14:1 (1972): 2–29; Armstrong, "Tsarist and Soviet Elite Administrators," *Slavic Review* 31:1 (1972): 1–28; M. Fainsod, "Bureaucracy and Modernization: The Russian and Soviet Case," in *Bureaucracy and Political Development,* ed. J. LaPalombara (Princeton, 1963), pp. 233–67; I. F. Gindin, "Sotsial'no-ekonomicheskie itogi razvitiia kapitalizma i predposylki revoliutsii v nashei strane," *Sverzhdenie samoderzhaviia: Sbornik statei* (Moscow, 1970), pp. 39–88; P. A. Zaionchkovskii, *Pravitel'stvennyi apparat samoderzhavnoi Rossii v XIX v.* (Moscow, 1978); V. R. Leikina-Svirskaia, *Intelligentsiia v Rossii vo vtoroi polovine XIX veka* (Moscow, 1971), esp. pp. 71–91; compare the discussion of the autocracy's social basis, the nature of absolutism, and the bureaucracy's relationship to both in *Istoriia SSSR,* beginning with A. Ia. Avrekh, "Russkii absolutizm i ego rol' v utverzhdenii kapitalizma v Rossii," 1968:2, pp. 82–104, and ending with, "K diskussii ob absoliutizme v Rossii," 1972:4, pp. 65–88. Also, see A. M. Davidovich, *Samoderzhavie v epokhu imperializma (Klassovaia su-*

shchnost' i evoliutsiia absoliutizma v Rossii) (Moscow, 1975); and P. Anderson, Lineages of the Absolutist State (London, 1974).

33. Recent works on the nobility are G. M. Hamburg, Politics of the Russian Nobility, 1881–1905 (New Brunswick, 1984); S. Becker, Nobility and Privilege in Late Imperial Russia (DeKalb, Ill.: 1985); Iu. B. Solov'ev, Samoderzhavie i dvorianstvo v kontse XIX veka (Leningrad, 1973); Solov'ev, Samoderzhavie i dvorianstvo v 1902–1907 gg. (Leningrad, 1981); A. P. Korelin, Dvorianstvo v poreformennoi Rossii 1861–1904 gg.: Sostav, chislennost', korporativnaia organizatsiia (Moscow, 1979).

34. The movement was divided between liberal/constitutional and populist/ socialist wings.

35. On the common origins of the intelligentsia and the bureaucracy, M. Raeff, Origins of the Russian Intelligentsia: The Eighteenth Century Nobility (New York, 1966).

36. The term opeka originated with government regulations for the care of orphans. It is similar in meaning and often interchangeable with the term popechitel'stvo, usually translated as "guardianship," which described the noble's traditional and patriarchal responsibilities toward his serfs prior to emancipation. At the end of the 1830s opeka was adapted to describe the supervisory and protective functions that were assigned to the new bureaucratic system of administration set up over the state peasants and aptly named "state feudalism." Druzhinin, Gosudarstvennye krest'iane, 1:193. After emancipation, opeka increasingly came to describe the bureaucracy's tutelary role and administrative responsibilities toward the nobility's former serfs. A. A. Rittikh, Krest'ianskii pravoporiadok, (SPB, 1904), pp. 293–320; Kovalevskii, "Sudby obshchinnago zemlevladeniia," pp. 71–73; A. A. Leont'ev, Krest'ianskoe pravo: Sistematicheskoe izlozhenie osobennostei zakonodatel'stva o krest'ianakh, 1st ed. (SPB, 1909), pp. 380–86; P. I. Liashchenko, Ocherki agrarnoi evoliutsii Rossii, vol. 1, Krest'ianskoe delo i poreformennaia zemleustroitel'naia politika, part 2, Regulirovanie krest'ianskogo zemlevladeniia (Tomsk, 1917), 1–43; P. S. Tsypkin, "Opeka v russkom krest'ianskom bytu," in Administrativnyi stroi russkago krest'ianina, ed. V. V. Tenishev, (SPB, 1908); D. Christian, "The Supervisory Function in Russian and Soviet History," Slavic Review 41:1 (1982): 73–90.

37. Compare the objections of the Chernigov Provincial Committee on the Needs of Agriculture to a government policy that it perceived as supporting a minimum standard of living for the peasantry. D. S. Fleksor, comp., Okhrana sel'skokhoziaistvennoi sobstvennosti (SPB, 1904), p. 11.

38. This correspondence between opeka and "state socialism" was made, for example, by Polovtsov, "Iz dnevnika A. A. Polovtsova," KA 67 (1934): 177, though he did not approve it. Others, however, saw it in a favorable light. See Stolypin's references to state socialism in Sbornik zakliuchenii po voprosam otnosiashchimsia k peresmotru Polozheniia 12 iiunia 1886 o naime na sel'skie raboty, (SPB, 1898): 2:30; and his 10 May 1907 speech to the Second Duma, in GDSO (1907): 2:443. Compare A. A. Kaufman, "Agrarnaia deklaratsiia P. A. Stolypina," Russkaia Mysl', 1907:6, part 2, p. 169; Kaufman, Voprosy ekonomiki i statistiki krest'ianskogo khoziaistva (Moscow, 1918), p. xii; P. Miliukov, Russia and Its Crisis (London, 1962), p. 255; P. P. Migulin, letter 2 November 1905 (Witte Archive, RACU); Migulin, "Dopolnitel'nyi nadel" in his Agrarnyi Vopros (Khar'kov, 1906), p. 44; S. Shidlovskii, "The Imperial Duma and the Land Settlement," Russian Review 1:1 (1912): 20–23. On the utopian aspects of various worldviews, see A. Walicki, The Slavophile Controversy: History of a Conservative Utopia in Nineteenth-Century Russian Thought (Oxford, 1975), esp. pp. 6–9; and

Zakharova "Pravitel'stvennaia programma," p. 43. On the theory of state socialism, A. I. Pashkov, ed., *Istoriia Russkoi ekonomicheskoi mysli*, vol. 2, p. 1 (Moscow, 1959), pp. 149–66.

39. A. von Haxthausen, *Studies on the Interior of Russia* (Chicago, 1972). See
S. F. Starr, "Introduction," pp. xxxiv–xli. C. A. Koefoed, *My Share in the Stolypin
Reforms* (Odense, 1985), p. 30.

40. This customary peasant institution is variously identified by the Russian
words *mir, obshchina*, or *sel'skoe obshchestvo*. The history of these Russian
terms is both complex and confusing and is concerned more with the misconcep-
tions of capital-city society and the aspirations of government legislators than
with either rural realities or peasant consciousness. See S. A. Grant, "*Obshchina*
and *Mir*," *Slavic Review* 35:4 (1976): 636–51; Y. Taniuchi, "Note on the Territo-
rial Relationship between Rural Societies, Settlements and Communes," *Discussion Papers*, RC/D:3 (Birmingham, 1966); Yaney, *Urge to Mobilize*, pp. 168–71.
On the discussions, see S. A. Grant, "The Peasant Commune in Russian Thought,
1861–1905" (Ph.D. diss., Harvard University, 1973). In addition, see *Trudy Osoboi Kommisii dlia sostavleniia proekt mestnago upravleniia*, (n.p., n.d.), pp. 1–
14; *Ocherk predpolozhenii bolshinstva chlenov Soveshchaniia Osoboi Kommisii
po sostavleniiu proektov mestnago upravleniia* (n.p., n.d.), pp. 7–20; and *Trudy
redkom*, 2:24–44. The literature on the peasant commune is immense, but see
especially K. R. Kachorovskii, *Russkaia obshchina. Vozmozhno li, zhelatel'no li
ee sokhranenie i razvitie?*, 2d ed. (Moscow, 1906); A. E. Voskresenskii, *Obshchinnoe zemlevladenie i krest'ianskoe malozemel'e* (SPB, 1903); P. Veniaminov,
*Krest'ianskaia obshchina: (Chto ona takoe, k chemu idet, chto daet i chto mozhet
dat' Rossii?)* (SPB, 1908); F. M. Watters, "The Peasant and the Village Commune,"
in W. S. Vucinich, ed., *The Peasant in Nineteenth-Century Russia* (Stanford: Stanford University Press, 1968), pp. 133–57; S. G. Pushkarev, *Krest'ianskaia
pozemel'no-peredel'naia obshchina v Rossii* (Newtonville, Mass., 1976); A. M.
Anfimov and P. N. Zyrianov, "Nekotorye cherty evoliutsii russkoi krest'ianskoi
obshchiny v poreformennyi period," *Istoriia SSSR*, 1980:4, pp. 26–41; B. Mironov,
"The Russian Peasant Commune after the Reforms of the 1860s," *Slavic Review*
44:3 (1985): 438–67; M. B. Petrovich, "The Peasant in Nineteenth-Century Historiography," in Vucinich, *The Peasant*, pp. 191–230; S. M. Dubrovskii, "Rossiiskaia obshchina v literature XIX i nachala XX v. (Bibliograficheskii obzor)," in
*Voprosy istorii sel'skogo khoziaistva, krest'ianstva i revoliutsionnogo dvizheniia
v Rossii* (Moscow, 1961), pp. 348–61; Dubrovskii, "K voprosu ob obshchine v
Rossii v nachale XX v.," in *EAIVE za 1960 g.* (Kiev, 1962), pp. 520–33.

41. See M. Raeff, "The Peasant Commune in the Political Thinking of Russian
Publicists: Laissez-faire Liberalism in the Reign of Alexander II" (Ph.D. diss.,
Harvard University, 1950), pp. 8–12; Raeff, "Some Reflections on Russian Liberalism," *Russian Review* 18:3 (1959): 218–30; V. V. Leontovitsch, *Geschichte des
Liberalismus in Russland* (Frankfurt-am-Main, 1957); S. Benson, "The Conservative Liberalism of Boris Chicherin," *FOG* 21 (1975): 17–104. I use this term to
refer to those who adhered to the political status quo yet favored social and economic change along individualistic, laissez-faire lines. Subsequently, the holders
of these ideas would come to favor government intervention, as we shall see. Cf.
M. Katz, *Mikhail N. Katkov: A Political Biography, 1818–1887* (The Hague, 1966),
pp. 15–43, who uses the similar term *conservative westerner*.

42. But see T. Shanin, ed., *Late Marx and the Russian Road: Marx and "The
Peripheries of Capitalism"* (New York, 1983).

43. Yaney, *The Urge to Mobilize*, calls this mobilization.

44. Rittikh, *Krest'ianskii pravoporiadok*, pp. 293–4.

45. K. P. Kachorovskii, "Biurokraticheskii zakon i krest'ianskaia obshchina," *Russkoe Bogatstvo*, 1910:7, p. 127.

46. A. A. Leont'ev, "Zakonodatel'stvo o krest'ianakh posle reformy," in *Velikaia reforma: Russkoe obshchestvo i krest'ianskii vopros v proshlom i nastoiashchem: Iubileinoe izdanie*, ed. A. K. Dzhivelegov et al. vol. 6 (Moscow, 1911), p. 199. Compare Rittikh, *Krest'ianskii pravoporiadok*, pp. 293–4.

47. T. S. Kuhn's *The Structure of Scientific Revolutions*, 2d ed. (Chicago, 1970), helped me achieve a more precise formulation of this concept.

48. Leont'ev, "Zakonodatel'stvo," p. 199.

Notes to Chapter 1

1. The Emancipation of 1861 affected only peasants owned by the nobility. *Udel* and State peasants were emancipated in 1863 and 1866, respectively.

2. A. S. Posnikov, "Agrarnyi vopros v tret'ei dume," *Vestnik Evropy* 1909:1, p. 233; V. Gerb'e, *Vtoroe raskreposhchenie, 19 fevralia 1861–14 iiunia 1910; obshchiia preniia po ukazu 9 noiabria 1906 g. v gosudarstvennoi dume i v gosudarstvennom sovete* (Moscow, 1911); Raeff, "Peasant Commune," pp. 7–8; Atkinson, *Russian Land Commune*, pp. 41–70.

3. P. I. Liashchenko, "Piat'desiat let nashego agrarno-ekonomicheskago zakonodatel'stva," *Vestnik Finansov*, 1911:8, pp. 330–36; "Osvobozhdenie krest'ian (19 fevralia 1861 g.–19 fevralia 1911 g.)," *IZO*, 1911:1, appendix; E. V[erpakhovskii]., comp., *Gosudarstvennaia deiatel'nost' predsedatelia soveta ministrov Stats-sekretaria Petra Arkad'evicha Stolypina, 1909–1911* (SPB, 1911), 2:35–37.

4. The term *enlightened bureaucrats* refers to a bloc of some sixteen government officials, led by N. A. Miliutin, deliberately assembled over the preceding two decades by some of the tsar's ministers in order to carry through their reform programs. They participated in numerous discussion circles and were familiar with the ideas of Westerners, Slavophiles, and Socialists. This group had particularly close associations with the reform-minded members of the tsarist family, Grand Duchess Elena Pavlovna and Grand Duke Konstantin Nikolaevich and considerable practical experience of administration and rural society. Many had participated in Kiselev's reform of the State Peasantry in 1837–1839 and the liberation of the Grand Duchess's serfs on her estate in Poltava Province in 1859. There are interesting parallels between this group and the new bureaucratic generation discussed in chapter 2. The Editing Commission included two other, smaller groups: a group of nonbureaucratic rural experts and noble landowners sympathetic to the reform, including the geographer and statistician P. P. Semenov (later Semenov-T'ian-Shanskii) and the liberal Slavophiles Iu. F. Samarin, Prince V. A. Cherkasskii, and A. I. Koshelev. The other group consisted of a rump of self-proclaimed defenders of the serf owners' interests and prerogatives. Its most outspoken members were two magnates, Counts F. I. Paskevich and P. A. Shuvalov. W. B. Lincoln, "The Editing Commissions of 1859–1860: Some Notes on Their Members' Backgrounds and Service Careers," SEER 56:3 (1978): 346–59; Lincoln, "The Genesis of an 'Enlightened' Bureaucracy in Russia," JGO 20:3 (1972): 321–30; Lincoln, *In the Vanguard*; and Lincoln, *Nikolai Miliutin: An Enlightened Russian Bureaucrat of the Nineteenth Century*, (Newtonville, Mass., 1977), pp. 30–62; P. P. Semenov-T'ian-Shanskii, *Memuary P. P. Semenova-T'ian-Shanskago. III, Epokha osvobozhdeniia krest'ian v Rossii (1857–1861 gg.) v vospominiakh*

P. P. Semenov-T'ian-Shanskago, (Petrograd, 1917) pp. 219–60, especially p. 219, fn. 1.

5. Raeff, "Peasant Commune," pp. 9–11; V. G. Chernukha uses the term *liberal conservatives* to describe the post-Emancipation faction of bureaucrats and dignitaries led by P. P. Shuvalov and P. A. Valuev in *Vnutrenniaia politika tsarizma s serediny 50kh do nachala 80kh gg. XIX v.* (Leningrad, 1978), p. 87.

6. Druzhinin, *Gosudarstvennye krest'iane*, 1:611–28, and 2:551–66; P. D. Kiselev, "O postepennom unichtozhenii rabstva v Rossii," in A. P. Zablotskii-Desiatovskii, *Graf P. D. Kiselev i ego vremia*, Vol. 4 (SPB, 1882), pp. 197–99; Semenov-T'ian-Shanskii, *Memuary*, 3:220, 222–23; S. V. Mironenko, "Sekretnyi komitet 1839–1842 gg i vopros ob osvobozhdenii krepostnykh krest'ian," VMUSI, 1977:3, pp. 25–43; P. A. Zaionchkovskii, *Otmena krepostnogo prava*, 3d ed. (Moscow, 1968), pp. 51–62; D. Field, *The End of Serfdom: Nobility and Bureaucracy in Russia, 1855–1861*, (Cambridge, Mass.: 1976), especially pp. 35–50; W. B. Lincoln, "Count P. D. Kiselev: A Reformer in Imperial Russia," *Australian Journal of Politics and History* 16:2 (1970), 177–88. See, too, L. G. Zakharova, *Samoderzhavie i otmena krepostnogo prava v Rossii, 1856–1861* (Moscow, 1984), pp. 24–135; T. Emmons, *The Russian Landed Gentry and the Peasant Emancipation of 1861* (Cambridge, 1968), pp. 47–205; E. N. Mukhina, "Nachalo podgotovki krest'ianskoi reformy v Rossii (1856–1857 gg.)," VMUSI, 1977:4, pp. 39–52.

7. *Zhurnaly sekretnago i glavnago komitetov po krest'ianskomu delu* (Petrograd, 1915), 1:5–26, 259–64; A. Skrebitskii, comp., *Krest'ianskoe delo v tsarstvovanie Imperatora Aleksandra II: Materialy dlia istorii osvobozhdeniia krest'ian* (Bonn, 1862), 1:908–25.

8. K. A. Sofronenko, comp., *Krest'ianskaia reforma v Rossii 1861 goda: Sbornik zakonodatel'nykh aktov*, (Moscow, 1954), p. 42.

9. Skrebitskii, *Krest'ianskoe delo*, vol. 1, pp. 31–56, 943–66; vol. 2, pt. 1 (Bonn, 1863), pp. 450–718, especially 515–29; and vol. 4 (Bonn, 1868), pp. 246–471, esp. 314–16; Reports Nos. 2 and 8 of the Juridical Section, and No. 8 of the Economic Section in *Pervoe izdanie materialov redaktsionnykh kommissii, dlia sostavleniia polozhenii o krest'ianakh vykhodiashchikh iz krepostnoi zavisimosti*, pt. 2 (SPB, 1859); Sofronenko, *Krest'ianskaia reforma*, pp. 37–80, 91–132.

10. D. P. Hammer, "Russia and the Roman Law," *Slavic Review* 16:1 (1957): 11–12; V. V. Leontovich, *Istoriia liberalizma v Rossii 1762–1914* (Paris, 1980), pp. 31–33, 136–37. Compare W. G. Wagner, "Legislative Reform of Inheritance in Russia, 1861–1914," in *Russian Law: Historical and Political Perspectives*, ed. W. E. Butler (Leiden, 1977), pp. 143–78.

11. R. Beerman, "Prerevolutionary Russian Peasant Laws," in *Russian Law*, ed. Butler, pp. 179–81; P. N. Zyrianov, "Obychnoe grazhdanskoe pravo v poreformennoi obshchine," in *Ezhegodnik po agrarnoi istorii*, vol. 6 (Vologda, 1976), pp. 91–101; M. Lewin, "Customary Law and Russian Rural Society in the Post-Reform Era" and discussion in *Russian Review* 44:1 (1985): 1–43; K. R. Kachorovskii, *Narodnoe pravo* (Moscow, 1906); O. A. Khauke, *Krest'ianskoe zemel'noe pravo* (Moscow, 1913); I. M. Strakhovskii, *Krest'ianskiia prava i uchrezhdeniia* (SPB, 1904).

12. This phrase was used repeatedly. Semenov-T'ian-Shanskii, *Memuary*, 3:1 224, 230, 241–42, 250; N. P. Semenov, *Osvobozhdenie krest'ian v tsarstvovanie Imperatora Aleksandra II: Khronika deiatel'nosti komissii po krest'ianskomu delu*, 3 vols. in 5 parts (SPB 1889–1891), vol. 2, pp. 324, 383, n., 393; vol. 3, pt. 2, pp. 63–64, 83; B. E. Nol'de, *Iurii Samarin i ego vremia* (Paris, 1978), pp. 116, 124. Miliutin noted that the best kind of "law" was that which reflected "existing facts," or custom. In this view, law was confined to the static function of describ-

ing existing reality rather than the dynamic one of prescribing it. The most the law could do was to prepare society for the future. However, any attempt to impose law on custom would provoke disorder and threaten the destruction of the law itself. It is remarkable that this historicism did not completely prevent any government actions whatever.

13. Juridical Section Report No. 2 in *Pervoe izdanie materialov*, pt. 2, especially pp. 6–7. Nol'de, *Iurii Samarin*, p. 80; Leontovich, *Istoriia liberalizma*, pp. 192–96.

14. S. I. Shidlovskii, comp., *Zemel'nye zakhvaty i mezhevoe delo* (SPB, 1904); A. Leont'ev, "Mezhevyia nuzhdy derevni," in *Nuzhdy derevni po rabotam komitetov o nuzhdakh sel'skokhoziaistvennoi promyshlennosti: Sbornik Statei* (SPB, 1904), 1:234–59.

15. Skrebitskii, *Krest'ianskoe delo*, vol. 2, pt. 1, pp. 480–86; Zaionchkovskii, *Otmena*, p. 78.

16. Skrebitskii, *Krest'ianskoe delo*, 4:295–97.

17. Ibid., vol. 2, pt. 1, pp. 478–80; Semenov, *Osvobozhdeniia*, 1:159–63.

18. Sofronenko, *Krest'ianskaia reforma*, p. 32.

19. Skrebitskii, *Krest'ianskoe delo*, 1:9–30, 832–33.

20. Skrebitskii, *Krest'ianskoe delo*, vol. 1, pp. 331–839, esp. 699–725 and 820–39; vol. 3 (Bonn, 1865–1866), chap. 16, esp. pp. 536–69; and *Pervoe izdanie materialov*, pt. 2, Reports Nos. 5 and 6 of the Administrative Section and No. 9 of the Economic Section; Sofronenko, *Krest'ianskaia reforma*, pp. 133–58; Semenov-T'ian-Shanskii, *Memuary* 3:240–60; and A. A. Kornilov, *Ocherki po istorii obshchestvennago dvizheniia i krest'ianskago dela v Rossii* (SPB, 1905), pp. 313–43.

21. Starr, *Decentralization*, especially pp. 138–62 and 175–91; V. V. Garmiza, *Podgotovka zemskoi reformy 1864 goda* (Moscow, 1957); Skrebitskii, *Krest'ianskoe delo*, 1:703–6, 714–15, 820–24, 838; Semenov, *Osvobozhdeniia*, vol. 2, p. 394; vol. 3, pt. 1, p. 317. The Special Commission on provincial and county institutions, formed within the Interior Ministry in 1859, produced both the 1861 Statute on local peasant administration and the 1864 Statute on the zemstvos. It continued in existence until the formation of the Kakhanov Commission in 1881 but achieved nothing.

22. Skrebitskii, *Krest'ianskoe delo*, 1:824, 838; Semenov, *Osvobozhdeniia*, vol. 3, pt. 1, p. 317.

23. Ibid., pt. 2, p. 76.

24. In fact, this reform was considerably more complicated and involved an attempt to separate the commune's administrative and judicial functions from its economic functions and to locate the former in a new administrative unit known as the "rural community" (sel'skoe obshchestvo). This aspect of the reform was, however, never realized; and although the government continued to use this terminology, the rural community was a fictitious unit. A commune did not necessarily coincide with the physical settlement or village. Some villages might be made up of several communes, and one commune might take in more than one settlement unit. *Trudy Redkom*, 2:24–28; Sofronenko, *Krest'ianskaia reforma*, pp. 47–80. See introduction, n. 40.

25. These institutions were modeled on similar ones established for the State Peasantry in the 1830s (Druzhinin, *Gosudarstvennye krest'iane*, 1:544–56), as was the rural community (ibid., 556–70).

26. The peace arbitrator was also modeled on a similar institution established over the State Peasantry. Semenov, *Osvobozhdeniia*, vol. 3, pt. 2, p. 76; Skrebitskii, *Krest'ianskoe delo*, vol. 1, 834–39. On the peace arbitrators, see *ibid.*, vol. 1, 706–8, 715–17; Sofronenko, *Krest'ianskaia reforma*, pp. 136–51; J. W. Rose, "The

Russian Peasant Emancipation and the Problem of Rural Administration: The Institution of the 'Mirovoi Posrednik,' " (Ph.D. diss., Kansas Univ., 1976), especially pp. 38–77; J. I. Mandel, "Paternalistic Authority in the Russian Countryside, 1856–1906" (Ph.D. diss., Columbia University, 1978), pp. 57–64; V. G. Chernukha, *Krest'ianskii vopros v pravitel'stvennoi politike (60–70 gody XIX v.)* (Leningrad, 1972), pp. 25–69, esp. 26–30; Zakharova, *Samoderzhavie*, pp. 214–21; Yaney, *Systematization*, pp. 364–67; Semenov, *Osvobozhdeniia*, vol. 3, pt. 1, 346–47.

27. D. P. Maliutin, *Oshibki, sdelannyia pri sostavlenii polozheniia o krest'ianakh 19 fevralia 1861 g. i ikh posledstviia* (SPB, 1895), p. 46.

28. This tradition was reinforced by the failure of Count Kiselev's attempt to abolish the commune among the state peasantry and his subsequent conviction that the commune had to be preserved as a guarantor of order. Druzhinin, "Kiselevskii opyt," pp. 351–72.

29. The idea of "invasion" is borrowed from K. S. Aksakov, "On the Internal State of Russia" in M. Raeff, ed., *Russian Intellectual History: An Anthology* (New York, 1966) p. 242.

30. Semenov, *Osvobozhdenie*, vol. 1, 196–97, 505–6, 529–30; vol. 2, 288–89, 324–25, 382–83; and vol. 3, pt. 2, 53–85, 226–29, 287–300; Skrebitskii, *Krest'ianskoe delo*, vol. 1, 9–30; vol. 2, pt. 1, 515–29, 541, 648–53, and Maliutin, *Oshibki*, p. 39.

31. See Article 36 of the Emancipation Statute in Sofronenko, *Krest'ianskaia reforma*, pp. 46–47; Semenov, *Osvobozhdeniia*, vol. 3, pt. 2, 227–29; Kachorovskii, "Biurokraticheskii zakon," 1910:7, p. 130.

32. Sofronenko, *Krest'ianskaia reforma*, pp. 207–8. These affected about 70 percent of the former serfs. Individual (hereditary-household) forms of tenure predominated in the western borderlands. By the turn of the century, repartitional tenure accounted for approximately 80 percent of the total.

33. Semenov, *Osvobozhdeniia*, vol. 3, pt. 2, 81–85, 227.

34. Sofronenko, *Krest'ianskaia reforma*, pp. 129–30. Miliutin supported the preservation of the state's land fund in order to satisfy any subsequent growth in the peasant population. L. G. Zakharova, "Dvorianstvo i pravitel'stvennaia programma otmeny krepostnogo prava v Rossii," *Voprosy Istorii*, 1973:9, p. 45. When the Emancipation's principles were extended to the state peasantry in 1866 this concern was reiterated.

35. Semenov, *Osvobozhdeniia*, vol. 3, pt. 2, 288–92, 298–300. A. I. Koshelev, *Zapiski, 1806–1883*, (Newtonville, Mass., 1976), appendix, p. 119.

36. Skrebitskii, *Krest'ianskoe delo*, vol. 2, pt. 1, 525–29, 650–51; Sofronenko, *Krest'ianskaia reforma*, p. 130.

37. Skrebitskii, *Krest'ianskoe delo*, 1:910; Semenov, *Osvobozhdenie*, vol. 3, pt. 2, 83, 288; Semenov-T'ian-Shanskii, *Memuary*, vol. 3, 232, n. 1; *Pervoe izdanie materialov*, Economic Section Report No. 8, p. 74.

38. P. Maslov, *Agrarnyi vopros v Rossii*, vol. 2 (SPB, 1908), 34–42; P. A. Zaionchkovskii, *Provedenie v zhizni krest'ianskoi reformy 1861 g.* (Moscow, 1958), pp. 40–87; Zaionchkovskii, *Otmena*, pp. 152–82; T. Emmons, "The Peasant and the Emancipation," in *The Peasant*, ed. Vucinich, pp. 41–71.

39. In addition to other works cited, the following have proved useful: V. Rozenberg, "Iz khroniki krest'ianksago dela," in *Ocherki po krest'ianskomu voprosu: Sobranie statei*, vol. 1, ed. A. A. Manuilov (Moscow, 1904), 1–227; F. Danilov, "Obshchaia politika pravitel'stva i gosudarstvennyi stroi k nachalu XX veka," in *Obshchestvennoe dvizhenie v Rossii v nachale XX-go veka*, vol. 1, ed. L. Martov et al. (SPB, 1909), 422–82; I. V. Chernyshev, "Klassovye interesy v zakondatel'stve ob obshchine," *Poznanie Rossii*, 1909:3, pp. 159–89; A. A. Kauf-

man, *Agrarnyi vopros v Rossii: Kurs Narodnago Universiteta*, 2d ed. (Moscow, 1919), pp. 89–133; B. D. Brutskus, *Agrarnyi vopros i agrarnaia politika* (Petrograd, 1922).

40. A. A. Kornilov, *Obshchestvennoe dvizhenie pri Aleksandra II (1855–1881): Istoricheskii ocherki* (Paris, 1905), especially pp. 58–83, 85–96; V. A. Kitaev, *Ot frondy k okhranitel'stvu: Iz istorii russkoi liberal'noi mysli 50–60 godov XIX veka* (Moscow, 1972); Emmons, *Russian Landed Gentry*, pp. 321–93.

41. Zaionchkovskii, *Provedenie*, pp. 88–364; V. G. Litvak, *Russkaia derevnia v reforme 1861 goda: Chernozemnyi tsentr 1861–1895 gg.* (Moscow, 1972).

42. Chernukha, *Vnutrenniaia politika*, pp. 15–118; Chernukha, "Sovet Ministrov v 1857–1861 gg." in VID, V (Leningrad, 1973), 120–37; and Chernukha, "Sovet ministrov v 1861–1881 gg." in VID, IX (Leningrad, 1978), 90–116.

43. P. A. Zaionchkovskii, "P. A. Valuev" in *Dnevnik P. A. Valueva ministra vnutrennikh del*, vol. 1 (Moscow, 1961) 23–28; Field, *End of Serfdom*, pp. 344–58; Nol'de, *Iurii Samarin*, pp. 134–45; A. Leroy-Beaulieu, *Un homme d'état Russe (Nicolas Miliutine): D'après sa correspondance inédite* (Hattiesburg, Miss., 1969), pp. 63–99; Koshelev, *Zapiski*, pp. 130–41; Lincoln, *Nikolai Miliutin*, p. 62; Orlovsky, *Limits of Reform*, especially pp. 123–69.

44. Garmiza, "Predlozheniia i proekty," p. 143.

45. His 1863 project is in M. Raeff, ed., *Plans for Political Reform in Imperial Russia, 1730–1905* (Englewood Cliffs, N.J., 1966), pp. 121–31.

46. On the problem of gathering information, Yaney, *Urge to Mobilize*, pp. 10–48.

47. *Chastnyia zametki chlenov kommissii* in *Doklad Vysochaishe uchrezhdennoi kommissii dlia izsledovaniia nyneshniago polozheniia sel'skago khoziaistva i sel'skoi proizvoditel'nosti v Rossii*, vol. 2 (SPB, 1873), appendix 3, pp. 1–8; Ia. St-k, "Valuevskaia kommissiia," *Russkaia Mysl'*, 1891:3, p. 13.

48. O. N. Shepeleva, "Zapiska P. A. Valueva Aleksandru II o provedenii reformy 1861 g.," *Istoricheskii Arkhiv*, 1961:1, p. 77.

49. Chernukha, *Vnutrenniaia politika*, p. 75.

50. N. M. Druzhinin, *Russkaia derevnia na perelome 1861–1880 gg.* (Moscow, 1978), pp. 25–44; N. M. Druzhinin, "Glavnyi Komitet ob ustroistve sel'skogo sostoianiia," in N. E. Nosov, ed., *Issledovaniia po sotsial'no-politicheskoi istorii Rossii: Sbornik statei* (Leningrad, 1971), pp. 269–86; J. W. Kipp, "The Grand Duke Konstantin Nikolaevich and the Epoch of the Great Reforms, 1855–1866" (Ph.D. diss., Pennsylvania State, 1970), pp. 265–301. This body was dominated by the enlightened bureaucrats. On the peace arbitrators, see Zaionchkovskii, *Provedenie*, pp. 88–135; Chernukha, *Krest'ianskii vopros*, pp. 25–69; Rose, "Russian Peasant Emancipation," pp. 136–77; T. S. Pearson, "Ministerial Conflict and Local Self-Government Reform in Russia, 1877–1890," (Ph.D. diss., Univ. of North Carolina at Chapel Hill, 1977) pp. 26–40; Mandel, "Paternalistic Authority," pp. 73–106; compare Valuev's 1863 proposal to draw gentry representatives into an advisory role in government and his 1864 proposal for the reform of local administration. P. Czap Jr., "P. A. Valuev's Proposal for a Vyt' Administration, 1864," SEER 45:105 (1967), pp. 391–410.

51. Chernukha, *Krest'ianskii vopros*, p. 65.

52. *Otchet za 1874* (SPB, 1876), pp. 10–19; Chernukha, *Krest'ianskii vopros*, pp. 61–69; Druzhinin, "Glavnyi komitet," pp. 282–83. The gap was partly filled by the expansion of the rural police force in 1878. PSZ (2d), LIII (1878) otd. 1, no. 58610, pp. 398–400 and appendix, pp. 336–44; R. Abbott, "Police Reform in the Russian Province of Iaroslavl, 1856–1876," *Slavic Review*, 32:2 (1973), 292–302; Mandel, "Paternalistic Authority," pp. 106–23.

53. Interior Minister Timashev had also expressed concern. P. A. Zaionchkov-

skii, ed., *Krest'ianskoe dvizhenie v Rossii v 1870–1880 gg.: Sbornik dokumentov* (Moscow, 1968), pp. 30–8, especially 30–2.

54. Confino, *Systèmes agraires*, especially pp. 157–221, 269; Yaney, *Urge to Mobilize*, pp. 163–77; compare McGrew, "Dilemmas of Development," p. 70.

55. Druzhinin, *Gosudarstvennye krest'iane*, vol. 2, 534.

56. "Chastnyia zametki," p. 5; Chernukha, *Krest'ianskii vopros*, p. 157.

57. "Chastnyia zametki," pp. 6–8; compare Koshelev, *Zapiski*, appendix, p. 119, and Mandel, "Paternalistic Authority," pp. 237–40 on traditional attitudes toward kulaks.

58. Cited in G. L. Freeze, "The *Soslovie* (Estate) Paradigm and Russian Social History," AHR 91:1 (1986), 26–27, n. 50. But compare "Sel'skoe obshchestvo," in *Ob"iasnitel'nyia zapiski k proektu polozhenii ob ustroistve mestnago upravleniia*, p. 13.

59. Shepeleva, "Zapiska P. A. Valueva," p. 80.

60. Chernukha, *Krest'ianskii vopros*, p. 162.

61. S. M. Seredonin, *Istoricheskii obzor deiatel'nosti Komiteta Ministrov*, vol. 3 (SPB, 1902), pt. 1, 99; pt. 2, 315; St-k, *Valuevskaia kommissiia*, 1891:4, pp. 25–29; Chernukha, *Krest'ianskii vopros*, pp. 163–64.

62. Ibid., p. 145.

63. According to N. Kh. Bunge in G. E. Snow, *The Years 1881–1894 in Russia: A Memorandum Found in the Papers of N. Kh. Bunge: A Translation and Commentary* (Philadelphia, 1981), p. 50. On the problem of governmental unity, Chernukha, *Vnutrenniaia politika*, pp. 170–98.

64. Chernukha blames the Russo-Turkish War and the political crisis at the end of the 1870s for the abandonment of the Commission's proposals. *Krest'ianskii vopros*, pp. 163–64. However, it seems more likely that the recommendation that completed projects subsequently be discussed in a Special Commission, under the Tsar's chairmanship, and with the participation of provincial marshals of the nobility and chairmen of provincial zemstvo executive boards as well as, where appropriate, members of city administrations and merchants (ibid., p. 315), was rejected as a political threat. Throughout the period down to the convocation of the Special Conference on the Needs of Agriculture in 1902, the government's need for information and knowledge about the real situation in the provinces was repeatedly undermined by its fear that such efforts would foster "constitutional" illusions within local society. See *Spravki MVD*, pp. 53–80. As an alternative, the government began to consult privately with individual groups. Compare Rieber, "Bureaucratic Politics," pp. 399–413. Interior Minister N. P. Ignat'ev noted that it was almost impossible to separate the question of administrative reform from the larger issue of Russia's constitutional structure. The subsequent Kakhanov Commission was in fact linked to Ignat'ev's own "constitutional project," calling for the establishment of a *zemskii sobor* modeled on the seventeenth century institution with the same name. P. A. Zaionchkovskii, *Krizis samoderzhaviia na rubezhe 1870–1880 godov* (Moscow, 1964), pp. 379–472; and Zaionchkovskii, "Popytka sozyva zemskogo sobora i padenie ministerstva N. P. Ignat'eva," *Istoriia SSSR*, 1960:5, pp. 126–39.

65. A. I. Koshelev, *Ob obshchinnom zemlevladenii v Rossii* (Berlin, 1875), as cited in H. Seton-Watson, *The Russian Empire, 1801–1917* (Oxford, 1967), p. 402.

66. In addition to works already cited, see A. M. Anfimov, "Krest'ianskoe dvizhenie v Rossii vo vtoroi polovine XIX veka," *Voprosy Istorii*, 1973:5, pp. 15–31; B. B. Veselovskii, *Istoriia zemstva za sorok let*, vol. 3 (SPB, 1911), 289–348; I. P. Belokonskii, *Zemstvo i konstitutsiia* (Moscow, 1910), pp. 5–30; R. Pipes, *Russia Under the Old Regime* (New York, 1974), esp. pp. 281–316; D. T. Orlovsky, "Ministerial Power and Russian Autocracy: The Ministry of Internal Affairs,

1802–1881" (Ph.D. diss., Harvard, 1976), pp. 287–339; and B. V. Anan'ich and R. Sh. Ganelin, "R. A. Fadeev, S. Iu. Witte i ideologicheskie iskaniia 'okhranitelei' v 1881–1883 gg.," in N. E. Nosov, ed., *Issledovaniia po sotsial'no-politicheskoi istorii* (Leningrad, 1971), pp. 299–326.

67. Chernukha, *Vnutrenniaia politika*, p. 81.

68. One of the first works to evaluate the economic impact of the Emancipation was Iu. E. Ianson, *Opyt statisticheskago izsledovaniia o krest'ianskikh nadelakh i platezhakh* (SPB, 1877). Compare N. M. Druzhinin, "Likvidatsiia feodal'noi sistemy v russkoi pomeshchich'ei derevne (1862–1882 gg.)," *Voprosy Istorii*, 1968:12, pp. 3–34.

69. Zaionchkovskii, *Krest'ianskoe dvizhenie*, pp. 378–82, 476 n. 376, 548–49.

70. Chernukha, "Problema politicheskoi reformy," p. 149. Compare Alexander III's opinion in *Svod vysochaishikh otmetok po vsepoddanneishim otchetam za 1881–1890 gg.* (SPB, 1893), p. 259; and Chicherin's in Benson, "Conservative Liberalism," p. 94.

71. Chernukha, *Krest'ianskii vopros*, pp. 70–122, 177–96; Chernukha, "Vsepoddanneishii doklad komissii P. A. Valueva ot 2 Aprelia 1872 g. kak isto-chnik po istorii podatnoi reformy v Rossii" in VID, II (Leningrad, 1969), 162–69; N. I. Anan'ich, "K istorii otmeny podushnoi podati v Rossii," IZ, 94 (1974) 183–212; J. L. Pesda, "N. K. Bunge and Russian Economic Development, 1881–1886" (Ph.D. diss., Kent State, 1971), pp. 51–62, 89–90; M. S. Simonova, "Otmena krugovoi poruki," IZ, 83 (1969), esp. pp. 159–69.

72. "Rech'" vel. kn. Konstantina Nikolaevicha 6 aprelia 1881 g.," *Golos Minuvshago*, 3:2 (1915), 211.

73. Compare Benson, "Conservative Liberalism," p. 93.

74. Zaionchkovskii, *Krest'ianskoe dvizhenie*, p. 382.

75. Orlovsky, *Limits of Reform*, pp. 170–96; Zaionchkovskii, *Krizis samoder-zhaviia*, pp. 207–11, 288. Loris-Melikov's "constitution" is in Raeff, *Plans for Political Reform*, pp. 132–40 and 37–39. On restrictions on peasant mobility, see F. X. Coquin, *La Siberie: peuplement et immigration paysanne au XIXe siècle* (Paris, 1969), pp. 223–55.

76. *Otchet za 1881 god* (SPB, 1883), pp. 122–45 and appendix no. 10, pp. 77–110; Zaionchkovskii, *Krizis samoderzhaviia*, pp. 344–50, 419–23.

77. Zaionchkovskii, *Krizis samoderzhaviia*, p. 349.

78. Five years later, the State Peasants were also finally transferred to obliga-tory redemption. A. M. Anfimov, "Preobrazovanie obrochnoi podati byvshikh gosudarstvennykh krest'ian v vykupnye platezhi," in *Iz istorii ekonomicheskoi i obshchestvennoi zhizni Rossii: Sbornik statei* (Moscow, 1976), pp. 27–43.

79. For a complete list of tax concessions: I. M. Strakhovskii, "Krest'ianskii vopros v zakondatel'stve i zakonosoveshchatel'nykh kommissiakh posle 1861 g." in P. D. Dolgorukov and S. L. Tolstoi, eds., *Krest'ianskii stroi*, vol. 1 (SPB, 1905), 413–19, 444; Simonova, "Otmena krugovoi poruka," pp. 163–69.

80. Druzhinin, "Glavnyi komitet," p. 286.

81. L. F. Skliarov, *Pereselenie i zemleustroistvo v Sibiri v gody Stolypinskoi agrarnoi reformy* (Leningrad, 1962), pp. 59–71; E. M. Brusnikin, "Pereselen-cheskaia politika tsarizma v kontse XIX veka," *Vosprosy Istorii*, 1965:1, pp. 28–34; M. S. Simonova, "Pereselencheskii vopros v agrarnoi politike samoderzhaviia v kontse XIX–nachale XX v.," *EAIVE za 1965* (Moscow, 1970), pp. 424–27; Co-quin, *La Siberie*, pp. 349–83, esp. 350–62; D. W. Treadgold, *The Great Siberian Migration: Government and Peasant in Resettlement from Emancipation to the First World War* (Princeton, 1957), pp. 73–80.

82. Compare Yaney, *Urge to Mobilize*, pp. 124–33; N. A. Iakimenko, "Agrarnye migratsii v Rossii (1861–1917 gg.)," *Voprosy Istorii*, 1983:3, p. 21.

83. Skliarov, *Pereselenie*, p. 64.

84. See A. N. Zak, *Krest'ianskii pozemel'nyi bank, 1883–1910* (Moscow, 1911), pp. 1–87; D. A. Baturinskii [Galprin], *Agrarnaia politika tsarskogo pravitel'stva i krest'ianskii pozemel'nyi bank* (Moscow, 1925), pp. 3–36; V. A. Vdovin, *Krest'ianskii pozemel'nyi bank (1883–1895 gg.)* (Moscow, 1959), pp. 7–37; and F. Voroponov, "Krest'ianskii bank i ego nachalo: Iz lichnykh vospominanii," *Vestnik Evropy*, 1905:12, pp. 507–59.

85. *Otchet za 1882* (SPB, 1884), pp. 157–68.

86. Ibid., p. 165.

87. Snow, *The Years 1881–1894*. Bunge is repeatedly cited as quoting the well-known saying "Give a man the secure possession of a bleak rock, and he will turn it into a garden; give him a nine years' lease of a garden, and he will convert it into a desert." Usually attributed to J. S. Mill, it originates with Arthur Young, *The Example of France a Warning to England* (London, 1793). A. A. Manuilov, "Noveishee zakonodatel'stvo o zemel'noi obshchine: Ego kharakteristika i rezultaty," *Vestnik Evropy*, 1912:11, p. 244; I. V. Sosnovskii, *Zemlevladenie* (SPB, 1904), p. 150; Chernukha, *Krest'ianskii vopros*, p. 195; I. V. Chernyshev, *Agrarno-krest'ianskaia politika Rossii za 150 let* (Petrograd, 1918), pp. 238–40. Compare J. S. Mill, *Principles of Political Economy with some of their Applications to Social Philosophy*, ed. Sir W. J. Ashley (London 1909; rpt. 1923), Book II, p. 283.

88. Seredonin, *Istoricheskii obzor*, vol. 4, 273; Anan'ich, "Otmena podushnoi podati," p. 202. Compare Snow, *The Years 1881–1894*, p. 60.

89. *Otchet za 1882*, p. 168.

90. Compare *Zakonadatel'nye materialy po voprosam, otnosiashchaia k ustroistvu sel'skago sostoianiia*, II, *Materialy po izdaniiu zakona 8 Iiunia 1893 goda o peredelakh mirskoi zemli . . .* (SPB, 1900) p. 28; Chernukha, *Krest'ianskii vopros*, p. 135.

91. V. V. Bol'shov, "Materialy senatorskikh revizii 1880–1881 gg. kak istochnik po istorii mestnogo upravleniia Rossii," VMUSI, 1976:4, pp. 46–54. Also see on the Kakhanov Commission, M. S. Islavin, ed., *Obzor trudov vysochaishii utverzhdenii pod predsedatel'stvom stats-sekretaria Kakhanov osoboi kommissii*, 2 parts (SPB, 1908); S. A. Korf, *Administrativnaia iustitsiia v Rossii* 1 (SPB, 1910), 353–418; F. W. Wcislo, "Bureaucratic Reform in Tsarist Russia: State and Local Society, 1881–1914" (Ph.D. diss., Columbia, 1984), pp. 7–86. The Kakhanov Commission took over the materials of the old Miliutin Commission. The members of the Kakhanov Commission included M. S. Kakhanov; five senators, four of whom had conducted the inspections for Loris-Melikov, including the new imperial secretary, A. A. Polovtsov; a representative from the *Udel* Department; and one academic expert. Other officials who participated included P. P. Semenov and I. N. Durnovo and V. K. [von] Pleve, both of whom later acquired notoriety as interior ministers.

92. *Ocherk predpolozhenii bol'shinstva chlenov Soveshchaniia* in *Trudy Osoboi Kommissii dlia sostavleniia proekt mestnago upravleniia* (SPB, n.d.), p. 8.

93. "Sel'skoe obshchestvo" and "Volostnoe upravlenie" in *Ob"iasnitel'nyia zapiski*, esp. "Sel'skoe obshchestvo," p. 12, and *Polozheniia ob ustroistve mestnago upravleniia*, in *Trudy Osoboi Kommissii*.

94. P. A. Zaionchkovskii, *Rossiiskoe samoderzhavie v kontse XIX stoletiia (Politicheskaia reaktsiia 80kh–nachale 90kh godov)* (Moscow, 1970), pp. 232–33.

95. T. S. Pearson, "Origins of Alexander III's Land Captains: A Reinterpretation," *Slavic Review*, 40:3 (1981), p. 399; Pearson, "Ministerial Conflict," pp. 195–207; *Ob"iasnitel'nyia zapiski*, untitled covering note, p. 2.

96. On the State Council, V. I. Gurko, *Features and Figures of the Past: Government and Opinion in the Reign of Nicholas II* (New York, rpt. 1970), pp. 22–34; Whelan, *Alexander III*, pp. 107–56.

97. On Alexander III's advisers, see Zaionchkovskii, *Rossiiskoe samoderzhavie*, pp. 35–81, esp. 53–65; Whelan, *Alexander III*, pp. 59–79. On Tolstoi, Pearson, "Origins of Land Captains," pp. 384–86, 395–403; Pearson, "Ministerial Conflict," pp. 195–207; Yaney, *Urge to Mobilize*, pp. 70–75; J. Taylor, Jr., "Dmitrii Andreevich Tolstoi and the Ministry of Interior, 1882–1889" (Ph.D. diss., New York Univ., 1970).

98. In addition to other works cited, on the land captains see P. A. Zaionchkovskii, "Zakon o zemskikh nachal'nikakh 12 Iiulia 1889 goda," *Nauchnye doklady vyshei shkoly*, 1961:2, pp. 42–72; M. M. Kataev, comp., *Mestnyia krest'ianskiia uchrezhdeniia, 1861, 1874 i 1889 (Istoricheskii ocherk ikh obrazovaniia i norm deiatel'nosti)*, pt. 3 (SPB, 1912), pp. 45–107. The law of 12 July 1889 is in PSZ, IX (1889) (SPB, 1891), no. 6196, pp. 508–35.

99. Yaney, *Urge to Mobilize*, p. 49.

100. B. N. Chicherin, *Vospominaniia Borisa Nikolaevicha Chicherina*, vol. 3 (Leningrad, 1929), p. 192.

101. Yaney, *Urge to Mobilize*, pp. 72, 74, 395. The first officials to serve in this post may actually have come close to fulfilling Tolstoi's expectations. *Svod za 1881–1890*, pp. 78–84.

102. Yaney, *Urge to Mobilize*, pp. 97–123; A. Borovskii, comp., *Nakaz zemskim nachal'nikam (utverzhden 11 avgusta, 1905 g.)* (Petrozavodsk, 1910); N. T. Volkov, *Nakaz zemskim nachal'nikam po administrativnym delam* (Moscow, 1907); and S. S. Usov, *Rukovodstvo dlia zemskikh nachal'nikov*, 2 vols. (SPB, 1910). The same dilemmas affected the task of reform at all levels of the administrative apparatus. See Korf's summary in *Administrativnaia iiustitsiia*, vol. 1, 527–28; and Yaney, *Systematization*.

103. Mandel, "Paternalistic Authority," p. 405.

104. P. N. Zyrianov, "Sotsial'naia struktura mestnogo upravleniia kapitalisticheskoi Rossii (1861–1914 gg.)," IZ, 107 (1982), 261–72; Mandel, "Paternalistic Authority," pp. 229–48.

105. In addition to works already cited on government policy, see E. M. Brusnikin, "Krest'ianskii vopros v Rossii v period politicheskoi reaktsii (80–90-e gody XIX veka)," *Voprosy Istorii*, 1970:2, pp. 34–47.

106. See, too, M. M. Kataev, comp., *Ocherki zakonopolozhenii o neotchuzhdaemosti nadel'nykh zemel'* (SPB, 1911), pp. 101–22; E. M. Brusnikin, "Podgotovka zakona 14/XII/93 goda 'o neotchuzhdaemosti krest'ianskikh zemel',' " *Uchenye Zapiski Gor'kovskogo Universiteta: Seriia istoriko-filologicheskaia*, 72 (1964), 345–75.

107. Snow, *The Years 1881–1894*, pp. 68–72. Compare Benson, "Conservative Liberalism," pp. 94–95. On the bureaucracy's anticapitalist views, Mosse, "Aspects of Tsarist Bureaucracy," p. 290.

108. PSZ, VI (1886) (SPB, 1888), no. 3578, pp. 116–17.

109. PSZ, XIII (1893) (SPB, 1897), no. 9754, pp. 425–27; and ibid., no. 10151, pp. 653–54. The legislation prohibiting the sale of allotment land was not, as one might have expected, directed against purchases by either nobles or merchants or even the village kulaks or *miroedy*. One must conclude, therefore, that it was directed at those universal "outsiders" and "aliens," the Jews. There is, however, no direct evidence of this in the sources. Nonetheless, the Valuev Commission was concerned to combat "alien and hostile outside elements" and "harmful influences" in the countryside: *Doklad Vysochaishe uchrezhdennoi kommissii*, vol. 2, appendix, p. 2. Compare Bunge in Snow, *The Years 1881–1894*, p. 32;

Assistant Interior Minister Lykoshin in GDSO, III:2, col. 2033; and Witte in GSSO, V, col. 1232, all of whom refer specifically to Jews.

110. G. P. Sazonov, *Neotchuzhdaemost' krest'ianskikh zemel' v sviazi s gosu-darstvenno-ekonomicheskoi programmoi* (SPB, 1889); L. Z. Slonimskii, *Okhrana krest'ianskago zemlevladeniia i neobkhodimyia zakondatel'nyia reformy* (SPB, 1891). On zemstvo petitions: M. Tolmachev, *Krest'ianskii vopros po vzgliadam zemstva i mestnykh liudei* (Moscow, 1903), pp. 10–13; Chernyshev, *Agrarno-krest'ianskaia politika*, pp. 211–32; and Veselovskii, *Istoriia zemstva*, vol. 3, 398–412. On the famine, see R. G. Robbins, Jr., *Famine in Russia 1891–1892: The Imperial Government Responds to a Crisis* (New York, 1975); Belokonskii, *Zemstvo i konstitutsiia*, pp. 31–38; Veselovskii, *Istoriia zemstva*, vol. 3, especially pp. 368–73; G. Fischer, *Russian Liberalism from Gentry to Intelligentsia* (Cambridge, Mass., 1958), pp. 72–82; S. Galai, *The Liberation Movement in Russia 1900–1905* (Cambridge, 1973), pp. 23–83, especially pp. 23–24, 62; N. M. Pirumova, *Zemskoe liberal'noe dvizhenie: Sotsial'nye korni i evoliutsiia do nachala XX veka* (Moscow, 1977), pp. 127–74.

111. *Otchet za 1893–1894* (SPB, 1894), vol. 1, 630–43. A. A. Polovtsov praised individual property ownership to Alexander III as a stimulus to agricultural intensification and increases in productivity and proposed replacing the commune with "household, family ownership" and terminating the existing policy of extensification. A. A. Polovtsov, *Dnevnik gosudarstvennogo sekretaria A. A. Polovtsova* vol. 2 (Moscow, 1966), 401–3. Other opponents included such unlikely bedfellows as Pobedonostsev, Durnovo, Ermolov, Witte, Ignat'ev, Vyshnegradskii, Krivoshein, Goremykin, and the future tsar Nicholas. Membership in the "liberal" minority was not, however, consistent, and several members changed sides at different times. Thus Bunge and Witte, and probably Ermolov as well, voted in favor of the law on repartitions since it was only intended to be a temporary measure, prior to a new round of more fundamental reforms. *Stenogrammy OSNSKhP* (SPB, n.d.), no. 13, pp. 14–16, and no. 14, pp. 2–8.

112. Also known as *sobirateli zemli*, they served a valuable function since they brought together otherwise unproductive and widely scattered strips, making their cultivation possible.

113. *Zakonodatel'nye materialy* II, 75–102; I. I. Vorontsov-Dashkov, *Zapiska Ministra dvora i udelov grafa Vorontsova-Dashkova ob unichtozhennii krest'ianskoi obshchiny i vozrazhenie na ee Ministra vnutrennikh del I. N. Durnovo* (Geneva, 1894); *Otchet za 1892–1893*, vol. 1 (SPB, 1893), 520.

114. *Zakonodatel'nyia materialy*, vol. 2, 99. He also proposed establishing a minimum size for such individual holdings and permitting the surplus population to migrate either to the east or to other *sosloviia*.

115. Ibid., pp. 102–42; the quotation is on p. 111. Three of the liberal minority's proposals were, however, acknowledged, leaving open at least a modest possibility for further changes. Thus, the Interior Ministry agreed to begin immediate discussion on a proposal to limit the area of land that could be owned by a single peasant as one way to prevent kulak exploitation—though nothing was to come of it until the Stolypin Reforms. In addition, sales of allotment land to nonpeasants were allowed where the purpose was to establish industrial undertakings. Finally, Durnovo acknowledged that any increase in small-scale credit would have to be provided by state rather than private institutions.

116. Ibid., pp. 27, 95, 104. Bunge also made that connection. Chernyshev, *Agrarno-krest'ianskaia politika*, p. 240.

117. *Zakonodatel'nye materialy*, vol. 2, especially 26–58, 103–42. The quotation is on p. 29.

118. Ibid., p. 27.

119. Ibid., p. 32.

120. Ibid., p. 36.

121. T. H. von Laue, *Sergei Witte and the Industrialization of Russia* (New York, 1969), especially pp. 71–119; T. M. Kitanina, *Khlebnaia torgovlia Rossii v 1875–1914 gg. (Ocherki pravitel'stvennoi politiki)* (Leningrad, 1978), pp. 170–243. Compare Crisp, *Studies in the Russian Economy.*

122. The impact of the grain price crisis on the peasantry depended on the degree of their involvement in the market. Those who produced grain for the market suffered a decline in income, thereby reducing their living standards and the government's tax receipts. Those who produced grain primarily for consumption tended to benefit from lower prices, though outside sources of income in both agriculture and industry also contracted. Nobles were similarly affected. In response, many returned to cheaper, more traditional agricultural methods, including renting land on a sharecropping basis or in return for labor services, usually to get in the harvest. N. A. Egiazarova, *Agrarnyi krizis kontsa XIX veka v Rossii* (Moscow, 1959); A. I. Chuprov and A. S. Postnikov, eds., *Vliianie urozhaev i khlebnykh tsen na nekotorye storony russkago narodnago khoziaistva,* 2 vols. (SPB, 1897); A. Gaister, "Sel'skoe khoziaistvo," in *1905,* ed. M. N. Pokrovskii, vol. 1 (Moscow-Leningrad, 1925), pp. 1–168; A. M. Anfimov, *Krupnoe pomeshchich'e khoziaistvo evropeiskoi Rossii (konets XIX–nachalo XX veka)* (Moscow, 1969); and B. N. Mironov, *Khlebnye tseny v Rossii za dva stoletiia (XVII–XIX vv.)* (Leningrad, 1985).

123. *Doklad predsedatelia vysochaishe uchrezhdennoi v 1888 godu kommisii po povodu padeniia tsen na sel'sko-khoziaistvennyia proizvedeniia v piatiletie (1883–1887)* (SPB, 1892), pp. 15, 137. The commission included representatives from the usual ministries; a variety of experts from public organizations involved in agriculture; some populist agricultural economists; Pazukhin and Bekhteev, who had been associated with Tolstoi and the passage of the land captain legislation; and A. A. Ermolov, from the Finance Ministry, and A. V. Krivoshein from Interior.

124. Ibid., pp. 33–56, 131–40.

125. *Otchet za 1893–1894,* vol. 1, 202–70.

126. Gurko, *Features and Figures,* p. 70.

127. S. Iu. Witte, *Vospominaniia: tsarstvovanie Nikolai II* (The Hague, 1968), vol. 1, 458–59. See Nicholas's comments on the provincial governors' reports. *Svod vysochaishikh otmetok po vsepoddaneishim otchetam za 1895–1901,* 7 vols. (SPB, 1897–1904). In general, Nicholas supported his father's policies concerning the agrarian problem. He even acknowledged the extreme seriousness of land-hunger. At the same time, he was abysmally ignorant of both real conditions in the countryside and the government's various measures to assist the peasantry. He was, however, familiar with early proposals to disperse large villages and form *khutora* in order to control rural fires and livestock diseases, raise economic productivity, and make the task of administrative supervision easier. Nicholas also urged the government to study the formation of small farms on state land for long-term rentals—a proposal similar to Witte's at the time of the revision of the Peasant Bank statute. Ultimately, however, Nicholas expressed his hope that agriculture would remain the principal source of peasant income for "a very long time."

128. K. F. Golovin, *Moi Vospominaniia,* vol. 2 (SPB, 1910), 249–50; also 237–40; P. Sokolov, "Aleksei Sergeevich Ermolov," *Istoricheskii Vestnik,* 1917:3, pp. 751–70; Gurko, *Features and Figures,* pp. 69–74.

129. See chapter 2.

130. The following is based on Anonymous [A. S. Ermolov], *Neurozhai i*

narodnoe bedstvie (SPB, 1892), pp. 70–82, 102–43, 251–70; Ermolov, Nash neurozhai i prodovol'stvennyi vopros, 2 vols. (SPB, 1909); Nash zemel'nyi vopros (SPB, 1906), pp. 177–207; Yermoloff, La Russie agricole devant la crise agraire (Paris, 1907), pp. 1–8, 280–81, 339–42; Solov'ev, Samoderzhavie i dvorianstvo v kontse XIX veka, pp. 276–78, 296, 298–300, 325–27, 332–33, 342–46. Compare Ermolov, Organizatsiia polevago khoziaistva; sistemy zemledeliia i sevooboroty, 1st ed. (SPB, 1879), 5th ed. (SPB, 1914).

131. B. B. Dubentsov, "Popytki preobrazovaniia organizatsii gosudarstvennoi sluzhby v kontse XIX v. (Iz praktiki ministerstva finansov)," in Problemy otechestvennoi istorii: Sbornik statei aspirantov i soiskatelei (Moscow-Leningrad, 1976), pp. 202–24, esp. p. 211; Lieven, "Russian Senior Officialdom," pp. 199–218.

132. Tolmachev, Krest'ianskii vopros, pp. 61–74; Veselovskii, Istoriia zemstva, vol. 3, 377–79; and Nuzhdy sel'skago khoziaistva i mery ikh udovletvorenniia po otzyvam zemskikh sobranii, 2d ed. (SPB, 1902).

133. Article 165 only applied to former serfs, who by the beginning of the twentieth century constituted only one-third of all peasants. For the remainder, mainly former State Peasants, the second part of the article remained in effect as Article 33 of the Statute on Former State Peasants. N. T. Volkov, Sbornik Polozhenii o sel'skom sostoianii, 2d ed. (SPB, 1910), p. 1578.

134. Svod zakliuchenii gubernskikh soveshchanii po voprosam otnosiashchimsia k peresmotru zakondatel'stve o krest'ianakh, vol. 3 (SPB, 1897), i–viii. There was considerable disagreement even within the Interior Ministry over these issues: Otchet za 1893–1894, p. 611. Although the questionnaire uses the terms zemlepol'zovanie and zemlevladenie interchangeably, it is clear that the focus is on problems of land utilization. During most of the nineteenth century, these two terms were virtually synonymous. It was only during the process of discussing these issues that the two terms became clearly distinguished. Thus zemlepol'zovanie came to be applied exclusively to the methods of land utilization, including both the agronomical aspects of land use and the technical problems associated with the configuration of open-field landholding patterns; zemlevladenie was restricted to the specifically juridical relationship of ownership. The failure to define the peasants' new relationship to the land after 1861 was a reflection of the government's ideology of opeka. The State Council specifically rejected the "west's" view of land, which treated it as a commodity. Otchet za 1893–1894, p. 646. Compare L. A. Kasso, Russkoe pozemel'noe pravo (Moscow, 1906), pp. 46–76; A. M. Kalandadze, "Zemel'nopravovoi rezhim tsarskoi Rossii nakanune velikoi oktiabr'skoi sotsialisticheskoi revoliutsii," Uchenye Zapiski Leningradskogo Universiteta, 1959:129, Seria iuridicheskikh nauk, vyp. 3, pp. 331–54; and Khauke, Krest'ianskoe zemel'noe pravo, pp. 1–31.

135. Tolmachev, Krest'ianskii vopros, pp. 46–54.

136. Otchet za 1895–1896 (SPB, 1896), p. 151; M. S. Simonova, "Krest'ianskii pozemel'nyi bank v sisteme obshchei agrarnoi politiki samoderzhaviia (1895–3 XI 1905 g.)," EAIVE za 1966 (Tallinn, 1971), pp. 471–84, esp. pp. 471–77.

137. On Witte's proposal, Otchet za 1895–1896, pp. 159, 166–67.

138. Ibid., pp. 175, 184–85, 205. The majority frankly acknowledged the inevitability of the nobility's demise as a soslovie and sought only to inhibit the process as much as possible. Ibid., pp. 173, 175.

139. Simonova, "Pereselencheskii vopros," pp. 428–34; Treadgold, Great Siberian Migration, pp. 108–27; Skliarov, Pereselenie, pp. 70–71. Proposals were submitted by N. Kh. Bunge and the Committee's administrator, and A. N. Kulomzin, who had himself just completed a trip to Siberia. They were supported by Witte, Ermolov, and even Durnovo.

140. Otchet za 1893–1894, vol. 1, 612–14, 606–8. The idea of such a review

originated with Tolstoi in January 1888. Polovtsov, *Dnevnik*, vol. 2, 479, n. 31. Tolstoi's call for a "Special Commission" appears to have been sidetracked into the Commission on the decline of grain prices, chaired by Pleve.

141. *Trudy Redkom*, vol. 1, 7; *Spravki MVD*, p. 112; and I. V. Nesterova, "Vopros o krest'ianskom nadel'nom zemlevladenii v redaktsionnoi komissii Ministerstva Vnutrennikh Del (1902–1904)," *Nauchnye doklady vyshei shkoly: Istoricheskie nauki*, 1960:2, p. 77.

142. Polovtsov, *Dnevnik*, vol. 2, 403. Durnovo was himself an opponent of the commune. Golovin, *Moi vospominaniia*, vol. 2, 245. Senator N. A. Khvostov was one of the commune's staunchest defenders. Given the important role Pleve played as assistant interior minister, it is conceivable that he was instrumental in obtaining the postponement. Alexander III himself apparently supported the initiative. Nicholas's comment is in *Svod za 1900*, p. 81.

143. This occurred during the Council of Ministers' discussion of the State Controller's 1896 report. *Spravki MVD*, p. 90.

144. The following views are based on Witte, *Vospominaniia*, vol. 1, 439–83; M. N. Enden, "Graf S. Iu. Witte: Glava chetvertaia: Ekonomika podchinennaia interesam natsii (prodolozhenie)," *Vozrozhenie*, 1971:228, pp. 84–111; M. de Enden, "The Roots of Witte's Thought," *Russian Review* 29:1 (1970), pp. 6–24; K., "Iz noveishei istorii krest'ianskago voprosa: Offitsial'nye proekty, soveshchaniia i zapiski 1897–1906 godov," *Vestnik Evropy*, 1909:4, pp. 621–37, and 1909:5, pp. 99–115, which was inspired by Witte himself; B. B. Glinskii, "Graf Sergei Iul'evich Vitte (Materialy dlia biografii)," *Istoricheskii Vestnik*, 141:2 (1915), 520–55, and 141:3 (1915), 893–97; T. B. Rainey, *Sergei Witte and the Peasant Problem* (Buffalo, 1973); and Witte's explanation of the controller's 1896 report together with relevant extracts from the minutes of the 1891 Special Conference on Grain Exports and the April 1893 discussions of the United Departments of the State Council in S. Iu. Witte, *Samoderzhavie i zemstvo*, 2d ed. (Stuttgart, 1903), pp. 213–24. The Council of Ministers' discussions are in *Spravki MVD*, pp. 87–107. The Controller's report, although detailing the successes of the tax collection program for 1896 in good bureaucratic fashion and expressing optimism for further improvements, nonetheless emphasized the weak taxpaying abilities of the peasants in the Central Agricultural Region. *Vsepoddanneishii otchet Gosudarstsvennago Kontrolera za 1896* (SPB, 1896). Von Laue is wrong in asserting that Witte's 1896 budget report implicitly favored the abolition of the commune and supported prosperous peasants. Witte's references to the latter were simply comments on his observations and did not imply any support. Von Laue, *Sergei Witte*, p. 116; compare *Vestnik Finansov*, 1895:53, pp. 1143–44; and 1897:1, pp. 4–5, for Witte's attitudes toward class differentiation within the peasantry. Several contemporaries branded Witte a "Marxist" or "socialist." Migulin, *Agrarnyi vopros*, p. 73; and Pobedonostsev in V. B. Lopukhin, "Liudi i politika (konets XIX–nachalo XXV)," *Voprosy Istorii*, 1966:9, p. 120.

145. S. Iu. Witte, *Po povodu natsionalizma: Natsional'naia ekonomiia i Fridrikh List*, 2d ed. (SPB, 1912); Von Laue, *Sergei Witte*, pp. 56–62.

146. "Natural economy" has been used to translate the Russian term *natural'noe khoziaistvo*, which is in turn a translation of the German term *Naturalwirtschaft*. The term is misleading to the extent that it implies that there were no monetary transactions whatsoever. The more common English term is *subsistence economy* though this implies that there was no surplus available for exchange—also an inaccurate portrayal. B. H. Slicher van Bath, *The Agrarian History of Western Europe A.D. 500–1800* (London, 1966), pp. 23–25; Nash, *Primitive Systems*, p. 22.

147. Witte, *Vospominaniia*, vol. 1, 471; compare A. S. Ermolov, *Narodnaia*

sel'skokhoziaistvennaia mudrost' v poslovitsakh, pogovorkakh i primetakh, vol. 2 (SPB, 1905), p. 158.

148. Compare his *Samoderzhavie i zemstvo*. The following is based on Solov'ev, *Samoderzhavie i dvorianstvo v kontse XIX veka*, pp. 252–377 and esp. pp. 280–305; Gurko, *Features and Figures*, pp. 52–68. The pronoble dimension of governmental policy was becoming increasingly moot. Compare the failure of the 1897 Special Conference on the Affairs of the Nobility, chaired by I. N. Durnovo. Solov'ev, *Samoderzhavie i dvorianstvo v kontse XIX veka*, pp. 345, 357–58.

149. The quotations are from Solov'ev, *Samoderzhavie i dvorianstvo v kontse XIX veka*, pp. 282, 289. Compare Witte's remarks to Polovtsov in "Dnevnik A. A. Polovtsova," *KA*, 3 (1923), 139; and Witte, *Vospominaniia*, vol. 1, 185. Compare "Dnevnik Kn. Ekateriny Alekseevny Sviatopolk Mirskoi za 1904–1905 gg," in *IZ*, 77 (1965), 266.

150. Solov'ev, *Samoderzhavie i dvorianstvo v kontse XIX veka*, pp. 282–91; Simonova, "Otmena krugovoi poruki," p. 176; N. K. Brzheskii, *Nedoimochnost' i krugovaia poruka sel'skikh obshchestv* (SPB, 1897), p. 403. Compare Vorontsov-Dashkov's position in Brusnikin, "Krest'ianskii vopros," pp. 42–43.

151. Glinskii, "Graf S. Iu. Witte," 141:3 (1915), 893. Compare S. E. Kryzhanovskii in P. E. Shchegolev, ed., *Padenie tsarskogo rezhima*, vol. 5 (Moscow-Leningrad, 1926), 386–87; A. Iswolsky, *The Memoirs of Alexander Iswolsky: Formerly Russian Minister of Foreign Affairs and Ambassador to France* (London, 1920), pp. 113, 118; and A. V. Peshekhonov, *Ekonomicheskaia politika samoderzhaviia (Tsentralizatsiia ekonomicheskoi vlasti)* (St. Petersburg, 1906).

152. *Vsepoddanneishii doklad ministra finansov i gosudarstvennoi rospisi dokhodov i raskhodov na 1883–1906 god* (SPB, 1883–1906), also published in *Vestnik Finansov*. Witte, *Vospominaniia*, vol. 1, 459–60.

153. Witte, *Vospominaniia*, vol. 1, 476. Pobedonostsev also shared this view. "Perepiska Vitte i Pobedonostseva (1895–1905)," *KA*, 30 (1928), pp. 97–99, 101, 107–9.

154. Witte, *Vospominaniia*, vol. 1, 446–47; Chernyshev, *Agrarno-krest'ianskaia politika*, pp. 246–55.

155. "Iz dnevnika A. A. Polovtsova," *KA*, 46 (1931), 128.

156. Witte, *Vospominaniia*, vol. 1, 467–73.

157. *Spravki MVD*, pp. 91–92. On Goremykin, see Gurko, *Features and Figures*, pp. 75–81; A. Kizevetter, *Na rubezhe dvukh stoletii, vospominaniia 1881–1914* (Prague, 1929), pp. 200–202, 252–53.

158. *Spravki MVD*, pp. 102–3.

159. Ibid., pp. 99–101, 104–7.

160. Witte, *Vospominaniia*, vol. 1, 469.

161. Ibid., p. 472.

162. *Spravki MVD.*, pp. 107–8; "Iz dnevnika Polovtsova," *KA*, 46 (1931), p. 118; A. V. Bogdanovich, *Tri poslednykh samoderzhtsa: Dnevnik A. V. Bogdanovicha* (Moscow-Leningrad, 1924), p. 226; Gurko, *Features and Figures*, pp. 79–80; Galai, *Liberation Movement*, pp. 49–50; Nesterova, "Vopros," p. 78. Goremykin, then interior minister, specifically rejected any reforms that would lead to the revision of the basic principles underlying the Emancipation Statutes. He was supported by Pobedonostsev.

163. On this conflict see C. N. Rosenthal, "Ministerial Conflict under Nicholas II: The Finance and Interior Ministries and the 'Peasant Question'" (M.A. and Certificate of the Russian Institute Essay, Columbia, 1969); Yaney, *Systematization*, pp. 286–318.

164. Gurko, *Features and Figures*, p. 111.

165. *Pamiati Viacheslava Konstantinovicha Pleve* (SPB, 1904); "Agrarnaia pro-

gramma G. F. Pleve," *Osvobozhdenie*, 20/21 (18 April 1903), pp. 349–52; "Rech' V. K. Pleve na stoletnem iubileinom torzhestve MVD," *Pravo*, (1 January 1903), cols. 35–37; S. E. Kryzhanovskii, "V. K. Pleve," *Novyi Zhurnal*, 1975:118, pp. 137–44; E. H. Judge, *Plehve: Repression and Reform in Imperial Russia, 1902–1904* (Syracuse, 1983).

166. Judge, *Plehve*, pp. 72–75, 82–87; Korf, *Administrativnaia iustitsiia*, pp. 423–54. However, Pleve did succeed in strengthening and bureaucratizing the lowest level of the police apparatus in 1903, doubling the rural police force.

167. N. B. Weissman, *Reform in Tsarist Russia: The State Bureaucracy and Local Government, 1900–1914* (New Brunswick, N.J., 1981), pp. 40–66; Judge, *Plehve*, pp. 175–79; Kryzhanovskii, in Shchegolev, *Padenie tsarskogo regima*, vol. 5, 378–79, saw it as a national institution of popular representation; I. V. Gessen, "Zakon 22 marta 1904 goda," *Pravo*, 18 (2 May 1904), cols. 1003–10, not only saw the Council as a meeting ground between government and society but also as a pool from which to select future government officials. This policy of Pleve's was responsible, in part, for the rapid promotion of one former marshal of the nobility, P. A. Stolypin.

168. See Wcislo, "Bureaucratic Reform," pp. 393–444; Weissman, *Reform in Tsarist Russia*, pp. 176–90.

169. Solov'ev, *Samoderzhavie i dvorianstvo v kontse XIX veka*, p. 295. The following is based on ibid., pp. 295–305; and "Pis'mo V. K. Pleve k A. A. Kireevu," KA, 18 (1926), 201–3. Pleve had long accepted the fact that Russia was in a state of transition from a natural to a money economy. *Doklad predsedatelia*, pp. 41, 55. At the end of 1904, Witte claimed that this transformation had already been completed. S. Iu. Witte, *Zapiska po krest'ianskomu delu* (SPB, 1904), p. 95; M. S. Simonova, "Politika tsarizma v krest'ianskom voprose nakanune revoliutsii 1905–1907 gg.," IZ, 75 (1965), 227. D. N. Shipov, in his *Vospominaniia i dumy o perezhitom* (Moscow, 1918), pp. 171–97, demonstrates the similarities between Witte and Pleve and their common desire to "retard" Russia's political development.

170. *Pamiati V. K. Pleve*, p. 16.

171. *Svod za 1881–1890*, p. 260.

172. The earlier attempts of Valuev and Bunge to moderate or eliminate mutual responsibility had failed because of the institution's links to the commune. Witte's ostensible motive was to improve the efficiency of tax collections. However, he soon came to see its abolition as a blow to the commune. "Dnevnik A. A. Polovtsova," KA 3 (1923), 126, 165: Witte, *Vospominaniia*, vol. 1, 453, 470, 474–75; *Stenogrammy OSNSKhP*, no. 19, p. 16. Vorontsov-Dashkov also considered the two institutions as interconnected: Vorontsov-Dashkov, *Zapiska*, pp. 13–15. In discussions of the 1899 law, ten members of the State Council, including Witte, Lobko, Semenov, Chikhachov, and Gerard, assumed a direct link between commune and mutual responsibility; eighteen conservative liberals, including Sol'ski, Polovtsov, Ermolov, Terner, and Kuropatkin, claimed there was no link. In 1903, the State Council as a body asserted that there was no organic connection between the two institutions. *Otchet za 1902–1903*, vol. 1 (SPB, 1903), 650–51. Opposition came primarily from Goremykin and the assistant interior minister, Sipiagin, though Goremykin seems to have been primarily motivated by a desire to maintain the predominance of the Interior Ministry's land captains over the Finance Ministry's tax inspectors. "Dnevnik A. A. Polovtsova," KA 3 (1923), 126, 136; Gurko, *Features and Figures*, pp. 86–88. On earlier efforts to abolish mutual responsibility, see Chernukha, *Krest'ianskii vopros*, pp. 196–204. On Witte's campaign: Simonova, "Otmena krugovoi poruki," pp. 158–95; *Sushchestvuiu-shchii poriadok vzimaniia okladnykh sborov s krest'ianin po svedeniiam dostav-*

lennym podatnymi inspektorami za 1887–1893 gg., 2 vols. (SPB, 1894–1895); Brzheskii, *Nedoimochnost'*, pp. 408–14; and A. Eropkin, "Otmena krugovoi poruki," *Narodnoe Khoziaistvo*, 4:3 (1903), 1–30; *Otchet za 1898–1899* (SPB, 1899), pp. 450–96; and *Otchet za 1902–1903*, vol. 1, 645–65.

173. D. N. Liubimov, "Russkaia smuta nachale deviatisotykh godov, 1902–1906" (ms., RACU and HIA), pp. 51–52; "Otryvki iz vospominanii D. N. Liubimova (1902–1904 gg.)," *Istoricheskii Arkhiv*, 1962:6, pp. 82–83. Pleve's Council on the Affairs of the Local Economy was established in 1904.

Notes to Chapter 2

1. Lokhtin, *Sostoianie sel'skago khoziaistva*, p. 307.

2. Recently, the existence of an agrarian crisis at the end of the nineteenth century has been challenged. J. Y. Simms, Jr., "The Crisis in Russian Agriculture at the End of the Nineteenth Century: A Different View," *Slavic Review*, 36:3 (1977), 377–98; Simms, "The Crop Failure of 1891: Soil Exhaustion, Technological Backwardness and Russia's 'Agrarian Crisis,'" *Slavic Review*, 41:2 (1982), 236–50; Simms, "The Economic Impact of the Russian Famine of 1891–92," *SEER* 60:1 (1982), 63–74; E. M. W. Wilbur, "Was Russian Peasant Agriculture Really That Impoverished? New Evidence from a Case Study from the 'Impoverished Center' at the End of the Nineteenth Century" and discussion in *Journal of Economic History*, 43:1 (1983), 137–47. For criticism: G. M. Hamburg, "The Crisis in Russian Agriculture: A Comment," *Slavic Review*, 37:3 (1978), 481–86; and J. T. Sanders, " 'Once More Into the Breach, Dear Friends': A Closer Look at Indirect Tax Receipts and the Condition of the Russian Peasantry, 1881–1899," *Slavic Review*, 43:4 (1984), 657–666. Also see P. R. Gregory, "Russian Living Standards During the Industrialization Era, 1885–1913," *Review of Income and Wealth*, 26 (1980), 87–103; Gregory, "Grain Marketings and Peasant Consumption, Russia, 1885–1913," *Explorations in Economic History*, 17 (1980), 135–64; and Gregory, *Russian National Income, 1885–1914* (Cambridge, 1982), which tend to support Simms's argument. Compare I. Koval'chenko and L. Milov, *Vserossiiskii agrarnyi rynok* (Moscow, 1974); S. M. Dubrovskii, *Sel'skoe khoziaistvo i krest'ianstvo Rossii v period imperializma* (Moscow, 1975); A. M. Anfimov, *Krest'ianskoe khoziaistvo Evropeiskoi Rossii, 1881–1904* (Moscow, 1980); Anfimov, *Ekonomicheskoe polozhenie i klassovaia bor'ba krest'ian Evropeiskoi Rossii, 1881–1904 gg.* (Moscow, 1984); Shanin, *Russia as a "Developing Society,"* pp. 150–74; and A. Kahan, "National Calamities and Their Effect upon the Food Supply in Russia (An Introduction to a Catalogue)," *JGO* 16:3 (1968), 374.

3. See, for example, P. I. Liashchenko, *Istoriia narodnogo khoziaistva SSSR*, 3d ed., vol. 2 (n.p., 1952), 68–71.

4. A. I. Shingarev, *Vymiraiushchaia derevnia: Opyt sanitarno-ekonomicheskago izsledovaniia dvukh selenii Voronezhskago uezda*, 2d ed. (SPB, 1907). Despite Shingarev's claims, the villages were not typical in that their peasants were *darstvenniki*. J. Maynard, *The Russian Peasant and Other Studies* (New York, 1962), pp. 62–70.

5. Robinson, *Rural Russia*, p. 138. Altogether, some thirty-eight thousand peasants from 174 communities participated. They were mainly either *darstvenniki* or former household serfs who had received no allotments at all and thus were also untypical. Most peasants in Poltava and Khar'kov provinces held their land in individual tenure. However, the disorders broke out in an area where communal tenure predominated. According to evidence given to the Special Confer-

ence, 179,000 out of a total of 191,000 desiatinas of peasant allotment land in Konstantinograd County, the center of the disturbances, was subject to yearly repartitions. *Stennogramy OSNSKhP*, no. 10, p. 21. Many bureaucrats, including Pleve, saw the root of the problem as lying with the repartitional commune and the absence of private property rights. Implicitly, this argument also saw the communal system as creating solidarity between different classes of peasants such that both rich and poor participated in the disturbances. *Krest'ianskoe dvizhenie v Poltavskoi i Khar'kovskoi guberniiakh v 1902 g.: Sbornik Dokumentov* (Khar'kov, 1961), pp. 79–82; and Gurko, *Features and Figures*, pp. 157, 172. Others, however, viewed the problem in terms of economic distress, and, in effect, perceived the poorest peasants as the principal participants in the disorders. *Krest'ianskoe dvizhenie v Poltavskoi i Khar'kovskoi*, pp. 112, 135–38, 147–48, 151–57. Subsequently, Pleve seemed to accept the latter interpretation, próposing changes in migration and Peasant Bank policy designed to address peasant land-hunger and poverty. Ibid., pp. 82, 138; V. A. Stepynin, "Iz istorii pereselencheskoi politiki samoderzhaviia v nachale XX veka (Pereselencheskii zakon 6 iiunia 1904 g)," *Istoriia SSSR*, 1960:5, p. 162. The evidence on participation is unclear. In 1902, it was the poorest peasants who mainly participated, stimulated by poverty and crop failure. In 1905, on the other hand, political factors played a greater role and all strata participated, though middle peasants predominated, at least in the agricultural center. Prosperous peasants tried to take material advantage of the activities of poorer fellow villagers. D. A. J. Macey, "The Peasantry, the Agrarian Problem, and the Revolution of 1905–1907," in A. W. Cordier, ed., *Columbia Essays in International Affairs*, vol. 7, *The Dean's Papers, 1971* (New York, 1972), pp. 14–22; C. M. Deane, "Poltava Guberniia, 1900–1917: A Case Study of Revolution in the Provinces" (M.A. essay, Columbia, 1966), pp. 1–54; P. Pomper, "The Peasant Disorders in Poltava and Khar'kov Provinces in 1902," (M.A. essay, Chicago, 1961); S. M. Dubrovskii and B. Grave, "Krest'ianskoe dvizhenie nakanune revoliutsii 1905 goda (1900–1904 gg.)," in Pokrovskii, *1905*, vol. 1, 233–392; B. B. Veselovskii, ed., *Krest'ianskoe dvizhenie 1902 goda* (Moscow-Leningrad, 1923); on 1905, see S. M. Dubrovskii, *Krest'ianskoe dvizhenie v revoliutsii 1905–1907 gg.* (Moscow, 1956), pp. 83–90; and M. Perrie, "The Russian Peasant Movement of 1905–1907: Its Social Composition and Revolutionary Significance," *Past and Present*, 57 (1972), pp. 123–55. In the course of 1908, sixteen of the twenty-three communities said to have communal tenure in Konstantinograd County, which included more than six thousand households and fifty-eight thousand desiatinas of land, transferred to individual ownership as a result of the Stolypin Reforms. The remainder were expected to transfer the following year. These figures do not agree with those cited previously. See Lykoshin, "Primeneniia zakona 9.XI.1906" in *Trudy s"ezda nepremennykh chlenov gubernskikh prisutstvii i zemleustroitel'nykh kommisii: 10–23 ianvaria 1909 g.* (SPB, 1909), p. 262. Since each household in this group averages slightly below 10 desiatinas each, it suggests that the villages involved in the disorders did not hold their land in communal tenure, thus invalidating the simplistic argument that equated communal tenure and agrarian disorders. Documents refer to family partitions, not communal repartitions. *Krest'ianskoe dvizhenie v Poltavskoi i Khar'kovskoi*, p. 152. The relationship was much more complex as the government's agrarian "experts" were aware.

6. Miliukov, *Russia and Its Crisis*, pp. 313, 316, 346–48; S. S. Oldenburg, *Last Tsar: Nicholas II, His Reign and His Russia*, 2 (Gulf Breeze, Fla., 1977), 7–9.

7. Lokhtin, *Sostoianie sel'skago khoziaistva*, p. 255.

8. See, for example, the changing opinions of zemstvo activists who were also directly involved in the modernization of their own estates: S. I. Shidlovskii,

Vospominaniia, vol. 1 (Berlin, 1923), 36–37; F. von Shlippe, "Memoirs" (unpub. ms., RACU), p. 58; Shlippe, *Ocherk krest'ianskago khoziaistva vereiskago uezde* (Moscow 1902); A. D. Golitsyn, "Vospominaniia" (unpub. ms., RACU), pp. 62–67. See, too, A. P. Nikol'skii, *Zemlia, obshchina i trud: Osobennosti krest'ianskago pravoporiadka, ikh proiskhozhdenie i znachenie* (SPB, 1902); F. Bar, *Krest'ianskoe obshchinnoe zemlevladenie v agrarnom i sotsial'nopoliticheskom otnosheniiakh* (Moscow, 1894). For a sketch of traditional noble attitudes, see Hamburg, *Politics of the Russian Nobility*, pp. 191–201.

9. *Spravki MVD*, pp. 121–23; G. G. Savich, *Novyi gosudarstvennyi stroi Rossii: Spravochnaia kniga* (SPB, 1907), pp. 4, 5, 8–10.

10. R. T. Manning, "The Russian Provincial Gentry in Revolution and Counterrevolution, 1905–1907" (Ph.D. diss., Columbia, 1975), pp. 1–107; Manning, *Crisis of the Old Order*, pp. 4–24. But compare Becker, *Nobility and Privilege*. On noble agriculture, see Anfimov, *Krupnoe pomeshchich'e khoziaistvo*; Dubrovskii, *Sel'skoe khoziaistvo*, pp. 268–96; and L. P. Minarik, *Ekonomicheskaia kharakteristika krupneishikh zemel'nykh sobstvennikov Rossii kontsa XIX–nachala XX v. Zemlevladenie, zemlepol'zovanie, sistema khoziaistva* (Moscow, 1971). A discussion of some of the problems is in N. B. Selunskaia, "Istochniko-vedcheskie problemy izucheniia pomeshchich'ego khoziaistva Rossii kontsa XIX–nachala XX veka," *Istoriia SSSR*, 1973:6, pp. 81–95.

11. Fisher, *Russian Liberalism*, pp. 72–82; Galai, *Liberation Movement*, pp. 23–83; Belokonskii, *Zemstvo i konstitutsiia*, pp. 31–38; Veselovskii, *Istoriia zemstva*, vol. 3, especially pp. 368–73; Pirumova, *Zemskoe liberal'noe dvizhenie*; T. Emmons, *The Formation of Political Parties and the First National Elections in Russia* (Cambridge, Mass., 1983); Solov'ev, *Samoderzhavie i dvorianstvo v 1902–1907 gg.*, chapter 1; and Hamburg, *Politics of the Russian Nobility*, pp. 214–24; T. Emmons and W. S. Vucinich, eds., *The Zemstvo in Russia: An Experiment in Local Self-government* (New York, 1982).

12. N. A. Pavlov, *Zapiski zemlevladel'tsa* (Petrograd, 1915); Gurko, *Features and Figures*, pp. 213, 307, 383–84, 643; Solov'ev, *Samoderzhavie i dvorianstvo v 1902–1907*, p. 199.

13. However, the Russian countryside remained "undergoverned." Starr, *Decentralization*, p. 48; H. Rogger, *Russia in the Age of Modernization and Revolution, 1881–1917* (New York, 1983), p. 49.

14. Veselovskii, *Istoriia zemstva*, vol. 3, 575–89; N. P. Diatlova, "Otchety gubernatorov kak istoricheskii istochnik" and R. Iu. Matskina, "Ministerskie otchety i ikh osobennosti kak istoricheskogo istochnika," in *Problemy arkhivovedeniia i istochnikovedeniie: Materialy* (Leningrad, 1964), pp. 227–46, 209–26.

15. Polovtsov was a particularly interesting figure. In addition to being a high ranking bureaucrat, he was deeply involved in commercial and industrial affairs. A long-time opponent of the commune and supporter of small-scale private peasant property, he proposed what was, indeed, a true program of "bourgeois" development. He even favored the differentiation of the peasantry into economic classes, which distinguished him from the "new generation." In contrast to the prevailing policies of "social-bureaucratism," as he called them, in June 1901 Polovtsov urged the tsar to encourage the formation of a class of laboring peasants who would be characterized by thrift and a commitment to order and would act as a social and political basis of support for the government. Polovtsov repeated his proposals to Witte in April 1902, emphasizing the political necessity of developing an alliance between such a class of peasants and the large landowners as a step toward eliminating the bureaucracy as a special *soslovie* and its

policy of administrative *opeka.* "Dnevnik A. A. Polovtsova," KA 3 (1923), 96, 98, 139, 144.

16. This group includes the following men, all of whom contributed to the development of a new government policy: V. I. Gurko (b. 1862); A. V. Krivoshein (b. 1858); N. N. Kutler (b. 1859); Prince B. A. Vasil'chikov (b. 1863); A. I. Putilov (b. 1866); A. A. Rittikh (b. 1868); P. A. Stolypin (b. 1862); A. I. Lykoshin (b. 1861); and V. I. Baftalovskii (b. 1864). D. I. Pestrzhetskii also belongs to the first group, though I have no data on him. Others of this or an even younger group who were also involved, though they did not become significant until after the Stolypin Reforms were enacted, included P. P. Zubovskii, N. N. Pokrovskii (b. 1865), A. A. Vishniakov, S. D. Rudin (b. 1860), E. A. Smirnov, G. E. Blosfel'dt, P. N. Miliutin (b. 1867), and G. V. Glinka. The following members of the older generation also played a role, though they were not actively involved in the reconceptualization: Vorontsov-Dashkov (b. 1837), Witte (b. 1849), Polovtsov (b. 1832), Ermolov (b. 1847), Ia. Ia. Litvinov (b. 1852), and A. P. Nikol'skii (b. 1851). In addition, Prince S. D. Sviatopolk-Mirskii, interior minister and chairman of the Council of Ministers at the end of 1904 and the beginning of 1905, was influenced by his experience in the western provinces to abandon the commune.

17. R. Edelman, *Gentry Politics on the Eve of the Russian Revolution: The Nationalist Party 1907–1917* (New Brunswick, 1980), chapter 1; and Edelman, "The Russian Nationalist Party and the Political Crisis of 1909," *Russian Review*, 34:1 (1975), pp. 22–30.

18. Yaney, *Urge to Mobilize*, pp. 124–33.

19. On the regional distribution of communal versus individual tenure, Dubrovskii, *Stolypinskaia zemel'naia reforma*, pp. 570–73. In Poland, only 430,000 of 5.5 million desiatinas were in communal ownership. V. I. Sharii, ed., *Statisticheskii Ezhegodnik na 1913 god* (SPB, 1913), pp. 14–15.

20. V. I. Gurko, *Ocherki privislian'ia* (Moscow, 1897), pp. 74–92, 377. On the emancipation of the Polish peasantry, Lincoln, *Nikolai Miliutin*, pp. 75–100. On the *gmina*, N. M. Korkunov, *Russkoe gosudarstvennoe pravo*, 7th ed., vol. 2 (SPB, 1913), 618–21.

21. Those associated with Witte included P. Lokhtin, A. A. Kofod (b. 1855), and N. K. Brzheskii (b. 1860), each of whom published important investigative works in the area of rural reform. In addition, A. P. Nikol'skii, N. N. Kutler, A. A. Rittikh, S. I. Shidlovskii (b. 1861), P. P. Migulin (b. 1870), F. G. Terner (b. 1833), and D. I. Mendeleev (b. 1834) contributed to Witte's campaign for rural reform. Equally important was a smaller group of officials brought together by Gurko within the Interior Ministry's Rural Section, including P. P. Zubovskii, A. I. Lykoshin, Ia. Ia. Litvinov, V. I. Baftalovskii, A. V. Krivoshein, and S. D. Rudin. Ermolov's agricultural ministry played only a secondary and supportive role in the struggle for reform, though it gained considerable importance after its reorganization in 1905 when it was placed in charge of implementing the Stolypin Reforms. Its members, however, seemed to be opposed to the commune primarily on agrotechnical grounds.

22. Gurko, *Features and Figures*, pp. 229–33; Golovin *Moi vospominaniia*, vol. 2, especially pp. 63–75, 100–104; von Laue, *Sergei Witte*, pp. 276–84.

23. See note 25.

24. Born in 1844, Bekhteev had lived in the countryside since 1862 and among other properties owned a model estate. *Opisaniia otdel'nykh russkikh khoziastv*, vol. 2 (SPB, 1897), 51–54. He was an active participant in the Eletskii County zemstvo in Orel Province, had been a justice of the peace after the Emancipation and a marshal of the nobility for fourteen years. He was an ardent critic

of the backwardness of noble agriculture and argued for the most complete modernization possible and the direct involvement of the nobility in running their properties. He was also a strong critic of government policies toward both peasant and noble agriculture. Insofar as the peasantry was concerned, however, Bekhteev's commitment to laissez-faire individualism was moderated by a continuing commitment to both the *soslovie* system and the commune—a stand that earned him the epithet "red." In his view, the agrarian problem was a product not of administrative, juridical or agrotechnical backwardness or even of land-hunger but of the sudden economic changes that followed from the development of a money economy, the decline of peasant handicrafts, the increased need for money, and the unavailability of outside earnings and, thus, of the totality of the peasants' economic way of life. Therefore, he did not see any particular benefits to be gained from a transfer from communal to individual ownership of land principally because that would take too long, agriculture was too backward, and peasant consciousness was insufficiently developed, either economically or juridically. On the contrary, he continued to see the commune as a form of insurance cooperative to which the peasant could return in his dotage and avoid becoming a burden to the state. He also continued to support restrictions on the disposability of peasant allotment land. His solution was to increase the productivity of both land and labor through agricultural diversification and specialization and an increase in zemstvo involvement in agricultural improvement. Since this too was a relatively long-term process, in the interim, he proposed what amounted to a return to a natural economy concomitant with both an expansion of handicraft industries and various measures to protect them from capitalist competition. S. S. Bekhteev, *Khoziaistvennyie itogi istekshago sorokapiatiletiia*, vol. 1 (SPB, 1902), 125–74, 216–360; *Zhurnal zasedaniia 10, 18, 20–24 oktiabria, 1903 vysochaishe uchrezhdennoi 16/XI/01 Kommissii . . .* (SPB, 1903), pp. 32, 52, 76, 81. Between 1902, when his first volume was published, and April 1906, when he completed the second volume, Bekhteev changed his mind about the commune and favored encouraging peasants to leave the commune and form *khutora* in order to stimulate the individualization and intensification of peasant agriculture. Bekhteev, *Khoziaistvennyie itogi istekshago sorokapiatiletiia*, vol. 2, *Zemel'nyi vopros* (SPB, 1906), 321–49; Golovin, *Moi vospominanii*, vol. 2, 102.

25. G. A. Evreinov, *Krest'ianskii vopros v ego sovremennoi postanovke*, 2d ed. (SPB, 1904); K. F. Golovin, *Nasha sel'skaia obshchina v literature i v deistvitel'-nosti* (SPB, 1885); P. D., *Russkii sotsializm i obshchinnoe zemlevladenie* (Moscow, 1899); P. D., *Vopros ob obshchine i uravnitel'nom zemlepol'zovanii* (Moscow, 1904). The identity of the author P. D. has not been definitively established. Most likely it is Prince Petr D. Dolgorukov, the rural expert and future founder of the Kadet party. Other possibilities are his brother, Prince Pavel D. Dolgorukov, or even a collaboration by the two brothers. In any event, the author of these books was a careful observer of rural life and an early opponent of the commune. Compare this author's other books: *Krest'ianskaia nadel'naia zemlia v proekte grazhdanskago ulozheniia* (Moscow, 1903); *Russkaia intelligentsiia i krest'ianstvo: Kriticheskii analiz trudov mestnykh komitetov o nuzhdakh sel'skokhoziaistvennoi promyshlennosti* (SPB, 1904); *Russkaia intelligentsiia i krest'ianstvo: Kriticheskii analiz mnenii chlenov Osobago Soveshchaniia po krest'ianskomu delu* (Moscow, 1906). In general, P. D. supported the ideas of A. A. Rittikh and was equally critical of both past government policy and established social attitudes toward the peasantry. The main difference was that P. D. was a supporter of large landed property. See *Nasha derevnia* (Moscow, 1900), pp.

110–11, and chapter 4. Petr Dolgorukov later adopted the Kadet program of land reform, which envisaged the expropriation of the nobility's lands, though he did not abandon his support of intensification. See his "Agrarnyi vopros s tochki zreniia krupnago zemlevladeniia" in P. D. Dolgorukov and I. I. Petrunkevich, eds., *Agrarnyi vopros: sbornik statei,* vol. 1, 1st ed. (Moscow, 1905), 1–10. Compare P. D. Dolgorukov, *Velikaia razrukha* (Madrid, 1964), pp. 318–63.

26. Other members included Senator N. A. Khvostov of the Second (Peasant) Department, who had been instrumental in strengthening the commune during the 1880s and who remained a supporter of the commune, and future state controller P. Kh. Shvanebakh, who, unlike the others, was not a hereditary noble. Like Polenov and Golovin, Shvanebakh published a number of scathing attacks on Witte's fiscal policies and their impact on the nobility and noble agriculture: Shvanebakh, *Denezhnoe preobrazovanie i narodnoe khoziaistvo* (SPB, 1901); Shvanebakh, *Nashe podatnoe delo* (SPB, 1903); A. D. Polenov, *Izsledovanie ekonomicheskago polozheniia tsentral'nykh chernozemnykh gubernii: Trudy osobago soveshchaniia 1899–1901 g.* (Moscow, 1901); K. F. Golovin, *Nasha finansovaia politika i zadachi budushchego* (SPB, 1899). Compare von Laue, *Sergei Witte,* pp. 276–84; G. Guroff, "The State and Industrialization in Russian Economic Thought, 1909–1914" (Ph.D. diss., Princeton, 1970), especially pp. 12–95; Kitanina, *Khlebnaia torgovlia,* pp. 170–243.

27. See Witte's speech in GDSO, V, col. 1145.

28. *Muzhik bez progressa ili progress bez muzhika (k voprosu ob ekonomicheskoi materializme)* (SPB, 1896). Golovin, *Moi Vospominanii,* vol. 2, 241–50.

29. *Vne partii: Opyt politicheskoi psikhologii* (SPB, 1905).

30. Ibid., pp. 274–319.

31. V. F. Karavaev, *Bibliograficheskii obzor zemskoi statistiki i otsenochnoi literatury (1864–1903),* 2 vols. (SPB, 1906–1913); Karavaev, ed., *Izdanie zemstv 34 gubernii po obshchei ekonomicheskoi i otsenochnoi statistike vyshedshie za vremia s 1864 g. po 1 ianvaria 1911 g.* (SPB, 1911); V. N. Grigor'ev, *Predmetnyi ukazatel' materialov v zemsko-statisticheskikh trudakh s 1860kh godov po 1917 g.,* 2 vols. (Moscow, 1926–27); Z. M. and N. A. Svavitskie, *Zemskie podvornye perepisi: Pouezdnye itogi 1880–1913 gg.* (Moscow, 1926); "Sistematicheskii ukazatel' izdanii Tsentral'nago Statisticheskago Komiteta s 1863 goda po 30e aprelia 1913 goda," in *Iubileinyi sbornik TsSK MVD 1863–1913 gg.* (SPB, 1913), appendix pp. 1–19; A. I. Gozulov, *Istoriia otechestvennoi statistiki (Kratkie ocherki)* (Moscow, 1957), pp. 5–81; A. A. Kaufman, "Russia" in *The History of Statistics,* ed. J. Koren (New York, 1918), pp. 469–534; A. Kahan, "Quantitative Data for the Study of Russian History" in *The Dimensions of the Past: Materials, Problems and Opportunities for Quantitative Work in History,* ed. V. R. Lorwin and J. M. Price (New Haven, 1972), pp. 361–430; I. D. Koval'chenko, *Massovye istochniki po sotsial'no-ekonomicheskoi istorii Rossii perioda kapitalizma* (Moscow, 1979), pp. 191–344.

32. Bar, *Krest'ianskoe obshchinnoe zemlevladenie,* p. 3; Witte in his 16 March 1910 speech in GDSO, V, col. 1230; compare D. Fanger, "The Peasant in Literature" in Vucinich, *The Peasant,* pp. 231–62.

33. Seredonin, *Istoricheskii obzor,* vol. 3, pt. 2, p. 287.

34. Compare A. Vucinich, *Social Thought in Tsarist Russia: The Quest for a General Science of Society, 1861–1917* (Chicago, 1976); J. F. Normano, *The Spirit of Russian Economics* (New York, 1945), pp. 12–81.

35. Wortman, *Russian Legal Consciousness,* pp. 43–45; Walicki, *Slavophile Controversy,* pp. 126–27; Benson, "Conservative Liberalism," pp. 19–28, 32–40; Chicherin, *Vospominaniia,* vol. 3, 9–22; N. L. Rubinshtein, *Russkaia Istoriogra-*

fiia (Moscow, 1941), chapters 13, 18, and 19; and R. Pipes, "Karamzin's Conception of the Monarchy," in *Essays on Karamzin: Russian Man of Letters, Political
Thinker, Historian, 1766–1826,* ed. J. L. Black (The Hague, 1975), pp. 105–26.

36. P. S. Shkurinov, *Positivizm v Rossii XIX veka* (Moscow, 1980); V. D.
Zor'kin, *Pozitivistskaia teoriia prava v Rossii* (Moscow, 1978).

37. A. Smith, *An Inquiry into the Nature and Causes of The Wealth of Nations,*
ed. B. Mazlish (Indianapolis, 1961), pp. 137–42, 218–48.

38. G. L. Yaney, "Bureaucracy and Freedom: N. M. Korkunov's Theory of the
State," AHR 71:2 (1966), p. 483; Yaney, "Law, Society and the Domestic Regime
in Russia, in Historical Perspective," *American Political Science Review,* 59 (June
1965), 379–90; A. F. Meiendorf, "Memoirs" (unpub. ms., RACU), pp. 5–7; R. F.
Byrnes, *Pobedonostsev: His Life and Thought* (Bloomington, 1968).

39. The image of the "tsar-peacemaker" underlines the attitudinal continuity
between the two generations of conservative liberal bureaucrats. He symbolized
decisiveness, authority, and will to both Witte and Gurko. S. Iu. Witte,
*Vospominaniia: Deststvo: Tsarstvovaniia Aleksandra II i Aleksandra III (1849–
1894)* (The Hague, 1968), pp. 365–409; Gurko, *Features and Figures,* pp. 16–21;
"Dnevnik Sviatopolk-Mirskaia," p. 264; also the commemorative volume by N. E.
Volkov, *Ocherk zakonodatel'noi deiatel'nosti tsarstvovanie Imperatora Aleksandra III, 1881–1894 gg.* (SPB, 1910). The role of the autocrat is finally achieving
greater attention as the object of scholarly study: Kipp and Lincoln, "Autocracy
and Reform," pp. 1–21; R. Wortman, "Power and Responsibility in the Upbring-
ing of the Nineteenth Century Russian Tsars," *Newsletter-Group for the Use of
Psychology in History,* 1976:4, pp. 18–27; Wortman, "The Russian Empress as
Mother," in *The Family in Imperial Russia: New Lines of Historical Research,*
ed. D. L. Ransel (Urbana, 1978), pp. 60–74; A. M. Verner, "Nicholas II and the
Role of the Autocrat During the First Russian Revolution, 1904–1907" (Ph.D.
diss., Columbia, 1984). Also see the recent studies of the autocratic idea by
Davidovich, *Samoderzhavie v epokhu imperializma;* and V. A. Tvardovskaia,
Ideologiia poreformennogo samoderzhaviia (M. N. Katkov i ego izdaniia)
(Moscow, 1978).

40. See chapter 1, note 145; Normano, *Russian Economics,* pp. 68–81; and
Pashkov, *Istoriia Russkoi ekonomicheskoi mysli,* vol. 2, pt. 1, pp. 47–236.
Mendeleev supported a strong and interventionist state, particularly in the realm
of economic development. D. I. Mendeleev, *Problemy ekonomicheskogo
razvitiia Rossii* (Moscow, 1960), pp. 478–83. However, Mendeleev always remained a supporter of the commune. See his report to Witte of April 1902 in
ibid., pp. 578–90. Gurko is wrong in citing Mendeleev as the source of Witte's
views on agriculture. Gurko, *Features and Figures,* pp. 60, 201. F. M. Stackenwalt,
"The Thought and Work of Dmitrii Ivanovich Mendeleev on the Industrialization
of Russia, 1867–1907" (Ph.D. diss., Illinois, 1976).

41. V. A. Maklakov, *Iz vospominaniia* (New York, 1954), pp. 125–26; Gurko,
Features and Figures, p. 172.

42. See chapter 1, note 87. Paradoxically, J. S. Mill was also a source of inspi-
ration to the populist N. G. Chernyshevskii, one of Lenin's ideological progeni-
tors. W. F. Woehrlin, *Chernyshevskii: The Man and the Journalist* (Cambridge,
Mass., 1971), pp. 219–24; F. Venturi, *Roots of Revolution: A History of the
Populist and Socialist Movements in Nineteenth Century Russia* (New York,
1966), pp. 165–66.

43. Compare A. A. Kaufman, "Ukaz 9 noiabria 1906 goda," *Russkaia Mysl',*
1908:1, pt. 2, p. 166.

44. *Spravki MVD,* pp. 113–14.

45. I. L. Goremykin, comp., *Svod uzakonenii i rasporiazhenii pravitel'stva ob ustroistve sel'skago sostoianiia*, 2 vols. (SPB, 1903).

46. *Spravki MVD*, p. 110, cites 1900 as the year of the tsar's request; *Trudy redkom*, vol. 1, 8, cites 1901. The latter is probably correct. Compare M. S. Simonova, "Bor'ba techenii v pravitel'stvom lagere po voprosam agrarnoi politiki v kontse XIX v.," *Istoriia SSSR*, 1963:1, p. 69.

47. *Spravki MVD*, pp. 108–116.

48. Savich, *Novyi gosudarstvennyi stroi*, p. 1.

49. Sipiagin had earlier opposed Witte's proposals to abolish mutual responsibility. Witte, *Vospominaniia*, vol. 1, 475–76; Gurko, *Features and Figures*, pp. 205–6.

50. On this alliance and Sipiagin's plans for a unified cabinet, see Gurko, *Features and Figures*, pp. 82–87; "Dnevnik A. N. Kuropatkina," KA 2 (1922), 11; "Perepiska Vitte i Pobedonostseva," p. 105. Compare Witte's plans in 1905, which were realized and which were then capitalized on by Stolypin. H. D. Mehlinger and J. M. Thompson, *Count Witte and the Tsarist Government in the 1905 Revolution* (Bloomington, 1972), pp. 29–46, 69; N. G. Koroleva, *Pervaia rossiiskaia revoliutsiia i tsarizm: Soviet ministrov Rossii v 1905–1907* (Moscow 1982), esp. pp. 27–44.

51. "Dnevnik A. A. Polovtsova," KA 3 (1923), 114–16; compare Witte's comments to the State Council concerning the 1903 budget, in *Ministr Finansov i Gosudarstvennyi Sovet o finansovom polozhenii Rossii: Zhurnal Obshchago Sobraniia Gosudarstvennago Soveta 30/XII/02* (Stuttgart, 1903).

52. "Dnevnik A. A. Polovtsova," KA 3 (1923), 117, 128; *Vsepoddanneishii otchet o deiatel'nosti Osobago Soveshchaniia 1902–1904* (SPB, 1904), p. 5. Von Laue is wrong in asserting that Sipiagin opposed this from the beginning. Von Laue, *Sergei Witte* p. 224. The translation of the relevant sections of Polovtsov's diary in S. R. Tomkins, "Why Witte Failed to Solve the Peasant Problem," JMH 4:2 (1932), 235–39 is unreliable.

53. See the following text.

54. Savich, *Novyi gosudarstvennyi stroi*, pp. 1–2. In addition to works cited throughout this chapter and in previous chapters, see G. M. Deich, "Osoboe soveshchanie o nuzhdakh sel'skokhoziaistvennoi promyshlennosti" (Kand. diss., Moscow, 1946); G. L. Yaney, "The Imperial Russian Government and the Stolypin Land Reform" (Ph.D. diss., Princeton, 1961), pp. 88–98.

55. Stishinskii had participated in drafting the land captain legislation in the late 1880s. Other officeholders who participated were V. N. Kokovtsov, imperial secretary and future minister of finance; A. Kh. Steven, an assistant agricultural minister, formerly active in zemstvo and noble affairs in Tauride Province; and A. N. Kulomzin, also of the agricultural ministry, who had served as administrator of the Committee of Ministers, was currently administrator of the Committee on the Siberian Railroad and member of the State Council, and was author of numerous books on economic and fiscal subjects including peasant agriculture and migration. To this core group were subsequently added Prince L. D. Viazemskii, a former county marshal of the nobility, who supervised the properties of the imperial family; Prince A. D. Obolenskii, assistant interior minister and senator, who had served for many years in the provinces and who sat concurrently on a commission that was reviewing the Peasant Bank Statute; and Shvanebakh, now also an assistant agricultural minister, though formerly of the Finance Ministry.

56. Others in this category were F. G. Terner, former assistant finance minister, member of the State Council, and author of the widely respected *Gosudarstvo*

i zemlevladenie: krest'ianskoe zemlevladenie, 2 vols. (SPB, 1896–1900), which favored private property at the expense of the commune; M. Chikhachev, formerly of the Naval Ministry and member of the State Council; P. A. Saburov, senator and state councilor; N. N. Gerard, also senator and state councilor; V. V. Kalachov, one of the first peace arbitrators, long active in provincial noble affairs and local administration, now also senator and state councilor; Prince V. S. Kochubei, former administrator of imperial properties and owner of some 67,000 desiatinas in Poltava Province, including the model estate "Dikan'ka"; Prince A. S. Dolgorukii, a member of the court and owner of over 63,000 desiatinas; Count M. P. Tolstoi, a future founder of the conservative United Nobility; Count S. D. Sheremetev, historian, archeologist, member of the State Council, and owner of over 150,000 desiatinas; Prince A. G. Shcherbatov, chairman of the Moscow Agricultural Society and author of numerous works advocating the modernization of noble agriculture and the individualization of peasant agriculture, most notably *Uporiadochenie obshchinnago krest'ianskago zemlevladeniia* (Moscow, 1902). But compare his comments in Tolmachev, *Krest'ianskii vopros,* p. 111.

57. Other experts who participated were Krivoshein; Litvinov, assistant head of the Interior Ministry's Rural Section; and S. N. Lenin, director of the Department of Agriculture in the agricultural ministry. Complete lists of members are in *Vsepoddanneishii otchet,* appendices 2–3, and on pp. 2–3.

58. "Dnevnik A. A. Polovtsova," KA 3 (1923), 120–21; Savich, *Novyi gosudarstvennyi stroi,* pp. 1–2; *Vsepoddanneishii otchet,* pp. 5–7; S. I. Shidlovskii, comp., *Obshchii obzor trudov mestnykh komitetov* (SPB, 1905), pp. 1–24.

59. K. K. Troitskii, "Iz vospominanii chinovnika osobykh poruchenii V kl. pri MVD," (unpub. ms., RACU), pt. 2, p. 26. At the time Gurko looked on the Special Conference favorably though in his memoirs he described the Conference's work as useless. Compare V. I. Gurko, *Ustoi narodnago khoziaistva Rossii: Agrarnoekonomicheskie etiudy* (SPB, 1902), pp. vii–viii, and *Features and Figures,* pp. 222–23. In fact, the Editing Commission frequently cited the publications of the Special Conference to support its arguments. However, the Commission completed its work before any of the summary volumes were compiled. Witte subsequently noted, in an acerbic session of the Committee of Ministers, that at least ten of these volumes touched on relevant portions of the peasant question. TsGAOR, f. 586, V. K. Pleve, op. 1, 1904, d. 432, l. 2 ob., "Proekt rezoliutsii po delo o poriadke predvaritel'nago obsuzhdeniia proektov novykh zakonopolozhenii o krest'ianakh." Pleve saw the Special Conference's work as a valuable source of information that would help resolve the "peasant question." *Printsipial'nye voprosy po krest'ianskomu delu s otvetami mestnykh sel'skokhoziaistvennykh komitetov* (SPB, 1904), p. 4; "Rech' V. K. Pleve," col. 37. Later, Pleve was less optimistic. TsGAOR, f. 586, op. 1 (1904), d. 432, l. 3.

60. Veselovskii, *Istoriia zemstva,* vol. 3, 545, 557–58.

61. "Dnevnik A. A. Polovtsova," KA 3 (1923), 120–21, 126–28; *Vestnik Finansov,* 20 (19 May 1902), pp. 274–75; Shidlovskii, *Obshchii obzor,* pp. 22–24; *Vsepoddanneishii otchet,* pp. 7–8, 56–57, and appendix 1. In general, the questions reflected the contemporary concerns of agricultural thought. Compare G. K. Gins and P. A. Shafranov, *Sel'sko-khoziaistvennoe vedomstvo za 75 let ego deiatel'nosti (1837–1912 gg.)* (Petrograd, 1914). They included questions concerning the spread of agricultural knowledge, reclamation, prevention of rural fires (introduced by the tsar and one of his special concerns), road construction, credit, cooperation, improved systems of rotation and methods of cultivation (on both noble and peasant lands), expansion of nongrain crops, production of agricultural machinery and fertilizer, trade, handicrafts, and migratory labor. Other concerns

were the protection of property from illegal acts—highlighted a few days later by the disorders in Poltava and Khar'kov provinces; the preservation of large properties from fragmentation; and the elimination of open fields between neighboring landowners.

62. "Dnevnik A. A. Polovtsova," KA 3 (1923), 144, 150. This department was a logical choice since it was directly concerned with the problem of tax arrears and had already compiled a number of statistical studies on the agrarian problem. The content of the project suggests that Rittikh may also have participated in drafting it.

63. Its full title was "Nekotoryia predpolozheniia o sposobakh uluchsheniia krest'ianskago zemlepol'zovaniia v sel'sko-khoziaistvennom otnoshenii." It was published in *Vestnik finansov*, 22 (2 June 1902), pp. 400–412. A report on the Special Conference's discussion of it is in ibid., 27 (7 July 1902), pp. 3–8; *Vsepoddanneishii otchet*, pp. 18–20.

64. Semenov's project was also considered by the Interior Ministry's Editing Commission. M. S. Simonova, "Krizis agrarnoi politike samoderzhaviia nakanune pervoi russkoi revoliutsii," in *EAIVE za 1962*, pp. 479–80; Nesterova, "Vopros," pp. 84–85.

65. The total number of males who would require resettlement was determined to be 1,663,500!

66. Semenov compiled a statistical study of peasant landownership and use for the Interior Ministry's Rural Section, *Statisticheskii ocherk krest'ianskago zemlevladeniia i zemlepol'zovaniia v Evropeiskoi Rossii* (SPB, 1904), that confirmed many of his assumptions. See, too, A. N. Kulomzin's report on his trip to Siberia to study migration. *Kolonizatsiia Sibiri v sviazi s obshchim pereselencheskim voprosam* (SPB, 1900). According to Rozenberg, "Iz khroniki," pp. 9–10, this report was the government's first *public* acknowledgment of the problem of land-hunger.

67. *Vestnik Finansov*, 22 (2 June 1902), pp. 407–8.

68. At last, the potential inherent in this post was being capitalized upon.

69. The problem of material cost, in terms of both finances and personnel, was a very real obstacle to action. The competition for scarce funds, as ever, was between the military and nonmilitary sectors of the economy. The issue of "costs" had been raised in 1893; see *Otchet za 1892–1893*, vol. 1, 522; it was again raised in 1905: *Otchet za 1905–1906*, pp. 220, 330, 335. Even after the Stolypin Reforms were adopted, they were continually plagued by budgetary problems and the opposition of Finance Minister Kokovtsov.

70. This faith was based on a biological model of evolution, though it lacked the extremist, Spencerian overtones of a socially beneficial "survival of the fittest." Compare the later proposals of G. I. Lisenkov, in his *Opyt sistematicheskago postroeniia agrarnoi programmy (Izsledovanie v piati chastiakh)* (SPB, 1906), p. 17. Lisenkov was upstaged by events, for he was only able to publish the first two of a projected five parts.

71. "Dnevnik A. A. Polovtsova," KA 3 (1923), 150; *Vestnik Finansov*, 27 (7 July 1902), pp. 3–8.

72. The two other opponents were S. N. Lenin and Nikol'skii, director of the State Savings Bank.

73. The other member was I. P. Shipov, director of the State Treasury.

74. *Vsepoddanneishii otchet*, pp. 18–20; J. R. Fisher, "The Witte Conference on the Needs of Agriculture in Russia: 1902–1905" (Ph.D. diss., Toronto, 1978), p. 116. The provinces were Vilno, Vladimir, Voronezh, Moscow, Saratov, Tavride, and Chernigov.

75. A. A. Rittikh, *Zavisimost' krest'ian ot obshchiny i mira* (SPB, 1903). Compare L. Slonimskii, "Noveishie protivniki obshchiny," *Vestnik Evropy,* 39:2 (1904), pp. 766–72.

76. *The London Times,* 19 June 1930, 9 g; *Vozrozhdenie,* no. 1842 (18 June 1930), 2:1–2.

77. Rittikh, *Zavisimost',* pp. 3–53.

78. See K. F. Golovin's review of books by P. Struve and A. Skvortsov, "Dva novykh protivniki obshchiny," *Russkii Vestnik,* 1894:12, pp. 311–29; and his *Muzhik bez progressa.* Also, E. Kingston-Mann, "Marxism and Russian Rural Development: Problems of Evidence, Experience, and Culture," AHR 86:4 (1981), 731–52, and "Transforming the Russian Countryside" (unpub. paper presented to National Seminar on Russian Social History in the Twentieth Century, Philadelphia, 1982); R. Kindersley, *The First Russian Revisionists: A Study of 'Legal Marxism' in Russia* (Oxford, 1962); R. Pipes, *Struve: Liberal on the Left, 1870–1905* (Cambridge, Mass., 1970), pp. 65–117; Walicki, *Controversy over Capitalism,* pp. 132–94.

79. This and subsequent pages are based on Rittikh *Zavisimost',* pp. 54–206.

80. See chapter 1. According to Sosnovskii, *Zemlevladenie,* p. 186, only eight of the Special Conference's local committees favored a restoration of Article 165.

81. Given the opposition to the land captains within the Finance Ministry, this decision was clearly dictated by necessity.

82. Rittikh, *Zavisimost',* pp. 180–81.

83. Ibid., pp. 185–86 quoting P. D., *Nasha derevnia,* p. 322.

84. Rittikh, *Zavisimost',* p. 184.

85. Ibid., p. 191.

86. The study of small-scale private property and the peasant family farm was only beginning to be a subject of academic interest and, while gathering momentum during the period prior to 1914, the ideologists of this form of peasant agriculture were only to achieve their full flowering during the NEP period of the 1920s. The stimulus was provided by the work of E. David and the Revisionist Marxists in Germany. After the Revolution of 1905–7 this trend was known as "Davidianstvo." A. Hussain and K. Tribe, *Marxism and the Agrarian Question,* vol. 1 *German Social Democracy and the Peasantry 1890–1917* (Atlantic Highlands, N.J., 1981), pp. 102–132; and E. David, *Sozialismus und Landwirtschaft* (Berlin, 1903). Early examples were N. N. Chernenkov, *K kharakteristike krest'ianskago khoziaistva,* 1st ed., 2 parts (Moscow, 1900–1902); N. A. Karyshev, *Iz literatury voprosa o krupnom i melkom sel'skom khoziaistve* (Moscow 1905); A. I. Chuprov, *Melkoe zemlevladenie i ego osnovykh nuzhdy,* 1st ed. (Moscow 1906); V. A. Kosinski, *K agrarnomu voprosu,* vol. 1, *Krest'ianskoe i pomeshchich'e khoziaistvo* (Odessa, 1906); N. Kablukov, *Ob usloviiakh razvitiia krest'ianskago khoziaistvo v Rossii* (Moscow, 1908); and *Bor'ba za zemliu (Induktivno-statisticheskoe izsledovanie),* vol. 1, pt. 1 (Moscow, 1908). See also the political discussions: A. Peshekhonov, "Iz teorii i praktiki krest'ianskago khoziaistva," *Russkoe Bogatstvo,* 1902:9, pp. 161–93; 1902:10, pp. 71–119; N. Oganovskii, *Zakonomernost' agrarnoi evoliutsii,* pt. 1, *Teorii kapitalisticheskago razvitiia: Obshchii khod i fazisy agrarnoi evoliutsii* (Saratov, 1909); N. N. Sukhanov, *K voprosu ob evoliutsii sel'skago khoziaistva: Sotsial'nyia otnosheniia v krest'ianskom khoziaistve Rossii* (Moscow, 1909); for a brief history, see S. G. Solomon, *The Soviet Agrarian Debate: A Controversy in Social Science, 1923–1929* (Boulder, 1977). Compare T. Shanin, *The Awkward Class: Political Sociology of Peasantry in a Developing Society: Russia, 1910–1925* (Oxford, 1972). On the "Organization-Production" school see B. Kerblay, "A. V. Chayanov: Life, Career, Works," in A.

V. Chayanov, *The Theory of Peasant Economy*, ed. D. Thorner et al. (Homewood, Ill., 1966), pp. xv–lxxv.

87. Rittikh, *Zavisimost'*, p. 195.

88. Compare the critique of social differentiation in Sosnovskii, *Zemlevladenie*, pp. 39–40, 62.

89. Compare Normano, *Russian Economics*, chapters V–VII; Kingston-Mann, "Transforming the Russian Countryside"; and B. Veselovskii, "Utopism i 'real'naia politika' v zemleustroistve," *Sovremennyi Mir*, 1910:1, pt. 2, pp. 1–17, who denies this possibility.

90. Rittikh, *Zavisimost'*, pp. 181, 199.

91. M. Steblev, *Zakon o krest'ianskoi razorenii* (SPB, 1909), p. 9, charges Stishinskii with having said; "We need kulaks! Without them we are lost!" J. Mavor, *An Economic History of Russia*, 2d ed. (New York, 1925), p. 349, cites the economist A. A. Chuprov to the same effect. Compare V. A. Butlerov's 1910 comments in the State Council in Kovalevskii, "Sud'by obshchinnago zemlevladeniia," p. 73, and the interpretation placed on those statements by Anfimov and Zyrianov, "Nekotorye cherty," p. 38. A representative sampling of critics who accused the government of trying to speed up the process of class differentiation and to create conflict between rich and poor peasants would include B. A. Brutskus, "K sovremennomu polozheniiu agrarnoi vopros" in his *Agrarnye voprosy v Rossii*, vol. 1 (Petrograd, 1917); I. V. Chernyshev, "Razsloenie sovremennoi derevni," *Sovremennyi Mir* 1908:6, pt. 2, pp. 46–69; N. N. Oganovskii, "Pervye itogi 'velikoi reformy,'" *Russkoe Bogatstvo*, 1911:10, pt. 1, pp. 124–62, 1911:11, pt. 1, pp. 67–98; A. Lositskii, *Raspadenie obshchiny* in *Trudy VEO*, 1912:1–2, pp. 1-60; Maslov, *Agrarnyi vopros*, vol. 2, 328–46. Chuprov later rejected the *divide et impera* interpretation of the government's agrarian policy: A. A. Tschuprow, "The Break-Up of the Village Community in Russia," *The Economic Journal*, 22 (June 1912), 196.

92. See chapter 1, note 150.

93. N. K. Brzheskii, *Obshchinnyi byt i khoziaistvennaia neobezpechennost' krest'ian: Po povodu predstoiashchago peresmotra krest'ianskikh polozhenii* (SPB, 1899).

94. Republished as N. K. Brzheskii, *Ocherki iuridicheskago byta krest'ian: Izsledovanie* (SPB, 1902). Brzheskii was also responsible for editing the 100th jubilee history of the Finance Ministry that was published in 1902.

95. P. Lokhtin, *Ob izmenenii velichiny posevnykh ploshchadei v Evropeiskoi Rossii za posledniia 20 let* (SPB, 1903).

96. P. Lokhtin, *Bezzemel'nyi proletariat v Rossii; opyt opredeleniia kolichestva bezzemel'nago proletariata, sozdannago sushchestvuiushchimi sposobami krest'ianskago zemlevladeniia* (Moscow, 1905); and *K voprosu o reforme sel'skago byta krest'ian* (SPB, 1902), which contained ideas very similar to Witte's.

97. A. A. Kofod, *Krest'ianskie khutora na nadel'noi zemel'*, 2 vols. (SPB, 1905). See, too, his valuable *Bor'ba chrezpolositseiu v Rossii i za granitseiu* (SPB, 1906) also issued under the title *Zemleustroistvo v Rossii i v drugikh stranakh* (SPB, 1906), which was based on research trips to the countries concerned that were financed by the Rural Section of the Interior Ministry. Koefoed, *My Share in the Stolypin Reforms*, pp. 64–65, 88–100; Shlippe, "Memoirs," pp. 95–96; A. Baker-Lampe, "A Danish Agronomist's View of the Russian Peasant Commune" (unpub. paper presented at 15th Annual Convention of AAASS, Kansas City, Mo., October 1983). See too Sosnovskii, *Zemlevladenie*, esp. pp. 142–202, which were devoted to *khutora*; B. Pares, *My Russian Memoirs* (London, 1931), pp. 214–15; Pares, "The Land Settlement in Russia," *Russian Review*, 1:1 (January

1912), 64–65; P. N. Pershin, *Uchastkovoe zemlepol'zovanie v Rossii* (Moscow 1922); Lositskii, "Raspadenie obshchiny," pp. 8–16.

98. Compare I. de Madariaga, *Russia in the Age of Catherine the Great* (New Haven, 1981), part 3.

99. Shidlovskii, *Obshchii obzor*, pp. 4, 7–13; *Vsepoddanneishii otchet*, pp. 70–72; S. N. Prokopovich, *Mestnye liudi o nuzhdakh Rossii* (SPB, 1904), p. 3.

100. M. S. Simonova, "Zemsko-liberal'naia fronda (1902–1903 gg.)," IZ 91 (1973), pp. 153–54.

101. Shidlovskii, *Obshchii obzor*, pp. 4–5; *Vsepoddanneishii otchet*, pp. 69–70, 73; *Pravitel'stvennyi Vestnik*, 69 (27 March 1902), and 109 (18 May 1902); and Witte's 9 August 1902 letter in *Vestnik Finansov*, 32 (11 August 1902), p. 286. Pleve had opposed the involvement of the zemstvos during the Special Conference's first session. By May, however, he expressed a desire to reduce the level of conflict between the Interior and Finance ministries and their two commissions. Dubrovskii, *Stolypinskaia zemel'naia reforma*, pp. 74–75; "Dnevnik A. A. Polovtsova," KA 3 (1923), pp. 121, 143; Judge, *Plehve*, pp. 65–71. There were, of course, also major differences between Witte and the zemstvo and liberal oppositions, for although they both regarded the integration of the peasantry into the general civil legal order as the primary means to achieve their goals, their goals differed. For Witte the goals were fiscal and economic; for the zemstvos, political. See, in addition to works cited earlier, Witte, *Vospominaniia*, vol. 1, 477–78; Gurko, *Features and Figures*, pp. 229–49, 691–703; D. N. Shipov, *Vospominaniia i dumy o perezhitom* (Moscow, 1918), pp. 156–97; Rozenberg, "Iz khroniki," pp. 201–16; Veselovskii, *Istoriia zemstva*, vol. 3, 551–75; P. N. Miliukov, "Vvedenie," in N. N. L'vov and A. A. Stakhovich, eds., *Nuzhdy derevni po rabotam komitetov o nuzhdakh sel'sko-khoziaistvennoi promyshlennosti: Sbornik statei*, vol. 1 (SPB, 1904), 1–40; Prokopovich, *Mestnye liudi*, pp. 1–47; articles by N. Cherevanin, "Dvizhenie intelligentsii (Do epokhi 'doveriia' Kn. Sviatopolka-Mirskago)," and B. B. Veselovskii, "Dvizhenie zemlevladel'tsev," in Martov, *Obshchestvennoe dvizhenie*, vol. 1, 286–90, 307–12; Simonova, "Zemsko-liberal'naia fronda," pp. 150–216. For the opposition's deepening involvement in the agrarian question, see Veselovskii, *Istoriia zemstva*, vol. 3, 690–96; Tolmachev, *Krest'ianskii vopros*, pp. 74–78; R. T. Manning, "The Zemstvo and Politics, 1864–1914," in Emmons and Vucinich, *Zemstvo in Russia*, pp. 133–76; and the movement's publication of numerous volumes on its various aspects.

102. Shidlovskii, *Obshchii obzor*, pp. 5–6, 13–15; *Vsepoddanneishii otchet*, pp. 69, 72–76.

103. *Trudy mestnykh komitetov*, 58 vols. (SPB, 1903). S. Iu. Lopatin, *Perechen' dokladov pomeshchennykh v trudakh mestnykh komitetov* (SPB, 1905). Because of Pleve's opposition, some reports could not be published. Some of these appeared in émigré publications such as *Osvobozhdenie* (Stuttgart and Paris, 1902–1905) and as individual pamphlets. On the distribution of the volumes, see *Vestnik Finansov*, 50 (14 December 1903), pp. 443–44; *Vsepoddanneishii otchet*, pp. 76–80 and appendix VI; and Shidlovskii, *Obshchii obzor*, pp. 15–16, 19–21.

104. *Svod trudov mestnykh komitetov po 49 gubernii Evropeiskoi Rossii*, 23 vols. (SPB, 1903–1905); a listing of the volumes and their titles is in Shidlovskii, *Obshchii obzor*, pp. 16–17; and *Vsepoddanneishii otchet*, appendix V. Also, see *Spisok otdelov svoda trudov mestnykh komitetov po Evropeiskoi Rossii (49 gubernii)* (SPB, 1904). Separate volumes were compiled by A. A. Kaufman and L. B. Skarzhinskii for the non-European regions and for Poland, respectively.

105. Shidlovskii, *Obshchii obzor*. The procedures followed in its composition are detailed in *ibid.*, p. 18; and *Vsepoddanneishii otchet*, pp. 77–78.

106. *Printsipial'nye voprosy*. The questions were, in fact, those compiled by the MVD's Editing Commission for its own provincial conferences.

107. Shidlovskii, *Vospominaniia*, vol. 1, 74.

108. A. A. Rittikh, comp., *Krest'ianskoe zemlepol'zovanie* (SPB, 1903); *Krest'ianskii pravoporiadok* (SPB, 1904).

109. A. A. Rittikh, *Krest'ianskoe delo: Kratkii svod trudov mestnykh komitetov (po otdelam svoda: "Krest'ianskoe zemlepol'zovanie" i "Krest'ianskii pravoporiadok")* (SPB, 1903). Written in November 1903, it was reprinted in *Spravki MVD*, pp. 133–57; as the introduction to Rittikh's *Krest'ianskii pravoporiadok*, pp. 1–13; and as an appendix to *Vestnik Finansov*, 51 (21 December 1903), pp. 1–5.

110. Rittikh, *Krest'ianskoe delo*, p. 13.

111. Shidlovskii, *Vospominaniia*, part 1.

112. S. I. Shidlovskii, *Zemstvo* (SPB, 1903); *Zemel'noe oblozhenie* (SPB, 1904); and *Zemel'nye zakhvaty i mezhevoe delo* (SPB, 1904). Compare Sosnovskii, *Zemlevladenie*, and Fleksor, *Okhrana sel'skokhoziaistvennoi sobstvennosti*, which reiterated the thesis that communal landownership undermined peasant respect for noble property rights and prevented them from developing a private-property consciousness.

113. Shidlovskii, *Obshchii obzor*, pp. 25–26. Compare Rittikh, *Krest'ianskoe zemlepol'zovanie*, pp. 69–77, on which Shidlovskii based his calculations concerning communal landownership.

114. Sosnovskii, *Zemlevladenie*, pp. 180–202.

115. Shidlovskii, *Obshchii obzor*, pp. 34–37. It is unlikely that the small numbers were a result of pressure from the Interior Ministry, since most of its efforts were directed against a comparatively small number of committees that explicitly utilized their position to make political demands. Thus, Prokopovich notes (*Mestnye liudi*, p. 256) that 70 percent of the county and 78 percent of the provincial level committees were able to express "liberal" tendencies on the issues of education, juridical structure, zemstvo self-government, financial policy, land-hunger, and agricultural workers. Had there been any greater concern about the commune, it would undoubtedly have found a way to express itself. The explanation seems rather to be lack of interest.

116. *Protokoly po krest'ianskomu delu*, no. 10 (15 January 1905), pp. 2–3; no. 14 (5 February 1905), p. 15; P. P. Semenov, comp., *Svod trudov mestnykh komitetov o nuzhdakh sel'skokhoziaistvennoi promyshlennosti (gubernii, sostoiashchikh na Velikorossiiskom polozhenii) po voprosu o krest'ianskom zemlepol'zovanii* (SPB, 1905). Stenogrammy OSNSKhP, 26 (22 March 1905), p. 23.

117. Tolmachev, *Krest'ianskii vopros*, p. 109.

118. Prokopovich, *Mestnye liudi*, pp. 256–59. On local attitudes toward land-hunger, *ibid.*, pp. 176–218. For other indications as to the nature of "liberal" concerns, see L'vov and Stakhovich, *Nuzhdy derevni*, 2 vols., which devoted its first volume to legal questions, relegating economic and social issues to the second; compare Dolgorukov and Petrunkevich, *Agrarnyi vopros*, 2 vols.; Manuilov, *Ocherki po krest'ianskomu voprosu*, 2 vols.; A. V. Peshekhonov, *Zemel'nye nuzhdy derevni i osnovnyia zadachi agrarnoi reformy*, 2d ed. (SPB, 1906), pp. 5–138; and A. D. Bilimovich, *Krest'ianskii pravoporiadok, po trudam mestnykh komitetov o nuzhdakh sel'skokhoziaistvennoi promyshlennosti* (Kiev, 1904). An important critique of the local committees and their members is P. D., *Russkaia intelligentsiia i krest'ianstvo* (1904). Another compilation is contained in P. A. Vikhliaev, *Pravo na zemliu* (Moscow, 1906), pp. 9–12. However, this author ignores the issues with which we are concerned here. However, he does

note that sixteen committees (including two provincial committees) supported compulsory alienation of private land and forty-five supported transfers of state land as a solution to land-hunger.

119. Chuprov and Postnikov, *Vliianie urozhaev.*

120. A. A. Chuprov, "Obshchinnoe zemlevladenie," in L'vov and Stakhovich, *Nuzhdy derevni*, vol. 2, 116–232, esp. pp. 116–26 and 204–14.

121. During the Conference's March 1905 discussions of these questions, Rittikh claimed that he had been very careful to avoid the accusation of prejudice in compiling his digest. Fisher, "The Witte Conference," pp. 279–340, tends to confirm Chuprov's analysis.

122. P. D., *Russkaia intelligentsiia i krest'ianstvo* (1904), p. 8. Compare P. D. Dolgorukov and D. I. Shakhovskoi, eds., *Melkaia zemskaia edinitsa; sbornik statei*, 2 vols. (SPB, 1903).

123. PSZ, 23 (1903), otd. 1 (SPB, 1905), no. 22581, pp. 113–14; Savich, *Novyi gosudarstvennyi stroi*, pp. 3–5; *Spravki MVD*, pp. 116–20. This section was apparently written by V. I. Gurko and edited by Pleve. Prince V. P. Meshcherskii also had a role. See Liubimov, "Russkaia smuta," p. 38; Gurko, *Features and Figures*, pp. 219–21. Iu. B. Solov'ev, "K istorii proiskhozhdeniia manifesta 26 fevralia 1903 g.," VID, 11, 192–205; and "Dnevnik Kuropatkina," KA 2 (1922), p. 38; on Meshcherskii, Witte, *Vospominaniia*, vol. 2, 509–26; K. A. Krivoshein, *A. V. Krivoshein (1857–1921 g.) Ego znachenie v istorii Rossii nachale XX veka* (Paris, 1973), pp. 154–62; I. Vinogradoff, "Some Russian Imperial Letters to Prince V. P. Mestchersky," *Oxford Slavonic Papers*, X (1962), pp. 105–58; Solov'ev, *Samoderzhavie i dvorianstvo v 1902–1907*, pp. 67–71, 89–91, 95–100, 115–18; and W. E. Mosse, "Imperial Favorite: V. P. Meshchersky and the *Grazhdanin*," SEER 59:4 (1981), 529–47.

124. Savich, *Novyi gosudarstvennyi stroi*, pp. 5–6. Witte was very disturbed by the 8 January 1904 ukaze according to Kuropatkin, "Dnevnik Kuropatkina," KA 2 (1922), 98.

125. Savich, *Novyi gosudarstvennyi stroi*, pp. 8–10.

126. Gurko, *Features and Figures*, pp. 221–25; Witte, *Vospominaniia*, vol. 1, 214–23; von Laue, *Sergei Witte*, pp. 231–61; V. N. Kokovtsov, *Iz moego proshlago: Vospominaniia 1903–1919 gg.* (Paris, 1933), vol. 1, 8–13.

127. Polenov, *Izsledovanie*, p. 1; M. S. Simonova, "Problema 'oskudeniia' tsentra i ee rol' v formirovanii agrarnoi politiki samoderzhaviia v 90-kh godakh XIX–nachale XX v," in *Problemy sotsial'no-ekonomicheskoi istorii Rossii: Sbornik statei* (Moscow, 1971), pp. 236–63. The results of the Kokovtsov Commission's work were published in *Materialy vysochaishe uchrezhdennoi 16/XI/01 Kommissii po izsledovaniiu blagosostoianiia sel'skago naseleniia srednezemledel'cheskikh gubernii*, 3 vols. (SPB, 1903). In fact, these two commissions were complementary, though the first is often ignored. The title by which the Kokovtsov Commission became known, "Commission on the Impoverishment of the Center," was in fact one that could with greater justice have been applied to the so-called Kovalevskii Commission.

128. Polenov, *Izsledovanie*; Simonova, "Problema 'oskudeniia' tsentra," pp. 239–46.

129. Polenov, *Izsledovanie*, pp. 68–70.

130. Future Kadets included N. V. Raevskii (Kursk), Prince G. E. L'vov (Tula), M. P. Kolobov (Tambov), S. M. Barataev (Simbirsk), A. A. Savel'ev (Nizhni Novgorod); future Octobrists included A. I. Urusul (Voronezh), A. A. Atryganev (Penza), V. F. Eman (Riazan), A. A. Ushakov (Samara), F. A. Lizogub (Poltava). Emmons, *Formation of Political Parties*, appendix, pp. 384–97.

131. "Zapiska predstavitelei zemskikh uchrezhdenii v komissiiu o tsentre," *Narodnoe Khozaiastvo*, 1903:6, pp. 201–23.

132. The criticisms are in "Zapiska," pp. 218–21; they were reflected in the commission's conclusions, *Zhurnal zasedaniia . . . 1903*, pp. 87–110. For the similarities with Witte's budget report, see "Zapiska," pp. 204–7. Compare *Rapport du Ministre des Finances a S. M. L'Empereur sur le budget de l' Empire pour l'exercice 1899* (SPB, 1898), pp. 16–26. Also see the reports for 1900 and 1902: *Rapport . . . pour l'exercice 1900* (SPB, 1899), pp. 22–28; and *Report of the Minister of Finance to H.M. the Emperor on the Budget of the Empire for 1902* (SPB, 1901), pp. 19–21. Witte's budget reports exhibit an internal contradiction. On the one hand, they minimize the poor state of agriculture, limiting those problems that did exist to the central and eastern provinces, and then only to individual villages. On the other hand, where they urged a study of the whole situation and the necessity of reforms, they emphasized agriculture's impoverishment and the necessity of improving it if the state's financial position were to be improved. Compare "Dnevnik A. A. Polovtsova," KA 3 (1923), pp. 103–5; "Iz dnevnika A. A. Polovtsova," 46 (1931), p. 128; and *Spravki MVD*, p. 103.

133. "Zapiska," pp. 210–18; *Zhurnal zasedanii . . . 1903*, p. 82.

134. *Zhurnal zasedanii . . . 1903*, pp. 18–19, 112.

135. Ibid., pp. 7–14, 17, 20–38, 43–44, 86–87, 112.

136. Ibid., pp. 17, 39–66, 112–113.

137. Ibid., pp. 23–24, 40; *Materialy . . . 16/XI/01 Kommissii*, vol. 3, 278–79; Simonova, "Problema 'oskudeniia' tsentra," p. 254.

138. *Zhurnal zasedanii . . . 1903*, pp. 23–24, 66–82, 113.

139. Ibid., pp. 21, 24–28, 112.

140. Ibid., p. 81.

141. Ibid., pp. 73, 75.

142. This development, of course, parallels the concomitant approach of the Interior Ministry to the urban labor problem and the separation of the economic and political spheres implicit in the *Zubatovshchina* and other measures. V. Ia. Laverychev, *Tsarizm i rabochii vopros v Rossii (1861–1917 gg.)* (Moscow, 1972), pp. 138–71.

143. Simonova, "Politika tsarizma," p. 215; Simonova, "Otmena krugovoi poruki," pp. 191–99; Simonova, "Problema 'oskudeniia' tsentra," p. 261; *Vsepoddanneishii otchet*, pp. 48–50. However, an imperial manifesto of 11 August 1904 abolishing corporal punishment also abolished arrears of redemption payments and other direct taxes accumulated up to 1 January 1904. IZO 1904:8 pp. 3–15; PSZ 24 (1904), otd. 1 (SPB, 1907), no. 25014, pp. 856–71.

144. Witte, *Vospominaniia*, I, 473–74, 478; Simonova, "Problema 'oskudeniia' tsentra," pp. 259-60; Gurko, *Features and Figures*, p. 232; "Zapiska," p. 220.

Notes to Chapter 3

1. Liashchenko, *Ocherki agrarnoi evoliutsii Rossii*, Vol. 2, *Krest'ianskoe delo i poreformennaia zemleustroitel'naia politika*, Part 2, *Regulirovanie krest'ianskago zemlevladeniia*, (Tomsk, 1917), pp. 131–46; Chernyshev, *Agrarno-krest'ianskaia politika*, pp. 267–73; Simonova, "Krizis agrarnoi politiki," pp. 475–88; Simonova, "Politika tsarizma," pp. 212–23; Nesterova, "Vopros," pp. 76–92; Rosenthal, "Ministerial Conflict," pp. 22–28; Yaney, "Imperial Russian Government," pp. 81–102; Rainey, *Sergei Witte*, pp. 25–39; Leontovitsch, *Geschichte des Liberalismus*, pp. 177–91; and K., "Iz noveishei istorii," pp. 99–104. Compare Miliukov

in Oldenburg, *Last Tsar*, vol. 3, 39; and S. E. Kryzhanovskii, *Vospominaniia* (Berlin, n.d.) pp. 215–16.

2. *Spravki MVD*, pp. 112–16.

3. Gurko, *Features and Figures*, pp. 131–36, 141, 153–57.

4. Ibid., pp. 35–51.

5. Ibid., p. v.

6. *Dvorianskoe zemlevladenie v sviazi s mestnoi reforme* (n.p., 1887); and *Ocherki privislian'ia* (Moscow, 1897).

7. They were reissued in book form under the title *Ustoi narodnago khoziaistva Rossii: Agrarno-ekonomicheskie etiudy* (SPB, 1902). In his memoirs, Gurko incorrectly dates the appearance of the articles to 1902–3. *Features and Figures,* p. 133. The following is based on *Ustoi narodnago khoziaistva*, especially pp. 183–96. The basic themes of this work were to be repeated with only minor changes in all of his subsequent writings. Compare *Otryvochnyia mysli po agrarnomu voprosu* (SPB, 1906); and *Nashe gosudarstvennoe i narodnoe khoziaistvo: Doklad predstavlennyi V-mu s"ezdu upol'nomochennykh ob"edinennykh dvorianskikh obshchestv* (SPB, 1909), especially pp. 42–80.

8. Compare *Materialy po peresmotru uzakonenii o vzimanii okladnykh sborov*, 2 vols. (SPB, 1894–95).

9. Compare Golovin, *Muzhik bez progressa*, p. 155.

10. The current system of direct taxation was in effect a poll tax and was independent of either the quantity of land owned or the income derived from it.

11. Some interpretations of Gurko's opinions exaggerate and take his statements out of context. See M. S. Simonova, "Agrarnaia politika samoderzhaviia v 1905 g.," *IZ* 81 (1968), 204, where it is wrongly implied that Gurko supported the "forcible abolition of the commune." True, in his memoirs (not cited by Simonova), he frequently refers to the "abolition" of the commune. However, these statements inadequately reflected the political constraints of the period. *Features and Figures*, pp. 311–12, 316–17. Compare his *Otryvochnyia mysli*, p. 38, and *Nashe gosudarstvennoe i narodnoe khoziaistvo*, p. 214. In 1917, Gurko supported the Kadet party's 1905 program, including the compulsory alienation of private lands. E. Chernevskii, *Agrarnyi vopros: Nastol'nyi spravochnik* (Petrograd, 1918), p. 22.

12. Gurko, *Ustoi narodnago khoziaistva*, pp. 196–201; Gurko, *Otryvochynia mysli*, pp. 39–42. Compare his admiration for the English system of local self-government, *Features and Figures*, p. 331; and Golovin, *Moi vospominanii*, vol. 2, 99–100.

13. *Zhurnal zasedaniia . . . 1903*, pp. 43, 55–56; Gurko, *Otryvochnyia mysli*, pp. 28–34; Simonova, "Problema 'oskudeniia' tsentra," p. 255.

14. *Nashe gosudarstvennoe i narodnoe khoziaistvo*, pp. 72, 78–79.

15. Gurko, *Features and Figures*, especially pp. 134–35, 138, 160.

16. Gurko, *Features and Figures*, pp. 134, 222–23, 296–97, 334. In his introduction to *Ustoi narodnago khoziaistva*, pp. vii–viii, Gurko referred very favorably to Witte's Special Conference, noting that the solution to the agrarian problem depended in large measure on its work. A complete set of the Special Conference's publications were in the Rural Section's library. Troitskii, "Iz vospominanii," pt. 2, p. 26. Compare Witte in GSSO, V, col. 1452.

17. The Commission drafted a total of six legislative projects. *Trudy redkom*, 6 vols. (SPB, 1903–4). Gurko, *Features and Figures*, pp. 161–63. *Novoe Vremia's* report on the project appeared on 7 December 1903, pp. 3–4, and saw it as providing for the gradual evolution of communal landownership and use. Senator G. A. Evreinov, a member of Witte's Special Conference, repeatedly criticized the Editing Commission's moderation. See TsGAOR, f. 586, op. 1 (1904), d. 431;

Evreinov, *Krest'ianskii vopros v ego sovremennoi postanovke* (SPB, 1904); and Evreinov, *Krest'ianskii vopros v trudakh obrazovannoi sostave MVD kommissii po peresmotru zakonopolozhenii o krest'ianakh* (SPB, 1904). Compare F. G. Terner, also a member of Witte's Conference, *Zamechaniia na trudy redaktsionnoi komissii MVD po peresmotru zakonopolozhenii krest'ianakh* (SPB, 1904). See, too, *Vestnik Evropy*, 1904:2, pp. 773–92; and *Russkaia Mysl'*, 1904:2, pt. 2, pp. 213–25; and the attacks by Minister of Justice Murav'ev and Kuropatkin in "Dnevnik Kuropatkina," *KA* 2 (1922), 84, 86. Only one liberal critic accused the Commission of trying to destroy communal landownership by supporting the prosperous minority at the expense of the peasantry as a whole. A. A. Manuilov, "Obshchinnoe zemlevladenie" in Manuilov, *Ocherki po krest'ianskomu voprosu*, vol. 1, 329–48. Neopopulist supporters of the commune were more alert to the Commission's innovations and criticized its work for undermining that institution. See "Iz russkoi zhizni: Krizis narodnago pravosoznaniia i neo-biurokraticheskie eksperimenty," *Revoliutsionnaia Rossiia*, 51 (August 1904), 6–7. On the reform of local administration, Weissman, *Reform in Tsarist Russia*, pp. 68–76.

18. Savich, *Novyi gosudarstvennyi stroi*, p. 4.

19. In discussing the Commission's work at one of the 1904 "economic banquets," Gurko made this connection explicit, *Features and Figures*, p. 170. On the original mandate and the later interpretation, see *Trudy redkom*, pp. 2–4; *Spravki MVD*, p. 114.

20. Gurko, *Features and Figures*, pp. 157–61.

21. *Trudy redkom*, vol. 1, 10–11. The program of questions later submitted to the provincial conferences stated that the "inviolability of communal landownership excludes not only its forcible break up but also any compulsory influence on its natural evolution." *Svod zakliuchenii gubernskikh soveshchanii po proektu polozheniia o nadel'nykh zemliakh. (Trudy redaktsionnoi kommisii, T. V.)*, (SPB, 1906), p. 615.

22. "Ocherk rabot redaktsionnoi kommisii," in *Trudy redkom*, vol. 1, 1–103. Many of the arguments are repeated and expanded upon in ibid., vol. 5, 171–78, 198–208, 210–12, 213–19, 329–44, 356–68, 382–91, 440–53, and 457–76.

23. Ibid., vol. 1, 86–87. Indeed, it was argued that no matter what laws were enacted the peasantry would be able to circumvent them and return to their customary order. Ibid., pp. 614–15. This fear that government laws would become "dead letters" was a familiar theme at the time. For example, Rittikh, *Zavisimost' krest'ian*, pp. 184, 186.

24. *Trudy redkom*, vol. 1, 16.

25. Subsequently, Gurko did support differentiation, as we shall see.

26. Article 5 of the principal local statute of Emancipation noted that peasant allotment land was intended to provide "For the security of the peasant way of life and the fulfillment of their responsibilities before the government and the landowning nobility. . . . " Sofronenko, *Krest'ianskaia reforma*, pp. 183, 246.

27. Gurko, *Nashe gosudarstvennoe i narodnoe khoziaistvo*, pp. 28, 63–64. The quotation is on p. 64.

28. *Trudy redkom*, vol. 1, 38–39; *Spravki MVD*, pp. 126–27.

29. Fleksor, *Okhrana sel'skokhoziaistvennoi sobstvennosti*.

30. *Trudy redkom*, vol. 1, 35–38. Compare B. N. Mironov, "Vliianie krespostnogo prava na otnoshenie russkogo krest'ianstva k trudu," in *Sovetskaia istoriografiia agrarnoi istorii SSSR (do 1917 g.)* (Kishinev, 1978), pp. 119–26.

31. *Trudy redkom*, vol. 5, 167–212, esp. 175–76, and 361; compare *Zakonodatel'nye materialy*, vol. 2, 125–29.

32. *Trudy redkom*, vol. 5, 361. The upsurge in repartitions in the 1880s seems to have been linked to a generational conflict between the "landless" youth, who

now demanded a share of the land, and their landowning "fathers," who coveted what they held. The conflict's appearance seems to be linked to the maturation of a new generation of male peasants born since the last revision in 1858.

33. Ibid., pp. 19–28. *Trudy redkom,* vol. 5, 1, sets forth the goals of the commission's project on allotment land as being "the establishment of regulations which will promote the development of individual initiative within the peasant population and encourage peasants to apply improved agricultural methods as well as to transfer to more improved forms of land-use."

34. Zubovskii was born in 1863 and attended the St. Petersburg Ecclesiastical Academy. In 1902 he was a junior assistant to the secretary of the Rural Section. In 1913, he transferred to the agricultural ministry, where he took over from Rittikh as the chief administrator of the Stolypin Reforms. Gurko, *Features and Figures,* pp. 148–49; Troitskii, "Iz vospominanii," pt. 1, p. 4.

35. Lykoshin was born in 1861. A member of the Ministry of Justice, he was appointed assistant interior minister in 1907, becoming the principal government defender of the Stolypin Reforms before the Duma and State Council. Gurko, *Features and Figures,* pp. 150–51; Shchegolev, *Padenie tsarskogo rezhima,* vol. 7, 370. Gurko's negative characterization seems unjustified. A. I. Lykoshin, "O semeinoi sobstvennosti u krest'ian," *Zhurnal Ministerstva Iustitsii,* 1900:5, pp. 108–43, and 1900:6, pp. 87–140.

36. At the time, Krivoshein was director of the Department of Migration. He was appointed agricultural minister in 1908. More biographical details will be given later. Rudin was born in 1860. From 1904, he was head of the Surveying Office in the Ministry of Justice. Others who participated in the Editing Commission's work were I. F. Tsyzyrev, another junior official within the Rural Section, who was also an assistant professor of constitutional law at St. Petersburg University; A. A. Bashmakov, an expert in peasant inheritance law and a conservative publicist whom Stolypin later appointed editor of *Pravitel'stvennyi Vestnik;* P. P. Shilovskii, a member of the Ministry of Justice, who in 1912 was appointed governor of Kostroma; G. G. Savich, the former head of the Rural Section; and V. G. Petrov, a recent university graduate and formerly of the agricultural ministry. In addition, there were a number of officials within the MVD's Rural Section who, although not participating directly in the Commission's work, belonged to the same generation and were sympathetic to rural reform. Among these were Ia. Ia. Litvinov, born in 1852 and thus a little older than the rest, a small landowner, former land captain, and zemstvo physician from Simbirsk Province, member of its provincial administration, appointed assistant director of the Rural Section in 1901. As Gurko's successor as head of the Rural Section, Litvinov supervised the Interior Ministry's contribution to the Stolypin Reforms. G. V. Glinka, a graduate of Moscow University, former member of the Smolensk provincial administration, and then successively assistant director of the Rural Section and of the Migration Section, director of the Migration Administration after its transfer to the GUZiZ in 1905, and from 1912 assistant GUZiZ; I. M. Strakhovskii, another assistant director of the Rural Section, associate of the liberal legal journal *Pravo,* and compiler of the first detailed set of regulations governing the land captains, which was issued in 1905; D. I. Pestrzhetskii, a junior official within the Rural Section, author of a number of important articles in 1905 and 1906 when he was politically active, later an assistant director of the Rural Section; V. I. Baftalovskii, born 1864, a member of the Special Board of the Saratov provincial administration, transferred to the Rural Section and subsequently responsible for initiating the publication of its journal, *Izvestiia Zemskago Otdela;* and Baron A. F. Meiendorff, born 1869, graduate of St. Petersburg University Law Faculty, and then an

assistant professor there, subsequently responsible for Baltic peasants within the Rural Section, a cousin and adviser to P. A. Stolypin, and later an Octobrist and vice-chairman of the Third Duma. Gurko, *Features and Figures*, pp. 141–53.

37. *Trudy redkom*, vol. 1, 84–98. *Svod zakliucheniia k T. V*, pp. 573–84, 614–19.

38. *Trudy redkom*, vol. 1, 90. Ibid., vol. 5, 467, cites Ermolov's *Neurozhai i narodnoe bedstvie* in support of such a policy.

39. *Trudy redkom*, vol. 1, 24–25. Compare Gurko, *Nashe gosudarstvennoe i narodnoe khoziaistvo*, pp. 64–66.

40. *Trudy redkom*, vol. 1, 27.

41. Ibid., p. 90.

42. Ibid., p. 91.

43. Ibid., p. 92. In his memoirs, however, Gurko relates a conversation with Pleve in which he spoke in support of encouraging the "strong" (including kulaks, whom he saw as having been forced into their role as moneylenders to and exploiters of their "weaker" neighbors by the commune) to separate and apply their talents directly to agriculture. However, Gurko had to moderate his views within the Editing Commission. Gurko, *Features and Figures*, pp. 171–72.

44. *Trudy redkom*, vol. 1, 94.

45. Ibid., p. 95.

46. Ibid., p. 96.

47. This is so, in particular, because, as Gurko points out (*Features and Figures*, pp. 159, 176–77), the Editing Commission's conclusions on such critical issues would be uncritically incorporated into the ukase of 9 November 1906. Most contemporary and subsequent interpretations of the Editing Commission have been based on a fundamental misunderstanding of this section of its work. Simonova, "Krizis agrarnoi politiki," p. 482; Simonova, "Politika tsarizma," pp. 217–18; and Nesterova, "Vopros," pp. 85–88. Compare Gurko's *Otryvochnyia mysli*, pp. 34–35, 38–39, 54–55, and his *Nashe gosudarstvennoe i narodnoe khoziaistvo*, pp. 64–67, which confirm the interpretation to be presented later. The following analysis is based primarily on *Trudy redkom*, vol. 5, 446–53.

48. Compare Witte's concern to retain as many peasants as possible "on the land" at this stage of Russia's economic development. Simonova, "Krest'ianskii pozemel'nyi bank," p. 476.

49. *Trudy redkom*, vol. 5, 362. Nesterova, "Vopros," p. 85, wrongly implies that this was a form of "interest politics."

50. *Trudy redkom*, vol. 5, 440–46.

51. Ibid., vol. 1, 98.

52. Ibid., vol. 5, 337–38, 368; compare ibid., vol. 1, 96.

53. Rittikh, *Zavisimost' krest'ian*, pp. 213–14.

54. Pleve made some minor editorial changes to the sections on peasant administration and courts. Gurko, *Features and Figures*, p. 163.

55. *Spravki MVD*, pp. 120–29.

56. The following discussion is based on "Proekt rezoliutsii po delo o poriadke predvaritel'nago obsuzhdeniia proektov novykh zakonopolozhenii o krest'ianakh" in TsGAOR, f. 586, op. 1 (1904), d. 432, ll. 1–7. Compare "Osobyi zhurnal komiteta ministrov 25 noiabria i 2 dekabria 1903 goda . . . " (Witte archive, RACU).

57. TsGAOR, f. 586, op. 1 (1904), d. 432, l. 4 ob. Bogdanovich, *Tri poslednykh samoderzhtsa*, p. 299.

58. Savich, *Novyi gosudarstvennyi stroi*, pp. 5–6. The second half of the report

appeared the following day. An incomplete version appeared in *Pravo*, 2 (11 January 1904), cols. 107–52. Gurko *Features and Figures*, p. 166; "Dnevnik Kuropatkina," KA 2 (1922), 98.

59. Gurko, *Features and Figures*, pp. 163–66, 169–74, 176–77.

60. Nesterova, "Vopros," p. 79.

61. Pleve disagreed with Gurko, who wanted the local nobility to select the zemstvo representatives as they had for Witte's Special Conference. Pleve, of course, was reluctant to repeat that process and required that they be selected by the governors. Gurko, *Features and Figures*, pp. 167–69; Bogdanovich, *Tri poslednykh samoderzhtsa*, p. 299; Simonova, "Politika tsarizma," p. 221; Dubrovskii, *Stolypinskaia zemel'naia reforma*, p. 71; *Svod zakliucheniia k T. V.*, p. viii. On the January Conference of governors in St. Petersburg, S. D. Urusov, *Memoirs of a Russian Governor*, pp. 173–75.

62. In addition to the already cited *Svod zakliuchenii k T. V.*, there was *Svod zakliuchenii gubernskikh soveshchanii po proektu pravil ob ogranichenii krest'ianskikh nadelov i ob razverstanii s chrezpolosnymi ugod'iami smezhnago vladeniia (Trudy red. kom. T. VI)* (SPB, 1906). They were published in reverse order. *Svod zakliuchenii k T. V.* included appendices of special opinions, a statistical table on communes that did not conduct repartitions based on information provided by the governors, data on membership in the responding commissions, and extracts from peasant responses to the project on allotment lands. These responses did not, however, address the question of the acceptability of *khutora*.

63. The specific figures are in *Svod zakliuchenii k T. V.*, pp. vii–xv.

64. The first question elicited forty responses, thirty-eight of which supported the Commission's proposal, thirty-three unanimously. Ibid., pp. 584–89. Support for the second question was also strongly favorable, though there was more disagreement within the conferences themselves. Of forty-one conferences responding, twenty-one expressed unanimous support, eleven majority support, and nine voted against it. There was no discernible geographical pattern to the responses. Ibid., pp. 614–29. Rittikh's proposal to divide the claiming of title and the physical consolidation into a two-stage process was specifically criticized as an obstacle to agricultural progress, as it would be repeatedly after it became part of the Stolypin Reforms.

65. Preliminary discussions of the general questions were completed by January 1905 though the subcommissions on specific questions reported their conclusions somewhat later: IZO 1905:1, p. 24. By May 1905, however, all work was virtually completed and several conferences had already closed: IZO 1905:7, p. 275. The government's attitude toward the peasant disorders during the early months of 1905 seems to have been a mixture of both fear and complacency. The first detailed analysis of the February–March disorders, compiled by Ia. Ia. Litvinov of the Rural Section and based on both provincial reports and a personal tour of inspection, was only submitted on 12 July 1905, four months later. The report was subsequently published in IZO 1906:1–3, pp. 33–38, 81–86, 148–54. It is reprinted in KA 73 (1935), 627–50. S. M. Sidel'nikov, *Agrarnaia reforma Stolypina (Uchebnoe posobie)* (Moscow, 1973), p. 300, n. 18.

66. At the upper levels of the central government, however, there was as yet no such agreement. In consequence, Gurko's preliminary summary of the local conferences' conclusions, published in the Rural Section's journal in early 1905, was less than candid. Instead of reporting the almost unanimous support for the development of *khutora*, it merely stated that a majority of the conferences (thirty-four) had unanimously agreed to the adoption of "special measures" to eliminate the open-field system of peasant allotment lands. The report added that thirty-

two conferences had recognized that such measures, even if requested by only one party, had to be obligatory on all other affected parties—a proposal that was not, in fact, included in the project itself: IZO 1905:1, pp. 24–26; and 1905:3, pp. 108–12. See, too, Liashchenko, *Regulirovaniia krestianskago zemlevladeniia*, pp. 143–44.

67. Skliarov, *Pereselenie*, pp. 71–77; Stepynin, "Iz istorii pereselencheskoi politiki," pp. 161–64; Treadgold, *Great Siberian Migration*, pp. 127–30; Yaney, *Urge to Mobilize*, pp. 124–33, 226–27; Simonova, "Politika tsarizma," pp. 222–23; Simonova, "Krizis agrarnoi politiki," pp. 484–86; Judge, *Plehve*, pp. 189–91. Compare S. N. Prokopovich, *Agrarnyi krizis i meropriatiia pravitel'stva* (Moscow, 1912), p. 176.

68. This article was actually preceded by a directive from the Interior Ministry's Migration Department in 1900 encouraging the formation of *khutora*, though to no practical avail. Yaney, *Urge to Mobilize*, pp. 226–27.

69. See the Conference on the Peasant Land Bank chaired by Witte's assistant, Prince A. D. Obolenskii, which met between January and April 1903, when the Special Conference was being eclipsed by the Interior Ministry's Editing Commission. Witte's goal was to permit the Bank, for the first time, to purchase land directly for resale to the peasantry. In response, Pleve criticized the Finance Ministry for its narrowly fiscal approach over the past two decades and for having favored more prosperous peasants as a better risk. Stimulated by the 1902 disorders, Pleve now expressed concern for the "most needy" and "land-hungry" peasants and the threat they posed to political order. Thus, he proposed transforming the Bank into an instrument of agrarian reform and shifting the focus of its activity toward the land-hungry by placing limits on the amount of land that could be purchased from the Bank, taking measures to prevent land speculation, and bringing the entire problem of peasant resettlement, whether on state or Bank land, under closer government control. These ideas were defended in the conference by the majority who saw the Bank's goal as "eliminating land-hunger." Even the minority, which included Gurko, Krivoshein, General A. P. Strukov, and Shul'ts, who considered farmer-type peasant farms economically progressive, opposed any specific government measures to facilitate their development. On the other hand, in the interests of encouraging the modernization of small- and medium-scale noble agriculture, they proposed limiting Bank activities in some twenty-seven provinces. Several attempts were also made to have the Bank encourage the formation of *otruba* and *khutora*, including one by Lokhtin, who proposed permitting mortgages against allotment land to that end. This won the support of a majority, including Gurko, Krivoshein, Kutler, General Strukov, and Nikol'skii. However, it was acknowledged that such a proposal would require the peasantry's integration into the general civil legal order. The conference quickly fell victim to the conflict between the two ministries and degenerated into a verbal confrontation between Gurko and Kutler even though, as Gurko acknowledged, they were in basic agreement on the underlying issues. In contrast to Gurko, Kutler defended the ideas of the former finance minister, Bunge, who had seen the Peasant Bank as a means of inculcating the concepts of private property in the peasantry, and insisted on continuing Bank policies of granting loans to those who could afford them. However, whether Kutler's dominant concern was to foster differentiation, to speed up the transfer of land from the nobility to the peasantry, or to preserve the Bank's fiscal integrity is unclear. Nothing, however, came of this conference. Gurko, *Features and Figures*, pp. 206–14; Witte, *Vospominaniia*, vol. 1, 462–64; Simonova, "Krest'ianskii pozemel'nyi bank," pp. 471–84; "Agrarnaia programma Pleve," pp. 349–52.

Notes to Chapter 4

1. In addition to works already cited on this period, see E. D. Chermenskii, *Burzhuaziia i tsarizma v pervoi russkoi revoliutsii*, 2d ed. (Moscow, 1970), pp. 12–48; and S. Harcave, *First Blood: The Russian Revolution of 1905* (New York, 1964), pp. 36–68; on Sviatopolk-Mirskii, see Gurko, *Features and Figures*, pp. 292–323; Witte, *Vospominaniia*, vol. 1, 288–303; Kokovtsov, *Iz moego proshlago*, vol. 1, 47–50.

2. Gurko, *Features and Figures*, pp. 292–98; Witte, *Vospominaniia*, vol. 1, 288–90; "Dnevnik Kn. E. A. Sviatopolk Mirskoi," pp. 240–42.

3. Veselovskii, *Istoriia zemstva*, vol. 3, p. 594.

4. Gurko, *Features and Figures*, p. 299.

5. "Dnevnik Kn. E. A. Sviatopolk Mirskoi," p. 254. Golovin, *Vne partii*, pp. 311–19.

6. Manning, *Crisis of the Old Order*, pp. 67–78.

7. Savich, *Novyi gosudarstvennyi stroi*, pp. 6–8; "Dnevnik Kn. E. A. Sviatopolk Mirskoi," pp. 253–67; Gurko, *Features and Figures*, pp. 300–304, 315–17; Witte, *Vospominaniia*, vol. 1, 294–301, 478; Kryzhanovskii, *Vospominaniia*, pp. 19–28, 215; Liubimov, "Russkaia smuta," pp. 150–58; P. P. Mendeleev, "Svet i teni v moei zhizni—(1864–1933 gg.): Otryvki vospominanii P. P. Mendeleeva" (typescript, RACU), book 2, chapter 6, pp. 34–54; Bogdanovich, *Tri poslednykh samoderzhtsa*, pp. 315–20. On the ukase's implementation, *Zhurnaly Komiteta Ministrov po ispol'neniiu Ukaza 12 dekabria 1904 g.* (SPB, 1905).

8. At the conference called to discuss Mirskii's proposals at the beginning of December, Witte, Kokovtsov, and the tsar had opposed electing representatives to the State Council. Gurko charges Witte with having excluded the proposal to begin the transfer of the peasantry to private property on the grounds that Witte had not yet conceived the necessity of this measure as a first step to create a "uniform social organization in Russia." This evaluation is manifestly inaccurate. Witte may have decided to exclude this point because it was just about to be taken up by his Special Conference. By 15 November 1904, Mirskii had already decided to transfer the peasant question back to Witte. Bogdanovich, *Tri poslednykh samoderzhtsa*, p. 307. Gurko, *Features and Figures*, p. 317fn; Solov'ev, *Samoderzhavie i dvorianstvo v 1902–1907*, pp. 133–36. "Dnevnik Kn. E. A. Sviatopolk-Mirskoi," pp. 261–62. Mirskii's report was subsequently passed on to Stolypin by Goremykin. According to Witte, the December conference also discussed the abolition of redemption payments, a program that many, including Witte, saw as a measure that would lead to the commune's eventual abolition, but that idea was quashed by Kokovtsov. Witte, *Vospominaniia*, vol. 1, 478.

9. Yaney, "The Imperial Russian Government," pp. 101–2. The Interior Ministry, however, saw the ukase as a threat to its work since it caused several of its provincial conferences to halt their review of the Editing Commission's projects. In response, the Interior Ministry dispatched a circular letter, drafted principally by Gurko, to the governors pointing out that the ukase did not preclude the preservation of the peasants' *soslovie* order insofar as it was the consequence of peculiarities in the traditional peasant way of life and their special forms of land use. As long as these peculiarities continued to exist, there could be no talk of abolishing the *soslovie* order. IZO 1905:1, pp. 17–18; Gurko, *Features and Figures*, pp. 332–33.

10. On this stage of the Conference see Chernyshev, *Agrarno-krest'ianskaia politika*, pp. 282–99.

11. Rittikh, *Zavisimost' krest'ian*, pp. 209–17.

12. *Printsipial'nye voprosy.*

13. *Vestnik Finansov,* 49 (5 December 1904), p. 390; *Protokoly po krest'ianskomu delu,* no. 1 (8 December 1904), pp. 1–2; Witte, *Vospominaniia,* vol. 1, 478–82; Gurko, *Features and Figures,* pp. 324–38.

14. Witte, *Zapiska,* also as an appendix to *Vestnik Finansov,* 49 (5 December 1904) and in a popular edition by a commercial publisher during 1905. Gurko, *Features and Figures,* p. 326; Simonova, "Zemsko-liberal'naia fronda," p. 152.

15. The following is based on Witte, *Zapiska,* pp. 81–93, 98.

16. Nikol'skii, *Zemlia, obshchina i trud,* pp. vii–ix, 158–71; B. N. Chicherin, *Kurs gosudarstvennoi nauki,* vol. 3 (Moscow, 1898), 358–59; P. D., *Russkii sotsializm;* and P. D., *Vopros ob obshchine,* chapter 2, pp. 23–53, entitled "Obshchina—'embrion' budushchago sotsial'nago poriadke." Though not himself a member of the "new generation" (he was born in 1851), Nikol'skii, in common with the bearers of the "perceptual revolution," argued in support of peasant integration, individualization, and private property as the sole means of raising labor productivity.

17. The *Memorandum* also asserted, again on the basis of local committees' opinions, that "at the present time . . . [a consciousness] that their right to allotment land is a valuable property right is firmly entrenched among the peasantry. . . ." Witte, *Zapiska,* p. 75; compare *Stenogrammy OSNSKhP,* 23 (12 March 1905), pp. 5–6.

18. Witte, *Zapiska,* pp. 100–101.

19. The Conference's membership during its final stage was essentially unchanged, but there were some notable additions, including the aging Goremykin, and the liberal Senator G. I. Evreinov, formerly marshal of the nobility from Sudzhansk County, Kursk Province. New advisory members included those ubiquitous bureaucratic experts, Gurko, Rittikh, and Krivoshein, as well as Lykoshin and Nikol'skii. On Evreinov, see "Dnevnik A. A. Polovtsova," KA 3 (1923), p. 134; and Simonova, "Zemsko-liberal'naia fronda," pp. 164–74. There were a total of thirty-one full members and eighteen advisory members during this phase of the conference, but only a few played a significant role. Polovtsov and Bulygin never attended; Murav'ev, Sheremetev, Vorontsov-Dashkov, Kokovtsov, and Kochubei attended sporadically and never spoke on the commune; Shvanebakh and Saburov spoke only once apiece. Among the advisory members, Krivoshein kept a perfect attendance record in accord with his reputation but spoke only once, on migration legislation. Counting multiple affiliations, the voting members included fifteen state councillors, twelve senators, thirteen members of government ministries, one governor, six generals, six members of the Tsar's court, and one ambassador. Twenty-eight of them belonged to the top four ranks of the civil or military tables of ranks. Among the advisory members, there were nine from the civil bureaucracy and six professors—the latter, curiously enough, all generally opposed to Witte's concept of reform. *Protokoly po krest'ianskomu delu,* pp. iii–vii; and Gurko, *Features and Figures,* p. 327. It is almost impossible to categorize the Conference's members as supporters or opponents of Witte's program, as will become clear. Witte's opponents are usually assumed to include Counts S. D. Sheremetev and M. P. Tolstoi, Prince A. G. Shcherbatov, Khvostov, Stishinskii, Gurko, Semenov-T'ian-Shanskii, Goremykin, Lobko, and Murav'ev. Witte, *Vospominaniia,* vol. 1, 479–80; "Perepiska Witte i Pobedonostseva," KA 30 (1928), 109; Gurko, *Features and Figures,* p. 327; Simonova, "Politika tsarizma," pp. 230–31; "Dnevnik Kuropatkina," KA 2 (1922), pp. 11, 13. However, the only implacable opponents seem to have been Khvostov, Sheremetev, and Shcherbatov. Shcherbatov's proposal to conduct a "poll" (opros) of the peasantry provoked a vitriolic exchange between him and Witte. Compare

Stenogrammy OSNSKhP, no. 26 (23 March 1905), pp. 29–36. When the Stolypin Reforms were before the State Council in early 1910, however, Witte criticized the government for not having consulted peasant opinion before enacting them into law. GSSO, V, cols. 1149, 1227–34.

20. The major exceptions were Stishinskii, now a member of the State Council, who continuously raised petty objections, and Khvostov. *Protokoly po krest'ianskomu delu*, no. 9 (12 January 1905) and no. 20 (2 March 1905) and appendix.

21. Ibid., no. 16 (12 February 1905), pp. 37–40 (appendix I). The editing commission was composed of Goremykin, Evreinov, Kutler, Gurko, and Rittikh—all supporters of Witte's proposals in various degrees. Ibid., no. 1 (9 December 1904), pp. 3–4. P. D. *Russkaia intelligentsiia i krest'ianstvo* (1906), pp. 1–69, argues that the question of the commune had been decided even before the first session on 8 December 1904.

22. "Dnevnik Kn. E. A. Sviatopolk Mirskoi," p. 259; Simonova, "Agrarnaia politika," p. 201.

23. Only Stishinskii, Khvostov, and Prince Shcherbatov voted against this point.

24. During the discussions of these points, Witte frequently criticized the Interior Ministry's passion for arbitrary control. Curiously, even though, or perhaps because, they were themselves members of that ministry, both Gurko and Lykoshin shared Witte's and Rittikh's desire to rely on the judicial system to resolve certain problems since the system of administrative justice frequently made such problems worse. *Protokoly po krest'ianskomu delu*, nos. 20–22 (2, 5, and 9 March 1905).

25. Ibid., nos. 24–26 (16, 19, and 22 March 1905). This issue was also a source of conflict during the State Council's discussions of the ukase of 9 November 1906, when it appeared to serve as a last battleground for opponents of reform. M. Kovalevskii, "Spor o sel'skoi obshchine v kommissii gosudarstvennago soveta" *Vestnik Evropy*, 1910:1, pp. 259–84; Kovalevskii, "Spor o semeinoi obshchine," *Vestnik Evropy*, 1910:3, pp. 259–72; Kovalevskii, "Sud'by obshchinnago zemlevladeniia," pp. 58–81. Presumably, the Editing Commission avoided this issue because of its sensitivity. Compare Witte, *Zapiska*, pp. 37–42, 93–97. Rittikh counted over one hundred local committees opposed to family ownership. *Stenogrammy OSNSKhP*, no. 26 (23 March 1905), pp. 28–29.

26. *Protokoly po krest'ianskomu delu*, no. 28 (30 March 1905).

27. Witte, *Vospominaniia*, vol. 1, 147–55, 480; Gurko, *Features and Figures*, pp. 75–81, 335–38; *Stenogrammy OSNSKhP*, no. 13 (12 February 1905), pp. 14–16; no. 14 (16 February 1905), pp. 2–8; "Iz dnevnika A. A. Polovtsova," KA 46 (1931), pp. 121, 124.

28. Bogdanovich, *Tri poslednykh samoderzhtsa*, p. 307.

29. Chernyshev, *Agrarno-krest'ianskaia politika*, p. 297.

30. Leont'ev, *Krestianskoe pravo*, 1st ed., pp. 272–85; A. S. Izgoev, *Obshchinnoe pravo (Opyt sotsial'no-iuridicheskago analiza obshchinnago zemlevladeniia, kak instituta grazhdanskago prava)* (SPB, 1906); Khauke, *Krest'ianskoe zemel'noe pravo*, pp. 32–81, 189–93. Zyrianov, "Obychnoe grazhdanskoe pravo," pp. 91–101. Senate decisions are contained in I. M. Tiutriumov, comp., *Praktika Pravitel'stvuiushchego Senata po krest'ianskim delam (1882–1914)* (SPB, 1914); and K. Abramovich, comp., *Krest'ianskoe pravo po resheniiam pravitel'stvuiushchego senata*, 2d ed. (SPB, 1912) and *Dopolnenie* (SPB, 1914).

31. Compare Witte's speeches in *Stenogrammy OSNSKhP*, no. 11 (1 January 1905), pp. 8–10; no. 13 (29 January 1905), p. 14 and pp. 2–21; and no. 19 (23 February 1905), pp. 24–28. On the commune see ibid., no. 19 (23 February 1905),

p. 15. On peasant attitudes to the commune see the fascinating evidence collected for the Special Conference in 1902 in Smolensk Province by I. V. Chernyshev, *Krest'iane ob obshchine nakanune 9 noiabria 1906: K voprosu ob obshchine* (SPB, 1911), which demonstrates, among other points, a widespread peasant recognition of the commune's disadvantages. Compare the same author's *Obshchina posle 9 noiabria 1906 po ankete Vol'nago Ekonomicheskago Obshchestva*, 2 vols. (Petrograd, 1917); *Materialy po voprosam zemel'nomu i krest'ianskomu: Vserossiiskii s''ezd staroobriadtsev v Moskve, 22–25 fevralia 1906 goda* (Moscow, 1906); and A. A. Kaufman's review in *Russkaia Mysl'*, 1907:2, pt. 2, pp. 26–45.

32. *Stenogrammy OSNSKhP*, no. 19 (23 February 1905), pp. 26–27. Kutler was one of only a few who held this opinion at the Conference, though his position was probably a question of equity rather than formal legal precedents.

33. Ibid., no. 18 (19 February 1905), p. 20.

34. Ibid., p. 21. On Stishinskii, see ibid., no. 19 (23 February 1905), p. 23; Bogdanovich, *Tri poslednykh samoderzhtsa*, p. 307. Lykoshin opposed forcible separations, against the commune's will, since it would lead to the artificial destruction of the commune and the development of strained relations, discord, and hostility between the two parties. *Stenogrammy OSNSKhP*, no. 19 (23 February 1905), pp. 12–13. On the other hand, Lykoshin, Ermolov, Gurko, and Rittikh were in the minority in their support of the dictatorship of the absolute majority over the existing requirement for a two-thirds majority for changes in tenure. Ibid., no. 16 (12 February 1905), pp. 10–14; no. 17 (16 February 1905), pp. 2–17.

35. *Protokoly po krest'ianskomu delu*, no. 13 (29 January 1905), pp. 2–3; *Stenogrammy OSNSKhP*, no. 18 (19 February 1905), p. 18; ibid., no. 9 (12 January 1905), p. 24.

36. *Stenogrammy OSNSKhP*, no. 10 (15 January 1905), p. 6.

37. Ibid., pp. 21–22; and ibid., no. 23 (12 March 1905), pp. 1–10.

38. Ibid., no. 23 (12 March 1905), pp. 5–6. Compare "S prosheniami i dokladnymi zapiskami ob uluchshenii byta krest'ian" in TsGIA SSSR, f. 1291, op. 122 (1905–6), d. 29; K. Sivkov, "Krest'ianskie prigovory 1905 goda," *Russkaia Mysl'*, 28:4 (1907), pt. 2, pp. 24–48; N. N. Vorob'ev, "Zemel'nyi vopros v zaiavleniiakh krest'ian i drugikh grupp naseleniia," in Dolgorukov and Petrunkevich, *Agrarnyi vopros*, vol. 2, 353–416; E. G. Vasilevskii, *Ideinaia bor'ba vokrug stolypinskoi agrarnoi reformy* (Moscow, 1960), pp. 11–15, 66–88; V. I. Mikhailova, "K voprosu ob otnoshenii krest'ian k I-i gosudarstvennoi dume (na materialakh Ukrainy)," in *Nekotorye problemy sotsial'no-ekonomicheskogo razvitiia Ukrainskoi SSR*, vol. 1 (Dneprepetrovsk, 1970), 123–30; A. I. Nil've, "Prigovory i nakazy krest'ian vo II Gosudarstvennuiu Dumu," *Istorii SSSR* 1975:5, pp. 99–109; B. G. Litvak, *Ocherki istochnikovedeniia massovoi dokumentatsii XIX nachala XX v.* (Moscow, 1979), pp. 259–85.

39. *Stenogrammy OSNSKhP*, no. 23 (12 March 1905), pp. 9, 31. Viazemskii also rejected an expansion of peasant landownership in favor of raising productivity. Ibid., no. 11 (22 January 1905), pp. 10–13. The discussants were also overwhelmingly concerned to prevent both the transfer of peasant land to nonpeasants and its concentration in the hands of kulaks; ibid., nos. 17–19 (16, 19, and 23 February 1905), and no. 28 (30 March 1905), pp. 17–28. Nationalistic factors played an important role, particularly in the western provinces; e.g., ibid., pp. 27–28.

40. Ibid., no. 24 (16 March 1905), pp. 25–26.

41. Ibid., no. 21 (5 March 1905), p. 29. For Lykoshin's opinions in general, see ibid., no. 10 (15 January 1905), pp. 10–18.

42. Ibid., no. 26 (23 March 1905), pp. 3–6. On Goremykin's support for individ-

ual private property and greater individual freedom, ibid., pp. 12–14 and no. 19 (23 February 1905), p. 26. Lykoshin, too, was abreast of the latest French and German agricultural studies, and he, too, noted the stability of small-scale peasant agriculture there. *Protokoly po krest'ianskomu delu*, no. 10 (15 January 1905), pp. 11–12. Prince A. D. Obolenskii also saw the Russian situation as a stable one. *Stenogrammy OSNSKhP*, no. 28 (30 March 1905), pp. 23–24.

43. *Stenogrammy OSNSKhP*, no. 11 (22 January 1905), pp. 2–8. This suggests that even Stishinskii supported Witte's program despite his strong defense of the commune and his desire to preserve some degree of administrative supervision. Compare ibid., no. 26 (23 March 1905), p. 3. Viazemskii, however, accused Stishinskii of insincerity, but the subsequent discussion did not bear him out; ibid., no. 11 (22 January 1905), pp. 10–13. Compare Kovalevskii, "Sud'by obshchinnago zemlevladeniia," pp. 62–63.

44. *Stenogrammy OSNSKhP*, no. 23 (12 March 1905), p. 9. Compare ibid., no. 10 (15 January 1905), pp. 23–25, where Kulomzin also rejects mere legislation.

45. Ibid., no. 11 (22 January 1905), p. 8.

46. Ibid., pp. 10–13.

47. Ibid., no. 23 (12 March 1905), pp. 5–6, and no. 26 (23 March 1905), pp. 3–4, for Witte; no. 12 (26 January 1905), p. 16, for Evreinov. Evreinov also emphasized the political benefits of a large class of conservative peasant proprietors and the identity that would develop between them and other property owners.

48. Ibid., no. 12 (26 January 1905), pp. 9–17.

49. Ermolov, *Narodnaia sel'skokhoziaistvennaia mudrost'*, vol. 2, p. 158. Compare Gurko's link between the "wealth" of the population and the development of a legal structure in *Protokoly po krest'ianskomu delu*, no. 11 (22 January 1905), p. 39; and Stolypin's 5 December 1908 speech to the Duma in which he uses the word *"bogatet' "* in referring to the improvement of peasant welfare and Russia's agricultural development. GDSO III: 2, vol. 1, col. 2280. The same sentiment was uttered by Bukharin in the very similar context of the New Economic Policy (NEP). A. Erlich, *The Soviet Industrialization Debate, 1924–1928* (Cambridge, Mass., 1960), pp. 16–17.

50. On this latter point, see Evreinov in *Stenogrammy OSNSKhP*, no. 12 (26 January 1905), p. 16; Lykoshin in ibid., no. 10 (15 January 1905), pp. 10–18; Gerard in ibid., no. 16 (12 February 1905), p. 7; and Obolenskii, ibid., p. 10.

51. Ibid., no. 16 (12 February 1905), pp. 5–10, 14.

52. Ibid., pp. 2–3.

53. He also cited the Populist, V. V[orontsov]'s description of peasant practices in his *Krest'ianskaia obshchina* (Moscow, 1892). *Stenogrammy OSNSKhP*, no. 22 (9 March 1905), pp. 10–11.

54. Ibid., no. 19 (23 February 1905), p. 3.

55. Ibid., p. 22.

56. Ibid., p. 23. For example, A. A. Kaufman, "Ukaz 9 noiabria 1906 goda," p. 163, who also quoted the well-known German expert Auhagen. Yaney's charge that the government's policy was contradictory is excessively formalistic. *Urge to Mobilize*, pp. 223–25, 262–63. Lositskii rejects the arguments of these critics and defends the procedure. "Raspadenie obshchiny," pp. 25–28. See TsGIA SSSR, f. 1291, op. 122 (1907), d. 72, ll. 151–3 for intrabureaucratic responses to critics.

57. *Protokoly po krest'ianskomu delu*, no. 11 (22 January 1905), pp. 28–40.

58. Ibid., p. 29.

59. The actual statistics are in *Svod zakliuchenii k T. V.*, p. 1021; reprinted in *IZO* 1905:3, pp. 108–9; and in part in Bekhteev, *Khoziaistvennye itogi*, vol. 2, 183. Khvostov attacked the validity of these data and even the possibility of obtaining

them; *Stenogrammy OSNSKhP*, no. 12 (26 January 1905), pp. 6–9. Professor A. S. Posnikov of the St. Petersburg Polytechnic Institute asserted that Gurko's figures agreed with those of K. R. Kachorovskii, who was a supporter of the commune and sympathetic to the Socialist-Revolutionary party. *Protokoly po krest'ianskomu delu* no. 12 (26 January 1905), p. 22. A summary of Kachorovskii's figures is in his *Narodnoe pravo*, pp. 77–79, 210. Compare Zyrianov, "Nekotory cherty," pp. 380–87; Lositskii, *Raspadenie obshchiny*, pp. 8–16. The Editing Commission had earlier regarded the lack of repartitions as a poor indicator of de facto ownership on household principles: *Trudy redkom*, vol. 5, 389–90.

60. *Protokoly po krest'ianskomu delu*, no. 11 (22 January 1905), p. 36. Compare Gurko, *Nashe gosudarstvennoe i narodnoe khoziaistvo*, pp. 84–113; Boserup, *The Conditions of Agricultural Growth*.

61. *Protokoly po krest'ianskomu delu*, p. 40.

62. Simonova, "Politika tsarizma," pp. 235–36, and "Krizis agrarnoi politiki," p. 487, is wrong to group Viazemskii and Evreinov with Gurko on this issue. Though more outspoken than other members, they both spoke against force. *Stenogrammy OSNSKhP*, no. 11 (22 January 1905), pp. 10–13, and no. 12 (26 January 1905), p. 17. They did, however, support government intervention. Sidel'nikov incorrectly includes Lykoshin in this group. *Agrarnaia reforma*, p. 303, n. 21. Both authors incorrectly identify government provision of agronomical aid or small-scale credit with force.

63. Snow, *The Years 1881–1894 in Russia*, pp. 68–72.

64. "Iz dnevnika A. A. Polovtsova," KA 46 (1931), p. 129.

65. See, for example, A. Peshekhonov's reference to atomization ("liudskii pyl'") in "Na ocherednyia temy: Iz krest'ianskikh pisem," *Russkoe Bogatstvo*, 1910:6, pt. 2, p. 105. A. Posnikov noted the apparent contradiction between the government's commitment to both the noninterventionism of "manchesterianism" and the bureaucracy's traditional policy of *opeka* in "Agrarnyi vopros v tret'ei dume ('Polozhenie o zemleustroistvo')," *Vestnik Evropy*, 1910:1, pp. 286–87.

Notes to Chapter 5

1. Goremykin, Krivoshein, the brothers D. F. and V. F. Trepov, and Count Sheremetev were immediately responsible for closing Witte's Conference. Krivoshein, *A. V. Krivoshein*, pp. 51–52 and 79; Witte, *Vospominaniia*, vol. 1, 480–83; Gurko, *Features and Figures*, pp. 335–38, with inaccuracies; F. G. Terner, *Vospominaniia zhizni F. G. Ternera* (SPB, 1911), vol. 2, 317; Dubrovskii, *Stolypinskaia zemel'naia reforma*, pp. 86–88; Mehlinger and Thompson, *Count Witte*, p. 186; Simonova, "Politika tsarizma," pp. 239–41; Simonova, "Agrarnaia politika," pp. 199–201. Witte's opposition to the Russo-Japanese War was also a factor in his dismissal.

2. B. Iurevskii, *Zemlia i obshchestvo* (SPB, 1912), p. 6.

3. Savich, *Novyi gosudarstvennyi stroi*, pp. 14–15; IZO 1905:4, pp. 129–30. A ukase of 6 May 1905 charged the Goremykin Conference with developing measures to consolidate peasant landownership and with compiling instructions concerning the expansion of peasant landownership for both the newly formed GUZiZ and the Peasant Bank. Savich, *Novyi gosudarstvennyi stroi*, pp. 35–37.

4. Dubrovskii, *Krest'ianskoe dvizhenie v 1905–1907*, pp. 42–43.

5. The strength and reality of this myth of peasant loyalty were manifest in the discussions preparatory to the publication of the election law of 6 August

1905 to the Bulygin Duma as well as in the structure of the electoral system established by the revised law of 11 December 1905. *Petergofskoe soveshchanie o proekte gosudarstvennoi dumy* (Berlin, n.d.), pp. 180–220; "Tsarskosel'skiia soveshchaniia: Protokoly," *Byloe*, 1917:3(25), pp. 235–65. The tsar was so convinced that he had a provision inserted requiring that the peasantry be guaranteed a minimum of one seat from each province. Illiteracy was specifically cited as guaranteeing a unified worldview. The peasantry were not, however, so illiterate as has traditionally been assumed. A. B. Eklof, "Peasant Sloth Reconsidered: Strategies of Education and Learning in Rural Russia before the Revolution," *Journal of Social History* 14:3 (1981), 355–85. On the electoral laws, Chermenskii, *Burzhuaziia i tsarizm*, pp. 105–13 and 211–14; and Mehlinger and Thompson, pp. 112–24. Chermenskii, pp. 106–7, claims Gurko subscribed to the myth of peasant loyalty and saw the peasantry as a source of social support. Two exceptions were Kokovtsov and Polovtsov. For a discussion of "peasant monarchism," Field, *Rebels*, pp. 208–15. The electoral laws are in F. I. Kalinichev, comp., *Gosudarstvennaia duma v Rossii v dokumentakh i materialakh* (Moscow, 1957), pp. 39–54 and 94–102.

6. Simonova, "Politika tsarizma," pp. 241–42; Simonova, "Agrarnaia politika," p. 200; Chermenskii, *Burzhuaziia i tsarizm*, pp. 49–78; Galai, *Liberation Movement*, pp. 245–67; V. V. Shelokhaev, "Agrarnaia programma kadetov v pervoi russkoi revoliutsii," *IZ* 86 (1970), 172–230; I. Fleischhauer, "The Agrarian Program of the Russian Constitutional Democrats," *CMRS* 20:2 (1979), 173–201; Belokonskii, *Zemstvo i konstitutsiia*, pp. 154–83; J. E. Zimmerman, "The Kadets and the Duma, 1905–1907," in *Essays on Russian Liberalism*, ed. C. E. Timberlake (Columbia, Mo., 1972), pp. 119–38; B. Dmytryshyn, ed., *Imperial Russia: A Source Book, 1700–1917* (New York, 1967), pp. 325–50. See Ermolov's report on the February disorders in *Nachalo pervoi russkoi revoliutsii: Ianvar'–mart 1905 goda* (Moscow, 1955), pp. 747–52; and the reports of I. A. Zvegintsev, dated 14 March 1905, and Ia. Ia. Litvinov, dated 12 July 1905, in *KA* 73 (1935), pp. 134–67. Ermolov, although noting the problem of peasant demands for land, however, only called—if urgently—for the formation of a new Special Conference. Ermolov's "reward" was his "retirement" to the State Council in May. On Ermolov's call for the "free development of rural landed relations," see "Dnevnik A. A. Polovtsova," *KA* 4 (1923), p. 93. The Interior Ministry's 15 April 1905 circular reemphasized these concerns and expressed the Ministry's faith in the majority of the peasantry. It also declared that the only possible solution to the problem of peasant land organization was migration to state lands or purchase of land through the Peasant Bank at market prices: *IZO* 1905:4, pp. 153–54; B. B. Veselovskii et al., eds., *Materialy po istorii krest'ianskikh dvizhenii v Rossii*, vypusk 4, *Agrarnyi vopros v sovete ministrov (1906)* (Moscow-Leningrad, 1924), pp. 82–88, cited hereafter as *Agrarnyi vopros v sovete ministrov*.

7. A. K. Drezen, ed., *Tsarizm v bor'be s revoliutsiei 1905–1907 gg.: Sbornik dokumentov* (Moscow, 1936), esp. pp. 110–31; Manning, *Crisis of the Old Order*, pp. 169–76; N. N. Polianskii, *Tsarskie voennye sudy v bor'be s revoliutsiei 1905–1907 gg.* (Moscow, 1958).

8. *IZO* 1905:4, p. 135; Simonova, "Agrarnaia politika," p. 202. Other members were Shvanebakh, A. S. Brianchaninov of the State Council, Senator Baron Iskul'-fon-Gil'denbandt, Count Golenishchev-Kutuzov of the Empress Maria Fedorovna's Chancellery, Baron Meller-Zakomel'skii of the Altai region administration, as well as Kutler, Putilov, Gurko, and Glinka. Terner, *Vospominaniia*, vol. 2, 246–47, doubted anything would result from the Goremykin Conference. Compare N. D. Chaplin's comments in Bogdanovich, *Tri poslednykh samoderzhtsa*, pp. 198,

199, 389; and ibid., p. 219, where Goremykin referred to the peasants as "cattle." See, too, Kizevetter, *Na rubezhe dvukh stoletii*, pp. 200–202, 252–53, 332; Iswolsky, *Memoirs*, pp. 92, 178; and V. B. Lopukhin, "Liudi i politika," pp. 128–29.

9. Simonova, "Agrarnaia politika," p. 203.

10. Ibid., p. 202.

11. For biographical details on Krivoshein, see chapter 6.

12. Witte, *Vospominaniia*, vol. 1, 309–18, 349; vol. 2, 67–73; Gurko, *Features and Figures*, pp. 360, 364–65, 482–85. As chief of police in Moscow from 1896 to 1905, Trepov had sponsored Colonel Zubatov's scheme for government-sponsored labor unions, known as "police socialism." This experiment ultimately led to the Bloody Sunday massacre. Deich, "Osoboe soveshchanie," pp. 212–15, ascribes the note "Zemel'naia politika i krest'ianskii vopros" to D. F. Trepov and thus sees Trepov as the initiator of the proposed reorganization and the creation of an expanded agricultural ministry. However, it is possible that Krivoshein was responsible. His links with Trepov and Goremykin are well known. After the GUZiZ's creation in May 1905, he was appointed assistant chief administrator. Subsequently, he authored a project on a united government. Krivoshein, *A. V. Krivoshein*, pp. 23–39 and 52–54. N. I. Vasil'eva et al., *Pervaia rossiiskaia revoliutsiia i samoderzhavie* (Leningrad, 1975), p. 127, n. 96, reject Chermenskii's claim (*Burzhuaziia i tsarizm*, p. 135) that Krivoshein was the author, on the basis of a statement by Kryzhanovskii, *Vospominaniia*, p. 51, which asserts that he himself had composed such a project. Kryzhanovskii's statement does not, however, preclude Krivoshein's having composed such a project. Compare Liubimov, "Russkaia smuta," pp. 298–99, who describes the appearance, after the October Manifesto, of a number of circles within the bureaucracy designed to support the government and submit memoranda and projects. One of these, formed at the invitation of Senator V. F. Trepov, included Liubimov, himself, D. F. Trepov, Krivoshein, and N. V. Pleve, the son of the late V. K. Pleve. They met twice a week in Trepov's apartment and worked out several projects on the instructions of D. F. Trepov. Among the projects Liubimov remembered were one on a unified government under a first minister, another on the reform of the State Council, and a third on the peasant question. Liubimov's timing does not preclude an earlier such association between Krivoshein and Trepov or earlier drafts of these projects. Compare TsGIA SSSR, f. 1571, op. 1, d. 28, which contains a document entitled "Dokladnaia zapiska (bez podpisi) o zemel'nom politike i krest'ianskago voprosa (bez kontsa)," which appears to have been authored by Krivoshein. It should be added that the idea for incorporating the Peasant Bank within an expanded agricultural ministry, supported in the Conference by Trepov but rejected by Goremykin, was repeatedly revived by Krivoshein over the next ten years, reflecting continued hostility toward the Finance Ministry. From 1906 to 1908, Krivoshein was head of the Land Banks and from 1908 chief administrator of the GUZiZ. In 1914, he finally forced Kokovtsov to resign from the post of finance minister. Krivoshein, *A. V. Krivoshein*, pp. 163–93; P. L. Bark, "Memoirs" (unpub. ms., RACU), chapter 4.

13. IZO 1905:12, pp. 478–79; Savich, *Novyi gosudarstvennyi stroi*, pp. 36–38; Yaney, "Imperial Russian Government," p. 108.

14. Savich, *Novyi gosudarstvennyi stroi*, pp. 35–37. See Yaney, "Imperial Russian Government," pp. 107–8 on the ministerial conflicts involved. Compare Golitsyn, "Vospominaniia," p. 181; and P. P. Migulin, "Russkaia agrarnaia problema i sel'sko-khoziaistvennaia katastrofa v sovetskoi Rossii" (unpub. ms., RACU), pp. 139–40.

15. The Editing Commission's project on the delimitation of peasant and noble lands was also transferred to the GUZiZ since it was agrotechnical in nature. Savich, *Novyi gosudarstvennyi stroi*, pp. 36, 38.

16. Compare Dolgorukov and Petrunkevich, *Agrarnyi vopros*, vol. 1, 84–127, 198–224, 299–355, which contains papers on land nationalization and the redemption operation by M. Ia. Gertsenshtein read at a conference on the agrarian question and the problem of land-hunger held in Moscow on 28/29 April 1905 and accounts of the subsequent discussion.

17. The instructions to the GUZiZ make clear the conference's opposition to granting an additional allotment and therefore a repeat of 1861. The GUZiZ was also charged with supporting and developing auxiliary industries to provide additional sources of peasant income. Simonova, "Agrarnaia politika," pp. 203–7.

18. Ibid., p. 207.

19. Ibid., p. 202. Trepov also expressed opposition to the commune, though it is not clear on what grounds. It is possible that his "Pavlia" estate in Orel was a model estate and that his beliefs derived from practical experience.

20. Ibid., pp. 204–5; Simonova, "Politika tsarizma," pp. 240, 241.

21. PSZ 24 (1904), otd. 1 (SPB, 1907), no. 24701, pp. 603–7; Savich, *Novyi gosudarstvennyi stroi*, pp. 242–49.

22. Payments on loans were lowered to 5.75 rubles per 100 over a 55½-year period. Savich, *Novyi gosudarstvennyi stroi*, pp. 222–23; and IZO 1905:8, p. 308.

23. Simonova, "Agrarnaia politika," p. 206; and Simonova, "Politika tsarizma," p. 240. The Goremykin Conference continued its dilatory and trivial activities of "regularization" into January of the following year, when, in a fitting reversal of roles, Witte gave this conference its coup de grace.

24. Kalinichev, *Gosudarstvennaia Duma*, pp. 90–91. Compare Witte's 17 October report in ibid., pp. 91–94.

25. Savich, *Novyi gosudarstvennyi stroi*, pp. 28–31; Koroleva, *Pervaia Rossiiskaia revoliutsiia* pp. 27–44.

26. "Kopiia zapiska, sostavlennoi N. I. Vuichem, o Manifeste 17 oktiabria 1905 g. meropriatiiakh po osushchestvleniiu nachal Manifesta 17 oktiabria i merakh k podavleniiu bezporiadkov" (Witte archive, RACU); Witte's 10 January 1906 report is in *Agrarnyi vopros v sovete ministrov*, pp. 70–80; compare his 23 December 1905 report in *Revoliutsiia 1905 goda i samoderzhavie* (Leningrad, 1928), pp. 33–34. Compare E. I. Bochkareva, "Iz istorii agrarnoi politiki tsarizma v gody pervoi russkoi revoliutsii," *Uchenyi Zapiski Leningradskogo Gosudarstvennogo Pedagogicheskogo Instituta A. I. Gertsena*, 61 (1947), pp. 32–36.

27. Dubrovskii, *Krest'ianskoe dvizhenie*, pp. 51–56; compare Witte's 15 December 1905 report in *Vysshii pod"em revoliutsii 1905–1907 gg.: Vooruzhennye vosstanniia: Noiabr'–dekabr' 1905 goda*, pt. 1 (Moscow, 1955), pp. 156–57.

28. In addition to works already cited on the political and constitutional events of this period, see Harcave, *First Blood*, pp. 164–244; Mehlinger and Thompson, *Count Witte*, esp. pp. 47–177; T. Riha, "Constitutional Developments in Russia," in *Russia under the Last Tsar*, ed. T. G. Stavrou (Minneapolis, 1969), pp. 87–116; L. Schultz, "Constitutional Law in Russia," in *Russia Enters the Twentieth Century, 1894–1917*, ed. E. Oberlander et al. (New York, 1971), pp. 34–59; E. Oberlander, "The Role of the Political Parties" in ibid., pp. 60–84; Zimmerman, "Kadets and the Duma, 1905–1907," pp. 119–38; M. Szeftel, "Nicholas II's Constitutional Decisions of October 17–19, 1905 and Sergius Witte's Role," in *Album J. Balon* (Namur, 1968), pp. 461–93; Chermenskii, *Burzhuaziia i tsarizm*, pp. 128–57; F. Dan, "Obshchaia politika pravitel'stva i izmeneniia v gosudarstvennoi organizatsii v period 1905–1907 gg." in Martov, *Obshchestvennoe dvizhenie*, vol. 4, pt. 1, pp. 279–392.

29. "Zapiska Witte ot 9 oktiabria," KA 11–12 (1925), pp. 51–61, esp. p. 58. G. S. Doctorow, "The Government Program of 17 October 1905," *Russian Review*, 34:2 (1975), 123–36; Witte, *Vospominaniia*, vol. 1, 497–98.

30. Witte, *Vospominaniia*, vol. 2, 174–91; Mendeleev, "Svet i teni," p. 69; Bogdanovich, *Tri poslednykh samoderzhtsa*, p. 364. Compare R. Hennessy, *The Agrarian Question in Russia, 1905–1907: The Inception of the Stolypin Reform* (Giessen, 1977), pp. 49–53, for a different explanation. On Witte's negotiations with the liberals, P. N. Miliukov, *Tri popytki (K istorii russkago lzhe-konstitutsionalizma)* (Paris, 1921), pp. 7–25.

31. Manning, *Crisis of the Old Order*, pp. 141–48, 177–79.

32. Witte, *Vospominaniia*, vol. 2, 172; *Agrarnyi vopros v sovete ministrov*, p. 3.

33. Migulin, "Russkaia agrarnaia problema," pp. 173, 184–85; Migulin, *Agrarnyi vopros*, p. 52; Witte, *Vospominaniia*, vol. 2, 172.

34. The Migulin memorandum is preserved in the Witte Archive (RACU). Compare Migulin, *Agrarnyi vopros*, p. ix. A slightly modified version of the memorandum, which was read at a congress of the Octobrist party on 9 February 1906, is in ibid., pp. 52–66. Compare Simonova, "Agrarnaia politika," pp. 208–10; Dubrovskii, *Stolypinskaia zemel'naia reforma*, pp. 90–91. The dating of the Migulin project's first appearance is confused. However, the similarity between Kuzmin-Karavaev's proposals incorporated in Witte's 9 October memorandum to the tsar and the subsequent Migulin project suggest that Migulin's project may have been circulating considerably earlier than either Witte and Migulin indicate in their respective memoirs. Migulin's chronology is particularly unreliable.

35. Migulin, *Agrarnyi vopros*, pp. 61–62. Compare Trepov's 17 November 1905 report in *Vysshii pod"em revoliutsii*, pt. 1, pp. 40–41.

36. Letters to *Slovo* of 19 November and 1 December 1905 in response to criticisms leveled by K. F. Golovin. Reprinted as "Polemika s K. F. Golovinym o zemel'nom voprose" in Migulin, *Agrarnyi vopros*, p. 72.

37. Migulin, *Agrarnyi vopros*, pp. 62–64. The summary of theses on pp. 65–66 was not a part of the original. Compare the copy in the Witte Archive (RACU).

38. Migulin, "Russkaia agrarnaia problema," pp. 173–84, 195. Migulin claimed that there was nothing new in his program. Indeed, it simply reflected the views of those circles in which it originated. Ibid., p. 181.

39. Migulin, *Agrarnyi vopros*, p. 52.

40. Ibid., pp. 53–56, 61.

41. It is this version of the project that was subsequently published. Ibid., p. 56, n. 1; p. 59, n. 1.

42. Witte, *Vospominaniia*, vol. 2, 172–73; Migulin, "Russkaia agrarnaia problema," pp. 184–86.

43. Witte, *Vospominaniia*, vol. 2, 172–73. Witte's words echo a section out of his later 10 January 1906 report to the tsar. Sidel'nikov, *Agrarnaia Reforma*, p. 55; They also repeat the wording of Vuich's "zapiska" cited previously in note 26.

44. Migulin, "Russkaia agrarnaia problema," pp. 188–91; compare Witte, *Vospominaniia*, vol. 2, 173.

45. Sidel'nikov, *Agrarnaia reforma*, p. 54. Witte opposed the abolition of redemption payments at this time. "Dnevnik A. A. Polovtsova," KA 4 (1923), p. 83.

46. PSZ 25 (1905), otd. 1 (SPB, 1908), no. 26872, p. 791; Savich, *Novyi gosudarstvennyi stroi*, pp. 259–60; Sidel'nikov, *Agrarnaia reforma*, p. 46; and IZO 1905:11, p. 429. Compare Dubrovskii, *Stolypinskaia zemel'naia reforma*, p. 90. Most sources, including even Migulin himself, consider the abolition of redemp-

tion payments as in some respects a quid pro quo for the Council of Ministers' having rejected the Migulin project. This is not the case, however, for the timing is wrong.

47. PSZ 25 (1905), otd. 1 (SPB, 1908), no. 26873, p. 791; Savich, *Novyi gosudarstvennyi stroi*, p. 224; IZO 1905:11, pp. 429–30; and Sidel'nikov, *Agrarnaia reforma*, p. 47.

48. PSZ 25 (1905), otd. 1 (SPB, 1908), no. 26871, p. 790; Savich, *Novyi gosudarstvennyi stroi*, pp. 192–93; IZO 1905:11, p. 426; and Sidel'nikov, *Agrarnaia reforma*, pp. 45–46.

49. Savich, *Novyi gosudarstvennyi stroi*, pp. 224–26; and IZO 1905:11, pp. 452–54. This step had been preceded by a letter dated 11 November 1905 from Kutler as chief administrator of the GUZiZ to the governors of twelve provinces with instructions regarding the sale of state lands to the peasantry. IZO 1905:12, pp. 506–9. Hennessy, *Agrarian Question*, pp. 29–52, sees these initiatives as the Finance Ministry's attempt to develop an independent agrarian program. Such, however, was not the case.

50. IZO 1905:11, pp. 452–53.

51. *Novoe Vremia*, no. 10746 (13 February 1906), pp. 3–4, notes the poor response. B. B. Veselovskii, *Krest'ianskii vopros i krest'ianskoe dvizhenie v Rossii (1902–1906 gg.)* (SPB, 1907), p. 53, includes a partial listing of responses.

52. Copy in Witte archive (RACU).

53. Migulin, *Agrarnyi vopros*, p. 52; Migulin, "Russkaia agrarnaia problema," pp. 173, 184–85.

54. Solov'ev, *Samoderzhavie i dvorianstvo v 1902–1907*, pp. 199–212. Other members of this influential group of noble landowners and dignitaries sympathetic to Migulin's proposals included Ermolov, Bekhteev, and N. A. Pavlov. Migulin, "Russkaia agrarnaia problema," pp. 186–88. Compare Strukov's 20 November 1905 report in *Vysshii pod"em revoliutsii*, pp. 141–44. He had also supported proposals to form *khutora* that were made in Kokovtsov's "Commission of the Center" at the end of 1903.

55. Witte, *Vospominaniia*, vol. 2, 127; "Konspekt k otchetu general-ad"iutanta Dubasova," KA 11–12 (1925), pp. 183–86.

56. "Zapiska upolnomochennykh simbirskago dvorianstva na vysochaishee imia ot 21 dekabria 1905 g.," in *Agrarnyi vopros v sovete ministrov*, pp. 23–27. One of the signatories was Ia. Ia. Litvinov of the Interior Ministry's Rural Section. Compare the 11 December 1905 telegram of the Don region's "Soiuz storonnikov mirnago razresheniia zemel'nago voprosa," in Sidel'nikov, *Agrarnaia reforma*, pp. 49–51, which proposed a similar program yet rejected the very notion of land-hunger as a motive for government policy and refused to support a policy of expropriation. Compare Gurko, *Nashe gosudarstvennoe i narodnoe khoziaistvo*, pp. 42–45; Mendeleev, "Svet i teni," pp. 55–84; Liubimov, "Russkaia smuta," pp. 297–98, 309–25.

57. Kaufman subsequently became a member of the Kadet party. His best known works are *Pereselenie i kolonizatsiia* (SPB, 1905) and *Agrarnyi vopros v Rossii: Kurs Narodnago Universiteta* (Moscow, 1908). Copies of the Kutler Project are preserved in the Witte Archive (RACU). The project and explanatory note were published in Dolgorukov and Petrunkevich, *Agrarnyi vopros*, vol. 2 (SPB, 1907), pp. 629–48 and 44–55, respectively.

58. Witte, *Vospominaniia*, vol. 2, 174–75.

59. *Agrarnyi vopros v sovete ministrov*, pp. 46, 48.

60. There was, however, no provision for this land to be transferred on private-property principles.

61. The preceding summary is based on ibid., pp. 4, 10–12, 29–51; compare Simonova, "Agrarnaia politika," p. 211.

62. Surveying work, however, would be performed by professional surveyors at government expense. Like the Special Conference, the project also proposed settling disputes by civil rather than administrative procedures. The project also blurred *soslovie* lines by permitting anyone whose "way of life was indistinguishable from that of the peasantry" to acquire land on the same principles. In addition, it sought to extend the provisions of the temporary regulations of 6 June 1904 on migration to allow peasants who resettled on newly acquired land to get compensation for those strips they left behind in the commune. P. P. Semenov-T'ian-Shanskii approved of these proposals. *Agrarnyi vopros v sovete ministrov*, p. 27, n. 1.

63. It was rejected by a near or possibly unanimous decision. Kutler dates the Council's session in a 13 January 1906 letter to Witte. Kutler, however, had been left out in the cold, for the first commission to be formed as a result of that meeting was headed by Gurko. *Agrarnyi vopros v sovete ministrov*, pp. 80–82. Details of the Council's argument are contained in Witte's 10 January 1906 report. *Novoe Vremia*, no. 10718, 15 January 1906, p. 5, reports on the imminent formation of a commission to discuss both Kutler and Migulin projects and three others.

64. Sidel'nikov, *Agrarnaia reforma*, p. 64.

65. See Migulin's polemic with Golovin, Migulin, *Agrarnyi vopros*, pp. 67–72.

66. "Zapiska o nedopustimosti dopolnitel'nago nadeleniia krest'ian" in *Agrarnyi vopros v sovete ministrov*, pp. 63–70. Simonova, "Agrarnaia politika," pp. 212–14 ascribes this note's authorship to Gurko, rejecting N. Karpov's assertion, *Agrarnaia politika Stolypina* (Leningrad, 1925), p. 162, that the author was Krivoshein. Judging by the specific arguments and the style, Simonova is undoubtedly correct.

67. Compare Gurko, *Ustoi narodnago khoziaistva*.

68. *Zhurnal zasedaniia s"ezda uchreditelei Vserossiiskago soiuza zemlevladel'tsev; 17 noiabria 1905 g.* (Moscow, 1906), pp. 21, 23, as cited in Simonova, "Agrarnaia politika," p. 215; Solov'ev, *Samoderzhavie i dvorianstvo v 1902–1907*, pp. 200–201. Compare V. Mech, *Sily reaktsii* (Moscow, 1907), pp. 29–34; V. Levitskii, "Pravyia partii," in Martov, *Obshchestvennoe dvizhenie*, vol. 3, 386–88; and Pavlov, *Zapiski zemlevladel'tsa*, p. 249.

69. There is little biographical information on Pestrzhetskii. He was, however, a member of the nobility. G. Simmonds, "The Congress of Representatives of the Nobles' Associations, 1906–1916" (Ph.D. diss., Columbia, 1964), p. 14. See, too, Gurko, *Features and Figures*, pp. 143–44. Pestrzhetskii became assistant head of the Rural Section after Gurko's dismissal, holding that post through 1914. *Russkii Kalendar' na 1908* (SPB, 1908), p. 586; and *Russkii kalendar' na 1914* (SPB, 1914), p. 529. After the Revolution he published *Okolo zemli: Iz kursa lektsii sel'sko-khoziastvennoi statistiki, chitannogo v 1921/2 gg. v Politekhnikume v Viunsdorfe bliz' Berlina (Y.M.C.A.)* (Berlin, 1922).

70. *Vestnik Finansov*, nos. 49–51, (4, 11, and 18 December 1905), pp. 302–17, 346–56 and 386–99.

71. D. I. Pestrzhetskii, *Opyt agrarnoi programmy* (SPB, 1906).

72. The first group was entitled "O prinuditel'nom otchuzhdenii chastnovladel'cheskikh zemel' dlia krest'ianskikh obshchestv," *Novoe Vremia*, nos. 10689–10690, 17 and 18 December 1905, pp. 3–4, and p. 4. These articles vigorously opposed compulsory expropriation except when necessary to provide water, facilitate the abolition of open fields and the claiming of title, or reinforce govern-

mental authority. The second group was entitled "Ocherki po krest'ianskomu voprosu," *Novoe Vremia*, nos. 10708–10710, 5, 6, and 7 January 1906, pp. 3, 3, and 3. These articles noted that the abolition of redemption payments had opened the path for claiming title to allotment lands. See also his three additional books on agrarian matters published the same year: *K vyiasneniiu agrarnago voprosa* (SPB, 1906); *Obzor agrarnago proekta K. D. partii* (SPB, 1906); and *Pishchevoe dovol'stvie krest'ian i prinuditel'noe otchuzhdenie* (SPB, 1906).

73. *Vestnik Finansov*, no. 49, 4 December 1905, pp. 311–16; IZO, 1906:1, pp. 42–43.

74. *Vestnik Finansov*, no. 49, 4 December 1905, pp. 316–17, on intensification; ibid., no. 50, 11 December 1905, pp. 346–56, on the survey of European agriculture and its relationship to Russia; the quotation appears on p. 354. Compare a lecture he read in September 1904 to the Imperial School of Jurisprudence and subsequently published in which he recognized that the evolution of the peasant economy from communal to *khutor* forms of landownership and land use was inevitable. *O prepodovanii uzakonenii o krest'ianakh* (SPB, 1905), pp. 18–27.

75. *Vestnik Finansov*, no. 50, 11 December 1905, pp. 354–56; the quotation appears on p. 356.

76. *Vestnik Finansov*, no. 51, 18 December 1905, pp. 386–94; the quotation appears on p. 394.

77. Ibid.

78. Ibid.

79. Ibid., p. 399; IZO 1906:1, p. 43. He also included provisions for the transfer of whole communities to individual ownership and use as well as for longer-term measures that would equalize peasant property rights with the general civil legislation and increase the spread of agrotechnical education among the peasantry. *Vestnik Finansov*, no. 51, 18 December 1905, p. 399; IZO 1906:1, pp. 43–44.

80. *Novoe Vremia*, no. 10710, 7 January 1906, p. 3.

81. "Bibliografiia," IZO 1906:1, pp. 42–44. Pestrzhetskii had also published a two-part article in *Vestnik Finansov* entitled "Otgranichenie krest'ianskikh nadelov," no. 19, 8 May 1905, pp. 215–19, and no. 32, 7 August 1906, pp. 169 ff. In January 1906, the tsar promoted Pestrzhetskii to the fourth rank in the table of ranks, a position that conferred hereditary nobility—thus, it would seem, confirming this interpretation. Yaney, *Urge to Mobilize*, p. 232. The January issue of IZO also saw the publication of the first installment of Litvinov's 12 July 1905 report on the February–March 1905 disorders. IZO 1906:1–3, pp. 33–38, 81–86, and 148–54. Its arguments are reminiscent of Gurko's. In it, Litvinov came out strongly for the speediest possible elimination of communal landownership and use and the transformation of the peasantry into individual landowners on private property principles.

82. *Otryvochnyia mysli po agrarnomu voprosu*. It was passed by the censorship on 14 March 1906.

83. Ibid., pp. 17–21.

84. Ibid., pp. 24–28.

85. Ibid., pp. 28–30. Compare *Nashe gosudarstvennoe i narodnoe khoziaistvo*, pp. 42–80. Compare his veiled attack on Rittikh in ibid., p. 44. Gurko's argument is to some extent a traditional noble argument but does not for that have to be rejected out of hand. Clearly this and other arguments warrant statistical examination.

86. Gurko, *Otryvochnia mysli*, pp. 30–32. The proportional distribution by country was given by Gurko, as follows:

	France, %	Germany, %	Russia, %
Small	35	28	60
Medium	40	47	3
Large	25	24	37
Of which over 1,000			
hectares or desiatinas	0	Insignificant	80

87. Ibid., pp. 32–33.

88. Ibid., pp. 33–35; the quotation appears on p. 35.

89. Ibid., p. 38.

90. Ibid., pp. 36–38. Gurko uses and quotes in support of the preceding arguments the work by Voskresenskii, *Obshchinnoe zemlevladenie*, an early opponent of the commune. Voskresenskii was a tax inspector in Dankovskii and Pronskii counties of Riazan Province. Like other members of the new generation of bureaucrats, Voskresenskii, too, had studied individual ownership in Poland for some 3½ years. He had also contributed to a publication on taxation and the economic situation of Polish peasants.

91. Gurko, *Otryvochnyia mysli*, pp. 38–43, 56.

92. Ibid., p. 42.

93. Ibid., pp. 56–57.

94. Ibid., p. 56. This analysis of "the wealth of nations" is of course the complete reverse of Adam Smith's. It does, however, share much with German images of economy and society whether Hegelian, Marxian, or Listian.

95. Witte, *Vospominaniia*, vol. 2, 174; Compare Dubrovskii, *Krest'ianskoe dvizhenie*, pp. 42–43, for statistical demonstration.

96. Witte, *Vospominaniia*, vol. 2, 174.

97. "Konspekt k otchetu general-ad"iutanta Panteleeva," KA 11–12 (1925), p. 192.

98. N. Karpov, *Krest'ianskoe dvizhenie v revoliutsii 1905 goda v dokumentakh* (Leningrad, 1926), pp. 268–73. However, Strukov continued to advocate the preservation of the peasant commune. Compare his reports on later disorders in Khar'kov, and in Tambov and Voronezh provinces in ibid., pp. 227–57 and 265–68.

99. TsGIA SSSR, f. 1276, op. 2 (1906), d. 2, l. 1 ob., point XII. Nicholas saw this resolution of 27 January 1906, ibid., l. 1; Sidel'nikov, *Agrarnaia reforma*, pp. 51–52.

100. Manning, *Crisis of the Old Order*, p. 224.

101. The circular, no. 244, was published in St. Petersburg in *Novoe Vremia*, no. 10737, 3 February 1906 as reprinted from *Kievlianin*. According to Migulin, "Russkaia agrarnaia problema," pp. 172–73, Witte had ordered Putilov to dispatch it. See the Kievan landowners' petition in KA 11–12 (1925), p. 156, as well as the various proposals to form local commissions to deal with the agrarian problem in *Agrarnyi vopros v sovete ministrov*, pp. 88–102. Compare Manning, *Crisis of the Old Order*, pp. 223–26. For the general rightward swing within the zemstvos, ibid., pp. 177–202.

102. Bogdanovich, *Tri poslednykh samoderzhtsa*, p. 364; Kokovtsov, *Iz moego proshlago*, vol. 1, 129.

103. *Agrarnyi vopros v sovete ministrov*, pp. 76, 78, 80; Sidel'nikov, *Agrarnaia reforma*, pp. 305–6, especially n. 43, 45, 50.

104. The speeches are reprinted in *Polnoe sobranie rechei Imperatora Nikolaia II: 1894–1906* (SPB, 1906), item no. 160, p. 70; no. 162, p. 71; no. 165, p. 72. Compare *Dnevnik imperatora Nikolaia II: 1890–1906 gg.* (Berlin, 1923), p. 234.

Dubrovskii, *Stolypinskaia zemel'naia reforma*, pp. 94–95 and n. 121;
Bochkareva, "Iz istorii," pp. 43–47.

105. In a conversation with the editor of *Moskovskie Vedomosti*, V. A.
Gringmut. Bogdanovich, *Tri poslednykh samoderzhtsa*, entry for 1 April 1906,
pp. 374–75.

106. Witte's explanation is in *Vospominaniia*, vol. 2, 174–91. Compare
Kokovtsov, *Iz moego proshlago*, vol. 1, 129–30; and Liubimov, "Russkaia smuta,"
p. 259. Mendeleev, "Svet i teni," p. 69, claimed that Witte had no definite views
for or against the project. Stishinskii and Nikol'skii confirm this evaluation.
Bogdanovich, *Tri poslednykh samoderzhtsa*, pp. 363–64. The tsar's letter of 29
January 1906 to Witte asking for Kutler's removal is preserved in the Witte Archive (RACU). Kutler's dismissal was reported to the State Council on 3
February. *Novoe Vremia*, no. 10739, 5 February 1906, p. 5. Compare Witte's 2
February 1906 letter to the tsar and the Kievan landowners' petition in "O petitsii
zemlevladel'tsev," KA 11–12 (1925), pp. 154–57. A copy of the letter is also pre-
served in the Witte archive (RACU).

107. Sidel'nikov, *Agrarnaia reforma*, pp. 55–57. See peasant petitions, though
from a later period, in ibid., pp. 19–28.

108. "Tsarskosel'skaia soveshchaniia," *Byloe*, 1917:4(26) p. 234; S. M. Sidel'-
nikov, *Obrazovanie i deiatel'nost' pervoi gosudarstvennoi dumy* (Moscow, 1962),
pp. 109–10.

109. See Yaney, *Urge to Mobilize*, pp. 242.

110. For example, N. A. Kriukov, director of the GUZiZ's Department of
Agriculture from 1907 and a member of the GUZiZ Council from 1909, published
Chem zhivet i na chem zizhdetsia sel'skoe khoziaistvo (Moscow, 1905), which
emphasized the importance of governmental aid and education in improving agriculture, and *Zemlia i kak s nei luchshe vsego rasporiadit'sia* (Moscow, 1906),
which argued in support of *khutora*. The administrator of the GUZiZ's Chancellery, G. I. Lisenkov, published *Opyt sistematicheskago postroeniia agrarnoi programmy*, pts. 1–2 (SPB, 1906). (Parts 3–5 were never published, because of
"circumstances beyond his control," meaning that they were irrelevant since the
Stolypin Reforms had already been adopted.) See introduction to Lisenkov,
*Zemel'nyi vopros (O tom, chto mozhno sdelat' dlia podniatiia blagosostoianii
krest'ian)* (SPB, 1907). See, too, the works of N. N. Zvorykin, a noble landowner
from the agricultural center, *Krest'ianskoe zemleustroistvo i neotlozhnaia agrarnaia reforma v Rossii* (SPB, 1905), and the pamphlet *Zhelatel'naia osnovaniia
krest'ianskago zemleustroistva* (SPB, 1906), in support of *khutora*; D. S. Kos-
sovich, an Orel noble who favored individual landownership and the expansion of extension services in *K resheniiu agrarnago voprosa: Formy melkago
zemlevladeniia v Rossii s sel'sko-khoziaistvennoi tochki zreniia* (Moscow, 1905);
P. M. Lokhtin, who wrote in support of individualization and land reorganization
in *Kak sdelat'sia krest'ianam bogache* (Kiev, 1906); I. I. Neikardt, in support of
intensification, in *K voprosu o krest'ianskom zemleustroistve* (SPB, 1905); E. A.
Shil'der-Shul'dner, "Krest'ianskie nadely i prichiny ikh maloi proizvoditel'nosti.
Pis'mo k redaktsiiu," *Vestnik Evropy*, 1906:8, pp. 722–86, reprinted as a pamphlet
in 1907, who favored individualization; K. Shirinkin, *K agrarnoi reforme* (Moscow, 1906), who supported a program very similar to the one adopted by the
government; I. A. Stebut, *Neskol'ko myslei i soobrazhenii po povodu agrarnago
voprosa* (SPB, 1906), a noble landowner and zemstvo activist from Bogoroditskii
County, Tula Province, supporting land reorganization and the expansion of extension services and rural handicrafts; Kruzhok Moskvichei, *Materialy po voprosu ob ukreplenii i rasshirenii krest'ianskago zemlevladeniia* (Moscow, 1906),
which contains articles by the Slavophiles D. A. Khomiakov and F. D. Samarin;

the geographer A. I. Skvortsov's *Agrarnyi vopros i Gosudarstvennaia Duma* (SPB, 1906), which demonstrated the irrelevance of an additional allotment; M. I. Goremykin, *Agrarnyi vopros; nekotoryia dannyia k obsuzhdeniiu ego v Gosudarstvennoi Dume* (SPB, 1907), which was completed on 21 November 1906 and published on the orders of the GUZiZ and was devoted to attacking all projects for compulsory alienation with statistical evidence; P. N. Sokovnin, *Kul'turnyi uroven' krest'ianskago polevodstva na nadel'noi zemle i ego znachenie v zemel'nom voprose* (SPB, 1906) published under the auspices of the Committee on Land-Organization Affairs; and G. Loganov, a member of the Interior Ministry, *Statistika zemlevladeniia Evropeiskoi Rossii po uezdam* (SPB, 1906). Stolypin also ordered the publication of the volume *Statistika zemlevladeniia 1905 g.: Svod dannykh po 50-ti guberniiam Evropeiskoi Rossii* (SPB, 1907) by the Interior Ministry's Central Statistical Committee.

111. Kaufman, "Agrarnaia deklaratsiia P. A. Stolypina," p. 172; Compare Chernyshev, *Agrarno-krest'ianskaia politika*, pp. 340–41.

112. Back in May 1905, when Shvanebakh was acting head of GUZiZ, he claimed that Nicholas was already a supporter of individualization and would introduce it in due course. D. Lieven, ed., *British Documents on Foreign Affairs, Russia, 1859–1914*, vol. 3 (n.p., 1983), pp. 120–121. This claim seems to be mere wishful thinking, however.

113. Gurko, *Features and Figures*, pp., 171–72.

Notes to Chapter 6

1. Sidel'nikov, *Agrarnaia reforma*, pp. 52–58. A complete version is in *Agrarnyi vopros v sovete ministrov*, pp. 70–80; *Vtoroi period revoliutsii: 1906–1907 gody*. pt. 1, *Ianvar'-aprel' 1906 goda*, book 1 (Moscow, 1957), pp. 77–83; and the Witte Archive (RACU). The memorandum was prepared by Vuich, V. K. Pleve's son-in-law. *Agrarnyi vopros v sovete ministrov*, p. 92, n. 1. Mendeleev, "Svet i teni," pp. 68–69, 72–74, puts Vuich among the supporters of the Kutler Project within the Council. Witte's 23 December 1905 report had already noted that the Council of Ministers had met three times and that a majority had decided to take no action before the Duma met. The next day the tsar directed the Council to discuss economic measures to eliminate the peasant disorders. *Revoliutsiia 1905 goda i samoderzhavie*, pp. 33–34.

2. See Witte's 16 March 1910 speech in GSSO, V, col. 1231.

3. Sidel'nikov, *Agrarnaia reforma*, p. 55.

4. Ibid., p. 57. Witte was clearly not completely hostile to the Interior Ministry.

5. Ibid., pp. 57–58.

6. See Witte's letters to Durnovo calling for the abolition of the land captains in TsGIA SSSR, f. 1291, op. 30 (1906), d. 71, ll. 12–14, dated 2 February and 22 June 1906.

7. S. M. Sidel'nikov, *Agrarnaia politika samoderzhaviia v period imperializma* (Moscow, 1980), pp. 65–66.

8. There were, in addition, a Finance Ministry commission to revise the Peasant Bank statute in conformity with the ukase of 3 November; the Rittikh commission in the GUZiZ to draft a project on the improvement and expansion of peasant landownership that began work in March; and the interdepartmental Nikol'skii Commission charged with coordinating the government's entire program.

9. Other members were Glinka, Prince V. S. Kochubei, and some new faces, E. A. Smirnov, assistant director of the Department of State Domains, A. N.

Verevkin of the Justice Ministry, and A. I. Putilov, head of the Land Banks and assistant finance minister. All were members of the new generation. Sidel'nikov, *Agrarnaia reforma*, pp. 57 and 306, n. 46; and the report in *Novoe Vremia*. no. 10718, 15 January 1906, p. 5. Compare the account in Krivoshein, *A. V. Krivoshein*, pp. 61–64.

10. *Novoe Vremia*, no. 10724, 21 January 1906, p. 1; no. 10738, 4 February 1906, p. 4; no. 10739, 5 February 1906, p. 5; no. 10750, 17 February 1906, p. 3; Krivoshein, *A. V. Krivoshein*, pp. 62–63.

11. *Novoe Vremia*, no. 10738, 4 February 1906, p. 4; no. 10741, 7 February 1906, p. 4; no. 10747, 14 February 1906, p. 4; Krivoshein, *A. V. Krivoshein*, p. 64. The commission was also renamed the "commission for the review of immediate measures for the organization of the peasants' landed way of life."

12. Among them were projects by Gurko; P. N. Durnovo; M. O. Men'shikov, a journalist for *Novoe Vremia*; and M. M. Fedorov, the recently appointed assistant minister of trade. *Agrarnyi vopros v sovete ministrov*, pp. 113–18.

13. *Novoe Vremia*, no. 10750, 17 February 1906, p. 3; P. P. Gronskii, "25-tiletie Ukaza 9 Noiabria," *Poslednie Novosti*, no. 3899, 25 November 1931, p. 3; Krivoshein, *A. V. Krivoshein*, pp. 64–65. The memorandum was entitled "Memorandum on Reforms in Peasant Organization and on Agrarian Measures." *Agrarnyi vopros v sovete ministrov*, pp. 105–10; Sidel'nikov, *Agrarnaia reforma*, pp. 47–49. The idea of forming local commissions to administer agrarian reform was in the air. *Agrarnyi vopros v sovete ministrov*, pp. 95–102. Compare the article by A. A. Stolypin, P. A. Stolypin's brother, on the problem of additional allotments in *Novoe Vremia*, no. 10738, 4 February 1906, p. 4, which suggests that the agrarian question be resolved on the local level.

14. The following is based on Krivoshein, *A. V. Krivoshein*, especially pp. 7–22, 40–83; and Gurko, *Features and Figures*, pp. 192–93, 593, n. 18.

15. Chernyshev, *Agrarno-krest'ianskaia politika*, pp. 306–8.

16. Gurko, *Features and Figures*, p. 194.

17. *Agrarnyi vopros v sovete ministrov*, pp. 3–4, 105, n. 2; Sidel'nikov, *Agrarnaia reforma*, p. 305, n. 34.

18. *Agrarnyi vopros v sovete ministrov*, p. 106.

19. Witte, *Vospominaniia*, vol. 2, 179–80, 184–88; Krivoshein, *A. V. Krivoshein*, pp. 63–64. Compare Witte's report dated 12 February 1906, p. 1 ob. (Witte Archive, RACU).

20. *Agrarnyi vopros v sovete ministrov*, pp. 106–8.

21. *Agrarnyi vopros v sovete ministrov*, pp. 107–9. Compare Gurko, *Nashe gosudarstvennoe i narodnoe khoziaistvo*, esp. pp. 114–55 on the problems of the state budget, and pp. 84–113 on the role of West European governments in stimulating agricultural development.

22. Krivoshein also shared the view that the ukase of 3 November 1905 abolishing redemption payments had predetermined the entire question of peasant rights. Thus he reiterated the Council of Ministers' call for immediate legislative action to restructure the existing system of communal landownership and use by granting peasants their allotments as private property, providing for an unrestricted personal right to depart from the commune with a share of the community allotment and to consolidate that share into a single compact plot. He also urged that these steps be enacted as soon as possible, before the convocation of the Duma, since they would help consolidate the peasants' respect for the principle of inviolability within a very brief span of time. He also proposed the unification of the two Land Banks into one state bank under the auspices of the GUZiZ. *Agrarnyi vopros v sovete ministrov*, pp. 109–10. Krivoshein was apparently also the author of the following anonymous articles: "Byt' ili ne byt' u nas

pravu sobstvennosti?" "Otkuda vzialsia vopros o 'prinuditel'nom otchuzhdenii' chastnykh zemel'?'" and "Malozemel'e i 'khronicheskoe golodanie'?'" which appeared in *Novoe Vremia*, no. 10711, 8 January 1906; no. 10714, 11 January 1906; and no. 10718, 15 January 1906, respectively. Krivoshein, A. V. Krivoshein, p. 62. On Krivoshein's commitment to a unification of Russia's "We and They"—a commitment that he shared with Gurko and Stolypin. Ibid., pp. 146–53. Compare Gurko, *Nashe gosudarstvennoe i narodnoe khoziaistvo*, p. 240.

23. *Agrarnyi vopros v sovete ministrov*, pp. 102–5; Sidel'nikov, *Agrarnaia reforma*, pp. 62–63, 307–8, n. 59 and 60.

24. *Agrarnyi vopros v sovete ministrov*, pp. 103–4; Sidel'nikov, *Agrarnaia reforma*, pp. 63–64.

25. *Agrarnyi vopros v sovete ministrov*, p. 105.

26. Ibid., pp. 102–5.

27. Ibid., p. 104. The proposal to unify the Land Banks under the GUZiZ was again rejected by the Council of Ministers. TsGIA SSSR f. 1291, op. 30 (1905), prilozhenie 4 v, ll. 56–58; *Agrarnyi vopros v sovete ministrov*, pp. 118–23. Krivoshein, it will be remembered, was acting chief administrator of the GUZiZ during most of February.

28. TsGIA SSSR f. 1291, op. 30 (1905), prilozhenie d. 4 v, ll. 56 ob.–57.

29. Ibid., ll. 57–58; *Agrarnyi vopros v sovete ministrov*, pp. 120–23; *Novoe Vremia*, no. 10746, 13 February 1906, pp. 3–4.

30. *Agrarnyi vopros v sovete ministrov*, pp. 122–23.

31. Ibid., p. 123. This suggests that his motive for transferring the Peasant Bank to the GUZiZ was not to subordinate its activities to noble interests as has commonly been assumed.

32. Ibid., pp. 126–31; Savich, *Novyi gosudarstvennyi stroi*, pp. 41–44.

33. *Agrarnyi vopros v sovete ministrov*, p. 127.

34. Ibid., p. 125. A. I. Putilov, in particular, seems to have had genuine respect for the Duma as well as a fear of offending local society and a desire to preserve his own bailiwick within the Finance Ministry. See his letter of 28 February 1906 to N. I. Vuich in ibid., pp. 146–47.

35. Ibid., pp. 127–31.

36. See his 9 October 1905 report to the tsar in KA 11–12 (1925), p. 59. Compare "Dnevnik A. A. Polotsova," KA 4 (1923), p. 98; Gurko, *Features and Figures*, pp. 454–55; and the tsar's letter to Witte of 15 April 1906 (Witte Archive, RACU) accepting the latter's resignation in which Nicholas blames the composition of the Duma upon the electoral law of 11 December 1905. Nonetheless, Nicholas still believed in the myth of a loyal peasantry since he also blamed the Duma's extremist (left) composition upon the "inertness of the conservative masses. . . ."

37. *Agrarnyi voprose v sovete ministrov*, pp. 144–46.

38. See Trepov's letter to Witte of 5 March 1906 in ibid., p. 147. The projects for both a ukase establishing the land-organization commissions and an imperial manifesto on peasant disorders or some combination statement by the tsar are in ibid., pp. 131–44. Although rejected, these documents all reflect the government's new-found confidence and its desire to express itself in decisive fashion. Compare ibid., pp. 110–18. The Council of Ministers' conclusions are in ibid., pp. 124–25. Some members also had their doubts about issuing such an overt challenge to the opposition.

39. Ibid., p. 124, n. 1; p. 126, n. 3. The project that was to serve as the basis for the 4 March 1906 ukase is in ibid., pp. 139–41. The ukase itself is in PSZ 26 (1906), otd. 1 (SPB, 1909), no. 27478, pp. 199–201; Savich, *Novyi gosudarstvennyi stroi*, pp. 38–41; and Sidel'nikov, *Agrarnaia reforma*, pp. 63–65.

40. Members of the Council of Ministers who participated in these discussions

were Witte; Count Lamsdorf, the minister of foreign affairs; P. N. Durnovo, interior minister; Count I. I. Tolstoi, minister of education; Prince A. D. Obolenskii, procurator of the Holy Synod; I. P. Shipov, finance minister, a Witte protégé and secretary for the Special Conference, but apparently, a supporter of the commune; K. Nessel'rode, unidentified but possibly a representative from the Ministry of Justice; Prince Kochubei; Krivoshein; and M. Fedorov, minister of trade and industry. The position of the various ministers is unknown with the exception of those of Obolenskii and Shipov, who had earlier been Witte men and who seem unlikely to have favored the Gurko/Krivoshein version of reform.

41. *Otchet za 1905–1906* (SPB, 1906), pp. 329–36.

42. Ibid., p. 332. To this group, the psychological impact of constructive government activity was extremely important.

43. Ibid., pp. 334–36 and 334, n. 1.

44. Ibid., p. 336; compare the report in *Izvestiia GUZiZ*, no. 42, 22 October 1906, p. 718, on the progress in their formation and the election of representatives from the zemstvos and the peasantry. Although noting that zemstvos refused to elect members to the land-organization commissions in 11 counties and that in 15 counties peasants refused to elect representatives, nevertheless the zemstvos had elected members in 170 counties and peasants in 153 counties. Evidence for both 1906 and 1907 demonstrates that peasant participation even when electing representatives was far from total. Sidel'nikov, *Agrarnaia reforma*, p. 324, n. 151, notes that in 34 counties, with a total of 7,560 cantons, 626 cantons had not elected representatives to the county commissions. In Simbirsk Province only 96 out of 137 cantons held elections. TsGIA SSSR f. 408, op. 1 (1906), d. 21, l. 87. For the whole of the Volga region the refusals were approximately 25 percent. V. V. Kostriukova, *Krest'iane Povolzh'ia v 1906–1916 gg* (Leningrad, 1953), p. 92. Such refusals could have been a result of ignorance about the reforms or revolutionary propaganda rather than hostility to the government's proposals. Compare K. P-v, "Krest'ianskii bank i krest'ianstvo," in *Narodno-Sotsialisticheskoe Obozrenie*, vol. 2 (1906), pp. 58–59.

45. *Sbornik zakonov i rasporiazhenii po zemleustroistvu (po 1 iiunia 1908 g.)* (SPB, 1908), p. 603.

46. Savich, *Novyi gosudarstvennyi stroi*, pp. 227–31; Hennessy, *Agrarian Question*, pp. 81–108.

47. *Otchet za 1905–6*, pp. 200–234, especially 207–8, 211–12.

48. Ibid., pp. 234–45.

49. Ibid., pp. 245–60.

50. Sidel'nikov, *Agrarnaia reforma*, pp. 58–61 and p. 307, n. 53–58. The Gurko Commission was first announced in *Novoe Vremia*, no. 10715, 12 January 1906, p. 3. Compare Kutler's letter of January 1906 in *Agrarnyi vopros v sovete ministrov*, pp. 81–82. It was actually formed on 24 or 25 January. *Novoe Vremia*, no. 10728, 25 January 1906, p. 3; Sidel'nikov, *Agrarnaia reforma*, pp. 306–7, n. 52. It met on 25, 27, 31 January and 4 and 7 February 1906. Extracts from the Council of Ministers "Memoriia" are in ibid., pp. 66–68; they were approved by the tsar 10 May 1906. Ibid., p. 308, n. 61.

51. There is no direct evidence concerning the views of the remaining five members, though it seems reasonable to assume that N. N. Pokrovskii and A. A. Vishniakov from the Finance Ministry and E. A. Smirnov from GUZiZ also favored individual private property, if only by reason of their membership in ministries whose superiors sought to recruit supporters of their own views. There is no basis at all for determining the opinions of G. E. Blosfel'dt, a representative from the State Chancellery, and P. N. Miliutin, from the Ministry of Justice, prior to their participation in the commission. However, it transpired that they too

shared the perceptions of the other members. Sidel'nikov, *Agrarnaia reforma*, pp. 59–61 and 307, n. 53.

52. TsGIA SSSR f. 1291, op. 122 (1906), d. 12, l. 58.

53. Sidel'nikov, *Agrarnaia reforma*, p. 58; Sofronenko, *Krest'ianskaia reforma*, pp. 46–47 and p. 130. The reader will recall that the right of the nobility's former serfs to claim a share of their community's land in private property had been restricted thirteen years earlier by the repeal of the second part of Article 165 of the Redemption Statute.

54. TsGIA SSSR f. 1291, op. 122 (1906), d. 12, ll. 58–58 ob.

55. The majority opinion is in ibid., ll. 60–62 ob.; that of Rittikh and Pokrovskii in ibid., ll. 62 ob.–63.

56. TsGIA SSSR f. 408, op. 1 (1906), d. 38, l. 123 ob. and 124.

57. TsGIA SSSR f. 1291, op. 122 (1906), d. 12, l. 65; compare the observations of Gurko's Editing Commission in 1903 in *Trudy redkom*, vol. 5, 389–90.

58. TsGIA SSSR f. 1291, op. 122 (1906), d. 12, ll. 66–68 ob.; the quotation is on l. 68 ob.

59. Ibid., l. 66.

60. Ibid., ll. 66–66 ob.

61. Ibid., ll. 68 ob.–70.

62. Ibid., ll. 70 ob.–71.

63. Ibid., l. 71.

64. Ibid., ll. 73 ob., 76–76 ob.

65. Ibid., ll. 76 ob.–77.

66. Ibid., l. 77.

67. Ibid., l. 77 ob.

68. Ibid., l. 41. Sidel'nikov, *Agrarnaia reforma*, p. 307, n. 58. Extracts from the Council of Ministers' "Memoriia" are in ibid., pp. 66–68. Obolenskii opposed publishing the project prior to the Duma's convocation.

69. Sidel'nikov, *Agrarnaia politika*, p. 71.

70. Ibid., p. 307, n. 58; "Dnevnik A. A. Polovtsova," KA 4 (1923), pp. 96–97; Gurko, *Features and Figures*, p. 451.

71. Sidel'nikov, *Agrarnaia politika*, p. 72, quoting TsGIA SSSR f. 1291, op. 122 (1906), d. 12, l. 197.

72. GSSO, V, col. 1451.

73. Gurko, *Features and Figures*, pp. 474–75. See Witte's comments on the problem of governmental disunity in his letter of resignation to the tsar of 14 April 1906 in specific reference to the agrarian question and to the conservative views of Interior Minister Durnovo—curious in that it had been Durnovo who had submitted the Gurko project to the Council of Ministers and who had presumably given it his support there. (Witte Archive, RACU). Compare Chaplin's comments in Bogdanovich, *Tri poslednykh samoderzhtsa*, p. 365; and Goremykin's in a memorandum of 19 July 1906 on his departure from the cabinet in TsGAOR f. 543, op. 1. d. 520, ll. 17–21.

74. Sidel'nikov, *Agrarnaia reforma*, pp. 67–68, p. 308, n. 63. See "Programma voprosov vnosimykh na razmotrenie Gosudarstvennoi Dumy" in the Witte Archive (RACU).

75. The members of this commission were I. M. Strakhovskii, the assistant head of the Interior Ministry's Rural Section; Lykoshin from the Ministry of Justice; Vishniakov, Liutsenskii, and Gorbunov from the Finance Ministry; and Krivoshein, Glinka, Rittikh, Smirnov, and N. V. Pleve from the GUZiZ. TsGIA SSSR f. 408, op. 1 (1906), d. 38, l. 4.

76. Ibid., ll. 4–4 ob.

77. Ibid., l. 7, l. 8 ob., l. 10 and l. 11.

78. Ibid., ll. 11 ob.–12 ob.
79. Ibid., l. 12 ob.
80. Ibid.
81. Ibid., ll. 12 ob.–13.
82. Ibid., l. 13.
83. Ibid.
84. GSSO, V, col. 1230; Otchet za 1905–1906, p. 220.
85. TsGIA SSSR f. 408, op. 1 (1906), d. 38, ll. 14 and 44. Even this commission expressed reservations about the costs of such a program. It also drafted a declaration to be presented to the Duma when it opened. The program was approved by Nicholas and after Witte's resignation passed to Goremykin. Sidel'nikov, Agrarnaia reforma, pp. 68–69, 308–9, n. 63–68.
86. Its members included Vishniakov, Liutsenskii, and Gorbunov from the Finance Ministry; Lykoshin and Rudin from the Ministry of Justice; Pestrzhetskii and Baftalovskii from the Interior Ministry; and nine members from the GUZiZ: Kofod, Kublitskii, Smirnov, Glinka, Zabello, Massal'skii, Pleve, Sumbatov, and Grudistov. Among the new names here cited, A.F. Kublitskii was the director of the Forestry Department and former director of the Department of State Landed Property; L. P. Zabello was the vice-director of the Department of State Landed Property; Prince V. I. Massal'skii was the assistant director of the Department of Agriculture and from June 1906 its director; N. V. Pleve was the head of the Department of Agricultural Economy and Agricultural Statistics; N. V. Grudistov was from 1912 the vice-director of the Forestry Department; Sumbatov is unidentified. V. I. Baftalovskii, meanwhile, was to transfer to the GUZiZ as assistant head of the Migration Administration in January 1910.
87. TsGIA SSSR f. 408, op. 1 (1906), d. 38, ll. 108–112. The materials for this conference are contained in ibid., ll. 45–367.
88. Ob''iasnitel'naia zapiska k proektu polozheniia ob uluchshenii i rasshirenii krest'ianskago zemlevladeniia (n.p., n.d.), p. 49.

Notes to Chapter 7

1. Witte, Vospominaniia, vol. 2, 289–310; Gurko, Features and Figures, pp. 450–58; V. N. Kokovtsov, Out of My Past: The Memoirs of Count Kokovtsov (Stanford, 1935), pp. 123–31; Iswolsky, Memoirs, pp. 113–38; E. J. Bing., ed., The Letters of Tsar Nicholas and Empress Marie (London, 1937), pp. 209–12; Bogdanovich, Tri poslednykh samoderzhtsa, p. 389; Chermenskii, Burzhuaziia i tsarizm, pp. 261–64; Solov'ev Samoderzhavie i dvorianstvo v 1902–1907, pp. 188–211; Mehlinger and Thompson, Count Witte, pp. 317–25; G. S. Doctorow, "The Fundamental State Laws of 23 April 1906," Russian Review: 35:1 (1976), 33–52.
2. Sidel'nikov, Agrarnaia reforma, pp. 308–9, n. 66; Dubrovskii, Stolypinskaia zemel'naia reforma, p. 101–2; Mehlinger and Thompson, Count Witte, pp. 314–17.
3. Witte, Vospominaniia, vol. 2, 296; Chermenskii, Burzhuaziia i tsarizm, p. 263. A copy of the letter is preserved in the Witte Archive (RACU).
4. Sidel'nikov, Obrazovanie pervoi dumy, esp. pp. 275–319, on the agrarian question; V. A. Maklakov, The First State Duma, Contemporary Reminiscences (Bloomington, 1964), esp. pp. 135–45; Chermenskii, Burzhuaziia i tsarizm, pp. 211–337, esp. pp. 275–83; Sidel'nikov, Agrarnaia reforma, pp. 70–80; Manning, Crisis of the Old Order, pp. 205–28.
5. Kokovtsov, Out of My Past, p. 127; Gurko, Features and Figures, pp. 75–81. A graduate of the Imperial School of Jurisprudence who had served for many years

in the Senate's Second (Peasant) Department, where he was in charge of the publication of the *Svod uzakonenii i rasporiazhenii pravitel'stva ob ustroistve sel'skago sostoianiia*, Goremykin was in fact a moderate monarchist. In the ongoing discussion within the government between the supporters of reform versus reaction, Duma versus dictatorship, he rejected the latter option. TsGAOR f. 543, op. 1, d. 520, ll. 22–25, esp. l. 22. Compare Iswolsky, pp. 92, 178; and "Dnevnik A. A. Polovtsova," KA 4 (1923), pp. 104–5. Goremykin's years as a commissar for peasant affairs in Poland may have inclined him toward the agrarian reforms that were being proposed within the bureaucracy. Goremykin expressed his support for the Stolypin Reforms publically after their adoption. Troitskii, "Iz vospominaii," pt. 1, p. 8.

6. Gurko, *Features and Figures*, pp. 448, 459–88. Durnovo was dismissed 22 April and Stolypin appointed 25 April. E. Amburger, *Geschichte der Behordenorganisation Russlands von Peter dem Grossen bis 1917* (Leiden, 1966), p. 137. Stolypin only assumed his post on 29 April 1906. Bogdanovich, *Tri poslednykh samoderzhtsa*, p. 381; M. P. Bok, *Vospominaniia o moem ottse P. A. Stolypine* (New York, 1953), pp. 159–61.

7. GDSO (1906), vol. 1 (SPB, 1906), pp. 239–41, 248–51. Compare Maklakov, *First State Duma*, especially pp. 66–83; Chermenskii, *Burzhuaziia i tsarizm*, pp. 275–83; Zimmerman, "Kadets and the Duma," pp. 119–38; P. Miliukov, *Political Memoirs 1905–1917*, (Ann Arbor, 1967), pp. 85–128; Sidel'nikov, *Obrazovanie pervoi dumy*, pp. 292–96.

8. Gurko, *Features and Figures*, pp. 471–73. Kryzhanovskii and P. P. Stremoukhov, the director of the Ministry of Internal Affairs' Department of General Affairs, also participated. Bogdanovich, *Tri poslednykh samoderzhtsa*, p. 384. Compare Maklakov, *First State Duma*, pp. 84–95, 136, and 248, n. 5; Kokovtsov, *Iz moego proshlago*, pp. 179–93; Witte, *Vospominaniia*, vol. 2, 311–23; and Dubrovskii, *Stolypinskaia zemel'naia reforma*, pp. 113–21. See the draft of a reply to the Duma prepared by the Nikol'skii Commission in Sidel'nikov, *Agrarnaia reforma*, pp. 68–69.

9. GDSO (1906) vol. 1, 322.

10. Ibid.

11. Ibid., p. 323; compare Sidel'nikov, *Agrarnaia reforma*, p. 68.

12. GDSO (1906) vol. 1, 324.

13. Maklakov, *The First State Duma*, p. 136.

14. GDSO (1906) vol. 1, 324. On *opeka*: "Equalization . . . must not deprive the governmental authority of the right and the obligation to display special solicitude for the needs of the agricultural peasantry." Compare Goremykin's memorandum of 19 July 1906 on the Council of Ministers as an institution of a supraclass government in TsGAOR f. 543, op. 1, d. 520, ll. 17–21.

15. Gurko, *Features and Figures*, pp. 474–78; Gurko, *Nashe gosudarstvennoe i narodnoe khoziaistvo*, p. 44.

16. Gurko, *Features and Figures*, pp. 383–84; *Trudy pervago s"ezda Upolnomochennykh Dvorianskikh Obshchestv 29 gubernii (21–28 maia, 1906)*, 1st ed. (SPB, 1906), p. 1; A. N. Naumov, *Iz utselevshikh vospominanii 1868–1917 v dvukh knigakh*, vol. 2 (New York, 1955), p. 76; Dubrovskii, *Stolypinskaia zemel'naia reforma*, p. 116.

17. GDSO (1906), vol. 1, 514. Compare the account by Tan (V. G. Bogoraz), *Muzhiki v gosudarstvennoi dume. Ocherki* (Moscow, 1907), pp. 27–30.

18. GDSO (1906), vol. 1, 516.

19. Gurko, *Features and Figures*, pp. 475–77; GDSO (1905), vol. 1, 517.

20. Ibid., p. 518.

21. Ibid.

22. Ibid., p. 519.
23. Ibid., p. 520.
24. Ibid.
25. Ibid., pp. 521–22.
26. Ibid., p. 522.
27. Ibid., pp. 522–23.
28. Ibid., p. 523. Such indeed was to be the course of events after 1917. G. L. Yaney, "Agricultural Administration in Russia from the Stolypin Land Reform to Forced Collectivization: An Interpretative Study," in *The Soviet Rural Community*, ed. J. R. Millar (Urbana, 1971), pp. 3–35; Yaney, *Urge to Mobilize*, chapters 10–12; Erlich, *Soviet Industrialization*; M. Lewin, *Russian Peasants and Soviet Power: A Study of Collectivization* (Evanston, 1968); D. J. Male, *Russian Peasant Organization before Collectivization: A Study of Commune and Gathering* (Cambridge, 1971); V. P. Danilov, et al., eds., *Sovetskoe krest'ianstvo, Kratkii ocherk istorii (1917–1970)*, 2d ed. (Moscow, 1973), esp. pp. 8–185, 206–92.

29. In addition to works already cited, on the United Nobility see I. D. Vaisberg, "Soviet ob"edinennogo dvorianstva i ego vliianie na politiku samoderzhaviia (1906–1914 gg.)" (Masterskaia diss., Moscow, 1956); Vaisberg, "Sovet ob"edinennogo dvorianstva i ego vliianie na politiku samoderzhaviia v 1906–1914 gg.," *Uchenye Zapiski Borisoglebskogo gosudarstvennogo pedagogicheskogo instituta*, vol. 2 (1957), 273–304; Simmonds, "Congress of Representatives"; M. M. Kovalevskii, *Chem Rossiia obiazana soiuzu ob"edinennago dvorianstva?* (Moscow, 1914), pp. 23–41; G. A. Hosking and R. T. Manning, "What Was the United Nobility," in *The Politics of Rural Russia, 1905–1914*, ed. L. H. Haimson (Bloomington, 1979), pp. 142–83; H. Rogger, "The Formation of the Russian Right 1900–1906," *California Slavic Studies*, 3 (1964), pp. 66–94; A. Levin, "Russian Bureaucratic Opinion in the Wake of the 1905 Revolution," JGO 11 (1963), 1–12. Also Gurko, *Nashe gosudarstvennoe i narodnoe khoziaistvo*, pp. 42–45; Liubimov, "Russkaia smuta," pp. 297–99; and Mendeleev, "Svet i teni," book 2, pp. 85–100.

30. Gurko, *Features and Figures*, pp. 381–87; Naumov, *Iz utselevshikh vospominanii*, vol. 2, 33, 45–46, 54–58, 63–64, 76–81; Solov'ev, *Samoderzhavie i dvorianstvo v 1902–1907*, pp. 199–200, 212; Mech, *Sily reaktsii*; Levitskii, "Pravyia partii," pp. 347–472.

31. The most important groups involved in this virtual coup d'état against the marshals were the All-Russian Union of Landowners, organized in Saratov and composed of both noble landowners and bureaucrats; the St. Petersburg Patriotic Union, made up almost exclusively of capital-city dignitaries; and the Golovin salon, which included noble landowners from Orel Province and bureaucrats and public figures from St. Petersburg. On the Volga group see *Programma i pervyi proekt ustava Russkago soiuza zemlevladel'tsev* (Saratov, 1905).

32. Students of modernization have judged such a fusion of old and new as more successful than earlier, naive theories of "total Westernization." C. E. Black, *The Dynamics of Modernization: A Study in Comparative History* (New York, 1966), esp. pp. 103–4, 119–23; Moore, *Social Origins*, pp. xv–xvi, 228–313, 433–52, and 453–83. Germany and Japan are the best examples. Compare C. E. Black et al., *The Modernization of Japan and Russia: A Comparative Study* (New York, 1975).

33. The composition of the organizing committees for the First Congress was critical because it was they who established the commissions that were to draft the Congress's program. The first of the planning committees met in Moscow between 20 and 23 April 1906. The majority of its twenty-six members were local

marshals of the nobility who had been associated with the January 1906 marshals' congress. The opening session was chaired by their leader, Prince Trubetskoi. Of the fourteen present, four are especially significant: S. N. Prutchenko, formerly of the Ministry of Education, now marshal of the nobility from Nizhnii-Novgorod, who represented the bureaucratic connection: A. N. Brianchaninov, a member of the Golovin circle, Pskov marshal of the nobility, an Octobrist and son of a former senator and governor; and two marshals from the Volga region, V. N. Oznobishin from Saratov and Kh. N. Sergeev from Astrakhan. The Volga contingent was later strengthened by the participation of N. A. Pavlov of Saratov and cofounder of the abortive Union of Landowners. Five additional members of the nobility joined the planning committee on 22 April: Golovin; Count A. A. Bobrinskii, of Kiev and St. Petersburg, member of the Imperial Court and State Council, senator, sugar manufacturer, and son-in-law of the former imperial secretary A. A. Polovtsov; Senator A. A. Naryshkin, a zemstvo activist from Orel Province, former assistant agricultural minister, elected member of the State Council, longtime friend of Ermolov and also a member of the Golovin circle; S. A. Volodomirov, a county marshal of the nobility, also from Orel Province; and the less well-known P. N. Semenov of the imperial court. After the cooptation of these men the planning committee decided to shift its headquarters and the site of the First Congress from the nobility's traditional home in Moscow to St. Petersburg, the center of government. Before the first committee disbanded, the secretary, Kh. N. Sergeev, proposed placing a question in the Congress's program about noble participation in the task of improving peasant welfare. Although rejected by ten votes to nine, it foreshadowed subsequent developments. *Trudy pervago s"ezda UDO*, 2d ed. (SPB, 1910), pp. 177–79. The second planning committee, which met in St. Petersburg on 16 May and functioned until the Congress itself opened on 21 May, was of a considerably different ideological hue from its predecessor. In the intervening month there had been a significant shift of political strength away from the marshals of the nobility, led by the liberal Trubetskoi, and toward those members of the nobility who had bureaucratic ties at the national level—particularly Bobrinskii and Naryshkin. Among the twenty-six members present at the first meeting of the second planning committee, there were two capital-city notables and former bureaucrats: A. A. Shul'ts, a member of the agricultural council of the GUZiZ, former vice-director of the Agriculture Department and landowner from Kazan Province; and A. B. Neidgardt of Nizhnii-Novgorod, Stolypin's brother-in-law, most recently one of Pleve's appointees as governor of Ekaterinoslav Province and an elected member of the State Council. In addition to Shul'ts, there were six other representatives from the Volga: V. N. Polivanov, a former marshal of the nobility in Simbirsk and an elected member of the State Council; A. A. Chemodurov, marshal of the nobility from Samara and also elected to the State Council; V. I. Denisov, the appointive marshal of the nobility from the Don, frequent participant in government trade commissions, author of a widely read book on forestry, *Lesa Rossii, ikh ekspluatatsiia i lesnaia torgovlia* (SPB, 1911), and an elected member of the State Council; Kh. N. Sergeev of Astrakhan, who was elected secretary of the planning committee; Count D. A. Olsuf'ev, chairman of the Saratov provincial zemstvo administrative board from 1902 to 1904, currently an Octobrist and an elected member of the State Council; and A. N. Naumov, marshal of the nobility from Samara, founder of a local law-and-order party and a future minister of agriculture. Finally, there were three members of the Golovin circle, Brianchaninov, Volodomirov, and Naryshkin. In addition, Bobrinskii attended this session and participated in the voting. Despite the decision to limit voting rights at the Congress to elected representatives of the nobility, this rule apparently did not hold for the planning committee. Thus, beginning with its very first session, it instituted a process of cooptation by which it sought to legitimize the role of the nonelected participants, though they had been granted only an advisory voice. One of the first invitations was extended to S. S. Bekhteev of Orel Province and the Golovin salon. Subsequently, both Gurko and Golovin himself were also invited to participate, along with Pestrzhetskii, Gurko's deputy in the Interior Ministry's Rural Section. Other cooptees included Bobrinskii, P. N. Semenov, Naryshkin, Volodomirov, and V. M. Vonliarliarskii, a retired general-lieutenant of the army and concessionaire on the Yalu who had been associated with Russia's ill-fated entry into the Russo-Japanese War. Beginning with the second evening session on 17 May, Gurko's associate Lykoshin, also a longtime acquaintance of Golovin, began attending sessions with Gurko. *Trudy pervago s"ezda UDO*, 2d ed., pp. 180–83.

34. The other members were Chemodurov; Denisov; Sergeev; Shul'ts; Zybin, a noble landowner from Nizhnii-Novgorod and future secretary of the United Nobility; Iu. B. Trubnikov, an economic expert and former bureaucrat active in noble and zemstvo affairs and in the running of his own estate in Spasskii County, Kazan Province, and also an elected member of the State Council; and, finally, Prince V. M. Volkonskii, a marshal of the nobility from Tambov and right-wing member of the Third and Fourth Dumas. Of these nine, five were from the Volga region; Bekhteev and Shul'ts were associated with the GUZiZ; Pestrzhetskii and Denisov with the Interior Ministry; Trubnikov had once been a bureaucrat. Both Pestrzhetskii and Bekhteev were coopted. All were acknowledged experts in agrarian or economic matters. Bekhteev, Shul'ts, and Pestrzhetskii each presented reports on the agrarian question at the council's evening session on 16 May and the morning session the next day. Bekhteev's was published as *Doklad o pod"eme blagosostoianiia krest'ianstva* (SPB, 1906). Needless to say, all three vigorously opposed expropriation and supported individualization and intensification. Subsequently, Olsuf'ev recommended that the agrarian commission review and discuss the projects already worked out by the Gurko and Rittikh commissions within the Goremykin government and urged the council to support them. *Trudy pervago s"ezda UDO*, 2d ed., pp. 181–83, 186.

35. The agrarian program is in ibid., pp. 152–56. The copy in Sidel'nikov, *Agrarnaia reforma*, pp. 80–84, is incorrectly identified as the version adopted by the First Congress itself.

36. *Trudy pervago s"ezda UDO*, 2d ed., p. 44.

37. Sidel'nikov, *Agrarnaia reforma*, pp. 82–83.

38. Ibid., p. 81.

39. Ibid., pp. 81, 84.

40. Compare Pavlov, *Zapiska zemlevladel'tsa*, pp. 249–53; Solov'ev, *Samoderzhavie i dvorianstvo v 1902–1907*, p. 207. The following members of the United Nobility were on the Union of Landed Proprietors' central committee: Bekhteev, Bobrinskii, Volkonskii, Golovin, Denisov, Neidgardt, Olsuf'ev, Pavlov, Polivanov, and Prutchenko. *Spisok chlenov Tsentral'nago Soveta Vserossiiskago Soiuza Zemel'nykh Sobstvennikov*.

41. *Trudy pervago s"ezda UDO*, 1st ed., pp. 5, 8, 14, 18.

42. Ibid., pp. 1–2.

43. Ibid., p. 18.

44. Ibid., p. 26.

45. Ibid., p. 29. Compare the discussion in ibid., pp. 67–74; and O. D. Durnovo's otherwise moderate speech. Ibid., pp. 32–33. The twin themes of urgency and action were also implicit in the repeated appeals to abolish the commune. For example, V. L. Kushelev of Pskov, ibid., p. 28.

46. Ibid., pp. 28–29, 41, and the comments of Prince A. P. Urusov of Tula,

p. 29; L. L. Kislovskii of Kazan, p. 35; and K. N. Grimm of St. Petersburg and Saratov, p. 38.

47. Ibid., p. 27.

48. Ibid., p. 28.

49. Ibid., p. 38–39.

50. Ibid., p. 27, 41 for Brianchaninov; p. 40 for Sheremetev.

51. Ibid., pp. 28–29. Compare Bekhteev, *Doklad o pod"eme blagosostoianiia krest'ianstva* (SPB, 1906). On the surface, it would seem impossible for members of the nobility to assert the existence of good relations between them and the peasantry, given that 75 percent of peasant actions during 1905–6 were directed against the landowning nobility. Dubrovskii, *Krest'ianskoe dvizhenie*, p. 65. That the nobility was suffering from a self-imposed delusion seems unlikely in the face of their demand for a new electoral law. Thus, notwithstanding the conflict over land, it is also necessary to acknowledge the very considerable degree of personal interdependence that could and did serve as a basis for good relations during nonrevolutionary periods. In a conversation held in Moscow in 1973, John Fisher, a student of Witte's Special Conference, on the basis of an examination of statements made to the local committees by peasants, suggested that the peasantry expressed greater hostility toward the governmental bureaucracy and the land captains than toward the nobility—and that despite the fact that those committees had considerable numbers of bureaucrats participating in their sessions.

52. *Trudy pervago s"ezda UDO*, 1st ed., p. 29.

53. See E. Vinogradoff, "The Russian Peasantry and the Election to the Fourth Duma: Estate Political Consciousness and Class Political Consciousness" (Ph.D. diss., Columbia, 1974), pp. 144–53.

54. *Trudy pervago s"ezda UDO*, 1st ed., p. 30. Compare the speeches of K. N. Grimm, p. 38; of N. Iu. Shil'dner-Shul'dner of Vitebsk, p. 40; N. E. Markov, p. 4; Lykoshin, pp. 86, 92; and Bobrinskii, p. 50. Compare Iu. Iu. Samorupo, ibid., p. 31.

55. Compare Pillar-fon-Pil'khau, who, like the government, felt that action spoke louder than words. Ibid., pp. 45–46; Pavlov, p. 62; and Markov, p. 63.

56. Ibid., pp. 35–38.

57. Ibid., p. 37. See chapter 1, n. 87.

58. *Trudy pervago s"ezda UDO*, 1st ed., pp. 37–38.

59. This involved Articles 1, 13, and 16. Ibid., pp. 41–50, 52–53, 64.

60. Ibid., p. 49.

61. Ibid., pp. 49–50, 52–53, 64.

62. Ibid., p. 53.

63. Ibid., pp. 49–50; and *Svod Postanovlenii I–X s"ezdov upolnomochennykh ob"edinennykh dvorianskikh obshchestv 1906–1914 gg.* (Petrograd, 1915), p. 1.

64. *Trudy pervago s"ezd UDO*, 1st ed., pp. 54–57. Compare Pavlov, who emphasized the need to provide a full range of agricultural extension services as a condition for the success of the other measures. Ibid., p. 62, and Markov, p. 63.

65. Ibid., pp. 57–59, and Pavlov, p. 62. See the discussions in the 3d Congress in *Trudy tret'ego s"ezda upolnomochennykh dvorianskikh obshchestv 32 gubernii (27/III–2/IV/1907)* (SPB, 1907), pp. 210–45, 271–98; and P. N. Semenov and A. A. Saltykov, *Krest'ianskii bank i budushchnost' russkago krest'ianstva* (SPB, 1907); and Semenov and Saltykov, "Zapiska tsentral'nago soveta soiuza zemel'nykh sobstvennikov o deiatel'nosti krest'ianskago banka" (SPB, 1907) in TsGIA SSSR f. 1291, op. 122 (1907), d. 72, ll. 33–47.

66. *Trudy pervago s"ezda UDO*, 1st ed., pp. 59–60.

67. Ibid., p. 60.

68. Ibid., p. 61.

69. Ibid., pp. 115–16.

70. *Svod Postanovlenii*, pp. 1–5, which contains a copy of the incompletely edited version.

71. This commission was also formed by the preparatory committee. Its members were Bobrinskii, Naryshkin, Prutchenko, D. D. Ivashintsov of Pskov, Bekhteev, Trubetskoi, Chemodurov, Oznobishin, and Zybin. Three of them had been coopted. Only Ivashintsov and Trubetskoi fell outside the parameters of those pressure groups that are our primary concern. *Trudy pervago s"ezda UDO*, 2d ed., p. 183.

72. *Trudy pervago s"ezda UDO*, 1st ed., pp. 115–18 and 67–84; and the discussion of *opeka* by Samorupo, Ia. N. Ofrosimov of Pskov, and Prince N. B. Shcherbatov of Poltava on pp. 63–64.

73. Their project of the address is in ibid., 2d ed., pp. 146–48.

74. *Inter alia* in *Pravo*, no. 23, 11 June 1906, cols. 2061–63.

75. *Trudy pervago s"ezda UDO*, 1st ed., p. 62, for Pavlov, p. 63 for Samorupo.

76. GDSO (1906), vol. 1, 560–62. On the Trudoviki, see D. A. Kolesnichenko, *Trudoviki v period pervoi rossiiskoi revoliutsii* (Moscow, 1985), pp. 28–91.

77. Miliukov, *Tri popytki*, pp. 26–60; Chermenskii, *Burzhuaziia i tsarizm*, pp. 283–302; V. I. Startsev, *Russkaia burzhuaziia i samoderzhavie v 1905–1917 gg.* (Leningrad, 1977), pp. 66–84.

78. Sidel'nikov, *Obrazovanie pervoi dumy*, pp. 316–17.

79. Ibid., pp. 302–3. The project is in GDSO (1906), vol. 2, 1153–56. It was the Socialist-Revolutionary party who came to symbolize the opposition in the government's eyes. A. Kleinbort, "Pravitel'stvo i partii ob agrarnom voprose," *Obrazovanie*, 1907:6, pp. 74–98; D. W. Treadgold, "Was Stolypin in Favor of Kulaks?" *American Slavic and East European Review* 17:1 (February 1965), 1–14. On the SRs, see S. N. Sletov, *K istorii vosniknoveniia P. S-R* (Petrograd, 1917); and O. H. Radkey, *The Agrarian Foes of Bolshevism: Promise and Default of the Russian Socialist Revolutionaries February to October 1917* (New York, 1958), especially pp. 3–87; A. Blakely, "The Socialist Revolutionary Party, 1901–1907: The Populists' Response to the Industrialization of Russia" (Ph.D. diss., Berkeley, 1971); M. Perrie, "The Social Composition and Structure of the SR Party before 1917," *Soviet Studies* (October 1972), pp. 223–50; Perrie, *The Agrarian Policy of the Russian Socialist-Revolutionary Party from Its Origins Through the Revolution of 1905–1907* (Cambridge, 1976); M. Hildermeier, "Neopopulism and Modernization: The Debate on Theory and Tactics in the Socialist Revolutionary Party, 1905–1914," *Russian Review*, 34:4 (October 1975), 453–75; and V. N. Ginev, *Bor'ba za krest'ianstvo i krizis russkogo neonarodnichestva 1902–1914 gg.* (Leningrad, 1983).

80. There were, of course, many other sources of pressure on the government. See, for example, N. L. Markov's 9 February 1906 memorandum on the Peasant Land Bank to Witte; N. A. Pavlov's report to the Union of Landowners on 12 February 1906, which contained most of the themes he later expressed at the First Congress of the United Nobility; the decrees of the "S"ezd Sel'skikh Khoziaev Po Zemel'nomu Voprosu," dated 26 February 1906 and signed by A. P. Meshcherskii, S. S. Bekhteev, N. A. Pavlov, P. P. Migulin, and A. A. Shul'ts among others; the 3 May 1906 telegram from the council of the Union of Russian Men urging immediate action; a project, echoing the Gurko/Pestrzhetskii formulae, from A. A. Dubenskii, a county marshal of the nobility, dated 31 May 1906; and a report from the governor-general of the southwest, Kleigel, dated 27 May 1906, also urging widespread and immediate reforms to intensify and rationalize peasant agriculture. *Agrarnyi vopros v sovete ministrov*, pp. 148–72.

81. GDSO (1906), vol. 2, 1086–87 and 1213.

82. The political problem would be further complicated by a new upsurge in peasant unrest during June that was only somewhat less severe than its previous high point in November of the previous year. Dubrovskii, *Krest'ianskoe dvizhenie*, pp. 42–43.

Notes to Chapter 8

1. Chermenskii, *Burzhuaziia i tsarizm*, pp. 283–302; Gurko, *Features and Figures*, pp. 480–83; Iswolsky, *Memoirs*, pp. 180–98; Kokovtsov, *Iz moego proshlago*, vol. 2, 194–219; Maklakov, *First State Duma*, pp. 184–204; Miliukov, *Political Memoirs*, pp. 103–28; P. N. Miliukov, "Moe svidanie s generalom Trepovym," *Rech'*, no. 46, 17 February 1909; Shipov, *Vospominaniia*, pp. 445–60; and J. E. Zimmerman, "Between Revolution and Reaction: The Russian Constitutional Democratic Party: October, 1905 to June, 1907" (Ph.D. diss., Columbia, 1967), pp. 254–58, 265–69.

2. "Dnevnik A. A. Polovtsova," KA 4 (1923), p. 114; "Tsarskosel'skiia soveshchaniia," pp. 234–35; Goremykin in TsGAOR f. 543, op. 1, d. 520, l. 23; and Goremykin's draft of his reply to the Duma, which included a reference to the necessity of revising the electoral law in ibid., l. 13; Witte, *Vospominaniia*, vol. 2, 311–19; Kokovtsov, *Iz moego proshlago*, vol. 1, 183–84, 194–219; Gurko, *Features and Figures*, pp. 459–60, 467–68, 469, 481–88; Iswolsky, *Memoirs*, pp. 168–98; Maklakov, *First State Duma*, pp. 12–31; Miliukov, *Political Memoirs*, pp. 103–16; Bing, *Letters*, pp. 228–29; Sidel'nikov, *Obrazovanie pervoi dumy*, pp. 333–34; Chermenskii, *Burzhuaziia i tsarizm*, pp. 234–35, 255–64, 283–302; Doctorow, "Fundamental State Laws," pp. 45–52; H. Heilbronner, "Piotr Khristianovich Schwanebach and the Dissolution of the First Two Dumas," *Canadian Slavonic Papers*, 11:1 (1969), pp. 31–37.

3. V. V. Shelokhaev, *Kadety—glavnaia partiia liberal'noi burzhuazii v bor'be s revoliutsiei 1905–1907 gg.* (Moscow, 1983), pp. 110–26.

4. GDSO (1906), vol. 2, 1086–87.

5. A. N. Brianchaninov, *Rospusk Gosudarstvennoi Dumy: Prichiny—posledstviia* (Pskov, 1906), p. 38. See, for example, *Russkiia Vedomosti*, which printed extracts from the explanatory note in nos. 161 and 164, 23 and 27 June 1906, p. 5 and p. 4, respectively; and from the project in nos. 172, 174, and 175, 6, 8, and 9 July 1906, p. 5, in each issue; *Novoe Vremia* no. 10862, 11 June 1906, p. 4, gave only a brief summary. Extracts from the explanatory note are reprinted in Sidel'nikov *Agrarnaia reforma*, pp. 31–40; compare, too, ibid., pp. 299–303, n. 13–24.

6. *Russkiia Vedomosti*, no. 161, 23 June 1906, p. 5:1. The commission's materials are in TsGIA SSSR f. 1291, op. 122 (1906), d. 12. Revised versions of both the project and the explanatory note were resubmitted to the Second Duma under the title of "Project on Peasant Landownership," GDSO (1907), vol. 1, 180, on 7 March 1907; "Osobyi zhurnal soveta ministrov" for 26 January 1907. The Second Duma took no action. It was resubmitted to the Third Duma on 15 November 1907, GDSO (1907–8), vol. 1, 600. The project was subsequently withdrawn from the Duma on 19 May 1909. GDSO (1908–9), vol. 4, 1439. It was never subsequently reintroduced, for its principal elements had by then been incorporated into other bills already enacted. The materials for the commission to reform village administration are in TsGIA SSSR f. 1291, op. 122 (1906), d. 46, pt. 1. It began its work about 12 April 1906. Copies of the projects on village, canton, *uchastok*, and county administrations as submitted to the Second Duma are reprinted in IZO 1907:3, pp. 96–115, 1907:4, pp. 142–51, 1907:5, pp. 187–93, and

1907:6, pp. 252–60 together with supporting materials. TsGIA SSSR f. 1291, op. 122 (1906), d. 72, ll. 394–411, contains the proposals as presented to the Council of Ministers on 11 December 1906. Compare an earlier draft in the materials of the Nikol'skii Commission, TsGIA SSSR f. 408, op. 1 (1906), d. 38, ll. 39–43. Clearly, these proposals and the projects themselves were no more Stolypin's own than was the ukase of 9 November 1906. Compare A. V. Zenkovskii, *Pravda o Stolyine* (New York, 1956).

7. *Russkiia Vedomosti*, no. 161, 23 June 1906, p. 5:2.

8. Ibid.

9. Ibid., p. 5:1. Such were the traditional and bureaucratic pressures upon the radical Gurko.

10. Ibid. There was no question, here, of a wager on the strong.

11. Ibid., p. 5:2. The use of the terms *melkie* and *srednie* was a clear reflection of Gurko's influence. Later speeches and references by bureaucrats would refer only to *melkie*.

12. *Russkiia Vedomosti*, no. 164, 27 June 1906, p. 4:4–5.

13. Ibid., cols. 5–6.

14. *Russkiia Vedomosti*, no. 172, 6 July 1906, p. 5:2.

15. Compare chapter 4, note 59. The government's critics at the time noted, accurately, that those villages owning land on an individual basis were usually smaller than the others. As a consequence, although half of all villages had not repartitioned, those villages included only about a third of the peasant population.

16. *Russkiia Vedomosti*, no. 164, 27 June 1906, p. 4:5. Of course, given that since the 1880s a growing number of communes had undertaken their first repartition, the reformers might appear to be in a race against time since the longer the proposed changes were delayed the fewer communes there would be in that category. However, as was made clear at the International Conference on the Russian Peasant Commune held in London in July 1986, there is considerable disagreement about the meaning of this development. More important, such a trend does not preclude the presence of individualistic attitudes toward land use. Certainly, during times of calm, peasant attitudes toward land seem to have been characterized more by egoism than by abstract concepts of egalitarianism or justice.

17. Ibid., no. 175, 9 July 1906, p. 5:5.

18. Ibid., no. 164, 27 June 1906, p. 4:5.

19. Ibid., col. 6. The Nikol'skii Commission was also preparing the abolition of this post. TsGIA SSSR f. 408, op. 1 (1906), d. 38, l. 40. The draft projects on the reform of local administration also assumed its abolition. *Russkiia Vedomosti*, no. 161, 23 June 1906, p. 5:6. The "rumor" spread consternation among the land captains and affected the execution of their responsibilities. Although Stolypin subsequently referred to the impending abolition of this post in his 6 March 1907 speech to the Duma, GDSO (1907), vol. 1, 113, he subsequently modified his position by claiming that what he intended was to reform this post. *Trudy s"ezda nepremennykh chlenov gubernskikh prisutstvii 24/X–1/XI/07*. (SPB, 1908), p. 4.

20. The twenty-four-year rule was included only in a modified form in the Law of 14 June 1910. On local reform, see V. A. Diakin, "Stolypin i dvorianstvo (Proval mestnoi reformy)," in *Problemy krest'ianskogo zemlevladeniia i vnutrennei politiki Rossii: Dooktiabr'skii period* (Leningrad, 1972), pp. 231–74; P. N. Zyrianov, "Krakh vnutrennei politika Tret'e-iiun'skoi monarkhii v oblasti mestnogo-upravleniia (1907–1914 gg.)" (Kand. diss., Moscow, 1972); Zyrianov, "Tret'ia Duma i vopros o reforme mestnogo suda i volostnogo upravleniia," *Istoriia SSSR*, 1969:6, pp. 45–62; Weissman, *Reform in Tsarist Russia*, pp. 124–

228; Wcislo, "Bureaucratic Reform," pp. 279–460; and Manning, *Crisis of the Old Order*, pp. 330–46.

21. GDSO (1906), vol. 2, 1213; TsGIA SSSR f. 408, op. 1 (1906), d. 38, ll. 298–99. The Rittikh commission materials are in ibid., ll. 53–367. The project and explanatory note are in TsGIA SSSR f. 1291, op. 122 (1907), d. 72, ll. 280–333. The project was reprinted in part in *Novoe Vremia*, nos. 10865–10868, 14–17 June 1906; and in *Izvestiia GUZiZ*, nos. 24–25, 18 and 25 June 1906. All citations will be to the bound archival copy preserved in the library of the Hoover Institution, Stanford, California: *Ob"iasnitel'naia zapiska k proektu polozheniia ob uluchshenii i rasshirenii krest'ianskago zemlevladeniia*. The project was subsequently replaced by the GUZiZ's Statute on Land-Organization, which was submitted on 15 March 1907 to the Second Duma, which ignored it. GDSO (1907), vol. 1, 537; and to the Third Duma on 16 November 1907. GDSO (1907–8), vol. 1, 291. This eventually became the Statute of 29 May 1911.

22. *Ob"iasnitel'naia zapiska*, pp. 1–11.

23. Ibid., p. 10.

24. Ibid., pp. 10–17, 25, 27, 78.

25. Ibid., pp. 11, 13, 15, 19.

26. Ibid., pp. 41–42.

27. Ibid., pp. 53, 59.

28. Ibid., pp. 42–43.

29. Ibid., p. 43.

30. Ibid., pp. 43–45.

31. Ibid., pp. 45–46. The government figure was based on figures developed by the Kadet party's agrarian expert A. A. Manuilov in *Pozemel'nyi vopros v Rossii: malozemel'e, dopolnitel'nyi nadel i arenda* (Moscow, 1905).

32. *Ob"iasnitel'naia zapiska*, p. 47.

33. Ibid., pp. 49, 51, 53.

34. Ibid., p. 51.

35. Ibid., pp. 53, 55, 57. The existing norms were twelve desiatinas per soul.

36. Ibid., pp. 63, 65, 67. Rittikh, too, had apparently been forced to abandon his earlier support of free disposability.

37. Ibid., pp. 75, 79. Financial cost was a continual obstacle to reform. Compare the State Council's January and February discussions concerning the grant of loans by the Noble and Peasant Land Banks in *Otchet za 1905–1906*, pp. 206, 220; and Stolypin's 24 October 1907 speech to the conference of Permanent Members of provincial executive boards, where he acknowledged the lack of staff in *Trudy s"ezda nepremennykh chlenov*, p. 4.

38. Of course, the principal problem with the government's agrarian program both at this stage of the "constitutional autocracy's" development, as well as later, was that it really only met the demands of the Octobrist party, though the Kadets were already beginning to move closer to their position. Manning, *Crisis of the Old Order*, pp. 216–17.

39. Savich, *Novyi gosudarstsvennyi stroi*, pp. 157–62; IZO 1906:6, pp. 245–48; compare Sidel'nikov, *Agrarnaia reforma*, pp. 309–13, n. 69, for the only discussion of the three projects submitted in June to the First Duma. On negotiations to form a coalition cabinet see chapter 7, note 77.

40. Sidel'nikov, *Agrarnaia reforma*, pp. 84–89.

41. Compare Goremykin's 19 July 1906 memorandum on the Council of Ministers as an institution in TsGAOR f. 543, op. 1, d. 520, ll. 17–21. On the dissolution, see "Dnevnik A. A. Polovtsova," KA 4 (1923), pp. 114, 116–17; P. Kh.

Shvanebakh, "Zapiska Shvanebakha, iiun' 1906 g.," *Golos Minuvshogo,* 1923:2(11), pp. 39–42; "Perepiska N. A. Romanova i P. A. Stolypina," KA 5 (1924), p. 102; Bogdanovich, *Tri poslednikh samoderzhtsa,* p. 386; Maklakov, *First State Duma,* pp. 205–17; Miliukov, *Political Memoirs,* pp. 117–28; Chermenskii, *Burzhuaziia i tsarizm,* pp. 305–11; Startsev, *Russkaia burzhuaziia,* pp. 84–109; Zimmerman, "Kadets and the Duma," p. 134; Manning, *Crisis of the Old Order,* pp. 239–43 and 256–61. The ukase of 8 July 1906 is in PSZ 26 (1906), otd. 1 (SPB, 1909), no. 28103, p. 738; and Savich, *Novyi gosudarstvennyi stroi,* p. 168; Gurko, in particular, had great contempt for the Duma's attempts to deal with the agrarian question and, as he relates, sat there and laughed openly at all who spoke on this question. Gurko, *Features and Figures,* p. 480.

Notes to Chapter 9

1. P. A. Tverskoi, "K istoricheskim materialam o pokoinoi P. A. Stolypine," *Vestnik Evropy,* 1912:4, p. 186.
2. Gurko, *Features and Figures,* pp. 484–87.
3. Ibid., pp. 491–515; Miliukov, *Political Memoirs,* pp. 139–40; Miliukov, *Tri popytki,* pp. 61–87; Kizevetter, *Na rubezhe dvukh stoletii,* pp. 440–41; Iswolsky, *Memoirs,* pp. 199–218; Chermenskii, *Burzhuaziia i tsarizm,* pp. 311–37; V. A. Maklakov, *Vtoraia gosudarstvennaia duma (Vospominaniia sovremennika)* (Paris, n.d.), pp. 5–17, 42–54; Startsev, *Russkaia burzhuaziia,* pp. 109–30; Manning, *Crisis of the Old Order,* pp. 260–92.
4. Gurko, *Features and Figures,* pp. 491–96; A. I. Guchkov, "Iz vospominanii A. I. Guchkova," *Poslednie Novosti,* no. 5623, 16 August 1936; "Iz dnevnika Konstantina Romanova," KA 45 (1931), p. 126.
5. Gins and Shafranov, *Sel'skokhoziaistvennoe vedomstvo,* prilozhenie, p. 15; Gurko, *Features and Figures,* p. 494. Guchkov, "Iz vospominanii," no. 5623, notes that the position was first offered to N. N. Lvov.
6. On the opposition's hopes, Mililukov, *Political Memoirs,* pp. 129–34; Maklakov, *First State Duma,* pp. 218–32.
7. "Perepiska Romanova i Stolypina," KA 5 (1924), pp. 102–3; Bing, *Letters,* p. 213; Guchkov, "Iz vospominaniia," no. 5623.
8. Compare M. E. Jones, "The Uses and Abuses of Article 87: A Study of the Development of Russian Constitutionalism, 1906–1917" (Ph.D. diss., Syracuse, 1975).
9. The principal sources are Bok, *Vospominaniia;* A. S. Izgoev, *P. A. Stolypin: Ocherk zhizni i deiatel'nosti* (Moscow, 1912); N. Savickij (Savitskii), "P. A. Stolypin," *Le monde slave* (November 1933), pp. 227–63, (December 1933), pp. 360–83, (December 1934), pp. 378–403, (April 1935), pp. 41–61, and (March 1936), pp. 341–81; A. P. Stolypin, *P. A. Stolypin, 1862–1911* (Paris, 1927); A. Stolypine (Stolypina), *L'homme du dernier tsar Stolypine: Souvenirs* (Paris, 1931); Zenkovskii, *Pravda o Stolypine;* L. M. Kliachko (L'vov), *Povesti proshlogo: Vremenshchiki konstitutsii: Dva prem'era: Evreiskoe schast'e* (Leningrad, 1929), pp. 25–39; I. F. Koshko, *Vospominaniia gubernatora (1905–1914 g.) Novgorod, Samara, Penza* (Petrograd, 1916), pp. 34, 39–44; F. A. Golovin, "Zapiski F. A. Golovin: P. A. Stolypin," KA 19 (1926), pp. 128–49; S. Syromatnikov, "Reminiscences of Stolypin," *Russian Review,* 1:2 (1912), 71–88; A. S. Izgoev, "P. A. Stolypin," *Russkaia Mysl',* 1907:12, pt. 2, pp. 129–52; Ia. Vechev, "Dela i dni. Ministerskaia kar'era P. A. Stolypina," *Sovremennik,* 1911:9, pp. 300–22; Tverskoi, "K istoricheskim materialam," pp. 183–201; Kryzhanovskii, *Vospominaniia,* especially pp. 209–21; A. V. Obolenskii, *Moi vospominaniia i razmyshleniia*

(Brussels, 1961), pp. 78–81; A. Meiendorf, "A Brief Appreciation of P. Stolypin's Tenure of Office" (unpub. ms., RACU); Troitskii, "Vospominaniia," pt. 2, pp. 1–34; Pares, *My Russian Memoirs*, esp. pp. 108–10; 120–29, 144–45, 175–76, 208–26. The major Western studies are Conroy, *Peter Arkad'evich Stolypin*, and G. Tokmakoff, *P. A. Stolypin and the Third Duma: An Appraisal of the Three Major Issues* (Washington, 1981).

10. Izgoev, *P. A. Stolypin*, pp. 5–12; Stolypin, *P. A. Stolypin*, pp. 5–6; Bok, *Vospominaniia*, 19–30; Savickij, "P. A. Stolypin," pp. 228–32.

11. Izgoev, *P. A. Stolypin*, pp. 7–20; Savickij, "P. A. Stolypin," pp. 229–33; Bok, *Vospominaniia*, pp. 31–38, 43–51, 78–79; Stolypin, *P. A. Stolypin*, p. 13; Savickij, "P. A. Stolypin," pp. 230–31. Obolenskii, *Moi vospominaniia*, pp. 78, 81; Syromatnikov, "Reminiscences," pp. 81–82; and I. S. Vasil'chikov, "Moe naznachenie gubernskim predvoditelem dvorianstva Kovenskoi gubernii" (unpub. ms., RACU), p. 3, concerning a project for the establishment of an agricultural school. Stolypin's cousin, the writer and positivist Dmitrii Arkad'evich, wrote widely on agriculture and the philosophy of science beginning in the 1870s and had early parceled up his properties in Tauride and Saratov provinces into small, individual peasant holdings—though unfortunately without success. On D. A. Stolypin see S. D. Sheremetev, *Dmitrii Arkad'evich Stolypin* (SPB, 1899).

12. Tverskoi, "K istoricheskim materialam," p. 186; Savickij, "P. A. Stolypin," pp. 228–31; Izgoev, *P. A. Stolypin*, pp. 12–14.

13. Vechev, "Dela i dni," p. 302; Izgoev, *P. A. Stolypin*, pp. 14–16; "Dopros Kryzhanovskogo," pp. 378–80; and Gessen, "Zakon 22 marta 1904," cols. 1007–9.

14. He was also the brother-in-law of the diplomat and future foreign minister S. D. Sazonov.

15. *Trudy mestnykh komitetov o nuzhdakh sel'skokhoziaistvennoi promyshlennosti*, vol. 11, *Grodenskaia guberniia* (SPB, 1903), 1, 32, 76; Bok, *Vospominaniia*, pp. 204–5. Nor was he alone. Compare Fisher, "Witte Conference," pp. 328–34.

16. *Trudy*, vol. 11, 32.

17. Bok, *Vospominaniia*, pp. 43–44.

18. *Trudy*, vol. 11, 1, 76.

19. "Vsepoddanneishii otchet saratovskogo gubernatora P. Stolypina za 1904 god," KA 17 (1926), p. 84. Versions of this quotation reappeared repeatedly in both his speeches and government documents in the post-1906 period. On Stolypin's Saratov period, Izgoev, *P. A. Stolypin*, pp. 20–24; Savickij, "P. A. Stolypin," pp. 234–52; and Bok, *Vospominaniia*, pp. 109–56.

20. "Vsepoddanneishii otchet," KA 17 (1926), pp. 84–85. These ideas caught the Tsar's attention. Ibid., p. 81.

21. Karpov, *Agrarnaia politika*, p. 173.

22. Ibid., pp. 172–73.

23. "Doklad MVD P. N. Durnovo Nikolaiu II ob otvetakh gubernatorov na zapros MVD otnositel'no prichin krest'ianskikh volnenii," in *Vtoroi period revoliutsii*, pt. 1, book 1, p. 97.

24. Ibid., p. 98.

25. Vechev, "Dela i dni," pp. 313, 302. On his assignment to St. Petersburg, see Bok, *Vospominaniia*, p. 157; V. A. Maevskii, *Borets za blago Rossii (K stoletiiu so dnia rozhdeniia)* (Madrid, 1962), p. 14; Gurko, *Features and Figures*, p. 461; A. Eropkin, *P. A. Stolypin i ukaz 9 Noiabria* (SPB, 1912), p. 2; and A. A. Oznobishin, *Vospominaniia chlena IV-i gosudarstvennoi dumy* (Paris, 1927), pp. 177–78, who quotes a letter to him from Stolypin that includes the phrase " . . . my whole life belongs to the *gosudariu* [tsar]." Oznobishin served under Stolypin in the western provinces.

26. *Nachalo pervoi russkoi revoliutsii*, pp. 747–48.

27. *Revoliutsiia 1905 goda i samoderzhavie*, pp. 99–103. For the opposition's account, Zheltagorskii, "Balashovskii geroi (P. A. Stolypin)," in *Sbornik "Izvestii krest'ianskikh deputatov" i "Trudovoi Rossii": Sbornik "Trudovoi gruppy" 2-i gosudarstvennoi dumy* (Moscow, 1906), pp. 107–8.

28. Izgoev, *P. A. Stolypin*, pp. 24–25; Savickij, "P. A. Stolypin," pp. 252–53; Bok, *Vospominaniia*, p. 144.

29. "Doklad Durnovo," p. 98.

30. Karpov, *Agrarnaia politika*, pp. 173–74. Compare Liubimov, "Russkaia smuta," p. 297; Gurko, *Nashe gosudarstvennoe i narodnoe khoziaistvo*, pp. 42–44; Tverskoi, "K istoricheskim materialam," p. 188.

31. "Doklad Durnovo," p. 98.

32. Bing, *Letters*, p. 220. Gurko has a different account: *Features and Figures*, pp. 460–61. Gurko has been quoted as saying that Stolypin had the reputation of a "fool [*durak*]." Bogdanovich, *Tri poslednikh samoderzhtsa*, p. 382.

33. The latest version is A. Solzhenitsyn, *Krasnoe Koleso: Avgust Chetyrnadsatogo*, Uzel 1, vol. 2 (Paris, 1983), chapters 63–74, esp. chapter 65.

34. Zenkovskii, *Pravda o Stolypine*.

35. Gurko, *Features and Figures*, pp. 462–63, 474–78.

36. "Programma voprosov, vnosimykh na razsmotrenie gosudarstvennoi dumy" (Witte Archive, RACU); and TsGIA SSSR f. 408, op. 1 (1906), d. 38.

37. In addition to works already cited, on Stolypin's ministry see A. Ia. Avrekh, *Stolypin i tret'iia Duma* (Moscow, 1968).

38. Bok, *Vospominaniia*, pp. 125, 128, 149; N. Semenov-T'ian-Shanskii, "Svetloi pamiati Petra Arkad'evicha Stolypina," *Vozrozhdeniia*, 1961:118, p. 81. Compare Guchkov, *Poslednie Novosti*, no. 5619, 12 August 1936, concerning Stolypin's relationship with N. N. L'vov, which originated in Saratov. Solov'ev, *Samoderzhavie i dvorianstvo v 1902–1907*, p. 226.

39. PSZ 26 (1906), otd. 1 (SPB, 1909), no. 28105, pp. 738–39; Kalinychev, *Gosudarstvennaia duma*, pp. 182–83; Savich, *Novyi gosudarstvennyi stroi*, pp. 168–69.

40. Bing, *Letters*, p. 213; "Perepiska Romanova i Stolypina," KA 5 (1924), pp. 102–3; Guchkov, *Poslednie Novosti*, no. 5623, 6 August 1936; Manning, *Crisis of the Old Order*, pp. 280–81 points to the important role of the United Nobility in dissuading the tsar from forming a coalition with members of the moderate parties.

41. "Iz dnevnika Konstantina Romanova," KA 45 (1931), p. 126; Gurko *Features and Figures*, p. 496; compare Izgoev, *P. A. Stolypin*, p. 37; and M. M. Kovalevskii, "P. A. Stolypin i ob"edinennoe dvorianstvo," *Vestnik Evropy*, 1913:10, pp. 406–23.

42. *Novoe Vremia*, no. 10896, 15 July 1906, p. 3.

43. Guchkov, *Poslednie Novosti*, no. 5623, 16 August 1936.

44. Ibid., no. 5633, 26 August 1936, p. 2:6.

45. Manning, *Crisis of the Old Order*, pp. 279–80.

46. Gurko, *Features and Figures*, pp. 500, 638, n. 7; Witte, *Vospominaniia*, vol. 2, 320–21; Prince I. S. Vasil'chikov, "Predki-Vasil'chikovy" (unpub. ms., RACU), p. 11. Vasil'chikov, like Sviatopolk-Mirskii, had apparently resigned as governor of Pskov Province because of his disagreements with Pleve.

47. Shchegolev, *Padenie*, vol. 7, 314.

48. *Svod za 1900*, p. 81.

49. See his speech to the agricultural ministry in *Novoe Vremia*, no. 10915, 3 August 1906, pp. 3–4.

50. See the report on his speech in *Novoe Vremia*, no. 10914, 2 August 1906, p. 4.

51. *Novoe Vremia*, no. 10915, 3 August 1906, pp. 3–4.

52. "Beseda s Kn. B. A. Vasil'chikov," *Novoe Vremia*, no. 10917, 5 August 1906, p. 3.

53. On the later conflict, see *TsGIA SSSR* f. 1276, op. 20 (1906), d. 4, ll. 64–68.

54. *Novoe Vremia*, no. 10917, 5 August 1906, p. 3.

55. Ibid. Gurko, *Nashe gosudarstvennoe i narodnoe khoziaistvo*, pp. 31–41 and 114–55. On these conflicts between Finance on the one hand and Interior and agriculture on the other, see G. L. Yaney, "Some Aspects of the Imperial Russian Government on the Eve of the First World War," SEER 43:100 (1964), 68–90; Krivoshein, *A. V. Krivoshein*, pp. 163–93; Gins and Shafranov, *Sel'skokhoziaistvennoe vedomstvo*, p. 397.

56. "Perepiska Romanova i Stolypina," KA 5 (1924), p. 104; and similar remarks in Bing, *Letters*, pp. 219–21.

57. P. G. Kurlov, *Gibel' imperatorskoi Rossii* (Berlin, 1923), pp. 67–68; Gurko, *Features and Figures*, pp. 497–98; Iswolsky, *Memoirs*, pp. 219–31; Oldenburg, *Last Tsar*, vol. 2, p. 217; *Dnevnik Imperatora Nikolaia II*, p. 251.

58. IZO 1906:7–8, p. 281. In addition to works already cited, on the 3 June system see A. Ia. Avrekh, *Tsarizm i tret'eiiun'skaia sistema* (Moscow, 1966); and Avrekh *Raspad tret'eiiun'skoi systemy* (Moscow, 1985).

59. IZO 1906:7–8, p. 281. Compare Stolypin's telegram to the provincial governors. *Pravo*, no. 28, 16 July 1906, col. 2373.

60. IZO 1906:7–8, p. 282.

61. Bogdanovich, *Tri poslednikh samoderzhtsa*, p. 387.

62. IZO 1906:7–8, p. 282.

63. Ibid., pp. 282–83. Compare "Dnevnik A. A. Polovtsova," KA 4 (1923), pp. 118–19.

64. The 12 August command is in Savich, *Novyi gosudarstvennyi stroi*, pp. 195–96; Sidel'nikov, *Agrarnaia reforma*, pp. 90–91. The regulations governing the transfer of these lands to the Peasant Land Bank are in Volkov, *Sbornik Polozhenii*, pp. 598–603. On government agrarian policy during this final period see Krivoshein, *A. V. Krivoshein*, pp. 71–77; Gurko, *Features and Figures*, pp. 499–503; Iswolsky, *Memoirs*, pp. 230–38; Kokovtsov, *Iz moego proshlago*, vol. 1, 224–29; Dubrovskii, *Stolypinskaia zemel'naia reforma*, pp. 121–29; Savickij, "P. A. Stolypin," pp. 366–74.

65. "Iz dnevnika Konstantina Romanova," KA 45 (1931), p. 126.

66. Ibid., p. 129; Grand Prince Nikolai Mikhailovich's letter in KA 15 (1926), p. 215; and Bogdanovich, *Tri poslednykh samoderzhtsa*, pp. 387–88.

67. PSZ 26 (1906), otd. 1 (SPB, 1909), no. 28315, pp. 846–47; Savich, *Novyi gosudarstvennyi stroi*, pp. 193–95; "Osobyi zhurnal soveta ministrov," 22 August 1906.

68. PSZ 26 (1906), otd. 1 (SPB, 1909), no. 28357, pp. 864–65; Savich, *Novyi gosudarstvennyi stroi*, pp. 196–97; "Osobyi zhurnal soveta ministrov," 1 September 1906. By a law of 9 May 1911 unsettled *kabinet* lands in the Altai region were transferred into the category of state property—with compensation to the *kabinet* at the rate of 22k. per desiatina per year for nine years—and placed at the disposal of the GUZiZ for settlement of migrants from European Russia. IZO 1911:8, p. 347.

69. PSZ 26 (1906) otd. 1 (SPB, 1909), no. 28474, pp. 931–32; Savich *Novyi gosudarstvennyi stroi*, pp. 198–200. Such was the end of those privileges so painfully won from the Conference on the Nobility at the end of the last century.

70. PSZ 26 (1906), otd. 1 (SPB, 1909), no. 28416, pp. 901–3; Savich *Novyi gosudarstvennyi stroi*, pp. 231–32; "Osobyi zhurnal soveta ministrov," 10 October 1906.

71. TsGIA f. 1291, op. 122 (1907), d. 72, ll. 420–31. Chaired by Pokrovskii, it included representatives from a variety of concerned departments including Krivoshein and Glinka from the GUZiZ; Gurko, Litvinov, and Zubovskii from the Interior Ministry; and from the Finance Ministry, Sosnovskii, now acting head of the Peasant Bank; Vishniakov, head of the Department of Direct Taxation; and two other Peasant Bank representatives.

72. PSZ 26 (1906), otd. 1 (SPB, 1909), no. 28547, pp. 980–82; Savich, *Novyi gosudarstvennyi stroi*, pp. 232–38. Curiously, when the Council of Ministers discussed this ukase, only Vasil'chikov defended the economic value of such loans. Stolypin, on the other hand, joined Kokovtsov and the other eight ministers to defend the Bank's fiscal integrity. "Osobyi zhurnal," 17 October 1906, p. 20. Later Stolypin would support the transfer of the Peasant Bank to the GUZiZ. Krivoshein, *A. V. Krivoshein*, p. 166; "Osobyi zhurnal," 28 September 1910.

73. See Article 54 of the Peasant Land Bank Charter in Volkov, *Sbornik Polozhenii*, pp. 604–5. When peasants purchased land directly from private landowners with the aid of a Bank loan, loans up to 90 percent of the land's value were available; if to be organized as an *otrub*, up to 95 percent; and if as a *khutor*, to the full 100 percent. Loans to communes for improving land use were available up to 85 percent of the cost and 90 percent when forming *khutora*. Otherwise limits were set at 80 percent. See the appendix to Article 97, note 2, *po prod.* 1908, to the Bank's Charter in ibid., pp. 689–91.

74. Fewer than ten thousand loans were granted under this law and its 5 July 1912 version, an average of about one thousand a year, averaging one thousand rubles each. Sidel'nikov, *Agrarnaia Reforma*, p. 170.

75. Ibid., pp. 93, 170–78; Dubrovskii, *Stolypinskaia zemel'naia reforma*, pp. 316–27.

76. Gurko, *Features and Figures*, p. 495.

77. TsGIA SSSR f. 1291, op. 122 (1906), d. 46, pt. 2, l. 2; Gurko, *Features and Figures*, pp. 500–502; Kryzhanovskii, *Vospominaniia*, pp. 93–94; Izgoev, *P. A. Stolypin*, p. 53; Troitskii, "Iz vospominanii," pt. 1, p. 4; pt. 2, pp. 23–26. The members of this commission included Rittikh and Glinka from the GUZiZ; Pokrovskii, Vishniakov, and Sosnovskii from the Finance Ministry; Chaplin, head of the Ministry of Justice's Surveying Section; Baron M. E. Nol'de, head of the Chancellery of the Ministry of Trade and Industry. G. B. Korob'in of the tsar's Chancellery, A. P. Talantov of the Ministry of Education, and E. N. Volkov of the Land Section of the tsar's *Kabinet* in the Ministry of. the Imperial Court were also members though they seldom attended. Lykoshin joined the conference on 14 September in its third and final stage; Krivoshein became a member only after it had finished most of its work at the end of September. Apparently, Pestrzhetskiǐ also participated in the commission's deliberations. TsGIA SSSR f. 1291 (1906), op. 122, d. 46, pt. 2, ll. 3, 6–8, 94, 107. The commission's name was changed according to the project it worked on.

78. Gurko, *Features and Figures*, pp. 159, 176–77, 499–502; Kokovtsov, *Out of My Past*, p. 161; Troitskii, "Iz vospominanii," pt. 1, p. 4.

79. *Novoe Vremia* no. 10918, 6 August 1906, p. 3, and no. 10925, 13 August 1906, p. 4.

80. Migulin, "Russkaia agrarnaia problema," pp. 210–12.

81. TsGIA SSSR f. 1291, op. 122 (1906), d. 46, pt. 2, ll. 17–18.

82. Gurko, *Features and Figures*, p. 499.

83. Manning, *Crisis of the Old Order*, pp. 286–88.

84. Migulin, "Russkaia agrarnaia problema," pp. 212–13.

85. In May 1907 a proposal that would provide special terms for *darstvenniki* to purchase land from the Peasant Bank was drafted though it was never submitted to the Duma. TsGIA SSSR f. 1291, op. 122 (1907), d. 72, ll. 412–19; compare O. N. Burdina, "Istochnikovedcheskie voprosy izucheniia sud'by darstvennikov v Rossii," in *Istochnikovedenie otechestvennoi istorii: Sbornik statei: 1979* (Moscow, 1980), pp. 177–91. Two factors seem to be responsible for its later abandonment: first, an unwillingness to enact a statute specifically devoted to "land-hungry" peasants; and second, a desire, similar to that expressed by the Nikol'skii Commission in March, to adopt legislation that could be applied to the peasant *soslovie* as a unified agricultural class. Fiscal limitations were also a factor: f. 1291, op. 122 (1907), d. 72, ll. 233–34 ob. Compare *Darstvennoe nadel'noe zemlevladenie krest'ian po obsledovaniiu 1907* (SPB, 1908).

86. Volkov, *Sbornik Polozhenii*, pp. 429–535; see, too, the joint Interior Ministry and GUZiZ Circular, no. 36, 14 June 1906 in IZO 1906:6, pp. 260–63. Hennessy, *Agrarian Question*, pp. 122–32; Yaney, *Urge to Mobilize*, pp. 267–72.

87. Compare S. Sternheimer, "Administering Development and Developing Administration: Organizational Conflict in Tsarist Bureaucracy, 1906–1914," CASS 9:3 (1975), pp. 277–301.

88. Manning, *Crisis of the Old Order*, pp. 177–202.

89. Volkov, *Sbornik polozhenii*, pp. 429–32.

90. Ibid., pp. 432–81.

91. The Bank's Temporary Instructions of 20 June 1907 emphasized that the goal was to form viable holdings. Each purchaser had to make a down payment in cash in order to discourage any impression that the land was free. Ibid., pp. 437–38. See, too, P. A. Stolypin, *Poezdka v Sibir' i Povolzh'e* in V(erpakhovskii), *Gosudarstvennaia deiatel'nost'*, vol. 1, 341, where the importance of this measure in combating ideas of compulsory expropriation is emphasized. Deposits were later set at 10 percent for communal and 5 percent for individual purchasers. The requirement was waived if the purchaser formed a *khutor*. To prevent peasants from accumulating surplus land, when the total of allotment and the purchased land exceeded the norm for the area, the surplus had to be sold within three years. Volkov, *Sbornik polozheniie*, p. 635.

92. Ibid., pp. 439, 475. On 12 March 1907, the GUZiZ granted landless peasants, including landless wage laborers, the right to purchase Bank land if the local land-organization commissions considered them capable of forming a stable economy even if they had no inventory. In practice, lower ranks from the Manchurian reserves were given precedence over even land-hungry peasants. Wherever possible Bank land was to be offered to local peasants first. Ibid., p. 440. Limits were placed on the quantity of Bank land that could be purchased. Ibid., pp. 665–77. They were lowered considerably by the Temporary Instructions of 19 February 1908. Ibid., pp. 639–52.

93. Ibid., pp. 442–44, 477–82. On 28 February 1907, the GUZiZ instructed the local commissions to encourage the following categories to migrate: *darstvenniki* and landless wage laborers unable to earn enough to ensure their day-to-day existence; individuals, associations, and whole communities whose departure would lead to a major improvement in the welfare and forms of land use of those who remained in the locality; and lower ranks who had fought in the Russo-Japanese War.

94. A. A. Kofod, *Khutorskoe rasselenie* (SPB, 1907). See Vasil'chikov's letter of 3 October 1906 to Stolypin concerning funds for "the publication of books and brochures establishing the correct view on the agrarian question and explaining

the essence of the government's decrees in the area of this question . . ." in Drezen, ed., *Tsarizm v bor'be s revoliutsiei*, pp. 127–28. See, too, "Sbornik retsenzii populiarnykh izdanii po sel'skomu khoziaistvu," *Trudy VEO*, 1912, vol. 2, kniga 5–6, pp. 1–52 and 1913, kniga 1, pp. 53–115, which lists some 134 items published between 1906 and 1912. There was, in addition, a flowering of agriculturally oriented newspapers both governmental and nongovernmental. Volkov, *Sbornik polozhenii*, pp. 482–90. Ibid., pp. 490–93, deals with procedures to be adopted when nonpeasant lands were involved. The partition of communal lands with the goal of transferring to multifield systems of crop rotation was subsequently eliminated from the concerns of local land-organization commissions. V. F. Safronov and A. A. Znosko-Borovskii, comps., *Kratkii ocherk deiatel'nosti zemleustroitel'nykh uchrezhdenii za pervoe desiatiletie, 1906–1916*, (n.p., n.d.), p. 20.

95. Volkov, *Sbornik polozhenii*, pp. 485–90. On procedures for communes holding land in individual tenure, ibid., p. 488.

96. Compare the Temporary Regulations of 19 March 1909 concerning the land reorganization of whole communities. Ibid., pp. 525–33.

97. Compare Terner's comment on land captains in *Vospominaniia*, vol. 2, p. 191. Aware of the problem, the Interior Ministry set up inspection procedures beginning 23 January 1908. IZO 1908:2, pp. 100–102. In February 1909, the GUZiZ established an inspectorate headed by A. A. Kofod. *Izvestiia GUZiZ*, no. 8, 22 February 1909, p. 157. The government also organized local and central conferences to educate local officials, raise admission standards, improve training, and establish incentives.

98. Stolypin, *Poezdka*, pp. 350–52.

99. Volkov, *Sbornik polozhenii*, pp. 490–93, 506–9.

100. For example, IZO 1909:1, pp. 17–19, 1909:3, p. 89, 1910:8, pp. 339–40, 348; Volkov, *Sbornik polozhenii*, pp. 512–14, 575–78.

101. Ibid., pp. 493–500, 653; Savich, *Novyi gosudarstvennyi stroi*, p. 39. On 10 January 1907, the Interior Ministry changed the election procedure for the three peasant members to ensure that the different agricultural zones of each county were represented. Volkov, *Sbornik polozhenii*, p. 494.

102. PSZ 26 (1906), otd. 1 (SPB, 1909), no. 28392, pp. 891–93; Savich, *Novyi gosudarstvennyi stroi*, pp. 174–82; "Osobyi zhurnal," 9 and 12 September 1906; Sidel'nikov, *Agrarnaia reforma*, pp. 95–99.

103. Compare L. G. Zakharova, *Zemskaia kontrreforma 1890 g.* (Moscow, 1968), pp. 91–165.

104. "Osobyi zhurnal," 9 and 12 September 1906, p. 2; Sidel'nikov, *Agrarnaia reforma*, p. 98; Volkov, *Sbornik polozhenii*, p. 98; Savich, *Novyi gosudarstvennyi stroi*, p. 174.

105. Sidel'nikov, *Agrarnaia reforma*, p. 96.

106. TsGIA SSSR f. 1291, op. 122 (1906), d. 46, pt. 2, l. 67 ob.; "Osobyi zhurnal," 9 and 12 September 1906, p. 2; Savich, *Novyi gosudarstvennyi stroi*, p. 175.

107. "Osobyi zhurnal," 10 October 1906, pp. 6–11.

108. Manning, *Crisis of the Old Order*, p. 288.

109. *Trudy vtorago s"ezda upolnomochennykh dvorianskikh obshchestv 31 gubernii 14–18 noiabria 1906* (SPB, 1906), esp. pp. 82–109. During the very first session, Prince A. P. Urusov and M. N. Golovin opposed the Congress's openly approving Stolypin's agrarian program. Ibid., p. 5. Meanwhile, Pestrzhetskii had reappeared in print with a series of articles entitled "O malozemel'e, kak prichine ekonomicheskago upadka zemledel'cheskago naseleniia," *Novoe Vremia*, nos. 10877, 10879, 10887, 26, 28 June and 6 July 1906, p. 2, p. 3, and p. 3, respectively, in which he again attacked the argument that blamed the agrarian problem on land-hunger.

110. PSZ 26 (1906), otd. 1, (SPB, 1909), no. 28528, pp. 970–74; Savich, *Novyi gosudarstvennyi stroi*, pp. 200–16; Volkov, *Sbornik Polozhenii*, pp. 348–428; and Sidel'nikov, *Agrarnaia reforma*, pp. 99–105. The explanatory note is also in TsGIA SSSR f. 1291, op. 122 (1906), d. 46, pt. 2; "Osobyi zhurnal," 10 October 1906. For a discussion of this law, see Dubrovskii, *Stolypinskaia zemel'naia reforma*, pp. 130–62; Leontovitsch, *Geschichte des Liberalismus*, pp. 213–31; Leont'ev, *Krest'ianskoe pravo*, 1st ed., pp. 272–309; 2d ed., pp. 269–95; Khauke, *Krest'ianskoe zemel'noe pravo*; Yaney, *Urge to Mobilize*, pp. 257–65 and 144–56.

111. Sidel'nikov, *Agrarnaia reforma*, p. 100.

112. Despite their relative moderation, these provisions of the 9 November ukase aroused much controversy during 1907 and 1908, accumulating some sixty interpolations and interpretations. Volkov, *Sbornik polozhenii*, pp. 352–61. In anticipation of this, the Interior Ministry's explanatory note to the Council of Ministers devoted some fourteen closely printed pages—mostly repeating discussions held back in March—to justifying them. Ibid., pp. 391–404. The Law of 14 June 1910 is in PSZ 30 (1910), otd. 1 (SPB, 1913), no. 33743, pp. 746–53. It is reprinted in Sidel'nikov, *Agrarnaia reforma*, pp. 112–23; and *Zakon 14 iiunia 1910 g. ob izmenenii i dopolnenii nekotorykh postanovlenii o krest'ianskom zemlevladenii* (SPB, 1911), pp. 1272–86. According to Article 1 of this law, all communities that held land in communal tenure and in which there had been no general repartition since the time of the initial allotment of land when that had occurred before 1 January 1887 were recognized as having transferred to individual ownership. Thus, for those communities the initial process of claiming title provided for in the ukase of 9 November was no longer required. Sidel'nikov, *Agrarnaia reforma*, pp. 112–13. See, too, IZO 1911:4, pp. 189–91, which contains an article explaining how Articles 1 through 8 were to be applied. Early versions of this law are in GDSO (1909–10) session 2, vol. 4, cols. 919–34, and appendix, vol. 2, no. 241; and Sidel'nikov, *Agrarnaia reforma*, pp. 105–12. Stolypin considered his ministry's version too radical and opposed the use of legislative coercion and the introduction of an automatically effective "twenty-four-year" article similar to the one proposed in June 1906 by Gurko: GSSO V, cols. 1138–1140. The final version was considerably modified under government pressure in the interests of avoiding force. Compare Shidlovskii, *Vospominaniia*, pt. 1, pp. 179–84; and Sidel'nikov, *Agrarnaia reforma*, pp. 316–17, n. 99; "Osobyi zhurnal," 28 October 1908.

113. Sidel'nikov, *Agrarnaia reforma*, pp. 100–101.

114. Volkov, *Sbornik polozhenii*, pp. 101–2.

115. "Osobyi zhurnal," 10 October 1906, p. 18.

116. There is no evidence to indicate that such was the government's intent. According to Dubrovskii, *Stolypinskaia zemel'naia reforma*, p. 212, only 26.6 percent of all title claims were by mutual consent. Compare ibid., pp. 175–82.

117. Sidel'nikov, *Agrarnaia reforma*, pp. 102–3; Volkov, *Sbornik polozhenii*, pp. 373–74, 392–406, and 410–15, where the "paramount state importance" of these articles is emphasized.

118. Sidel'nikov, *Agrarnaia reforma*, pp. 103–4.

119. Sidel'nikov, *Agrarnaia reforma*, p. 104; Volkov, *Sbornik polozhenii*, pp. 421–26.

120. Gurko, *Features and Figures*, p. 501. Compare Stolypin's speeches to the State Council on 15 and 26 March 1910, in GSSO V, cols. 1136–1145 and 1601–1607. Compare, too, Leontovitsch, *Geschichte des Liberalismus*, pp. 217–29; Dubrovskii, *Stolypinskaia zemel'naia reforma*, pp. 153–62.

121. Sidel'nikov, *Agrarnaia reforma*, p. 105; Volkov, *Sbornik polozhenii*, pp. 426–27.

122. D. A. J. Macey, "The Stolypin Land Reform: Its Formation and Develop-

ment" (unpub. ms., 1971); compare Yaney, "Imperial Russian Government," pp. 146–268; and Yaney, *Urge to Mobilize*, pp. 161–94, 274–400.

123. According to the Fundamental Laws, measures adopted under Article 87 had subsequently to be submitted for approval by both the Duma and the State Council. However, the Second Duma, which met for the first time on 20 February 1907, had been elected on essentially the same basis as the First. As a result, neither its composition nor its agrarian program had changed. Yet, although Stolypin instructed Kryzhanovskii to draft a new electoral law, even before the Second Duma had begun to meet, he had not completely given up hope for this Duma session: "Perepiska Romanova i Stolypina," KA 5 (1924), pp. 108–14; Kryzhanovskii, *Vospominaniia*, pp. 107–9; Kokovtsov, *Iz moego proshlago*, vol. 1, 232–35; Shvanebakh, "Zapiska sanovnika," p. 120; Heilbronner, "Piotr Khristianovich von Schwanebach," pp. 31–55; Kryzhanovskii in Shchegolev, *Padenie tsarskogo rezhima*, vol. 5, pp. 416–23; Chermenskii, *Burzhuaziia i tsarizm*, pp. 399–416; Hosking, *Russian Constitutional Experiment*, pp. 14–55; A. Levin, *The Second Duma: A Study of the Social-Democratic Party and the Russian Constitutional Experiment*, 2d ed. (Hamden, Conn., 1966), pp. 307–49; Levin, *The Third Duma, Election and Profile* (Hamden, Conn., 1973); Maklakov, *Vtoraia gosudarstvennaia duma*, pp. 224–48; Zimmerman, "The Kadets and the Duma," pp. 119–28; Manning, *Crisis of the Old Regime*, pp. 293–321. The Second Duma formed its agrarian commission on 26 March 1907. Its chairman was none other than Kutler. On 13 April the government presented the ukase of 9 November to the Duma. On 14 April a special subcommission consisting of eleven members formed to discuss it. The subcommission began meeting on 3 May and held a total of nine sessions: GDSO (1907), 1, 1754; GDSO (1907), *Obzor deiatel'nosti komissii i otdelov* (SPB, 1907), pp. 69–87 and 453–98; Levin, *Second Duma*, pp. 156–99; and Manning, *Crisis of the Old Order*, pp. 317–18. During its eighth session, at the end of May, and after some disagreement, it rejected the ukase and called on the government to terminate all attempts to implement it: *Obzor deiatel'nosti*, p. 78, 463–70. Meanwhile not only had the full agrarian commission just voted in favor of a compulsory expropriation of private lands (ibid., pp. 73–74), but the Duma's general assembly had been spending most of its time discussing projects that involved greater or lesser assaults on the inviolability of the nobility's private-property rights. Compare Levin, *Second Duma*, pp. 166–92; Chermenskii, *Burzhuaziia i tsarizm*, pp. 384–99. Thus, it became clear, the Second Duma, like the First, could not survive, and it was dissolved on 3 June 1907. Simultaneously, a new Electoral Law designed to increase the representation of the landowning nobility while reducing that of the peasantry, was published: PSZ 26 (1907), otd. 1 (SPB, 1910), no. 29242, pp. 321–35. See V. V. Vorovskii, *Sochineniia*, vol. 3 (Moscow, 1933), 286–91; S. N. Harper, *The New Electoral Law for the Russian Duma* (Chicago, 1908); M. Szeftel, "The Reform of the Electoral Law to the State Duma on June 3, 1907: A New Basis for the Formation of the Russian Parliament," in *Liber Memorialis Georges de Lagarde: Studies presented to the International Commission for the History of Representative and Parliamentary Institutions*, 38, London, 1969. (Louvain/Paris, 1970), pp. 326–45; Levin, *Third Duma*; L. H. Haimson, "Introduction: The Landed Nobility," in Haimson, *Politics of Rural Russia*, pp. 9–24; Edelman, *Gentry Politics*, pp. 30–49. The tsar's manifesto explaining the dissolution avoided any mention of the agrarian question: PSZ 27 (1907), otd. 1 (SPB, 1910), no. 29240, pp. 319–20. However, in a note dated 31 March 1907 to Stolypin, Nicholas noted the extremism of the speeches on the agrarian question, their publication and distribution across the country, and the danger that they represented "for the calm of the countryside." "Perepiska Romanova i Stolypina," KA 5 (1942), p. 110. Thus ended the government's brief

experiment in trying to constitute itself as a *muzhik*-state, based on a supposedly conservative peasantry. However, as we have already shown, this did not mean that the Stolypin government intended to create a new social and political order based on a wager on the "strong and sober" peasant. Nor did the revised electoral law make any special provisions for these so-called Stolypin peasants, continuing to group them with other peasants as a separate *soslovie:* Levin, *The Third Duma,* p. 81. On the contrary, the government pursued the path of compromise. In the tradition of *opeka* and a supraclass conception of government, it attempted to withdraw from the political fray in order to mediate between the conflicting claims of its various constituencies—in the *national* interest. At the same time, it sought to use the agencies of the bureaucracy and the electoral mechanism to create a new social basis for itself, consisting of the new agrarian constituency of noble and peasant agriculturalists, on the one hand, and the emergent and recently politicized bourgeoisie, on the other. This attempt to resolve the old problem of the government's relationship to its social basis was, however, no more successful than earlier ones.

Notes to Chapter 10

1. The phrase a "wager on the strong" was just one example of Stolypin's skillful use of propaganda. It was designed to appeal to the Octobrist party, his new-found ally and the linchpin of the 3 June system while it lasted. Indeed, they were far more zealous in their desire to place a wager on the strong than the government. S. G. Pushkarev, *Rossiia v XIX veke (1801–1914)* (New York, 1956), p. 425, n. 31; Kaufman, "Ukaz 9 noiabria 1906," pp. 158–59; and N. P. Oganovskii, "Pervye itogi 'velikoi reformy,' " p. 127. Even Gurko did not believe Stolypin's propaganda: Gurko, *Nashe gosudarstvennoe i narodnoe khoziaistvo,* pp. 63–64. Although Stolypin may have been a natural "poser" (Vechev, "Dela i dni," pp. 302 and 313), his "phrases" were written by I. Ia. Gurliand, a former professor of constitutional law, member of the Council of the Interior Ministry and of the State Council's right-wing faction, and from 1907 editor of the newspaper *Rossiia,* Mendeleev, "Svet i teni," book 2, p. 99.

2. In fact, the focus was on economic classes as defined by the division of labor. As Stolypin noted, one of his goals was the development of a "cult of labor" within the peasantry. Stolypin, *Poezdka,* p. 341.

3. IZO 1907:9, p. 383.

4. Ibid., p. 391.

5. *Zakon 14 iiunia 1910,* p. 14.

6. Yaney, "Imperial Russian Government," pp. 118–19.

7. Thus strips held as "personal" property would have to be relocated when an entire village transferred to *otruba* or *khutora.* IZO 1909:1, p. 15.

8. IZO 1907:9, pp. 383, 387–91.

9. "Osobyi zhurnal," 10 October 1906, p. 17.

10. Kofod, *Khutorskoe rasselenie,* pp. 8–11.

11. This will be the subject of a subsequent volume. Compare D. A. J. Macey, "Bureaucratic Solutions to the Peasant Problem: Before and After Stolypin," in *Russian and East European History: Selected Papers from the Second World Congress for Soviet and East European Studies,* ed. R. C. Elwood (Berkeley, 1984), pp. 73–95.

12. N. P. Oganovskii, "K peresmotru agrarnoi problemy," *Zavety,* 1912:5 (August), pp. 1–37; Oganovskii, *S nebes' na zemliiu; Sbornik statei* (Moscow, 1917), pp. 22–23; B. A. Brutskus, "K sovremennomu polozheniiu agrarnoi voprosa," in

Agrarnye voprosy v Rossii, vol. 1 (Petrograd, 1917), pp. 22–23; Lositskii, "Raspadenie obshchiny," p. 44; I. V. Chernyshev, "Pazsloenie sovremennoi derevni," Sovremennyi mir, 1908:6, pt. 2, pp. 68–69; B. Chernenkov, "Peremena fronta v bor'be s obshchinoi," Sovremennik, 1911:9, pp. 240–41.

13. See Krivoshein's speech of 10 November 1908 in GDSO (1908–9), vol. 1 col. 1036; and Rittikh's in ibid., col. 2484. Compare A. A. Kofod, Russkoe zemleustroistvo, 2d ed. (SPB, 1914), pp. 104–5.

14. For one of the first signs, see IZO 1908:6, pp. 294–96.

15. IZO 1909:1, p. 12. Compare S. M. Dubrovskii, Stolypinskaia reforma: Kapitalizatsiia sel'skogo khoziastva v XX veke (Leningrad, 1925), pp. 60–71; Dubrovskii, Stolypinskaia zemel'naia reforma, pp. 175–82. Yaney, Urge to Mobilize, pp. 186–92.

16. Kofod, Russkoe zemleustroistvo, pp. 60–69. See Krivoshein's 17 May 1911 speech to a conference on land reorganization in IZO 1911:5, pp. 220–22.

17. See the Temporary Regulations on the dispersion of whole communities dated 19 March 1909 in Volkov, Sbornik polozhenii, pp. 525–33.

18. Ibid; and chapter 1 of the 29 May 1911 statute on land organization in Polozhenie o zemleustroistve, s zakondatel'nymi motivami i raz''iasneniami, ed. A. A. Znosko-Borovskii (SPB, 1912). Also Lykoshin in GDSO (1908–9), vol. 3, 2901–2.

19. See Krivoshein's 10 November 1908 speech in GDSO (1908–9), vol. 1, 1043.

20. See, for example, Stolypin's Circular Telegram of 19 September 1909 in IZO 1909:10, pp. 312–13.

21. See Trudy I-go Vserossiiskago sel'sko-khoziaistvennago s''ezda v Kieve 1-10 sentiabria 1913g, Vyp. 1 (n.p., n.d.); and TsGIA SSSR, f. 395, op. 1, d. 2433.

22. Osobyi zhurnal, 28 September 1910, pp. 4, 30–31. The original proposal is in Agrarnyi vopros v soveta ministrov, p. 103.

23. See Stolypin's 15 March 1910 speech in GSSO V, col. 171–74.

24. Znosko-Borovskii, Polozhenie o zemleustroistve.

25. Krivoshein's speech of 12 October 1909 in GDSO (1909-10), vol. 1, col. 59.

26. Dorner, Land Reform; K. Griffin, The Political Economy of Agrarian Change: An Essay on the Green Revolution (Cambridge, Mass., 1974); Boserup, Conditions of Agricultural Growth. Compare E. H. Jacoby, "Has Land Reform Become Obsolete?" in Peasants in History: Essays in Honor of Daniel Thorner, ed. E. J. Hobsbawm et al. (Calcutta, 1980), pp. 296–305.

27. Yaney, "Agricultural Administration," pp. 3–35. Compare Yaney, Urge to Mobilize, pp. 462–557.

28. "Iz dnevnika A. A. Polovtsova," KA 46 (1931), p. 128.

29. Koefoed, My Share; A. Baker-Lampe, "A Danish Agronomist's View."

30. Kaufman, "Ukaz 9 noiabria," pp. 158–75; and A. E. Lositskii, "Raspadenie obshchiny," p. v.

31. Compare L. H. Haimson, "The Problem of Social Stability in Urban Russia, 1905–1917" and discussion in Slavic Review, 23:4 (1964), 619–42, and 24:1 (1965), 1–65; Haimson, Politics of Rural Russia; G. L. Yaney, "Social Stability in Pre-Revolutionary Russia: A Critical Note," Slavic Review, 24:3 (1965), 521–27; A. Levin, "More on Social Stability, 1905–1917," Slavic Review, 25:1 (1966), 149–54; H. Rogger, "Russia in 1914," Journal of Contemporary History, 1:4 (1966), 95–119; A. Mendel, "On Interpreting the Fate of Imperial Russia," in Stavrou, Russia Under the Last Tsar, pp. 13–41; G. F. Kennan, "The Breakdown of Tsarist Autocracy" and discussion in R. Pipes, ed., Revolutionary Russia (Cambridge, Mass., 1968), pp. 1–25; M. Malia, Comprendre la revolution russe (Paris, 1980).

GLOSSARY

Committee of
Ministers

Prior to 17 October 1905, this was a body in which
the various ministers, one of whom served as the
chairman, discussed policy issues. However, the
chairman had no special authority and no power to
impose a unity on the other members, who were his
equals before the tsar.

Council of
Ministers

Created in October 1905 as part of the effort to form
a unified government. The chairman, also known as
premier or prime minister, had more power than the
chairman of the Committee of Ministers. However,
this change did not effectively create a unified government since there were many other forces influencing the tsar.

darstvennik[i]

Peasants who at the time of the Emancipation
accepted one-quarter of the standard allotment. As a
result they did not have to pay redemption. By 1906
there were approximately 250,000 households (2 percent of the total) in this category, who were widely
recognized as those suffering most from land-hunger.
Their holdings are sometimes referred to as dwarf
holdings or beggarly allotments.

desiatina

An area equaling 2.7 acres or 1.09 hectares.

dvorianin

See *pomeshchik.*

fronde/frondeur

The noble reaction at the beginning of the twentieth
century. Although this term technically refers to nobles who take up arms against the king, as in seventeenth century France, in the contemporary Russian
context this term was used to describe a phenomenon similar to the social and political movements of
noble reaction in eighteenth century France.

GUZiZ

Glavnoe Upravlenie Zemleustroistva i Zemledeliia:
Main Administration of Land Organization and
Agriculture. Formed in 1905, it was the successor
to the Ministry of Agriculture and State Domains,
formed in 1894, which was itself the successor of the

Ministry of State Domains. Because the two earlier bodies were not strictly ministries of agriculture, and because the GUZiZ was not a ministry, the head of these bodies will be referred to as the *agricultural minister*. The predecessors of the GUZiZ will be referred to as *agricultural ministries*.

khutor[a]   Peasant farm with land consolidated into a single, compact, or integral parcel that was separated from the commune's land and on which the peasant's cottage and other farm buildings were located.

khutorizatsiia   The policy of transforming all traditional forms of peasant habitation and cultivation into *khutora*.

krugovaia poruka   Mutual responsibility: the system of making the commune responsible for the payment of taxes and the fulfillment of duties by its members.

kulak   Lit. "fist": the top 1 or 2 percent of a peasant village that engages primarily in moneylending or other nonagricultural activities such as running the local tavern as well as renting or letting land. Speculator.

mir   Commune or peasant community as an administrative unit. The other meanings of this word have significance for the social psychology of the peasant community: "world" and "peace."

mirovoi posrednik   Peace arbitrator: officials established at the time of the Emancipation to implement its provisions.

muzhik   The traditional term for the Russian peasant.

nad-soslovie   Supraestate, supraclass. The traditional ideology of tsarism in which the government was independent of and above particular social or class interests. In the modern period this was gradually coming to mean a "national" perspective.

obshchina   Commune: the peasant community as an economic unit. Usually associated with periodical repartitions of land and with communal ownership.

opeka   Tutelage, guardianship, especially as applied to administrative or bureaucratic tutelage over the affairs of the peasantry. Insofar as the peasantry was concerned, there were two forms during the period under consideration: a more traditional, protective, paternalistic, passive, and regulatory form that did not intervene in the peasants' economic life and that was similar to *nadzor* or supervision; and a new, more active, manipulative, interventionist form that developed with the creation of the land captains in 1889 and that laid the basis for government intervention in their economic life. The two functions were often combined. See Introduction for more details.

otrub[a]	A peasant farm consisting of one to three or four plots of arable land in different locations and separate from grazing land. The peasant cottage and other farm buildings remain in the core village or some other central location.
podvornoe	Applied to land within a commune that was owned on a hereditary and household or family basis. Usually translated as "individual" where it is contrasted to communal ownership and that is the meaning intended. When contrasting family and individual ownership, however, it will be translated as "household." As with other terms, its use was not very precise in the period being considered.
pomeshchik	Noble: used to translate both the terms *dvorianin* and *pomeshchik*. When there is a need to emphasize the landowning characteristics of the nobility then they will be referred to as *noble landowners*. Much has been written about the respective merits of the English terms *noble* and *gentry*. Here *gentry* will be used only rarely to refer to the gentry reaction—a movement originating in the provinces—as distinguished from the "noble reaction," which was more associated with the capitals.
Pugachevshchina	Refers to the "evil times" of Emelian Pugachev's peasant and cossack revolt, 1773–75.
sanovnik[i]	High dignitary in the imperial court and the government. Notable.
soslovie [*sosloviia*]	A legal or social estate or class. There were several estates in Russia. The nobility constituted the first estate; the clergy, the second. In addition there were separate estates for town dwellers, peasants, and others. Each estate had its own set of laws defining its rights and obligations.
State Council	Legislative institution made up of former officeholders appointed by the tsar and current ministers, ex officio. Laws generally get sent to this body for discussion. Its opinion is not binding, however, and the tsar could and did approve the minority opinion. Laws generally went first to one of its departments, and from there to a meeting of the United Departments, and then on to the General Assembly. From 1906, made up of 50 percent appointive and 50 percent elected members and transformed into the upper house of the legislature.
uezd	County: administrative division intermediate between the province and the canton.
Udel	A term used to describe properties owned by

members of the royal family other than the tsar.
These lands were administered by a Ministry of
Udel lands.

ukreplenie Title claim (lit. "consolidation"): process by which
peasants claimed title to their strips within the commune. Distinguished from consolidating strips into a
single parcel.

volost' Canton: administrative division between commune
and the county.

vydel Separation (to one place): the act of consolidating
one's strips and transferring to a *khutor.*

zemlepol'zovanie Land use—sometimes translated as "landownership"
where that is the meaning intended. See
zemlevladenie.

zemleustroistvo Land organization or land reorganization: a neutral
term used to encompass both intensification and
extensification; the entire process of agricultural
rationalization. By 1906 it meant more specifically
the reorganization of landholding patterns and the
elimination of open-field ownership and use.

zemlevladenie Landownership: sometimes translated as "land use"
where that is the intent. This term and the term for
land use *(zemlepol'zovanie)* were interchangeable
right up to 1905. The distinction in meaning was
only established as a result of the perceptual revolution itself. See chapter 1, note 134.

zemskii nachal'nik Land captain: post in the Interior Ministry's bureaucratic hierarchy closest to the peasantry.

zemstvo The local, elective form of all-class self-government.

SELECT LIST OF WORKS CONSULTED

The following list represents only the most significant sources consulted in the course of preparing this book. It is neither a comprehensive bibliography, nor a list of works cited. For a more complete list of works consulted through 1976, see the author's Ph.D. dissertation: "The Russian Bureaucracy and the 'Peasant Problem': The Pre-History of the Stolypin Reforms, 1861–1907," Columbia University, 1976.

Unpublished Materials

Archives

Tsentral'nyi Gosudarstvennyi Istoricheskii Arkhiv SSSR v Leningrade (TsGIA SSSR)
    fond 408 Komitet po Zemleustroitel'nym Delam
    fond 1276 Sovet Ministrov
    fond 1291 Ministerstvo Vnutrennikh Del, Zemskii Otdel
    fond 1571 A. V. Krivoshein
Tsentral'nyi Gosudarstvennyi Arkhiv Oktiabr'skoi Revoliutsii (TsGAOR)
    fond 543 Tsarsko-Sel'skii Aleksandrovskii Dvorets
    fond 586 V. K. Pleve
Russian Archive, Columbia University, New York, NY
    Golitsyn, Prince A. D.
    Koshko, I. F.
    Kryzhanovskii, S. E.
    Liubimov, D. N.
    Maiborodov, V.
    Meiendorf, A.
    Mendeleev, P. P.
    Migulin, P. P.
    Semenov, N. D. (nee N. Kh. Bark)
    Shlippe, F. V. fon
    Troitskii, K. K.
    Vasil'chikov, Prince I. S.
    Witte, S. Iu.
    Zenkovskii, A. V.

Hoover Institution Archive, Stanford, California
Gurko, V. I.
Liubimov, D. N.

Other Unpublished Papers and Dissertations

Deich, G. M. "Osoboe Soveshchanie o nuzhdakh sel'skokhoziaistvennoi pro-myshlennosti," Kandidatskaia dissertatsiia, Moscow University, 1946.
Fisher, J. R. "The Witte Conference on the Needs of Agriculture in Russia: 1902–1905," Ph.D. dissertation, University of Toronto, 1978.
Kingston-Mann, E. "Transforming the Russian Countryside," unpub. paper presented to the National Seminar on Russian Social History in the 20th Century, Philadelphia, 1982.
Mandel, J. I. "Paternalistic Authority in the Russian Countryside, 1856–1906," Ph.D. dissertation, Columbia University, 1978.
Pearson, T. S. "Ministerial Conflict and Local Self-Government Reform in Russia, 1877–1890," Ph.D. dissertation, University of North Carolina, 1977.
Raeff, M. "The Peasant Commune in the Political Thinking of Russian Publicists: Laissez-faire Liberalism in the Reign of Alexander II," Ph.D. dissertation, Harvard University, 1950.
Rose, J. W. "The Russian Peasant Emancipation and the Problem of Rural Administration: The Institution of the 'Mirovoi Posrednik,' " Ph.D. dissertation, University of Kansas, 1976.
Rosenthal, C. N. "Ministerial Conflict under Nicholas II: The Finance and Interior Ministries and the 'Peasant Question,' " M.A. thesis and Certificate of the Russian Institute Essay, Columbia University, 1969.
Shapkarin, A. V. "Stolypinskaia agrarnaia reforma," 3 volumes, Doktorskaia dissertatsiia, Akademiia Nauk SSSR, Moscow, 1954.
Simmonds, G. "The Congress of Representatives of the Nobles' Association, 1906–1916: A Case Study in Russian Conservatism," Ph.D. dissertation, Columbia University, 1964.
Vaisberg, I. D. "Sovet ob"edinennogo dvorianstva i ego vliianie na politiku samoderzhaviia (1906–1914 gg)," Kandidatskaia dissertatsiia, Moscow University, 1956.
Zyrianov, P. N. "Krakh vnutrennei politiki tret'e-iiun'skoi monarkhii v oblasti mestnogo-upravleniia (1907–1914)," Kandidatskaia dissertatsiia, Moscow University, 1972.

Published Materials

Anan'ich, N. I. "K istorii otmeny podushnoi podati v Rossii," IZ, 94 (1974), 183–212.
Anfimov, A. M. *Ekonomicheskoe polozhenie i klassovaia bor'ba krest'ian Evropeiskoi Rossii, 1881–1904 gg.* Moscow, 1984.
———. "Krest'ianskoe dvizhenie v Rossii vo vtoroi polovine XIX veka." *Voprosy Istorii*, 1973:5, pp. 15–31.
———. *Krest'ianskoe khoziaistvo Evropeiskoi Rossii, 1881–1904.* Moscow, 1980.

————. *Krupnoe pomeshchich'e khoziaistvo Evropeiskoi Rossii (Konets XIX– nachalo XX veka)*. Moscow, 1969.

————. "Preobrazovanie obrochnoi podati byvshikh gosudarstvennykh krest'ian v vykupnye platezhi." *Iz istorii ekonomicheskoi i obshchestvennoi zhizni Rossii. Sbornik statei*. Moscow, 1976, pp. 27–43.

Anfimov, A. M., and P. N. Zyrianov. "Nekotorye cherty evoliutsii russkoi krest'ianskoi obshchiny v poreformennyi period." *Istoriia SSSR*, 1980:4, pp. 26–41.

Armstrong, J. A. *The European Administrative Elite*. Princeton, N.J., 1973.

————. "Old-Regime Administrative Elites. Prelude to Modernization in France, Prussia, and Russia." *International Review of Administrative Sciences*, 38:1 (1972), 21–40.

————. "Old-Regime Governors: Bureaucratic and Patrimonial Attitudes." *CSSH*, XIV:1 (1972), 2–29.

————. "Tsarist and Soviet Elite Administrators." *Slavic Review*, 31:1 (1972), 1–28.

Atkinson, D. *The End of the Russian Land Commune, 1905–1930*. Stanford, 1983.

Avrekh, A. Ia. *Tsarizm i tret'eiiunskaia sistema*. Moscow, 1966.

Bar, F. *Krest'ianskoe obshchinnoe zemlevladenie v agrarnom i sotsial' no-politicheskom otnosheniiakh*. Moscow, 1894.

Baturinskii (Galprin), D. A. *Agrarnaia politika tsarskogo pravitel'stva i krest'ianskii pozemel'nyi bank*. Moscow, 1925.

Becker, S. *Nobility and Privilege in Late Imperial Russia*. DeKalb, 1985.

Bekhteev, S. S. *Doklad o pod"eme blagosostoianiia krest'ianstva*. SPB, 1906.

————. *Khoziaistvennye itogi istekshago sorokapiatiletiia i mery k khoziaistvennomu pod"emu*. 3 vols. SPB, 1902–1911.

Belokonskii, I. P. *Zemstvo i konstitutsiia*. Moscow, 1910.

Bilimovich, A. D. *Krest'ianskii pravoporiadok po trudam mestnykh komitetov o nuzhdakh sel'skokhoziaistvennoi promyshlennosti*. Kiev, 1904.

————. "The Land Settlement in Russia and the War." In *Russian Agriculture during the War*. Ed. by N. Antsiferov et al. New Haven, 1930; New York, 1968, pp. 301–88.

Bing, E. J., ed. *The Letters of Tsar Nicholas and Empress Marie*. London, 1937.

Bochkareva, E. I. "Iz istorii agrarnoi politiki tsarizma v gody pervoi russkoi revoliutsii," *Uchenye Zapiski Leningradskogo Gosudarstsvennogo Pedagogicheskogo Instituta imeni A. I. Gertsena*, 61 (1947), 25–47.

Bogdanovich, A. V. *Tri poslednikh samoderzhtsa. Dnevnik A. V. Bogdano-vich*. Moscow–Leningrad, 1924.

Boianus, A. K., comp. *Otchet po zemskomu otdelu. Kratkii obzor ego sovremennago deiatel'nosti. 19/II/1861–19/II/1911*. SPB, 1911.

Bok, M. P. *Vospominaniia o moem ottse P. A. Stolypine*. New York, 1953.

Bol'shov, V. V. "Materialy senatorskikh revizii 1880–1881 gg. kak istochnik po istorii mestnogo upravleniia Rossii." *VMUSI*, 1976:4, pp. 38–54.

Brusnikin, E. M. "Krest'ianskii vopros v Rossii v period politicheskoi reaktsii (80–90-e gody XIX veka)." *Voprosy Istorii*, 1970:2, pp. 34–47.

————. "Pereselencheskaia politika tsarizma v kontse XIX veka." *Voprosy Istorii*, 1965:1, pp. 28–38.

———. "Podgotovka zakona 14/XII/93 goda 'o neotchuzhdaemosti krest'ian-skikh zemel',' " *Uchenye Zapiski Gor'kovskogo Universiteta. Seriia is-toriko-filologicheskaia.* Vol. 72, 345–75.

Brutskus, B. D. "K sovremennomu polozheniiu agrarnogo voprosa." In *Agrarnye voprosy v Rossii.* Ed. by B. D. Brutskus. Vyp. I. Petrograd, 1917.

Brzheskii, N. K. *Nedoimochnost' i krugovaia poruka sel'skikh obshchestv. Istoriko-kriticheskii obzor deistvuiushchago zakondatel'stva, v sviazi s praktikoiu krest'ianskago podatnago dela.* SPB, 1897.

———. *Obschchinnyi byt i khoziaistvennaia neobezpechennost' krest'ian. Po povodu predstoiashchago peresmotra krest'ianskikh polozhenii.* SPB, 1899.

———. *Ocherki iuridicheskago byta krest'ian. Izsledovanie.* SPB, 1902.

Chayanov, A. V. *A. V. Chayanov on The Theory of Peasant Economy.* Ed. by D. Thorner et al. Homewood, Ill., 1966.

Cherevanin, N. "Dvizhenie intelligentsii. (Do epokhi 'doveriia' kn. Sviato-polka-Mirskago)." In *Obshchestvennoe dvizhenie v Rossii v nachale XX-go veka.* Ed. by L. Martov et al. Vol. I. SPB, 1909; The Hague, 1968, pp. 259–90.

Chermenskii, E. D. *Burzhuaziia i tsarizm v pervoi russkoi revoliutsii.* 2d ed. Moscow, 1970.

Chernenkov, B. "Peremena fronta v bor'be s obshchinoi." *Sovremennik,* 1911:9, pp. 221–41.

Chernukha, V. G. *Krest'ianskii vopros v pravitel'stvennoi politike Rossii (60–70 gody XIX v.).* Leningrad, 1962.

———. *Vnutrenniaia politika tsarizma s serediny 50kh do nachala 80kh gg. XIX v.* Leningrad, 1978.

———. "Vsepoddanneishii doklad komissii P. A. Valueva ot 2 aprelia 1872 g. kak istochnik po istorii podatnoi reformy v Rossii," VID, II (1969), 262–9.

Chernyshev, I. V. *Agrarno-krest'ianskaia politika Rossii za 150 let.* Petrograd, 1918.

———. "Klassovye interesy v zakonodatel'stve ob obshchine." *Poznanie Rossii,* 1909:3, pp. 159–89.

———. *Krest'iane ob obshchine nakanune 9 noiabria 1906. K voprosu ob obshchine.* SPB, 1911.

———. *Obshchina posle 9 noiabria 1906 po ankete Vol'nago Ekonomiches-kago Obshchestva.* 2 vols. Petrograd, 1917.

———. "Razsloenie sovremennoi derevni." *Sovremennyi Mir,* 1908:6, part 2, pp. 46–69.

Christian, D. "The Supervisory Function in Russian and Soviet History." *Slavic Review,* 41:1 (1982), 73–90.

Chuprov [Tschuprow], A. A. "The Break-Up of the Village Community in Russia." *The Economic Journal,* 22 (June 1912), pp. 173–97.

———. "Obshchinnoe zemlevladenie." In *Nuzhdy derevni po rabotam kom-itetov o nuzhdakh sel'skokhoziaistvennoi promyshlennosti. Sbornik statei.* Ed. by N. N. L'vov and A. A. Stakhovich. Vol. II. SPB, 1904, pp. 116–232.

Confino, M. *Domaines et seigneurs en Russie vers la fin du XVIIIe siècle. Étude de structures agraires et de mentalités économiques.* Paris, 1963.

———. *Systèmes agraires et progrès agricole. L'assolement triennal en Russie aux XVIIIe–XIXe siècles. Étude d'economie et de sociologie rurales.* Paris, 1969.

Conroy, M. S. *Peter Arkad'evich Stolypin: Practical Politics in Late Tsarist Russia.* Boulder, Co., 1976.

Coquin, F. –X. *La Siberie. Peuplement et immigration paysanne au XIXe siècle.* Paris, 1969.

Crisp, O. *Studies in the Russian Economy Before 1914.* London, 1976.

Czap, P., Jr. "P. A. Valuev's Proposal for a Vyt' Administration, 1864." SEER, 45:105 (1967), 391–410.

D., P. *Krest'ianskaia nadel'naia zemlia v proekte grazhdanskago ulozheniia.* Moscow, 1903.

———. *Nasha derevnia.* Moscow, 1900.

———. *Russkaia intelligentsiia i krest'ianstvo. Kriticheskii analiz mnenii chlenov Osobago Soveshchaniia po krest'ianskomu delu.* Moscow, 1906.

———. *Russkaia intelligentsiia i krest'ianstvo. Kriticheskii analiz trudov mestnykh komitetov o nuzhdakh sel'skokhoziaistvennoi promyshlennosti.* SPB, 1904.

———. *Russkii sotsializm i obshchinoe zemlevladenie.* Moscow, 1899.

———. *Vopros ob obshchine i uravnitel'nom zemlepol'zovanii.* Moscow, 1904.

Dan, F. "Obshchaia politika pravitel'stva i izmeneniia v gosudarstvennoi organizatsii v period 1905–1907 gg." In *Obshchestvennaia dvizhenie v Rossii v nachale XX–go veka.* Ed. by L. Martov et al. Vol. IV, part I. SPB, 1912; The Hague, 1968, 279–392.

Danilov, F. "Obshchaia politika pravitel'stva i gosudarstvennyi stroi k nachalu XX veka," In *Obshchestvenoe dvizhenie v Rossii v nachale XX–go veka.* Ed. by L. Martov et al. Vol. I. SPB, 1909, pp. 422–82.

Darstvennoe nadel'noe zemlevladenie krest'ian po obsledovaniiu 1907. SPB, 1908.

Demey, J. *De l'institution sous le tsar Alexandre III des zemskie natchalniki (Étude de droit public Russe).* Roubaix, 1908.

Diakin, V. A. "Stolypin i dvorianstvo (Proval mestnoi reformy)." In *Problemy krest'ianskogo zemlevladeniia i vnutrennei politiki Rossii. Dooktiabr'skii period.* Leningrad, 1972, 231–74.

Dnevnik Imperatora Nikolaia II. Berlin, 1923.

Doctorow, G. S. "The Fundamental State Laws of 23 April 1906." *Russian Review,* 35:1 (1976), 33–52.

———. "The Government Program of 17 October 1905." *Russian Review,* 34:2 (1975), 123–36.

Doklad predsedatelia vysochaishe uchrezhdennoi v 1888 godu kommisii po povodu padeniia tsen na sel'skokhoziaistvennyia proizvodeniia v piatiletie (1883–1887). SPB, 1892.

Doklad Vysochaishe uchrezhdennoi kommissii dlia izsledovaniia nyneshniago polozheniia sel'skago khoziaistva i sel'skoi proizvoditel'nosti v Rossii. 2 vols. SPB, 1873.

Dolgorukov, P. D. "Agrarnyi vopros s tochki zreniia krupnago zemlevladeniia." In *Agrarnyi vopros: Sbornik statei*. Ed. by P. D. Dolgorukov and I. I. Petrunkevich. Vol. I. 1st ed. Moscow, 1905, 1–10.

———. *Velikaia razrukha*. Madrid, 1964.

Drezen, A. K., ed. *Tsarizm v bor'be s revoliutsiei 1905–1907g. Sbornik dokumentov*. Moscow, 1936.

Druzhinin, N. M. "Glavnyi komitet ob ustroistve sel'skogo sostoianiia." In *Issledovaniia po sotsial'no-politicheskoi istorii Rossii. Sbornik statei pamiati B. A. Romanova*. Ed. by N. E. Nosov. Leningrad, 1971, pp. 269–86.

———. *Gosudarstvennye krest'iane i reforma P. D. Kiseleva*. 2 vols. Moscow, 1946–58.

———. "Kiselevskii opyt likvidatsii obshchiny." In *Akademiku Borisu Dmitrievichu Grekovu ko dniu semidesiatiletiia. Sbornik statei*. Moscow, 1952, pp. 351–72.

———. "Likvidatsiia feodal'noi sistemy v russkoi pomeshchich'ei derevene (1862–1882 gg.)." *Voprosy Istorii*, 1968:12, pp. 3–34.

———. *Russkaia derevnia na perelome 1861–1880 gg*. Moscow, 1978.

Dubentsov, B. B. "Popytki preobrazovaniia organizatsii gosudarstvennoi sluzhby v kontse XIX v. (Iz praktiki ministerstva finansov)." In *Problemy otechestvennoi istorii: Sbornik statei aspirantov i soiskatelei*. Moscow–Leningrad, 1976, pp. 202–24.

Dubrovskii, S. M. *Krest'ianskoe dvizhenie v revoliutsii 1905–1907 gg*. Moscow, 1956.

———. "K voprosu ob obshchine v Rossii v nachale XX v." *EAIVE za 1960*. Kiev, 1962, pp. 520–33.

———. "Rossiiskaia obshchina v literature XIX-nachale XX veka (bibliograficheskii obzor)." In *Voprosy istorii sel'skogo khoziaistva, krest'ianstva i revoliutsionnogo dvizheniia v Rossii. Sbornik statei k 75-letiiu Akademika N. M. Druzhinina*. Moscow, 1961, pp. 348–61.

———. *Sel'skoe khoziaistvo i krest'ianstvo Rossii v period imperializma*. Moscow, 1975.

———. *Stolypinskaia reforma. Kapitalizatsiia sel'skogo khoziaistva v XX veke*. 1st ed. Leningrad, 1925; 2nd ed. Moscow, 1930.

———. *Stolypinskaia zemel'naia reforma. Iz istorii sel'skogo khoziaistva i krest'ianstva Rossii v nachale XX veka*. Moscow, 1963.

Dubrovskii, S. M., and B. Grave, eds. *Agrarnoe dvizhenie v 1905–1907 gg. Materialy i dokumenty*. In *1905. Materialy i dokumenty*. Ed. by M. N. Pokrovskii. Vol. 1. Moscow–Leningrad, 1925.

———. "Krest'ianskoe dvizhenie nakanune revoliutsii 1905 goda (1900–1904 gg.)." In *1905*. Ed. by M. N. Pokrovskii. Vol. 1. *Predposylki revoliutsii*. Moscow–Leningrad, 1925, 233–392.

Dzhivelegov, A. K., et al., eds. *Velikaia Reforma. Russkoe obshchestvo i krest'ianskii vopros v proshlom i nastoiashchem. Iubileinoe izdanie*. 6 vols. Moscow, 1911.

Egiazarova, N. A. *Agrarnyi krizis kontse XIX veka v Rossii*. Moscow, 1959.

Emmons, T. "The Peasant and the Emancipation." In *The Peasant in Nineteenth-Century Russia*. Ed. by W. S. Vucinich. Stanford, Calif., 1970, pp. 41–71.

———. *The Russian Landed Gentry and the Peasant Emancipation of 1861.* Cambridge, 1968.

Enden, M. N. "Graf S. Iu. Vitte," *Vozrozhdenie,* #228 (January 1971), pp. 84–111.

———. [de Enden]. "The Roots of Witte's Thought." *Russian Review,* 29:1 (1970), 6–24.

Entsiklopedicheskii Slovar' Granata. Vol. 17 (biographies of members of First, Second and Third Dumas); vol. 23 (biographies of members of the State Council, 1801–1914).

Ermolov, A. S. *Narodnaia sel'skokhoziaistvennaia mudrost' v poslovitsakh, pogovorkakh i primetakh.* 4 vols. SPB, 1905.

———. *Nash neurozhai i prodovol'stvennyi vopros.* 2 vols. SPB, 1909.

———. *Nash zemel'nyi vopros.* SPB, 1906.

———. *Neurozhai i narodnoe bedstvie.* SPB, 1892.

———. *Organizatsiia polevago khoziaistva; sistemy zemledeliia i sevooboroty.* 1st ed. SPB, 1879; 5th ed. SPB, 1914.

———. [Yermoloff]. *La Russie agricole devant la crise agraire.* Paris, 1907.

Eropkin, A. "Otmena krugovoi poruki." *Narodnoe Khoziaistvo,* 4:3 (1903), 1–30.

———. *P. Stolypin i ukaz 9-go noiabria. Lektsiia.* SPB, 1911.

Eroshkin, N. P. *Istoriia gosudarstvennykh uchrezhdenii dorevoliutsionnoi Rossii.* 2d ed. Moscow, 1968.

Evreinov, G. A. *Krest'ianskii vopros v ego sovremennoi postanovke.* 2nd ed. SPB, 1904.

———. *Krest'ianskii vopros v trudy obrazovannoi v sostave MVD kommissii po peresmotru zakonopolozhenii o krest'ianakh.* SPB, 1904.

Fainsod, M. "Bureaucracy and Modernization: The Russian and Soviet Case." In *Bureaucracy and Political Development.* Ed. by J. LaPalombara. Princeton, N.J., 1963, pp. 233–67.

Field, D. *The End of Serfdom. Nobility and Bureaucracy in Russia, 1855–1861.* Cambridge, Mass., 1976.

———. *Rebels in the Name of the Tsar.* Boston, 1976.

Fischer, G. *Russian Liberalism. From Gentry to Intelligentsia.* Cambridge, Mass., 1958.

Fleksor, D. S., comp. *Okhrana sel'skokhoziaistvennoi sobstvennosti.* SPB, 1904.

Gaister, A. "Sel'skoe khoziaistvo." In *1905.* Ed. by M. N. Pokrovskii. Vol. I. *Predposylki revoliutsii.* Moscow–Leningrad, 1925, 1–168.

Galai, S. *The Liberation Movement in Russia 1900–1905.* Cambridge, 1973.

Garmiza, V. V. *Podgotovka zemskoi reformy 1864 goda.* Moscow, 1957.

———. "Predlozheniia i proekty P. A. Valueva po voprosam vnutrennei politiki (1862–1866 gg.)." *Istoricheskii Arkhiv,* 4:1 (1958), 138–53.

Gershenkron, A. *Continuity in History and Other Essays.* Cambridge, Mass., 1968.

———. *Economic Backwardness in Historical Perspective. A Book of Essays.* Cambridge, Mass., 1962; New York, 1965.

———. "The Rate of Industrial Growth in Russia since 1885." *Journal of Economic History.* Supplement VII (1947). *The Tasks of Economic History.*

Gins, G. K. and P. A. Shafranov. *Sel'skokhoziaistvennoe vedomstvo za 75 let ego deiatel'nosti (1837–1912 gg.)* Petrograd, 1914.

Glinskii, B. B. "Graf Sergei Iul'evich Vitte (Materialy dlia biografii)." *Istoricheskii Vestnik*, 140 (1915): April, pp. 232–79; May, pp. 573–89; 141 (1915), July, pp. 204–33; August, pp. 520–55; September, pp. 893–906; 142 (1915), November, pp. 592–609; December, pp. 893–907.

Goldsmith, R. W. "The Economic Growth of Tsarist Russia 1860–1913." *Economic Development and Cultural Change*, 9:3 (1961), 441–75.

Golos Minuvshego. 1913–1923.

Golovin, F. A. "Zapiski." *KA*, 19 (1926), 110–49.

Golovin, K. F. "Dva novykh protivnikov obshchiny." *Russkii Vestnik*, 1894:12, pp. 311–29.

———. *Moi vospominaniia.* 2 vols. SPB, 1908–1910.

———. *Muzhik bez progressa ili progress bez muzhika (K voprosu ob ekonomicheskoi materializme).* SPB, 1896.

———. *Nasha finansovaia politika i zadachi budushchago.* SPB, 1899.

———. *Nasha sel'skaia obshchina v literatura i v deistvitel'nosti.* SPB, 1885.

———. *Vne partii. Opyt politicheskoi psikhologii.* SPB, 1905.

Goremykin, I. L., ed. *Svod uzakonenii i rasporiazhenii pravitel'stva ob ustroistve sel'skago sostoianiia.* 2 vols. SPB, 1903.

Goremykin, M. I. *Agrarnyi vopros; nekotoryia dannyia k obsuzhdeniiu ego v gosudarstvennoi dume.* SPB, 1907.

Grant, S. A. "*Obshchina* and *Mir.*" *Slavic Review*, 35:4 (1976), 636–51.

Gregory, P. "Economic Growth and Structural Change in Tsarist Russia: A Case of Modern Economic Growth?" *Soviet Studies*, XXIII:1 (1972), 418–34.

———. "Grain Marketings and Peasant Consumption, Russia, 1885–1913." *Explorations in Economic History*, 17 (1980), 135–64.

———. "Russian Industrialization and Economic Growth: Results and Perspectives of Western Research." *JGO*, 25:2 (1977), 200–18.

———. "Russian Living Standards During the Industrialization Era, 1885–1913." *Review of Income and Wealth*, 26 (1980), 87–103.

———. *Russian National Income, 1885–1914.* Cambridge, 1982.

Guchkov, A. I. "Iz vospominanii A. I. Guchkova," *Poslednie Novosti*, August 9–September 30, 1936.

Gurko, V. I. *Dvorianskoe zemlevladenie v sviazi s mestnoi reforme.* n.p., 1887.

———. *Features and Figures of the Past. Government and Opinion in the Reign of Nicholas II.* Tr. L. Matveev. Stanford, Calif., 1939; New York, 1970.

———. *Nashe gosudarstvennoe i narodnoe khoziaistvo. Doklad predstavlennyi V-mu s"ezdu upolnomochennykh ob"edinennykh dvorianskikh obshchestv.* SPB, 1909.

———. [V. Romeiko-Gurko]. *Ocherki privislian'ia.* Moscow, 1897.

———. *Otryvochnyia mysli po agrarnomu voprosu.* SPB, 1906.

———. *Ustoi narodnago khoziaistva Rossii. Agrarno-ekonomicheskie etiudy.* SPB, 1902.

Haimson, L. H., ed. *The Politics of Rural Russia.* Bloomington, 1979.

———. "The Problem of Social Stability in Urban Russia, 1905–1917." *Slavic Review*, 23:4 (1964), 619–42; 24:1 (1965), 1–65.

Hamburg, G. M. *Politics of the Russian Nobility, 1881–1905.* New Brunswick, N.J., 1984.

Harper, S. N. *The New Electoral Law for the Russian Duma.* Chicago, 1908.

———. *The Russia I Believe in. The Memoirs of Samuel N. Harper, 1902–1941.* Chicago, 1945.

Heilbronner, H. "Piotr Khristianovich von Schwanebach and the Dissolution of the First Two Dumas." *Canadian Slavonic Papers*, XI:1 (1969), 31–55.

Hennessy, R. *The Agrarian Question in Russia, 1905–1907: The Inception of the Stolypin Reform.* Giessen, 1977.

Hildermeier, M. "Neopopulism and Modernization: The Debate on Theory and Tactics in the Socialist Revolutionary Party, 1905–1914." *Russian Review*, 34:4 (1975), 453–75.

Hosking, G. A., and R. T. Manning. "What Was the United Nobility?" In *The Politics of Rural Russia, 1905–1914.* Ed. by L. H. Haimson. Bloomington, 1979, pp. 142–83.

Ianson, Iu. E. *Opyt statisticheskago izsledovaniia o krest'ianskikh nadelakh i platezhakh.* 1st ed. SPB, 1877.

Islavin, M. S., ed. *Obzor trudov vysochaishe utverzhdenii pod predsedatel'stvom stats-sekretaria Kakhanov osoboi kommissii.* 2 vols. SPB, 1908.

Iswolsky (Izvolskii), A. *The Memoirs of Alexander Iswolsky: Formerly Russian Minister of Foreign Affairs and Ambassador to France.* Ed. and tr. by C. L. Seeger. London, 1920; Gulf Breeze, Fla., 1974.

Iurevskii, B. *Zemlia i obshchestvo.* SPB, 1912.

Izgoev, A. S. *Obshchinnoe pravo. (Opyt sotsial'no-iuridicheskago analiza obshchinnago zemlevladeniia, kak institut grazhdanskago prava.* SPB, 1906.

———. "P. A. Stolypin." *Russkaia Mysl'*, 28:12 (1907), part 2, pp. 129–52.

———. *P. A. Stolypin. Ocherk zhizni i deiatel'nosti.* Moscow, 1912.

Izvestiia Glavnago Upravleniia Zemeleustroistva i Zemledeliia. 1905–1906.

Izvestiia Zemskago Otdela. 1904–1917.

Judge, E. H. *Plehve: Repression and Reform in Imperial Russia, 1902–1904.* Syracuse, 1983.

K. "Iz noveishei istorii krest'ianskago voprosa. Offitsial'nye proekty, soveshchaniia i zapiski 1897–1906 godov." *Vestnik Evropy*, 1909:4, pp. 621–37; 1909:5, pp. 99–115.

Kachorovskii, K. R. "Biurokraticheskii zakon i krest'ianskaia obshchina." *Russkoe Bogatstvo*, 1910:7, pp. 121–42; 1910:8, pp. 44–62.

———. *Narodnoe Pravo.* Moscow, 1906.

———. *Russkaia obshchina. Vozmozhno li, zhelatel'no li ee sokhranenie i razvitie?* 2d ed. Moscow, 1906.

Kahan, A. "Government Policies and the Industrialization of Russia." *Journal of Economic History*, 27:4 (1967), 460–77.

———. "National Calamities and their Effect upon the Food Supply in Russia (An Introduction to a Catalogue)." *JGO*, 16:3 (1968), 353–77.

Kalinichev, F. I., comp. *Gosudarstvennaia Duma v Rossii v dokumentakh i materialakh*. Moscow, 1957.

Karpov, N. *Agrarnaia politika Stolypina*. Leningrad, 1925.

———. *Krest'ianskoe dvizhenie v revoliutsii 1905 goda v dokumentakh*. Leningrad, 1926.

Kataev, M. M. *Mestnyia krest'ianskiia uchrezhdeniia, 1861, 1874, i 1889 (Istoricheskii ocherk ikh obrazovaniia i norm deiatel'nosti)*. 3 parts. SPB, 1911–1912.

———. comp. *Ocherki zakonopolozhenii o neotchuzhdaemosti nadel'nykh zemel'*. SPB, 1911.

Kaufman, A. A. "Agrarnaia deklaratsiia P. A. Stolypina." *Russkaia Mysl'*, 1907:6, part 2, pp. 169–76.

———. *Agrarnyi vopros v Rossii. Kurs Narodnago Universiteta*. 2d ed. Moscow, 1919.

———. "Ukaz 9 noiabria 1906 goda." *Russkaia Mysl'*, 1908:1, part 2, pp. 158–75.

———. *Voprosy ekonomiki i statistiki krest'ianskogo khoziaistva*. Moscow, 1918.

Kautsky, J. H. *The Politics of Aristocratic Empires*. Chapel Hill, 1982.

———. "Revolutionary and Managerial Elites in Modernizing Regimes." *Comparative Politics*, July 1969, pp. 441–66.

Khauke, O. A. *Krest'ianskoe zemel'noe pravo. Podrobnoe sistematicheskoe posobie k izucheniiu deistvuiushchego zakonodatel'stva i praktiki po voprosam krest'ianskago zemlevladeniia*. Moscow, 1913, 1914.

Kingston-Mann, E. *Lenin and the Problem of Marxist Peasant Revolution*. New York, 1983.

———. "Marxism and Russian Rural Development: Problems of Evidence, Experience, and Culture." AHR, 86:4 (1981), 731–52.

Kipp, J. W. "M. Kh. Reitern on the Russian State and Economy: A Liberal Bureaucrat during the Crimean Era, 1854–1860." JMH, 47:3 (1975), 437–59.

Kipp, J. W., and W. B. Lincoln. "Autocracy and Reform: Bureaucratic Absolutism and Political Modernization in Nineteenth-Century Russia." *Russian History*, 6:1 (1979), 1–21.

Kizevetter, A. A. *Na rubezhe dvukh stoletii (Vospominaniia 1881–1914)*. Prague, 1929; Cambridge, Mass., 1974.

Kleinbort, A. "Pravitel'stvo i partii ob agrarnom voprose." *Obrazovanie*, 1907:6, pp. 74–98.

Koefoed, C. A. [A. A. Kofod]. *My Share in the Stolypin Reforms*. Odense, 1985.

Kofod, A. A. *Bor'ba s chrezpolositseiu v Rossii i za granitseiu*. (Also published under the title: *Zemleustroistvo v Rossii i v drugikh stranakh*.) SPB, 1906.

———. *Khutorskoe rasselenie*. SPB, 1906.

———. *Krest'ianskie khutora na nadel'noi zemel'*. 2 vols. SPB, 1905.

———. *Russkoe zemleustroistvo*. 2d ed. SPB, 1914.

Kokovtsov, V. N. *Iz moego proshlago. Vospominaniia 1903–1919 gg.* 2 vols. Paris, 1933; The Hague, 1969.

Kolesnichenko, D. A. *Trudoviki v period pervoi rossiiskoi revoliutsii.* Moscow, 1985.

Kolonizatsiia Sibiri v sviazi s obshchim pereselencheskim voprosom. SPB, 1900.

Korelin, A. P. *Dvorianstvo v poreformennoi Rossii 1861–1904 gg. Sostav, chislennost', korporativnaia organizatsiia.* Moscow, 1979.

Korf, S. A. *Administrativnaia iustitsiia v Rossii.* 2 vols. SPB, 1910.

Korkunov, N. M. *Russkoe gosudarstvennoe pravo.* 7th. ed. 2 vols. SPB, 1913.

Kornilov, A. A. *Obshchestvennoe dvizhenie pri Aleksandra II (1855–1881). Istoricheski ocherki.* Paris, 1905.

———. *Ocherki po istorii obshchestvennago dvizheniia i krest'ianskago dela v Rossii.* SPB, 1905.

Koroleva, N. G. *Pervaia rossiiskaia revoliutsiia i tsarizm. Sovet ministrov Rossii v 1905–1907.* Moscow, 1982.

Koshelev, A. I. *Zapiski, 1806–1883.* Newtonville, Mass., 1976.

Koshko, I. F. *Vospominaniia gubernatora (1905–1914 g.) Novgorod, Samara, Penza.* Petrograd, 1916.

Kostriukova, V. V. *Krest'iane Povolzh'ia v 1906–1916 gg.* Leningrad, 1953.

Kovalevskii, M. M. *Chem Rossiia obiazano Soiuzu Ob"edinennago Dvorianstva.* Moscow, 1914.

———. "P. A. Stolypin i ob"edinennoe dvoriansto." *Vestnik Evropy,* 1913:10, pp. 406–23.

———. "Spor o sel'skoi obshchine v kommissii gosudarstvennago soveta." *Vestnik Evropy,* 1910:1, pp. 259–84.

———. "Sudby obshchinnago zemlevladeniia v nashei verkhnei palate." *Vestnik Evropy,* 1910:6, pp. 58–81.

Krasnyi Arkhiv. 1922–1941.

Krest'ianskoe dvizhenie v Poltavskoi i Khar'kovskoi guberniakh v 1902 g. Sbornik Dokumentov. Khar'kov, 1961.

Kriukov, N. A. *Chem zhivet i na chem zizhdetsia sel'skoe khoziaistvo.* Moscow, 1905.

———. *Zemlia i kak s nei luchshe vsego rasporiadit'sia.* Moscow, 1906.

Krivoshein, K. A. *A. V. Krivoshein (1857–1921 g.) Ego znachenie v istorii Rossii nachale XX veka.* Paris, 1973.

Kryzhanovski, S. E. "Dopros S. E. Kryzhanovskogo 10 iiulia 1917 goda." In *Padenie tsarskogo rezhima.* Ed. by P. E. Shchegolev. Vol. V. Moscow–Leningrad, 1926, 376–443.

———. "V. K. Pleve." *Novyi Zhurnal,* 1975:118, pp. 137–44.

———. *Vospominaniia.* Berlin, n.d.

Kurlov, P. G. *Gibel' Imperatorskoi Rossii.* Berlin, 1923.

Kuropatkin, A. N. "Dnevnik A. N. Kuropatkina," KA, 2 (1922), 5–117.

Laue, T. H. von. "Imperial Russia at the Turn of the Century: The Cultural Slope and the Revolution from Without." *Comparative Studies in Society and History,* 3 (July 1961), 353–67.

———. *Sergei Witte and the Industrialization of Russia.* New York, 1963, 1969.

Leikina-Svirskaia, V. R. *Intelligentsiia v Rossii vo vtoroi polovine XIX veka.* Moscow, 1971.

Lenin, V. I. "The Agrarian Program of Social Democracy in the First Russian Revolution." In *V. I. Lenin. Collected Works*. Vol. 13. 4th ed. Moscow, 1962, 217–431.

———. "The Agrarian Question in Russia Towards the Close of the Nineteenth Century." In *V. I. Lenin. Collected Works*. Vol. 15. 4th ed. Moscow, 1963, 69–147.

Leont'ev, A. A. *Krest'ianskoe pravo. Sistematicheskoe izlozhenie osobennostei zakonodatel'stva o krest'ianakh*. 1st ed. SPB, 1909; 2d ed. SPB, 1914.

———. "Mezhevyia nuzhdy derevni." In *Nuzhdy derevni po rabotam komitetov o nuzhdakh sel'skokhoziaistvennoi promyshlennosti. Sbornik statei*. Vol. II. SPB, 1904, 234–59.

———. "Zakonodatel'stvo o krest'ianakh posle reformy." In *Velikaia Reforma; Russkoe obshchestvo i krest'ianskii vopros v proshlom i nastoiashchem. Iubileinoe izdanie*. Ed. by A. K. Dzhivelegov et al. Vol. VI. Moscow, 1911, pp. 158–99.

Leontovitsch, V. *Geschichte des Liberalismus in Russland*. Frankfort-am-Main, 1957.

Leroy-Beaulieu, A. *The Empire of the Tsars and the Russians*. Tr. by Z. Ragozin. 3 vols. New York, 1902–5, 1969.

———. *Un homme d'état Russe (Nicholas Miliutine). D'après sa correspondance inédite*. Hattiesburg, 1969.

Levin, A. "More on Social Stability, 1905–1917." *Slavic Review*, 25:1 (1966), 149–54.

———. "Russian Bureaucratic Opinion in the Wake of the 1905 Revolution." *JGO*, 11 (1963), 1–12.

———. *The Second Duma. A Study of the Social-Democratic Party and the Russian Constitutional Experiment*. 2d ed. Hamden, Conn., 1966.

———. *The Third Duma, Election and Profile*. Hamden, Conn., 1973.

Levitskii, V. "Pravyia partii." In *Obshchestvennoe dvizhenie v Rossii v nachale XX-go veka*. Ed. by L. Martov et al. Vol. 3, kn. 5 (SPB, 1914), 347–472.

Liashchenko, P. I. *Istoriia narodnogo khoziaistvo SSSR*. 3 vols. 3rd ed. Moscow, 1952–56.

———. *Ocherki agrarnoi evoliutsii Rossii*. 2 vols. in 3 parts. SPB, 1908; SPB, 1913 (1924); Tomsk, 1917.

———. "Piat'desiat let nashego agrarno-ekonomicheskago zakonodatel'-stva." *Vestnik Finansov*, 1911:8, pp. 330–36.

Lieven, D. C. B. *British Documents on Foreign Affairs, Russia, 1859–1914*. Vol. 3. n.p., 1983.

———. "Bureaucratic Authoritarianism in Late Imperial Russia: The Personality, Career and Opinions of P. N. Durnovo." *The Historical Journal*, 26:2 (1983), 392–402.

———. "Bureaucratic Liberalism in Late Imperial Russia: The Personality, Career and Opinions of A. N. Kulomzin." *SEER*, 60:3 (1982), 413–31.

———. "The Russian Civil Service under Nicholas II: Some Variations on the Bureaucratic Theme." *JGO*, 29:3 (1981), 366–403.

———. "Russian Senior Officialdom under Nicholas II: Careers and Mentalités." *JGO*, 32:2 (1984), 199–223.

Lincoln, W. B. *In the Vanguard of Reform: Russia's Enlightened Bureaucrats, 1825–1861.* DeKalb, 1982.

———. *Nikolai Miliutin: An Enlightened Russian Bureaucrat of the Nineteenth Century.* Newtonville, Mass., 1977.

Lisenkov, G. I. *Opyt sistematicheskago postroeniia agrarnoi programmy (Izsledovanie v piati chastiakh).* Parts 1–2. SPB, 1906.

———. *Zemel'nyi vopros (O tom, chto mozhno sdelat' dlia podniatiia blasgosostoianiia krest'ian).* SPB, 1907.

Liubimov, D. N. "Otryvki iz vospominanii D. N. Liubimova (1902–1904 gg.)." *Istoricheskii Arkhiv,* 1962:6, pp. 69–84.

Loganov, G. *Statistika zemlevladeniia Evropeiskoi Rossii po uezdam.* SPB, 1906.

Lokhtin, P. M. *Bezzemel'nyi proletariat v Rossii. Opyt opredeleniia kolichestva bezzemel'nago proletariata, sozdannago sushchestsvuiushchimi sposobami krest'ianskago zemlevladeniia.* Moscow, 1905.

———. *K voprosu o reforme sel'skago byta krest'ian.* SPB, 1902.

———. *Kak sdelat'sia krest'ianam bogache.* Kiev, 1906.

———. *Ob izmenenii velichiny posevnykh ploshchadei v Evropeiskoi Rossii za posledniia 20 let.* SPB, 1903.

———. *Sostoianie sel'skago khoziaistva v Rossii sravnitel'no s drugimi stranami. Itogi k XX-mu veka.* SPB, 1901.

Lopatin, S. Iu. *Perechen' dokladov pomeshchennykh v trudakh mestnykh komitetov.* SPB, 1905.

Lopukhin, V. B. "Liudi i politika (konets XIX-nachalo XX v.)." *Voprosy Istorii,* 1966:9, pp. 120–36.

Lositskii, A. *Raspadenie obshchiny, Trudy VEO,* 1912:1–2, pp. 1–60.

L'vov, N. N., and A. A. Stakhovich, eds. *Nuzhdy derevni po rabotam komitetov o nuzhdakh sel'skokhoziaistvennoi promyshlennosti. Sbornik statei.* 2 vols. SPB, 1904.

Lykoshin, A. I. "O semeinoi sobstvennosti u krest'ian." *Zhurnal Ministerstva Iustitsii,* 1900:5, pp. 108–43; 1900:6, pp. 87–140.

Macey, D. A. J. "Agriculture." In *Dictionary of the Russian Revolution.* Ed. by G. D. Jackson and R. Devlin. Westport, Conn., forthcoming.

———. "Bureaucratic Solutions to the Peasant Problem: Before and After Stolypin." In *Russian and East European History: Selected Papers from the Second World Congress for Soviet and East European Studies.* Ed. by R. C. Elwood. Berkeley, 1984, pp. 73–95.

———. "The Peasantry, the Agrarian Problem, and the Revolution of 1905–1907." In *Columbia Essays in International Affairs.* Vol. VII. Ed. by A. W. Cordier. New York, 1972, pp. 1–35.

Maklakov, V. "The Agrarian Problem in Russia Before the Revolution." *Russian Review,* 9:1 (1950), 3–15.

———. *The First State Duma. Contemporary Reminiscences.* Tr. by M. Belkin. Bloomington, 1964.

———. "The Peasant Question and the Russian Revolution." *Slavonic Review,* II (December 1923), 225–48.

———. *Vtoraia gosudarstvennaia duma (Vospominaniia sovremennika).* Paris, n.d.

Maliutin, D. P. *Oshibki, sdelannyia pri sostavlenii polozheniia o krest'-ianakh 19 fevralia 1861 g. i ikh posledstviia.* SPB, 1895.

Manning, R. T. *The Crisis of the Old Order in Russia: Gentry and Government.* Princeton, 1982.

———. "The Zemstvo and Politics, 1864–1914." In *The Zemstvo in Russia: An Experiment in Local Self-Government.* Ed. by T. Emmons and W. S. Vucinich. New York, 1982, pp. 133–76.

Manuilov, A. A. "Obshchinnoe zemlevladenie." In *Ocherki po krest'-ianskomu voprosu.* Ed. by A. A. Manuilov. Vol. I. Moscow, 1904, 329–48.

———. "Noveishee zakonodatel'stvo o zemel'noi obshchine. Ego kharakteristika i rezultaty." *Vestnik Evropy,* 1912:11, pp. 243–67.

———. "Pozemel'nyi vopros v Rossii." In *Agrarnyi vopros. Sbornik statei.* Ed. by P. D. Dolgorukov and I. I. Petrunkevich. Vol. I. Moscow, 1905, pp. 11–83.

———. *Pozemelnyi vopros v Rossii. Malozemel'e, dopolnitel'nyi nadel i arenda.* Moscow, 1905.

———. "The Stolypin Reforms (Agrarian Reform in Russia)." *Russian Review,* I:4 (1912), 131–49.

———. "Zametki ob obshchinnom zemlevladenii." In *Ocherki po krest'-ianskomu voprosu.* Ed. by A. A. Manuilov. Vol. I. Moscow, 1904, 256–85.

Maslov, P. *Agrarnyi vopros v Rossii.* 2 vols. SPB, 1908.

Materialy Kakhanovskoi kommisii. 8 vols. SPB, n.d.

Materialy po peresmotru uzakonenii o vzimanii okladnykh sborov. 2 vols. SPB, 1894–5.

Materialy postupivshie v Osoboe Soveshchanie o nuzhdakh sel'skokhoziaistvennoi promyshlennosti. 7 vols. SPB, 1902.

Materialy po voprosam zemel'nomu i krest'ianskomu. Vserossiiskii s"ezd staroobriadtsev v Moskve, 22–25 fevralia 1906 goda. Moscow, 1906.

Materialy vysochaishe uchrezhdennoi 16/XI/01 Kommissii po izsledovaniiu voprosa o dvizhenii s 1861 po 1900 g. blagosostoianiia sel'skago naseleniia srednezemledel'cheskikh gubernii, sravnitel'no s drugimi mestnostiami Evropeiskoi Rossii. 3 vols. SPB, 1903.

Mavor, J. *An Economic History of Russia.* 2d ed. New York, 1925.

McGrew, R. E. "Dilemmas of Development: Baron Heinrich Friedrich Storch (1766–1835) on the Growth of Imperial Russia." JGO, 24:1 (1976), 31–71.

Mech, V. *Sily reaktsii.* Vyp. 1. *Bor'ba obshchestvennykh sil v russkoi revoliutsii v 1905 i 1906 gg.* Ed. by V. Mech et al. Moscow, 1907.

Mehlinger, H. D., and J. M. Thompson. *Count Witte and the Tsarist Government in the 1905 Revolution.* Bloomington, 1972.

Mendeleev, D. I. "O nuzhdakh russkago sel'skago khoziaistva." In D. I. Mendeleev. *Problemy ekonomicheskogo razvitiia Rossii.* Moscow, 1960, pp. 578–90.

Migulin, P. P. *Agrarnyi vopros.* Khar'kov, 1906.

———. *Vykupnye platezhi. K voprosu o ikh ponizhenii.* Khar'kov, 1904.

Mikheev, N. M. *Bibliograficheskii ukazatel' sel'skokhoziaistvennoi literatury 1783–1966.* 2d ed. Moscow, 1968.

Miliukov, P. N. *Political Memoirs. 1905–1917.* Tr. by C. Goldberg. Ann Arbor, 1967.

———. *Tri popytki. K istorii russkago lzhe-konstitutionalizma.* Paris, 1921.

———. "Vvedenie." In *Nuzhdy derevni po rabotam komitetov o nuzhdakh sel'skokhoziaistvennoi promyshlennosti. Sbornik statei.* Ed. by N. N. L'vov and A. A. Stakhovich. Vol. I. SPB, 1904, 1–40.

Ministr Finansov i Gosudarstvennyi Sovet o finansovom polozhenii Rossii; zhurnal obshchago sobraniia gosudarstvennago soveta 30 dekabria 1902 g. Stuttgart, 1903.

Mironov, B. "The Russian Peasant Commune After the Reforms of the 1860s." *Slavic Review*, 44:3 (1985), 438–67.

———. "Vliianie krepostnogo prava na otnoshenie russkogo krest'ianstva k trudu." In *Sovetskaia istoriografiia agrarnoi istorii SSSR (do 1917 g.).* Kishinev, 1978, pp. 119–27.

Mosse, W. E. "Aspects of Tsarist Bureaucracy: Recruitment to the Imperial State Council, 1855–1914." SEER, 57:2 (1979), 240–54.

———. "Aspects of Tsarist Bureaucracy: the State Council in the Late 19th Century." *English Historical Review*, April 1980, pp. 268–92.

———. "Bureaucracy and Nobility at the End of the Nineteenth Century." *The Historical Journal*, 24:3 (1981), 605–28.

———. "Imperial Favorite: V. P. Mestchersky and the *Grazhdanin*." SEER, 59:4 (1981), 529–47.

———. "Russian Bureaucracy at the End of the Ancien Regime: The Imperial State Council, 1897–1915." *Slavic Review*, 39:4 (1980), 616–32.

———. "Russian Provincial Governors at the End of the Nineteenth Century." *The Historical Journal*, 27:1 (1984), 225–40.

———. "The Tsarist Ministerial Bureaucracy 1882–1904: Its Social Composition and Political Attitudes." CASS, 18:3 (1984), 249–67.

Mukhina, E. N. "Nachalo podgotovki krest'ianskoi reformy v Rossii (1856–1857 gg.)." VMUSI, 1977:4, pp. 39–52.

Nesterova, I. V. "Vopros o krest'ianskom nadel'nom zemlevladenii v redaktsionnoi komissii Ministerstva Vnutrennikh Del (1902–1904 gg.)." *Nauchnye doklady vysshei shkoly. Istoricheskie Nauki.* 1960:2, pp. 76–92.

Nikol'skii, A. P. *Zemlia, obshchina i trud. Osobennosti krest'ianskago pravoporiadka, ikh proiskhozhdenie i znachenie.* SPB, 1902.

Nol'de, B. E. *Iurii Samarin i ego vremia.* Paris, 1978.

Normano, J. F. *The Spirit of Russian Economics.* New York, 1945.

Nötzold, J. *Wirtschaftspolitische Alternativen der Entwicklung Russlands in der Ära Witte and Stolypin.* Berlin, 1966.

Novikov, A. I. *Zapiska zemskago nachal'nika.* SPB, 1899; Newtonville, Mass., 1980.

Novoe Vremia. 1904–1906.

Nuzhdy sel'skago khoziaistva i mery ikh udovletvoreniia po otzyvam zemskikh sobranii. 2d ed. SPB, 1902.

Ob"iasnitel'naia zapiska k proektu polozheniia ob uluchenii i rasshirenii krest'ianskago zemlevladeniia. n.p., n.d.

Obolenskii, A. V. *Moi vospominaniia i razmyshleniia.* Brussells, 1961.

Obzor deiatel'nosti komissii i otdelov Gosudarstvennoi Dumy Vtorago Sozyva. SPB, 1907.

Obzor trudov vysochaishe uchrezhdennoi pod predsedatel'stvom stats-sekretaria Kakhanova osoboi komissii. Vol. 1. SPB, 1908.

Ocherk predpolozhenii bolshinstva chlenov Soveshchaniia Osoboi Kommisii po sostavleniiu proektov mestnago upravleniia. n.p., n.d.

Oganovskii, N. P. "K peresmotru agrarnoi problemy." *Zavety,* 1912:V (August), pp. 1–37.

———. "Pervye itogi 'velikoi reformy.' " *Russkoe Bogatstvo,* 1911:10, part 2, pp. 124–62; 1911:11, part 1, pp. 67–98.

———. *S nebes' na zemliu; sbornik statei.* Moscow, 1917.

Ol'denburg, S. S. *Tsartsvovanie Imperatora Nikolaia II.* 2 vols. Belgrade, 1939; Munchen, 1949.

Opisanie otdel'nykh russkikh khoziaistv. Vol. 2. SPB, 1897.

Orlovsky, D. T. *The Limits of Reform: The Ministry of Internal Affairs in Imperial Russia, 1802–1881.* Cambridge, Mass., 1981.

———. "Recent Studies of the Russian Bureaucracy." *Russian Review,* 35:4 (1976), 448–67.

Osobye zhurnaly Soveta Ministrov. 1906–1917. (n.p., n.d.)

Osvobozhdenie. 1902–1904.

Otchet po deloproizvodstvu Gosudarstvennago Soveta. 1874–1906. SPB, 1876–1906.

Owen, L. A. *The Russian Peasant Movement 1906–1917.* n.p., 1937; New York, 1963.

Oznobishin, A. A. *Vospominaniia chlena IV-i Gosudarstvennoi Dumy.* Paris, 1927.

Pamiati Viacheslava Konstantinovicha Pleve. SPB, 1904.

Pares, B. "The Land Settlement in Russia." *Russian Review,* I:1 (1912), 56–74.

———. *My Russian Memoirs.* London, 1931.

———. "The Peterhof Conference of 1905." *Russian Review,* II:4 (1913), 87–102.

———. *A Wandering Student: The Story of a Purpose.* Syracuse, 1948.

Pashkov, A. I., ed. *Istoriia russkoi ekonomicheskoi mysli.* 3 vols. in 5. Moscow, 1955–1966.

Pavlov, N. A. *Zapiski zemlevladel'tsa.* Petrograd, 1915.

Pavlovsky, G. *Agricultural Russia on the Eve of Revolution.* London, 1930; New York, 1968.

Pearson, T. S. "Origins of Alexander III's Land Captains: A Reinterpretation." *Slavic Review,* 40:3 (1981), 384–403.

Pedashenko, A. D., ed. *Ukazatel' knig, zhurnal'nykh i gazetnykh statei po sel'skomu khoziaistvu za 1889, 1891–1911.* SPB, 1890–1915.

Perrie, M. *The Agrarian Policy of the Russian Socialist-Revolutionary Party from Its Origins Through the Revolution of 1905–1907.* Cambridge, 1976.

Pershin, P. N. *Agrarnaia revoliutsiia v Rossii. Istoriko-ekonomicheskoe issledovanie v dvukh knigakh.* Moscow, 1966.

———. *Uchastkovoe zemlepol'zovanie v Rossii. Khutora i otruba, ikh rasprostranenie za desiatiletie 1907–1916. Sud'by vo vremia revoliutsii (1917–1920 gg.).* Moscow, 1922.

Pervoe izdanie materialov redaktsionnykh kommissii, dlia sostavleniie polozhenii o krest'ianakh vykhodiashchikh iz krepostnoi zavisimosti. 18 vols. SPB, 1859–60.

Peshekhonov, A. V. *Economicheskaia politika samoderzhaviia (Tsentralizatsiia ekonomicheskoi vlasti).* SPB, 1906.

———. "Na ocherednyia temy. Iz krest'ianskikh pisem." *Russkoe Bogatstvo,* 1910:6, part 2, pp. 105–27; 1910:7, pp. 1–19.

———. "Ukaz 9 noiabria o vydelenii iz obshchiny." *Trudy VEO,* 2:6 (1906), pp. 5–9.

———. *Zemel'nyia nuzhdy derevni i osnovnyia zadachi agrarnoi reformy.* 2d ed. SPB, 1906.

Pestrzhetskii, D. I. *K vyiasneniiu agrarnago voprosa.* SPB, 1906.

———. *O prepodovanii uzakonenii o krest'ianakh.* SPB, 1905.

———. *Obzor agrarnago proekta K. D. partii.* SPB, 1906.

———. *Okolo zemli. Iz kursa lektsii sel'sko-khoziaistvennoi statistiki, chitannogo v 1921/2 gg. v Politekhnikume v Viunsdorfe bliz' Berlina (Y.M.C.A.).* Berlin, 1922.

———. *Opyt agrarnoi programmy.* SPB, 1906.

———. *Pishchevoe dovol'stvie krest'ian i prinuditel'noe otchuzhdenie.* SPB, 1906.

Petergofskoe soveshchanie o proekte gosudarstvennoi dumy. Berlin, n.d.

Petrovich, M. B. "The Peasant in Nineteenth-Century Historiography." In *The Peasant in Nineteenth-Century Russia.* Ed. by W. S. Vucinich. Stanford, Calif., 1970, pp. 191–230.

Pintner, W. M., and D. K. Rowney, eds. *Russian Officialdom: The Bureaucratization of Russian Society from the Seventeenth to the Twentieth Century.* Chapel Hill, 1980.

Pirumova, N. M. *Zemskoe liberal'noe dvizhenie. Sotsial'noe korni i evoliutsiia do nachala XX veka.* Moscow, 1977.

Polenov, A. D. *Izsledovanie ekonomicheskago polozheniia tsentral'-nochernozemnykh gubernii. Trudy Osobago Soveshchaniia 1899–1901 gg.* Moscow, 1901.

Pol'ianskii, N. N. *Tsarskie voennye sudy v bor'be s revoliutsii 1905–1907 gg.* Moscow, 1958.

Polnoe sobranie rechei Imperatora Nikolaia II, 1894–1906 gg. Sostavleno po offitsial'nym dannym "Pravitel'stvennago Vestnika." SPB, 1906.

Polnoe Sobranie Zakonov Rossiiskoi Imperii. Vtoroe sobranie. 55 vols. 1830–1884.

———. Tretee sobranie. 33 vols. 1885–1916.

Polovtsov, A. A. "Dnevnik A. A. Polovtsova (1901–1903)." *KA,* 3 (1923), 75–112.

———. "Dnevnik A. A. Polovtsova (1905–1908)." *KA,* 4 (1923), 63–128.

———. *Dnevnik gosudarstvennogo sekretaria A. A. Polovtsova. V. dvukh tomakh. 1883–1892.* Moscow, 1966.

———. "Iz dnevnika A. A. Polovtsova (1894)." *KA,* 67 (1934), 168–86.

———. "Iz dnevnika A. A. Polovtsova (1895–1900 gg.)." *KA,* 46 (1931), 110–32.

Posnikov, A. S. "Agrarnyi vopros v tret'ei dume (Malozemel'e i dopolnitelnoe nadelenie)." *Vestnik Evropy,* 1909:1, pp. 233–48.

————. "Agrarnyi vopros v tret'ei dume ('Polozhenie o zemleustroistvo')." *Vestnik Evropy*, 1910:1, pp. 285–97.

Presniakov, A. "Samoderzhavie Aleksandr II." *Russkoe Proshloe*, 1923:4, pp. 3–20.

Printsipial'nye voprosy po krest'ianskomu delu s otvetami mestnykh sel'skokhoziaistvennykh komitetov. SPB, 1904.

Programma i pervyi proekt ustava russkago soiuza zemlevladel'tsev. Saratov, 1905.

Prokopovich, S. N. *Agrarnyi krizis i meropriatiia pravitel'stva.* Moscow, 1912.

————. *Mestnye liudi o nuzhdakh Rossii.* SPB, 1904.

Protokoly po krest'ianskomu delu. Zasedaniia s 8 dekabria 1904 goda—30 marta 1905 goda. SPB, 1905.

Pushkarev, S. G. *Krest'ianskaia pozemel'no-peredel'naia obshchina v Rossii.* Newtonville, Mass., 1976.

————. *Rossiia v XIX veka (1801–1914).* New York, 1956.

Raeff, M. "The Bureaucratic Phenomenon of Imperial Russia." AHR, 84:2 (1979), 399–411.

————. *Comprendre l'Ancien Régime Russe. État et société en Russie imperiale. Essai d'interpretation.* Paris, 1982.

————. "L'état, le gouvernement et la tradition politique en Russie imperiale avant 1861." *Revue d'Histoire Moderne et Contemporaine*, IX (October–December 1962), 295–307.

————. "Georges Samarin et la commune paysanne après 1861." *Revue des Études Slaves*, 29 (1952), 71–81.

————. *Origins of the Russian Intelligentsia. The Eighteenth Century Nobility.* New York, 1966.

————. ed. *Plans for Political Reform in Imperial Russia, 1730–1905.* Englewood Cliffs, N.J., 1966.

————. "The Russian Autocracy and Its Officials." *Harvard Slavic Studies*, IV (1957), 77–91.

————. "Some Reflections on Russian Liberalism." *Russian Review*, 18:3 (1959), 218–30.

————. "The Well-Ordered Police State and the Development of Modernity in Seventeenth– and Eighteenth–Century Europe: An Attempt at a Comparative Approach." AHR, 80:5 (1975), 1221–43.

————. *The Well-Ordered Police State: Social and Institutional Change through Law in the Germanies and Russia, 1600–1800.* New Haven, 1983.

Rainey, T. B. *Sergei Witte and the Peasant Problem, 1901–1905.* Buffalo, 1973.

Rapport du Ministre des Finances à S. M. l'Empereur sur le budget de l'Empire pour l'excercice 1899–1900. SPB, 1898–1899.

Report of the Minister of Finance to H. M. the Emperor on the Budget of the Empire for 1902. SPB, 1902.

Revoliutsiia 1905 goda i samoderzhavie. Moscow, 1928.

Revoliutsiia 1905–1907 gg. v Rossii. Dokumenty i materialy. 18 vols. Moscow, 1955–1965.

Rieber, A. J. "Alexander II: A Revisionist View." JMH, 43:1 (1971), 42–58.

————. "Bureaucratic Politics in Imperial Russia." *Social Science History*, 2:4 (1978), 399–413.

Rittikh, A. A., comp. *Krest'ianskii pravoporiadok*. SPB, 1904.

————. comp. *Krest'ianskoe delo*. *Kratkii svod trudov mestnykh komitetov (po otdelam svoda: "Krest'ianskoe zemlepol'zovanie" i "Krest'ianskii pravoporiadok")*. SPB, 1903.

————. comp. *Krest'ianskoe zemlepol'zovanie*. SPB, 1903.

————. *Zavisimost' krest'ian ot obshchiny i mira*. SPB, 1903.

Robbins, R. G., Jr. "Choosing the Russian Governors: The Professionalization of the Gubernatorial Corps." *SEER*, 58:4 (1980), 541–60.

————. *Famine in Russia, 1891–1892. The Imperial Government Responds to a Crisis*. New York, 1975.

Robinson, G. T. *Rural Russia under the Old Regime. A History of the Land-lord–Peasant World and a Prologue to the Peasant Revolution of 1917*. New York, 1932; Berkeley, 1967.

Rogger, H. "The Formation of the Russian Right, 1900–1906." *California Slavic Studies*, 3 (1964), 66–94.

Rowney, D. K. "Higher Civil Servants in the Russian Ministry of Internal Affairs: Some Demographic and Career Characteristics, 1905–1916." *Slavic Review*, 31:1 (1972), 101–10.

————. "The Study of the Imperial Ministry of Internal Affairs in the Light of Organization Theory." In *The Behavioral Revolution and Communist Studies*. Ed. by R. Kanet. New York, 1971, pp. 209–31.

Rozenberg, V. "Iz khroniki krest'ianskago dela." In *Ocherki po krest'ianskomu voprosu. Sbornik statei*. Ed. by A. A. Manuilov. Vol. I. Moscow, 1904, 1–227.

Rudin, S. D. *Mezhevoe zakonodatel'stvo i deiatel'nost' mezhevoi chasti v Rossii za 150 let. 19 sentiabria 1765–1915*. Petrograd, 1915.

Russkii Kalendar' na 1900–1912 A. Suvorina. SPB, 1902–14.

Safronov, V. F., and A. A. Znosko-Borovskii, comps. *Kratkii ocherk deiatel'-nosti zemleustroitel'nykh uchrezhdenii za pervoe desiatiletie, 1906–1916*. n.p., n.d.

Savich, G. G. *Novyi gosudarstvennyi stroi Rossii. Spravochnaia kniga*. SPB, 1907.

Savickij, N. "P. A. Stolypine." *Le monde slave*, November 1933, pp. 227-63; December 1933, pp. 360–83; December 1934, pp. 378–403; April 1935, pp. 41–61; March 1936, pp. 341–81.

Sazonov, G. P. *Neotchuzhdaemost' krest'ianskikh zemel' v sviazi s gosudarst-venno-ekonomicheskoi programmoi*. SPB, 1889.

"Sbornik retsenzii populiarnykh izdanii po sel'skomu khoziaistvu." *Trudy VEO*, 2:5–6 (1912), 1–52, and 3:1 (1913), 53–115.

Sbornik zakliuchenii po voprosam otnosiashchimsia k peresmotru Polozheniia 12 iiunia 1886 goda o naime na sel'skie raboty. Vol. II. Osobye mneniia i zakliucheniia. SPB, 1898.

Sbornik zakonov i rasporiazhenii po zemleustroistvu (po 1 iiunia 1908 g.). SPB, 1908.

Semenov, D. P. *Statisticheskii ocherk krest'ianskago zemlevladeniia i zem-lepol'zovaniia v Evropeiskoi Rossii*. SPB, 1904.

Semenov, N. P. *Osvobozhdenie krest'ian v tsarstvovanie Imperatora Aleksandra II. Khronika deiatel'nosti komissii po krest'ianskomu delu.* 3 vols. in 5 parts. SPB, 1889–1891.

Semenov, P. N., and A. A. Saltykov. *Krest'ianskii bank i budushchnost' russkago krest'ianstva.* SPB, 1907.

Semenov-T'ian-Shanskii, N. "Svetloi pamiati Petra Arkad'evicha Stolypina." *Vozrozhdenie,* 118 (October 1961), pp. 79–100.

Semenov-T'ian-Shanskii, P. P. *Memuary P. P. Semenova-T'ian-Shanskago.* Vols. 3 and 4. *Epokha osvobozhdeniia krest'ian v Rossii (1857–1861 gg.) v vospominaniiakh P. P. Semenov-T'ian-Shanskago.* Petrograd, 1911–16.

———. *Svod trudov mestnykh komitetov o nuzhdakh sel'skokhoziaistvennoi promyshlennosti (gubernii, sostoiashchikh na Velikorossiiskom polozhenii) po voprosu o krest'ianskom zemlepol'zovanii.* SPB, 1905.

Seredonin, S. M. *Istoricheskii obzor deiatel'nosti Komiteta Ministrov. K stoletiiu Komiteta Ministrov (1801–1902).* 5 vols. in 8. SPB, 1902–1903.

Shanin, T. *The Awkward Class. Political Sociology of Peasantry in a Developing Society: Russia, 1910–1925.* Oxford, 1972.

———. ed. *Peasants and Peasant Societies.* Baltimore, Md., 1971.

———. *The Roots of Otherness: Russia's Turn of Century.* 2 vols. London, 1985–6.

Shchegolev, P. E., ed. *Padenie tsarskogo rezhima. Stenograficheskie otchety doprosov i pokazanii, dannykh v 1917 g. v chrezvychainoi sledstvennoi kommissii vremennogo pravitel'stva.* Vol. VII. Moscow–Leningrad, 1927.

Shelokhaev, V. V. "Agrarnaia programma kadetov v pervoi russkoi revoliutsii." *IZ,* 86 (1970), 172–230.

Shepeleva, O. N. "Zapiska P. A. Valueva Aleksandru II o provedenii reformy 1961 g." *Istoricheskii Arkhiv,* 1961:1, pp. 66–81.

Sheremetev, S. D. *Dmitrii Arkad'evich Stolypin.* SPB, 1899.

Shidlovskii, S. I. "The Imperial Duma and the Land Settlement." *Russian Review,* I:1 (1912), 18–26.

———. comp. *Obshchii obzor trudov mestnykh komitetov.* SPB, 1905.

———. comp. *Zemel'noe oblozhenie.* SPB, 1904.

———. comp. *Zemel'nye zakhvaty i mezhevoe delo.* SPB, 1904.

———. comp. *Zemstvo.* SPB, 1903.

Shingarev, A. I. *Vymiraiushchaia derevnia. Opyt sanitarno-ekonomicheskago izsledovaniia dvukh selenii Voronezhskago uezda.* 2d ed. SPB, 1907.

Shipov, D. N. *Vospominaniia i dumy o perezhitom.* Moscow, 1918.

Sidel'nikov, S. M. *Agrarnaia politika samoderzhaviia v period imperializma.* Moscow, 1980.

———. *Agrarnaia reforma Stolypina (Uchebnoe posobie).* Moscow, 1973.

———. *Obrazovanie i deiatel'nost' pervoi gosudarstvennoi dumy.* Moscow, 1962.

Simms, J. Y., Jr. "The Crisis in Russian Agriculture at the End of the Nineteenth Century: A Different View." *Slavic Review,* 36:3 (1977), 377–98.

———. "The Crop Failure of 1891: Soil Exhaustion, Technological Backwardness and Russia's 'Agrarian Crisis.'" *Slavic Review,* 41:2 (1982), 236–50.

————. "The Economic Impact of the Russian Famine of 1891–92." SEER, 60:1 (1982), 63–74.

Simonova, M. S. "Agrarnaia politika samoderzhaviia v 1905 g." IZ, 81 (1968), 199–215.

————. "Bor'ba techenii v pravitel'stvennom lagera po voprosam agrarnoi politiki v kontse XIX v." Istoriia SSSR, 1963:1, pp. 65–82.

————. "Krest'ianskii pozemel'nyi bank v sisteme obshchei agrarnoi politiki samoderzhaviia (1895–3.XI.1905 g.)." EAIVE za 1966. Tallinn, 1971, pp. 471–84.

————. "Krizis agrarnoi politiki samoderzhaviia nakanune pervoi russkoi revoliutsii." EAIVE za 1962. Moscow, 1964, pp. 465–88.

————. "Otmena krugovoi poruki." IZ, 83 (1969), 159–95.

————. "Pereselencheskii vopros v agrarnoi politike samoderzhaviia v kontse XIX-nachale XX v." EAIVE za 1965. Moscow, 1970, pp. 424–32.

————. "Politika tsarizma v krest'ianskom voprose nakanune revoliutsii 1905–1907 gg." IZ, 75 (1965), 212–242.

————. "Problema 'oskudeniia' Tsentra i ee rol' v formirovanii agrarnoi politiki samoderzhaviia v 90-kh godakh XIX-nachale XX v." In Problemy sotsial'no-ekonomicheskoi istorii Rossii. Sbornik statei k 85-letiiu so dnia rozhdeniia Akademika N. M. Druzhinina. Moscow, 1971, pp. 236–63.

————. "Zemsko-liberal'naia fronda (1902–1903 gg.)." IZ, 91 (1973), 150–216.

Skerpan, A. A. "The Russian National Economy and Emancipation." In Essays in Russian History. A Collection Dedicated to George Vernadsky. Ed. by A. D. Ferguson and A. Levin. Hamden, Conn., 1964, pp. 161–229.

Skliarov, L. F. Pereselenie i zemleustroistvo v Sibiri v gody stolypinskoi agrarnoi reformy. Leningrad, 1962.

Skrebitskii, A., comp. Krest'ianskoe delo v tsarstvovanie Imperatora Aleksandra II. 4 vols. in 5. Bonn, 1862–1868.

Skvortsov, A. I. Agrarnyi vopros i gosudarstvennaia duma. SPB, 1906.

Slonimski, L. "Noveishie protivniki obshchiny." Vestnik Evropy, 1904:2, pp. 756–72.

————. Okhrana krest'ianskago zemlevladeniia i neobkhodimyia zakonodatel'nyia reformy. SPB, 1891.

Snow, G. E. The Years 1881–1894 in Russia: A Memorandum Found in the Papers of N. Kh. Bunge. A Translation and Commentary. Philadelphia, 1981.

Sofronenko, K. A., comp. Krest'ianskaia reforma v Rossii 1861 goda. Sbornik zakonodatel'nykh aktov. Moscow, 1954.

Sokolov, P. "Aleksei Sergeevich Ermolov." Istoricheskii Vestnik, 1917:3, pp. 751–70.

Sokovnin, P. N. Kul'turnyi uroven' krest'ianskago polevodstva na nadel'noi zemle i ego znachenie v zemel'nom voprose. SPB, 1906.

Solov'ev, Iu. B. "K istorii proiskhozhdeniia manifesta 26 fevralia 1903 g." VID, XI, 192–205.

————. Samoderzhavie i dvorianstvo v kontse XIX veka. Leningrad, 1973.

————. Samoderzhavie i dvorianstvo v 1902–1907 gg. Leningrad, 1981.

Sosnovskii, I.V., comp. *Zemlevladenie.* SPB, 1904.

Spisok chlenov Tsentral'nago Soveta Vserossiiskago Soiuza Zemel'nykh Sobstvennikov. n.p., n.d.

Spisok grazhdanskim chinam pervykh trekh klassov. Ispravlen po 1–2e oktiabria 1905 goda. SPB, 1905.

Spisok otdelov svoda trudov mestnykh komitetov po Evropeiskoi Rossii (49 gubernii). SPB, 1904.

Spravki k vnesennomu Ministrom Vnutrennikh Del, 27 oktiabria 1903 g. za No. 29157, delu o poriadke predvaritel'nago obsuzhdeniia proektov novykh zakonopolozhenii o krest'ianakh. SPB, 1903.

Spravochnaia knizhka dlia chlenov Departamenta Gosudarstvennykh Zemel'nykh Imushchestv i Kantseliarii Komiteta po Zemleustroitel'nym Delam. SPB, 1914.

Starr, S. F. *Decentralization and Self-Government in Russia, 1830–1870.* Princeton, N.J., 1972.

Statistika zemlevladeniia 1905 g. Svod dannykh po 50 gubernii evropeiskoi Rossii. 50 vyp. i svod. SPB, 1907.

Stenograficheskie Otchety Gosudarstvennoi Dumy Pervago Sozyva. 2 vols. SPB, 1906.

Stenograficheskie Otchety Gosudarstvennoi Dumy Tret'ego Sozyva. 18 vols. SPB, 1907–1912.

Stenograficheskie Otchety Gosudarstvennoi Dumy Vtorago Sozyva. 2 vols. SPB, 1907.

Stenograficheskie Otchety Gosudarstvennago Soveta. 6 vols. SPB, 1906–1911.

Stenogrammy suzhdenii Osobago Soveshchaniia o nuzhdakh sel'skokhoziaistvennoi promyshlennosti po krest'ianskomu delu. ##1–28, sessii LXXI–XCVIII, 8/XII/04–30/III/05. n.p., n.d.

Stepynin, V. A. "Iz istorii pereselencheskoi politiki samoderzhaviia v nachale XX veka (pereselencheskii zakon 6 iiunia 1904 g.)." *Istoriia SSSR,* 1960:5, pp. 161–4.

St-k. "Valuevskaia kommissiia." *Russkaia Mysl',* 1891:3, pp. 1–29.

Stolypin, A. P. *P. A. Stolypin, 1862–1911.* Paris, 1927.

Stolypin, P. A. *Poezdka v Sibir' i Povolzh'e.* In *Gosudarstvennaia deiatel'nost' predsedatelia soveta ministrov Stats-sekretaria Petra Arkadeevicha Stolypina, 1909–1911.* Comp. by E. V(erpakhovskii). Vol. I. SPB, 1911. pp. 195–360.

Stolypine (Stolypina), A. *L'homme du dernier tsar, Stolypine. Souvenirs.* Paris, 1931.

Strakhovskii, I. M. "Krest'ianskii vopros v zakonodatel'stve i zakonosoveshchatel'nykh kommissiiakh posle 1861 g." In *Krest'ianskii stroi. Sbornik statei.* Ed. by P. D. Dolgorukov and S. L. Tolstoi. SPB, 1905, pp. 371–455.

―――. *Krest'ianskiia prava i uchrezhdeniia.* SPB, 1904.

Sushchestvuiushchii poriadok vzimaniia okladnykh sborov s krest'ianin po svedeniiam, dostavlennym podatnymi inspektorami za 1887–1893 gg. 2 vols. n.p., n.d.

Sviatopolk-Mirskaia, E. A. "Dnevnik Kn. Ekateriny Alekseevny Sviatopolk Mirskoi za 1904–1905 gg." IZ, 77 (1965), pp. 236–93.

Svod postanovlenii I–X s"ezdov upol'nomochennykh dvorianskikh obshchestv, 1906–1914 gg. Petrograd, 1915.

Svod trudov mestnykh komitetov po 49 guberniiam Evropeiskoi Rossii. 22 vols. SPB, 1903–1905.

Svod vysochaishikh otmetok po vsepoddanneishim otchetam za 1881–1890 gg. SPB, 1893.

Svod vysochaishikh otmetok po vsepoddanneishim otchetam za 1895–1901. 7 vols. SPB, 1897–1904.

Svod zakliuchenii gubernskikh soveshchanii po proektu polozheniia o nadel'nykh zemliakh (Trudy red. kom. T. 5.). SPB, 1906.

Svod zakliuchenii gubernskikh soveshchanii po proektu pravil ob ogranichenii krest'ianskikh nadelov i ob ikh razverstanii s cherespolosnymi ugod'iami smezhnago vladeniia (Trudy red. kom. T. 6.) SPB, 1906.

Svod zakliuchenii gubernskikh soveshchanii po voprosam otnosiashchimsia k peresmotru zakonodatel'stva o krest'ianakh. 3 vols. SPB, 1897.

Szeftel, M. "Nicholas II's Constitutional Decisions of October 17–19, 1905 and Sergius Witte's Role." In *Album J. Balon.* Namur, 1968, pp. 461–93.

———. "Reform of the Electoral Law to the State Duma on June 3, 1907: A New Basis for the Formation of the Russian Parliament." In *Liber Memorialis Georges de Lagarde. Studies Presented to the International Commission for the History of Representative and Parliamentary Institutions.* Vol. 38. London, 1968; Louvain/Paris, 1970, pp. 319–67.

Tarnovskii, K. N. "Problema agrarnoi istorii Rossii period imperializma v sovetskoi istoriografii." IZ, 78 (1965), 31–62; 83 (1969), 196–221.

———. "Problema agrarnoi istorii Rossii period imperializma v sovetskoi istoriografii (diskussii nachala 1960-kh godov)." In *Problemy sotsial'noekonomicheskoi istorii Rossii. Sbornik statei k 85-letiiiu so dnia rozhdeniia Akademika N. M. Druzhinina.* Moscow, 1971, pp. 264–311.

Terner, F. G. *Vospominaniia zhizni F. G. Ternera.* 2 vols. SPB, 1910–1911.

———. *Zamechaniia na trudy redaktsionnoi komissii Ministerstva Vnutrennikh Del po peresmotru zakonopolozhenii o krest'ianakh.* SPB, 1904.

Tiutchev, A. P. *Semeinye razdely u krest'ian.* SPB, 1912.

Tolmachev, M. *Krest'ianskii vopros po vzgliadam zemstva i mestnykh liudei.* Moscow, 1903.

Tomkins, S. R. "Why Witte Failed to Solve the Peasant Problem," JMH, 4:2 (1932), 235–39.

Treadgold, D. W. *The Great Siberian Migration. Government and Peasant in Resettlement from Emancipation to the First World War.* Princeton, N.J., 1957.

———. "Was Stolypin in Favor of Kulaks?" *Slavic Review,* 17:1 (1965), 1–14.

Trudy mestnykh komitetov Osobago Soveshchaniia o nuzhdakh sel'skokhoziaistvennoi promyshlennosti. 58 vols. SPB, 1903.

Trudy Osoboi Kommisii dlia sostavleniia proekt mestnago upravleniia. SPB, n.d.

Trudy pervago s"ezda upolnomochennykh dvorianskikh obshchestv 29 gubernii 21–28 maia 1906 g. 1st ed. SPB, 1906; 2d ed. SPB, 1910.

Trudy redaktsionnoi komissii po peresmotru zakonopolozhenii o krest'ianikh. 6 vols. SPB, 1903–1904.

Trudy s''ezda nepremennykh chlenov gubernskikh prisutstvii. 24/X–1/XI, 1907 g. SPB, 1908.

Trudy tret'ego s''ezda upolnomochennykh dvorianskikh obshchestv 32 gubernii s 27 marta po 2 aprelia 1907 g. SPB, 1907.

Trudy vtorago s''ezda upolnomochennykh dvorianskikh obshchestv 31 gubernii 14–18 noiabria 1906 g. SPB, 1906.

"Tsarskosel'skiia Soveshchaniia. Po voprosu o rasshirenii izbiratel'nago prava." *Byloe,* #25 (September 1917), pp. 217–65.

———. "Po peresmotru osnovnykh zakonov." *Byloe,* #26 (October 1917), pp. 183–245.

———. "Po vyrabotke uchrezhdenii gosudarstvennoi dumy i gosudarstvennago soveta." *Byloe,* ##27–28 (November-December 1917), pp. 289–318.

Tverskoi, P. "K istoricheskim materialam o pokoinom P. A. Stolypine." *Vestnik Evropy,* 1912:4, pp. 183–201.

Urusov, S. D. *Memoirs of a Russian Governor.* New York, 1908; New York, 1970.

Usov, S. S. *Rukovodstvo dlia zemskikh nachal'nikov.* 2 vols. SPB, 1910.

Vaisberg, I. D. "Sovet ob''edinennogo dvorianstva i ego vliianie na politiku samoderzhaviia v 1906–1914 gg." *Uchenye Zapiski Borisoglebskogo Gosudarstvennogo Pedagogicheskogo Instituta,* vyp. 2 (1957) pp. 273–304.

Vasil'eva, N. I., et al. *Pervaia rossiiskaia revoliutsiia i samoderzhavie (Gosudarstvenno-pravovye problemy).* Leningrad, 1975.

Vasilevskii, E. G. *Ideinaia bor'ba vokrug stolypinskoi agrarnoi reformy.* Moscow, 1960.

Vdovin, V. A. *Krest'ianskii pozemel'nyi bank (1883–1895 gg.).* Moscow, 1959.

Vechev, Ia. "Dela i Dni. Ministerskaia kar'era P. A. Stolypina." *Sovremennik,* 1911:9, pp. 300–22.

Veniaminov, P. *Krest'ianskaia obshchina. (Chto ona takoe, k chemu idet, chto daet i chto mozhet dat' Rossii?)* SPB, 1908.

V(erpakhovskii), E., comp. *Gosudarstvennaia deiatel'nost' predsedatelia soveta ministrov Stats-sekretaria Petra Arkad'evicha Stolypina, 1909–1911.* 3 vols. SPB, 1911.

———. *Predsedatel' soveta ministrov, Petr Arkad'evich Stolypin.* SPB, 1909.

Veselovskii, B. B., ed. *Agrarnyi vopros v sovete ministrov (1906).* Vol. 4. *Materialy po istorii krest'ianskikh dvizhenii Rossii.* Ed. by B. B. Veselovskii et al. Moscow-Leningrad, 1924.

———. "Dvizhenie zemlevladel'tsev." In *Obshchestvenoe dvizhenie v Rossii v nachale XX-go veka.* Ed. by L. Martov et al. Vol. I. SPB, 1909; The Hague, 1968, pp. 291–312.

———. *Istoriia zemstva za sorok let.* 4 vols. SPB, 1909–1911; Cambridge, Mass., 1973.

———. *Krest'ianskii vopros i krest'ianskoe dvizhenie v Rossii (1902–1906 gg.).* SPB, 1907.

———. ed. *Krest'ianskoe dvizhenie 1902 goda.* Vol. 3. *Materialy po istorii krest'ianskikh dvizhenii v Rossii.* Ed. by B. B. Veselovskii et al. Moscow-Leningrad, 1923.

———. "Utopism i real'naia politika v zemleustroistva." *Sovremennyi Mir,* 1910:1, part 2, pp. 1–17.

Vestnik finansov, promyshlennosti i torgovli. 1902–1905.

Vikhliaev, P. A. *Pravo na zemliu.* Moscow, 1906.

Volin, L. *A Century of Russian Agriculture from Alexander II to Khrushchev.* Cambridge, Mass., 1970.

Volkov, N. E. *Ocherk zakonodatel'noi deiatel'nosti v tsarstvovanie Imperatora Aleksandra III 1881–1894 gg.* SPB, 1910.

Volkov, N. T. *Nakaz zemskim nachal'nikam po administrativnym delam.* Moscow, 1907.

———. *Sbornik Polozhenii o sel'skom sostoianii.* 2d ed. SPB, 1910.

Vorob'ev, N. N. "Zemel'nyi vopros v zaiavleniiakh krest'ian i drugikh grupp naseleniia." In *Agrarnyi vopros. Sbornik statei.* Ed. by P. D. Dolgorukov and I. I. Petrunkevich. Vol. II. Moscow, 1907, pp. 353–416.

Vorontsov-Dashkov, I. I. *Zapiska Ministra dvora i udelov grafa Vorontsova-Dashkova ob unichtozhenii krest'ianskoi obshchiny.* Geneva, 1894.

Voroponov, F. "Krest'ianskii bank i ego nachalo: iz lichnykh vospominanii." *Vestnik Evropy,* 1905:12, pp. 507–59.

Voskresenskii, A. E. *Obshchinnoe zemlevladenie i krest'ianskoe malozemel'e.* SPB, 1903.

Vsepoddanneishii doklad Ministra Finansov i gosudarstvennoi rospisi dokhodov i raskhodov na 1883–1906 godov. SPB, 1883–1906.

Vsepoddanneishii Otchet Gosudarstvennago Kontrolera za 1896 g. SPB, 1897. *Vsepoddanneishii otchet o deiatel'nosti Osobago Soveshchaniia, 1902–1904.* SPB, 1904.

Vucinich, A. *Science in Russian Culture, 1861–1917.* Stanford, Calif., 1970.

Walicki, A. *The Controversy over Capitalism. Studies in the Social Philosophy of the Russian Populists.* Oxford, 1969.

———. *The Slavophile Controversy: History of a Conservative Utopia in Nineteenth-Century Russian Thought.* Oxford, 1975.

Watters, F. M. "The Peasant and the Village Commune." In *The Peasant in Nineteenth-Century Russia.* Ed. by W. S. Vucinich. Stanford, Calif., 1970, pp. 133–57.

Weissman, N. B. *Reform in Tsarist Russia: The State Bureaucracy and Local Government, 1900–1914.* New Brunswick, N.J., 1981.

Whelan, H. *Alexander III and the State Council: Bureaucracy and Counter-Reform in Late Imperial Russia.* New Brunswick, N.J., 1982.

Wilbur, E. M. W. "Was Russian Peasant Agriculture Really That Impoverished? New Evidence from a Case Study from the 'Impoverished Center' at the End of the Nineteenth Century." *Journal of Economic History,* XLIII:1 (1983), 137–47.

Witte, S. Iu. *Konspekt lektsii o narodnom i gosudarstvennom khoziaistve, chitannykh ego Imperatorskomu Vysochestvu Velikomu Kniaziu Mikhailu Aleksandrovichu v 1900–1902 gg.* 2d ed. SPB, 1912.

———. *The Memoirs of Count Witte.* Tr. by A. Yarmolinsky. New York, 1920, 1967.

———. *Po povodu natsionalizma: Natsional'naia ekonomika i Fridrikh List.* 2d ed. SPB, 1912.

————. *Samoderzhavie i zemstvo.* 2d ed. Stuttgart, 1903.

————. *Vospominaniia: Detstvo. Tsarstvovaniia Aleksandra II i Aleksandra III (1849–1894)* Berlin, 1923; The Hague, 1968.

————. *Vospominaniia: Tsarstvovanie Nikolaia II.* 2 vols. Berlin, 1922; The Hague, 1968.

————. *Zapiska po krest'ianskomu delu.* SPB, 1904, 1905.

Wortman, R. S. *The Development of a Russian Legal Consciousness.* Chicago, 1976.

Yaney, G. L. "Agricultural Administration in Russia from the Stolypin Land Reform to Forced Collectivization: An Interpretative Study." In *The Soviet Rural Community.* Ed. by J. R. Millar. Urbana, Ill., 1971, pp. 3–35.

————. "Bureaucracy and Freedom: N. M. Korkunov's Theory of the State." AHR, 71:2 (1966), 468–86.

————. "The Concept of the Stolypin Land Reform." *Slavic Review,* 23:2 (1964), 275–93.

————. "Law, Society and the Domestic Regime in Russia in Historical Perspective." *American Political Science Review,* 59 (June 1965), 379–90.

————. "Social Stability in Pre-Revolutionary Russia: A Critical Note." *Slavic Review,* 24:3 (1965), 521–7.

————. "Some Aspects of the Imperial Russian Government on the Eve of the First World War." SEER, 43:100 (1964), 68–90.

————. *The Systematization of Russian Government: Social Evolution in the Domestic Administration of Imperial Russia, 1711–1905.* Urbana, Ill., 1973.

————. *The Urge to Mobilize: Agrarian Reform in Russia, 1861–1930.* Urbana, Ill., 1982.

————. "War and the Evolution of the Russian Government." *South Atlantic Quarterly,* 66 (Summer 1967), 291–306.

Zaionchkovskii P. A., ed. *Krest'ianskoe dvizhenie v Rossii v 1870–1880 gg. Sbornik dokumentov.* Moscow, 1968.

————. *Krizis samoderzhaviia na rubezhe 1870–1880-kh godov.* Moscow, 1964.

————. *Otmena krepostnogo prava v Rossii.* 3d ed., Moscow, 1968.

————. "P. A. Valuev." In *Dnevnik P. A. Valueva Ministra Vnutrennikh Del v dvukh tomakh.* Ed. by P. A. Zaionchkovskii. Vol. I. Moscow, 1961, pp. 17–54.

————. "Popytka sozyva zemskogo sobora i padenie ministerstva N. P. Ignat'eva." *Istoriia SSSR,* 1960:5, pp. 126–39.

————. *Pravitel'stvennyi apparat samoderzhavnoi Rossii v XIX v.* Moscow, 1978.

————. *Provedenie v zhizn' krest'ianskoi reformy 1861 g.* Moscow, 1958.

————. *Rossiiskoe samoderzhavie v kontse XIX stoletiia (Politicheskaia reaktsiia 80-kh-nachale 90-kh godov).* Moscow, 1970.

————. ed. *Spravochniki po istorii dorevoliutsionnoi Rossii. Spravochnik,* Moscow, 1971.

————. "Zakon o zemskikh nachal'nikakh 12 Iulia 1889 goda." *Nauchnye doklady vysshei shkoly,* 1961:2, pp. 42–72.

Zak, A. N. *Krest'ianskii pozemel'nyi bank, 1883–1910.* Moscow, 1911.

Zakharova, L. G. "Dvorianstvo i pravitel'stvennaia programma otmeny krepostnogo prava v Rossii." *Voprosy Istorii*, 1973:9, pp. 32–51.

———. "Pravitel'stvennaia programma otmeny krepostnogo prava v Rossii." *Istoriia SSSR*, 1975:2, pp. 22–47.

———. "Redaktsionnye komissii 1859–1860 godov: uchrezhdenie, deiatel'nost'. (K istorii 'krizisa verkhov')." *Istoriia SSSR*, 1983:3, pp. 53–71.

———. *Samoderzhavie i otmena krepostnogo prava v Rossii, 1856–1861.* Moscow, 1984.

———. *Zemskaia kontrreforma 1890 g.* Moscow, 1968.

Zakon 14 iiunia 1910 g. ob izmenenii i dopolnenii nekotorykh postanovlenii o krest'ianskom zemlevladenii. SPB, 1911.

Zakonodatel'nye materialy po voprosam, otnosiashchaia k ustroistvu sel'skago sostoianiia. 2 vols. SPB, 1899–1900.

"Zapiska zemskago nachal'nika." *Russkaia Mysl'*, 1917:7–8, pp. 59–90; 1917:9–10, pp. 17–46.

Zemel'noe delo bez dumy; sbornik statei. Moscow, 1906.

Zemskii otdel Ministerstva Vnutrennikh Del. 1858 4/X 1908. Kratkii ocherk vozniknoveniia i razvitiia vazhneishikh faktov deiatel'nosti zemskago otdela MDV (K 50-letiiu ego sushchestsvovaniia). SPB, 1908.

Zen'kovskii, A. V. *Pravda o Stolypine.* New York, 1956.

Zhurnal zasedaniia 10, 18, 20–24 oktiabria 1903 g. vysochaishe uchrezhdennoi 16/XI/01 Kommissii po izsledovaniiu voprosa o dvizhenii s 1861 po 1900 g. blagosostoianiia sel'skago naseleniia srednezemledel'cheskikh gubernii, sravnitel'no s drugimi mestnostiami Evropeiskoi Rossii. SPB, 1903.

Zhurnal zasedaniia s"ezda uchreditelei Vserossiiskago soiuza zemlevladel'tsev, 17 noiabria 1905 g. Moscow, 1906.

Zhurnaly Komiteta Ministrov po ispol'neniu ukaza 12 dekabria 1904 g. SPB, 1905.

Zhurnaly sekretnago i glavnago komitetov po krest'ianskomu delu. 2 vols. Petrograd, 1915.

Zimmerman, J. E. "The Kadets and the Duma, 1905–1907." In *Essays on Russian Liberalism.* Ed. by C. E. Timberlake. Columbia, Miss., 1972, pp. 119–38.

Znosko-Borovskii, A. A., ed. *Polozhenie o zemleustroistve, s zakonodatel'nymi motivami i raz"iasneniiami.* SPB, 1912.

Zvorykin, N. N. *Krest'ianskoe zemleustroistvo i neotlozhnaia agrarnaia reforma v Rossii.* SPB, 1905.

———. *Zhelatel'naia osnovaniia krest'ianskago zemleustroistva.* SPB, 1906.

Zyrianov, P. N. "Nekotorye cherty evoliutsii krest'ianskogo 'mira' v poreformennuiu epokhu." In *EAIVE za 1971.* Vil'nius, 1974, pp. 380–7.

———. "Obychnoe grazhdanskoe pravo v poreformennoi obshchine." *Ezhegodnik po agrarnoi istorii.* Vol. VI. Vologda, 1976. pp. 91–101.

———. "Sotsial'naia struktura mestnogo upravleniia kapitalisticheskoi Rossii (1861–1914 gg.)." *IZ*, 107 (1982), 261–72.

———. "Tret'ia duma i vopros o reforme mestnogo suda i volostnogo upravleniia." *Istoriia SSSR*, 1969:6, 45–62.

INDEX

This book forms part of the STUDIES OF THE HARRIMAN INSTITUTE, successor to:

STUDIES OF THE RUSSIAN INSTITUTE

ABRAM BERGSON, *Soviet National Income in 1937* (1953).

ERNEST J. SIMMONS, JR., ed., *Through the Glass of Soviet Literature: Views of Russian Society* (1953).

THAD PAUL ALTON, *Polish Postwar Economy* (1954).

DAVID GRANICK, *Management of the Industrial Firm in the USSR: A Study in Soviet Economic Planning* (1954).

ALLEN S. WHITING, *Soviet Policies in China, 1917–1924* (1954).

GEORGE S. N. LUCKYJ, *Literary Politics in the Soviet Ukraine, 1917–1934* (1956).

MICHAEL BORO PETROVICH, *The Emergence of Russian Panslavism, 1856–1870* (1956).

THOMAS TAYLOR HAMMOND, *Lenin on Trade Unions and Revolution, 1893–1917* (1956).

DAVID MARSHALL LANG, *The Last Years of the Georgian Monarchy, 1658–1832* (1957).

JAMES WILLIAM MORLEY, *The Japanese Thrust into Siberia, 1918* (1957).

ALEXANDER G. PARK, *Bolshevism in Turkestan, 1917–1927* (1957).

HERBERT MARCUSE, *Soviet Marxism: A Critical Analysis* (1958).

CHARLES B. MCLANE, *Soviet Policy and the Chinese Communists, 1931–1946* (1958).

OLIVER H. RADKEY, *The Agrarian Foes of Bolshevism: Promise and Defeat of the Russian Socialist Revolutionaries, February to October, 1917* (1958).

RALPH TALCOTT FISHER, JR., *Pattern for Soviet Youth: A Study of the Congresses of the Komsomol, 1918–1954* (1959).

ALFRED ERICH SENN, *The Emergence of Modern Lithuania* (1959).

ELLIOT R. GOODMAN, *The Soviet Design for a World State* (1960).

JOHN N. HAZARD, *Settling Disputes in Soviet Society: The Formative Years of Legal Institutions* (1960).

DAVID JORAVSKY, *Soviet Marxism and Natural Science, 1917–1932* (1961).

MAURICE FRIEDBERG, *Russian Classics in Soviet Jackets* (1962).

ALFRED J. RIEBER, *Stalin and the French Communist Party, 1941–1947* (1962).

THEODORE K. VON LAUE, *Sergei Witte and the Industrialization of Russia* (1962).

JOHN A. ARMSTRONG, *Ukrainian Nationalism* (1963).

OLIVER H. RADKEY, *The Sickle under the Hammer: The Russian Socialist Revolutionaries in the Early Months of Soviet Rule* (1963).

KERMIT E. MCKENZIE, *Comintern and World Revolution, 1928–1943: The Shaping of Doctrine* (1964).

HARVEY L. DYCK, *Weimar Germany and Soviet Russia, 1926–1933: A Study in Diplomatic Instability* (1966).

(Above titles published by Columbia University Press.)

HAROLD J. NOAH, *Financing Soviet Schools* (Teachers College, 1966).

JOHN M. THOMPSON, *Russia, Bolshevism, and the Versailles Peace* (Princeton, 1966).

PAUL AVRICH, *The Russian Anarchists* (Princeton, 1967).

LOREN R. GRAHAM, *The Soviet Academy of Sciences and the Communist Party, 1927–1932* (Princeton, 1967).

ROBERT A. MAGUIRE, *Red Virgin Soil: Soviet Literature in the 1920's* (Princeton, 1968).

T. H. RIGBY, *Communist Party Membership in the U.S.S.R., 1917–1967* (Princeton, 1968).

RICHARD T. DE GEORGE, *Soviet Ethics and Morality* (University of Michigan, 1969).

JONATHAN FRANKEL, *Vladimir Akimov on the Dilemmas of Russian Marxism, 1895–1903* (Cambridge, 1969).

WILLIAM ZIMMERMAN, *Soviet Perspectives on International Relations, 1956–1967* (Princeton, 1969).

PAUL AVRICH, *Kronstadt, 1921* (Princeton, 1970).

EZRA MENDELSOHN, *Class Struggle in the Pale: The Formative Years of the Jewish Workers' Movement in Tsarist Russia* (Cambridge, 1970).

EDWARD J. BROWN, *The Proletarian Episode in Russian Literature* (Columbia, 1971).

REGINALD E. ZELNIK, *Labor and Society in Tsarist Russia: The Factory Workers of St. Petersburg, 1855–1870* (Stanford, 1971).

PATRICIA K. GRIMSTED, *Archives and Manuscript Repositories in the USSR: Moscow and Leningrad* (Princeton, 1972).

RONALD G. SUNY, *The Baku Commune, 1917–1918* (Princeton, 1972).

EDWARD J. BROWN, *Mayakovsky: A Poet in the Revolution* (Princeton, 1973).

MILTON EHRE, *Oblomov and His Creator: The Life and Art of Ivan Goncharov* (Princeton, 1973).

HENRY KRISCH, *German Politics Under Soviet Occupation* (Columbia, 1974).

HENRY W. MORTON AND RUDOLPH L. TÖKÉS, eds., *Soviet Politics and Society in the 1970's* (Free Press, 1974).

WILLIAM G. ROSENBERG, *Liberals in the Russian Revolution* (Princeton, 1974).

RICHARD G. ROBBINS, JR., *Famine in Russia, 1891–1892* (Columbia, 1975).

VERA DUNHAM, *In Stalin's Time: Middleclass Values in Soviet Fiction* (Cambridge, 1976).

WALTER SABLINSKY, *The Road to Bloody Sunday* (Princeton, 1976).

WILLIAM MILLS TODD III, *The Familiar Letter as a Literary Genre in the Age of Pushkin* (Princeton, 1976).

ELIZABETH VALKENIER, *Russian Realist Art. The State and Society: The Peredvizhniki and Their Tradition* (Ardis, 1977).

SUSAN SOLOMON, *The Soviet Agrarian Debate* (Westview, 1978).

SHEILA FITZPATRICK, ed., *Cultural Revolution in Russia, 1928–1931* (Indiana, 1978).

PETER SOLOMON, *Soviet Criminologists and Criminal Policy: Specialists in Policy-Making* (Columbia, 1978).

KENDALL E. BAILES, *Technology and Society under Lenin and Stalin: Origins of the Soviet Technical Intelligentsia, 1917–1941* (Princeton, 1978).

LEOPOLD H. HAIMSON, ed., *The Politics of Rural Russia, 1905–1914* (Indiana, 1979).

THEODORE H. FRIEDGUT, *Political Participation in the USSR* (Princeton, 1979).

SHEILA FITZPATRICK, *Education and Social Mobility in the Soviet Union, 1921–1934* (Cambridge, 1979).

WESLEY ANDREW FISHER, *The Soviet Marriage Market: Mate Selection in Russia and the USSR* (Praeger, 1980).

JONATHAN FRANKEL, *Prophecy and Politics: Socialism, Nationalism, and the Russian Jews, 1862–1917* (Cambridge, 1981).

ROBIN FEUER MILLER, *Dostoevsky and the Idiot: Author, Narrator, and Reader* (Harvard, 1981).

DIANE KOENKER, *Moscow Workers and the 1917 Revolution* (Princeton, 1981).

PATRICIA K. GRIMSTED, *Archives and Manuscript Repositories in the USSR: Estonia, Latvia, Lithuania, and Belorussia* (Princeton, 1981).

EZRA MENDELSOHN, *Zionism in Poland: The Formative Years, 1915–1926* (Yale, 1982).

HANNES ADOMEIT, *Soviet Risk-Taking and Crisis Behavior* (George Allen & Unwin, 1982).

SEWERYN BIALER AND THANE GUSTAFSON, eds., *Russia at the Crossroads: The 26th Congress of the CPSU* (George Allen & Unwin, 1982).

ROBERTA THOMPSON MANNING, *The Crisis of the Old Order in Russia: Gentry and Government* (Princeton, 1983).

ANDREW A. DURKIN, *Sergei Aksakov and Russian Pastoral* (Rutgers, 1983).

BRUCE PARROTT, *Politics and Technology in the Soviet Union* (MIT Press, 1983).

SARAH PRATT, *Russian Metaphysical Romanticism: The Poetry of Tiutchev and Boratynskii* (Stanford, 1984).

Studies of the Harriman Institute

ELIZABETH KRIDL VALKENIER, *The Soviet Union and the Third World: An Economic Bind* (Praeger, 1983).

JOHN LEDONNE, *Ruling Russia: Politics and Administration in the Age of Absolutism 1762–1796* (Princeton, 1984).

RICHARD E. GUSTAFSON, *Leo Tolstoy: Resident and Stranger* (Princeton, 1986).

DIANE GREENE, *Insidious Intent: A Structural Analysis of Fedor Sologub's Petty Demon* (Slavica, 1986).

WILLIAM CHASE, *Workers, Society, and the State: Labor and Life in Moscow, 1918–1929* (University of Illinois Press, 1987).

JOHN MALMSTAD, ed., *Andrey Bely: Spirit of Symbolism* (Cornell University Press, 1987).

DATE DUE

MAY 2 4 2001	
DEC 1 4 2009	